Honda VTR1000F FireStorm (Super Hawk) & XL1000V Varadero
Service and Repair Manual

by Matthew Coombs

Models covered
VTR1000F. 996cc. 1997 to 2007
XL1000V. 996cc. 1999 to 2008
XL1000VA. 996cc. 2004 to 2008

(3744-328-5AH3)

ABCDE
FGHIJ
K

© Haynes Publishing 2008

A book in the **Haynes Service and Repair Manual Series**

All rights reserved. No part of this book may be reproduced or transmitted in any form or by any means, electronic or mechanical, including photocopying, recording or by any information storage or retrieval system, without permission in writing from the copyright holder.

ISBN 978 1 84425 771 3

Library of Congress Control Number 2008926893

British Library Cataloguing in Publication Data
A catalogue record for this book is available from the British Library

Printed in the USA

Haynes Publishing
Sparkford, Yeovil, Somerset BA22 7JJ, England

Haynes North America, Inc
861 Lawrence Drive, Newbury Park, California 91320, USA

Haynes Publishing Nordiska AB
Box 1504, 751 45 UPPSALA, Sweden

Contents

LIVING WITH YOUR HONDA VTR/XL

Introduction
The Birth of a Dream	Page	0•4
Acknowledgements	Page	0•8
About this manual	Page	0•8
Frame and engine numbers	Page	0•9
Model development	Page	0•9
Safety first!	Page	0•10

Daily (pre-ride checks)
Engine/transmission oil level check	Page	0•11
Legal and safety checks	Page	0•11
Brake fluid level checks	Page	0•12
Clutch fluid level check – VTR models	Page	0•14
Suspension, steering and drive chain checks	Page	0•14
Coolant level check	Page	0•15
Tyre checks	Page	0•16

MAINTENANCE

Routine maintenance and servicing
Specifications	Page	1•1
Recommended lubricants and fluids	Page	1•2
Maintenance schedule	Page	1•3
Component locations	Page	1•4
Maintenance procedures	Page	1•6

Contents

REPAIRS AND OVERHAUL

Engine, transmission and associated systems

Engine, clutch and transmission	Page	2•1
Cooling system	Page	3•1
Fuel and exhaust systems – carburettor models	Page	4A•1
Fuel system – fuel injection models	Page	4B•1
Ignition system	Page	5•1

Chassis components

Frame, suspension and final drive	Page	6•1
Brakes, wheels and tyres	Page	7•1
Fairing and bodywork	Page	8•1

Electrical system

	Page	9•1

Wiring diagrams

	Page	9•29

REFERENCE

Dimensions and Weights	Page	REF•1
Tools and Workshop Tips	Page	REF•2
Lubricants and fluids	Page	REF•20
Conversion factors	Page	REF•23
MOT Test Checks	Page	REF•24
Storage	Page	REF•29
Fault Finding	Page	REF•32
Fault Finding Equipment	Page	REF•41
Technical Terms Explained	Page	REF•45

Index

	Page	REF•49

Introduction

The Birth of a Dream

by Julian Ryder

There is no better example of the Japanese post-war industrial miracle than Honda. Like other companies which have become household names, it started with one man's vision. In this case the man was the 40-year old Soichiro Honda who had sold his piston-ring manufacturing business to Toyota in 1945 and was happily spending the proceeds on prolonged parties for his friends. However, the difficulties of getting around in the chaos of post-war Japan irked Honda, so when he came across a job lot of generator engines he realised that here was a way of getting people mobile again at low cost.

A 12 by 18-foot shack in Hamamatsu became his first bike factory, fitting the generator motors into pushbikes. Before long he'd used up all 500 generator motors and started manufacturing his own engine, known as the 'chimney', either because of the elongated cylinder head or the smoky exhaust or perhaps both. The chimney made all of half a horsepower from its 50 cc engine but it was a major success and became the Honda A-type.

Less than two years after he'd set up in Hamamatsu, Soichiro Honda founded the Honda Motor Company in September 1948. By then, the A-type had been developed into the 90 cc B-type engine, which Mr Honda decided deserved its own chassis not a bicycle frame. Honda was about to become Japan's first post-war manufacturer of complete motorcycles. In August 1949 the first prototype was ready. With an output of three horsepower, the 98 cc D-type was still a simple two-stroke but it had a two-speed transmission and most importantly a pressed steel frame with telescopic forks and hard tail rear end. The frame was almost triangular in profile with the top rail going in a straight line from the massively braced steering head to the rear axle. Legend has it that after the D-type's first tests the entire workforce went for a drink to celebrate and try and think of a name for the bike. One man broke one of those silences you get when people are thinking, exclaiming 'This is like a dream!' 'That's it!' shouted Honda, and so the Honda Dream was christened.

> 'This is like a dream!'
> 'That's it'
> shouted Honda

Mr Honda was a brilliant, intuitive engineer and designer but he did not bother himself with the marketing side of his business. With hindsight, it is possible to see that employing Takeo Fujisawa who would both sort out the home market and plan the eventual expansion into overseas markets was a masterstroke. He arrived in October 1949 and in 1950 was made Sales Director. Another vital new name was Kiyoshi Kawashima, who along with Honda himself, designed the company's first four-stroke after Kawashima had told them that the four-stroke opposition to Honda's two-strokes sounded nicer and therefore sold better. The result of that statement was the overhead-valve 148 cc E-type which first ran in July 1951 just two months after the first drawings were made. Kawashima was made a director of the Honda Company at 34 years old.

The E-type was a massive success, over 32,000 were made in 1953 alone, a feat of mass-production that was astounding by the

Honda C70 and C90 OHV-engined models

Introduction

standards of the day given the relative complexity of the machine. But Honda's lifelong pursuit of technical innovation sometimes distracted him from commercial reality. Fujisawa pointed out that they were in danger of ignoring their core business, the motorised bicycles that still formed Japan's main means of transport. In May 1952 the F-type Cub appeared, another two-stroke despite the top men's reservations. You could buy a complete machine or just the motor to attach to your own bicycle. The result was certainly distinctive, a white fuel tank with a circular profile went just below and behind the saddle on the left of the bike, and the motor with its horizontal cylinder and bright red cover just below the rear axle on the same side of the bike. This was the machine that turned Honda into the biggest bike maker in Japan with 70% of the market for bolt-on bicycle motors, the F-type was also the first Honda to be exported. Next came the machine that would turn Honda into the biggest motorcycle manufacturer in the world.

The C100 Super Cub was a typically audacious piece of Honda engineering and marketing. For the first time, but not the last, Honda invented a completely new type of motorcycle, although the term 'scooterette' was coined to describe the new bike which had many of the characteristics of a scooter but the large wheels, and therefore stability, of a motorcycle. The first one was sold in August 1958, fifteen years later over nine-million of them were on the roads of the world. If ever a machine can be said to have brought mobility to the masses it is the Super Cub. If you add in the electric starter that was added for the C102 model of 1961, the design of the Super Cub has remained substantially unchanged ever since, testament to how right Honda got it first time. The Super Cub made Honda the world's biggest manufacturer after just two years of production.

The CB250N Super Dream became a favorite with UK learner riders of the late seventies and early eighties

Honda's export drive started in earnest in 1957 when Britain and Holland got their first bikes, America got just two bikes the next year. By 1962 Honda had half the American market with 65,000 sales. But Soichiro Honda had already travelled abroad to Europe and the USA, making a special

The GL1000 introduced in 1975, was the first in Honda's line of GoldWings

Introduction

Carl Fogarty in action at the Suzuka 8 Hour on the RC45

An early CB750 Four

point of going to the Isle of Man TT, then the most important race in the GP calendar. He realised that no matter how advanced his products were, only racing success would convince overseas markets for whom 'Made in Japan' still meant cheap and nasty. It took five years from Soichiro Honda's first visit to the Island before his bikes were ready for the TT. In 1959 the factory entered five riders in the 125 class. They did not have a massive impact on the event being benevolently regarded as a curiosity, but sixth, seventh and eighth were good enough for the team prize. The bikes were off the pace but they were well engineered and very reliable.

The TT was the only time the West saw the Hondas in '59, but they came back for more the following year with the first of a generation of bikes which shaped the future of motorcycling – the double-overhead-cam four-cylinder 250. It was fast and reliable – it revved to 14,000 rpm – but didn't handle anywhere near as well as the opposition. However, Honda had now signed up non-Japanese riders to lead their challenge. The first win didn't come until 1962 (Aussie Tom Phillis in the Spanish 125 GP) and was followed up with a world-shaking performance at the TT. Twenty-one year old Mike Hailwood won both 125 and 250 cc TTs and Hondas filled the top five positions in both races. Soichiro Honda's master plan was starting to come to fruition, Hailwood and Honda won the 1961 250 cc World Championship. Next year Honda won three titles. The other Japanese factories fought back and inspired Honda to produce some of the most fascinating racers ever seen: the awesome six-cylinder 250, the five-cylinder 125, and the 500 four with which the immortal Hailwood battled Agostini and the MV Agusta.

When Honda pulled out of racing in '67 they had won sixteen rider's titles, eighteen manufacturer's titles, and 137 GPs, including 18 TTs, and introduced the concept of the modern works team to motorcycle racing. Sales success followed racing victory as Soichiro Honda had predicted, but only because the products advanced as rapidly as the racing machinery. The Hondas that came to Britain in the early '60s were incredibly sophisticated. They had overhead cams where the British bikes had pushrods, they had electric starters when the Brits relied on the kickstart, they had 12V electrics when even the biggest British bike used a 6V system. There seemed no end to the technical wizardry. It wasn't that the technology itself was so amazing but just like that first E-type, it was the fact that Honda could mass-produce it more reliably than the lower-tech competition that was so astonishing.

When in 1968 the first four-cylinder CB750 road bike arrived the world of motorcycling changed for ever, they even had to invent a new word for it, 'Superbike'. Honda raced again with the CB750 at Daytona and won the

Introduction 0•7

World Endurance title with a prototype DOHC version that became the CB900 roadster. There was the six-cylinder CBX, the CX500T – the world's first turbocharged production bike, they invented the full-dress tourer with the GoldWing, and came back to GPs with the revolutionary oval-pistoned NR500 four-stroke, a much-misunderstood bike that was more a rolling experimental laboratory than a racer. Just to show their versatility Honda also came up with the weird CX500 shaft-drive V-twin, a rugged workhorse that powered a new industry, the courier companies that oiled the wheels of commerce in London and other big cities.

It was true, though, that Mr Honda was not keen on two-strokes – early motocross engines had to be explained away to him as lawnmower motors! However, in 1982 Honda raced the NS500, an agile three-cylinder lightweight against the big four-cylinder opposition in 500 GPs. The bike won in its first year and in '83 took the world title for Freddie Spencer. In four-stroke racing the V4 layout took over from the straight four, dominating TT, F1 and Endurance championships with the RVF750, the nearest thing ever built to a Formula 1 car on wheels. And when Superbike arrived Honda were ready with the RC30. On the roads the VFR V4 became an instant classic while the CBR600 invented another new class of bike on its way to becoming a best-seller. The V4 road bikes had problems to start with but the VFR750 sold world-wide over its lifetime while the VFR400 became a massive commercial success and cult bike in Japan. The original RC30 won the first two World Superbike Championships is 1988 and '89, but Honda had to wait until 1997 to win it again with the RC45, the last of the V4 roadsters. In Grands Prix, the NSR500 V4 two-stroke superseded the NS triple and became the benchmark racing machine of the '90s. Mick Doohan secured his place in history by winning five World Championships in consecutive years on it.

In yet another example of Honda inventing a new class of motorcycle, they came up with the astounding CBR900RR FireBlade, a bike with the punch of a 1000 cc motor in a package the size and weight of a 750. It became a cult bike as well as a best seller, and with judicious redesigns continues to give much more recent designs a run for their money.

When it became apparent that the high-tech V4 motor of the RC45 was too expensive to produce, Honda looked to a V-twin engine to power its flagship for the first time. Typically, the VTR1000 FireStorm was a much more rideable machine than its opposition and once accepted by the market formed the basis of the next generation of Superbike racer, the VTR-SP-1.

One of Mr Honda's mottos was that technology would solve the customers' problems, and no company has embraced

The CX500 – Honda's first V-Twin and a favorite choice of dispatch riders

cutting-edge technology more firmly than Honda. In fact Honda often developed new technology, especially in the fields of materials science and metallurgy. The embodiment of that was the NR750, a bike that was misunderstood nearly as much as the original NR500 racer. This limited-edition technological tour-de-force embodied many of Soichiro Honda's ideals. It used the latest techniques and materials in every component, from the oval-piston, 32-valve V4 motor to the titanium coating on the windscreen, it was – as Mr Honda would have wanted – the best it could possibly be. A fitting memorial to the man who has shaped the motorcycle industry and motorcycles as we know them today.

The VFR400R was a cult bike in Japan and a popular grey import in the UK

0•8 Introduction

Honda's First Fast Twin

Honda had never made a V-twin sportster before 1997 when the VTR1000 arrived. There had of course been V-twins, notably that couriers' favourite the CX500, but no-way could they be have been defined as sports bikes. More importantly, there were no V-twins in the golden era of racing when Honda kept the four-stroke flying against the new generation of two-strokes. That meant more cylinders and gears, hence such glorious bikes as the 250-6 and the five-cylinder 125, and definitely no V-twins. So why did Honda deviate from their heritage in the shape of the straight-four of the FireBlade or the V4 of the RC45 for their new flagship?

Cynics will give the pat answer that they had to copy Ducati to win World Superbike races. This is, of course, not true. The Ducati uses a steel lattice frame to house a fuel-injected motor with Desmodromic valve actuation, whereas the Honda uses an aluminium diamond frame to house a carburetted motor with conventional valve operation. Sure, they both have twin-cylinder motors and two wheels but the resemblance ends right there. Long before the end of the RC45's life, we were being told by very senior Honda management that it was too expensive to make, and on the grounds that it was £6000 more expensive than the Ducati 916 when it was launched, who can argue?

Hence Honda went the V-twin route, but their first big Vee wasn't a Superbike homologation machine (that came later) it was the FireStorm. Here was a bike that delivered all the Honda virtues as best demonstrated in the VFR, attention to detail, innovative design and usability. And all at the right price, too.

When unveiled, it was only a couple of kilos heavier than the 916 Biposto and was scheduled to be a massive £5000 cheaper - and because it was a Honda you knew it would be reliable. The lightness is achieved by

the minimalist frame that doesn't include a swinging arm pivot, the crankcases do that job. Front forks are conventional, not upside down, and the swinging arm is a conventional twin-sided arrangement. The motor is standard-issue Honda four-valve-heads with chain-driven double overhead camshafts. Carburettors are fitted, probably as part of the cost-cutting efforts. The only unusual thing about the motor is that as well as acting as a major stressed member of the frame it also incorporates the swinging arm pivot as on the VFR800.

A V-twin is of course inherently narrow when mounted with the crank across the frame, add in the slimline frame, side-mounted radiators and small tank and you have an amazingly thin motorcycle. However, the VTR was never meant to be a race replica better suited to track days than road work. However, the motor's state of tune gave it much better top-gear roll-on performance than even the VFR800 or that other much more sporty V-twin launched at the same time, Suzuki's TL1000. The roadtests all agreed, the FireStorm was very rideable and great fun, only losing out to the opposition at the very extremes of performance. But Honda had an answer for that and they saved it for the 2000 World Superbike season: the SP-1. However, that bike shares nothing of importance with the FireStorm, not the frame, not the bore, not the stroke, not even the method of cam operation.

The bike that does share its motor with the FireStorm is much stranger, it's the Varadero. It seems silly to call a bike this size an off-roader, the name Honda invented for the Transalp – Rally Tourer – seems much more suitable. It is an attempt to take some of the sales the BMW GS has racked up over the years. The FireStorm motor gets smaller carbs and a heavier flywheel for even more torque and low-down driveability. The chassis is conventional tubular steel.

Acknowledgements

Our thanks are due to Bransons Motorcycles of Yeovil and Fowlers of Bristol who supplied the machines featured in the illustrations throughout this manual. We would also like to thank NGK Spark Plugs (UK) Ltd for supplying the colour spark plug condition photos, the Avon Rubber Company for supplying information on tyre fitting, and Draper Tools Ltd for some of the workshop tools.

Thanks are also due to Honda (UK) Ltd for supplying model photographs.

The introduction 'The Birth of a Dream' was written by Julian Ryder.

About this Manual

The aim of this manual is to help you get the best value from your motorcycle. It can do so in several ways. It can help you decide what work must be done, even if you choose to have it done by a dealer; it provides information and procedures for routine maintenance and servicing; and it offers diagnostic and repair procedures to follow when trouble occurs.

We hope you use the manual to tackle the work yourself. For many simpler jobs, doing it yourself may be quicker than arranging an appointment to get the motorcycle into a dealer and making the trips to leave it and pick it up. More importantly, a lot of money can be saved by avoiding the expense the shop must pass on to you to cover its labour and overhead costs. An added benefit is the sense of satisfaction and accomplishment that you feel after doing the job yourself.

References to the left or right side of the motorcycle assume you are sitting on the seat, facing forward.

We take great pride in the accuracy of information given in this manual, but motorcycle manufacturers make alterations and design changes during the production run of a particular motorcycle of which they do not inform us. No liability can be accepted by the authors or publishers for loss, damage or injury caused by any errors in, or omissions from, the information given.

Illegal Copying

It is the policy of Haynes Publishing to actively protect its Copyrights and Trade Marks. Legal action will be taken against anyone who unlawfully copies the cover or contents of this Manual. This includes all forms of unauthorised copying including digital, mechanical, and electronic in any form. Authorisation from Haynes Publishing will only be provided expressly and in writing. Illegal copying will also be reported to the appropriate statutory authorities.

Identification numbers 0•9

Frame and engine numbers

The frame serial number is stamped into the right-hand side of the steering head. The engine number is stamped into the top of the crankcase behind the rear cylinder. Both of these numbers should be recorded and kept in a safe place so they can be furnished to law enforcement officials in the event of a theft and they should also be kept handy to that they are available when purchasing spare parts. Each carburettor/throttle body carries an identification number (see Chapters 4A or 4B) and there is a colour code label on the left-hand frame rail of the rear subframe.

The procedures in this manual identify the bikes by type (i.e. VTR or XL), then if necessary by model code (eg X, meaning a 1999 production year model). The model code or production year is printed on the colour code label.

Model	Year		
VTR1000F-V	1997	XL1000V-1	2001
VTR1000F-W	1998	XL1000V-2	2002
VTR1000F-X	1999	XL1000V-3	2003
VTR1000F-Y	2000	XL1000V-4	2004
VTR1000F-1	2001	XL1000VA-4	2004
VTR1000F-2	2002	XL1000V-5	2005
VTR1000F-3	2003/4	XL1000VA-5	2005
VTR1000F-5	2005	XL1000V-6	2006
VTR1000F-6	2006/7	XL1000VA-6	2006
		XL1000V-7	2007
		XL1000VA-7	2007
XL1000V-X	1999	XL1000V-8	2008
XL1000V-Y	2000	XL1000VA-8	2008

1 The frame number is stamped into the right-hand side of the steering head

2 The engine number is stamped into the top of the crankcase behind the rear cylinder

3 The colour code label is on the top left-hand rail on the rear subframe on VTR models (shown), and on the bottom rail on XL models

Model development

VTR1000F models

The VTR1000F was launched in 1997 in Europe as the FireStorm, and in 1998 in the US as the Super Hawk.

The engine/transmission unit is a liquid-cooled 90°V-twin. The eight valves are operated by double overhead camshafts which are chain driven off the crankshaft. The hydraulically-actuated clutch is a wet multi-plate unit with conventional springs. The transmission is a six-speed constant-mesh unit. Twin CV carburettors feed the engine.

It has an aluminium trellis-type frame which uses the engine as a stressed member. Front suspension is by a pair of oil-damped telescopic forks with cartridge dampers that are adjustable for spring pre-load and rebound damping. At the rear, an alloy swingarm acts on a single shock absorber via a three-way linkage. The swingarm is mounted directly onto the back of the engine. The shock absorber is adjustable for spring preload and rebound damping.

Final drive to the rear wheel is by chain and sprockets. Cast alloy wheels are fitted with tubeless tyres.

Both front and rear brakes are hydraulically operated disc brakes. The front brakes have twin opposed piston calipers and the rear brake has a single piston sliding caliper.

An immobiliser system (HISS) was added in 2001, and the front brake and clutch master cylinders were changed from remote to integral reservoir type in 2005. Otherwise, and apart from colour options, the design changed very little over the ten years of its production life.

XL1000V models

The XL1000V Varadero was launched in 1999 and sold in Europe only.

Using the engine/transmission unit of the VTR1000, it differed in its use of a five-speed gearbox and cable-operated clutch.

The engine is housed in an aluminium trellis-type frame which uses the engine as a stressed member. Front suspension is by a pair of oil-damped telescopic forks with conventional dampers and are not adjustable. At the rear, an alloy swingarm acts on a single shock absorber via a three-way linkage. The swingarm is mounted directly onto the back of the engine. The shock absorber is adjustable for spring pre-load.

Final drive to the rear wheel is by chain and sprockets. Cast alloy wheels are fitted with tubeless tyres.

Front and rear brakes are hydraulically operated disc brakes and use triple piston sliding calipers. All models are fitted with Honda's dual combined braking system (Dual-CBS) which applies both front and rear brakes irrespective of whether the front brake lever or rear brake pedal is applied.

The Varadero was given an overhaul in 2003, when it was fitted with fuel injection, six-speed gearbox, a new fairing and new instruments. The XL1000VA, launched in 2004, had an anti-lock braking system (ABS), and the left-hand fork had a cartridge damper that was adjustable for rebound damping.

A further overhaul in 2007 resulted in revised throttle bodies for the fuel injection system, and a host of styling updates.

Safety first!

Professional mechanics are trained in safe working procedures. However enthusiastic you may be about getting on with the job at hand, take the time to ensure that your safety is not put at risk. A moment's lack of attention can result in an accident, as can failure to observe simple precautions.

There will always be new ways of having accidents, and the following is not a comprehensive list of all dangers; it is intended rather to make you aware of the risks and to encourage a safe approach to all work you carry out on your bike.

Asbestos

● Certain friction, insulating, sealing and other products - such as brake pads, clutch linings, gaskets, etc. - contain asbestos. Extreme care must be taken to avoid inhalation of dust from such products since it is hazardous to health. If in doubt, assume that they do contain asbestos.

Fire

● Remember at all times that petrol is highly flammable. Never smoke or have any kind of naked flame around, when working on the vehicle. But the risk does not end there - a spark caused by an electrical short-circuit, by two metal surfaces contacting each other, by careless use of tools, or even by static electricity built up in your body under certain conditions, can ignite petrol vapour, which in a confined space is highly explosive. Never use petrol as a cleaning solvent. Use an approved safety solvent.

● Always disconnect the battery earth terminal before working on any part of the fuel or electrical system, and never risk spilling fuel on to a hot engine or exhaust.
● It is recommended that a fire extinguisher of a type suitable for fuel and electrical fires is kept handy in the garage or workplace at all times. Never try to extinguish a fuel or electrical fire with water.

Fumes

● Certain fumes are highly toxic and can quickly cause unconsciousness and even death if inhaled to any extent. Petrol vapour comes into this category, as do the vapours from certain solvents such as trichloro-ethylene. Any draining or pouring of such volatile fluids should be done in a well ventilated area.
● When using cleaning fluids and solvents, read the instructions carefully. Never use materials from unmarked containers - they may give off poisonous vapours.
● Never run the engine of a motor vehicle in an enclosed space such as a garage. Exhaust fumes contain carbon monoxide which is extremely poisonous; if you need to run the engine, always do so in the open air or at least have the rear of the vehicle outside the workplace.

The battery

● Never cause a spark, or allow a naked light near the vehicle's battery. It will normally be giving off a certain amount of hydrogen gas, which is highly explosive.

● Always disconnect the battery ground (earth) terminal before working on the fuel or electrical systems (except where noted).
● If possible, loosen the filler plugs or cover when charging the battery from an external source. Do not charge at an excessive rate or the battery may burst.
● Take care when topping up, cleaning or carrying the battery. The acid electrolyte, evenwhen diluted, is very corrosive and should not be allowed to contact the eyes or skin. Always wear rubber gloves and goggles or a face shield. If you ever need to prepare electrolyte yourself, always add the acid slowly to the water; never add the water to the acid.

Electricity

● When using an electric power tool, inspection light etc., always ensure that the appliance is correctly connected to its plug and that, where necessary, it is properly grounded (earthed). Do not use such appliances in damp conditions and, again, beware of creating a spark or applying excessive heat in the vicinity of fuel or fuel vapour. Also ensure that the appliances meet national safety standards.
● A severe electric shock can result from touching certain parts of the electrical system, such as the spark plug wires (HT leads), when the engine is running or being cranked, particularly if components are damp or the insulation is defective. Where an electronic ignition system is used, the secondary (HT) voltage is much higher and could prove fatal.

Remember...

✗ **Don't** start the engine without first ascer-taining that the transmission is in neutral.

✗ **Don't** suddenly remove the pressure cap from a hot cooling system - cover it with a cloth and release the pressure gradually first, or you may get scalded by escaping coolant.

✗ **Don't** attempt to drain oil until you are sure it has cooled sufficiently to avoid scalding you.

✗ **Don't** grasp any part of the engine or exhaust system without first ascertaining that it is cool enough not to burn you.

✗ **Don't** allow brake fluid or antifreeze to contact the machine's paintwork or plastic components.

✗ **Don't** siphon toxic liquids such as fuel, hydraulic fluid or antifreeze by mouth, or allow them to remain on your skin.

✗ **Don't** inhale dust - it may be injurious to health (see Asbestos heading).

✗ **Don't** allow any spilled oil or grease to remain on the floor - wipe it up right away, before someone slips on it.

✗ **Don't** use ill-fitting spanners or other tools which may slip and cause injury.

✗ **Don't** lift a heavy component which may be beyond your capability - get assistance.

✗ **Don't** rush to finish a job or take unverified short cuts.

✗ **Don't** allow children or animals in or around an unattended vehicle.

✗ **Don't** inflate a tyre above the recommended pressure. Apart from overstressing the carcass, in extreme cases the tyre may blow off forcibly.

✔ **Do** ensure that the machine is supported securely at all times. This is especially important when the machine is blocked up to aid wheel or fork removal.

✔ **Do** take care when attempting to loosen a stubborn nut or bolt. It is generally better to pull on a spanner, rather than push, so that if you slip, you fall away from the machine rather than onto it.

✔ **Do** wear eye protection when using power tools such as drill, sander, bench grinder etc.

✔ **Do** use a barrier cream on your hands prior to undertaking dirty jobs - it will protect your skin from infection as well as making the dirt easier to remove afterwards; but make sure your hands aren't left slippery. Note that long-term contact with used engine oil can be a health hazard.

✔ **Do** keep loose clothing (cuffs, ties etc. and long hair) well out of the way of moving mechanical parts.

✔ **Do** remove rings, wristwatch etc., before working on the vehicle - especially the electrical system.

✔ **Do** keep your work area tidy - it is only too easy to fall over articles left lying around.

✔ **Do** exercise caution when compressing springs for removal or installation. Ensure that the tension is applied and released in a controlled manner, using suitable tools which preclude the possibility of the spring escaping violently.

✔ **Do** ensure that any lifting tackle used has a safe working load rating adequate for the job.

✔ **Do** get someone to check periodically that all is well, when working alone on the vehicle.

✔ **Do** carry out work in a logical sequence and check that everything is correctly assembled and tightened afterwards.

✔ **Do** remember that your vehicle's safety affects that of yourself and others. If in doubt on any point, get professional advice.

● If in spite of following these precautions, you are unfortunate enough to injure yourself, seek medical attention as soon as possible.

Daily (pre-ride) checks 0•11

1 Engine/transmission oil level check

Note: *The daily (pre-ride) checks outlined in the owner's manual covers those items which should be inspected on a daily basis.*

Before you start:
✔ Take the motorcycle on a short run to allow it to reach normal operating temperature.

Caution: Do not run the engine in an enclosed space such as a garage or workshop.

✔ Stop the engine and support the motorcycle in an upright position, using an auxiliary stand if required. Allow it to stand undisturbed for a few minutes to allow the oil level to stabilise. Make sure the motorcycle is on level ground.

Bike care:
● If you have to add oil frequently, check whether you have any oil leaks from the engine joints, seals and gaskets. If not, the engine could be burning oil, in which case there will be white smoke coming out of the exhaust (see *Fault Finding*).

The correct oil
● Modern, high-revving engines place great demands on their oil. It is very important that the correct oil for your bike is used.
● Always top up with a good quality motorcycle oil of the specified type and viscosity and do not overfill the engine.

Oil type	API grade SG, JASO MA
Oil viscosity	SAE 10W40

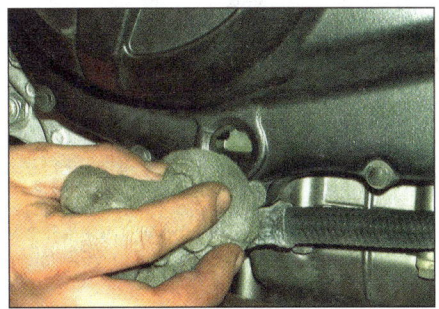
1 Wipe the oil level inspection window, located on the right-hand side of the engine, so that it is clean.

2 With the motorcycle vertical, the oil level should lie between the maximum and minimum level lines on the window

3 If the level is below the minimum line, remove the filler cap from the top of the clutch cover

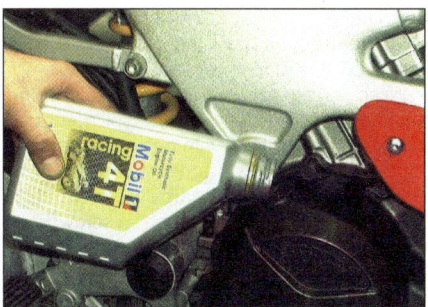
4 Top the engine up with the recommended grade and type of oil to bring the level up to the maximum level on the window.

2 Legal and safety checks

Lighting and signalling:
● Take a minute to check that the headlight, tail light, brake light, instrument lights and turn signals all work correctly.
● Check that the horn sounds when the switch is operated.
● A working speedometer is a statutory requirement in the UK.

Safety:
● Check that the throttle grip rotates smoothly and snaps shut when released, in all steering positions. Also check for the correct amount of freeplay (see Chapter 1).
● Check that the engine shuts off when the kill switch is operated.
● Check that sidestand return spring holds the stand securely up when retracted.

Fuel:
● This may seem obvious, but check that you have enough fuel to complete your journey. If you notice signs of fuel leakage – rectify the cause immediately.
● Ensure you use the correct unleaded fuel – see Chapter 4 Specifications.

3 Brake fluid level check

> **Warning:** Brake hydraulic fluid can harm your eyes and damage painted surfaces, so use extreme caution when handling and pouring it and cover surrounding surfaces with rag. Do not use fluid that has been standing open for some time, as it absorbs moisture from the air which can cause a dangerous loss of braking effectiveness.

Before you start:
✔ Support the motorcycle in an upright position, using an auxiliary stand if required, and turn the handlebars until the top of the front brake master cylinder is as level as possible. The rear master cylinder reservoir is located on the right-hand side of the machine.
✔ Make sure you have the correct hydraulic fluid. DOT 4 is recommended.
✔ Wrap a rag around the reservoir being worked on to ensure that any spillage does not come into contact with painted surfaces.
✔ On VTR models, access to the front reservoir cap screws is partially restricted by the windshield. If a short or angled screwdriver is not available, angle the reservoir to access the screws – it is rubber mounted and there is enough flex to provide clearance without stressing the mounts.

Bike care:
● The fluid in the front and rear brake master cylinder reservoirs will drop slightly as the brake pads wear down.
● If any fluid reservoir requires repeated topping-up there could be an hydraulic leak somewhere in the system, which must be investigated immediately.
● Check for signs of fluid leakage from the hydraulic hoses and components – if found, rectify immediately (see Chapter 7).
● Check the operation of both brakes before taking the machine on the road; if there is evidence of air in the system (spongy feel to lever or pedal), it must be bled (see Chapter 7).

FRONT BRAKE FLUID LEVEL – VTR1000F-V TO F-3 MODELS

1 The front brake fluid level is visible through the reservoir body - it must be between the UPPER and LOWER level lines.

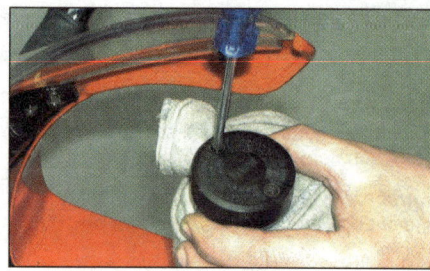

2 If the level is below the LOWER level line, undo the two reservoir cap screws and remove the cap, diaphragm plate and diaphragm.

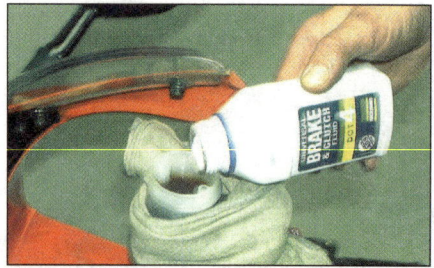

3 Top up with new clean hydraulic fluid of the recommended type, until the level is up to the UPPER level line. Take care to avoid spills (see **Warning** above).

4 Ensure that the diaphragm is correctly seated before installing the plate and cap.

FRONT BRAKE FLUID LEVEL – XL MODELS, AND VTR1000F-5 AND F-6

5 The front brake fluid level is visible through the window in the reservoir body - it must be above the LOWER level line.

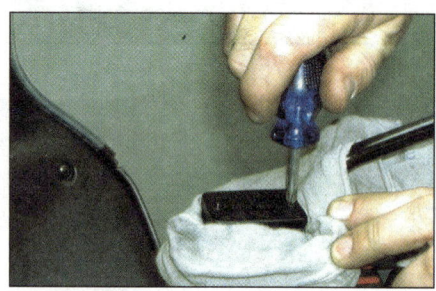

6 If the level is below the LOWER level line, undo the two reservoir cover screws and remove the cover, diaphragm plate and diaphragm.

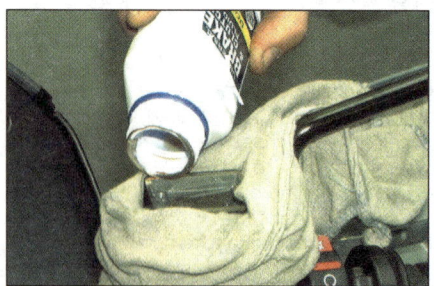

7 Top up with new clean hydraulic fluid of the recommended type, until the level is up to the UPPER level line, marked on the inside of the reservoir. Take care to avoid spills (see **Warning** above).

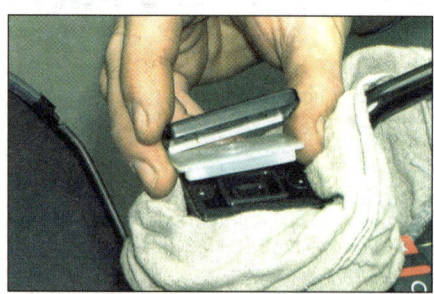

8 Ensure that the diaphragm is correctly seated before installing the plate and cover.

Daily (pre-ride) checks 0•13

REAR BRAKE FLUID LEVEL – VTR MODELS

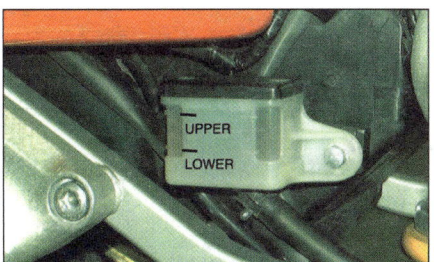

9 On VTR models, the rear brake fluid level is visible through the reservoir body - it must be above the LOWER level line.

10 If the level is below the LOWER level line, remove the bolt securing the reservoir and draw the reservoir out.

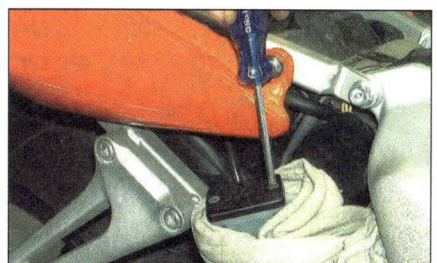

11 Undo the two reservoir cover screws and remove the cover, diaphragm plate and diaphragm. Take care to avoid spills (see **Warning** on page 12).

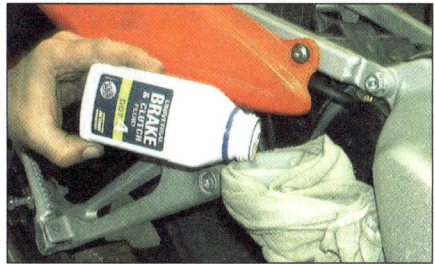

12 Top up with new clean hydraulic fluid of the recommended type, until the level is up to the UPPER level line.

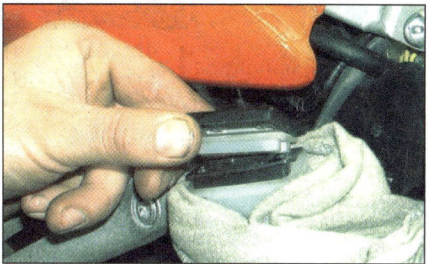

13 Ensure that the diaphragm is correctly seated before installing the plate and cover. Remount the reservoir and tighten the bolt securely.

REAR BRAKE FLUID LEVEL – XL MODELS

14 On XL models, the rear brake fluid level is visible through the reservoir body - it must be above the LOWER level line. On models with ABS, view the level through the slot in the side cover.

15 If the level is below the LOWER level line, remove the right-hand side cover (see Chapter 8, Section 4). Unscrew the reservoir cap (arrowed) and remove the diaphragm plate and diaphragm.

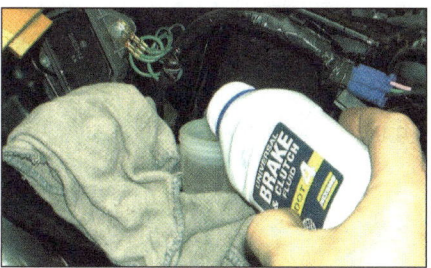

16 Top up with new clean hydraulic fluid of the recommended type, until the level is up to the UPPER level line. Take care to avoid spills (see **Warning** on page 12). Ensure that the diaphragm is correctly seated

17 before installing the plate and cap. Tighten the cap securely.

0•14 Daily (pre-ride) checks

4 Clutch fluid level check – VTR models

Note: *VTR1000F-V to F-3 models are fitted with a circular clutch fluid reservoir as shown the accompanying four photos. VTR1000F-5 and F-6 models have an integral rectangular reservoir – refer to photos 5 to 8 on page 0.12 for level checking and top-up.*

> ⚠ **Warning:** Hydraulic fluid can harm your eyes and damage painted surfaces, so use extreme caution when handling and pouring it and cover surrounding surfaces with rag. Do not use fluid that has been standing open for some time, as it absorbs moisture from the air which can cause a dangerous loss of braking and clutch effectiveness.

Before you start:
✔ Support the motorcycle in an upright position, using an auxiliary stand if required. Turn the handlebars until the top of the clutch master cylinder is as level as possible.
✔ Make sure you have the correct hydraulic fluid. DOT 4 is recommended.
✔ Wrap a rag around the reservoir being worked on to ensure that any spillage does not come into contact with painted surfaces.

Bike care:
● If the fluid reservoir requires repeated topping-up there could be an hydraulic leak somewhere in the system, which must be investigated immediately.
● Check for signs of fluid leakage from the hydraulic hose and components - if found, rectify immediately.
● Check the operation of the clutch; if there is evidence of air in the system (spongy feel to the lever), bleed the clutch as described in Chapter 2, Section 17.

1 The clutch fluid level is visible through the reservoir body - it must be above the LOWER level line.

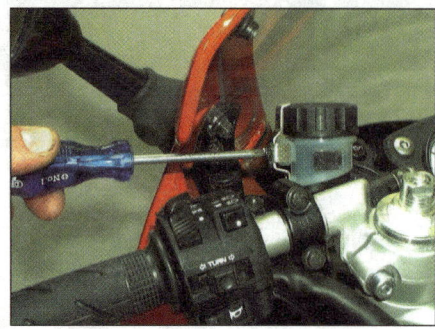

2 If the level is below the LOWER level line, slacken the reservoir cap clamp screw and displace the clamp, then unscrew the cap and remove the diaphragm plate and the diaphragm.

3 Top up with new clean hydraulic fluid of the recommended type, until the level is up to the UPPER level line. Take care to avoid spills (see **Warning** above).

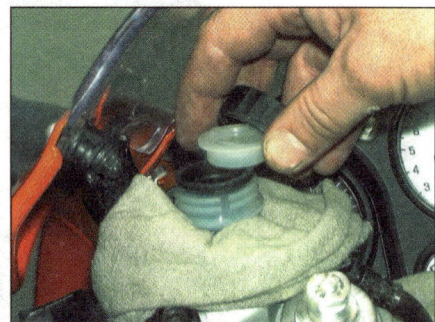

4 Ensure that the diaphragm is correctly seated before installing the plate and cap. Secure the cap with its clamp.

5 Suspension, steering and drive chain checks

Suspension and steering:
● Check that the front and rear suspension operates smoothly without binding.
● Check that the suspension is adjusted as required.

● Check that the steering moves smoothly from lock-to-lock.

Drive chain:
● Check that the drive chain slack isn't excessive, and adjust if necessary (see Chapter 1).
● If the chain looks dry, lubricate it (see Chapter 1).

Daily (pre-ride) checks

6 Coolant level check

> ⚠️ **Warning: DO NOT remove the radiator pressure cap to add coolant. Topping up is done via the coolant reservoir tank filler. DO NOT leave open containers of coolant about, as it is poisonous.**

Before you start:
✔ Make sure you have a supply of coolant available (a mixture of 50% distilled water and 50% corrosion inhibited ethylene glycol anti-freeze is needed).
✔ Always check the coolant level when the engine is at normal working temperature. Take the motorcycle on a short run to allow it to reach normal temperature.

Caution: Do not run the engine in an enclosed space such as a garage or workshop.

✔ Support the motorcycle in an upright position, using an auxiliary stand if required, whilst checking the level. Make sure the motorcycle is on level ground.

Bike care:
● Use only the specified coolant mixture. It is important that anti-freeze is used in the system all year round, and not just in the winter. Do not top the system up using only water, as the system will become too diluted.
● Do not overfill the reservoir tank. If the coolant is significantly above the UPPER level line at any time, the surplus should be siphoned or drained off to prevent the possibility of it being expelled out of the overflow hose.
● If the coolant level falls steadily, check the system for leaks (see Chapter 1, Section 13). If no leaks are found and the level continues to fall, it is recommended that the machine is taken to a Honda dealer for a pressure test.

VTR MODELS

1 The coolant reservoir is located on the right-hand side between the engine cylinders. The coolant UPPER and LOWER level lines (arrowed) are marked on the back of the reservoir.

2 If the coolant level is not in between the UPPER and LOWER markings, remove the reservoir filler cap.

3 Top the coolant level up with the recommended coolant mixture. Fit the cap securely.

XL MODELS

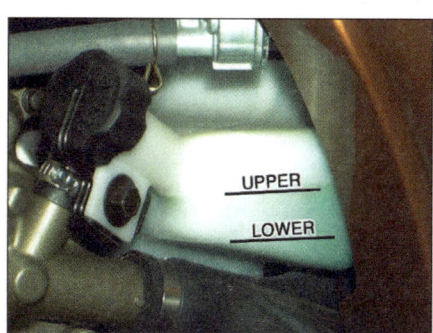

4 The coolant reservoir is located on the right-hand side below the fuel tank. The coolant UPPER and LOWER level lines are marked on the outside of the reservoir.

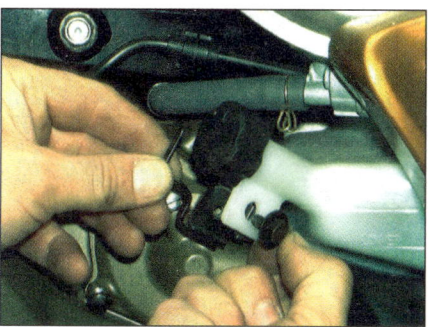

5 If the coolant level is not in between the UPPER and LOWER markings, remove the reservoir filler cap – it is secured by a clamp, which is released by unscrewing the bolt.

6 Top the coolant level up with the recommended coolant mixture. Fit the cap securely.

0•16 Daily (pre-ride) checks

7 Tyre checks

Tyre care:
● Check the tyres carefully for cuts, tears, embedded nails or other sharp objects and excessive wear. Operation of the motorcycle with excessively worn tyres is extremely hazardous, as traction and handling are directly affected.

● Check the condition of the tyre valve and ensure the dust cap is in place.

● Pick out any stones or nails which may have become embedded in the tyre tread. If left, they will eventually penetrate through the casing and cause a puncture. If a nail has punctured the tyre, leave the nail in place to make it easier to find the hole if a repair is possible.

● If tyre damage is apparent, or unexplained loss of pressure is experienced, seek the advice of a tyre fitting specialist without delay.

Tyre tread depth:
● At the time of writing UK law requires that tread depth must be at least 1 mm over 3/4 of the tread breadth all the way around the tyre, with no bald patches. Many riders, however, consider 2 mm tread depth minimum to be a safer limit. Honda recommend a minimum of 1.5 mm on the front and 2 mm on the rear.

● Many tyres now incorporate wear indicators in the tread. Identify the location marking on the tyre sidewall to locate the indicator bar and replace the tyre if the tread has worn down to the bar.

The correct pressures:
● The tyres must be checked when **cold**, not immediately after riding. Note that low tyre pressures may cause the tyre to slip on the rim or come off. High tyre pressures will cause abnormal tread wear and unsafe handling.

● Use an accurate pressure gauge. Many forecourt gauges are wildly inaccurate. If you buy your own, spend as much as you can justify on a quality gauge.

● Proper air pressure will increase tyre life and provide maximum stability and ride comfort.

VTR models		
Loading	**Front**	**Rear**
Rider only	36 psi (2.50 bar)	42 psi (2.90 bar)
Rider and passenger	36 psi (2.50 bar)	42 psi (2.90 bar)
XL models		
Loading	**Front**	**Rear**
Rider only	36 psi (2.50 bar)	36 psi (2.50 bar)
Rider and passenger	36 psi (2.50 bar)	41 psi (2.80 bar)

1 Check the tyre pressures when the tyres are **cold** and keep them properly inflated.

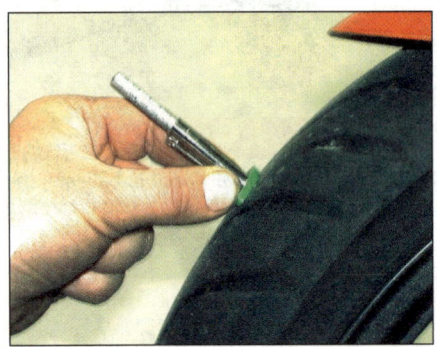

2 Measure tread depth at the centre of the tyre using a tread depth gauge.

3 Tyre tread wear indicator bar and its location marking (usually either an arrow, a triangle or the letters TWI) on the sidewall (arrowed).

Chapter 1
Routine maintenance and servicing

Contents

Air filter – renewal	22	Evaporative emission control (EVAP) system – check	
Battery – charging	see Chapter 9	(California VTR models)	23
Battery – check	10	Front forks – oil change	38
Battery – removal, installation, inspection and		Fuel hoses – renewal	35
maintenance	see Chapter 9	Fuel system – check	9
Brake caliper and master cylinder seals – renewal	33	Headlight aim – check and adjustment	15
Brake fluid – change	24	Idle speed – check and adjustment	2
Brake hoses – renewal	34	Nuts and bolts – tightness check	19
Brake pads – wear check	3	Pulse secondary air injection (PAIR) system – check	21
Brake system – check	14	Sidestand – check	16
Carburettors – synchronisation	12	Sidestand, lever pivots and cables – lubrication	7
Clutch – check and adjustment	4	Spark plugs – gap check and adjustment	5
Clutch fluid – change (VTR models)	25	Spark plugs – renewal	6
Clutch hose – renewal (VTR models)	36	Steering head bearings – freeplay check and adjustment	18
Clutch master and release cylinder seals – renewal		Steering head bearings – re-greasing	31
(VTR models)	37	Suspension – check	17
Cooling system – check	13	Swingarm and suspension linkage bearings – re-greasing	32
Cooling system – draining, flushing and refilling	27	Throttle and choke cables – check	11
Cylinder compression – check	28	Valve clearances – check and adjustment	26
Drive chain and sprockets – check, adjustment and lubrication	1	Wheels and tyres – general check	20
Engine oil pressure – check	29	Wheel bearings – check	30
Engine/transmission oil – change and filter renewal	8		

Degrees of difficulty

Easy, suitable for novice with little experience		**Fairly easy,** suitable for beginner with some experience		**Fairly difficult,** suitable for competent DIY mechanic		**Difficult,** suitable for experienced DIY mechanic		**Very difficult,** suitable for expert DIY or professional	

Specifications

Engine
Spark plugs
  Type
    VTR models .... NGK DPR9EVX-9
    XL-X, Y, 1 and 2 models .... NGK DPR8EVX-9
    XL-3 models onward .... NGK IJR8B9
  Electrode gap .... 0.8 to 0.9 mm
Engine idle speed
  VTR-V models .... 1100 ± 100 rpm
  All other VTR models .... 1200 ± 100 rpm
  XL-X, Y, 1 and 2 models .... 1200 ± 50 rpm
  XL-3 to 6 models .... 1200 ± 100 rpm
  XL-7 models onward .... 1300 ± 100 rpm
Carburettor synchronisation – max. difference between carburettors .. 20 mm Hg
Valve clearances (COLD engine)
  Intake valves .... 0.13 to 0.19 mm
  Exhaust valves .... 0.28 to 0.34 mm
Cylinder compression
  VTR models .... 167 psi (11.5 bar) @ 350 rpm
  XL-X, Y, 1 and 2 models .... 174 psi (12.0 bar) @ 300 rpm
  XL-3 models onward .... 192 psi (13.5 bar) @ 300 rpm
Oil pressure (with engine warm) .... 87 psi (6.0 bar) @ 5000 rpm, oil @ 80°C

Specifications

Miscellaneous
Drive chain slack
   VTR models .... 30 to 40 mm
   XL models .... 35 to 45 mm
Clutch cable freeplay – XL models .... 10 to 20 mm at lever end
Throttle cable freeplay .... 2 to 6 mm
Tyre pressures (cold) .... see *Daily (pre-ride) checks*

Recommended lubricants and fluids
Engine/transmission oil type .... API grade SG, JASO MA motorcycle oil
Engine/transmission oil viscosity .... SAE 10W40
Engine/transmission oil capacity
   VTR models
      Oil change .... 3.7 litres
      Oil and filter change .... 3.9 litres
      Following engine overhaul – dry engine, new filter ..... 4.5 litres
   XL models
      Oil change .... 3.4 litres
      Oil and filter change .... 3.6 litres
      Following engine overhaul – dry engine, new filter ..... 4.1 litres
Coolant type .... 50% distilled water, 50% corrosion inhibited ethylene glycol anti-freeze
Coolant capacity
   Radiator and engine .... 2.86 litres
   Reservoir
      VTR models .... 0.7 litre
      XL models .... 0.5 litre
Brake fluid .... DOT 4
Clutch fluid – VTR models .... DOT 4
Drive chain .... SAE 80 or 90 gear oil or chain lubricant suitable for O-ring chains
Steering head bearings .... Molybdenum disulphide grease
Swingarm pivot bearings .... Molybdenum disulphide grease
Suspension linkage bearings .... Molybdenum disulphide grease
Bearing seal lips .... Molybdenum disulphide grease
Gearchange lever/clutch lever/rear brake pedal pivots .... Molybdenum disulphide grease
Front brake lever pivot and piston tip .... Molybdenum disulphide grease
Cables .... Cable lubricant
Sidestand pivot .... Molybdenum disulphide grease
Throttle grip .... Multi-purpose grease or dry film lubricant

Torque settings
Rear axle nut .... 93 Nm
Spark plugs .... 14 Nm
Engine/transmission oil drain plug .... 30 Nm
Engine/transmission oil filter
   VTR models .... 10 Nm
   XL-X, Y, 1 and 2 models .... 10 Nm
   XL-3 models onward .... 26 Nm
Steering head bearing adjuster nut .... 25 Nm
Steering stem nut .... 103 Nm
Top yoke fork clamp bolts
   VTR models .... 23 Nm
   XL models .... 22 Nm
Timing inspection cap .... 10 Nm
Crankshaft end-cap .... 15 Nm

Maintenance schedule

Note: *The daily (pre-ride) checks outlined in the owner's manual covers those items which should be inspected on a daily basis. Always perform the pre-ride inspection at every maintenance interval (in addition to the procedures listed). The intervals listed below are the intervals recommended by the manufacturer for each particular operation during the model years covered in this manual. Your owner's manual may have different intervals for your model.*

Daily (pre-ride)
- [ ] See *Daily (pre-ride) checks* at the beginning of this manual.

After the initial 600 miles (1000 km)
Note: *This check is usually performed by a Honda dealer after the first 600 miles (1000 km) from new. Thereafter, maintenance is carried out according to the following intervals of the schedule.*

Every 600 miles (1000 km)
- [ ] Check, adjust and lubricate the drive chain (Section 1)

Every 4000 miles (6000 km) or 6 months (whichever comes sooner)
- [ ] Check and adjust the idle speed (Section 2)
- [ ] Check the brake pads (Section 3)
- [ ] Check and adjust the clutch (Section 4)

Every 8000 miles (12,000 km) or 12 months (whichever comes sooner)
Carry out all the items under the 4000 mile (6000 km) check, plus the following
- [ ] Check the spark plugs – UK carburettor models (Section 5)
- [ ] Renew the spark plugs – US carburettor models (Section 6)
- [ ] Lubricate the clutch/gear change/brake lever/brake pedal/sidestand pivots and the throttle/choke/clutch cables (Section 7)
- [ ] Renew the engine oil and filter (Section 8)
- [ ] Check the fuel system and hoses (Section 9)
- [ ] Check the battery terminals (Section 10)
- [ ] Check and adjust the throttle and choke cables (Section 11)
- [ ] Check/adjust the carburettor synchronisation (Section 12)
- [ ] Check the cooling system (Section 13)
- [ ] Check the brake system and brake light switch operation (Section 14)
- [ ] Check and adjust the headlight aim (Section 15)
- [ ] Check the sidestand (Section 16)
- [ ] Check the suspension (Section 17)
- [ ] Check and adjust the steering head bearings (Section 18)
- [ ] Check the tightness of all nuts, bolts and fasteners (Section 19)
- [ ] Check the condition of the wheels and tyres (Section 20)
- [ ] Check the pulse secondary air injection (PAIR) system – US VTR models and all XL models (Section 21)

Every 12,000 miles (18,000 km) or 18 months (whichever comes first)
Carry out all the items under the 4000 mile (6000 km) check, plus the following
- [ ] Renew the air filter element (Section 22)
- [ ] Check the evaporative emission control (EVAP) system hoses – California VTR models (Section 23)

Every 12,000 miles (18,000 km) or two years (whichever comes first)
- [ ] Change the brake fluid (Section 24)
- [ ] Change the clutch fluid – VTR models (Section 25)

Every 16,000 miles (24,000 km) or two years (whichever comes sooner)
Carry out all the items under the 8000 mile (12,000 km) check, plus the following
- [ ] Check and adjust the valve clearances (Section 26)
- [ ] Renew the spark plugs – UK carburettor models (Section 6)
- [ ] Check the spark plugs – fuel injection models (Section 5)

Every 24,000 miles (36,000 km) or two years (whichever comes sooner)
Carry out all the items under the 8000 mile (12,000 km) and 12,000 mile (18,000 km) checks, plus the following:
- [ ] Change the coolant (Section 27)

Every 32,000 miles (48,000 Km)
- [ ] Renew the spark plugs – fuel injection models (Section 6)

Non-scheduled maintenance
- [ ] Check the cylinder compression (Section 28)
- [ ] Check the engine oil pressure (Section 29)
- [ ] Check the wheel bearings (Section 30)
- [ ] Re-grease the steering head bearings (Section 31)
- [ ] Re-grease the swingarm and suspension linkage bearings (Section 32)
- [ ] Renew the brake master cylinder and caliper seals (Section 33)
- [ ] Renew the brake hoses (Section 34)
- [ ] Renew the fuel hoses (Section 35)
- [ ] Renew the clutch hose – VTR models (Section 36)
- [ ] Renew the clutch master and slave cylinder seals – VTR models (Section 37)
- [ ] Change the front fork oil (Section 38)

1•4 Component locations

VTR1000F left-hand view

1. Clutch fluid reservoir
2. Steering head bearing adjuster
3. Clutch release cylinder
4. Battery
5. Oil drain bolt
6. Crankshaft end cap
7. Timing inspection cap

VTR1000F right-hand view

1. Rear brake fluid reservoir
2. Idle speed adjuster
3. Air filter
4. Front brake fluid reservoir
5. Radiator pressure cap
6. Engine oil filter
7. Coolant reservoir
8. Engine oil level window
9. Engine oil filler

Component locations 1•5

XL1000V left-hand view

1. Clutch cable upper adjuster
2. Steering head bearing adjuster
3. Clutch cable lower adjuster
4. Battery
5. Engine oil drain bolt
6. Crankshaft end cap
7. Timing inspection cap
8. Fuel filter
9. Secondary master cylinder (D-CBS)

XL1000V right-hand view

1. Rear brake fluid reservoir
2. Idle speed adjuster
3. Coolant reservoir
4. Air filter
5. Front brake fluid reservoir
6. Radiator pressure cap
7. Engine oil filter
8. Engine oil level window
9. Engine oil filler

1•6 Introduction

1 This Chapter is designed to help the home mechanic maintain the motorcycle for safety, economy, long life and peak performance.
2 Deciding where to start or plug into the routine maintenance schedule depends on several factors. If your motorcycle has been maintained according to the warranty standards, you may want to pick up routine maintenance as it coincides with the next mileage or calendar interval. If you have owned the machine for some time but have never performed any maintenance on it, then you may want to start at the nearest interval and include some additional procedures to ensure that nothing important is overlooked. If you have just had a major engine overhaul, then you may want to start the maintenance routine from the beginning. If you have a used machine and have no knowledge of its history or maintenance record, you may desire to combine all the checks into one large service initially and then settle into the maintenance schedule prescribed.
3 Before beginning any maintenance or repair, the machine should be cleaned thoroughly, especially around the oil filter, spark plugs, valve covers, body panels, carburettors, etc. Cleaning will help ensure that dirt does not contaminate the engine and will allow you to detect wear and damage that could otherwise easily go unnoticed.
4 Certain maintenance information is sometimes printed on decals attached to the motorcycle. If the information on the decals differs from that included here, use the information on the decal.

Every 600 miles (1000 km)

1 Drive chain and sprockets – check, adjustment and lubrication

Check

1 A neglected drive chain won't last long and can quickly damage the sprockets. Routine chain adjustment and lubrication isn't difficult and will ensure maximum chain and sprocket life.
2 To check the chain, place the bike on its sidestand and shift the transmission into neutral. Make sure the ignition switch is OFF.
3 Push up on the bottom run of the chain and measure the slack midway between the two sprockets, then compare your measurement to that listed in this Chapter's Specifications **(see illustration)**. As the chain stretches with wear, adjustment will periodically be necessary (see below). Since the chain will rarely wear evenly, roll the bike forwards so that another section of chain can be checked; do this several times to check the entire length of chain.
4 In some cases where lubrication has been neglected, corrosion and galling may cause the links to bind and kink, which effectively shortens the chain's length. Such links should be thoroughly cleaned and worked free. If the chain is tight between the sprockets, rusty or kinked, it's time to replace it with a new one. If you find a tight area, mark it with felt pen or paint, and repeat the measurement after the bike has been ridden. If the chain's still tight in the same area, it may be damaged or worn. Because a tight or kinked chain can damage the transmission bearings, it's a good idea to replace it with a new one.
5 Check the entire length of the chain for damaged rollers, loose links and pins, and missing O-rings and replace it with a new one if damage is found. **Note:** *Never install a new chain on old sprockets, and never use the old chain if you install new sprockets – replace the chain and sprockets as a set.*
6 Remove the front sprocket cover (see Chapter 6, Section 16). Check the teeth on the front sprocket and the rear sprocket for wear **(see illustration)**.
7 Inspect the drive chain slider on the swingarm for excessive wear and damage. There are wear limit lines marked on the front of the slider. Replace it with a new one if necessary (see Chapter 6, Section 13).

Adjustment

8 Rotate the rear wheel until the chain is positioned with the tightest point at the centre of its bottom run, then place the machine on its sidestand.
9 Slacken the axle nut **(see illustration)**.
10 Turn the adjuster on each side of the swingarm evenly until the amount of freeplay specified at the beginning of the Chapter is obtained at the centre of the bottom run of the chain **(see illustration)**. Following adjustment, check that each chain adjustment marker is in the same position in relation to the mark on the swingarm. It is important the index line on the swingarm aligns with the same notch on each adjuster; if not, the rear wheel will be out of alignment with the front.
11 If there is a discrepancy in the chain adjuster positions, adjust one of them so that its position is exactly the same as the other. Check the chain freeplay as described above and readjust if necessary.
12 Also check the alignment of the wear decal on the left-hand adjustment marker with the index line on the swingarm **(see**

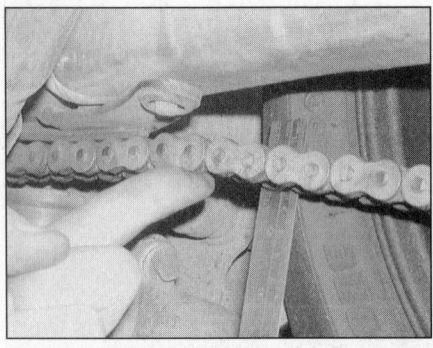

1.3 Push up on the chain and measure the slack

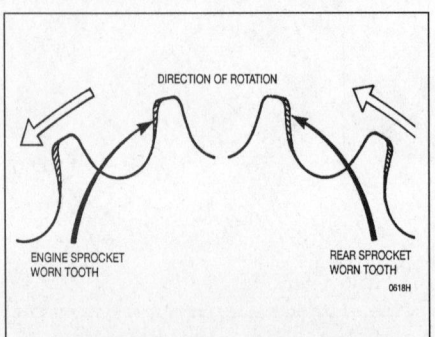

1.6 Check the sprockets in the areas indicated to see if they are worn excessively

1.9 Slacken the axle nut (arrowed)

1.10 Turn each adjuster by an equal amount then check the alignment marks as described

Every 600 miles

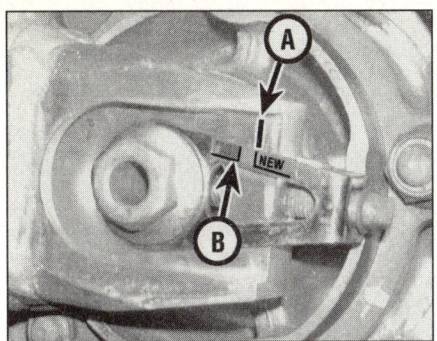

1.12 When the index line (A) meets the red zone (B), replace the chain with a new one

1.13 Tighten the axle nut to the specified torque

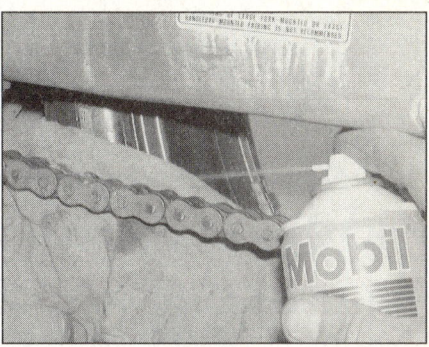

1.15 Apply the lubricant to the overlap in the sideplates

illustration). When the index line meets the red REPLACE CHAIN zone, the drive chain has stretched excessively and must be replaced with a new one.

13 Counter-hold the axle head and tighten the axle nut to the torque setting specified at the beginning of the Chapter (see illustration). Recheck the adjustment, and spin the wheel to make sure it runs freely.

Lubrication

14 If required, wash the chain in paraffin (kerosene), then wipe it off and allow it to dry, using compressed air if available. If the chain is excessively dirty it should be removed from the machine and allowed to soak in the paraffin (see Chapter 6).
Caution: Don't use petrol (gasoline), solvent or other cleaning fluids which might damage the internal sealing properties of the chain. Don't use high-pressure water to clean the chain. The entire process shouldn't take longer than ten minutes, otherwise the O-rings could be damaged.
15 For routine lubrication, the best time to lubricate the chain is after the motorcycle has been ridden. When the chain is warm, the lubricant will penetrate the joints between the sideplates better than when cold. **Note:** *Honda specifies SAE 80 to SAE 90 gear oil or* an aerosol chain lube that it is suitable for O-ring or X-ring (sealed) chains; do not use any other chain lubricants – the solvents could damage the chain's sealing rings. Apply the oil to the area where the sideplates overlap – not the middle of the rollers (see illustration).

> **HAYNES HiNT** *Apply the lubricant to the top of the lower chain run, so centrifugal force will work the oil into the chain when the bike is moving. After applying the lubricant, let it soak in a few minutes before wiping off any excess.*

Every 4000 miles (6000 km) or 6 months

2 Idle speed – check and adjustment

All VTR models and XL-X to XL-6 models

1 The idle speed should be checked and adjusted before and after the carburettors or starter valves (according to model) are synchronised (balanced) and when it is obviously too high or too low. Before adjusting the idle speed, check throttle cable freeplay, the spark plugs, the air filter and the valve clearances. Also, turn the handlebars back-and-forth and see if the idle speed changes as this is done. If it does, the throttle cables may not be adjusted or routed correctly, or may be worn out. This is a dangerous condition that can cause loss of control of the bike. Be sure to correct this problem before proceeding.

2 The engine should be at normal operating temperature, which is usually reached after 10 to 15 minutes of stop-and-go riding. Place the motorcycle on its sidestand, and make sure the transmission is in neutral.

3 The idle speed adjuster is located on the right-hand side (see illustrations). With the

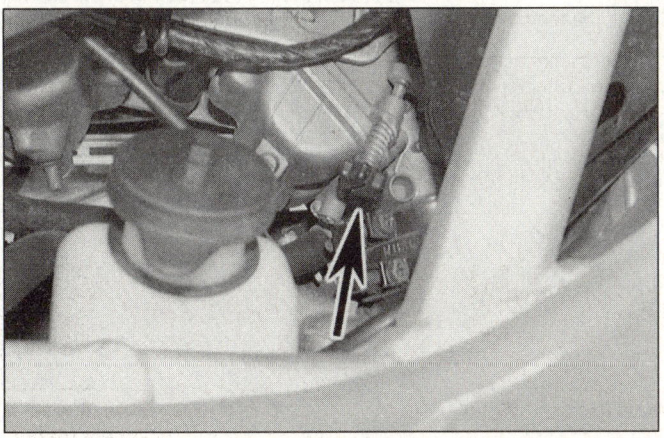

2.3a Idle speed adjuster (arrowed) – VTR models

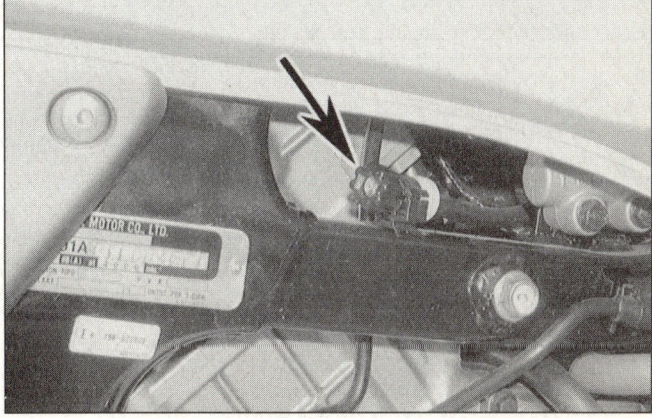

2.3b Idle speed adjuster (arrowed) – XL models

1•8 Every 4000 miles

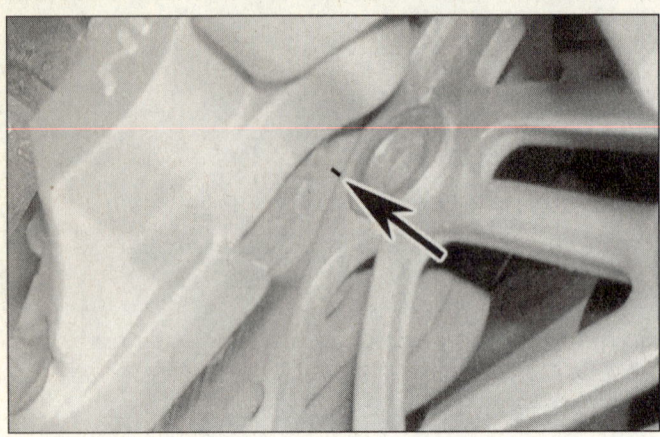

3.1a Front brake pad wear indicator (arrowed) – VTR models

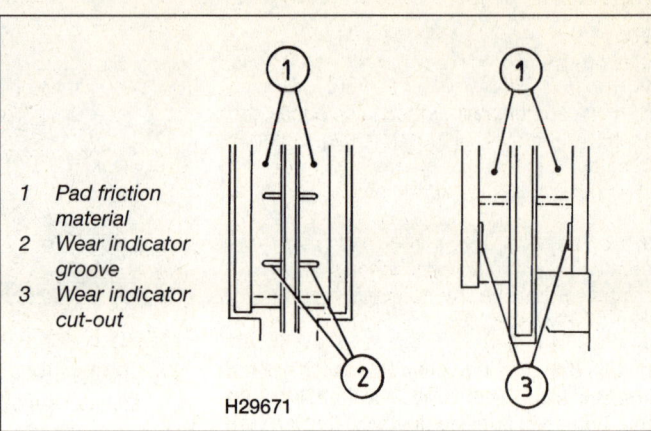

1 Pad friction material
2 Wear indicator groove
3 Wear indicator cut-out

3.1b Brake pad wear indicators

engine idling, adjust the idle speed by turning the adjuster screw until the idle speed listed in this Chapter's Specifications is obtained. Turn the screw clockwise to increase idle speed, and anti-clockwise to decrease it.
4 Snap the throttle open and shut a few times, then recheck the idle speed. If necessary, repeat the adjustment procedure.
5 If a smooth, steady idle can't be achieved, on carburettor models the fuel/air mixture may be incorrect (see Chapter 4A) or the carburettors may need synchronising (see Section 12). On models with fuel injection check the starter valves and fast idle cable (see Chapter 4B). On all models also check the intake manifold rubbers for cracks or a loose clamp which will cause an air leak, resulting in a weak mixture.

XL-7 models onward

6 The idle speed is set automatically by the ECU which controls the intake air control valve (IACV) on the rear throttle body. The idle speed should be checked with the engine warm, and after checking throttle cable freeplay, the spark plugs, the air filter and the valve clearances. Also, turn the handlebars back-and-forth and see if the idle speed changes as this is done. If it does, the throttle cables may not be adjusted or routed correctly, or may be worn out. This is a dangerous condition that can cause loss of control of the bike. Be sure to correct this problem before proceeding.
7 The engine should be at normal operating temperature, which is usually reached after 10 to 15 minutes of stop-and-go riding. Place the motorcycle on its sidestand, and make sure the transmission is in neutral.
8 Start the engine and allow it idle, then check the speed is as specified at the beginning of the Chapter. If the correct, smooth and steady idle can't be achieved check the intake manifold rubbers for cracks or a loose clamp which will cause an air leak, resulting in a weak mixture. If they are good, check the intake air control valve (see Chapter 4B).
9 Pull the clutch in and select a gear – the idle speed should increase by 100 rpm. Reselect neutral – the idle speed should drop by 100

rpm. If not, check the neutral switch and its diode (see Chapter 9). If they are good, check the intake air control valve (see Chapter 4B).

3 Brake pads – wear check

1 Each brake pad has wear indicators in the form of cut-outs or grooves in the friction material **(see illustrations)**. The wear indicators should be plainly visible by looking at the edges of the friction material from the best vantage point, although an accumulation of road dirt and brake dust could make them difficult to see. If the indicators aren't visible, then the amount of friction material remaining should be, and it will be obvious when the pads need replacing. Honda do not specify a minimum thickness for the friction material, but anything less than 1 mm should be considered worn. **Note:** *Some after-market pads may use different indicators to those on the original equipment.*
2 If the pads are worn to or beyond the wear indicator (i.e. the bottom of the groove or the beginning of the cut-out) or there is little friction material remaining, they must be replaced with new ones, though it is advisable to replace the pads before they become this worn. If the pads are dirty or if you are in doubt as to the amount of friction material remaining, remove them for inspection (see Chapter 7). If the pads are excessively worn, check the brake discs (see Chapter 7).
3 Refer to Chapter 7 for details of pad replacement.

4 Clutch – check and adjustment

VTR models

1 All models are fitted with an hydraulic clutch, for which there is no method of adjustment.

2 Check the fluid level in the reservoir (see *Daily (pre-ride) checks*).
3 Inspect the hose and its connections for signs of fluid leakage, cracking, deterioration and wear. The clutch fluid should be changed every two years (see Section 25), and the hose replaced with a new one either if damaged or deteriorated, or every few years irrespective of condition (see Section 36). The master and slave cylinder seals should be changed every two years, or if leakage from them is evident (see Section 37).
4 Check the operation of the clutch. If there is evidence of air in the system (spongy feel to the lever), bleed the clutch (see Chapter 2, Section 17). If the lever feels stiff or sticky, overhaul the release mechanism (see Chapter 2).
5 The clutch lever has a span adjuster which alters the distance of the lever from the handlebar. Each setting is identified by a notch in the adjuster which aligns with the arrow on the lever bracket. Turn the adjuster ring until the setting which best suits the rider is obtained **(see illustration)**.

XL models

6 Check that the clutch cable operates smoothly and easily.
7 If the clutch lever operation is heavy or stiff, remove the cable (see Chapter 2, Section 17) and lubricate it (see Section 7). If the cable is still stiff, replace it with a new one. Install the lubricated or new cable (see Chapter 2).

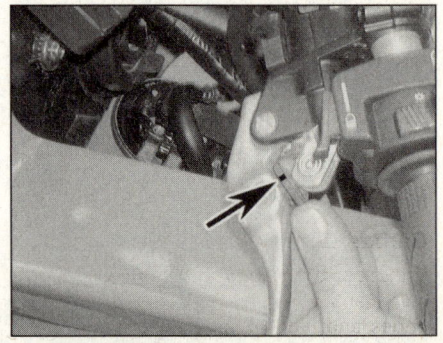

4.5 Adjusting the clutch lever span

Routine maintenance and servicing

8 With the cable operating smoothly, check that the clutch lever is correctly adjusted. Periodic adjustment is necessary to compensate for wear in the clutch plates and stretch of the cable. Check that the amount of freeplay at the clutch lever end is within the specifications listed at the beginning of the Chapter.

9 If adjustment is required, pull the rubber boot back off the adjuster at the lever end of the cable. Loosen the adjuster lockring and turn the adjuster in or out until the required amount of freeplay is obtained **(see illustration)**. To increase freeplay, turn the adjuster clockwise. To reduce freeplay, turn the adjuster anti-clockwise. Tighten the lockring securely.

10 If all the adjustment has been taken up at the lever, reset the adjuster to give the maximum amount of freeplay, then set the correct amount of freeplay using the adjuster on the clutch end of cable. The adjuster is set

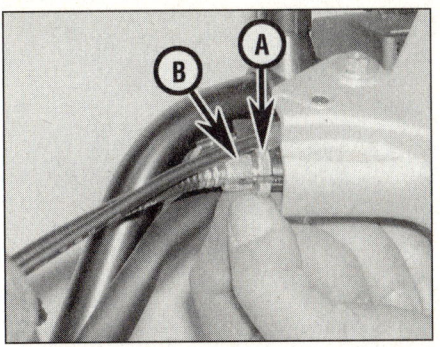

4.9 Slacken the lockring (A) and turn the adjuster (B) in or out as required

in a bracket on the alternator cover on the left-hand side of the engine. Use the nuts on each end of the threaded section in the cable to adjust freeplay **(see illustration)**. To increase freeplay, slacken the front nut and tighten the rear nut until the freeplay is as

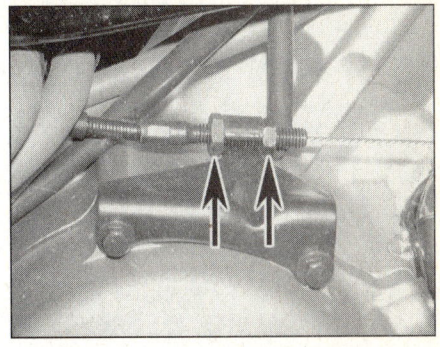

4.10 Clutch cable lower adjuster nuts (arrowed)

specified, then tighten the front nut. To reduce freeplay, slacken the rear nut and tighten the front nut until the freeplay is as specified, then tighten the rear nut. Subsequent adjustments can now be made using the lever adjuster only.

Every 8000 miles (12,000 km) or 12 months

Carry out all the items under the 4000 mile (6000 km) check, plus the following:

5 Spark plugs – gap check and adjustment

Removal

1 Make sure your spark plug socket is the correct size before attempting to remove the plugs – a suitable one is supplied in the motorcycle's tool kit which is stored under the seat.

2 To access the rear cylinder spark plug, raise the rear of the fuel tank (see Chapter 4A).

3 Clean the area around the plug caps to prevent any dirt falling into the spark plug channels.

4 Check that the cylinder location is marked on each plug lead, then pull the spark plug cap off each spark plug **(see illustrations)**. Clean the area around the base of the plugs to prevent any dirt falling into the engine. Using either the plug removing tool supplied in the bike's toolkit or a deep socket type wrench, unscrew the plugs from the cylinder head **(see illustrations)**. Lay each plug out in relation to its cylinder; if any plug shows up a problem it will then be easy to identify the troublesome cylinder.

Inspection

Carburettor models

5 Inspect the electrodes for wear. Both the centre and side electrodes should have square edges and the side electrodes should be of uniform thickness. Look for excessive deposits and evidence of a cracked or chipped insulator around the centre electrode. Compare your spark plugs to the colour spark plug reading chart at the end of this manual. Check the threads, the washer and the ceramic insulator body for cracks and other damage.

6 If the electrodes are not excessively worn, if no cracks or chips are visible in the insulator,

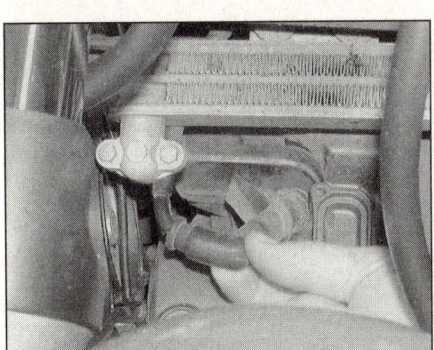

5.4a Removing the front cylinder spark plug cap

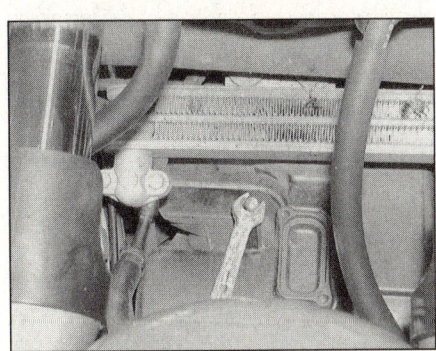

5.4c Unscrew the spark plug using the tool provided in the kit or a suitable alternative . . .

and if the deposits can be easily removed with a wire brush, the plugs can be re-gapped and re-used. If in doubt concerning the condition of the plugs, replace them with new ones, as the expense is minimal.

7 Cleaning spark plugs by sandblasting is

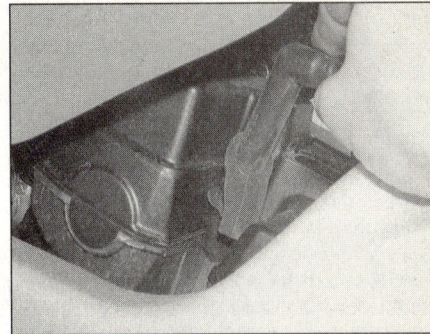

5.4b Removing the rear cylinder spark plug cap

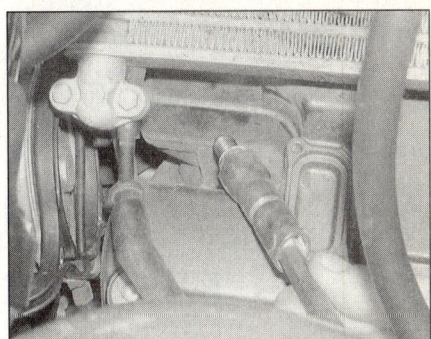

5.4d . . . and remove it from the cylinder

1•10 Routine maintenance and servicing

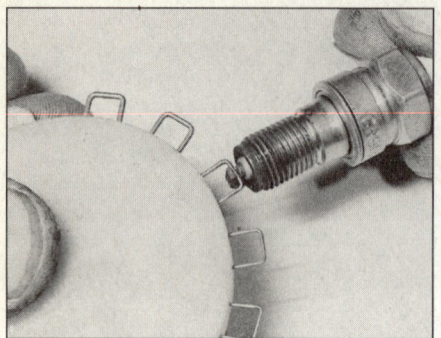

5.8a Using a wire type gauge to measure the spark plug electrode gap

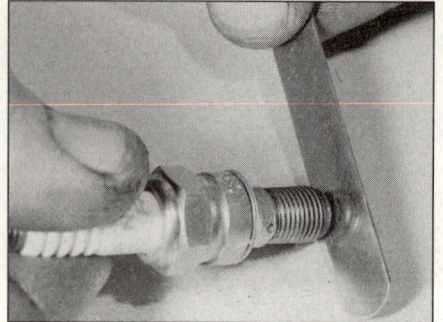

5.8b Using a feeler gauge to measure the spark plug electrode gap

5.8c Adjust the electrode gap by bending the side electrode only

permitted, provided you clean the plugs with a high flash-point solvent afterwards.

8 Before installing the plugs, make sure they are the correct type and heat range and check the gap between the electrodes **(see illustrations)**. Compare the gap to that specified; if the gap must be adjusted, bend the side electrodes only and be very careful not to chip or crack the insulator nose **(see illustration)**. Make sure the washer is in place before installing each plug.

Fuel injection models

Note: *Fuel injection models are equipped with plugs that have an iridium coated centre electrode. The plugs must be treated differently to conventional plugs.*

9 Check the condition of the electrodes, referring to the spark plug reading chart at the end of this manual if signs of contamination are evident. Note that contaminated iridium plugs should not be cleaned – discard them and install new ones.

10 Examine the pointed iridium-tipped centre electrode; if the tip has rounded off, the plug is worn **(see illustration)**. Measure the gap between the two electrodes with a wire type gauge only **(see illustration)** – do not use blade type feeler gauges because the iridium tip might be damaged. The gap should be as given in the Specifications at the beginning of this chapter; if the electrodes have worn and the gap is wider than it should be, or for some reason the gap is narrower than it should be a new plug must be installed. Do not bend the outer electrode to adjust the gap.

Installation

11 Since the cylinder head is made of aluminium, which is soft and easily damaged, thread the plugs into the heads turning the tool by hand **(see illustration)**. Once the plugs are finger-tight, the job can be finished with a spanner on the tool supplied or a socket drive **(see illustration 5.4c)**. If a torque wrench can be applied, tighten the spark plugs to the torque setting specified at the beginning of the Chapter. Otherwise tighten them according the instructions on the box, or by 1/4 to 1/2 turn after they have been fully hand tightened and have seated. Do not over-tighten them.

 **HAYNES HiNT** *As the plugs are quite recessed, slip a short length of hose over the end of the plug to use as a tool to thread it into place. The hose will grip the plug well enough to turn it, but will start to slip if the plug begins to cross-thread in the hole – this will prevent damaged threads.*

12 Reconnect the spark plug caps, making sure they are securely connected to the correct cylinder. Install all other components previously removed.

 **HAYNES HiNT** *Stripped plug threads in the cylinder head can be repaired with a Heli-Coil insert – see Tools and Workshop Tips in the Reference section.*

6 Spark plugs – renewal

1 Remove the old spark plugs as described in Section 5 and install new ones, ensuring the gaps are correctly set.

7 Sidestand, lever pivots and cables – lubrication

1 Since the controls, cables and various other components of a motorcycle are exposed to the elements, they should be lubricated periodically to ensure safe and trouble-free operation.

2 The footrests, clutch and brake levers, brake pedal, gearchange lever and linkage, and sidestand pivot should be lubricated frequently. In order for the lubricant to be applied where it will do the most good, the component should

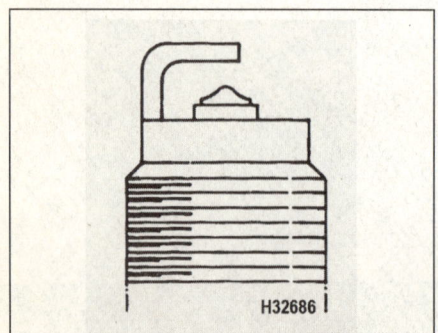

5.10a The iridium tip should be sharply pointed, not rounded as shown

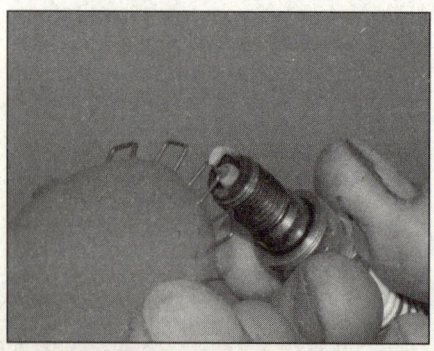

5.10b Measure the gap using a wire gauge only

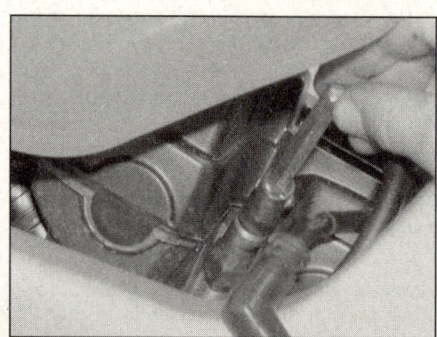

5.11 Thread the plug as far as possible turning the tool by hand

Routine maintenance and servicing

be disassembled. However, if chain and cable lubricant is being used, it can be applied to the pivot joint gaps and will usually work its way into the areas where friction occurs. If motor oil or light grease is being used, apply it sparingly as it may attract dirt (which could cause the controls to bind or wear at an accelerated rate). **Note:** *One of the best lubricants for the control lever pivots is a dry-film lubricant (available from many sources by different names).*

3 To lubricate the cables, disconnect the relevant cable at its upper end, then lubricate the cable with a pressure adapter and aerosol lubricant, or if one is not available, using the set-up shown **(see illustrations)**. See Chapter 2 for the clutch cable, Chapter 4A for the choke cable on carburettor models and for the throttle cables on all models, and Chapter 4B for the fast idle cable on XL-3 to 6 models.

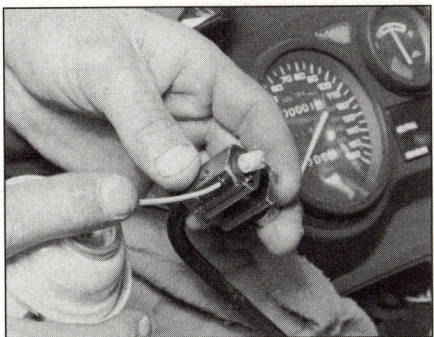

7.3a Lubricating a cable with a pressure lubricator. Make sure the tool seals around the inner cable

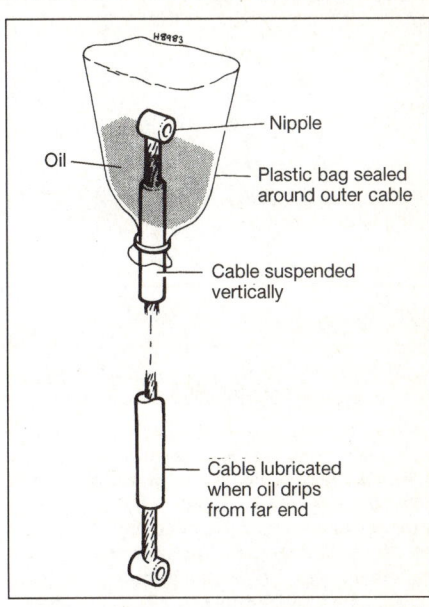

7.3b Lubricating a cable with a makeshift funnel and motor oil

8 Engine/transmission oil – change and filter renewal

> **Warning:** *Be careful when draining the oil, as the exhaust pipes, the engine, and the oil itself can cause severe burns.*

1 Consistent routine oil and filter changes are the single most important maintenance procedure you can perform on a motorcycle. The oil not only lubricates the internal parts of the engine, transmission and clutch, but it also acts as a coolant, a cleaner, a sealant, and a protectant. Because of these demands, the oil takes a terrific amount of abuse and should be replaced often with new oil of the recommended grade and type. The oil filter should be changed with every oil change.

2 Before changing the oil, warm up the engine so the oil will drain easily. Remove the belly-pan (see Chapter 8).

3 Put the motorcycle on its sidestand, and position a clean drain tray below the engine. Unscrew the oil filler cap from the clutch cover to vent the crankcase and to act as a reminder that there is no oil in the engine **(see illustration)**.

4 Next, unscrew the oil drain plug from the rear of the left-hand side of the engine and allow the oil to flow into the drain tray **(see illustrations)**. Check the condition of the sealing washer on the drain plug and replace it with a new one if damaged or worn – it is advisable to use a new one whatever the condition of the old one.

5 When the oil has completely drained, fit the plug to the sump, using a new sealing washer if necessary, and tighten it to the torque setting specified at the beginning of the Chapter **(see illustrations)**. Avoid overtightening, as damage to the sump will result.

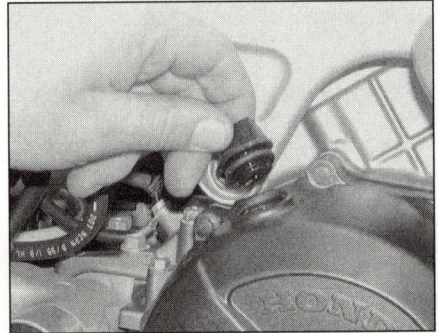

8.3 Unscrew the oil filler cap . . .

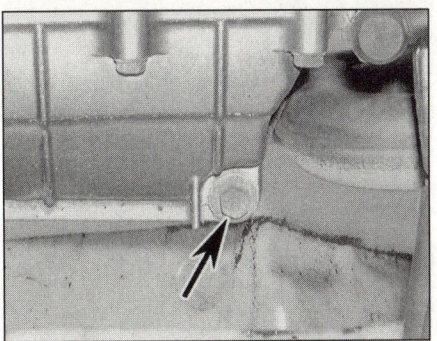

8.4a . . . and the oil drain plug (arrowed) . . .

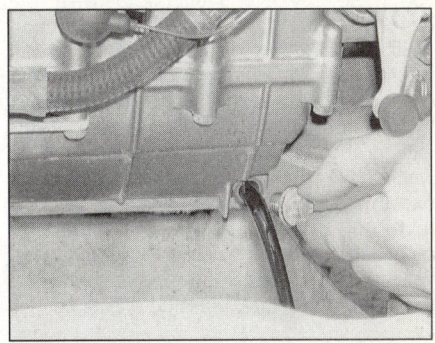

8.4b . . . and allow the oil to completely drain

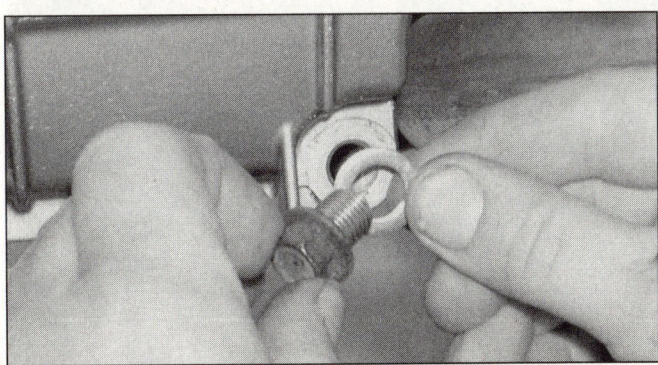

8.5a Install the drain plug, using a new sealing washer if necessary . . .

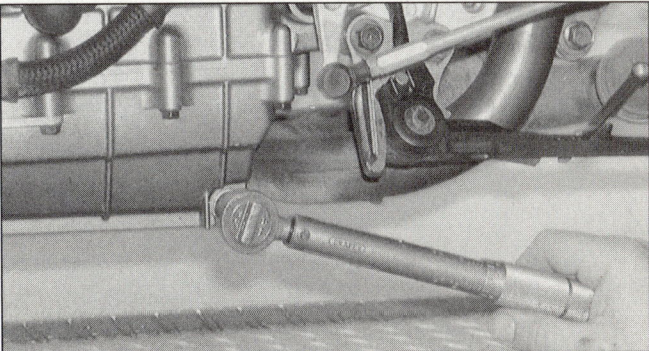

8.5b . . . and tighten it to the specified torque setting

1•12 Every 8000 miles

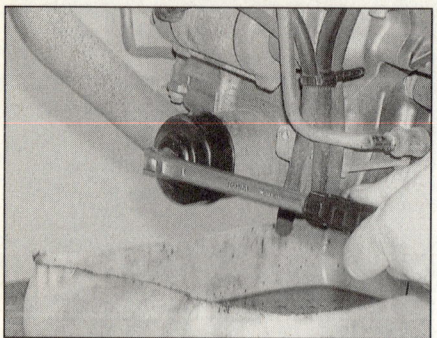

8.6a Unscrew the filter using a filter removing tool . . .

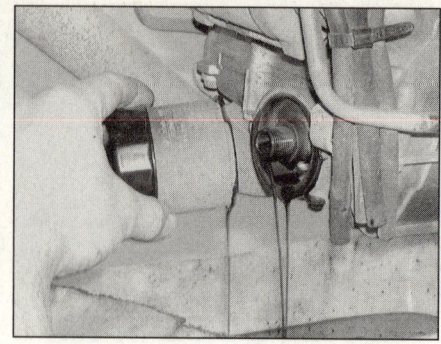

8.6b . . . and allow the oil to drain

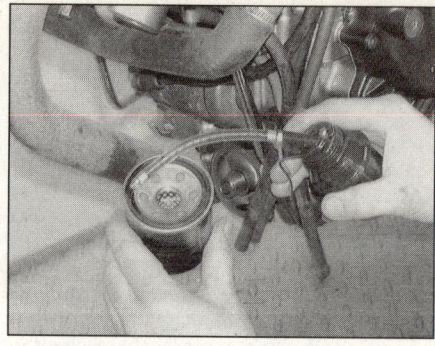

8.7a Smear clean oil onto the seal . . .

6 Now place the drain tray below the oil filter. Unscrew the oil filter using a filter removing strap- or chain-wrench and tip any residual oil into the drain tray **(see illustrations)**.

7 Smear clean engine oil onto the rubber seal on the new filter and thread it onto the engine **(see illustrations)**. Tighten it to the specified torque setting using a filter wrench, or if one is not available, tighten the filter as tight as possible by hand, or by the number of turns specified on the filter or its packaging **(see illustration)**. **Note:** *Do not use a strap or chain filter removing tool to tighten the filter as you will damage it.*

8 Refill the engine to the proper level using the recommended type and amount of oil (see *Daily (pre-ride) checks*). With the motorcycle vertical, the oil level should lie between the upper and lower level lines on the inspection window (see *Daily (pre-ride) checks*). Install the filler cap **(see illustration 8.3)**. Start the engine and let it run for two or three minutes (make sure that the oil pressure light extinguishes after a few seconds). Shut it off, wait a few minutes, then check the oil level. If necessary, add more oil to bring the level up to the upper level line. Check around the drain plug and the oil filter for leaks. Install the belly-pan (see Chapter 8).

9 The old oil drained from the engine cannot be re-used and should be disposed of properly. Check with your local refuse disposal company, disposal facility or environmental agency to see whether they will accept the used oil for recycling. Don't pour used oil into drains or onto the ground.

> **HAYNES HINT** *Saving a little money on the difference between good and cheap oils won't pay off if the engine is damaged as a result.*

> **HAYNES HINT** *Check the old oil carefully – if it is very metallic-coloured, then the engine is experiencing wear from running-in (new engine) or from insufficient lubrication. If there are flakes or chips of metal in the oil, then something is drastically wrong internally and the engine will have to be disassembled for inspection and repair. If there are pieces of fibre-like material in the oil, the clutch is experiencing excessive wear and should be checked.*

9 Fuel system – check

⚠️ **Warning:** *Petrol (gasoline) is extremely flammable, so take extra precautions when you work on any part of the fuel system. Don't smoke or allow open flames or bare light bulbs near the work area, and don't work in a garage where a natural gas-type appliance is present. If you spill any fuel on your skin, rinse it off immediately with soap and water. When you perform any kind of work on the fuel system, wear safety glasses and have a fire extinguisher suitable for a Class B type fire (flammable liquids) on hand.*

Check

1 Remove the fuel tank (see Chapter 4A) and check the tank, the fuel tap(s) and the fuel hoses for signs of leakage, deterioration or damage; in particular check that there is no leakage from the fuel hoses. On VTR models, also check the vacuum hose. Replace any hoses which are cracked or deteriorated with new ones.

2 If the fuel tap is leaking, tighten the

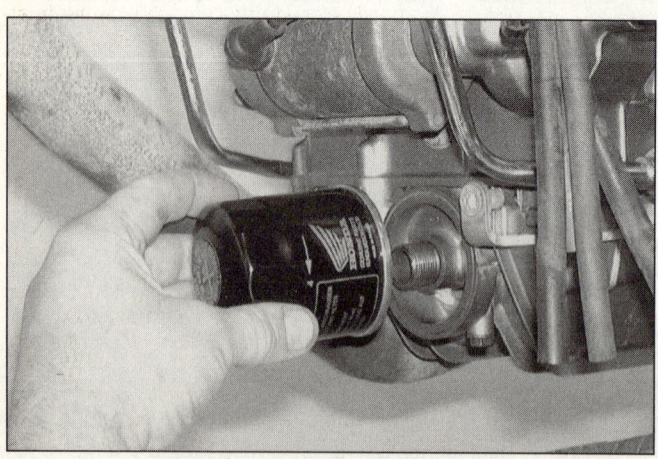

8.7b . . . then install the filter . . .

8.7c . . . and tighten it as described

Every 8000 miles 1•13

9.4a Check the hoses (arrowed) to and from the pump

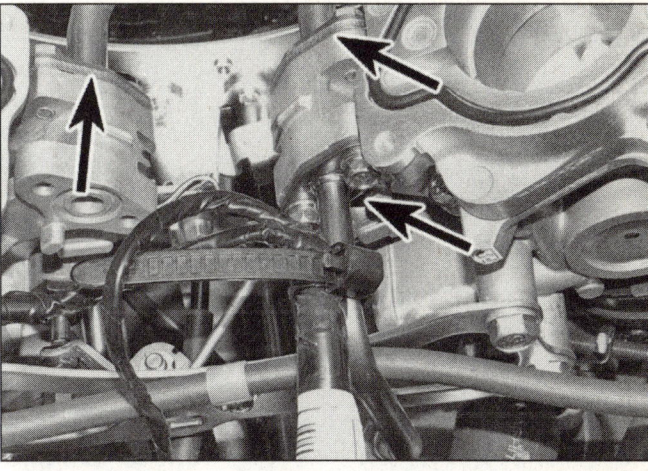

9.4b On XL-3 to 6 models check the delivery pipe and fuel rail joints (arrowed)

assembly screws (see Chapter 4A). If leakage persists undo the screws and disassemble the tap, noting how the components fit. Inspect and clean all components and rebuild the tap. If leakage persists, replace the whole tap with a new one – individual components are not available.

3 If carburettor gaskets are leaking, the carburettors should be disassembled and rebuilt using new gaskets and seals (see Chapter 4A).

4 On models with fuel injection check the hose connections to the fuel pump on the front of the engine for leakage, and also check the connection to the throttle bodies **(see illustrations)**.

Filter cleaning

5 Cleaning or replacement of the fuel filter(s) is advised after a particularly high mileage has been covered. It is also necessary if fuel starvation is suspected, or if the filter looks clogged or dirty. Honda do not specify a replacement interval – fuel is so clean now that this may not always be necessary. Check the condition of the inside of your tank – if it is old and there is evidence of rust, remove, drain and clean the tank and tap (see Chapter 4A), and fit a new filter afterwards.

6 A fuel filter is mounted in the tank and is integral with the fuel tap(s). Remove the fuel tank and the fuel tap (see Chapter 4A). Clean the gauze filter to remove all traces of dirt and fuel sediment. Check the gauze for holes. If any are found, a new filter should be fitted. Check the condition of the O-ring and replace it with a new one if it is in any way damaged or deteriorated.

7 On XL models, an in-line fuel filter is fitted in the hose from the fuel tap to the fuel pump. To replace the filter, remove the belly-pan (see Chapter 8, Section 4). Have a rag handy to soak up any residual fuel, then release the clamps and disconnect the hoses from the filter, noting which fits where **(see illustration)**.

9.4c On XL-7 models onward check the supply and distribution hoses (arrowed)

Release the filter from its holder and discard it. Install the new filter so that its arrow points in the direction of fuel flow (i.e. towards the pump). Fit the hoses to the unions on the filter and secure them with the clamps. The hose from the fuel tap goes on the inlet end, and the hose to the pump goes on the outlet (lipped) end. Install the fuel tank (see Chapter 4A). Start the engine and check that there are no leaks.

10 Battery – check

1 All models covered in this manual are fitted with a sealed battery, and therefore require no maintenance. **Note:** *Do not attempt to remove the battery caps to check the electrolyte level or battery specific gravity. Removal will damage the caps, resulting in electrolyte leakage and battery damage.* All that should be done is to check that its terminals are clean and tight and that the casing is not damaged or leaking. See Chapter 9 for further details.

2 If the machine is not in regular use, disconnect the battery and give it a refresher

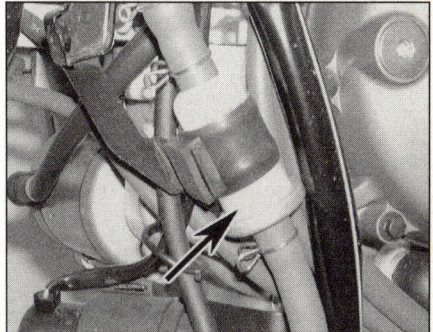

9.7 Fuel filter (arrowed) – XL-X, Y, 1 and 2 models

charge every month to six weeks, as described in Chapter 9.

11 Throttle and choke cables – check

Throttle cables

1 Make sure the throttle grip rotates easily from fully closed to fully open with the front wheel turned at various angles. The grip should return automatically from fully open to fully closed when released.

2 If the throttle sticks, this is probably due to a cable fault. Remove the cables (see Chapter 4A) and lubricate them (see Section 7). Install the cables, making sure they are correctly routed. If this fails to improve the operation of the throttle, the cables must be replaced with new ones. Note that in very rare cases the fault could lie in the carburettors or throttle bodies rather than the cables, necessitating their removal for inspection of the throttle linkage (see Chapter 4A).

3 With the throttle operating smoothly, check for a small amount of freeplay in the cables, measured in terms of the amount of twistgrip rotation before the throttle

1•14 Every 8000 miles

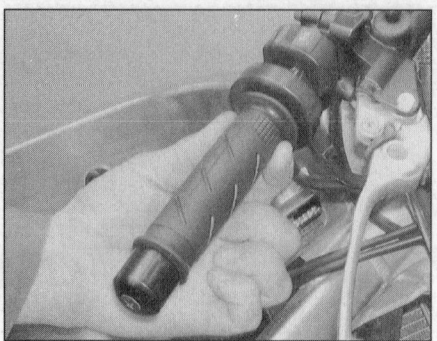

11.3 Throttle cable freeplay is measured in terms of twistgrip rotation

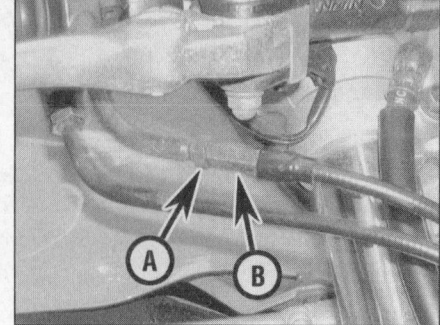

11.4 Throttle cable adjuster locknut (A) and adjuster (B) - throttle end

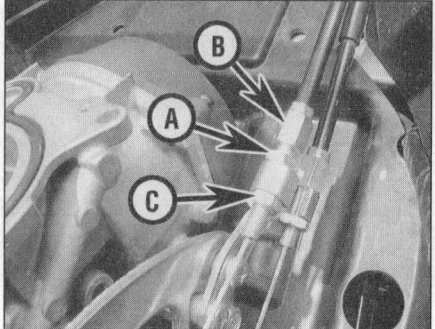

11.5 Throttle cable adjuster locknut (A), adjuster (B) and lower nut (C) - carburettor end

opens, and compare the amount to that listed in this Chapter's Specifications (see illustration). If it's incorrect, adjust the cables to correct it.

4 Freeplay adjustments can be made at the throttle end of the cable. Loosen the locknut on the accelerator cable where it leaves the handlebar (see illustration). Turn the adjuster until the specified amount of freeplay is obtained (see this Chapter's Specifications), then retighten the locknut.

5 If the adjuster has reached its limit of adjustment, reset it so that the freeplay is at a maximum, then remove the fuel tank and air filter housing (see Chapter 4A or B) and adjust the cable at the carburettor or throttle body end. The adjuster is on the upper cable in the bracket. Slacken the adjuster locknut, then screw the adjuster in or out as required, making sure the lower nut remains captive in the bracket, then tighten the locknut. Further adjustments can now be made at the throttle end. If the cable cannot be adjusted correctly, replace it with a new one (see Chapter 4A).

⚠ **Warning: Turn the handlebars all the way through their travel with the engine idling. Idle speed should not change. If it does, the cables may be routed incorrectly. Correct this condition before riding the bike.**

6 Check that the throttle twistgrip operates smoothly and snaps shut quickly when released.

Choke/fast idle cable

7 If the mechanism does not operate smoothly this is probably due to a cable fault. Remove the cable (see Chapter 4A or B) and lubricate it (see Section 7). Install the cable, routing it so it takes the smoothest route possible.

8 If this fails to improve the operation of the mechanism, the cable must be replaced with a new one. Note that in very rare cases the fault could lie in the carburettors or throttle bodies rather than the cable, necessitating their removal for inspection of the choke plungers or starter valves (see Chapter 4A or B).

12 Carburettors – synchronisation

⚠ **Warning: Petrol (gasoline) is extremely flammable, so take extra precautions when you work on any part of the fuel system. Don't smoke or allow open flames or bare light bulbs near the work area, and don't work in a garage where a natural gas-type appliance is present. If you spill any fuel on your skin, rinse it off immediately with soap and water. When you perform any kind of work on the fuel system, wear safety glasses and have a fire extinguisher suitable for a Class B type fire (flammable liquids) on hand.**

⚠ **Warning: Take great care not to burn your hand on the hot engine unit when accessing the gauge take-off points on the intake manifolds. Do not allow exhaust gases to build up in the work area; either perform the check outside or use an exhaust gas extraction system.**

Note: *On XL-3 to 6 models with fuel injection refer to Chapter 4B for synchronisation of the throttle body starter valves if required, but note that it is not a regular maintenance item and need only be carried out if the starter valves are removed.*

1 Carburettor synchronisation is simply the process of adjusting the carburettors so they pass the same amount of fuel/air mixture to each cylinder. This is done by measuring the vacuum produced in each cylinder. Carburettors that are out of synchronisation will result in decreased fuel mileage, increased engine temperature, less than ideal throttle response and higher vibration levels. Before synchronising the carburettors, make sure the valve clearances are properly set.

2 To properly synchronise the carburettors, you will need a set of vacuum gauges or calibrated tubes to indicate engine vacuum. The equipment used should be suitable for a twin cylinder engine and come complete with the necessary adapters and hoses to fit the take-off points. **Note:** *Because of the nature of the synchronisation procedure and the need for special instruments, most owners leave the task to a Honda dealer.*

⚠ **Warning: The engine and carburettors will be hot. With the restricted access to the screws, great care must be taken not to burn yourself while synchronising the carburettors.**

3 On VTR models, raise the fuel tank at the rear (see Chapter 4A). Start the engine and let it run until it reaches normal operating temperature. When it is hot and while still running, clamp the fuel tap vacuum hose, then stop the engine (see illustration). This ensures the fuel tap remains open and can supply fuel to the carburettors. Trace the vacuum hose and disconnect it from the rear cylinder take-off point (see illustration). On UK and

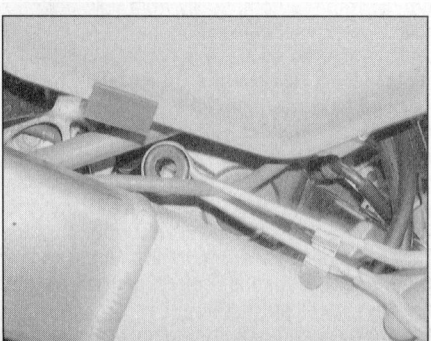

12.3a Clamp the fuel tap vacuum hose

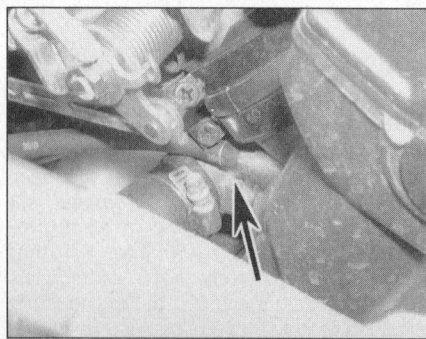

12.3b Detach the vacuum hose from its union (arrowed) and fit the gauge hose onto it

Every 8000 miles 1•15

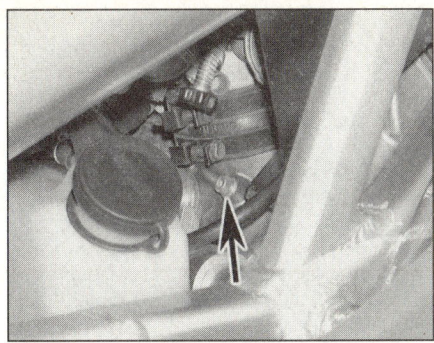

12.3c Remove the blanking bolt (arrowed) . . .

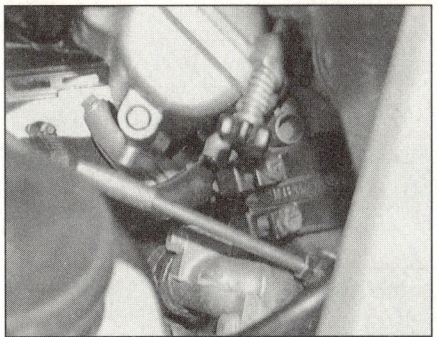

12.3d . . . and thread in a suitable adapter

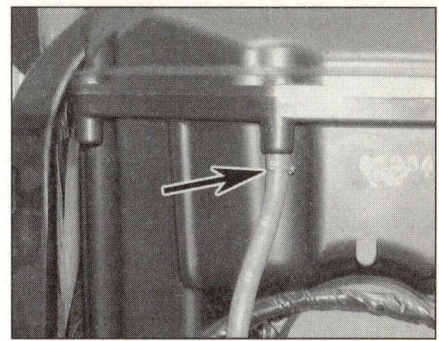

12.4a Disconnect the vacuum hoses (arrowed) from the air filter housing . . .

12.4b . . . and the PAIR valve

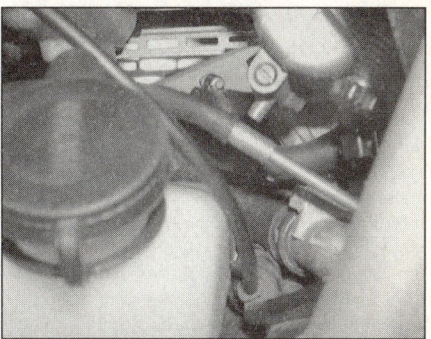

12.5 Connect the vacuum gauge hoses as described

US 49 State models, remove the blanking bolt from the front cylinder take-off point and screw in a suitable adapter piece **(see illustrations)**. On California models, disconnect the No. 10 vacuum hose from the front cylinder take-off point.

4 On XL models, start the engine and let it run until it reaches normal operating temperature. Raise the fuel tank at the rear (see Chapter 4A) and disconnect the vacuum hoses from the air filter housing and the PAIR control valve **(see illustrations)**.

5 Connect the vacuum gauge hoses to the take-off points on VTR models, and to the vacuum hoses on XL models using suitable joining pieces **(see illustration)**. Make sure they are a good fit because any air leaks will result in false readings.

6 Start the engine and adjust the idle speed (see Section 2). If using vacuum gauges fitted with damping adjustment, set this so that the needle flutter is just eliminated but so that they can still respond to small changes in pressure.

7 The vacuum reading for each cylinder should be the same. If the vacuum readings vary, adjust the carburettors by turning the synchronising screw situated in the throttle linkage on the left-hand side until the readings are the same **(see illustrations)**. **Note:** *Do not press up on the screw whilst adjusting it, otherwise a false reading will be obtained.*

8 When the carburettors are synchronised, open and close the throttle quickly to settle the linkage, and recheck the gauge readings, readjusting if necessary.

9 When the adjustment is complete, recheck the vacuum readings, then adjust the idle speed by turning the throttle stop screw (see Section 2) until the idle speed listed in this Chapter's Specifications is obtained. Stop the engine.

10 Remove the vacuum gauges and any adapters, then reconnect the hoses previously detached. On UK and US 49 State VTR models install the blanking bolt and release the clamp on the fuel tap vacuum hose.

13 Cooling system – check

Warning: *The engine must be cool before beginning this procedure.*

1 Check the coolant level (see *Daily (pre-ride) checks*).

2 On VTR models remove the fairing, and on XL models remove the fairing side panels (see Chapter 8). The entire cooling system should be checked for evidence of leakage. Examine each rubber coolant hose along its entire

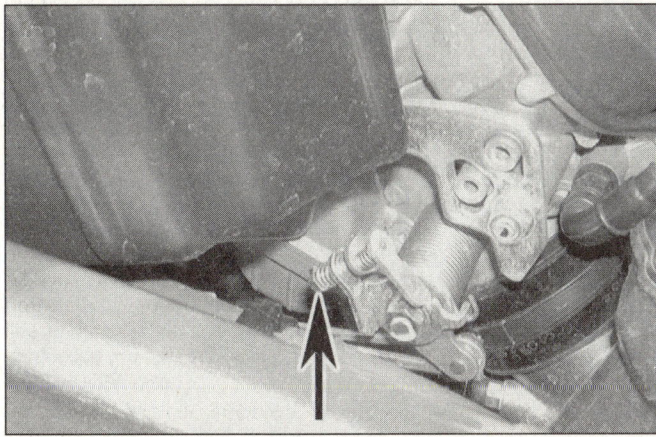

12.7a Adjust the carburettors using the synchronisation screw (arrowed) . . .

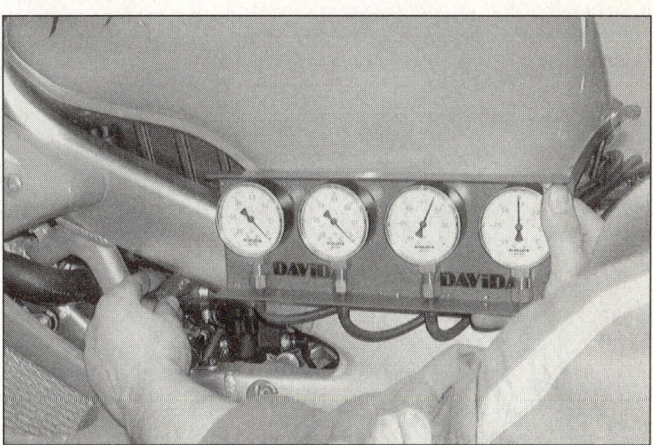

12.7b . . . until the gauge readings are the same

1•16 Every 8000 miles

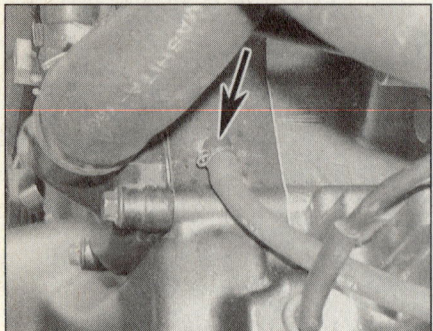

13.4 Check the drain hose (arrowed) for leakage

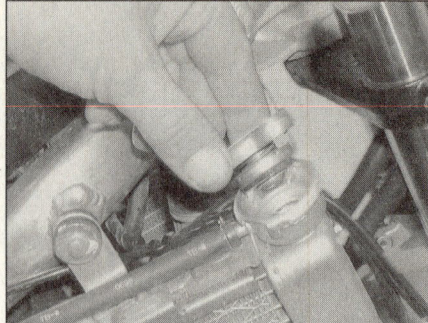

13.8 Remove the pressure cap as described

length. Look for cracks, abrasions and other damage. Squeeze each hose at various points. They should feel firm, yet pliable, and return to their original shape when released. If they are dried out or hard, replace them with new ones.

3 Check for evidence of leaks at each cooling system joint and around the pump cover on the right-hand side of the engine. Tighten the hose clips carefully to prevent future leaks. If the cover is leaking, check that the bolts are tight. If they are, replace the O-ring in the cover with a new one (see Chapter 3).

4 To prevent leakage of water from the cooling system to the lubrication system and *vice versa*, two seals are fitted on the pump shaft. On the front of the pump housing there is also a drain hose **(see illustration)**. If either seal fails, the drain allows the coolant or oil to escape and prevents them mixing. The seal on the water pump side is of the mechanical type which bears on the rear face of the impeller. The second seal, which is mounted behind the mechanical seal is of the normal feathered lip type. If on inspection the drain hose shows signs of coolant leakage, remove the pump and replace the mechanical seal with a new one. If it is oil that is leaking, replace the oil seal with a new one. If the leakage is white and with the texture of emulsion, replace both seals with new ones. Refer to Chapter 3, Section 8, for seal replacement.

5 Check the radiators for leaks and other damage. Leaks in the radiators leave tell-tale scale deposits or coolant stains on the outside of the core below the leak. If leaks are noted, remove the radiator (see Chapter 3) and have it repaired or replace it with a new one.

Caution: *Do not use a liquid leak stopping compound to try to repair leaks.*

6 Remove the radiator grilles and check the radiator fins for mud, dirt and insects, which may impede the flow of air through the radiator. If the fins are dirty, remove the radiators (see Chapter 3) and clean them using water or low pressure compressed air directed through the fins from the inner side of the radiator. If the fins are bent or distorted, straighten them carefully with a screwdriver. If the air flow is restricted by bent or damaged fins over more than 20% of the radiator's surface area, replace the radiator with a new one.

7 On VTR models, check the oil cooler and its pipes/hoses in a similar manner to the Steps above.

8 Remove the pressure cap from the right-hand radiator filler neck by turning it anti-clockwise until it reaches a stop **(see illustration)**. If you hear a hissing sound (indicating there is still pressure in the system), wait until it stops. Now press down on the cap and continue turning the cap until it can be removed. Check the condition of the coolant in the system. If it is rust-coloured or if accumulations of scale are visible, drain, flush and refill the system with new coolant (See Section 27). Check the cap seal for cracks and other damage. If in doubt about the pressure cap's condition, have it tested by a Honda dealer or replace it with a new one. Install the cap by turning it clockwise until it reaches the first stop then push down on the cap and continue turning until it can turn no further.

9 Check the anti-freeze content of the coolant with an anti-freeze hydrometer. Sometimes coolant looks like it's in good condition, but might be too weak to offer adequate protection. If the hydrometer indicates a weak mixture, drain, flush and refill the system (see Section 27).

10 Start the engine and let it reach normal operating temperature, then check for leaks again. As the coolant temperature increases, the fan should come on automatically and the temperature should begin to drop. If it does not, refer to Chapter 3 and check the fan and fan circuit carefully.

11 If the coolant level is consistently low, and no evidence of leaks can be found, have the entire system pressure checked by a Honda dealer.

14 Brake system – check

General check – all models

1 A routine general check of the brake system will ensure that any problems are discovered and remedied before the rider's safety is jeopardised.

2 Check the brake lever and pedal for loose connections, improper or rough action, excessive play, bends, and other damage. Replace any damaged parts with new ones (see Chapter 7).

3 Make sure all brake fasteners are tight. Check the brake pads for wear (see Section 3) and make sure the fluid level in the reservoirs is correct (see *Daily (pre-ride) checks*). Look for leaks at the hose connections and check for cracks in the hoses **(see illustration)**. If the lever or pedal is spongy, bleed the brakes (see Chapter 7).

4 Make sure the brake light operates when the front brake lever is pulled in. The front brake light switch, mounted on the underside of the master cylinder, is not adjustable. If it fails to operate properly, check it (see Chapter 9).

5 Make sure the brake light is activated just before the rear brake takes effect. If adjustment is necessary, hold the switch and turn the adjuster ring on the switch body until the brake light is activated when required **(see illustration)**. The switch is mounted on the inside of the rider's right-hand footrest bracket, just ahead of the master cylinder. If the brake light comes on too late, turn the ring clockwise. If the brake light comes on too soon or is permanently on, turn the ring anti-clockwise. If the switch doesn't operate the brake light, check it (see Chapter 9).

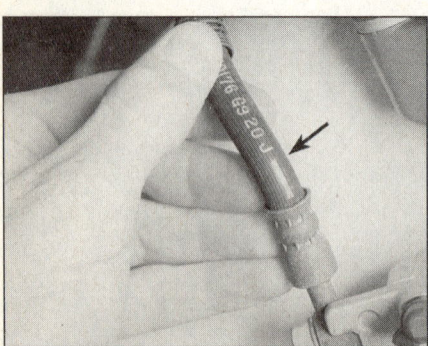

14.3 Flex the hoses and check for cracks, bulges and leaking fluid

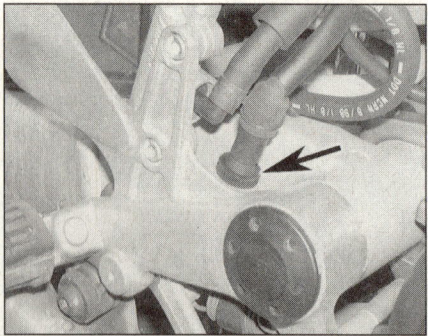

14.5 Rear brake light switch adjuster ring (arrowed)

Every 8000 miles 1•17

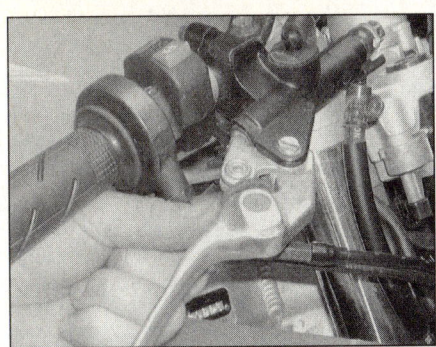
14.6 Adjusting the front brake lever span

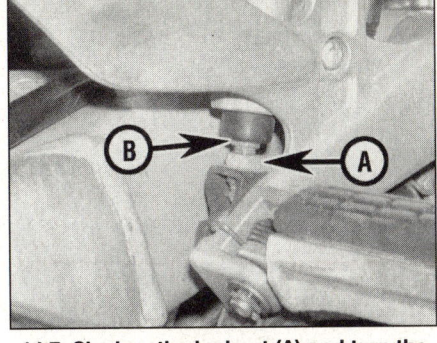
14.7 Slacken the locknut (A) and turn the pushrod using the hex (B)

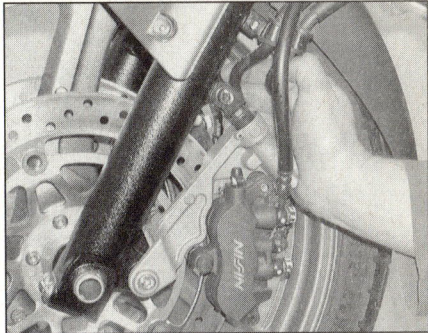
14.8 Measure the amount of stroke in the secondary master cylinder pushrod

6 The front brake lever has a span adjuster which alters the distance of the lever from the handlebar (see illustration). Each setting is identified by a notch in the adjuster which aligns with the arrow on the lever. Turn the adjuster ring until the setting which best suits the rider is obtained.

7 The height of the rear brake pedal can be adjusted to suit the rider's preference. Slacken the clevis locknut on the master cylinder pushrod, then turn the pushrod using a spanner on the hex at the top of the rod until the pedal is at the desired height (see illustration). On completion tighten the locknut securely. Adjust the rear brake light switch after adjusting the pedal height (see Step 5).

Dual-CBS (Combined Brake System) check – XL models

8 Lift the left-hand front brake caliper up so that the secondary master cylinder pushrod is activated and measure the amount of stroke in the pushrod (see illustration). It should be less than 4 mm. If it is more than 4 mm, check for leaks in the system as described above, then bleed the system (see Chapter 7). With the caliper raised, check that the rear wheel is locked by the brake. If the wheel can be turned, the Dual-CBS system is faulty and must be overhauled (see Chapter 7). Also check that the linkage between the left-hand caliper and the secondary master cylinder pushrod moves smoothly and freely.

9 Press the rear brake pedal down and check that the front wheel is locked by the brake. If the wheel can be turned, the Dual-CBS system is faulty and must be overhauled (see Chapter 7).

15 Headlight aim – check and adjustment
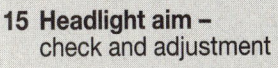

Note: *An improperly adjusted headlight may cause problems for oncoming traffic or provide poor, unsafe illumination of the road ahead. Before adjusting the headlight aim, be sure to consult with local traffic laws and regulations – for UK models refer to MOT Test Checks in the Reference section.*

1 The headlight beam can adjusted both horizontally and vertically. Before making any adjustment, check that the tyre pressures are correct and the suspension is adjusted as required. Make any adjustments to the headlight aim with the machine on level ground, with the fuel tank half full and with an assistant sitting on the seat. If the bike is usually ridden with a passenger on the back, have a second assistant to do this.

2 On VTR models, vertical adjustment is made by turning the adjuster screw on the top left corner of the headlight unit (see illustration). Turn it clockwise to move the beam up, and anti-clockwise to move it down. Horizontal adjustment is made by turning the adjuster screw on the bottom right corner of the headlight unit (see illustration). Turn it clockwise to move the beam to the left, and anti-clockwise to move it to the right.

3 On XL models, vertical adjustment is made by turning the adjuster screw on the top outer corner of each headlight unit (see illustration). Remove the rubber blanking cap in the cockpit trim and access the adjuster with a screwdriver inserted in the hole (see illustration). Turn the adjuster clockwise to move the beam up, and anti-clockwise to move it down. Horizontal adjustment is made by turning the adjuster screw on the bottom inner corner of each headlight unit (see illustration 15.3a). Access the adjusters with a screwdriver inserted in the hole in the underside of the fairing.

15.2a Headlight beam vertical adjustment screw (arrowed) – VTR models

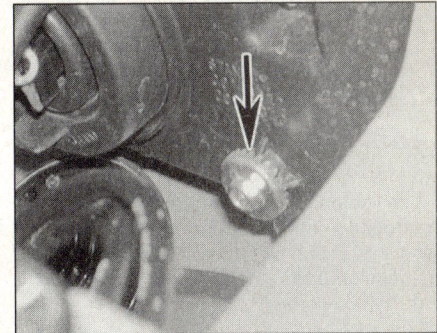
15.2b Headlight beam horizontal adjustment screws (arrowed) – VTR models

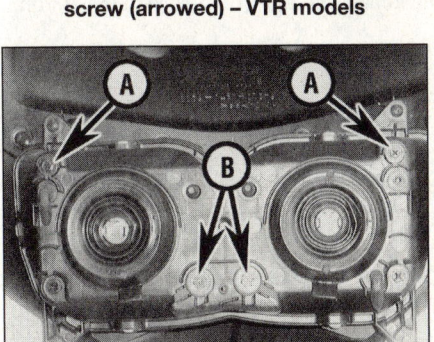
15.3a Headlight beam vertical adjustment screws (A), horizontal adjustment screws (B) – XL models

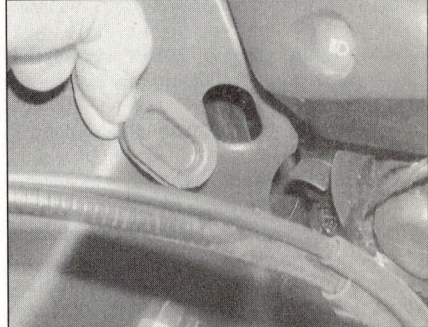
15.3b Access the vertical adjusters by removing the blanking plugs – XL models

1•18 Every 8000 miles

17.3 Check above and below the dust seal for signs of fluid leakage

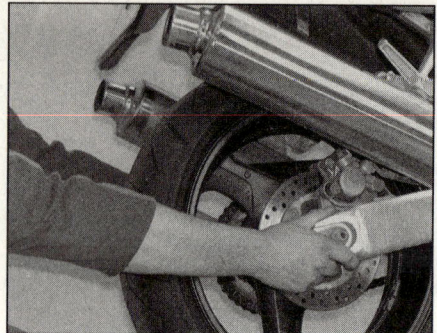

17.7a Checking for play in the swingarm bearings

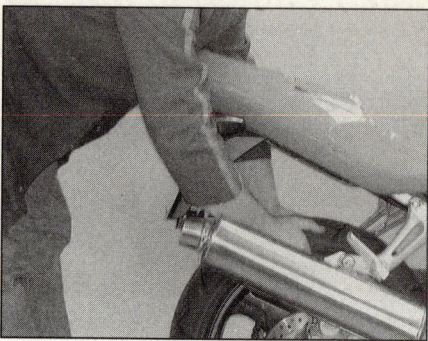

17.7b Checking for play in the rear shock mountings and suspension linkage bearings

16 Sidestand – check
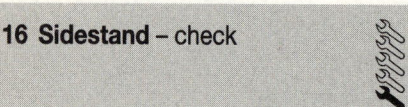

1 The sidestand return spring must be capable of retracting the stand fully and holding the stand retracted when the motorcycle is in use. If the spring is sagged or broken it must be replaced with a new one.
2 Lubricate the sidestand pivot regularly (see Section 7).
3 Check the operation of the sidestand switch by shifting the transmission into neutral, retracting the stand and starting the engine. Pull in the clutch lever and select a gear. Extend the sidestand. The engine should stop as the sidestand is extended. If the sidestand switch does not operate as described, check its circuit (see Chapter 9).

17 Suspension – check
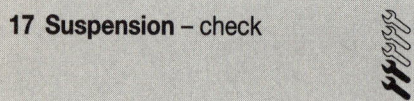

1 The suspension components must be maintained in top operating condition to ensure rider safety. Loose, worn or damaged suspension parts decrease the motorcycle's stability and control.

Front suspension

2 While standing alongside the motorcycle, apply the front brake and push on the handlebars to compress the forks several times. See if they move up-and-down smoothly without binding. If binding is felt, the forks should be disassembled and inspected (see Chapter 6).
3 Inspect the area around the dust seal for signs of oil leakage, then carefully lever up the dust seal using a flat-bladed screwdriver and inspect the area around the fork seal **(see illustration)**. If leakage is evident, the seals must be replaced with new ones (see Chapter 6).
4 Check the tightness of all suspension nuts and bolts to be sure none have worked loose.

Rear suspension

5 Inspect the rear shock for fluid leakage and tightness of its mountings. If leakage is found, the shock should be replaced with a new one (see Chapter 6).
6 With the aid of an assistant to support the bike, compress the rear suspension several times. It should move up and down freely without binding. If any binding is felt, the worn or faulty component must be identified and checked (see Chapter 6). The problem could be due to either the shock absorber, the suspension linkage components or the swingarm components.
7 Support the motorcycle using an auxiliary stand so that the rear wheel is off the ground. Grab the swingarm and rock it from side to side – there should be no discernible movement at the rear **(see illustration)**. If there's a little movement or a slight clicking can be heard, inspect the tightness of all the rear suspension mounting bolts and nuts, referring to the torque settings specified at the beginning of Chapter 6, and re-check for movement. Next, grasp the top of the rear wheel and pull it upwards – there should be no discernible freeplay before the shock absorber begins to compress **(see illustration)**. Any freeplay felt in either check indicates worn bearings in the suspension linkage or swingarm, or worn shock absorber mountings. The worn components must be replaced with new ones (see Chapter 6).
8 To make an accurate assessment of the swingarm bearings, remove the rear wheel (see Chapter 7) and the bolt securing the suspension linkage assembly to the swingarm (see Chapter 6). Grasp the rear of the swingarm with one hand and place your other hand at the junction of the swingarm and the frame. Try to move the rear of the swingarm from side-to-side. Any wear (play) in the bearings should be felt as movement between the swingarm and the frame at the front. If there is any play the swingarm will be felt to move forward and backward at the front (not from side-to-side). Next, move the swingarm up and down through its full travel. It should move freely, without any binding or rough spots. If there is any play in the swingarm or if it does not move freely, remove the bearings for inspection (see Chapter 6).

18 Steering head bearings – freeplay check and adjustment

1 This motorcycle is equipped with caged ball steering head bearings which can become dented, rough or loose during normal use of the machine. In extreme cases, worn or loose steering head bearings can cause steering wobble – a condition that is potentially dangerous.

Check

2 Support the motorcycle in an upright position using an auxiliary stand. Raise the front wheel off the ground either by having an assistant push down on the rear or by placing a support under the engine.
3 Point the front wheel straight-ahead and slowly move the handlebars from side-to-side. Any dents or roughness in the bearing races will be felt and the bars will not move smoothly and freely.
4 Next, grasp the bottom of the forks and try to move them forward and backward **(see illustration)**. Any looseness in the steering head bearings will be felt as front-to-rear movement of the forks. If play is felt in the bearings, adjust the steering head as follows.

18.4 Checking for play in the steering head bearings

 *Freeplay in the fork due to worn fork bushes can be misinterpreted for steering head bearing play – do not confuse the two.*

Every 8000 miles 1•19

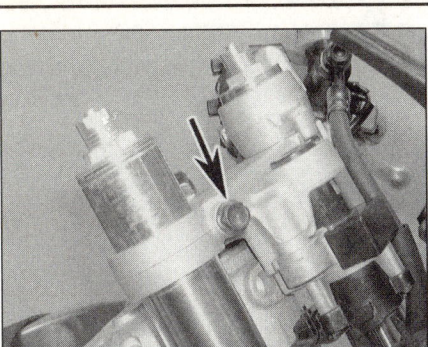

18.7 Slacken the fork clamp bolt (arrowed) on each side

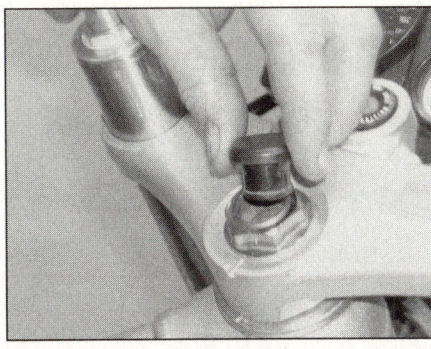

18.8 Prise off the cap and unscrew the nut

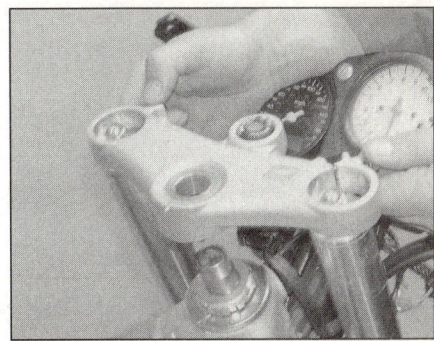

18.9 Gently ease the yoke up off the forks

Adjustment

5 Remove the fuel tank (see Chapter 4A) and the fairing (see Chapter 8). This will prevent the possibility of damage should a tool slip.
6 Displace the handlebars from the top yoke (see Chapter 6). Support them so the master cylinder is upright to prevent the possibility of fluid leakage. There is no need to remove assemblies from the handlebars.
7 Slacken the fork clamp bolts in the top yoke **(see illustration)**.
8 On VTR models, prise the cap off the steering stem nut. Unscrew the nut using a 30 mm socket or spanner, and on XL models remove the washer **(see illustration)**.
9 Gently ease the top yoke up off the fork tubes and position it clear of the head bearings, using a rag to protect other components **(see illustration)**.
10 Bend the lockwasher tabs out of the notches in the locknut **(see illustration)**. Unscrew the locknut using either a C-spanner or a suitable drift located in one of the notches **(see illustration)**. Remove the lockwasher, bending up the remaining tabs to release it from the adjuster nut if necessary **(see illustration)**. Inspect the tabs for cracks or signs of fatigue. If there are any, discard the lockwasher and use a new one; otherwise the old one can be re-used.
11 Using either the C-spanner or drift, slacken the adjuster nut slightly until pressure

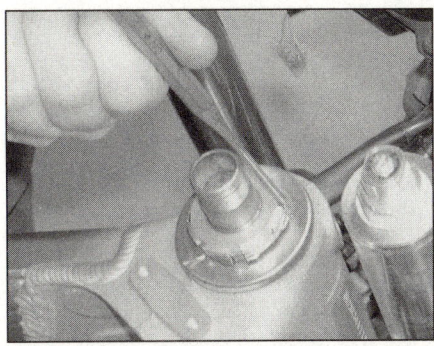

18.10a Bend down the tabs securing the locknut . . .

is just released, then tighten it until all freeplay is removed, yet the steering is able to move freely **(see illustration)**. The object is to set the adjuster nut so that the bearings are under a very light loading, just enough to remove any freeplay. If the correct tools are available, tighten the adjuster nut to the torque setting specified at the beginning of the Chapter, then turn the steering from lock-to-lock five times and recheck the torque setting. If the bearings cannot be correctly adjusted, disassemble the steering head and check the bearings and races (see Chapter 6).

Caution: Take great care not to apply excessive pressure because this will cause premature failure of the bearings.

12 With the bearings correctly adjusted,

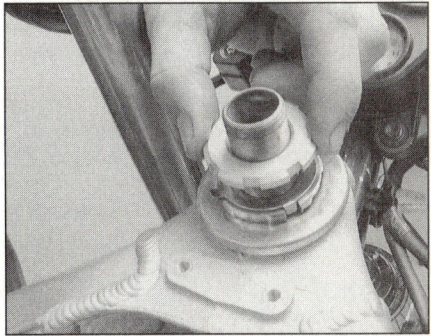

18.10b . . . then unscrew the locknut . . .

install the lockwasher, using a new one if the tabs are weakened or cracked, onto the adjuster nut and fit two tabs into the slots in the adjuster nut **(see illustration 18.10c)**.
13 Hold the adjuster nut to prevent it from moving, then install the locknut and tighten it finger-tight **(see illustration 18.10b)**. Tighten the locknut further (but no more than 90°) until its notches align with the remaining lockwasher tabs. Secure the locknut in position by bending up the lock washer tabs into its notches **(see illustration)**.
14 Fit the top yoke onto the steering stem **(see illustration 18.9)**. Install the nut, not forgetting the washer on XL models, and tighten it to the torque setting specified at the beginning of the Chapter (see

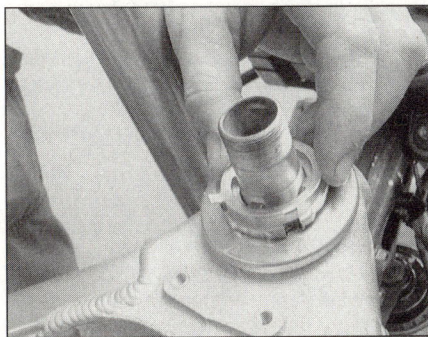

18.10c . . . and remove the lockwasher

18.11 Adjust the bearings as described using either a C-spanner or a drift

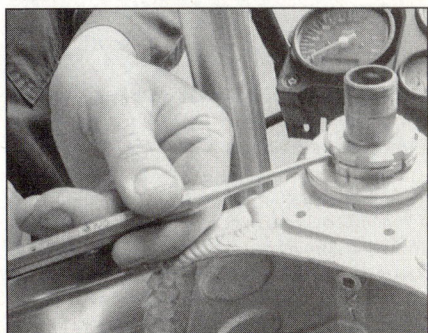

18.13 Bend the tabs up into the notches in the locknut

1•20 Every 8000 miles

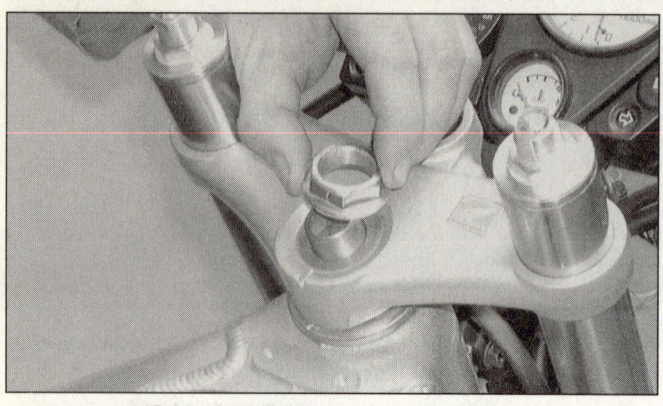

18.14a Install the steering stem nut . . .

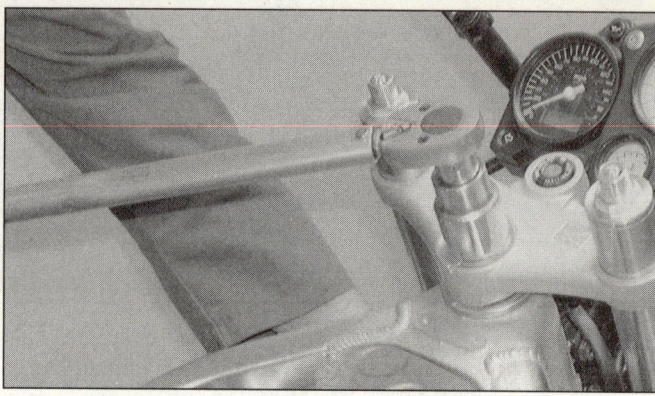

18.14b . . . and tighten it to the specified torque

illustrations). Now tighten both the fork clamp bolts to the specified torque (see illustration 18.7).
15 Check the bearing adjustment as described above and re-adjust if necessary.
16 Install the handlebars (see Chapter 6), the fuel tank (see Chapter 4A) and the fairing (see Chapter 8). On VTR models, fit the cap over the stem nut (see illustration 18.8).

19 Nuts and bolts – tightness check

1 Since vibration of the machine tends to loosen fasteners, all nuts, bolts, screws, etc. should be periodically checked for proper tightness.
2 Pay particular attention to the following:
Spark plugs
Engine oil drain plug
Lever and pedal bolts
Footrest and stand bolts
Engine mounting bolts
Shock absorber and suspension linkage bolts and swingarm pivot bolts
Handlebar clamp bolts
Front axle bolt and axle clamp bolts
Front fork clamp bolts (top and bottom yoke)
Rear axle nut
Brake caliper mounting bolts
Brake hose banjo bolts and caliper bleed valves
Brake disc bolts
Exhaust system bolts/nuts
3 If a torque wrench is available, use it along with the torque specifications at the beginning of this and other Chapters.

20 Wheels and tyres – general check

Tyres
1 Check the tyre condition and tread depth thoroughly – see *Daily (pre-ride) checks*.

Wheels
2 Cast wheels are virtually maintenance free, but they should be kept clean and checked periodically for cracks and other damage. Also check the wheel runout and alignment (see Chapter 7). Never attempt to repair damaged cast wheels; they must be replaced with new ones. Check the valve rubber for signs of damage or deterioration and have it replaced if necessary. Also, make sure the valve stem cap is in place and tight.

21 Pulse secondary air injection (PAIR) system – check

1 A PAIR system is fitted to all models except European market VTR1000F-V, W, X and Y models. Remove the fuel tank (see Chapter 4A) and visually inspect all the system hoses for kinks and splits and any other damage or deterioration – refer to illustration 16.1a in Chapter 4A. Make sure that the hoses are securely connected with a clamp on each end. Replace any hoses that are damaged or deteriorated with new ones.
2 See Chapter 4A for further information and tests on the system.

Every 12,000 miles (18,000 km) or 18 months

Carry out all the items under the 4000 mile (6000 km) check, plus the following:

22 Air filter – renewal

Caution: *If the machine is continually ridden in wet or dusty conditions, the filter should be replaced more frequently.*

1 Remove the fuel tank (see Chapter 4A).
2 On VTR models and XL-X, Y, 1 and 2 models undo the screws securing the air filter housing cover and remove it – the filter element comes away with the cover (see illustrations). Remove the element from the cover, noting how it fits, and discard it (see illustration). Fit the new filter element into the cover, making sure it is properly seated, then install the cover.
3 On XL-3 models onward undo the air filter housing cover screws and remove the cover (see illustration). Undo the filter element screws and remove the element (see illustrations). Fit the new filter element, making sure it is properly seated, then fit the cover.
4 Install the fuel tank (see Chapter 4A).
5 To clean the filter in between replacement intervals, tap it on a hard surface to dislodge any dirt and use compressed air to clear the element, directing the air in the opposite way to normal flow. Do not use any solvents or cleaning agents on the element as it is pre-treated with a dust adhesive. There are also two sub-air cleaner elements which should also be checked and cleaned if required (see illustration).

23 Evaporative emission control (EVAP) system – check (California VTR models)

1 Visually inspect all the system hoses for kinks and splits and any other damage or deterioration. Make sure that the hoses are securely connected with a clamp on each end. Replace any hoses that are damaged or deteriorated.
2 Check the EVAP canister and the two valves for cracks or other damage.
3 See Chapter 4A for further information and tests on the system.

Routine maintenance and servicing 1•21

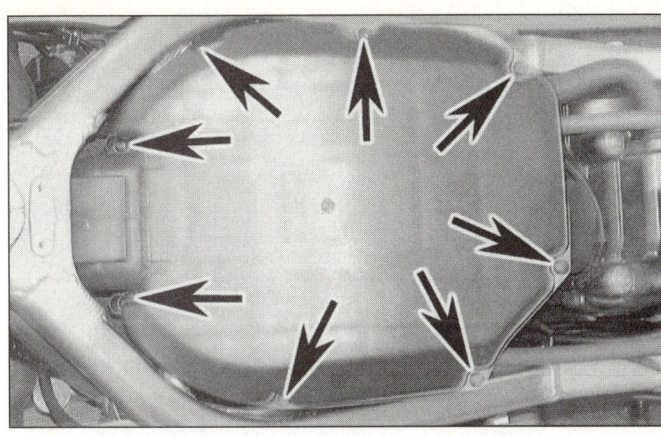

22.2a Remove the cover screws (arrowed) . . .

22.2b . . . then lift off the cover . . .

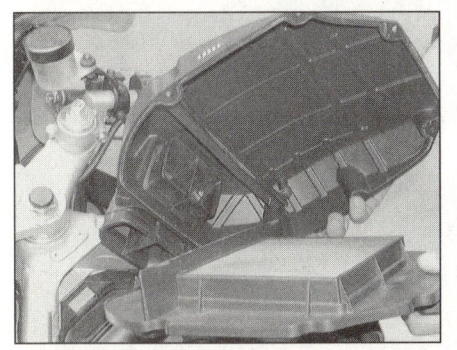

22.2c . . . and separate the filter from it

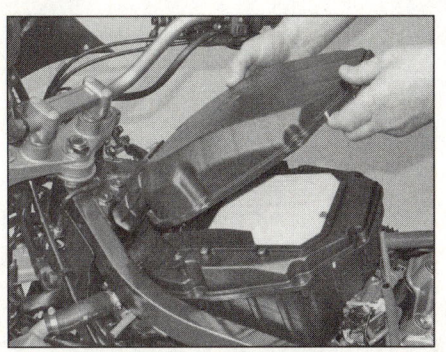

22.3a Remove the cover . . .

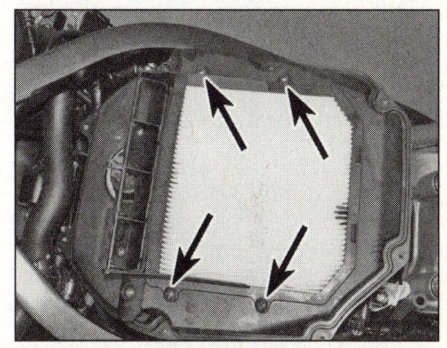

22.3b . . . then undo the screws (arrowed) . . .

22.3c . . . and remove the filter element

22.5 Check and clean the sub-air cleaner elements (arrowed)

Every 12,000 miles (18,000 km) or two years

24 Brake fluid – change

1 The brake fluid should be replaced at the prescribed interval or whenever a master cylinder or caliper overhaul is carried out. Refer to the brake bleeding section in Chapter 7, noting that all old fluid must be pumped from the fluid reservoir and hydraulic lines before filling with new fluid.

HAYNES HiNT Old brake/ hydraulic fluid is invariably much darker in colour than new fluid, making it easy to see when all old fluid has been expelled from the system.

25 Clutch – fluid change (VTR models)

1 The clutch fluid should be replaced at the prescribed interval or whenever a master or release cylinder overhaul is carried out. Refer to the clutch bleeding section in Chapter 2, Section 17, noting that all old fluid must be pumped from the fluid reservoir and hydraulic lines before filling with new fluid.

1•22 Every 16,000 miles

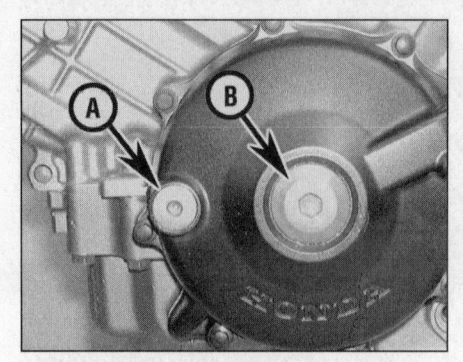

26.5a Remove the timing inspection cap (A) and crankshaft end cap (B)

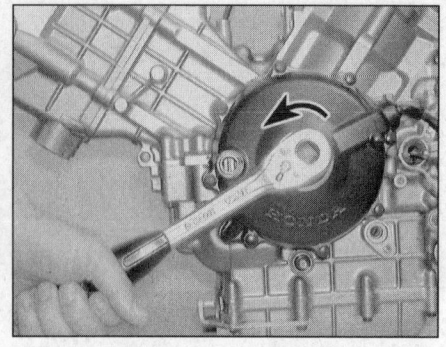

26.5b Turn the engine anti-clockwise using a 17 mm socket on the starter clutch bolt

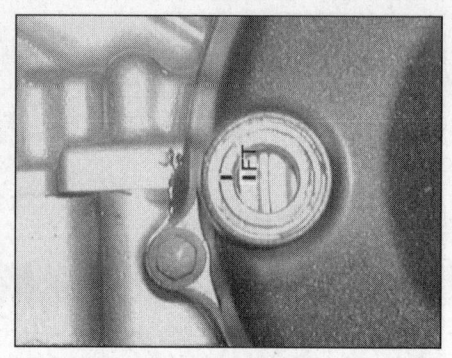

26.6a Turn the engine until the FT mark aligns with the static mark . . .

26.6b . . . the camshaft sprocket marks face away from each other . . .

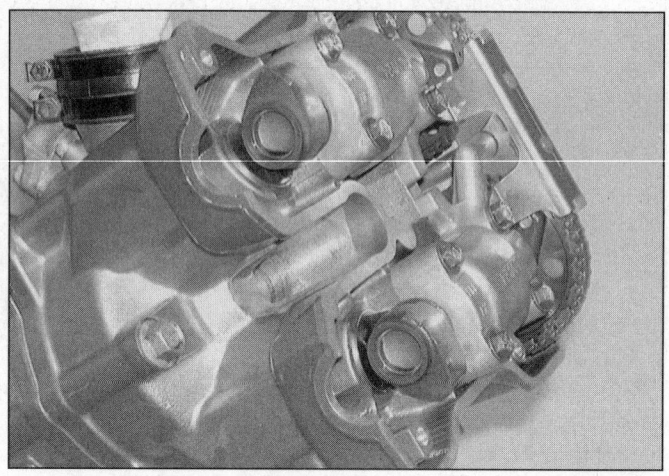

26.6c . . . and the camshaft lobes are positioned as shown

Every 16,000 miles (24,000 km) or two years

Carry out all the items under the 8000 mile (12,000 km) check, plus the following:

26 Valve clearances – check and adjustment

1 The engine must be completely cool for this maintenance procedure, so let the machine stand overnight before beginning.
2 Remove the spark plugs (see Section 5).
3 Remove the valve covers (see Chapter 2).
4 Make a chart or sketch of all valve positions so that a note of each clearance can be made against the relevant valve.
5 Unscrew the timing inspection cap and crankshaft end-cap from the left-hand crankcase cover **(see illustration)**. Discard the cap O-rings as new ones should be used. The engine can be turned using a 17 mm spanner or socket on the alternator bolt and turning it in an anti-clockwise direction only **(see illustration)**. Alternatively, place the motorcycle on an auxiliary stand so that the rear wheel is off the ground, select a high gear and rotate the rear wheel by hand in its normal direction of rotation.
6 Turn the engine until the FT mark on the rotor aligns with the static timing mark on the crankcase cover, and the FI and FE marks on the intake and exhaust camshaft sprockets respectively are facing away from each other, and are flush with the cylinder head top surface (in this position the camshaft lobes will pointing away from each other) **(see illustrations)**. If the marks and lobes are facing towards each other, rotate the engine clockwise one full turn until the FT mark again aligns with the static timing mark. The sprocket marks and camshaft lobes will now be facing away and the front cylinder is at TDC on the compression stroke.
7 With the front cylinder at TDC on the compression stroke, check the clearances on the inlet and exhaust valves. Insert a feeler gauge of the same thickness as the correct valve clearance (see Specifications) between the camshaft lobe and follower of each valve and check that it is a firm sliding fit – you should feel a slight drag when the you pull the gauge out **(see illustration)**. If not, use the feeler gauges to obtain the exact clearance. Record the measured clearance on the chart.
8 Now rotate the engine 270° anti-clockwise until the RT mark on the rotor aligns with the

26.7 Measure the valve clearance using a feeler gauge as shown

Every 16,000 miles 1•23

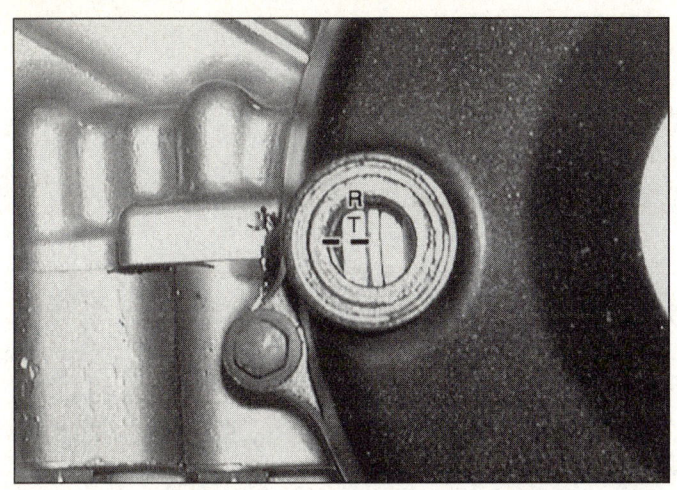

26.8a Turn the engine until the RT mark aligns with the static mark . . .

26.8b . . . the camshaft sprocket marks face away from each other . . .

static timing mark on the crankcase cover **(see illustration)**. The RI and RE marks on the intake and exhaust camshaft sprockets respectively will be facing away from each other and flush with the cylinder head top surface, and the camshaft lobes will pointing toward each other as shown **(see illustrations)**. The rear cylinder is now at TDC on the compression stroke. Measure the clearance of the valves using the method described in Step 7.

9 When all clearances have been measured and charted, identify whether the clearance on any valve falls outside the specified range. If any do, the shim must be replaced with one of a thickness which will restore the correct clearance.

10 Shim replacement requires removal of the camshafts (see Chapter 2). There is no need to remove both camshafts if shims from only one side of the cylinder need replacing. Place rags over the spark plug holes and the cam chain tunnel to prevent a shim from dropping into the engine on removal.

11 With the camshaft removed, remove the cam follower of the valve in question, then retrieve the shim from the inside of the follower **(see illustrations)**. If it is not in the follower, pick it out of the top of the valve spring retainer using either a magnet, a small screwdriver with a dab of grease on it (the shim will stick to the grease), or a screwdriver and a pair of pliers **(see illustration 26.14)**. Do not allow the shim to fall into the engine.

12 A size mark should be stamped on one face of the shim – a shim marked 175 is 1.75 mm thick. If the mark is not visible the shim thickness will have to be measured. It is recommended that the shim is measured anyway to check that it has not worn **(see illustration)**.

13 Calculate the required replacement shim by using the formula a = b – c + d, where a is the required shim size, b is the measured valve clearance, c is the specified valve clearance, and d is the existing shim thickness. For example:

The measured clearance of an inlet valve is 0.20 mm, so b = 0.20.
The specified clearance range for an inlet valve is 0.13 to 0.19 mm, the mid-point being 0.16 mm, so c = 0.16.
The thickness of the existing shim is 2.20 mm, so d = 2.2.
Therefore, the required replacement shim a = 0.20 – 0.16 + 2.2 (a = 2.24 mm)

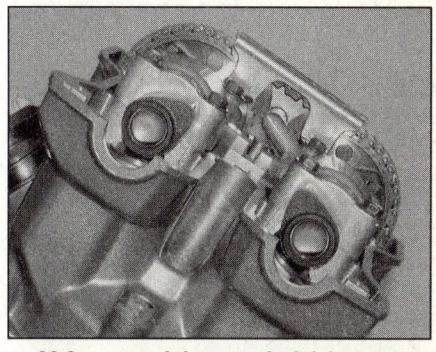

26.8c . . . and the camshaft lobes are positioned as shown

Note: *If the required replacement shim is greater than 2.450 mm (the largest available), the valve is probably not seating correctly due to a build-up of carbon deposits and should be checked and cleaned or resurfaced as required (see Chapter 2).*

14 Shims are available in 0.025 mm increments from 1.200 mm to 2.450 mm. Obtain the replacement shim, then lubricate it with molybdenum disulphide oil (a 50/50 mixture of molybdenum disulphide grease and engine oil) and fit it into the recess in the top

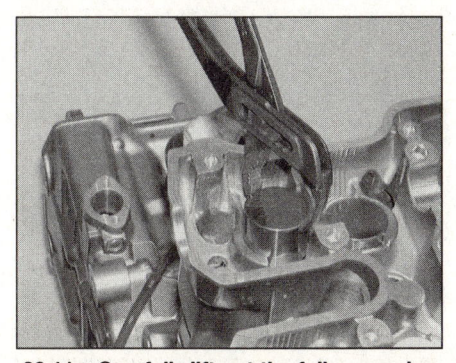

26.11a Carefully lift out the follower using grips or a magnet . . .

26.11b . . . and retrieve the shim from inside it

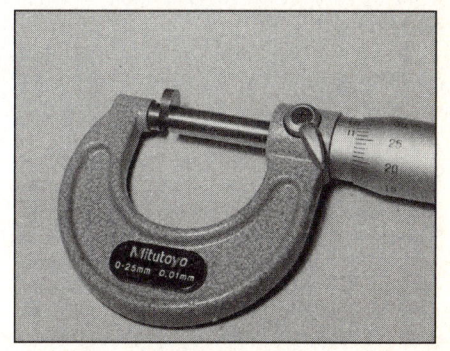

26.12 Measure the shim using a micrometer

1•24 Every 16,000 miles

26.14 Install the shim using a magnet or a screwdriver with a dab of grease . . .

26.15 . . . then install the follower

26.17 Fit the caps using new O-rings and smear them and the threads with grease

of the valve spring retainer with the size mark facing up **(see illustration)**,
15 Check that the shim is correctly seated, then lubricate the follower with molybdenum disulphide oil and install it onto the valve **(see illustration)**. Repeat the process for any other valves until the clearances are correct, then install the camshafts (see Chapter 2).
16 Rotate the crankshaft several turns to seat the new shim(s), then check the clearances again.
17 Install all disturbed components in a reverse of the removal sequence. Install the timing inspection cap and the crankshaft end-cap using new O-rings, and smear them and the cap threads with grease **(see illustration)**. Tighten the caps to the torque settings specified at the beginning of the Chapter.

Every 24,000 miles (36,000 km) or two years

Carry out all the items under the 8000 mile (12,000 km) and 12,000 mile (18,000 km) checks, plus the following:

27 Cooling system – draining, flushing and refilling

⚠️ *Warning: Allow the engine to cool completely before performing this maintenance operation. Also, don't allow anti-freeze to come into contact with your skin or the painted surfaces of the motorcycle. Rinse off spills immediately with plenty of water. Anti-freeze is highly toxic if ingested. Never leave anti-freeze lying around in an open container or in puddles on the floor; children and pets are attracted by its sweet smell and may drink it. Check with local authorities (councils) about disposing of anti-freeze. Many communities have collection centres which will see that anti-freeze is disposed of safely. Anti-freeze is also combustible, so don't store it near open flames.*

Draining

1 On VTR models remove the fairing (see Chapter 8). On XL models remove the right-hand fairing side panel and the belly-pan (see Chapter 8, Section 4).
2 Remove the pressure cap from the top of the right-hand radiator by turning it anti-clockwise until it reaches a stop **(see illustration 13.8)**. If you hear a hissing sound (indicating there is still pressure in the system), wait until it stops. Now press down on the cap and continue turning the cap until it can be removed.
3 Position a suitable container beneath the right-hand radiator. Slacken the clamp on the hose coming out of the bottom of the radiator. Detach the hose and allow the coolant to completely drain from the system **(see illustration)**.
4 Remove the cap from the coolant reservoir. Detach the reservoir hose from the radiator filler neck, then position it below the level of the reservoir and allow it to drain into the container **(see illustrations)**.
5 Position the container beneath the front cylinder, then remove the drain plug and sealing washer and allow the coolant to completely drain from the cylinder **(see illustration)**. Retain the old sealing washer for use during flushing.

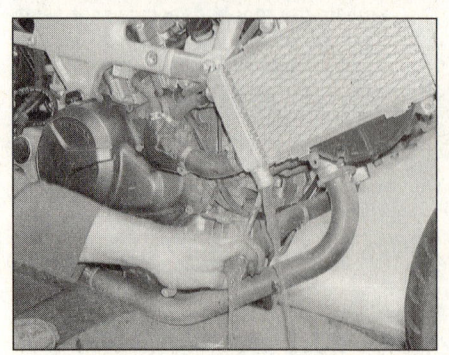

27.3 Detach the bottom hose from the radiator and allow the coolant to drain

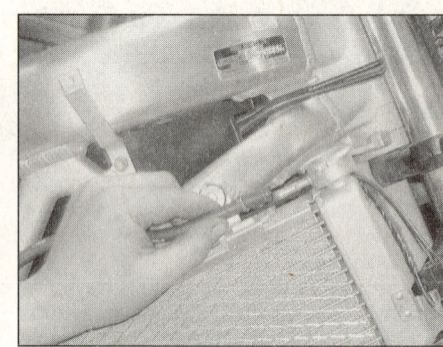

27.4a Detach the reservoir hose . . .

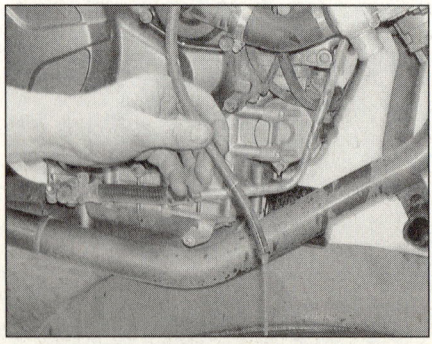

27.4b . . . and drain the reservoir

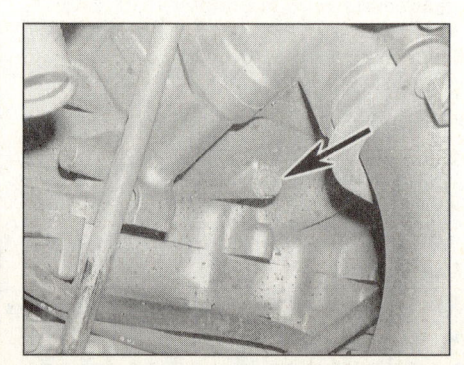

27.5 Remove the drain plug (arrowed) and drain the front cylinder

Routine maintenance and servicing

Flushing

6 Flush the system with clean tap water by inserting a garden hose in the radiator filler neck. Allow the water to run through the system until it is clear and flows out cleanly. If the radiator is extremely corroded, remove it (see Chapter 3) and have it cleaned by a specialist.

7 Connect the hose to the radiator and tighten the clamp. Also connect the reservoir hose to the union on the filler neck **(see illustration 27.4a)**. Clean the drain hole in the front cylinder bock then install the drain plug using the old sealing washers.

8 Fill the cooling system with clean water mixed with a flushing compound. Make sure the flushing compound is compatible with aluminium components, and follow the manufacturer's instructions carefully.

9 Start the engine and allow it to reach normal operating temperature. Let it run for about ten minutes.

10 Stop the engine. Let it cool for a while, then cover the pressure cap with a heavy rag and turn it anti-clockwise to the first stop, releasing any pressure that may be present in the system. Once the hissing stops, push down on the cap and remove it completely.

11 Drain the system once again.

12 Fill the system with clean water and repeat the procedure in Steps 6 to 10.

Refilling

13 Fit a new sealing washer onto the drain plug and tighten it securely.

14 Fill the system with the proper coolant mixture (see this Chapter's Specifications). **Note:** *Pour the coolant in slowly to minimise the amount of air getting trapped in the system.*

15 When the system is full (all the way up to the base of the upper radiator filler neck), start the engine and allow it to idle for 2 to 3 minutes. Flick the throttle twistgrip part open 3 or 4 times, so that the engine speed rises to approximately 4000 – 5000 rpm, then stop the engine. This process will bleed any trapped air bubbles from the system.

16 If necessary, top up the coolant level to the base of the upper radiator filler neck and install the pressure cap. Also top up the coolant reservoir to the UPPER level mark (see *Daily (pre-ride) checks*).

17 Start the engine and allow it to reach normal operating temperature, then shut it off. Let the engine cool then remove the pressure cap as described in Step 2. Check that the coolant level is still up to the base of the upper radiator filler neck. If it's low, add the specified mixture until it reaches the base of the filler neck. Refit the cap.

18 Check the coolant level in the reservoir and top up if necessary.

19 Check the system for leaks.

20 Do not dispose of the old coolant by pouring it down the drain. Instead pour it into a heavy plastic container, cap it tightly and take it into an authorised disposal site or service station – see *Warning* at the beginning of this Section.

Non-scheduled maintenance

28 Cylinder compression – check

1 Among other things, poor engine performance may be caused by leaking valves, incorrect valve clearances, a leaking head gasket, or worn pistons, rings and/or cylinder walls. A cylinder compression check will help pinpoint these conditions and can also indicate the presence of excessive carbon deposits in the cylinder heads.

2 The only tools required are a compression gauge and a spark plug wrench. A compression gauge with a threaded end for the spark plug hole is preferable to the type which requires hand pressure to maintain a tight seal. Depending on the outcome of the initial test, a squirt-type oil can may also be needed.

3 Make sure the valve clearances are correctly set (see Section 26) and that the cylinder head nuts are tightened to the correct torque setting (see Chapter 2).

4 Refer to *Fault Finding Equipment* in the Reference section for details of the compression test. Refer to the specifications at the beginning of the Chapter for compression figures.

29 Engine oil pressure – check

1 The oil pressure warning light should come on when the ignition (main) switch is turned ON and extinguish a few seconds after the engine is started – this serves as a check that the warning light bulb is sound. If the oil pressure light comes on whilst the engine is running, low oil pressure is indicated – stop the engine immediately and carry out an oil level check *(see Daily (pre-ride) checks)*.

2 An oil pressure check must be carried out if the warning light comes on when the engine is running yet the oil level is good (Step 1). It can also provide useful information about the condition of the engine's lubrication system.

3 To check the oil pressure, a suitable gauge and adapter (which screws into the crankcase) will be needed. Honda provide a tool for this purpose, or one can be obtained commercially.

4 Warm the engine up to normal operating temperature then stop it.

5 Remove the oil pressure switch (see Chapter 9) and swiftly screw the adapter into the crankcase threads. Connect the oil pressure gauge to the adapter.

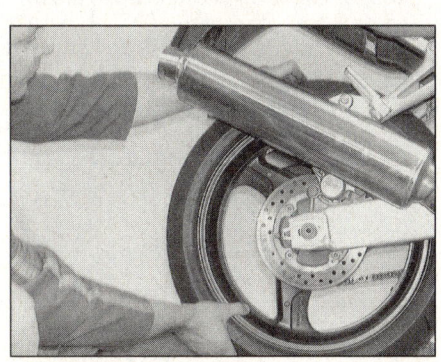

30.2 Checking for play in the wheel bearings

6 Start the engine and briefly increase the engine speed to 5000 rpm whilst watching the gauge reading. The oil pressure should be similar to that given in the Specifications at the start of this Chapter.

7 If the pressure is significantly lower than the standard, either the pressure relief valve is stuck open, the oil pump or its drive mechanism is faulty, the oil strainer or filter is blocked, or there is other engine damage. Also make sure the correct grade oil is being used. Begin diagnosis by checking the oil filter, strainer and relief valve, then the oil pump (see Chapter 2). If those items check out okay, chances are the bearing oil clearances are excessive and the engine needs to be overhauled.

8 If the pressure is too high, either an oil passage is clogged, the relief valve is stuck closed or the wrong grade of oil is being used.

9 Stop the engine and unscrew the gauge and adapter from the crankcase.

10 Install the oil pressure switch (see Chapter 9). On XL models, install the bolt and its washer. Check the oil level (see *Daily (pre-ride) checks*).

30 Wheel bearings – check

1 Wheel bearings will wear over a period of time and result in handling problems.

2 Support the motorcycle upright using an auxiliary stand so that the wheel being checked is off the ground Check for any play in the bearings by pushing and pulling the wheel against the axle **(see illustration)**. Also

Non-scheduled maintenance

rotate the wheel and check that it rotates smoothly.

3 If any play is detected in the hub, or if the wheel does not rotate smoothly (and this is not due to brake or transmission drag), the wheel bearings must be removed and inspected for wear or damage (see Chapter 7).

31 Steering head bearings – re-greasing

1 Over a period of time the grease will harden or may be washed out of the bearings by incorrect use of jet washes.
2 Disassemble the steering head for re-greasing of the bearings. Refer to Chapter 6 for details.

32 Swingarm and suspension linkage bearings – re-greasing

1 Over a period of time the grease will harden or dirt will penetrate the bearings due to failed dust seals.
2 The suspension is not equipped with grease nipples. Remove the swingarm and suspension linkage as described in Chapter 6 for greasing of the bearings.

33 Brake caliper and master cylinder seals – renewal

1 Brake seals will deteriorate over a period of time and lose their effectiveness, leading to sticking operation or fluid loss, or allowing the ingress of air and dirt. Refer to Chapter 7 and dismantle the components for seal renewal.

34 Brake hoses – renewal

1 The hoses will in time deteriorate with age and should be renewed regardless of their apparent condition.
2 Refer to Chapter 7 and disconnect the brake hoses from the master cylinders and calipers. Always replace the banjo union sealing washers with new ones.

35 Fuel hoses – renewal

⚠️ **Warning: Petrol (gasoline) is extremely flammable, so take extra precautions when you work on any part of the fuel system. Don't smoke or allow open flames or bare light bulbs near the work area, and don't work in a garage where a natural gas-type appliance is present. If you spill any fuel on your skin, rinse it off immediately with soap and water. When you perform any kind of work on the fuel system, wear safety glasses and have a fire extinguisher suitable for a Class B type fire (flammable liquids) on hand.**

1 The fuel delivery and vacuum hoses should be renewed regardless of their condition.
2 Remove the fuel tank (see Chapter 4A). Disconnect the fuel hoses from the fuel tap and from the carburettors, noting the routing of each hose and where it connects (see Chapter 4A if required). It is advisable to make a sketch of the various hoses before removing them to ensure they are correctly installed.
3 Secure each new hose to its unions using new clamps. Run the engine and check for leaks before taking the machine out on the road.

36 Clutch hose – renewal (VTR models)

1 The hose will in time deteriorate with age and should be renewed regardless of its apparent condition.
2 Refer to Chapter 2, Section 17, and disconnect the hose from the master and release cylinders. Always replace the banjo union sealing washers with new ones.

37 Clutch master and release cylinder seals – renewal (VTR models)

1 The seals will deteriorate over a period of time and lose their effectiveness, leading to sticking operation or fluid loss, or allowing the ingress of air and dirt. Refer to Chapter 2, Section 17, and dismantle the components for seal renewal.

38 Front forks – oil change

1 Fork oil degrades over a period of time and loses its damping qualities. To change the oil, refer to Chapter 6, Section 6 and remove the fork legs from the machine.
2 Referring to Section 7 of the same chapter, on XL models follow steps 3 to 6 to drain the oil and steps 25 to 27 to replenish it. On VTR models, follow steps 32 to 36 to drain the oil and steps 55 to 59 to replenish it. The forks do not need to be completely dismantled.
3 Fork oil details are given in Chapter 6 Specifications.

Chapter 2
Engine, clutch and transmission

Contents

Alternator – removal and installation . . . . see Chapter 9	Oil and filter – change. . . . . see Chapter 1
Cam chain tensioners – removal and installation. 9	Oil cooler and pipes – removal and installation (VTR models). 7
Cam chain, tensioner blade and guide blades – removal,	Oil level – check . . . . see *Daily (pre-ride) checks*
inspection and installation 11	Oil pressure – check. . . . . see Chapter 1
Camshafts and followers – removal, inspection and installation . . . 10	Oil pressure switch – check, removal and installation . . . see Chapter 9
Clutch – check . . . . see Chapter 1	Oil pump – removal, inspection and installation. 19
Clutch – removal, inspection and installation. 16	Oil sump, oil strainer and pressure relief valve –
Clutch release mechanism – removal, overhaul and installation . . . 17	removal, inspection and installation 18
Connecting rods – removal, inspection and installation. 25	Operations possible with the engine in the frame 2
Crankcase halves – separation and reassembly 22	Operations requiring engine removal 3
Crankcase halves and cylinder bores – inspection and servicing . . 23	Piston rings – inspection and installation. 27
Crankshaft and main bearings – removal, inspection	Pistons – removal, inspection and installation. 26
and installation 28	Pulse generator coil assembly – removal and
Cylinder compression – check. see Chapter 1	installation. . . . . see Chapter 5
Cylinder head and valves – disassembly, inspection	Recommended running-in procedure 33
and reassembly 14	Selector drum and forks – removal, inspection and installation . . . 31
Cylinder heads – removal and installation 12	Spark plug gap – check and adjustment . . . . see Chapter 1
Engine – removal and installation. 5	Starter clutch – check, removal, inspection and installation 15
Engine disassembly and reassembly – general information 6	Starter motor – removal and installation . . . . see Chapter 9
Gearchange mechanism – removal, inspection and installation . . . 20	Timing rotor and primary drive gear – removal and installation. . . . 21
General information 1	Transmission shafts – disassembly, inspection and reassembly . . . 30
Idle speed – check and adjustment . . . . see Chapter 1	Transmission shafts and bearings – removal and installation 29
Initial start-up after overhaul 32	Valve clearances – check and adjustment . . . . see Chapter 1
Main and connecting rod bearings – general note. 24	Valve covers – removal and installation 8
Major engine repair – general note. 4	Valves/valve seats/valve guides – servicing. 13
Neutral switch – check, removal and installation. . . . . . . see Chapter 9	

Degrees of difficulty

Easy, suitable for novice with little experience	Fairly easy, suitable for beginner with some experience	Fairly difficult, suitable for competent DIY mechanic	Difficult, suitable for experienced DIY mechanic	Very difficult, suitable for expert DIY or professional

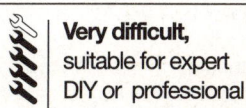

Specifications

General

Type	Four-stroke 90° V-twin
Capacity	995.7 cc
Bore	98.0 mm
Stroke	66.0 mm

Compression ratio
- VTR models .... 9.4 to 1
- XL-X, Y, 1 and 2 models .... 9.0 to 1
- XL-3 models onward .... 9.8 to 1

Valve timing
- VTR models
  - Inlet valve opens .... 20° BTDC
  - Inlet valve closes .... 45° ABDC
  - Exhaust valve opens .... 50° BBDC
  - Exhaust valve closes .... 15° ATDC
- XL models
  - Inlet valve opens .... 15° BTDC
  - Inlet valve closes .... 30° ABDC
  - Exhaust valve opens .... 40° BBDC
  - Exhaust valve closes .... 5° ATDC

Cooling system .... Liquid cooled
Clutch .... Wet multi-plate

Transmission
- VTR models .... Six-speed constant mesh
- XL-X, Y, 1 and 2 models .... Five-speed constant mesh
- XL-3 models onward .... Six-speed constant mesh

Final drive .... Chain

Camshafts and followers

	Standard	Service limit (min)
Inlet lobe height – VTR models and XL-X, Y, 1 and 2 models	40.080 to 40.240 mm	39.780 mm
Exhaust lobe height – VTR models and XL-X, Y, 1 and 2 models	40.230 to 40.390 mm	39.930 mm
Inlet lobe height – XL-3 models onward	38.680 to 38.840 mm	38.380 mm
Exhaust lobe height – XL-3 models onward	38.830 to 38.990 mm	38.530 mm

Oil clearance
- VTR models
  - Standard .... 0.020 to 0.062 mm
  - Service limit (max) .... 0.088 mm
- XL models
  - Standard .... 0.020 to 0.062 mm
  - Service limit (max) .... 0.10 mm

Camshaft runout (max) .... 0.05 mm

Camshaft follower diameter
- Standard .... 33.978 to 33.993 mm
- Service limit (min) .... 33.97 mm

Camshaft follower bore diameter
- Standard .... 34.010 to 34.026 mm
- Service limit (min) .... 34.04 mm

Cylinder head

Warpage (max) .... 0.10 mm

Valves, guides and springs

Valve clearances .... See Chapter 1

Inlet valve
- Stem diameter
  - Standard .... 5.975 to 5.990 mm
  - Service limit (min) .... 5.965 mm
- Guide bore diameter
  - Standard .... 6.000 to 6.012 mm
  - Service limit (max) .... 6.040 mm
- Stem-to-guide clearance
  - Standard .... 0.010 to 0.037 mm
  - Service limit (max) .... 0.075 mm
- Seat width
  - Standard .... 1.10 to 1.30 mm
  - Service limit (max) .... 1.70 mm
- Valve guide height above cylinder head .... 14.0 to 14.2 mm

Exhaust valve
  Stem diameter
    Standard... 5.965 to 5.980 mm
    Service limit (min)................................. 5.955 mm
  Guide bore diameter
    Standard... 6.000 to 6.012 mm
    Service limit (max)................................ 6.040 mm
  Stem-to-guide clearance
    Standard... 0.020 to 0.047 mm
    Service limit (max)................................ 0.085 mm
  Seat width
    Standard... 1.30 to 1.50 mm
    Service limit (max)................................ 1.90 mm
  Valve guide height above cylinder head............... 14.0 to 14.2 mm
Valve spring free length (inlet and exhaust)
  VTR models
    Inner spring
      Standard... 37.0 mm
      Service limit (min).............................. 36.0 mm
    Outer spring
      Standard... 41.9 mm
      Service limit (min).............................. 40.9 mm
  XL models
    Standard... 43.9 mm
    Service limit (min)................................ 42.9 mm

Starter clutch
Starter driven gear hub OD
  Standard... 57.749 to 57.768 mm
  Service limit (min).................................. 57.639 mm

Clutch
Friction plates.. 10
Plain plates... 9
Friction plate thickness
  Standard... 3.72 to 3.88 mm
  Service limit (min).................................. 3.5 mm
Plain plate warpage (max).............................. 0.3 mm
Spring free length
  Standard... 49.6 mm
  Service limit (min).................................. 46.6 mm
Clutch guide OD
  Standard... 34.975 to 34.991 mm
  Service limit (min).................................. 34.965 mm
Clutch guide ID
  Standard... 28.000 to 28.021 mm
  Service limit (max)................................. 28.031 mm
Input shaft OD at clutch guide
  Standard... 27.980 to 27.993 mm
  Service limit (max)................................. 27.970 mm

Clutch release mechanism – VTR models
Master cylinder bore diameter
  Standard... 14.000 to 14.043 mm
  Service limit (max)................................. 14.055 mm
Master cylinder piston diameter
  Standard... 13.957 to 13.984 mm
  Service limit (min).................................. 13.945 mm
Clutch fluid... DOT 4

Lubrication system
Oil pressure.. see Chapter 1
Oil pump
  Inner rotor tip-to-outer rotor clearance
    Standard... 0.15 mm
    Service limit (max)............................... 0.20 mm
  Outer rotor-to-body clearance
    Standard... 0.15 to 0.21 mm
    Service limit (max)............................... 0.35 mm
  Rotor end-float
    Standard... 0.02 to 0.09 mm
    Service limit (max)............................... 0.12 mm

2•4 Engine, clutch and transmission

Cylinder bores
Bore
    Standard.. 98.005 to 98.025 mm
    Service limit (max) .... 98.100 mm
Warpage (max)... 0.05 mm
Ovality (out-of-round) (max)................................. 0.10 mm
Taper (max)... 0.10 mm
Cylinder compression... see Chapter 1

Pistons
Piston diameter (measured 20 mm up from skirt, at 90° to piston pin axis)
    VTR models
        Standard.. 97.965 to 97.985 mm
        Service limit (min) .... 97.900 mm
    XL models
        Standard.. 97.983 to 97.985 mm
        Service limit (min) .... 97.900 mm
Piston-to-bore clearance
    VTR models
        Standard.. 0.020 to 0.060 mm
        Service limit (max)....................................... 0.20 mm
    XL models
        Standard.. 0.010 to 0.055 mm
        Service limit (max)....................................... 0.20 mm
Piston pin diameter
    Standard.. 23.994 to 24.000 mm
    Service limit (min) .... 23.984 mm
Piston pin bore diameter in piston
    Standard.. 24.002 to 24.008 mm
    Service limit (max).. 24.03 mm
Piston pin-to-piston pin bore clearance
    VTR models
        Standard.. 0.002 to 0.014 mm
        Service limit (max)....................................... 0.046 mm
    XL models
        Standard.. 0.002 to 0.014 mm
        Service limit (max)....................................... 0.055 mm

Piston rings
Ring end gap (installed)
    VTR models
        Top ring
            Standard.. 0.25 to 0.40 mm
            Service limit (max)................................... 0.55 mm
        Second ring
            Standard.. 0.40 to 0.55 mm
            Service limit (max)................................... 0.70 mm
        Oil ring side-rail
            Standard.. 0.20 to 0.70 mm
            Service limit (max)................................... 0.90 mm
    XL models
        Top ring
            Standard.. 0.25 to 0.40 mm
            Service limit (max)................................... 0.55 mm
        Second ring
            Standard.. 0.40 to 0.55 mm
            Service limit (max)................................... 0.70 mm
        Oil ring side-rail
            Standard.. 0.425 to 0.475 mm
            Service limit (max)................................... 0.70 mm
Ring-to-groove clearance
    Top ring
        Standard.. 0.065 to 0.100 mm
        Service limit (max)....................................... 0.115 mm
    Second ring
        Standard.. 0.035 to 0.070 mm
        Service limit (max)....................................... 0.085 mm
Ring identification
    Top ring... R (facing up)
    2nd ring... RN (facing up)

Connecting rods
Small-end internal diameter
    Standard... 24.020 to 24.041 mm
    Service limit (max) .... 24.051 mm
Small-end-to-piston pin clearance
    Standard... 0.020 to 0.047 mm
    Service limit (max) .... 0.067 mm
Big-end side clearance
    Standard... 0.1 to 0.3 mm
    Service limit (max) .... 0.4 mm
Big-end oil clearance
    Standard... 0.032 to 0.050 mm
    Service limit (max) .... 0.060 mm

Crankshaft and bearings
Main bearing oil clearance
    Standard... 0.020 to 0.038 mm
    Service limit (max) .... 0.048 mm
Runout (max) .... 0.10 mm

Transmission – VTR models
Gear ratios (no. of teeth)
    Primary reduction.................................... 1.682 to 1 (74/44T)
    Final reduction .... 2.562 to 1 (41/16T)
    1st gear... 2.733 to 1 (41/15T)
    2nd gear .... 1.812 to 1 (29/16T)
    3rd gear .... 1.428 to 1 (30/21T)
    4th gear .... 1.206 to 1 (35/29T)
    5th gear .... 1.080 to 1 (27/25T)
    6th gear .... 0.961 to 1 (25/26T)
Input shaft 5th and 6th gears ID
    Standard... 31.000 to 31.016 mm
    Service limit (max) .... 31.04 mm
Input shaft 5th and 6th gears bush OD
    Standard... 30.955 to 30.980 mm
    Service limit (min) .... 30.93 mm
Input shaft 5th and 6th gears gear-to-bush clearance
    Standard... 0.020 to 0.061 mm
    Service limit (max) .... 0.10 mm
Input shaft 5th gear bush ID
    Standard... 27.985 to 28.006 mm
    Service limit (max) .... 28.02 mm
Input shaft OD at 5th gear bush point
    Standard... 27.967 to 27.980 mm
    Service limit (min) .... 27.94 mm
Input shaft-to-bush clearance at 5th gear bush point
    Standard... 0.005 to 0.039 mm
    Service limit (max) .... 0.06 mm
Output shaft 2nd, 3rd and 4th gears ID
    Standard... 33.000 to 33.025 mm
    Service limit (max) .... 33.05 mm
Output shaft 2nd, 3rd and 4th gears bush OD
    Standard... 32.955 to 32.980 mm
    Service limit (min) .... 32.93 mm
Output shaft 2nd, 3rd and 4th gears gear-to-bush clearance
    Standard... 0.020 to 0.070 mm
    Service limit (max) .... 0.11 mm
Output shaft 2nd gear bush ID
    Standard... 29.985 to 30.006 mm
    Service limit (max) .... 30.02 mm
Output shaft OD at 2nd gear bush point
    Standard... 29.950 to 29.975 mm
    Service limit (min) .... 29.92 mm
Output shaft-to-bushing clearance at 2nd gear bush point
    Standard... 0.010 to 0.056 mm
    Service limit (max) .... 0.06 mm

2•6 Engine, clutch and transmission

Transmission – XL-X, Y, 1 and 2 models
Gear ratios (no. of teeth)
    Primary reduction . . . . 1.682 to 1 (74/44T)
    Final reduction . . . . 2.938 to 1 (47/16T)
    1st gear. . . . . 2.571 to 1 (36/14T)
    2nd gear . . . . 1.706 to 1 (29/17T)
    3rd gear . . . . 1.318 to 1 (29/22T)
    4th gear . . . . 1.111 to 1 (30/27T)
    5th gear . . . . 0.961 to 1 (25/26T)
Input shaft 4th and 5th gears ID
    Standard. . . . . 31.000 to 31.016 mm
    Service limit (max) . . . . 31.04 mm
Input shaft 4th and 5th gears bush OD
    Standard. . . . . 30.955 to 30.980 mm
    Service limit (min) . . . . 30.93 mm
Input shaft 4th and 5th gears gear-to-bush clearance
    Standard. . . . . 0.020 to 0.061 mm
    Service limit (max) . . . . 0.10 mm
Input shaft 4th gear bush ID
    Standard. . . . . 27.985 to 28.006 mm
    Service limit (max) . . . . 28.02 mm
Input shaft OD at 4th gear bush point
    Standard. . . . . 27.967 to 27.980 mm
    Service limit (min) . . . . 27.94 mm
Input shaft-to-bush clearance at 4th gear bush point
    Standard. . . . . 0.005 to 0.039 mm
    Service limit (max) . . . . 0.06 mm
Output shaft 1st gear ID
    Standard. . . . . 26.000 to 26.021 mm
    Service limit (max) . . . . 26.04 mm
Output shaft 2nd and 3rd gears ID
    Standard. . . . . 33.000 to 33.025 mm
    Service limit (max) . . . . 33.05 mm
Output shaft 2nd and 3rd gears bush OD
    Standard. . . . . 32.955 to 32.980 mm
    Service limit (min) . . . . 32.93 mm
Output shaft 2nd and 3rd gears gear-to-bush clearance
    Standard. . . . . 0.020 to 0.070 mm
    Service limit (max) . . . . 0.11 mm
Output shaft 2nd gear bush ID
    Standard. . . . . 29.985 to 30.006 mm
    Service limit (max) . . . . 30.02 mm
Output shaft OD at 2nd gear bush point
    Standard. . . . . 29.967 to 29.980 mm
    Service limit (min) . . . . 29.92 mm
Output shaft-to-bushing clearance at 2nd gear bush point
    Standard. . . . . 0.010 to 0.056 mm
    Service limit (max) . . . . 0.06 mm

Transmission – XL-3 models onward
Gear ratios (no. of teeth)
    Primary reduction . . . . 1.682 to 1 (74/44T)
    Final reduction . . . . 2.938 to 1 (47/16T)
    1st gear. . . . . 2.571 to 1 (36/14T)
    2nd gear . . . . 1.684 to 1 (32/19T)
    3rd gear . . . . 1.292 to 1 (31/24T)
    4th gear . . . . 1.100 to 1 (33/30T)
    5th gear . . . . 1.969 to 1 (31/32T)
    6th gear . . . . 0.853 to 1 (29/34T)
Input shaft 5th and 6th gears ID
    Standard. . . . . 31.000 to 31.016 mm
    Service limit (max) . . . . 31.04 mm
Input shaft 5th gear bush OD
    Standard. . . . . 30.955 to 30.980 mm
    Service limit (min) . . . . 30.93 mm
Input shaft 6th gear bush OD
    Standard. . . . . 30.950 to 30.975 mm
    Service limit (min) . . . . 30.93 mm

… Engine, clutch and transmission 2•7

Transmission – XL-3 models onward (continued)

Input shaft 5th gear gear-to-bush clearance
    Standard.. 0.020 to 0.065 mm
    Service limit (max) .... 0.10 mm
Input shaft 6th gear gear-to-bush clearance
    Standard.. 0.020 to 0.061 mm
    Service limit (max) .... 0.10 mm
Input shaft 5th gear bush ID
    Standard.. 27.985 to 28.006 mm
    Service limit (max) .... 28.02 mm
Input shaft OD at 5th gear bush point
    Standard.. 27.967 to 27.980 mm
    Service limit (min) .... 27.96 mm
Input shaft-to-bush clearance at 5th gear bush point
    Standard.. 0.005 to 0.039 mm
    Service limit (max) .... 0.06 mm
Output shaft 1st gear ID
    Standard.. 26.000 to 26.021 mm
    Service limit (max) .... 26.04 mm
Output shaft 2nd, 3rd and 4th gears ID
    Standard.. 33.000 to 33.025 mm
    Service limit (max) .... 33.05 mm
Output shaft 2nd, 3rd and 4th gears bush OD
    Standard.. 32.955 to 32.980 mm
    Service limit (min) .... 32.93 mm
Output shaft 2nd, 3rd and 4th gears gear-to-bush clearance
    Standard.. 0.020 to 0.070 mm
    Service limit (max) .... 0.11 mm
Output shaft 2nd gear bush ID
    Standard.. 29.985 to 30.006 mm
    Service limit (max) .... 30.02 mm
Output shaft OD at 2nd gear bush point
    Standard.. 29.950 to 29.975 mm
    Service limit (min) .... 29.92 mm
Output shaft-to-bushing clearance at 2nd gear bush point
    Standard.. 0.010 to 0.056 mm
    Service limit (max) .... 0.06 mm

Selector drum and forks

Selector fork end thickness
    Standard.. 5.93 to 6.00 mm
    Service limit (min) .... 5.90 mm
Selector fork bore ID
    Standard.. 12.000 to 12.021 mm
    Service limit (max) .... 12.03 mm
Selector fork shaft OD
    Standard.. 11.957 to 11.968 mm
    Service limit (min) .... 11.95 mm

Torque settings

Engine mountings
  VTR models
    Middle mounting bolts .... 39 Nm
    Adjuster bolts .... 3 Nm
    Adjuster bolt locknuts
      Indicated.. 49 Nm
      Actual .... 54 Nm
    Front and rear mounting bolt nuts .... 64 Nm
Engine mountings (continued)
  XL models
    Middle mounting bolts .... 39 Nm
    Adjuster bolts .... 3 Nm
    Adjuster bolt locknuts
      Indicated.. 49 Nm
      Actual .... 54 Nm
    Front and rear mounting bolt nuts .... 64 Nm

2•8 Engine, clutch and transmission

Torque settings (continued)

Suspension linkage arm/sidestand bracket nuts	
VTR models	44 Nm
XL-X, Y, 1 and 2 models	
12 mm bolt	54 Nm
14 mm bolt	59 Nm
XL-3 models onward	
12 mm bolt	64 Nm
14 mm bolt	74 Nm
Valve cover bolts	10 Nm
Camshaft holder bolts (7 mm)	21 Nm
Camshaft sprocket bolts	20 Nm
Timing inspection cap	10 Nm
Crankshaft end-cap	15 Nm
Cam chain tensioner blade and guide blade pivot bolts	23 Nm
Cylinder head 10 mm bolts	53 Nm
Starter clutch bolts	23 Nm
Oil pump driven sprocket bolt	15 Nm
Clutch nut	127 Nm
Clutch spring bolts	12 Nm
Clutch hose banjo bolt	34 Nm
Clutch release cylinder bleed valve	9 Nm
Oil pump assembly bolts	
VTR models	12 Nm
XL models	13 Nm
Oil pump mounting bolts	12 Nm
Selector drum cam bolt	23 Nm
Primary drive gear bolt	88 Nm
Crankcase	
6 mm bolts	10 Nm
8 mm bolts	22 Nm
Lower crankcase 10 mm bolts	42 Nm
Upper crankcase 10 mm bolt	39 Nm
Connecting rod bolts	29 Nm + 120° (see text)

1 General information

The engine/transmission unit is a liquid-cooled 90°V-twin. The eight valves are operated by double overhead camshafts which are chain driven off the crankshaft. The engine/transmission assembly is constructed from aluminium alloy. The crankcase is divided horizontally.

The crankcase incorporates a wet sump, pressure-fed lubrication system which uses a dual rotor oil pump that is chain-driven off the back of the clutch. The system has an oil filter, an oil pressure switch, and two pressure relief valves. The main relief valve is in the feed to the oil filter, the second valve is in the feed to the oil cooler. The oil pump has a second rotor which feeds the oil through a cooler mounted on the front of the engine.

The alternator is on the left-hand end of the crankshaft and has the starter clutch mounted behind it. The water pump is chain driven off the right-hand end of the crankshaft. The pulse generator coil and ignition rotor are also on the right-hand end of the crankshaft.

Power from the crankshaft is routed to the transmission via the clutch. The clutch is of the wet, multi-plate type and is gear-driven off the crankshaft. The clutch is operated hydraulically on VTR models, and by cable on XL models. The transmission is a six-speed constant-mesh unit on all VTR models and XL models from 2003-on, and a five-speed unit on XL models up to 2002. Final drive to the rear wheel is by chain and sprockets.

2 Operations possible with the engine in the frame

The components and assemblies listed below can be removed without having to remove the engine/transmission assembly from the frame. If, however, a number of areas require attention at the same time, removal of the engine is recommended.

Valve cover
Cam chain tensioners and blades
Camshafts and cam chains
Cylinder heads
Ignition rotor and pulse generator coil assembly
Clutch
Gearchange mechanism
Alternator
Oil filter and oil cooler
Oil sump, oil pump, oil strainer and oil pressure relief valves
Starter motor
Starter clutch
Water pump
Selector drum and forks

3 Operations requiring engine removal

It is necessary to remove the engine/transmission assembly from the frame to gain access to the following components.
Pistons, piston rings and cylinder bores
Transmission shafts
Crankshaft and bearings
Connecting rods and bearings

4 Major engine repair – general note

1 It is not always easy to determine if an engine should be completely overhauled, as a number of factors must be considered.
2 High mileage is not necessarily an indication that an overhaul is needed, while low mileage, on the other hand, does not preclude the need for an overhaul. Frequency of servicing is probably the single most important consideration. An engine that has regular and frequent oil and filter changes, as well as other required maintenance, will most likely give many miles of reliable service. Conversely, a neglected engine, or one which has not been run-in properly, may require an overhaul very early in its life.
3 Exhaust smoke and excessive oil

Engine, clutch and transmission 2•9

consumption are both indications that piston rings and/or valve guides are in need of attention, although make sure that the fault is not due to oil leakage.

4 If the engine is making obvious knocking or rumbling noises, the connecting rods and/or main bearings are probably at fault.

5 Loss of power, rough running, excessive valve train noise and high fuel consumption rates may also point to the need for an overhaul, especially if they are all present at the same time. If a complete tune-up does not remedy the situation, major mechanical work is the only solution.

6 An engine overhaul generally involves restoring the internal parts to the specifications of a new engine. The piston rings and main and connecting rod bearings are usually replaced and the cylinder walls honed or, if necessary, re-bored, during a major overhaul. Generally the valve seats are re-ground, since they are usually in less than perfect condition at this point. The end result should be a like-new engine that will give as many trouble-free miles as the original.

7 Before beginning the engine overhaul, read through the related procedures to familiarise yourself with the scope and requirements of the job. Overhauling an engine is not all that difficult, but it is time-consuming. Plan on the motorcycle being tied up for a minimum of two weeks. Check on the availability of parts and make sure that any necessary special tools, equipment and supplies are obtained in advance.

8 Most work can be done with typical workshop hand tools, although a number of precision measuring tools are required for inspecting parts to determine if they must be replaced. Often a dealer will handle the inspection of parts and offer advice concerning reconditioning and replacement. As a general rule, time is the primary cost of an overhaul so it does not pay to install worn or substandard parts.

9 As a final note, to ensure maximum life and minimum trouble from a rebuilt engine, everything must be assembled with care in a spotlessly clean environment.

5 Engine – removal and installation

Caution: The engine is very heavy. Engine removal and installation should be carried out with the aid of at least one assistant; personal injury or damage could occur if the engine falls or is dropped.

Removal

1 Support the bike securely in an upright position using an auxiliary stand. Work can be made easier by raising the machine to a suitable working height on an hydraulic ramp or a suitable platform. Make sure the motorcycle is secure and will not topple over (see *Tools and Workshop Tips* in the Reference section).

2 If the engine is dirty, particularly around its mountings, wash it thoroughly before starting any major dismantling work. This will make work much easier and rule out the possibility of caked on lumps of dirt falling into some vital component.

3 Remove the fairing, fairing side panels (XL models), belly-pan and front mudguard (see Chapter 8). Remove the fairing/radiator brackets on the front cylinder. On VTR models, there are also two brackets bolted to the frame (the left-hand one secured by the front cylinder coil rear mounting bolt) which have extremely sharp edges. It is advisable to remove these as it is all to easy to knock your head against them when working around the engine. Note how they fit when removing them, and which fits where.

4 Drain the engine oil and the cooling system (see Chapter 1).

5 Remove the fuel tank (see Chapter 4).

6 Remove the radiators along with their hoses (see Chapter 3). On VTR models, also remove the oil cooler along with its pipes/hoses (see Section 7).

7 Remove the exhaust system (see Chapter 4).

8 Remove the carburettors (see Chapter 4A) or throttle bodies (see Chapter 4B) according to model. Plug the engine inlet manifolds with clean rag.

9 Remove the thermostat housing (see Chapter 3).

10 Disconnect the negative (–ve) lead from the battery. Feed the lead through to the engine and coil it on the crankcase.

11 On VTR models, disconnect the alternator, sidestand switch and speed sensor wiring connectors – they are housed inside the rubber boot near the battery **(see illustration)**. Also disconnect the ignition pulse generator wiring connector, which is located under the left-hand side of the frame **(see illustration)**. Release the wiring from any clips or ties, noting its routing, and feed it through to its source so that it does not impede engine removal.

12 On XL models, disconnect the wiring connectors housed inside the rubber boot on the left-hand side **(see illustration)**. On XL-3 models onward remove the side covers and also disconnect the alternator wiring connector on the left-hand side and the speed sensor

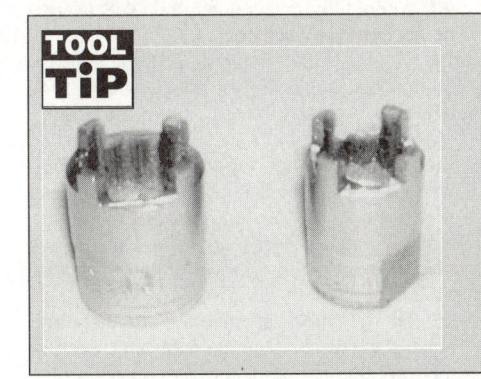

TOOL TiP

On all models a peg spanner is required to slacken and tighten the adjuster bolt locknuts on two of the engine mounting bolts. If the Honda service tool (Part no 07VMA-MBB0100) is not available, a suitable one will have to fabricated out of a piece of steel tubing, or an old 19 mm socket (right). On VTR models a second similar tool (Part no. 07HMA-MR70200) is required for one of the other mounting bolts – this can be made out of a 22 mm socket (left).

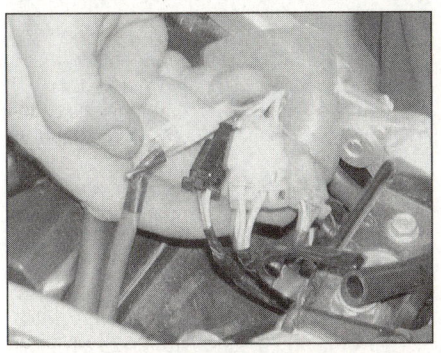

5.11a Disconnect the relevant wiring connectors in the boot . . .

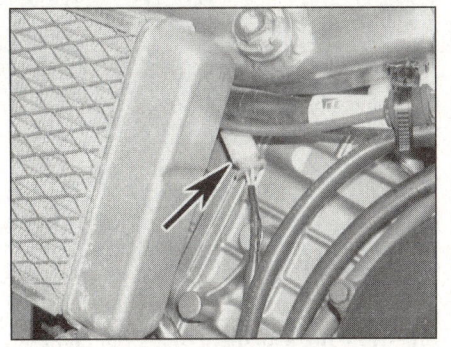

5.11b . . . and the pulse generator coil wiring connector (arrowed)

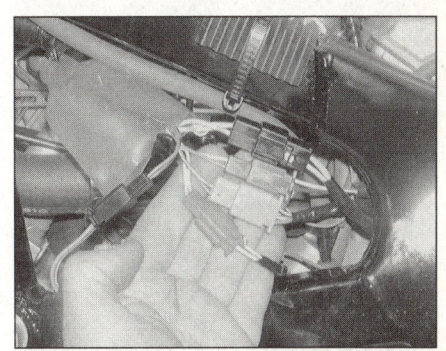

5.12a Disconnect the relevant wiring connectors in the boot

2•10 Engine, clutch and transmission

5.12b Disconnect the alternator wiring connector (arrowed) . . .

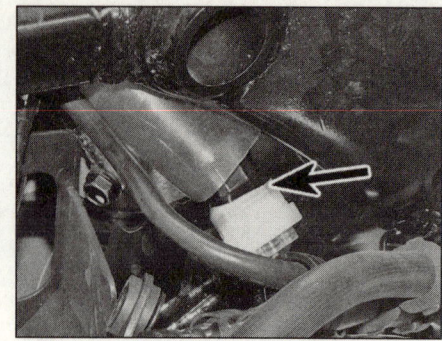

5.12c . . . and the speed sensor wiring connector (arrowed) . . .

5.12d . . . displacing the ABS modulator to access it

wiring connector on the right **(see illustrations)** – on models equipped with ABS the rear modulator blocks access to the speed sensor wiring connector, so you need to displace it (see Chapter 7 – there is no need to drain the brake fluid or disconnect the brake hoses). Release the wiring from any clips or ties, noting its routing, and feed it through to its source so that it does not impede engine removal.

13 Pull back the rubber boot on the oil pressure switch, then undo the screw and detach the wiring connector **(see illustration)**. Disconnect the wiring connector from the neutral switch **(see illustration)**. On XL models, if access is restricted by the front sprocket cover, disconnect it after removing the cover (Step 17).

14 Pull back the rubber cover on the starter motor terminal, then unscrew the nut and disconnect the lead **(see illustration)**.

15 Disconnect the HT leads from the spark plugs and secure them clear of the engine. If the HT leads don't have their cylinder identity marked on them, label each lead to ensure correct reconnection.

16 Note how the punchmark on the gearchange shaft aligns with either the slot in the linkage arm or the punchmark on the arm, where marked. Unscrew the linkage arm pinch bolt and slide the arm off the shaft **(see illustration)**.

17 If required, remove the front sprocket (see Chapter 6). Alternatively, remove the clutch release cylinder (VTR models, see Section 17)

and the front sprocket cover (see Chapter 6), then slip the chain off the sprocket once the swingarm has been removed.

18 Support the motorcycle using either a hoist attached to the frame from above, or by using two tall axle stands with a metal bar between them, with the bar under the frame. Remove the rear wheel, suspension linkage, footrest brackets and swingarm (see Chapters 7 and 6).

19 Remove the sidestand (see Chapter 6). If required, unscrew the nuts and withdraw the bolts securing the suspension linkage arm/sidestand bracket(s) – on VTR models there is a bracket on each side located by two dowels **(see illustration)**, on XL models it is a one-piece assembly with spacers on the right-hand side. Take care not to lose the dowels or spacers.

20 Where fitted, disconnect the PAIR system hoses from the valve covers.

21 At this point, position an hydraulic or mechanical jack under the engine with a block of wood between the jack head and sump. Make sure the jack is centrally positioned so the engine will not topple in any direction when the last mounting bolt is removed. Take the weight of the engine on the jack.
Note: *It may be necessary to adjust the jack height to ease the removal of the mounting bolts.*

22 On VTR models, unscrew the nuts and remove the washers on the right-hand ends of the front and rear engine mounting bolts **(see**

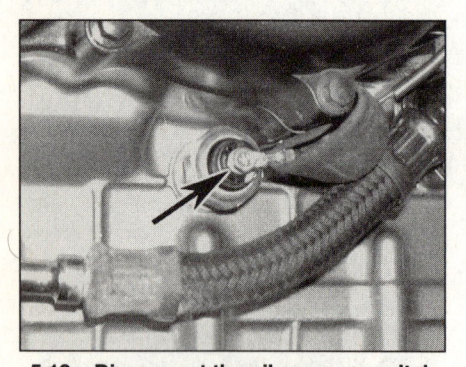

5.13a Disconnect the oil pressure switch wiring connector (arrowed) . . .

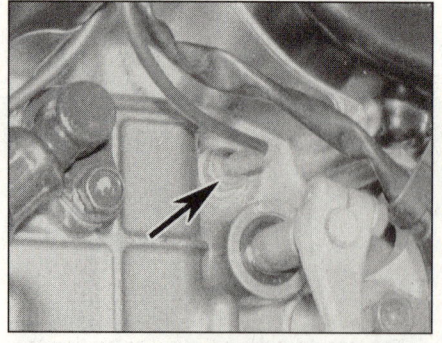

5.13b . . . and the neutral switch wiring connector (arrowed)

5.14 Pull back the cover and remove the nut securing the starter motor lead

5.16 Note the alignment of the punchmark, then remove the bolt (arrowed) and slide the arm off the shaft – VTR models

5.19 Removing the sidestand/suspension linkage bracket – VTR models

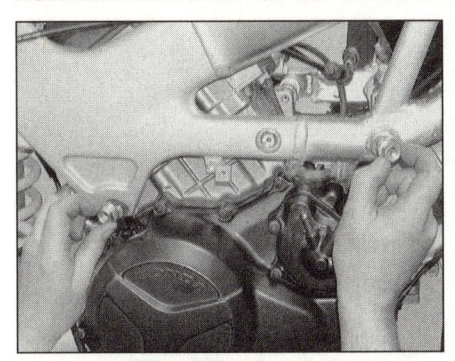

Engine, clutch and transmission 2•11

5.22a Unscrew the nuts and remove the washers . . .

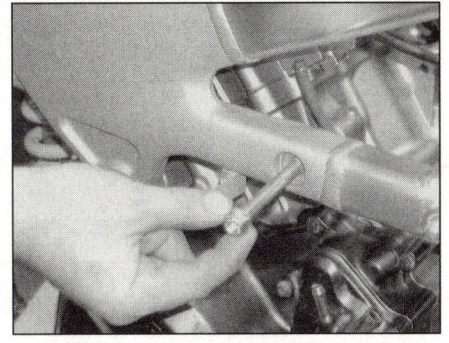

5.22b . . . then remove the middle mounting bolt

5.22c Unscrew the locknuts (arrowed) . . .

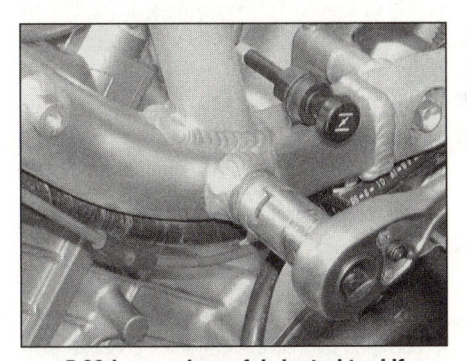

5.22d . . . using a fabricated tool if necessary

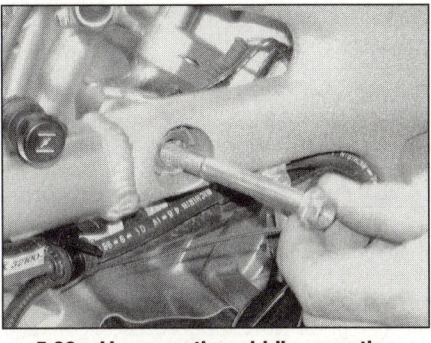

5.22e Unscrew the middle mounting bolt . . .

5.22f . . . and remove the spacer

5.22g Unscrew the adjuster bolt using the mounting bolt

5.22h Withdraw the front mounting bolt

5.23a Engine left-hand mounts – XL models

5.23b Engine right-hand mounts – XL models

illustration). Unscrew and remove the middle mounting bolt on the right-hand side **(see illustration)**. Slacken the adjuster bolt locknuts on the left-hand mounting bolts using a suitable peg spanner **(see *Tool Tip* on page 2•8) (see illustrations)**. Unscrew and remove the centre bolt, then unscrew the adjuster bolt until it is flush with the inside of the frame and remove the spacer from between it and the frame **(see illustrations)**. Partially unscrew the rear adjuster bolt using an Allen key in the mounting bolt head, which engages with the adjuster bolt, until the adjuster is flush with the inside of the frame **(see illustration)**. Withdraw the front mounting bolt **(see illustration)**.

23 On XL-X, Y, 1 and 2 models, unscrew the nuts and remove the washers on the right-hand end of the front and rear engine mounting bolts **(see illustrations)**. Unscrew and remove the middle mounting bolt on each side and remove the spacers from between the engine and frame, noting which fits where. Unscrew the adjuster bolt locknuts on the front and rear left-hand mounting bolts using a suitable peg spanner **(see *Tool Tip* on page 2•8)**. Unscrew the front and rear adjuster bolts using an Allen key in the mounting bolt head, which engages with the adjuster bolt, until the adjusters are flush with the inside of the frame. Withdraw the front mounting bolt and remove the spacer from between the engine and frame on the right-hand side.

24 On XL-3 models onward, remove the

2•12 Engine, clutch and transmission

5.24a Remove the blanking cap from each side

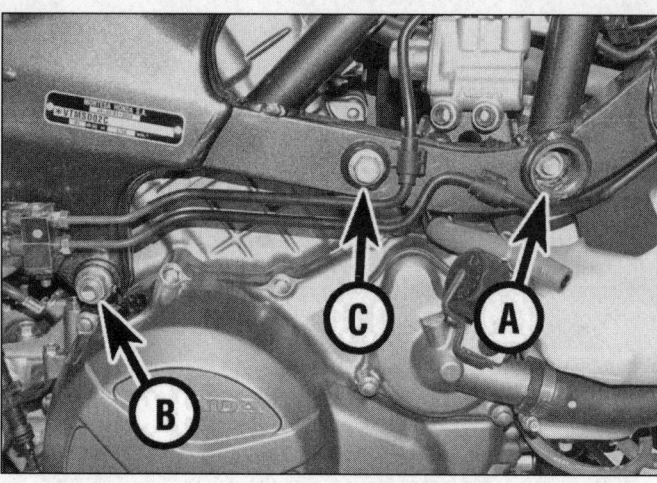

5.24b Front mounting bolt nut (A), rear mounting bolt nut (B), middle mounting bolt (C)

blanking cap from each side of the rear engine mounting bolt, then unscrew the nuts and remove the washers on the right-hand end of the front and rear engine mounting bolts **(see illustrations)**. Unscrew and remove the middle mounting bolt on each side and remove the spacers from between the engine and frame, noting which fits where. Withdraw the front mounting bolt and remove the spacers from between the engine and frame on each side, noting which fits where.

25 The engine can now be removed from the frame (see **Caution** above). Check that all wiring, cables and hoses are well clear, move the jack out of the way, then carefully pivot the front of the engine down using the rear mounting bolt as the pivot, until the rear cylinder is just upright (so that it is clear of the mounting bolt lugs on the inside of the frame), then either place a support between the bottom of the engine and the ground/ramp or lower the rear of the bike until the engine rests on the sump. Now support the engine and withdraw the rear mounting bolt, then raise the frame up off the engine, making sure the lugs on the inside of the frame do not touch it **(see illustrations)**. Support the frame in the raised position and manoeuvre the engine from under it **(see illustration)**. If required (and where fitted), remove the adjuster bolts from the frame – remove the front one from the inside **(see illustration)**.

Installation

26 If removed, thread the adjuster bolts into the frame – fit the front one from the inside and thread it as far into the frame as possible **(see illustration 5.24d)**. Fit the others from the outside of the frame and thread them in until they are flush with the inside of the frame.

27 Manoeuvre the engine into position under the frame and tilt it forward until the rear cylinder is just upright as on removal **(see illustrations 5.25c and b)**. In this position the front cylinder conveniently rests against the front tyre while the rear mounting bolt hole should just about be vertically in line with the corresponding holes in the frame. Carefully lower and guide the frame down onto the engine, making sure the lugs on the inside of the frame do not contact it, until the rear mounting bolt holes align, then install the rear bolt, on all except XL-3 models onward aligning the flats on the bolt head so it engages with the adjuster bolt **(see illustration 5.25a)**. Now pivot the front of the engine up until the front mounting bolt holes align, then install the front mounting bolt, on XL-X, Y, 1 and 2 models not forgetting the spacer between the right-hand side of the engine and the frame **(see illustration 5.22h)**, and on XL-3 models onward not forgetting the short spacer on the left-hand side and the long spacer on the right between the engine and frame. Make sure no wires, cables or hoses become trapped between the engine and the frame. Install and tighten the remaining mounting bolt assemblies in the order described below.

28 On VTR models, install the middle right-hand bolt and tighten it to the torque setting specified at the beginning of the Chapter **(see illustration 5.22b)**. Fit the spacer between the middle left-hand adjuster bolt and the engine **(see illustration 5.22f)**,

5.25a Withdraw the rear mounting bolt . . .

5.25b . . . then raise the frame off the engine . . .

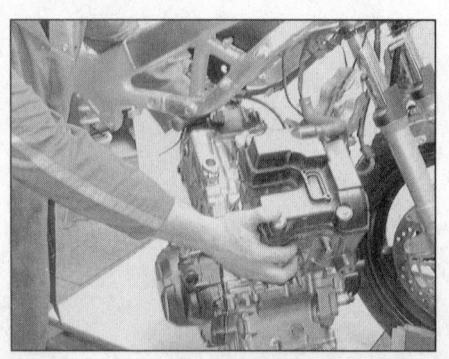

5.25c . . . and manoeuvre the engine out

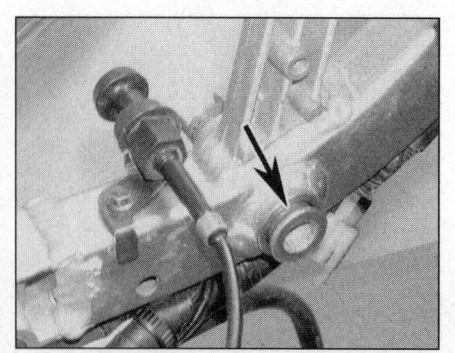

5.25d Remove the front adjuster bolt (arrowed) from the inside of the frame

Engine, clutch and transmission 2•13

5.28a Fit the locknut . . .

5.28b . . . and tighten it to the specified torque as described

is the reverse of removal, noting the following points:

a) If removed, tighten the suspension linkage arm/sidestand bracket(s) nuts to the specified torque settings, not forgetting the dowels (VTR) or spacers (XL) – see Step 19.
b) Use new gaskets on the exhaust pipe connections.
c) Align the punchmark on the gearchange shaft with the slit in the linkage arm when installing the arm onto the shaft, and tighten the pinch bolt securely **(see illustration 5.16)**.
d) Make sure all wires, cables and hoses are correctly routed and connected, and secured by any clips or ties.
e) Refill the engine with oil and coolant (see Chapter 1).
f) Adjust the throttle cable freeplay, and on XL models clutch cable freeplay.
g) Adjust the drive chain (see Chapter 1).
h) Start the engine and check that there are no oil or coolant leaks. Adjust the idle speed (see Chapter 1).

6 Engine disassembly and reassembly – general information

Disassembly

1 Before disassembling the engine, thoroughly clean and degrease its external surfaces. This will prevent contamination of the engine internals, and will also make working a lot easier and cleaner. A high flash-point solvent, such as paraffin (kerosene) can be used, or better still, a proprietary engine degreaser. Use old paintbrushes and toothbrushes to work the solvent into the various recesses of the engine casings. Take care to exclude solvent or water from the electrical components and inlet and exhaust ports.

> **Warning: The use of petrol (gasoline) as a cleaning agent should be avoided because of the risk of fire.**

2 When clean and dry, position the engine on the workbench, leaving suitable clear area for

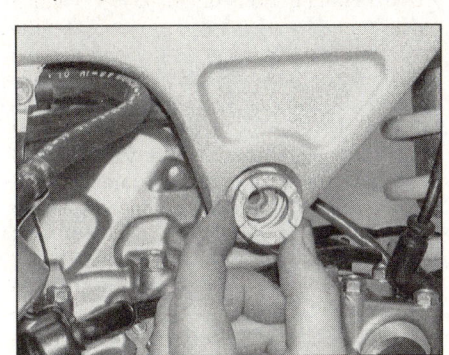

then tighten the adjuster bolt to the specified torque. Fit the locknut onto the adjuster bolt and tighten the locknut to the specified torque, making sure the adjuster bolt does not turn **(see illustrations)**. If the Honda special tool is being used, tighten the locknut to the indicated torque setting specified. If a home-made tool is being used, tighten it to the actual torque setting specified. If the special tool is used, the adjuster bolt can be counter-held to prevent it from moving, otherwise make a reference mark between the adjuster bolt and the frame and check that it has not moved after tightening. Now install the middle left-hand mounting bolt and tighten it to the specified torque **(see illustration 5.22e)**. Tighten the rear adjuster bolt to the specified torque using an Allen key in the mounting bolt head **(see illustration 5.22g)**, then install the locknut and tighten it in the same way as the middle locknut, according to your tools **(see illustration)**. Tighten the front adjuster bolt and locknut in the same way **(see illustrations)**. Finally fit the washers and nuts onto the right-hand ends of the front and rear mounting bolts, then counter-hold the bolts and tighten the nuts to the specified torque **(see illustration 5.22a)**.

29 On XL-X, Y, 1 and 2 models, install the middle mounting bolts with their spacers (long spacer on the left-hand side, short spacer on the right) and tighten them to the torque setting specified at the beginning of the Chapter **(see illustrations 5.23a and 5.23b)**.

Tighten the rear and front adjusting bolts to the specified torque using an Allen key in the mounting bolt head. Fit the locknuts onto the adjusting bolts and tighten the locknuts to the specified torque, making sure the adjuster bolts do not turn. If the Honda special tool is being used, tighten the locknuts to the indicated torque setting specified. If a home-made tool is being used, tighten them to the actual torque setting specified. If the special tool is used, the adjusting bolts can be counter-held to prevent it from moving, otherwise make a reference mark between the adjuster bolts and the frame and check that they have not moved after tightening. Finally fit the washers and nuts onto the right-hand ends of the front and rear mounting bolts, then counter-hold the bolts and tighten the nuts to the specified torque.

30 On XL-3 models onward, install the middle mounting bolts with their spacers (long spacer on the left-hand side, short spacer on the right) and tighten them finger-tight **(see illustration 5.24b)**. Fit the washers and nuts onto the right-hand ends of the front and rear mounting bolts. First tighten the right-hand middle mounting bolt to the torque setting specified at the beginning of the Chapter, then tighten the left-hand middle bolt. Next tighten the nut on the rear mounting bolt to the specified torque, counter-holding the bolt head, and then repeat for the front mounting bolt. Fit the blanking cap into each side of the frame **(see illustration 5.24a)**.

31 The remainder of the installation procedure

5.28c Fit the locknut onto the rear adjuster bolt

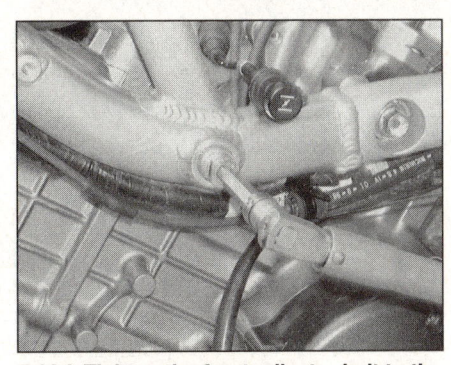

5.28d Tighten the front adjuster bolt to the specified torque . . .

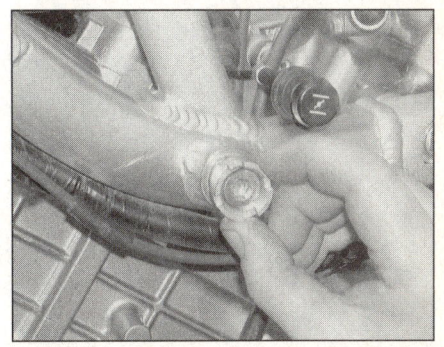

5.28e . . . then fit and tighten the locknut to the specified torque

2•14 Engine, clutch and transmission

6.4 An engine support made from pieces of 2 x 4 inch wood

working. Gather a selection of small containers, plastic bags and some labels so that parts can be grouped together in an easily identifiable manner. Also get some paper and a pen so that notes can be taken. You will also need a supply of clean rag, which should be as absorbent as possible.

3 Before commencing work, read through the appropriate section so that some idea of the necessary procedure can be gained. When removing components note that great force is seldom required, unless specified. In many cases, a component's reluctance to be removed is indicative of an incorrect approach or removal method – if in any doubt, re-check with the text.

4 An engine support stand made from short lengths of 2 x 4 inch wood bolted together into a rectangle will help support the engine

7.3a Unscrew the bolts (arrowed) and detach the pipe from the cooler

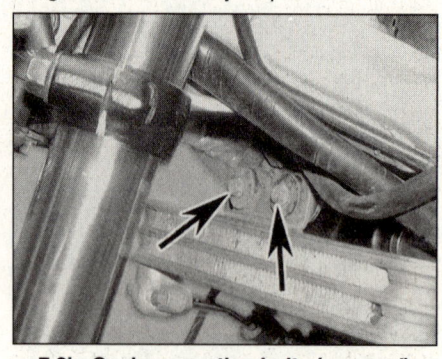

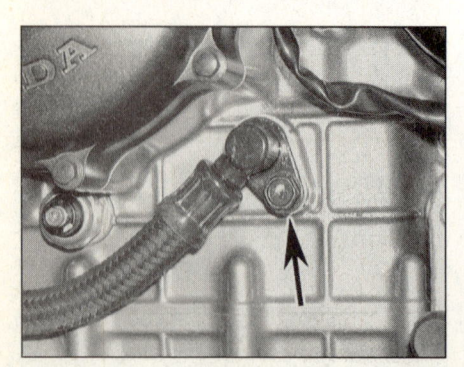

7.4 Unscrew the bolt (arrowed) and detach the hose

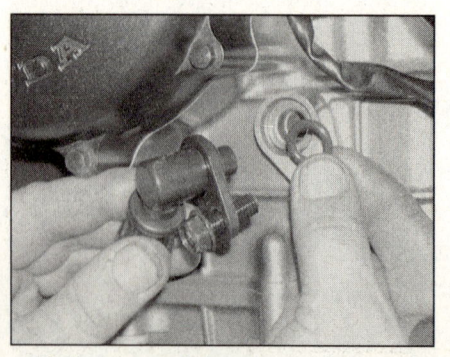

(see illustration). The perimeter of the mount should be just big enough to accommodate the sump within it so that the engine rests on its crankcase.

5 When disassembling the engine, keep 'mated' parts together (including gears, cylinder bores, pistons, connecting rods, valves, etc. that have been in contact with each other during engine operation). These 'mated' parts must be reused or replaced as an assembly.

6 A complete engine/transmission disassembly should be done in the following general order with reference to the appropriate Sections.

Remove the valve covers
Remove the cylinder heads
Remove the clutch cover/water pump/pulse generator coil assembly
Remove the clutch
Remove the alternator/starter clutch (see Chapter 9)
Remove the starter motor (see Chapter 9)
Remove the gearchange mechanism
Remove the cams chains and blades
Remove the oil sump
Remove the oil pump
Separate the crankcase halves
Remove the connecting rods and pistons
Remove the crankshaft
Remove the transmission shafts
Remove the selector drum and forks

Reassembly

7 Reassembly is accomplished by reversing the general disassembly sequence.

7.3b Cooler mounting bolts (arrowed)

7.6 Use a new O-ring on each hose and pipe union

7 Oil cooler and pipes – removal and installation (VTR models)

Note: *The oil cooler can be removed with the engine in the frame. If the engine has been removed, ignore the steps which do not apply.*

Removal

1 Remove the fairing (see Chapter 8).
2 Drain the engine oil (see Chapter 1).
3 To remove the cooler without its feed and return pipes, unscrew the bolts securing the cooler to the pipe unions and detach the pipes **(see illustration)**. Discard the union O-rings as new ones must be used. Now unscrew the cooler mounting bolts, noting the collars, and remove the cooler **(see illustration)**.
4 To remove the cooler with its feed and return pipes, unscrew the bolt securing each hose union to the crankcase and detach the hoses from the engine **(see illustration)**. Discard the union O-rings as new ones must be used. Now unscrew the cooler mounting bolts, noting the collars, and remove the cooler and pipes **(see illustration 7.3b)**.
5 To remove the pipes/hoses but leave the cooler in place, unscrew the bolts securing the pipe unions to the cooler **(see illustration 7.3a)**, then unscrew the bolt securing each hose union to the crankcase **(see illustration 7.4)**, then detach the pipes/hoses from the engine and cooler and remove them. Discard the union O-rings as new ones must be used.

Installation

6 Installation is the reverse of removal, noting the following:
a) Always use new O-rings on the pipe and hose unions and smear them with clean oil **(see illustration)**.
b) Check the condition of the cooler mounting grommets and replace them if they are damaged or deteriorated.
c) Fill the engine with oil (see Chapter 1).

8 Valve covers – removal and installation

Note: *The valve covers can be removed with the engine in the frame. If the engine has been removed, ignore the steps which do not apply.*

Removal

1 On VTR models, to access the front cylinder valve cover remove the fairing (see Chapter 8). Unscrew the two oil cooler mounting bolts, noting the collars, and displace the cooler forward **(see illustration 7.3b)**. There is no need to detach the pipes. Also remove the bolts securing the cooler mounting bracket to the frame and remove the bracket.
2 On XL models, to access the front cylinder valve cover remove the fairing side panels (see Chapter 8). Also remove the trim clips securing

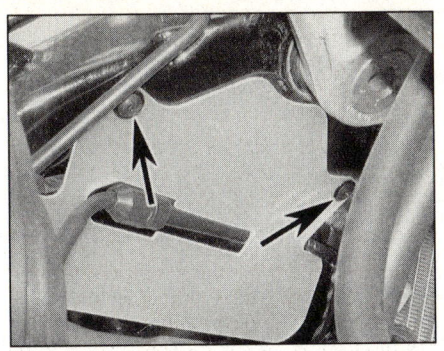

Engine, clutch and transmission 2•15

8.2 Release the trim clips (arrowed) and remove the shield

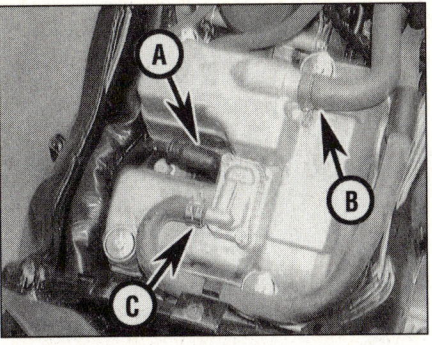

8.5 Pull off the spark plug cap (A), detach the breather hose (B), and on US VTR and all XL models the PAIR hose (C)

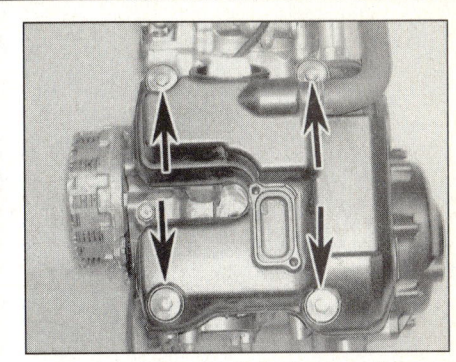

8.6a Unscrew the bolts (arrowed)...

8.6b ...and remove the cover

8.7 Make sure the gasket locates in the groove and stays there

the heat shield above the valve cover and remove the shield **(see illustration)**. To release the trim clips unscrew the centre of the clip, then pull the body of the clip out.

3 On all models, to access the rear cylinder valve cover remove the fuel tank (see Chapter 4).

4 Pull the spark plug cap off the plug and secure it clear of the cover.

5 Release the breather hose clamp and detach the hose from the valve cover **(see illustration)**. Where fitted, release the PAIR system hose clamp and detach the hose from the reed valve assembly on the cover.

6 Unscrew the valve cover bolts and lift the cover off the cylinder head **(see illustrations)**. If it is stuck, do not try to lever it off with a screwdriver. Tap it gently around the sides with a rubber hammer or block of wood to dislodge it. Note the rubber washers fitted in the cover and remove them if they are loose **(see illustration 8.9a)**. The rubber gasket is normally glued into the groove in the cover, and is best left there if it is reusable. If the gasket is in any way damaged, deformed or deteriorated, remove it and use a new one. On US VTR models and all XL models, remove the O-ring and dowel from the cylinder head or valve cover for safekeeping.

Installation

7 Examine the valve cover gasket for signs of damage or deterioration and replace it with new one if necessary. If a new one is used, clean all traces of the old glue from the groove in the cover and clean it and the cylinder head mating surface with solvent. Fit the new gasket into the groove, using a suitable glue, sealant or grease to hold it in place **(see illustration)**. Also apply sealant to the cut-outs in the cylinder head.

8 On US VTR models and all XL models, fit the dowel into the cylinder head then fit a new O-ring around it.

9 Position the valve cover on the cylinder head, making sure the gasket stays in place **(see illustration 8.6b)**. If removed, fit the rubber washers into the cover, using new ones if required, and making sure they are installed with the UP mark facing up **(see illustration)**. Install the cover bolts and tighten them to the torque setting specified at the beginning of the Chapter **(see illustration)**.

10 Install the remaining components in the reverse order of removal.

9 Cam chain tensioners – removal and installation

Removal

1 To access the front cylinder tensioner, remove the air filter housing (see Chapter 4). To access the rear cylinder tensioner, on XL models remove the right-hand side cover (see Chapter 8, Section 4).

2 Unscrew the tensioner cap bolt and remove the sealing washer **(see illustration)**.

3 If the Honda tensioner locking key is

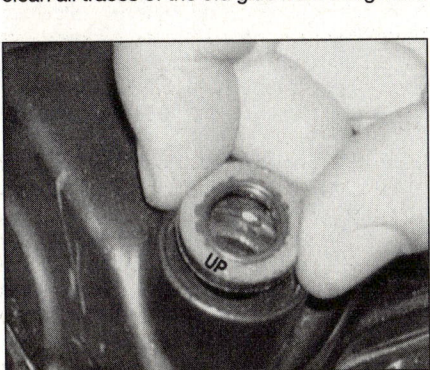

8.9a Make sure the UP mark on the washers faces up...

8.9b ...then install the bolts and tighten them to the specified torque

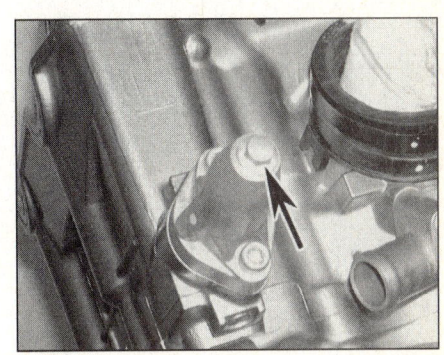

9.2 Unscrew the cap bolt (arrowed) and remove the washer

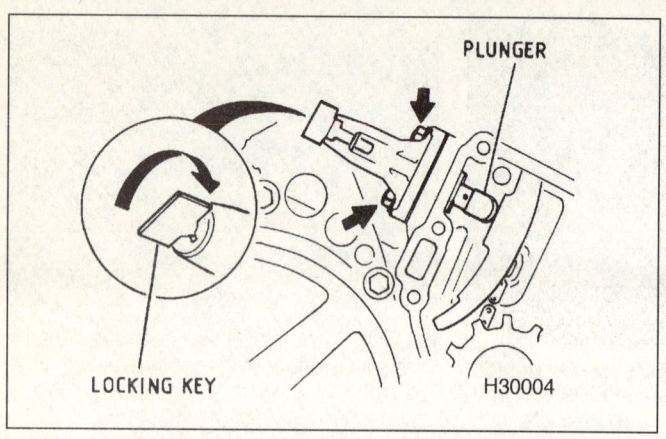

2•16 Engine, clutch and transmission

9.3a Honda locking key in position with tensioner plunger retracted. Tensioner mounting bolts arrowed

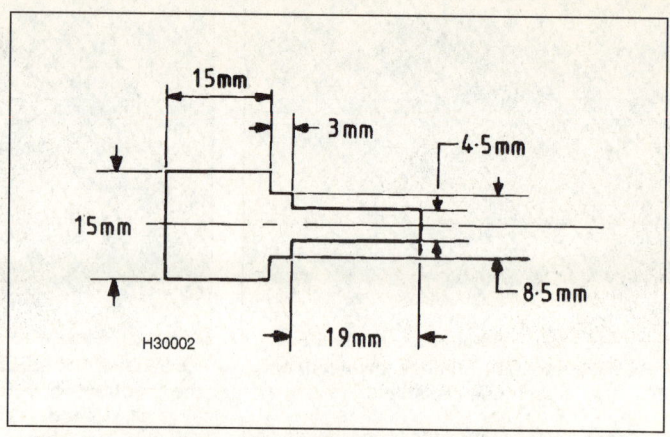

9.3b A copy of Honda's locking key can be made using 1 mm thick steel cut to the dimensions shown

available, insert it in the end of the tensioner so that it engages the slotted plunger, turn it clockwise until the plunger is fully retracted, then push the key into the slots in the end of the tensioner body to lock it **(see illustration)**. Unscrew the tensioner mounting bolts and withdraw the tensioner from the engine. If the Honda tool is not available, a home-made equivalent can be easily made out of a piece of 1 mm steel plate cut to the dimensions shown **(see illustration)**.

4 If a locking key is not available, first slacken the tensioner mounting bolts slightly **(see illustration)**. Insert a small flat-bladed screwdriver in the end of the tensioner so that it engages the slotted plunger. Turn the screwdriver clockwise until the plunger is fully retracted and hold it in this position while unscrewing the tensioner mounting bolts **(see illustration)**. Withdraw the tensioner from the engine, then release the screwdriver – the plunger will spring back out once the screwdriver is removed, but can be easily reset on installation.

5 Discard the gasket as a new one must be used on installation. Do not dismantle the tensioner.

Installation

6 Check that the plunger moves smoothly when pressed into the tensioner and springs back out freely when released. Ensure the tensioner and cylinder block surfaces are clean and dry and fit a new gasket onto the tensioner **(see illustration)**.

7 If the locking key described above is being used, insert it in the end of the tensioner so that it engages the slotted plunger and turn it clockwise until the plunger is fully retracted, then push the key into the slotted end of the tensioner body to lock it in this position **(see illustrations 9.3a and 9.3b)**. Apply a suitable non-permanent thread locking compound to the tensioner mounting bolt threads. Install the tensioner and tighten the bolts to the torque setting specified at the beginning of the Chapter. Remove the key, then install the tensioner end bolt with a new sealing washer and tighten it securely **(see illustration 9.8c)**.

8 If the key is not available, first apply a suitable non-permanent thread locking compound to the tensioner mounting bolt threads. Now insert a small flat-bladed screwdriver in the end of the tensioner so that it engages the slotted plunger **(see illustration)**. Turn the screwdriver clockwise until the plunger is fully retracted and hold it in this position whilst the tensioner and its bolts are installed **(see illustration and**

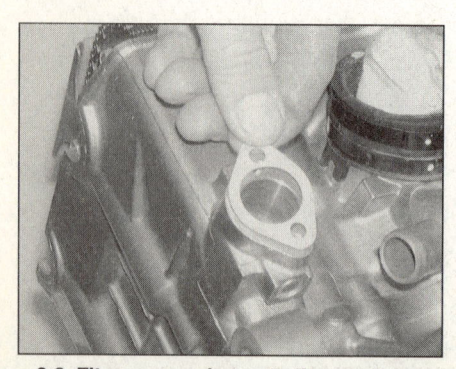

9.4a Slacken the mounting bolts (arrowed) slightly . . .

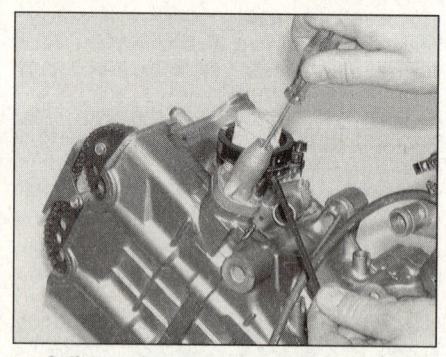

9.4b . . . then insert the screwdriver, retract the tensioner and unscrew the mounting bolts

9.6 Fit a new gasket onto the tensioner flange

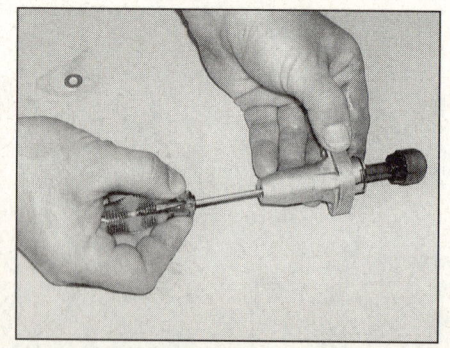

9.8a Insert the screwdriver and retract the plunger . . .

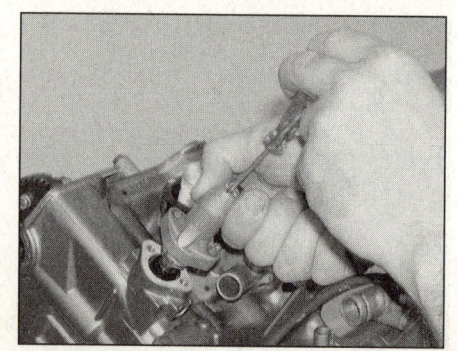

9.8b . . . then install the tensioner

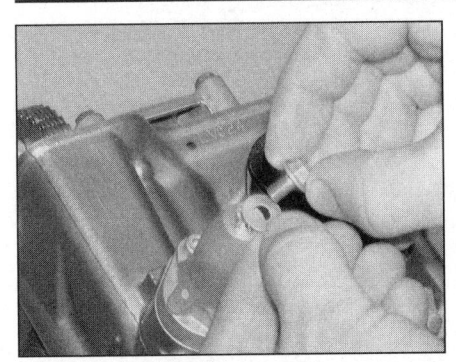

Engine, clutch and transmission 2•17

9.8c Install the cap bolt using a new sealing washer

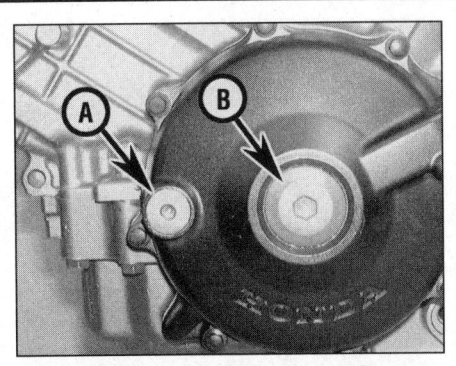

10.2a Remove the timing inspection cap (A) and crankshaft end cap (B)

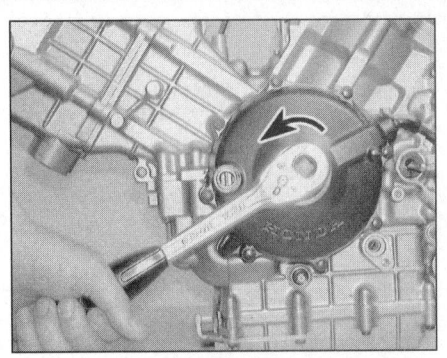

10.2b Turn the engine anti-clockwise using a 17 mm socket on the alternator rotor bolt

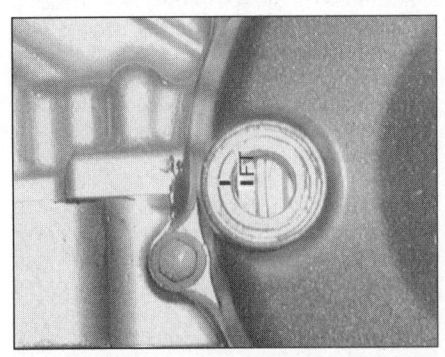

illustration 9.4b). Release and remove the screwdriver, then install the tensioner end bolt with a new sealing washer and tighten it securely **(see illustration)**.

9 Install the remaining components.

10 Camshafts and followers – removal, inspection and installation

Note: *The camshafts can be removed with the engine in the frame. Place clean rags over the spark plug holes and the cam gear train holes to prevent any component from dropping into the engine on removal. To make installation and setting the timing easier, it is advised that the front and rear cylinders are worked on separately, i.e. the camshafts are not all removed at the same time.*

Removal

1 Remove the valve cover(s) (see Section 8). Access to the front cylinder camshafts is greatly improved by also removing the air filter housing and the carburettors or throttle bodies (see Chapter 4A or B), and one or both radiators (see Chapter 3).

2 Unscrew the timing inspection cap and crankshaft end-cap from the left-hand crankcase cover **(see illustration)**. Discard the cap O-rings as new ones should be used. The engine can be turned using a 17 mm spanner or socket on the alternator bolt and turning it in an anti-clockwise direction only **(see illustration)**. Alternatively, place the motorcycle on an auxiliary stand so that the rear wheel is off the ground, select a high gear and rotate the rear wheel by hand in its normal direction of rotation (removing the spark plugs first will make this a lot easier – see Chapter 1).

3 To remove the front cylinder head camshafts, turn the engine until the FT mark on the rotor aligns with the static timing mark on the crankcase cover, and the FI and FE marks on the intake and exhaust camshaft sprockets respectively are facing away from each other and are flush with the cylinder head top surface (in this position the camshaft lobes will pointing away from each other as shown) **(see illustrations)**. If the sprocket marks are facing towards each other, rotate the engine anti-clockwise one full turn until the FT mark again aligns with the static timing mark. The sprocket marks will now be facing away and

10.3a Turn the engine until the FT mark aligns with the static mark . . .

the front cylinder is at TDC on the compression stroke.

4 To remove the rear cylinder head camshafts, turn the engine until the RT mark on the rotor aligns with the static timing mark on the crankcase cover, and the RI and RE marks on the intake and exhaust camshaft sprockets respectively are facing away from each other and are flush with the cylinder head top surface (in this position the camshaft lobes will pointing toward each other as shown) **(see**

10.3b . . . the camshaft sprocket marks face away from each other . . .

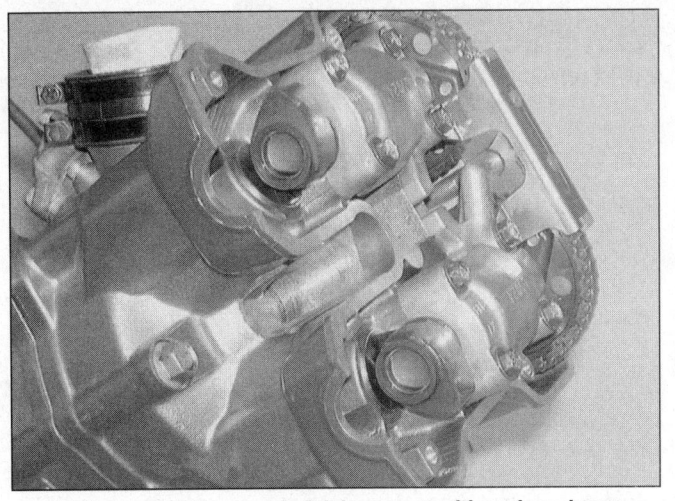

10.3c . . . and the camshaft lobes are positioned as shown

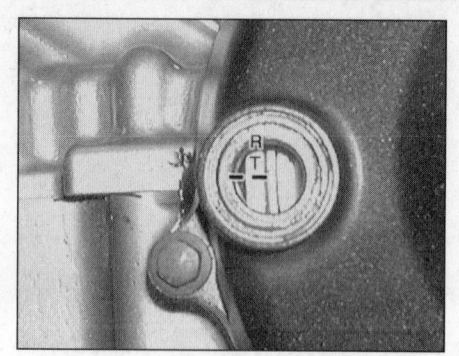

2•18 Engine, clutch and transmission

10.4a Turn the engine until the RT mark aligns with the static mark . . .

10.4b . . . the camshaft sprocket marks face away from each other . . .

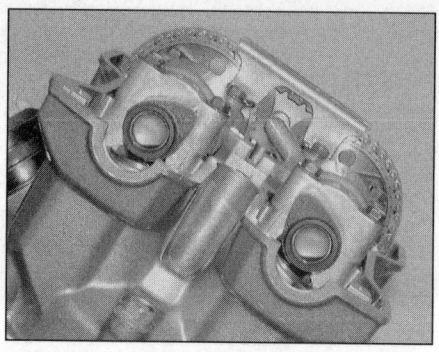

10.4c . . . and the camshaft lobes are positioned as shown

illustrations). If the sprocket marks are facing towards each other, rotate the engine anti-clockwise one full turn until the RT mark again aligns with the static timing mark. The sprocket marks will now be facing away and the rear cylinder is at TDC on the compression stroke.

5 If both sets of camshafts are being removed, remove the front cylinder ones first, then turn the engine as described and remove the rear ones. When turning the engine with one set of camshafts removed, hold the cam chain taut to prevent it binding around the bottom of the crankshaft.

6 Either remove the cam chain tensioner for the cylinder being worked on (see Section 9), or if you prefer, fabricate the tensioner locking tool, then retract and lock the tensioner plunger using the special tool as described in Section 9, Steps 2 and 3. Also unscrew the bolts securing the top cam chain guide, noting that two of them are common to the camshaft holders, and remove the guide **(see illustration)**.

7 Before disturbing the camshaft holders, check for identification markings. For each cylinder head, the inlet camshaft holders are marked IN and the exhaust camshaft holders are marked EX **(see illustration)**. To distinguish between the front and rear cylinders, either mark the holders F and R respectively, or note the matching code markings on the holders and on the cylinder head itself – on the model stripped down the front cylinder holders and head are marked LVO24 and the rear cylinder ones are marked LVO55 **(see illustrations)**. These markings ensure that the holders can be matched up to their original locations on installation. If no markings are visible, mark your own using a felt pen. If necessary, make a sketch of the layout as a further aid for installation.

8 Unscrew the remaining camshaft holder bolts for the camshaft being worked on, slackening them evenly and a little at a time **(see illustration)**. Remove the bolts and lift off the camshaft holders, noting how they fit **(see illustration)**. Retrieve the dowels from either the holder or the cylinder head if they are loose.

9 Carefully lift the camshaft off the head and disengage the sprocket from the chain **(see**

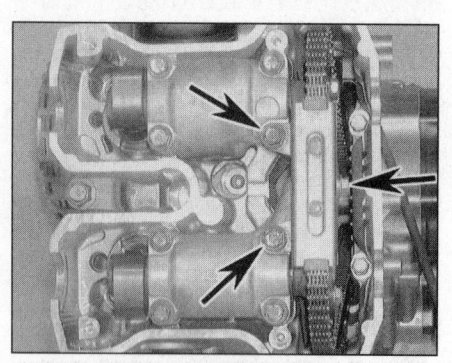

10.6 Unscrew the bolts (arrowed) and remove the top guide

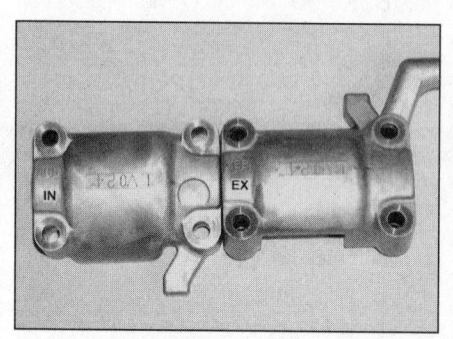

10.7a Note the markings on the holders to distinguish between intake and exhaust camshaft . . .

10.7b . . . and the markings to match front cylinder components . . .

10.7c . . . and rear cylinder components

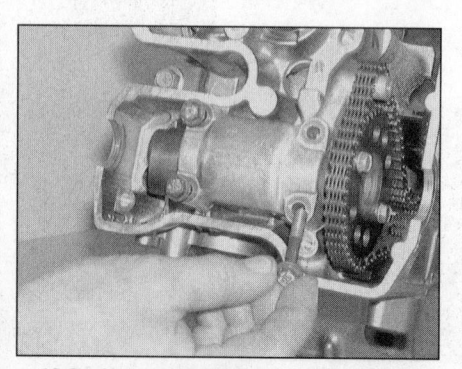

10.8a Unscrew and remove the holder bolts . . .

10.8b . . . and remove the holder

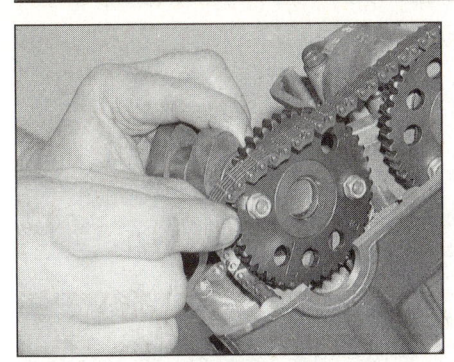

Engine, clutch and transmission 2•19

10.9 Lift the camshaft and disengage the chain from the sprocket

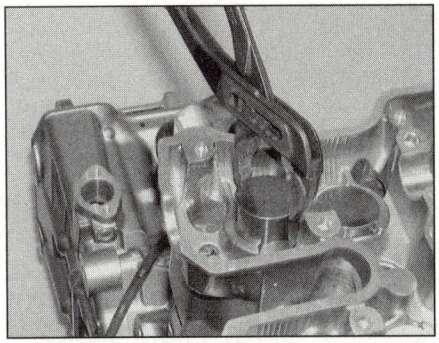

10.10a Carefully lift out the follower using grips or a magnet . . .

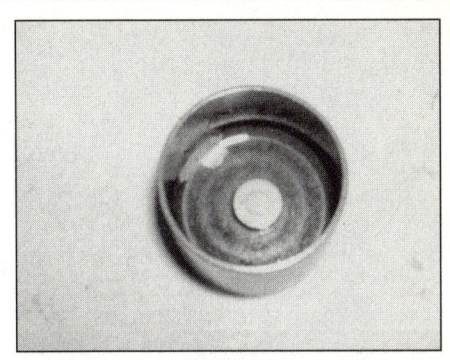

10.10b . . . and retrieve the shim from inside it

illustration). The camshafts are marked for identification. For the front cylinder head, the inlet camshaft is marked FR IN and the exhaust camshaft is marked FR EX. For the rear cylinder head the inlet camshaft is marked RR IN and the exhaust camshaft is marked RR EX. If the marks aren't clear make your own as the camshafts must be installed in their original location. While the camshafts are out, don't allow the cam chain to go slack and do not rotate the crankshaft – the chain may drop down and bind between the crankshaft and case, which could damage these components. Wire the chain to another component or secure it using a rod of some sort to prevent it from dropping.

10 If the followers and shims are being removed from the cylinder head, obtain a container which is divided into eight compartments, and label each compartment with the location of a valve, i.e. front or rear cylinder head, intake or exhaust camshaft, left or right valve. If a container is not available, use labelled plastic bags (egg cartons also do very well!). Remove the cam follower of the valve in question, then retrieve the shim from the inside of the follower **(see illustrations)**. If it is not in the follower, pick it out of the top of the valve spring retainer using either a magnet, a small screwdriver with a dab of grease on it (the shim will stick to the grease), or a screwdriver and a pair of pliers **(see illustration 10.24a)**. Do not allow the shim to fall into the engine.

11 The sprockets can be separated from the camshafts if required by removing the two bolts that hold them. All the sprockets are identical and are therefore interchangeable, but mark the sprockets according to their camshaft so they can be installed in their original position. Also make alignment marks between the sprocket and the camshaft so that the sprocket can be installed the correct way round to avoid confusion when setting up the timing. Alternatively, make a drawing of each camshaft showing the positions of the lobes relative to the marks on the sprocket.

Inspection

12 Inspect the bearing surfaces of the camshaft holders and cylinder heads and the corresponding journals on the camshaft. Look for score marks, deep scratches and evidence of spalling (a pitted appearance) **(see illustrations)**.

13 Check the camshaft lobes for heat discoloration (blue appearance), score marks, chipped areas, flat spots and spalling **(see illustration)**. Measure the height of each lobe with a micrometer **(see illustration)** and

10.12a Check the bearing surfaces of the camshaft holder and cylinder head . . .

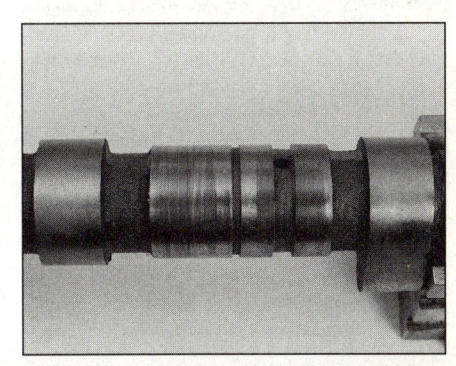

10.12b . . . and the camshaft journals for scratches or wear

10.13a Check the lobes of the camshaft for wear – here's an example of damage requiring camshaft repair or renewal

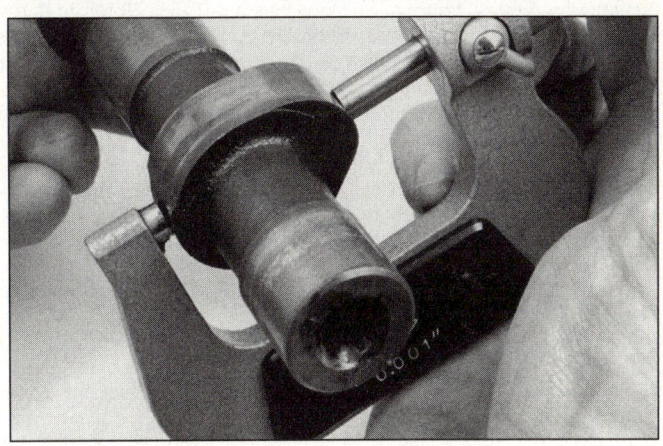

10.13b Measure the height of the camshaft lobes with a micrometer

2•20 Engine, clutch and transmission

10.16 Lay a strip of plastigauge across each bearing journal, parallel with the camshaft centreline

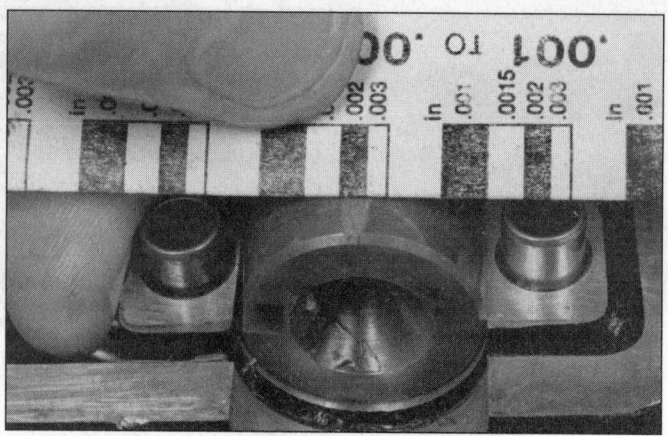

10.18 Compare the width of the crushed Plastigauge to the scale printed on the container

compare the results to the minimum height listed in this Chapter's Specifications. If damage is noted or wear is excessive, the camshaft must be replaced with a new one.

14 Check the amount of camshaft runout by supporting each end on V-blocks, and measuring any runout using a dial gauge. If the runout exceeds the specified limit the camshaft must be replaced with a new one.

> **HAYNES HiNT** Refer to Tools and Workshop Tips in the Reference section for details of how to read a micrometer and dial gauge.

15 Next, check the camshaft journal oil clearances. Check each camshaft in turn rather than at the same time. Clean the camshaft and the bearing surfaces in the cylinder head and camshaft holders with a clean lint-free cloth, then lay the camshaft in its correct location in the cylinder head (see Step 9).

16 Cut some strips of Plastigauge and lay one piece on each journal, parallel with the camshaft centreline **(see illustration)**. Make sure the camshaft holder dowels are installed, and lay the holders in their correct place in the case (see Step 7) **(see illustration 10.30b)**. Install all the holder bolts and tighten them evenly and a little at a time in a criss-cross pattern to the torque setting specified at the beginning of the Chapter. Whilst tightening the bolts, make sure the holders are being pulled squarely down and are not binding on the dowels. While doing this, don't let the camshaft rotate.

Caution: The holders are likely to break if they are not tightened down evenly and squarely.

17 Now unscrew the bolts evenly and a little at a time in a criss-cross pattern and carefully lift off the camshaft holders.

18 To determine the oil clearance, compare the crushed Plastigauge (at its widest point) on each journal to the scale printed on the Plastigauge container **(see illustration)**. Compare the results to this Chapter's Specifications. If the oil clearance is greater than specified, replace the camshaft with a new one and recheck the clearance. If the clearance is still too great, also replace the cylinder head and holders with new ones.

> **HAYNES HiNT** Before replacing the camshafts, cylinder head or holders because of damage, check with local machine shops specialising in motorcycle engine work. In the case of the camshafts, it may be possible for cam lobes to be welded, reground and hardened, at a cost far lower than that of a new camshaft. If the bearing surfaces in the case or holders are damaged, it may be possible for them to be bored out to accept bearing inserts. Due to the cost of new components it is recommended that all options be explored before condemning them as trash!

19 Except in cases of oil starvation, the cam chain should wear very little. If the chain has stretched excessively, which makes it difficult to maintain proper tension, or if it is stiff or the links are binding or kinking, replace it with a new one. Refer to Section 11 for replacement.

20 Check the sprockets for wear, cracks and other damage. If the sprockets are worn, the cam chain is also worn, and so probably is the sprocket on the crankshaft. If severe wear is apparent, the entire engine should be disassembled for inspection.

21 Inspect the cam chain guides and tensioner blade (see Section 11).

22 Inspect the outer surface of each cam follower for evidence of scoring or other damage. If a follower is in poor condition, it is probable that the bore in the cylinder head in which it works is also damaged. Check for clearance between each follower and its bore. Measure the outer diameter of each follower and the inner diameter of its bore and compare the results to the Specifications **(see illustration)**. If any follower is worn beyond its service limit replace it with a new one. If any bore is worn beyond its limit, is seriously out-of-round or tapered, replace the cylinder head with a new one.

Installation

23 If separated, fit the sprockets onto the camshafts, making sure they are installed the correct way round and in their original location as identified by the marks made on removal (Step 11). Alternatively the relative positions of the camshafts and sprockets can be worked out from the information in Steps 3 and 4 and the accompanying illustrations. Apply a suitable non-permanent thread locking compound to the sprocket bolts and tighten them to the torque setting specified at the beginning of the Chapter.

24 If removed, lubricate each shim and its follower with molybdenum disulphide oil (a 50/50 mixture of molybdenum disulphide grease and engine oil). Fit each shim into its recess in the top of the valve spring retainer with the size mark facing up, making sure it is

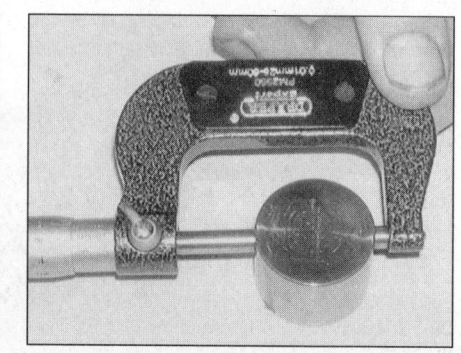

10.22 Measure the diameter of each follower

Engine, clutch and transmission 2•21

10.24a Install the shim using a magnet or a screwdriver with a dab of grease . . .

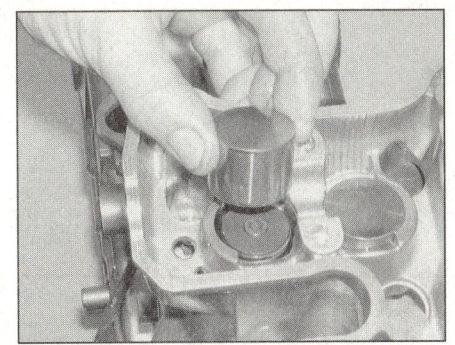

10.24b . . . then install the follower

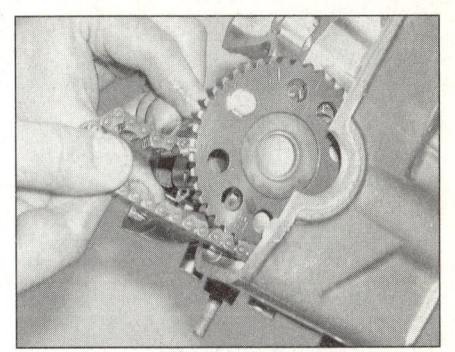

10.30a Install the front cylinder exhaust camshaft as described . . .

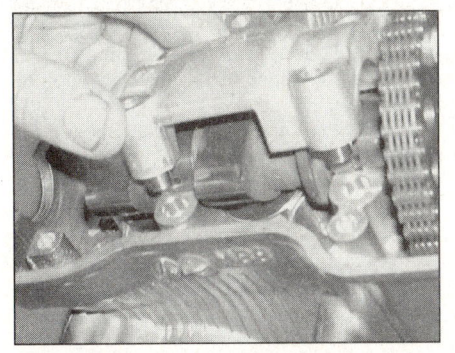

10.30b . . . then fit the holder

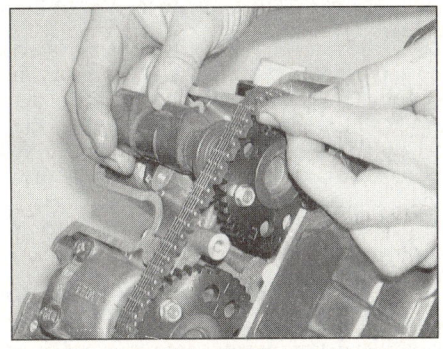

10.30c Install the intake camshaft as described . . .

10.30d . . . then fit the holder

correctly seated **(see illustration)**. **Note:** *It is most important that the shims and followers are returned to their original valves otherwise the valve clearances will be inaccurate.* Install each follower, making sure it fits squarely in its bore **(see illustration)**.

25 Make sure the bearing surfaces on the camshafts and in the holders and cylinder head are clean, then apply molybdenum disulphide oil to each of them. Also apply it to the camshaft lobes.

26 The camshafts and holders must be installed in their correct location according to their identification marks (see Steps 9 and 7).

27 To install the front cylinder camshafts when the rear cylinder shafts are in place, first remove the rear cylinder valve cover (see Section 8). Turn the engine so that the RT mark on the rotor aligns with the static timing mark on the crankcase cover, and the RI and RE marks on the rear cylinder intake and exhaust camshaft sprockets respectively are facing away from each other and are flush with the cylinder head top surface (in this position the camshaft lobes will pointing toward each other as shown) **(see illustrations 10.4a, 10.4b and 10.4c)**. Now turn the engine 450° (1 and 1/4 turns) anti-clockwise until the FT mark on the rotor aligns with the static timing mark on the crankcase cover **(see illustration 10.3a)**. Install the front cylinder camshafts as described in Step 30.

28 To install the rear cylinder camshafts when the front cylinder shafts are in place, first remove the front cylinder valve cover (see Section 8). Turn the engine so that the FT mark on the rotor aligns with the static timing mark on the crankcase cover, and the FI and FE marks on the front cylinder intake and exhaust camshaft sprockets respectively are facing away from each other and are flush with the cylinder head top surface (in this position the camshaft lobes will pointing away from each other as shown) **(see illustrations 10.3a, 10.3b and 10.3c)**. Now turn the engine 270° (3/4 turn) anti-clockwise until the RT mark on the rotor aligns with the static timing mark on the crankcase cover **(see illustration 10.4a)**. Install the rear cylinder camshafts as described in Step 31.

29 If the camshafts have been removed from both heads, install the front ones first with the marks aligned as described in Step 3, then turn the engine 270° (3/4 turn) anti-clockwise until the RT mark on the rotor aligns with the static timing mark on the crankcase cover, and install the rear camshafts with the marks aligned as described in Step 4.

30 To install the front cylinder camshafts, first fit the exhaust camshaft onto the head, aligning the marks as described in Step 3. Fit the cam chain around the exhaust sprocket, pulling up on the chain to remove all slack in the front run between the crankshaft and the camshaft **(see illustration)**. Fit the exhaust camshaft holder dowels into the head or holder if removed, then install the holder (see Step 7) and tighten its bolts finger-tight, leaving out the bolt that also holds the top cam chain guide **(see illustration and illustration 10.8a)**. Now fit the intake camshaft onto the head, aligning the marks as described in Step 3. Fit the cam chain around the exhaust sprocket, pulling on it to remove all slack from between the two camshaft sprockets **(see illustration)**. Any slack in the chain must lie in the rear run of the chain between the intake camshaft and the crankshaft so that it is later taken up by the tensioner. Fit the intake camshaft holder dowels into the head or holder if removed, then install the holder (see Step 7) and tighten its bolts finger-tight, leaving out the bolt that also holds the top cam chain guide **(see illustration)**.

31 To install the rear cylinder camshafts, first fit the intake camshaft onto the head, aligning the marks as described in Step 4. Fit the cam chain around the intake sprocket, pulling up on the chain to remove all slack in the front run between the crankshaft and the camshaft **(see illustration)**. Fit the intake camshaft holder dowels into the head or holder if

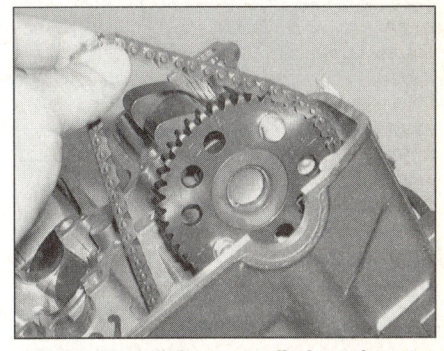

10.31a Install the rear cylinder exhaust camshaft as described . . .

2•22 Engine, clutch and transmission

10.31b ... then fit the holder

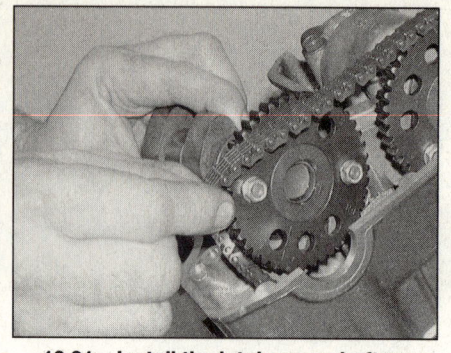

10.31c Install the intake camshaft as described ...

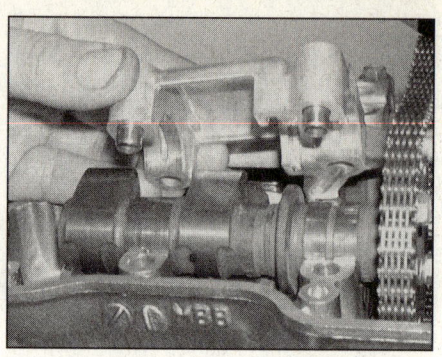

10.31d ... then fit the holder

removed, then install the holder (see Step 7) and tighten its bolts finger-tight, leaving out the bolt that also holds the top cam chain guide **(see illustration)**. Now fit the exhaust camshaft onto the head, aligning the marks as described in Step 4. Fit the cam chain around the exhaust sprocket, pulling on it to remove all slack from between the two camshaft sprockets **(see illustration)**. Any slack in the chain must lie in the rear run of the chain between the exhaust camshaft and the crankshaft so that it is later taken up by the tensioner. Fit the exhaust camshaft holder dowels into the head or holder if removed, then install the holder (see Step 7) and tighten its bolts finger-tight, leaving out the bolt that also holds the top cam chain guide **(see illustration)**.

32 Fit the top cam chain guide and tighten all the 7 mm thread size camshaft holder bolts evenly and a little at a time in a criss-cross pattern to the torque setting specified at the beginning of the Chapter **(see illustration)**. Whilst tightening the bolts, make sure the holders are being pulled squarely down and are not binding on the dowels. Fit the 6 mm thread size bolt to the side of the top cam chain guide and tighten it securely - no specific torque setting is available.

Caution: The holders are likely to break if they are not tightened down evenly and squarely.

33 Using a piece of wooden dowel, press on the back of the cam chain tensioner blade via the tensioner bore in the cylinder block to ensure that any slack in the cam chain is taken up and transferred to the rear run of the chain (where it will later be taken up by the tensioner). At this point check that all the timing marks are still in **exact** alignment as described in Steps 3 and 4. Note that it is easy to be slightly out (one tooth on the sprocket) without the marks appearing drastically out of alignment. If the marks are out, verify which sprocket is misaligned, then unscrew its bolts and slide it off the camshaft, then disengage it from the chain. Move the camshaft round as required, then fit the sprocket back into the chain and onto the camshaft, and check the marks again. With everything correctly aligned, apply a suitable non-permanent thread locking compound to the sprocket bolts and tighten them to the torque setting specified at the beginning of the Chapter.

Caution: If the marks are not aligned exactly as described, the valve timing will be incorrect and the valves may strike the pistons, causing extensive damage to the engine.

34 Either install the cam chain tensioner (see Section 9), or remove the tensioner locking tool, according to the method you used earlier. Turn the engine anti-clockwise through two full turns and check again that all the timing marks still align (see Steps 3 and 4).

35 Check the valve clearances and adjust them if necessary (see Chapter 1).

36 Install the timing inspection cap and the crankshaft end-cap using new O-rings, and smear them and the cap threads with grease **(see illustration)**. Tighten the caps to the torque settings specified at the beginning of the Chapter.

37 Install the valve covers (see Section 8), and any other components or assemblies previously removed.

11 Cam chain, tensioner blade and guide blades – removal, inspection and installation

Removal

Front cylinder cam chain

1 Remove the front cylinder camshafts (see Section 10).

2 Remove the alternator/starter clutch assembly (see Chapter 9).

3 Draw the cam chain off its sprocket and out of the engine **(see illustration)**.

Front cylinder tensioner blades and guide blades

4 Remove the front cylinder camshafts (see Section 10) – this procedure involves removing the top cam chain guide.

5 Remove the alternator/starter clutch assembly (see Chapter 9).

6 Unscrew the pivot bolts securing the blades to the crankcase and draw the blades out of the engine **(see illustration)**. Note the collars for the pivot bolts.

10.32 Install the top cam chain guide, then tighten all the holder bolts as described

10.36 Fit the caps using new O-rings and smear them and the threads with grease

11.3 Slip the cam chain off the sprocket and draw it out of the engine

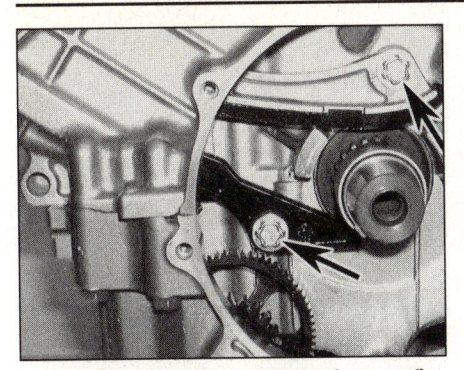

Engine, clutch and transmission 2•23

11.6 Unscrew the pivot bolts (arrowed) and remove the blades

11.9 Remove the water pump chain and sprocket . . .

11.10 . . . then slip the cam chain off the sprocket (arrowed) and draw it out of the engine

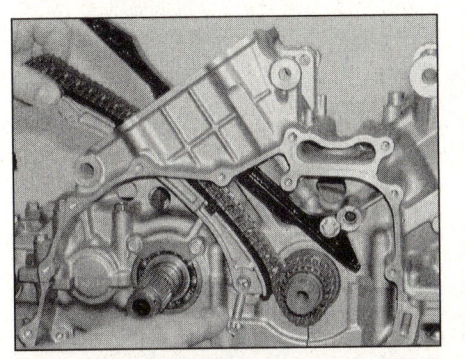

11.14 Unscrew the pivot bolts and remove the blades

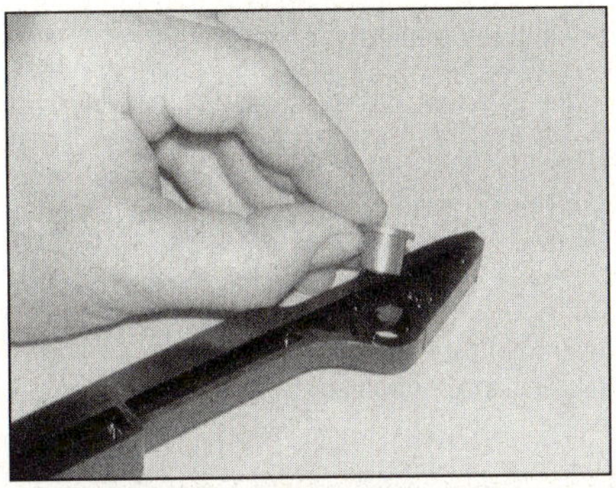

11.17 Fit the collars into the inside of the blades

Rear cylinder cam chain

7 Remove the rear cylinder camshafts (see Section 10).
8 Remove the timing rotor and primary drive gear (see Section 21).
9 Remove the water pump driven sprocket and its chain (see illustration).
10 Draw the cam chain off its sprocket and out of the engine (see illustration).

Rear cylinder tensioner blades and guide blades

11 Remove the rear cylinder camshafts (see Section 10) – this procedure involves removing the top cam chain guide.
12 Remove the timing rotor and primary drive gear (see Section 21).
13 Remove the water pump driven sprocket and its chain (see illustration 11.9).
14 Unscrew the pivot bolts securing the blades to the crankcase and draw the blades out of the engine (see illustration). Note the collars for the pivot bolts.

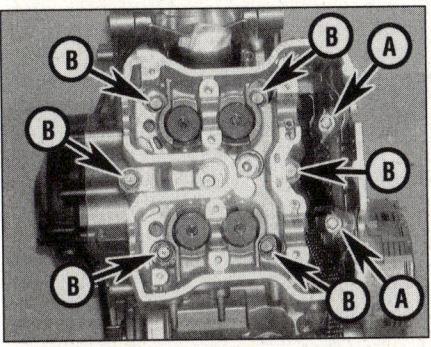

Inspection

Cam chain

15 Check the chain for binding, kinks and any obvious damage and replace it with a new one if necessary. Check the camshaft and crankshaft sprocket teeth for wear and renew the cam chain, camshaft sprockets and crankshaft as a set if necessary.

Tensioner and guide blades

16 Check the sliding surface and edges of the blades for excessive wear, deep grooves, cracking and other obvious damage, and replace them with new ones if necessary. Also check the condition of the pivot bolt collars.

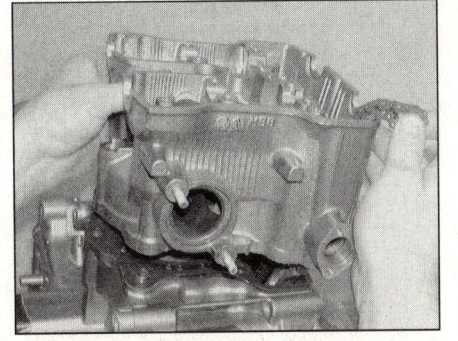

Installation

17 Installation of the chains and blades is the reverse of removal. Do not omit the collars for the blade pivot bolts, and install them from the inside of the blade so the flanged end faces the engine (see illustration). Apply a suitable non-permanent thread locking compound to the pivot bolts and tighten them to the torque setting specified at the beginning of the Chapter.

12 Cylinder heads – removal and installation

Caution: *The engine must be completely cool before beginning this procedure or the cylinder heads may become warped.*
Note: *The cylinder heads can be removed with the engine in the frame. If the engine has been removed, ignore the steps which don't apply.*

Removal

1 Remove the carburettors or throttle bodies (see Chapter 4A or 4B).
2 Remove the exhaust system (see Chapter 4A).
3 Remove the camshafts (see Section 10). If the cam chain tensioner body was not removed, and the engine is in the frame, remove the body to provide extra clearance (see Section 9).
4 Slacken the clamp securing the coolant hose to the outlet union on the head and detach the hose.
5 Each cylinder head is secured by two 6 mm bolts and six 10 mm bolts (see illustration). First unscrew and remove the 6 mm bolts. Now unscrew and remove the 10 mm bolts, slackening them evenly and a little at a time in a criss-cross pattern until they are all loose.
6 Hold the cam chain up and pull the cylinder head up off the block, then pass the cam chain down through the tunnel (see illustration). Do not let the chain fall into the crankcase – secure it with a piece of wire or

12.5 Cylinder head 6 mm bolts (A) and 10 mm bolts (B)

12.6a Lift the head up off the block

2•24 Engine, clutch and transmission

12.6b Use a screwdriver in the leverage cut-out (arrowed) if necessary

12.11 Install the dowels (arrowed) then lay the new gasket on the block

12.13 Tighten the cylinder head bolts to the specified torque

metal bar to prevent it from doing so. If the head is stuck, tap around the joint faces with a soft-faced mallet, then insert a screwdriver into the leverage cut-out and carefully lever the head up until the seal breaks **(see illustration)**. Do not attempt to free the head by inserting a screwdriver between the head and block mating surfaces – you'll damage them.

7 Remove the old cylinder head gasket and discard it as a new one must be used. If they are loose, remove the dowels from the cylinder block or the underside of the cylinder head **(see illustration 12.11)**. On VTR-5 and 6 models and XL-3/4 models onward remove the special collar with its O-ring, noting which way up it fits. Check the condition of the O-ring and replace it with a new one if it is deformed or damaged.

8 Check the cylinder head gasket and the mating surfaces on the cylinder head and crankcase for signs of leakage, which could indicate warpage. Refer to Section 14 and check the flatness of the cylinder head.

9 Clean all traces of old gasket material from the cylinder head and crankcase. If a scraper is used, take care not to scratch or gouge the soft aluminium. Be careful not to let any of the gasket material fall into the crankcase, the cylinder bore or the oil and coolant passages.

Installation

10 Lubricate the cylinder bore with engine oil. If removed, fit the dowels into the cylinder block **(see illustration 12.11)**. On VTR-5 and 6 models and XL-3/4 models onward fit the O-ring onto the special collar if removed, then fit the collar into its hole with the O-ring at the top.

11 Ensure both cylinder head and crankcase mating surfaces are clean, then lay the new head gasket over the cam chain and blades and into place on the cylinder block, making sure all the holes are correctly aligned **(see illustration)**. Never re-use the old gasket.

12 Carefully fit the cylinder head onto the block, making sure it locates correctly onto the dowels **(see illustration 12.6a)**. Feed the cam chain up through the tunnel as you install the head, then secure it in place with a piece of wire to prevent it from falling back down.

13 Apply some clean engine oil to the threads and the underside of the heads of the six 10 mm bolts. Install the bolts and tighten them all finger-tight **(see illustration 12.5)**. Now tighten them evenly and a little at a time in a criss-cross pattern to the torque setting specified at the beginning of the Chapter **(see illustration)**. Now install the 6 mm bolts and tighten them securely **(see illustration 12.5)**.

14 Install the remaining components in a reverse of their removal sequence, referring to the relevant Sections or Chapters (see Steps 1 to 4).

13 Valves/valve seats/valve guides – servicing

1 Because of the complex nature of this job and the special tools and equipment required, most owners leave servicing of the valves, valve seats and valve guides to a professional. However, you can make an initial assessment of whether the valves are seating, and therefore sealing, correctly by pouring a small amount of solvent into each of the valve ports. If the solvent leaks past any valve into the combustion chamber area the valve is not seating and sealing correctly.

2 You can also remove the valves from the cylinder head, clean the components, check them for wear to assess the extent of the work needed, and, unless a valve service is required, grind in the valves (see Section 14). The head can then be reassembled.

3 The dealer service department will remove the valves and springs, replace the valves and guides, recut the valve seats, check and replace the valve springs, spring retainers and collets (as necessary), replace the valve seals with new ones and reassemble the valve components.

4 After the valve service has been performed, the head will be in like-new condition. When the head is returned, be sure to clean it again very thoroughly before installation on the engine to remove any metal particles or abrasive grit that may still be present from the valve service operations. Use compressed air, if available, to blow out all the holes and passages.

14 Cylinder head and valves – disassembly, inspection and reassembly

1 As mentioned in the previous section, valve overhaul should be left to a Honda dealer. However, disassembly, cleaning and inspection of the valves and related components can be done (if the necessary special tools are available) by the home mechanic. This way no expense is incurred if the inspection reveals that overhaul is not required at this time.

2 To disassemble the valve components without the risk of damaging them, a valve spring compressor is absolutely essential. Make sure it is suitable for motorcycle work.

Disassembly

3 Before proceeding, arrange to label and store the valves along with their related components in such a way that they can be returned to their original locations without getting mixed up **(see illustration)**. A good way to do this is to use the same container as the followers and shims are stored in (see Section 10), or to obtain a separate container which is divided into eight compartments, and label each compartment with the location of a valve, i.e. front or rear cylinder head, intake or exhaust camshaft, left or right valve. If a container is not available, use labelled plastic bags (egg cartons also do very well).

4 Clean all traces of old gasket material from the cylinder head. If a scraper is used, take care not to scratch or gouge the soft aluminium.

> **HAYNES HiNT** *Refer to Tools and Workshop Tips for details of gasket removal methods.*

5 Compress the valve spring on the first valve with a spring compressor, making sure it is correctly located onto each end of the valve assembly **(see illustrations)**. On the underside of the head make sure the plate on the compressor only contacts the valve and not the soft aluminium of the head – if the plate is

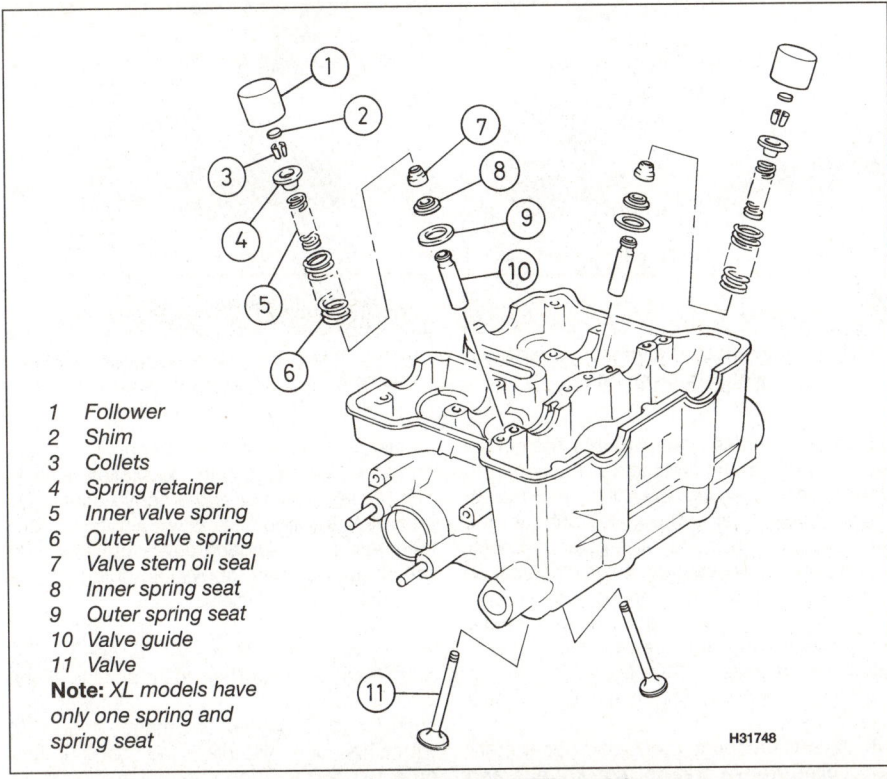

Engine, clutch and transmission 2•25

1 Follower
2 Shim
3 Collets
4 Spring retainer
5 Inner valve spring
6 Outer valve spring
7 Valve stem oil seal
8 Inner spring seat
9 Outer spring seat
10 Valve guide
11 Valve

Note: XL models have only one spring and spring seat

14.3 Valve components – VTR models

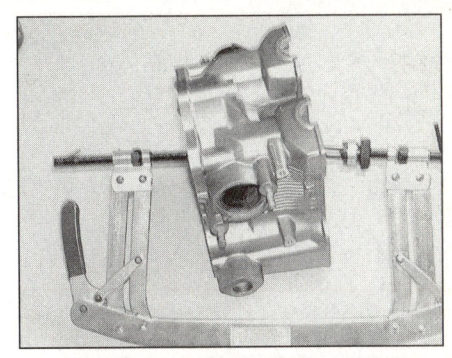

14.5a Compressing the valve springs using a valve spring compressor

14.5b Make sure the compressor locates correctly both top . . .

14.5c . . . and bottom

14.5d Remove the collets with needle-nose pliers, tweezers, a magnet or a screwdriver with a dab of grease on it

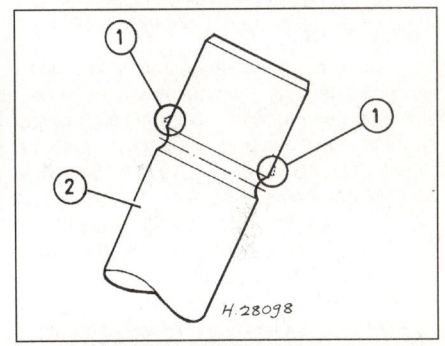

14.5e If the valve stem (2) won't pull through the guide, deburr the area above the collet groove (1)

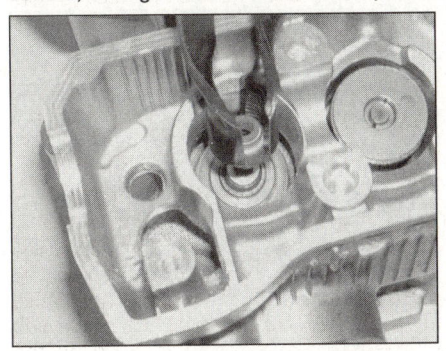

14.6a Pull the seal off the valve stem

14.6b Using a magnet to lift off the spring seats

too big for the valve, use a spacer between them. Do not compress the springs any more than is absolutely necessary. Remove the collets, using either needle-nose pliers, tweezers, a magnet or a screwdriver with a dab of grease on it **(see illustration)**. Carefully release the valve spring compressor and remove the spring retainer, noting which way up it fits, and the spring(s) (VTR models have two springs per valve, XL models have one) from the top of the head, and the valve from the underside of the head **(see illustration 14.3)**. If the valve binds in the guide (won't pull through), push it back into the head and deburr the area around the collet groove with a very fine file or whetstone **(see illustration)**.

6 Once the valve has been removed and labelled, pull the valve stem seal off the top of the valve guide with pliers and discard it (the old seals should never be reused) **(see illustration)**. Now remove the spring seat(s) – VTR models have two seats (one for each spring) while XL models have one **(see illustration)**.

7 Repeat the procedure for the remaining valves. Remember to keep the parts for each

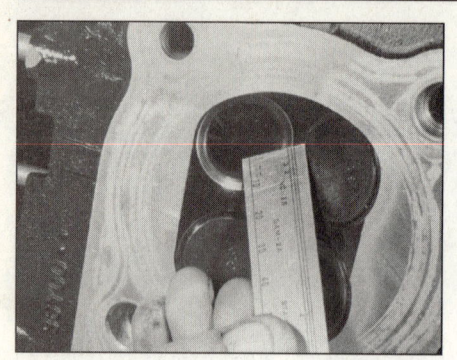

2•26 Engine, clutch and transmission

14.13 Measure the valve seat width with a ruler (or for greater precision use a vernier caliper)

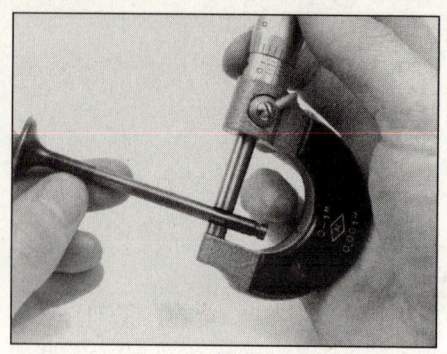

14.14a Measure the valve stem diameter with a micrometer

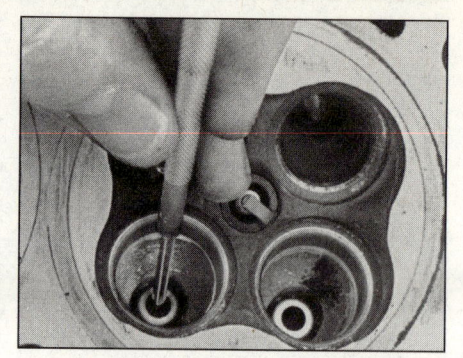

14.14b Insert a small hole gauge into the valve guide and expand it so there's a slight drag when it's pulled out

valve together and in order so they can be reinstalled in the same location.

8 Next, clean the cylinder head with solvent and dry it thoroughly. Compressed air will speed the drying process and ensure that all holes and recessed areas are clean.

9 Clean all of the valve springs, collets, retainers and spring seats with solvent and dry them thoroughly. Do the parts from one valve at a time so they don't get mixed up.

10 Scrape off any deposits that may have formed on the valve, then use a motorised wire brush to remove deposits from the valve heads and stems. Again, make sure the valves do not get mixed up.

Inspection

11 Inspect the head very carefully for cracks and other damage. If cracks are found, a new head will be required. Check the cam bearing surfaces for wear and evidence of seizure. Check the camshafts for wear as well (see Section 10).

12 Using a precision straight-edge and a feeler gauge set to the warpage limit listed in the specifications at the beginning of the Chapter, check the head gasket mating surface for warpage. Refer to *Tools and Workshop Tips* in the Reference section for details of how to use the straight-edge.

13 Examine the valve seats in the combustion chamber. If they are pitted, cracked or burned, the head will require work beyond the scope of the home mechanic. Measure the valve seat width and compare it to this Chapter's Specifications **(see illustration)**. If it exceeds the service limit, or if it varies around its circumference, valve overhaul is required. If available, use Prussian blue to determine the extent of valve seat wear. Uniformly coat the seat with the Prussian blue, then install the valve and rotate it back and forth using a lapping tool. Remove the valve and check whether the ring of blue on the valve is uniform and continuous around the valve, and of the correct width as specified.

14 Measure the valve stem diameter **(see illustration)**. Clean the valve guides to remove any carbon build-up, then measure the inside diameters of the guides (at both ends and the centre of the guide) with a small hole gauge and micrometer **(see illustrations)**. The guides are measured at the ends and at the centre to determine if they are worn in a bell-mouth pattern (more wear at the ends). Subtract the stem diameter from the valve guide diameter to obtain the valve stem-to-guide clearance. If the stem-to-guide clearance is greater than listed in this Chapter's Specifications, renew whichever components are worn beyond their specification limits. If the valve guide is within specifications, but is worn unevenly, it should be renewed.

15 Carefully inspect each valve face, stem and collet groove area for cracks, pits and burned spots **(see illustration)**.

16 Rotate the valve and check for any obvious indication that it is bent, in which case it must be replaced with a new one. Check the end of the stem for pitting and excessive wear. The presence of any of the above conditions indicates the need for valve servicing. The stem end can be ground down, provided that the amount of stem above the collet groove after grinding is sufficient.

17 Check the end of each valve spring for wear and pitting. Measure the spring free lengths and compare them to the specifications **(see illustration)**. If any spring is shorter than specified it has sagged and must be replaced with a new one. Also place the spring upright on a flat surface and check it for bend by placing a ruler against it **(see illustration)**. If the bend in any spring is excessive, it must be replaced with a new one.

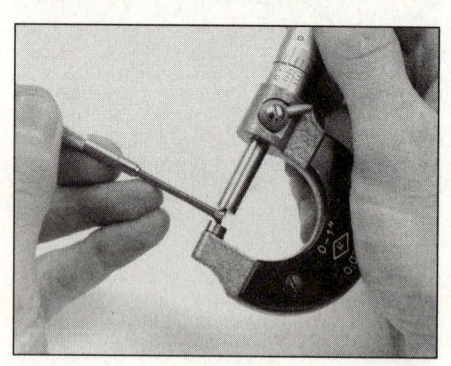

14.14c Measure the small hole gauge with a micrometer

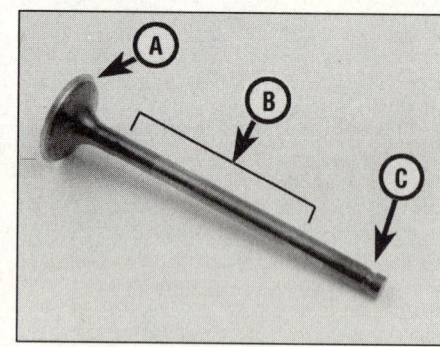

14.15 Check the valve face (A), stem (B) and collet groove (C) for signs of wear and damage

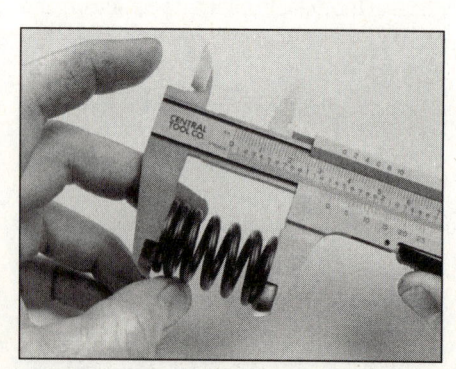

14.17a Measure the free length of the valve springs

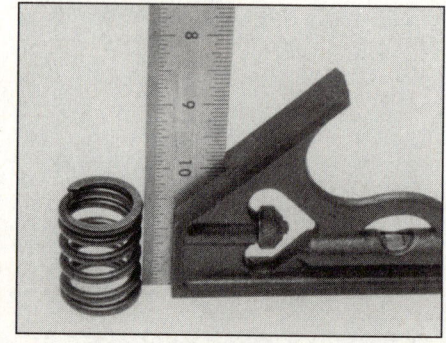

14.17b Check the valve springs for squareness

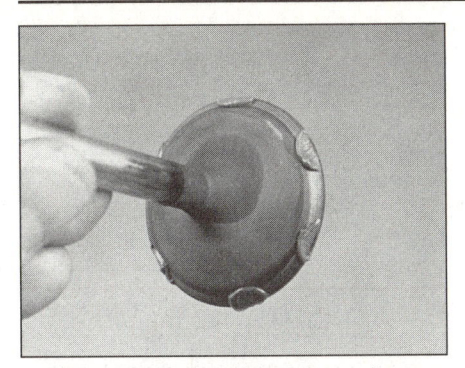

Engine, clutch and transmission 2•27

14.21 Apply the lapping compound very sparingly, in small dabs, to the valve face only

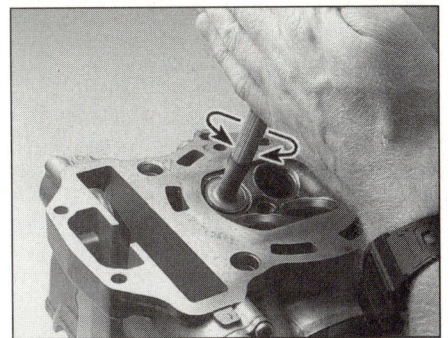

14.22a Rotate the valve grinding tool back and forth between the palms of your hands

14.22b The valve face and seat should show a uniform unbroken ring . . .

18 Check the spring retainers and collets for obvious wear and cracks. Any questionable parts should not be reused, as extensive damage will occur in the event of failure during engine operation.

19 If the inspection indicates that no overhaul work is required, the valve components can be reinstalled in the head.

Reassembly

20 Unless a valve service has been performed, before installing the valves in the head they should be ground in (lapped) to ensure a positive seal between the valves and seats. This procedure requires coarse and fine valve grinding compound and a valve grinding tool. If a grinding tool is not available, a piece of rubber or plastic hose can be slipped over the valve stem (after the valve has been installed in the guide) and used to turn the valve.

21 Apply a small amount of coarse grinding compound to the valve face and some molybdenum disulphide oil (a 50/50 mixture of molybdenum disulphide grease and engine oil) to the valve stem, then slip the valve into the guide **(see illustration)**. Note: *Make sure each valve is installed in its correct guide and be careful not to get any grinding compound on the valve stem.*

22 Attach the grinding tool (or hose) to the valve and rotate the tool between the palms of your hands. Use a back-and-forth motion (as though rubbing your hands together) rather than a circular motion (i.e. so that the valve rotates alternately clockwise and anti-clockwise rather than in one direction only) **(see illustration)**. Lift the valve off the seat and turn it at regular intervals to distribute the grinding compound properly. Continue the grinding procedure until the valve face and seat contact area is of uniform width and unbroken around the entire circumference of the valve face and seat **(see illustrations)**.

23 Carefully remove the valve from the guide and wipe off all traces of grinding compound. Use solvent to clean the valve and wipe the seat area thoroughly with a solvent soaked cloth.

24 Repeat the procedure with fine valve grinding compound, then repeat the entire procedure for the remaining valves.

25 Working on one valve at a time, lay the spring seat(s) in place in the cylinder head. On VTR models, install the outer seat first, then the inner, making sure they fit correctly, with the shouldered side on the inner seat facing up so that it fits into the spring **(see illustrations)**. On XL models, fit the seat with its shouldered side up so that it fits into the spring.

26 Using a stem seal fitting tool or an appropriate size deep socket, fit a new valve stem seal onto the guide, using the tool or socket to push the seal over the end of the valve guide until it is felt to clip into place **(see illustrations)**. Don't twist or cock the seal, or it will not seal properly against the valve stem. Also, don't remove it or it will be damaged.

27 Coat the valve stem with molybdenum

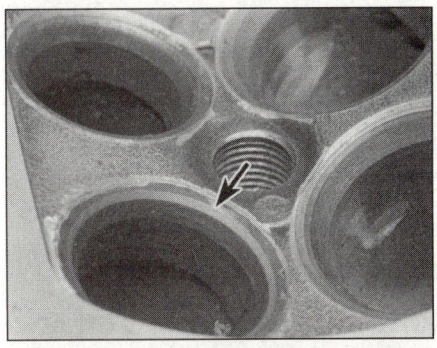

14.22c . . . and the seat (arrowed) should be the specified width all the way round

14.25a Fit the outer spring seat . . .

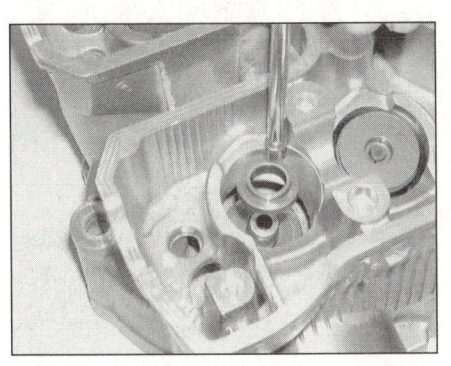

14.25b . . . followed by the inner spring seat

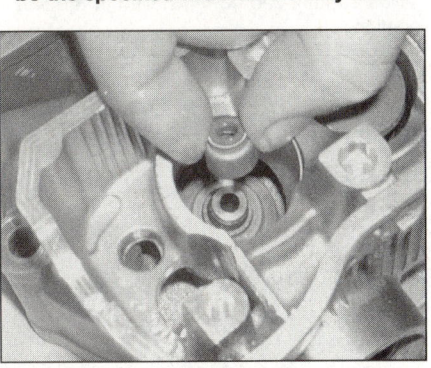

14.26a . . . Fit a new valve stem seal . . .

14.26b . . . using the special tool shown or a deep socket to press it squarely into place

2•28 Engine, clutch and transmission

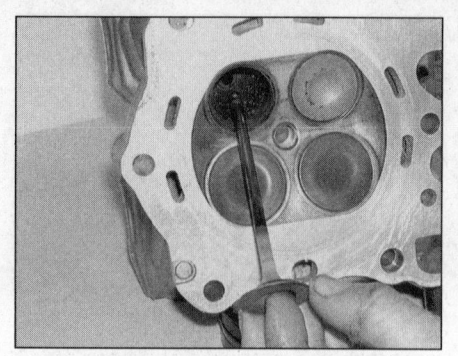

14.27 Lubricate the stem and slide the valve into its correct location

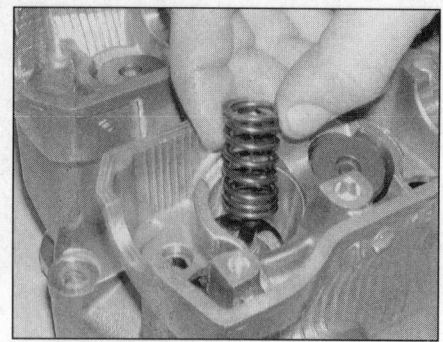

14.28a Fit the inner valve spring . . .

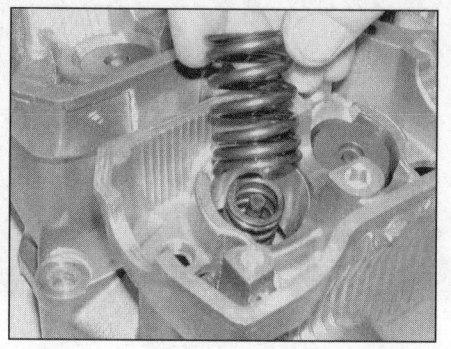

14.28b . . . and the outer valve spring, with their closer wound coils facing down . . .

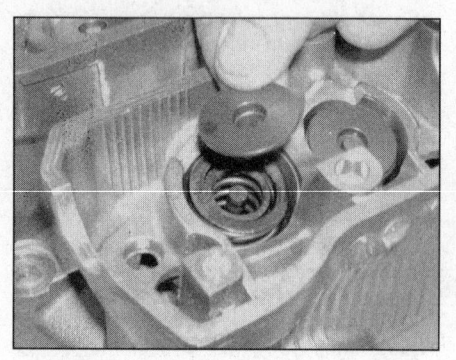

14.28c . . . then fit the spring retainer

14.29a A small dab of grease will help to keep the collets in place on the valve while the spring is released

14.29b Compress the springs and install the collets, making sure they locate in the groove

disulphide oil (a 50/50 mixture of molybdenum disulphide grease and engine oil), then install it into its guide, rotating it slowly to avoid damaging the seal **(see illustration)**. Check that the valve moves up and down freely in the guide.

28 Next, install the spring(s) (two per valve on VTR models, one on XL models), with the closer-wound coils facing down into the cylinder head, followed by the spring retainer, with its shouldered side facing down so that it fits into the top of the spring **(see illustrations)**.

29 Compress the valve spring with a spring compressor, making sure it is correctly located onto each end of the valve assembly **(see illustrations 14.5a, 14.5b and 14.5c)**. On the underside of the head make sure the plate on the compressor only contacts the valve and not the soft aluminium of the head – if the plate is too big for the valve, use a spacer between them. Do not compress the springs any more than is necessary to slip the collets into place. Apply a small amount of grease to the collets to help hold them in place **(see illustration)**. Locate each collet in turn into the groove in the valve stem, then carefully release the compressor, making sure the collets seat and lock as you do **(see illustration)**. Check that the collets are securely locked in the retaining groove

30 Support the cylinder head on blocks so the valves can't contact the workbench top, then very gently tap the valve stem with a soft-faced hammer **(see illustration)**. This will help seat the collets in the groove.

HAYNES HiNT Check for proper sealing of the valves by pouring a small amount of solvent into each of the valve ports. If the solvent leaks past any valve into the combustion chamber area the valve grinding operation on that valve should be repeated.

31 Repeat the procedure for the remaining valves. Remember to keep the parts for each valve together and separate from the other valves so they can be reinstalled in the same location.

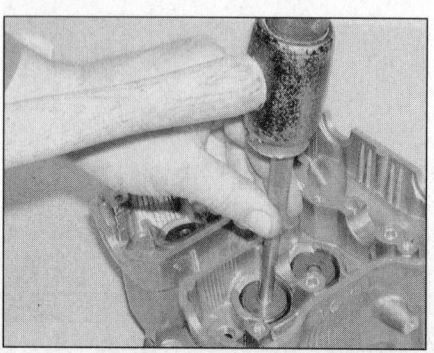

14.30 Tap the top of the valve stem to fully seat the collets

15 Starter clutch – check, removal, inspection and installation

Check

1 The operation of the starter clutch can be checked while it is *in situ*. Remove the starter motor (see Chapter 9). Check that the idle/reduction gear is able to rotate freely anti-clockwise as you look at it via the starter motor aperture, but locks when rotated clockwise **(see illustration)**. If not, the starter clutch is faulty and should be removed for inspection.

Removal

2 Remove the alternator – the starter clutch is

15.1 Check the starter clutch as described

Engine, clutch and transmission 2•29

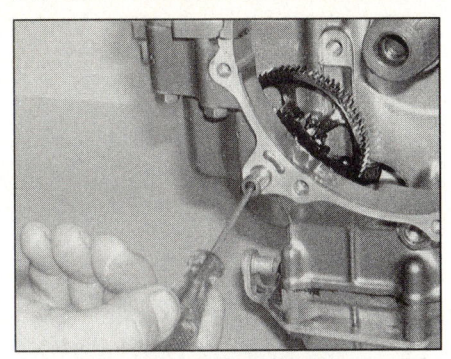

15.3 Withdraw the shaft and remove the idle/reduction gear (arrowed)

15.4 The driven gear should turn freely anti-clockwise

15.5a Draw the gear out of the clutch...

15.5b ... and remove the needle bearing

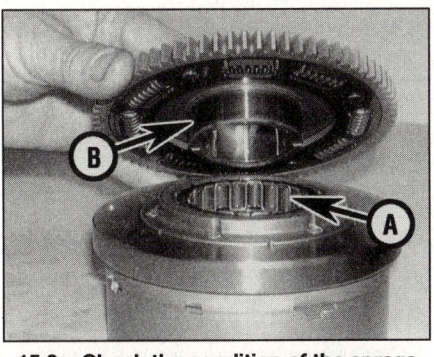

15.6a Check the condition of the sprags (A) and the driven gear hub (B)

15.6b Unscrew the bolts (arrowed) ...

mounted on the back of it (see Chapter 9). If the starter driven gear does not come away with the starter clutch, slide it off the crankshaft.
3 Withdraw the idle/reduction gear shaft from the crankcase and remove the gear **(see illustration)**.

Inspection

4 With the alternator rotor face down on a workbench, check that the starter driven gear rotates freely in an anti-clockwise direction and locks against the rotor in a clockwise direction **(see illustration)**. If it doesn't, the starter clutch should be dismantled for further investigation.
5 Withdraw the starter driven gear from the starter clutch **(see illustration)**. If the gear appears stuck, rotate it anti-clockwise as you withdraw it to free it from the starter clutch. Withdraw the needle bearing from the centre of the driven gear **(see illustration)**.
6 Check the condition of the sprags inside the clutch body and the corresponding surface on the driven gear hub **(see illustration)**. If they are damaged, marked or flattened at any point, they should be replaced with new ones. Measure the outside diameter of the hub and check that it has not worn beyond the service limit specified. To remove the sprag assembly, hold the rotor using a holding strap and unscrew the six bolts inside the rotor **(see illustration)**. Separate the sprag holder from the rotor, then remove the sprag assembly from the inside of the holder, noting how it fits **(see illustrations)**. Install the new components in a reverse sequence. Apply clean engine oil to the sprag assembly. Apply a suitable non-permanent thread locking compound to the bolts and tighten them to the torque setting specified at the beginning of the Chapter **(see illustrations)**.

15.6c ... and remove the sprag holder ...

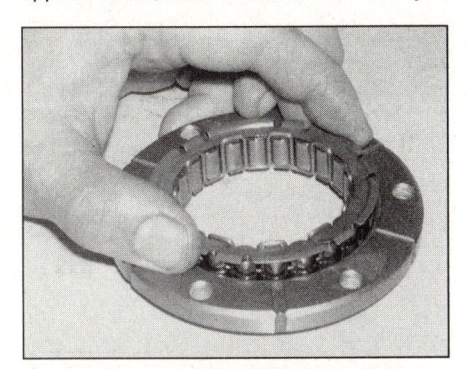

15.6d ... then separate the sprag assembly

15.6e Apply a threadlock to the bolts ...

15.6f ... and tighten them to the specified torque, holding the rotor using a strap

2•30 Engine, clutch and transmission

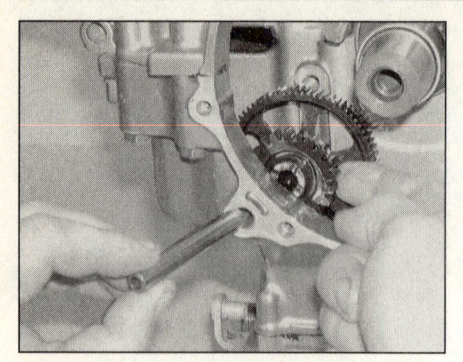

15.9 Fit the idle/reduction gear with the smaller pinion on the outside

7 Check the needle roller bearing and the bearing surfaces in the starter driven gear hub and on the crankshaft **(see illustration 15.5b)**. If the bearing surface shows signs of excessive wear or the bearing itself is worn or damaged, they should be replaced with new ones.
8 Check the teeth of the starter idle/reduction gear and the corresponding teeth of the starter driven gear and starter motor drive shaft. Replace the gears and/or starter motor if worn or chipped teeth are discovered on related gears. Also check the idle/reduction gear shaft for damage, and check that the gear is not a loose fit on the shaft. Replace the shaft with a new one if necessary.

Installation

9 Lubricate the idle/reduction gear shaft with clean engine oil. Position the gear in the crankcase, making sure the smaller pinion faces outwards, and the teeth of the larger pinion mesh correctly with the teeth of the starter motor shaft, then slide the shaft into the gear **(see illustration)**.
10 Lubricate the needle roller bearing with clean engine oil and fit into the inside of the starter driven gear hub **(see illustration 15.5b)**. Lubricate the outside of the starter driven gear hub with clean engine oil, then fit the gear into the clutch, rotating it anti-clockwise as you do so to spread the sprags and allow the hub to enter **(see illustration 15.5a)**.
11 Install the alternator (see Chapter 9).

16 Clutch – removal, inspection and installation

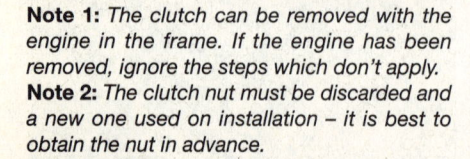

Note 1: *The clutch can be removed with the engine in the frame. If the engine has been removed, ignore the steps which don't apply.*
Note 2: *The clutch nut must be discarded and a new one used on installation – it is best to obtain the nut in advance.*

Removal

1 Remove the water pump cover and water pump housing, which is integral with the clutch cover (see Chapter 3). There is no need

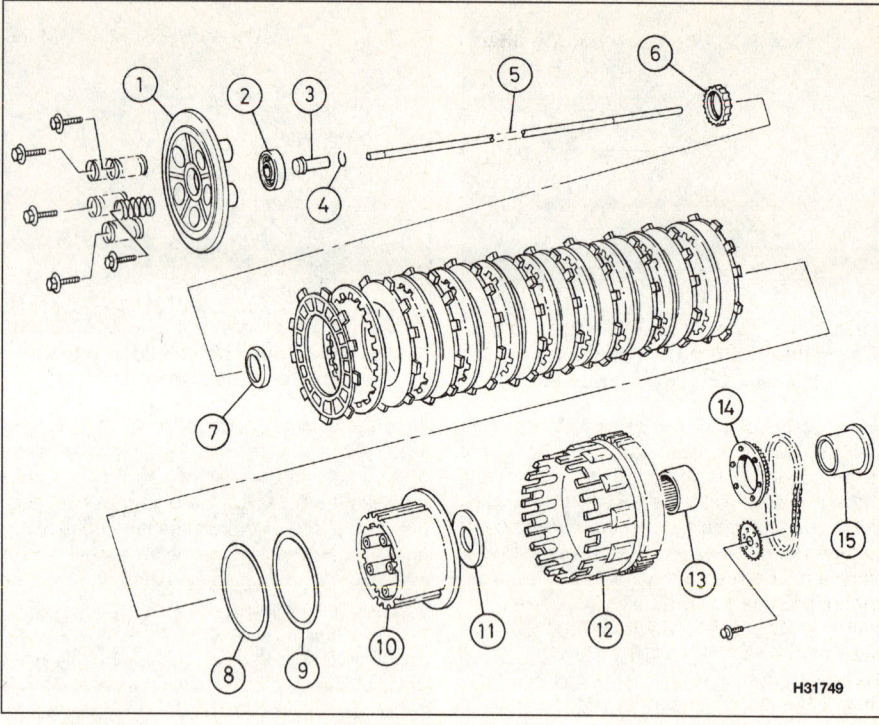

16.1 Clutch assembly

1 Pressure plate
2 Bearing
3 Pushrod end-piece
4 Ring
5 Pushrod
6 Clutch nut
7 Washer
8 Anti-judder spring
9 Spring seat
10 Clutch centre
11 Thrust washer
12 Clutch housing
13 Needle bearing
14 Oil pump drive sprocket, chain and driven sprocket
15 Housing guide

to remove any of the pump components from the housing **(see illustration)**.
2 Working in a criss-cross pattern, gradually slacken the clutch spring bolts until spring pressure is released **(see illustration)**. To prevent the assembly from turning, cover it with a rag and hold it securely – the bolts are not very tight. If available, have an assistant to hold the clutch while you unscrew the bolts. Remove the bolts and springs, then remove the clutch pressure plate **(see illustrations 16.26b and 16.26a)**. Remove the pushrod end-piece from either the back of the pressure plate or the end of the shaft **(see illustration 16.25b)**. If required also withdraw the pushrod

from inside the shaft – you may need a magnet or magnetised screwdriver to draw it out **(see illustration 16.25a)**. Otherwise, remove the front sprocket cover (see Chapter 6, Section 16), then withdraw the pushrod from the left-hand side **(see illustration)**. Note the differences in the ends of the pushrod and which way round it fits.
3 Grasp the complete set of clutch plates and remove them as a pack if possible, though it is difficult to get them all out in one go **(see illustration)**. It may be necessary to hook out the innermost plates with a piece of wire bent over at the end, especially if the oil is making them stick together. Unless the plates are

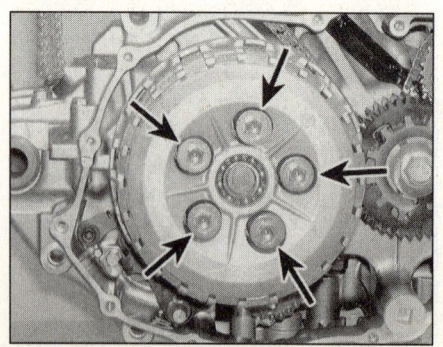

16.2a Unscrew the pressure plate bolts (arrowed) and remove the springs

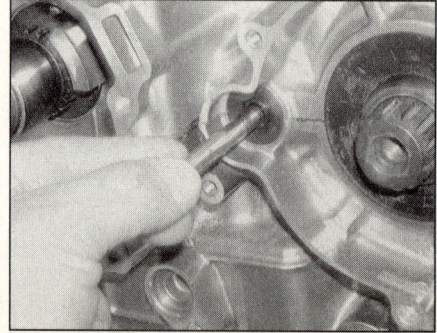

16.2b Withdraw the pushrod from the left-hand side if necessary

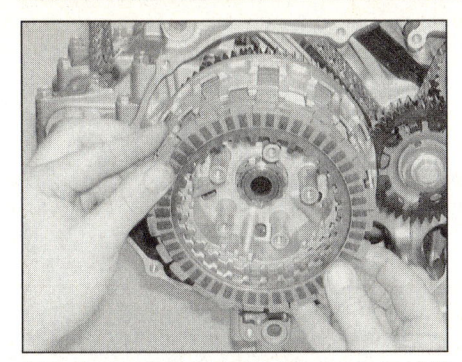

Engine, clutch and transmission 2•31

16.3 Draw off the clutch plates as a pack if possible

16.4a Unstake the nut . . .

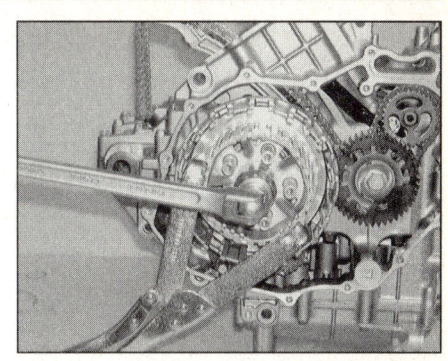

16.4b . . . then unscrew it as described and remove the washer

being replaced with new ones, keep them in their original order. Note how the tabs on the outer friction plate locate in the shallow slots in the housing, while the rest sit in the deep slots. On XL models, note the difference in surface texture between the outermost plain plate and the rest. Remove the anti-judder spring and the spring seat from the clutch centre, noting which way round they fit **(see illustrations 16.23b and 16.23a)**.

4 The clutch nut is staked against the input shaft. Unstake the nut using a screwdriver, a punch, or a suitable grinding tool – take care not to damage the threads on the end of the shaft **(see illustration)**. To remove the clutch nut, the input shaft must be locked. This can be done in several ways. If the engine is in the frame, engage 1st gear and have an assistant hold the rear brake on hard with the rear tyre in firm contact with the ground. Alternatively, the Honda service tool (Pt. No. 07724-0050002), or a similar commercially available or home-made tool **(see Tool tip)**, can be used to stop the clutch centre from turning whilst the nut is slackened **(see illustration)**. Unscrew the nut and remove the washer from the input shaft **(see illustration 16.22c and 16.22b)**. Discard the nut as a new one must be used on installation.

5 Remove the clutch centre and the thrust washer from the shaft **(see illustrations 16.22a and 16.21)**. At this point, if required, slacken the oil pump driven sprocket bolt.

This needs to be done if the clutch housing guide is being checked, for a full disassembly of the engine, or for removal of the oil pump. The same applies to the primary drive gear bolt in the end of the crankshaft, if either the gear or the timing rotor is being removed, or a cam chain or its blades are being replaced, or for a full disassembly of the engine. To do this the clutch housing must be locked to prevent it turning. The best way is to lock the primary drive gear and the primary driven gear on the back of the clutch housing together using either the special tool (Part no. 07724-0010100), or a stout piece of cloth, such as denim, jammed between them, without the risk of any damage should the bolt prove tight **(see illustration)**.

6 To remove the clutch housing it is necessary to align the primary drive sub-gear teeth with the main gear. To do this, locate a suitable screwdriver or rod in the holes in the gears and twist it to align them **(see illustration)**. Alternatively locate a large, flat-bladed screwdriver in-between the gear teeth and lever against the spring pressure to bring the teeth into alignment. Slide the clutch housing off the shaft, noting how it engages with the oil pump drive sprocket **(see illustration)**.

7 Note how the pins on the oil pump drive sprocket behind the clutch housing locate in the holes in the back of the housing. If required, unscrew the oil pump driven sprocket bolt and remove the driven sprocket, the chain and the

TOOL TIP

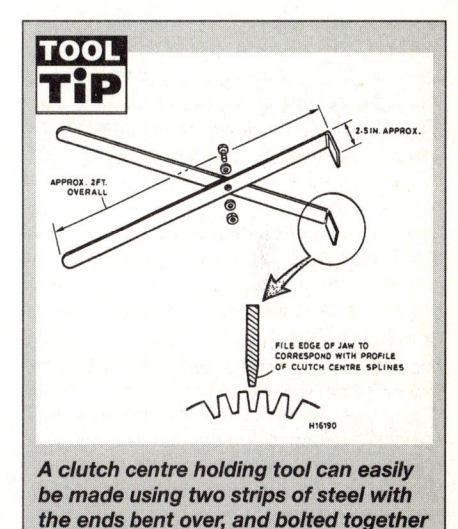

A clutch centre holding tool can easily be made using two strips of steel with the ends bent over, and bolted together in the middle

drive sprocket **(see illustrations 16.19c, 16.19b and 16.19a)**. If the sprocket bolt was not previously slackened, lock the sprocket to prevent it from turning (see Step 5). Also remove the clutch housing guide from the input shaft **(see illustration 16.18)**.

Inspection

8 After an extended period of service the clutch friction plates will wear and promote clutch slip. Measure the thickness of each friction plate using a vernier caliper **(see**

16.5 A piece of cloth can be used as shown to lock the gears when slackening the timing rotor/primary drive gear bolt or the oil pump sprocket bolt (arrowed)

16.6a Align the main and sub-gear teeth as shown . . .

16.6b . . . and draw the housing off the shaft

2•32 Engine, clutch and transmission

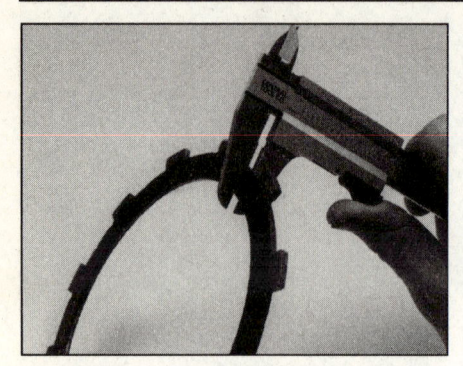

16.8 Measuring clutch friction plate thickness

16.9 Check the plain plates for warpage

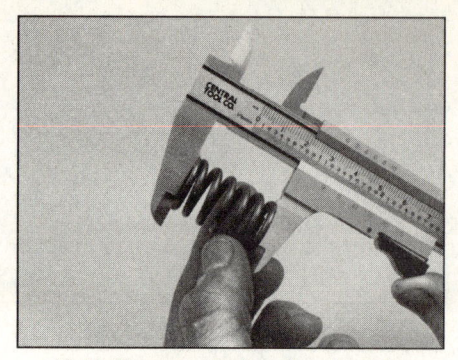

16.10 Measure the free length of the springs as shown

illustration). If any plate has worn to or beyond the service limits given in the Specifications at the beginning of the Chapter, the friction plates must be renewed as a set. Also, if any of the plates smell burnt or are glazed, they must be renewed as a set.

9 The plain plates should not show any signs of excess heating (bluing). Check for warpage using a flat surface and feeler gauges **(see illustration)**. If any plate exceeds the maximum permissible amount of warpage, or shows signs of bluing, all plain plates must be renewed as a set.

10 Measure the free length of each clutch spring using a vernier caliper **(see illustration)**. If any spring is below the service limit specified, renew all the springs as a set. Also check the anti-judder spring and spring seat for damage or distortion and replace them with new ones if necessary.

11 Inspect the clutch assembly for burrs and indentations on the edges of the protruding tangs of the friction plates and/or slots in the edge of the housing with which they engage. Similarly check for wear between the inner tongues of the plain plates and the slots in the clutch centre. Wear of this nature will cause clutch drag and slow disengagement during gear changes as the plates will snag when the pressure plate is lifted. With care a small amount of wear can be corrected by dressing with a fine file, but if this is excessive the worn components should be renewed.

12 Inspect the clutch housing guide bearing surface and the needle roller bearing in the clutch housing. If there are any signs of wear, pitting or other damage the affected parts must be renewed. The bearing is a press fit in the housing – refer to *Tools and Workshop Tips* in the Reference Section for details on bearing removal and installation. When installing the new bearing, align it so that its inner end is flush with the back of the clutch housing.

13 Check the pressure plate and its bearing for signs of wear or damage and roughness **(see illustration)**. Check that the bearing outer race is a tight fit in the centre of the lifter, and that the inner race rotates freely without any rough spots. Check the pushrod end piece for signs of wear or damage. Replace any parts, if necessary, with new ones.

14 Check the release mechanism (see Section 17). Also check that the pushrod is straight by rolling it on a flat surface – if it is bent, replace it with a new one. Check the pushrod oil seal in the left-hand side of the crankcase for signs of leakage and replace it if necessary. To replace it, first remove the front sprocket cover and the pushrod (if not already done – see Chapter 6, Section 16) **(see illustration 16.2b)**. Lever out the old seal using a screwdriver. Apply grease to the lips of the new seal, then drive it squarely into place. Install the front sprocket cover (see Chapter 6).

15 Using a vernier caliper, measure the internal and external diameter of the clutch housing guide, and the external diameter of the input shaft. Compare the measurements to the Specifications at the beginning of the Chapter and renew any components that are worn beyond their service limit. Also check all the above components for signs of damage or scoring, and renew if necessary.

16 Check the teeth of the primary driven gear on the back of the clutch housing and the corresponding teeth of the primary drive gear on the end of the crankshaft. Renew the clutch housing and/or drive gear if worn or chipped teeth are discovered (see Section 21 for removal of the primary drive gear). The primary drive sub-gear can be separated from the main gear by lifting it off if required – note how the tabs on the inside of the sub-gear locate against the spring ends, and how the holes align, and how the spring washer (where present) fits with its raised outer edge facing out **(see illustration)**.

Installation

17 Remove all traces of old gasket from the crankcase and clutch cover surfaces.

18 If removed, smear the inside and outside of the clutch housing guide with molybdenum disulphide oil (a 50/50 mixture of molybdenum disulphide grease and engine oil), then slide the guide onto the input shaft with the flanged end inwards **(see illustration)**.

19 Slide the oil pump drive sprocket over the guide, making sure the pins face out, and slip the chain onto the sprocket **(see illustrations)**. Engage the driven sprocket with the chain, then locate the sprocket on the oil pump, making

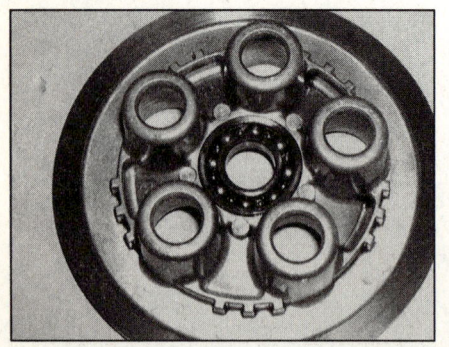

16.13 Check the bearing in the pressure plate

16.16 Separate the sub-gear from the main gear if required

16.18 Slide the guide onto the shaft . . .

Engine, clutch and transmission 2•33

16.19a . . . then slide the drive sprocket over it

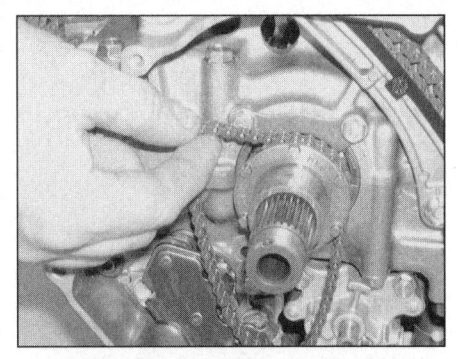

16.19b Slip the chain onto the drive sprocket . . .

16.19c . . . then engage and install the driven sprocket

sure the scribed lines on the driven sprocket face the engine **(see illustration)**. Apply a suitable non-permanent thread locking compound to the sprocket bolt and tighten it to the torque setting specified at the beginning of the chapter **(see Tool Tip)**, not forgetting its washer. Alternatively, tighten the bolt after the housing has been installed so that the method used on removal can again be used to prevent the sprocket turning (see Step 5, but note that the rag must be on the other bottom of the gear mesh as the gears will turn the other way).

> **TOOL TiP** *Insert a screwdriver through one of the holes in the sprocket and lock it against the crankcase to prevent the sprocket from turning whilst tightening the bolt.*

20 To install the clutch housing it is necessary to align the primary drive sub-gear teeth with the main gear using the method employed on removal (see Step 6). Slide the clutch housing over the housing guide on the input shaft, making sure that the pins on the oil pump drive sprocket locate in the holes in the rear of the housing **(see illustration)**. At this point, if required, tighten the oil pump driven sprocket bolt and/or primary drive gear bolt to the specified torque setting, using the same locking method as on removal, but noting that the gears will be turning the other way **(see illustration 21.6)**.
21 Slide the thrust washer onto the shaft **(see illustration)**.
22 Slide the clutch centre onto the shaft

16.20 Locate the pins on the drive sprocket in the holes in the back of the clutch housing

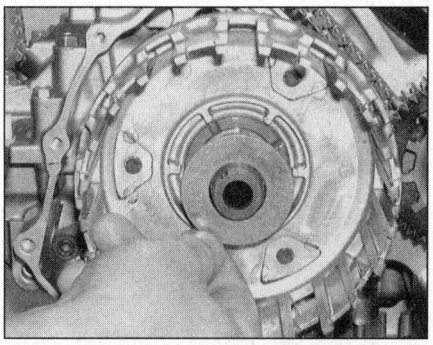

splines **(see illustration)**, then install the washer **(see illustrations)**. Install the new clutch nut and, using the method employed on

16.21 Fit the thrust washer . . .

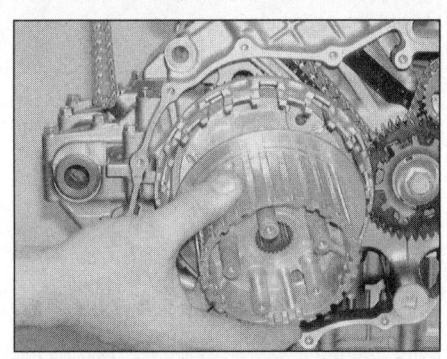

removal to lock the input shaft (see Step 4), tighten the nut to the torque setting specified at the beginning of the Chapter **(see illustration)**. Stake the collar of the nut into the indent on the end of the shaft **(see illustration)**.

16.22a . . . and the clutch centre

16.22b Fit the clutch nut washer . . .

16.22c . . . and a new clutch nut . . .

16.22d . . . and tighten it to the specified torque

16.22e Stake the nut against the detent in the shaft end

2•34 Engine, clutch and transmission

16.23a Fit the anti-judder spring seat . . .

16.23b . . . and the spring

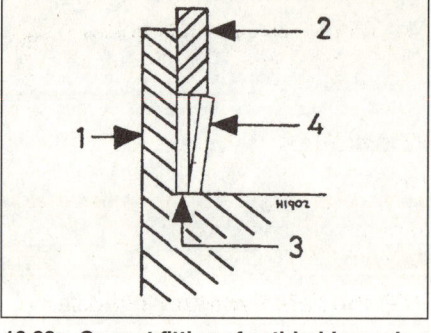

16.23c Correct fitting of anti-judder spring
1 Clutch centre   3 Spring seat
2 Friction plate   4 Anti-judder spring

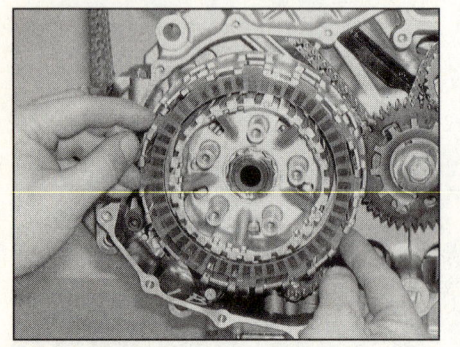

16.24a Fit a friction plate first . . .

16.24b . . . then a plain plate, and so on . . .

16.24c . . . fitting the tabs on the final friction plate into the shallow slots in the housing

23 Fit the anti-judder spring seat into the clutch centre, then fit the spring so that the outer edge is raised and facing outwards **(see illustrations)**.

16.25a Install the pushrod . . .

24 Coat each clutch plate with engine oil prior to installation. Build up the plates as follows: first fit a friction plate, then a plain plate, then alternate friction and plain plates until all are installed, making sure the outermost friction plate is installed with its tabs fitting into the shallow slots in the housing **(see illustrations)**. On XL models make sure the plain plate with the different surface texture to the rest is fitted outermost.

25 Lubricate the pressure plate bearing, the pushrod end-piece and the pushrod with molybdenum disulphide oil (a 50/50 mixture of molybdenum disulphide grease and engine oil). Note the differences in the end sections of the clutch pushrod – the longer end section faces the left-hand side of the engine (towards the release mechanism), the shorter end section faces the right-hand side (towards the clutch). Slide the pushrod into the shaft **(see illustration)** – if the sprocket cover has been removed it can be inserted from the left-hand side **(see illustration 16.2b)**. Fit the pushrod end-piece into the shaft **(see illustration)**.

26 Fit the pressure plate onto the clutch **(see illustration)**. Install the springs and the bolts and tighten them evenly in a criss-cross sequence to the specified torque setting **(see illustration)**. Counter-hold the clutch housing to prevent it turning when tightening the spring bolts.

27 Install the water pump housing, which is integral with the clutch cover, and the water pump cover (Chapter 3). If removed, install the front sprocket cover (Chapter 6, Section 16).

28 Fill the engine with oil and coolant (see Chapter 1).

16.25b . . . and its end-piece

16.26a Fit the pressure plate . . .

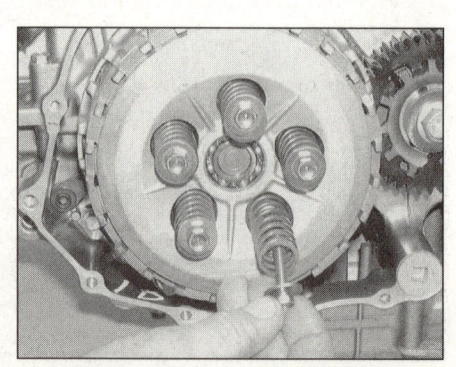

16.26b . . . then install the springs and tighten the bolts as described

Engine, clutch and transmission 2•35

17 Clutch release mechanism – removal, overhaul and installation

VTR models

1 All VTR models have an hydraulic clutch release mechanism consisting of a master cylinder and a release cylinder linked by an hydraulic hose.

VTR models – master cylinder

2 If the master cylinder is leaking fluid, or if the clutch does not work properly when the lever is applied, bleeding the system does not help (see below), and the hydraulic hoses are all in good condition, then master cylinder overhaul is recommended.

3 Before disassembling the master cylinder, read through the entire procedure and make sure that you have the correct rebuild kit **(see illustration)**. Also, you will need some new DOT 4 hydraulic brake and clutch fluid, some clean rags and internal circlip pliers. **Note:** *To prevent damage to the paint from spilled brake fluid, always cover the fuel tank and fairing when working on the master cylinder.*
Caution: *Disassembly, overhaul and reassembly of the master cylinder must be done in a spotlessly clean work area to avoid contamination and possible failure of the hydraulic system.*

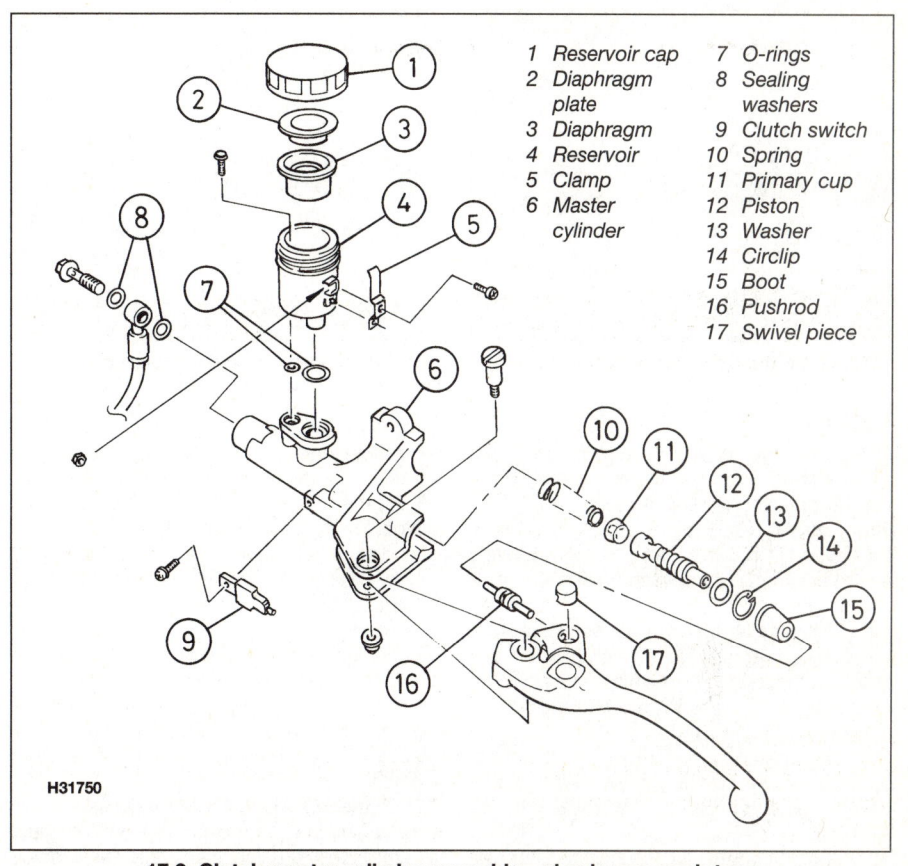

Removal

Note: *If the master cylinder is being displaced from the handlebar and not being removed completely or overhauled, follow Steps 5 and 8 only.*

4 On models with a circular reservoir slacken the reservoir cap clamp screw, then displace the clamp and partially unscrew the cap **(see illustration)**. On all other models slacken the reservoir cover screws.

5 Disconnect the clutch switch wiring connectors **(see illustration)**. If required, remove the clutch switch (see Chapter 9).

6 If the master cylinder is being overhauled, remove the clutch lever (see Chapter 6, Section 5). If it is just being displaced it can remain *in situ*.

7 If the master cylinder is being completely removed or overhauled, unscrew the clutch hose banjo bolt and separate the hose from the master cylinder, noting its alignment **(see illustration 17.5)**. Discard the sealing washers as they must be replaced with new ones. Wrap the end of the hose in a clean rag and suspend in an upright position or bend it down carefully and place the open end in a clean container. The objective is to prevent excessive loss of hydraulic fluid, fluid spills and system contamination. If the master cylinder is just being displaced and not completely removed or overhauled, do not disconnect the brake hose.

8 Unscrew the master cylinder clamp bolts, noting how the UP mark faces up and the top mating surfaces of the clamp align with the punchmark on the handlebar, then lift the master cylinder away from the handlebar **(see illustration 17.4)**.

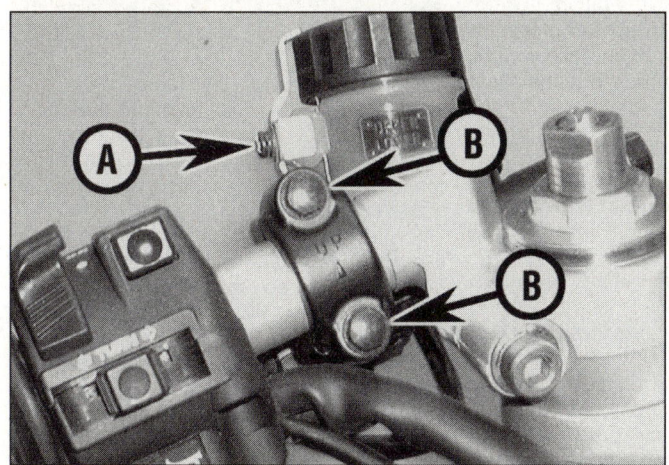

1 Reservoir cap
2 Diaphragm plate
3 Diaphragm
4 Reservoir
5 Clamp
6 Master cylinder
7 O-rings
8 Sealing washers
9 Clutch switch
10 Spring
11 Primary cup
12 Piston
13 Washer
14 Circlip
15 Boot
16 Pushrod
17 Swivel piece

17.3 Clutch master cylinder assembly – circular reservoir type

17.4 Reservoir clamp screw (A), master cylinder clamp bolts (B)

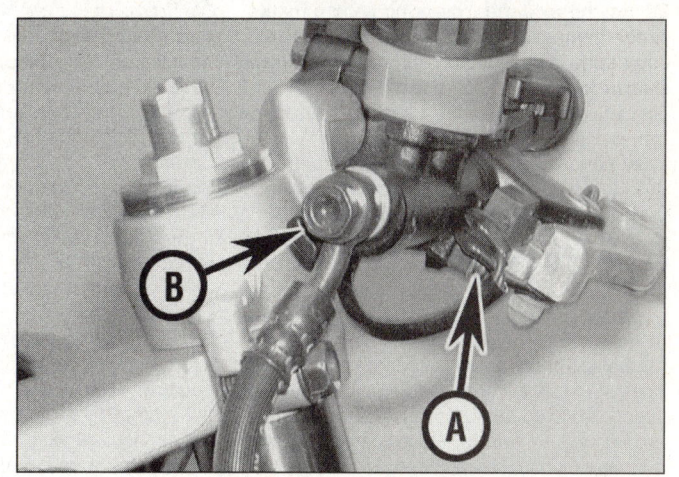

17.5 Clutch switch wiring connectors (A), clutch hose banjo bolt (B)

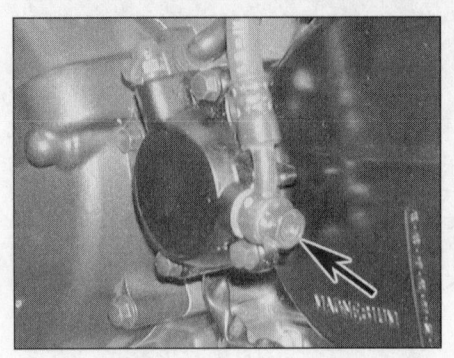

2•36 Engine, clutch and transmission

17.30 Clutch hose banjo bolt (arrowed)

17.31 Release cylinder mounting bolts (arrowed)

Overhaul

9 Remove the reservoir cap or cover and remove the diaphragm plate and the rubber diaphragm, and where fitted the float (see illustration 17.3). Drain the brake fluid from the reservoir into a suitable container. Wipe any remaining fluid out of the reservoir with a clean rag.

10 On models with a circular reservoir remove the screw on the inside of the reservoir and separate the reservoir from the master cylinder by easing it off. Discard the two O-rings as new ones must be used.

11 Draw the pushrod out of the master cylinder, noting how it locates in the rubber boot – the boot may come away with the pushrod.

12 If it didn't come with the pushrod, remove the rubber boot from the end of the piston in the cylinder.

13 Using circlip pliers, remove the circlip, then slide out the washer, piston assembly, primary cup and spring, noting how they fit. Lay the parts out in the proper order and way round to prevent confusion during reassembly.

14 Clean all parts with clean brake fluid.

Caution: Do not, under any circumstances, use a petroleum-based solvent to clean brake parts.

15 Check the master cylinder bore for corrosion, scratches, nicks and score marks. If the necessary measuring equipment is available, compare the dimensions of the piston and bore to those given in the Specifications Section of this Chapter. If damage or wear is evident, the master cylinder must be replaced with a new one. If the master cylinder is in poor condition, then the release cylinder should be checked as well. Check that the fluid inlet and outlet ports in the master cylinder are clear.

16 The dust boot, circlip, washer, piston assembly, primary cup and spring are included in the rebuild kit. Use all of the new parts, regardless of the apparent condition of the old ones. If the seal is not already on the piston, fit it according to the layout of the old piston assembly. Lubricate the piston assembly and primary cup with clean hydraulic fluid.

17 Fit the spring into the master cylinder so that its narrow end faces out. Slip the primary cup into the bore with the cupped side innermost and locate it against the spring, making sure the lips do not turn inside out.

18 Fit the washer onto the outer end of the piston. Fit the piston assembly into the master cylinder, making sure it is the correct way round. Depress the piston and install the new circlip, making sure that it locates in the groove.

19 Install the rubber dust boot, making sure the lip is seated correctly in the groove.

20 Apply some silicone grease to the pushrod. Fit the pushrod into the end of the master cylinder, making sure the rubber boot locates in the groove.

21 On models with a circular reservoir fit new O-rings smeared with clean brake/clutch fluid into the reservoir union, then press the reservoir into the master cylinder and secure it with the screw, taking care not to overtighten it.

22 Inspect the reservoir cap rubber diaphragm and renew it if it is damaged or deteriorated.

Installation

23 Attach the master cylinder to the handlebar and fit the clamp with its UP mark facing up, aligning the top mating surfaces of the clamp with the punchmark on the handlebar (see illustration 17.4). Tighten the upper bolt first, then the lower bolt.

24 If detached, connect the clutch hose to the master cylinder, using new sealing washers on each side of the union, and aligning the hose as noted on removal (see illustration 17.5). Tighten the banjo bolt to the torque setting specified at the beginning of the Chapter.

25 If removed, install the clutch switch (see Chapter 9). Otherwise, connect the clutch switch wiring connectors (see illustration 17.5).

26 If removed, install the clutch lever (see Chapter 6).

27 Fill the fluid reservoir with new DOT 4 hydraulic fluid as described in *Daily (pre-ride) checks*. Refer below and bleed the air from the system.

28 On models with a circular reservoir fit the rubber diaphragm, making sure it is correctly seated, the diaphragm plate and the cap onto the master cylinder reservoir, then fit the cap clamp (see illustration 17.4). On models with a rectangular reservoir fit the float into the reservoir, then fit the rubber diaphragm, making sure it is correctly seated, the diaphragm plate and the cover onto the master cylinder reservoir, and secure the cover with the screws.

29 Check the operation of the clutch before riding the motorcycle.

VTR models – release cylinder
Removal

30 If the release cylinder is just being displaced and not completely removed or overhauled, do not disconnect the clutch hose. Otherwise, unscrew the clutch hose banjo bolt and separate the hose from the release cylinder, noting its alignment (see illustration). Plug the hose end or wrap a plastic bag around it to minimise fluid loss and prevent dirt entering the system. Discard the sealing washers as new ones must be used on installation. *Note: If you're planning to overhaul the release cylinder and don't have a source of compressed air to blow out the piston, just loosen the banjo bolt at this stage and retighten it lightly. The hydraulic system can then be used to force the piston out of the body once the cylinder has been unbolted. Disconnect the hose once the piston has been sufficiently displaced.*

31 Unscrew the three bolts securing the release cylinder to the sprocket cover and remove the cylinder (see illustration). Remove the gasket and discard it. Retrieve the two dowels if they are loose. If required, withdraw the pushrod, noting which way round it fits. Do not operate the clutch lever with the release cylinder removed.

> **HAYNES HiNT**: *If the release cylinder is not being disassembled, the piston can be prevented from creeping out of the release cylinder by restraining it with a couple of cable ties passed through the mounting bolt holes.*

Overhaul

32 Have a supply of clean rags on hand, then pump the clutch lever to expel the piston under hydraulic pressure. If the hose has already been detached, use a jet of compressed air directed into the fluid inlet to expel the piston.

⚠️ *Warning: Use only low air pressure, otherwise the piston may be forcibly expelled causing injury. Wrap the cylinder in a rag before applying the air.*

33 Remove the spring from the piston (see illustration).

34 Using a plastic or wooden tool, remove the piston seal from the groove in the piston. Also remove the pushrod seal from the front of the piston by levering it out with a screwdriver. Discard both seals as new ones must be used.

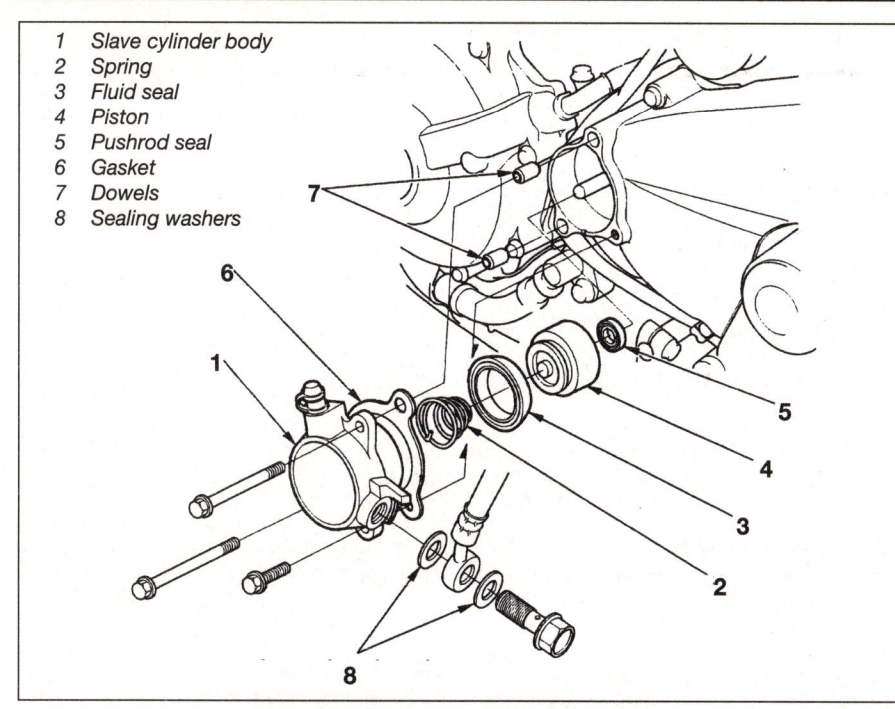

Engine, clutch and transmission 2•37

1 Slave cylinder body
2 Spring
3 Fluid seal
4 Piston
5 Pushrod seal
6 Gasket
7 Dowels
8 Sealing washers

17.33 Clutch release cylinder components

35 Clean the piston and release cylinder bore with clean hydraulic fluid.

Caution: Do not, under any circumstances, use a petroleum-based solvent to clean hydraulic parts.

36 Inspect the piston and release cylinder bore for signs of corrosion, nicks and burrs and loss of plating. If surface defects are found, the piston and cylinder should be replaced with new ones. If the release cylinder is in poor condition the master cylinder should also be overhauled (see above).

37 Check that the pushrod is straight by rolling it on a flat surface – if it is bent, replace it with a new one.

38 Lubricate the new piston seal with clean hydraulic fluid and fit it into the groove in the piston so that its narrow end butts against the rim of the piston. Fit the narrow end of the spring over the lug on the inner end of the piston. Smear a new pushrod seal with grease and press it into the outer end of the piston. Lubricate the piston and seal with clean hydraulic fluid and insert the assembly into the cylinder. Use your thumbs to press it fully in.

Installation

39 If removed, lubricate the pushrod with molybdenum disulphide oil (a 50/50 mixture of molybdenum disulphide grease and engine oil). Note the differences in the end sections of the clutch pushrod – the longer end section faces the left-hand side of the engine (towards the release mechanism), the shorter end section faces the right-hand side (towards the clutch). Slide the pushrod into the sprocket cover and through the engine. Wipe the outer end of the pushrod clean and smear some silicon grease onto it.

40 Fit the dowels into the sprocket cover if removed, then fit a new gasket onto the dowels **(see illustration)**. Remove the cable ties if used, then install the release cylinder and tighten the bolts securely **(see illustration)**.

41 If the hydraulic hose was disconnected, use a new sealing washer on each side of the banjo union. Position the union as noted on removal and tighten the banjo bolt to the specified torque setting **(see illustration 17.30)**.

42 Slacken the reservoir cap clamp screw, then displace the clamp, unscrew the cap, and remove the diaphragm plate and diaphragm **(see illustrations 17.3 and 17.4)**. Fill the reservoir with new hydraulic fluid (see *Daily (pre-ride) checks*) and bleed the system as described below. Check for fluid leaks.

VTR models – clutch bleeding

43 Bleeding the clutch is simply the process of removing all the air bubbles from the master cylinder, the hydraulic hose and the release cylinder. Bleeding is necessary whenever a clutch system hydraulic connection is loosened, when a component or hose is replaced, or when the master cylinder or release cylinder is overhauled. Leaks in the system may also allow air to enter, but leaking hydraulic fluid will reveal its presence and warn you of the need for repair.

44 To bleed the clutch, you will need some new DOT 4 hydraulic fluid, a length of clear vinyl or plastic tubing, a small container partially filled with clean fluid, a supply of clean rags and a spanner to fit the bleed valve.

45 Cover the fuel tank and other painted components to prevent damage in the event that fluid is spilled.

46 Position the bike so that the master cylinder is level. On models with a circular reservoir slacken the reservoir cap clamp screw, then displace the clamp, unscrew the cap, and remove the diaphragm plate and diaphragm **(see illustrations 17.3 and 4)**. On models with a rectangular reservoir undo the cover screws and remove the cover, diaphragm plate and float. Slowly pump the clutch lever a few times until no air bubbles can be seen floating up from the bottom of the reservoir. Doing this bleeds air from the master cylinder end of the hose.

Caution: Do not pump the lever too quickly as fluid could spurt out of the reservoir and onto a painted component.

47 Pull the dust cap off the bleed valve on the release cylinder and attach one end of the clear tubing to the valve **(see illustration)**. Submerge the other end in the fluid in the

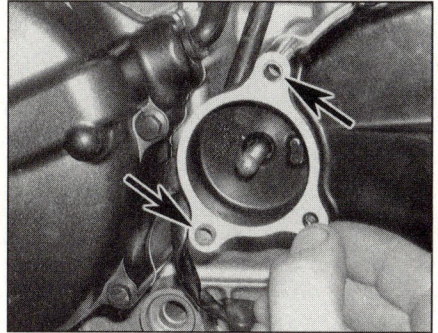

17.40a Locate the new gasket onto the dowels (arrowed) . . .

17.40b . . . then fit the release cylinder

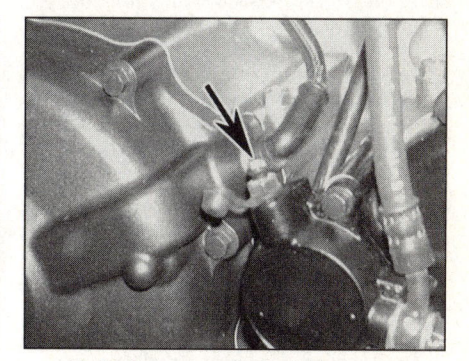

17.47 Release cylinder bleed valve (arrowed)

2•38 Engine, clutch and transmission

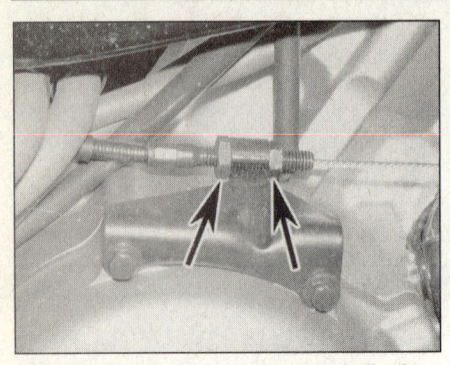

17.52a Slacken the rear nut and slip the cable out of the bracket . . .

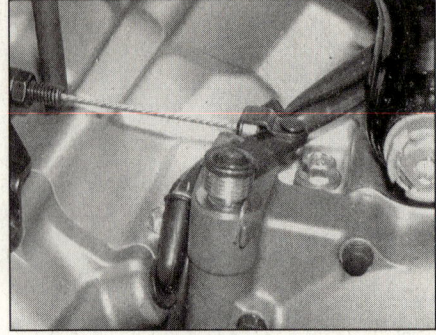

17.52b . . . and detach it from the release lever

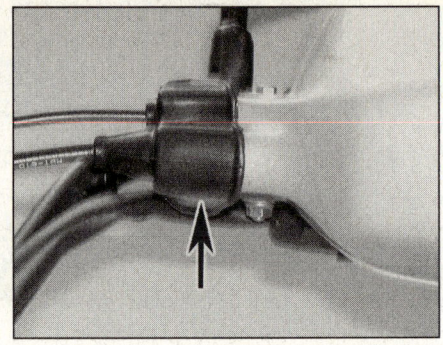

17.53a Pull back the rubber boot (arrowed) . . .

container. Check the fluid level in the reservoir. Do not allow it to drop below the lower mark during the bleeding process.

48 Pump the clutch lever slowly three or four times and hold it in against the handlebar, then open the bleed valve. When the valve is opened, fluid will flow out of the release cylinder into the clear tubing.

49 Tighten the bleed valve, then release the lever gradually. Repeat the process until no air bubbles are visible in the fluid leaving the release cylinder and the clutch action feels smooth and progressive. On completion, tighten the bleed valve to the torque setting specified at the beginning of the Chapter.

50 Ensure that the fluid is above the lower level mark on the reservoir. On models with a circular reservoir fit the rubber diaphragm, making sure it is correctly seated, the diaphragm plate and the cap onto the master cylinder reservoir, then fit the cap clamp **(see illustration 17.4)**. On models with a rectangular reservoir fit the float into the reservoir, then fit the rubber diaphragm, making sure it is correctly seated, the diaphragm plate and the cover onto the master cylinder reservoir, and secure the cover with the screws. Wipe up any spilled fluid and check that there are no leaks from the system when activated. Refit the dust cap over the bleed valve.

XL models

51 All XL models have a cable type release mechanism consisting of a lever and a release mechanism in the front sprocket cover linked by a cable.

XL models – cable replacement

52 Working at the lower end of the clutch cable, slacken the rear adjuster nut and slip the threaded section out of the cable bracket on the alternator cover **(see illustration)**. Disconnect the cable end from the clutch release mechanism arm, noting how it fits **(see illustration)**.

53 Pull the rubber boot off the clutch cable adjuster. Slacken the adjuster lockring and thread the adjuster fully into the bracket to provide maximum freeplay in the cable **(see illustrations)**.

54 Unscrew the nut and remove the collar on the underside of the handguard. Unscrew the bolt securing the top of the handguard and remove the guard, noting how it fits **(see illustration)**.

55 Align the slots in the adjuster and lockwheel with that in the lever bracket, then pull the outer

> **HAYNES HiNT** Before removing the cable from the bike, tape the lower end of the new cable to the upper end of the old cable. Slowly pull the lower end of the old cable out, guiding the new cable down into position. Using this method will ensure the cable is routed correctly.

cable end from the socket in the adjuster and release the inner cable from the lever. Remove the cable from the machine, noting its routing through the guide on the top yoke.

56 Installation is the reverse of removal. Apply grease to the cable ends. Make sure the cable is correctly routed. Adjust the amount of clutch lever freeplay (see Chapter 1).

XL models – release mechanism

57 Detach the clutch cable from the release mechanism arm (see above). Unscrew the bolts securing the front sprocket cover to the crankcase and draw the cover away from the engine **(see illustration)**. Note the position of the shorter bolt with the cable guide. Remove the dowels if they are loose.

58 Check the clutch release mechanism for smooth operation and any signs of wear or damage.

59 Turn the release mechanism arm and remove the releaser rod, noting how it fits. Draw the release mechanism shaft with its return spring and washer out of the cover, noting how the return spring ends locate. Check the shaft and release rod for signs of wear and damage and replace them with new ones if necessary. Also check the return spring for fatigue and damage, and the dust seal on the release rod for deterioration, cracks and any other damage.

60 Check the condition of the dust seal in the top of the cover for damage and deterioration

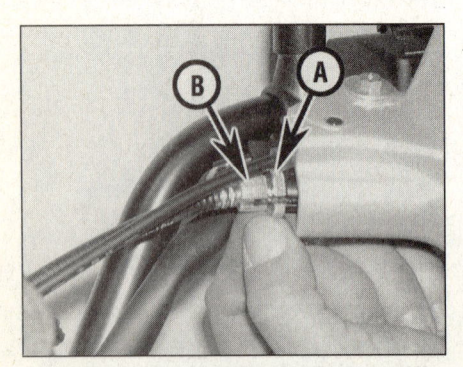

17.53b . . . then slacken the lockring (A) and thread the adjuster (B) in

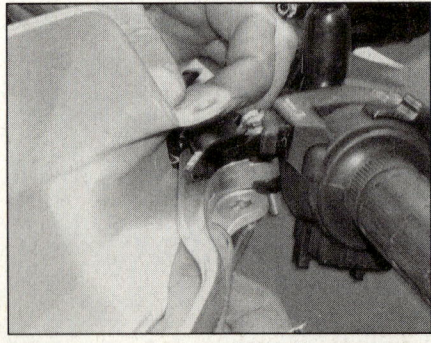

17.54 Remove the handguard as described

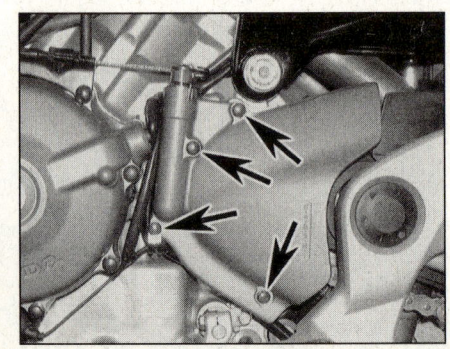

17.57 Unscrew the bolts (arrowed) and remove the cover

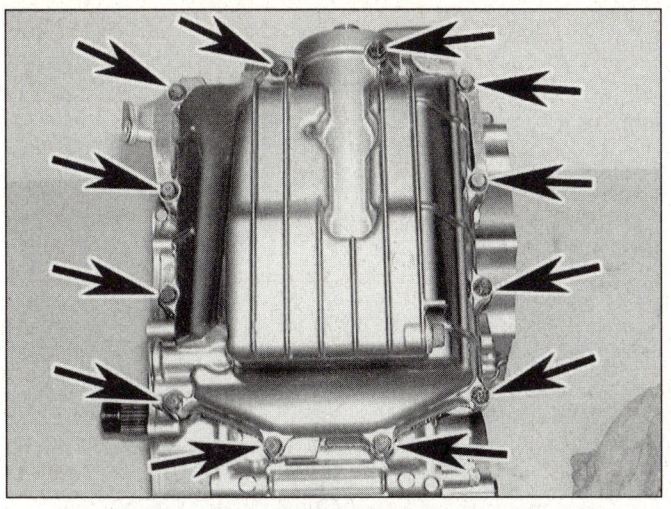

Engine, clutch and transmission 2•39

18.3a Unscrew the bolts (arrowed) and remove the sump

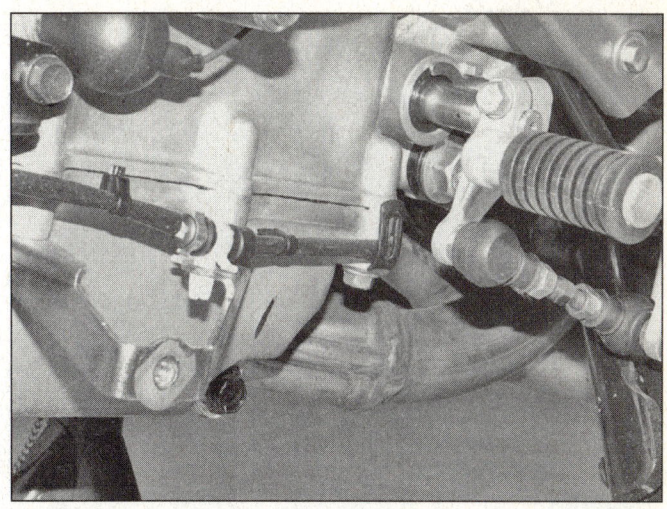

18.3b On XL-7 models onward note how the wiring is secured

18.4 Pull the strainer off the pump – it is a push-fit

18.5 Remove the dowels and O-rings (arrowed)

and replace it with a new one if necessary. Lever out the old seal using a flat-bladed screwdriver, then press the new one in so that it is flush with the top of the cover.

61 If the action of the release mechanism has been rough or tight, remove the dust seal (see above) and check the condition of the two needle bearings which the shaft turns in. Clean the bearings and smear them with grease, then insert the shaft and recheck the action. If new bearings are required, refer to *Tools and Workshop Tips* in the Reference Section for details of bearing removal and installation methods.

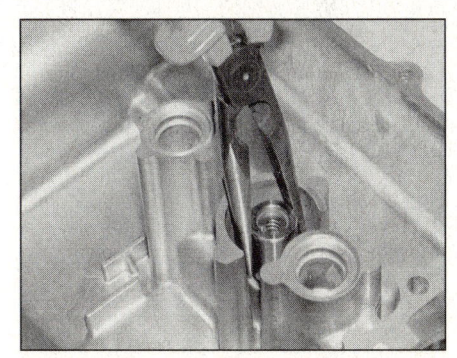

62 On assembly, align the shaft so that the release rod fits into the cut-out. Refit the cover, making sure the bolts are in their correct location. Connect the clutch cable.

18 Oil sump, oil strainer and pressure relief valve – removal, inspection and installation

Note: *The oil sump, strainer and pressure relief valve can be removed with the engine in the frame. If the engine has been removed, ignore the steps which don't apply.*

18.6 Pull the relief valve out of its socket

Removal

1 Drain the engine oil (see Chapter 1).
2 While the oil is draining, remove the exhaust system (see Chapter 4).
3 Unscrew the sump bolts, slackening them evenly in a criss-cross sequence to prevent distortion, and remove the sump, noting the positions of the belly-pan brackets, and on XL-7 models onward the wiring clamp **(see illustrations)**.
4 Remove the oil strainer from the oil pump – it is a push-fit **(see illustration)**. Remove the rubber seal and discard it as a new one must be used.
5 Remove the dowels and O-rings from the sump or crankcase – there are three of each on VTR models, and two on XL models **(see illustration)**.
6 Remove the pressure relief valve – it is a push-fit into its socket in the crankcase **(see illustration)**. Remove and discard the O-ring as a new one must be used.

2•40 Engine, clutch and transmission

18.9a Remove the circlip (arrowed) ...

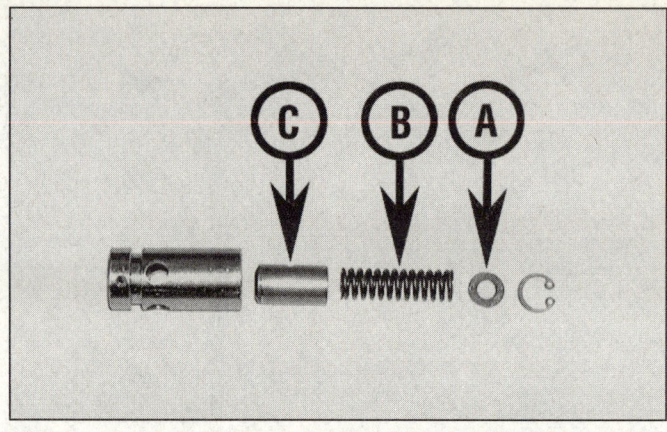

18.9b ... and draw out the spring seat (A), spring (B) and plunger (C)

Inspection

7 Remove all traces of sealant from the sump and crankcase mating surfaces, and clean the inside of the sump with solvent. Blow through all the oil passages with compressed air if available.
8 Clean the oil strainer in solvent and remove any debris caught in the mesh. If the strainer gauze is damaged, replace the strainer with a new one.
9 Push the relief valve plunger into the valve body and check that it moves smoothly and freely against spring pressure. If not, remove the circlip, noting that it is under spring pressure, then remove the spring seat, spring and plunger **(see illustrations)**. Clean all components in solvent, then check the plunger and the valve body for evidence of scoring, wear and any other damage. If any is found, replace the relief valve with a new one – individual components are not available. Otherwise, coat the plunger with oil and fit it back into the valve and recheck the movement. If it is good, install the spring and spring seat and secure them with the circlip.

Installation

10 Fit a new O-ring onto the relief valve and smear it with clean oil, then push the valve into its socket in the sump **(see illustration)**.
11 Fit the dowels into the sump (three on VTR models, two on XL models), then smear the new O-rings with clean oil and fit them around the dowels **(see illustration 18.5)**.
12 Fit a new rubber seal into the strainer orifice in the oil pump **(see illustration)**. Do not fit it onto the strainer as it will distort when the strainer is fitted onto the pump. Fit the strainer onto the pump, locating the cut-out in the strainer base over the lug on the pump **(see illustration)**.
13 Clean the mating surfaces of the sump and crankcase with solvent. Apply a suitable sealant to the sump mating surface. Position the sump onto the crankcase and install the bolts finger-tight, not forgetting the belly-pan brackets, and on XL-7 models onward the wiring clamp **(see illustration)**. Tighten the bolts evenly and a little at a time in a criss-cross pattern.
14 Install the exhaust system, but do not yet fit the belly-pan (see Chapter 4).
15 Fill the engine with the correct type and quantity of oil as described in Chapter 1. Start the engine and check that there are no leaks around the sump.
16 Install the belly-pan (see Chapter 8, Section 4).

19 Oil pump – removal, inspection and installation

Note: *The oil pump can be removed with the engine in the frame. If the engine has been removed, ignore the steps which don't apply.*

Removal

1 Remove the sump and oil strainer (see Section 18).
2 Remove the clutch, along with the oil pump drive and driven sprockets (see Section 16).
3 Unscrew the three bolts securing the pump to the crankcase, then remove the pump, noting how it fits **(see illustration)**. Remove the dowels from either the crankcase or the pump if they are loose.

Inspection

Note: *On VTR models, when removing the rotors from the oil pump, note the punchmark*

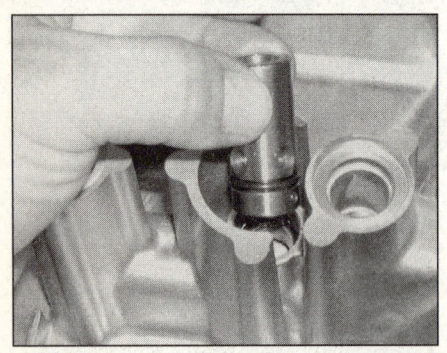

18.10 Install the relief valve using a new O-ring

18.12a Fit the rubber seal into the pump ...

18.12b ... then install the strainer, aligning the cut-out with the lug (arrowed)

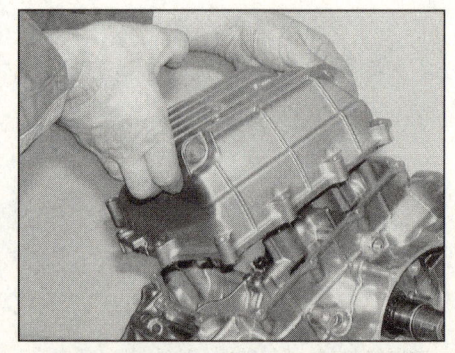

18.13 Install the sump, making sure it locates correctly onto the dowels

Engine, clutch and transmission 2•41

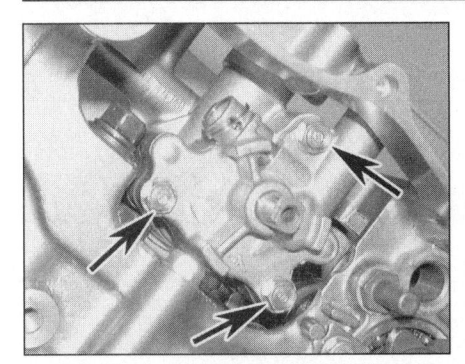

19.3 Unscrew the bolts (arrowed) and remove the pump

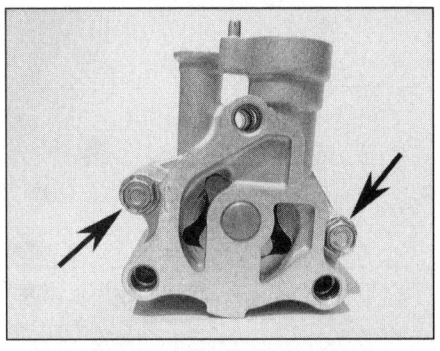

19.4a Unscrew the bolts (arrowed) . . .

19.4b . . . and remove the outer cover, noting the dowels (arrowed)

in each outer rotor and which way it faces, as the rotors must be installed the same way round. Honda specify that the punchmark on the feed circuit rotor should face the centre of the pump, while the punchmark on the cooling circuit rotor should face the outside of the pump. On the models we stripped down this was not the case, and the cooling circuit rotor punchmark also faced the centre. The important thing is to install the rotors the same way round as they were removed, so that mated surfaces continue to run together.

4 On VTR models, unscrew the bolts securing the covers to the pump body, then remove the outer (cooling circuit) cover **(see illustrations)**. Remove the cover dowels if they are loose. Remove the outer and inner rotors, noting which way round they fit and how the inner rotor locates over the drive pin **(see illustration)**. Withdraw the drive pin from the shaft **(see illustration)**. Hold the pump body and push the shaft through to separate the body from the inner (feed circuit) cover **(see illustration)**. Remove its dowels if they are loose. Withdraw the shaft and inner rotor from the cover, then remove the outer rotor, noting which way round it fits **(see illustrations)**. Remove the thrust washer from the end of the shaft, then slide the inner rotor off the shaft, and remove the drive pin **(see illustrations)**.

5 On XL models, unscrew the bolts securing the cover to the pump body, then hold the

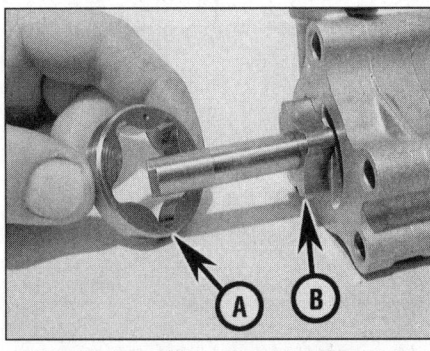

19.4c Remove the outer rotor (A) and the inner rotor (B), noting how it fits . . .

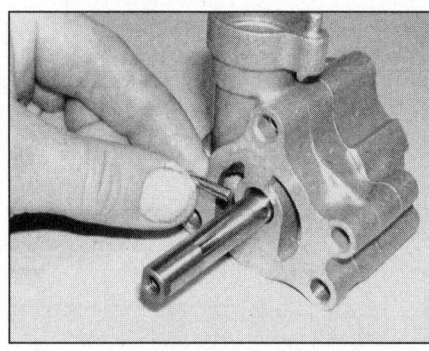

19.4d . . . and the drive pin

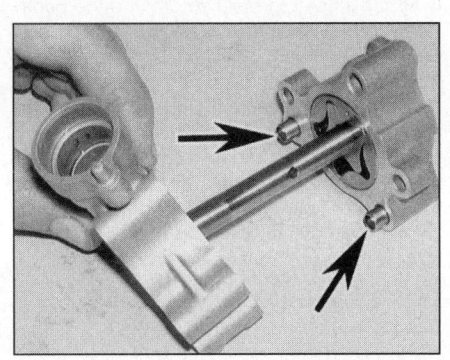

19.4e Separate the body and inner cover, noting the dowels (arrowed)

19.4f Remove the shaft and inner rotor from the cover . . .

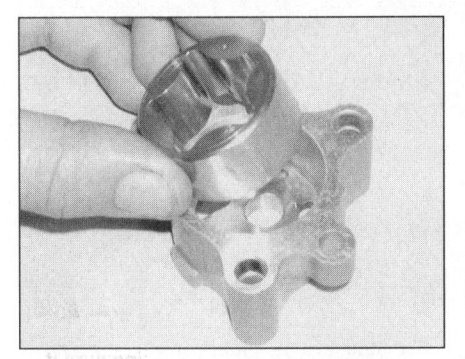

19.4g . . . then remove the outer rotor

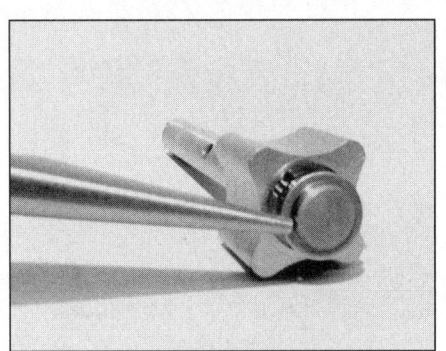

19.4h Remove the thrust washer . . .

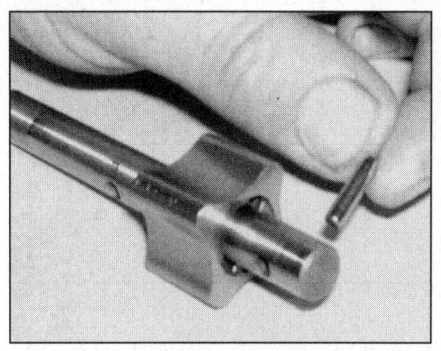

19.4i . . . and the drive pin, then slide the inner rotor off

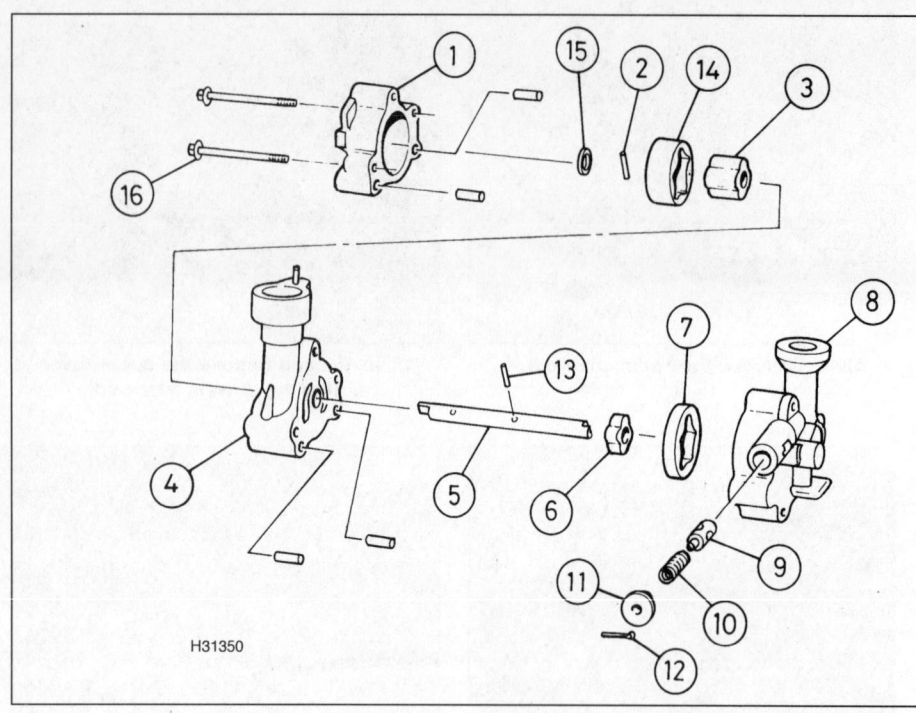

2•42 Engine, clutch and transmission

1 Main pump housing
2 Drive pin
3 Main pump inner rotor
4 Main pump housing
5 Driveshaft
6 Oil cooler pump inner rotor
7 Oil cooler pump outer rotor
8 Oil cooler pump housing
9 Oil cooler relief valve piston
10 Spring
11 Spring retainer
12 Split pin
13 Drive pin
14 Main pump outer rotor
15 Thrust washer
16 Bolts

19.4j Oil pump components – VTR models

pump body and pull the shaft to separate the cover from the body **(see illustration)**. Remove the cover dowels if they are loose. Note which way round the driveshaft fits in the pump. Withdraw the shaft from the inner side of the cover and remove the drive pin and thrust washer. Remove the outer and inner rotors, noting which way round they fit – it is best to mark one face of the outer rotor so that it can installed the same way round. This keeps mated surfaces running together.

6 Clean all the components in solvent.

7 Inspect the pump body and rotors for scoring and wear. If any damage, scoring or uneven or excessive wear is evident, replace the pump (individual components are not available) **(see illustration)**.

8 Fit the inner and outer rotors into the pump body (on VTR models with the dual circuit pump, make sure the thinner rotors are fitted in the cooling circuit side, and the thicker rotors in the feed side). Measure the clearance between the inner rotor tip and the outer rotor with a feeler gauge and compare it to the service limit listed in the specifications at the beginning of the Chapter **(see illustration)**. If the clearance measured is greater than the maximum listed, replace the pump with a new one.

9 Measure the clearance between the outer rotor and the pump body with a feeler gauge and compare it to the maximum clearance

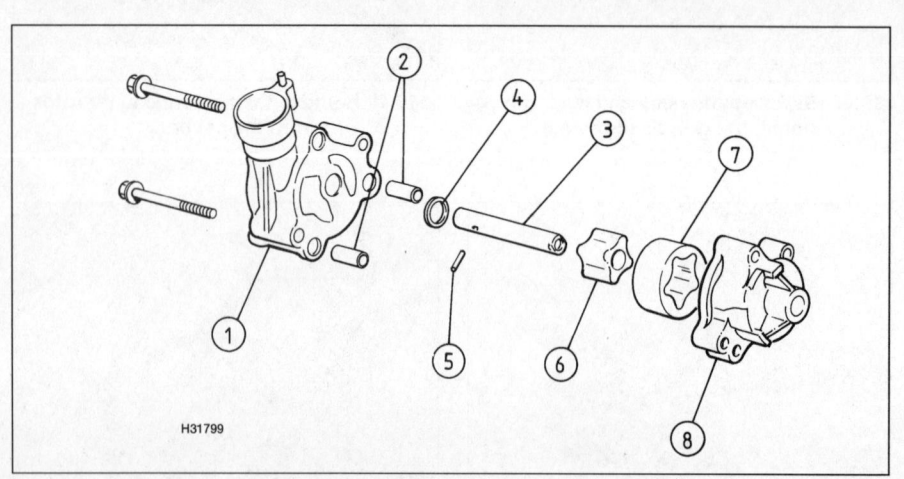

19.7 Look for scoring and wear, such as on this outer rotor

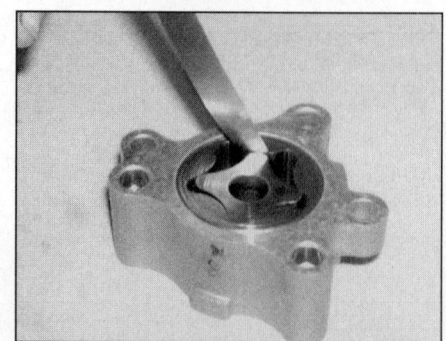

19.8 Measure the inner rotor tip-to-outer rotor clearance as shown (inner cover shown removed for clarity)

19.5 Oil pump components – XL models

1 Oil pump body
2 Dowel pin
3 Oil pump shaft
4 Washer
5 Drive pin
6 Inner rotor
7 Outer rotor
8 Oil pump cover

Engine, clutch and transmission 2•43

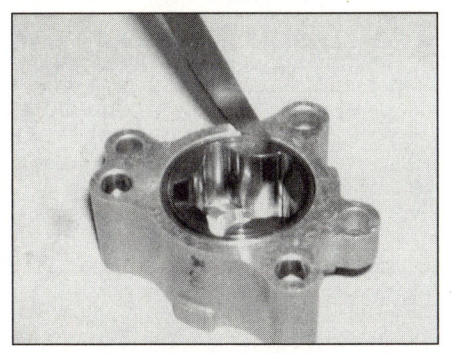

19.9 Measure the outer rotor-to-body clearance as shown

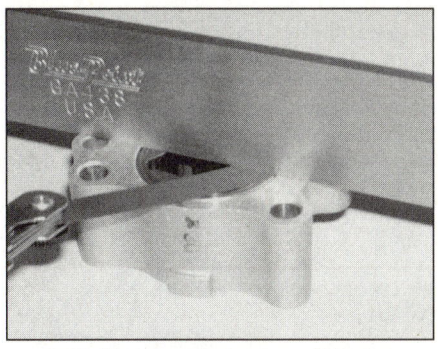

19.10 Measure the rotor end-float as shown

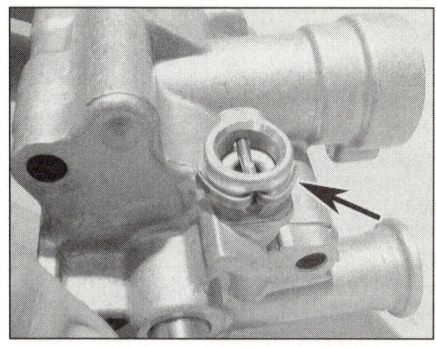

19.12a Remove the split pin (arrowed) ...

listed in the specifications at the beginning of the Chapter **(see illustration)**. If the clearance measured is greater than the maximum listed, replace the pump with a new one.

10 Lay a straight-edge across the rotors and the pump body and, using a feeler gauge, measure the rotor end-float (the gap between the rotors and the straight-edge **(see illustration)**. If the clearance measured is greater than the maximum listed, replace the pump with a new one.

11 Check the pump drive chain and drive and driven sprockets for wear or damage, and renew them as a set if necessary.

12 On VTR models, withdraw the split pin securing the cooling circuit pressure relief valve, noting that it is under spring pressure, then remove the spring seat, spring and plunger **(see illustrations)**. Clean all components in solvent, then check the plunger and the valve body for evidence of scoring, wear and any other damage. If any is found, replace the oil pump with a new one – individual components are not available. Otherwise, coat the plunger with oil and fit it back into the valve and recheck the movement. If it is good, install the spring and spring seat and secure them with the circlip.

13 If the pump is good, make sure all the components are clean, then lubricate them with new engine oil.

14 On VTR models, slide the feed circuit drive pin into its hole in the end of the driveshaft **(see illustration 19.4i)**, then slide the feed circuit inner rotor onto the shaft so that the cut-outs on the inside of the rotor locate over the ends of the drive pin **(see illustration)**. Remember that the feed circuit rotors are thicker than the cooling circuit rotors. Slide the thrust washer onto the shaft so it covers the drive pin **(see illustration 19.4h)**. Fit the feed circuit outer rotor into the inner cover with the punchmark facing the same way as noted on removal (see **Note** and Step 4) **(see illustration 19.4g)**. Fit the drive shaft with the inner rotor into the outer rotor and cover **(see illustration 19.4f)**. Fit the dowels into the cover if removed, then slide the pump body down the shaft and fit it onto the dowels **(see illustration 19.4e)**. Fit the cooling circuit drive pin into the hole in the driveshaft **(see illustration 19.4d)**, then slide the inner rotor onto the shaft so that the cut-outs on the inside of the rotor locate over the ends of the drive pin **(see illustration)**. Fit the outer rotor over the inner rotor with the punchmark facing the same way as noted on removal **(see illustration 19.4c)**. Fit the dowels into the body if removed, then slide the outer cover down the shaft and fit it onto the dowels **(see illustration 19.4b)**. Install the bolts and tighten them to the torque

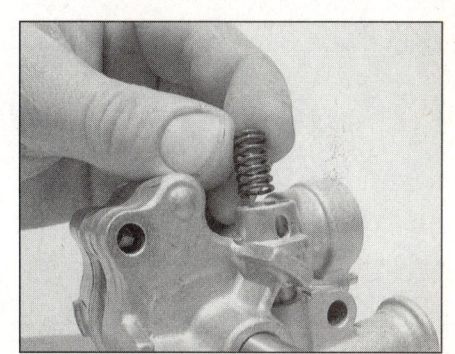

19.12b ... the spring seat ...

19.12c ... the spring ...

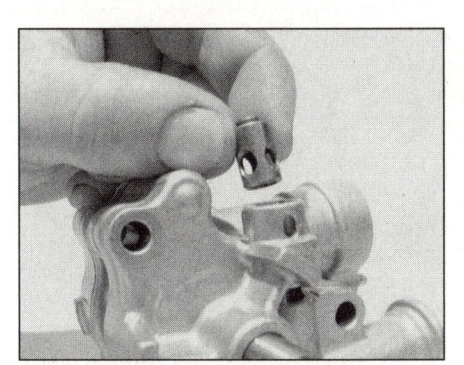

19.12d ... and the plunger

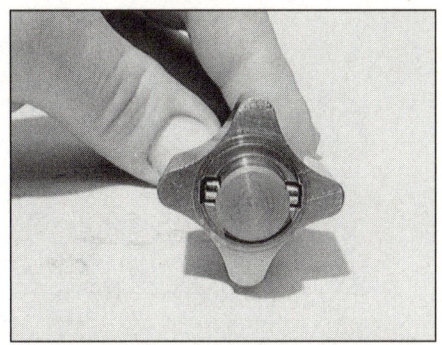

19.14a Locate the cut-outs in the feed circuit rotor over the drive pin ends

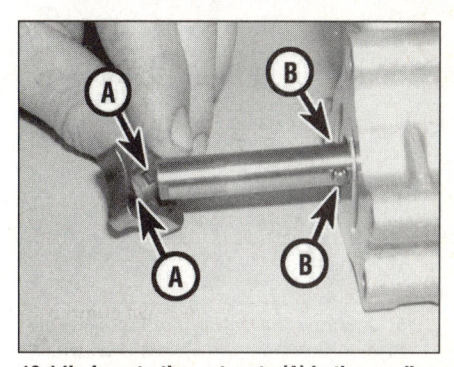

19.14b Locate the cut-outs (A) in the cooling circuit rotor over the drive pin ends (B)

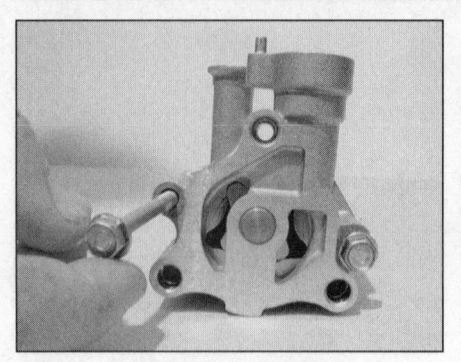

2•44 Engine, clutch and transmission

19.14c Install the bolts and tighten them to the specified torque

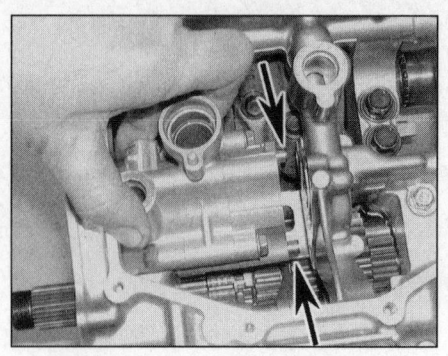

19.18 Install the pump, making sure the dowels (arrowed) locate correctly

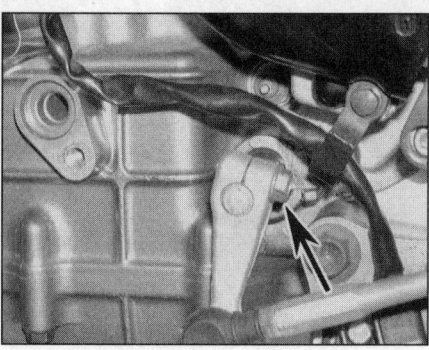

20.2 Note the alignment of the punchmark, then remove the bolt (arrowed) and slide the arm off the shaft – VTR models

setting specified at the beginning of the Chapter **(see illustration)**.
15 On XL models, fit the outer and inner rotors into the cover, with the outer rotor facing the same way as noted on removal and the cut-outs in the inner rotor facing out **(see illustration 19.5)**. Fit the drive pin into the hole in the inner end of the driveshaft, then slide the driveshaft through the rotors and cover and locate the drive pin into the cut-outs in the inner rotor. Fit the thrust washer over the drive pin. Fit the dowels if removed, then fit the pump body onto the cover and tighten the bolts to the torque setting specified at the beginning of the Chapter.
16 Rotate the pump shaft by hand and check that the rotors turn smoothly and freely.

Installation
17 If removed, fit the pump dowels into the crankcase. Pour some oil into the pump and rotate the shaft to distribute it.
18 Manoeuvre the pump into position, making sure it locates correctly onto the dowels **(see illustration)**. Fit the pump mounting bolts and tighten them to the torque setting specified at the beginning of the Chapter **(see illustration 19.3)**.
19 Install the pump drive and driven sprockets and chain, and the clutch (see Section 16).
20 Install the oil strainer and sump (see Section 18).

20 Gearchange mechanism – removal, inspection and installation

Note: *The gearchange mechanism can be removed with the engine in the frame. If the engine has been removed, ignore the steps which don't apply.*

Removal
1 Make sure the transmission is in neutral. Remove the clutch (see Section 16). There is no need to remove the oil pump drive, and driven sprockets and chain.
2 Note how the punchmark on the gearchange shaft aligns with either the slot in the linkage arm or the punchmark on the arm, where

marked. Unscrew the linkage arm pinchbolt and slide the arm off the shaft **(see illustration)**.
3 Wrap a single layer of thin insulating tape around the gearchange shaft splines to protect the oil seal lips as the shaft is removed.
4 Note how the gearchange shaft centralising spring ends fit on each side of the locating pin in the casing, and how the pawls on the selector arm locate onto the pins on the end of the selector drum **(see illustration 20.10)**. Grasp the end of the shaft and withdraw the shaft/arm assembly **(see illustration)**. Retrieve the washer from the crankcase if it didn't come with the shaft.
5 If required, note how the stopper arm spring ends locate and how the roller on the arm locates in the neutral detent on the selector drum cam, then unscrew the stopper arm bolt and remove the arm, the washer and the spring, noting how they fit **(see illustration)**.

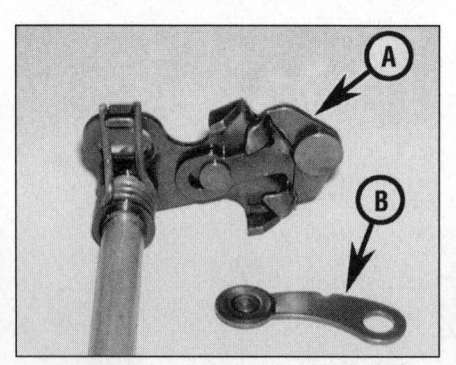

Inspection
6 Check the selector arm for cracks, distortion and wear of its pawls, and check for any corresponding wear on the pins on the selector drum cam **(see illustration)**. Also check the stopper arm roller and the detents in the selector drum cam for any wear or damage, and make sure the roller turns freely. Replace any components that are worn or damaged with new ones. Remove the selector drum cam by unscrewing the bolt in its centre **(see illustration)**. Note the locating pin in the

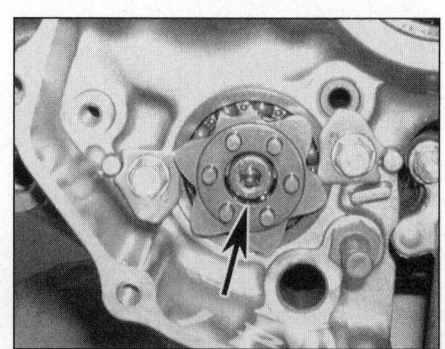

20.4 Withdraw the shaft/arm assembly, noting how it fits

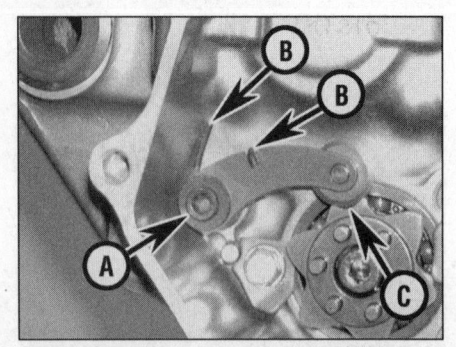

20.5 Unscrew the bolt (A) and remove the arm, noting how the spring ends (B) locate, and how the roller sits in the neutral detent (C)

20.6a Check the selector arm (A) and stopper arm (B) as described

20.6b Selector drum cam bolt (arrowed)

Engine, clutch and transmission 2•45

20.9a Fit the bolt, washer and spring onto the arm . . .

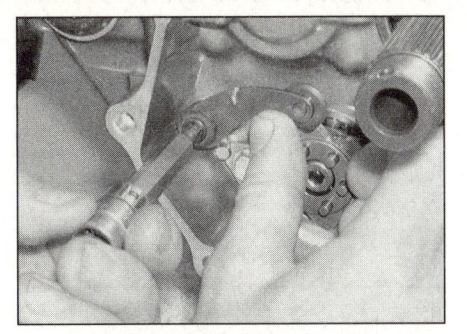

20.9b . . . then install the arm

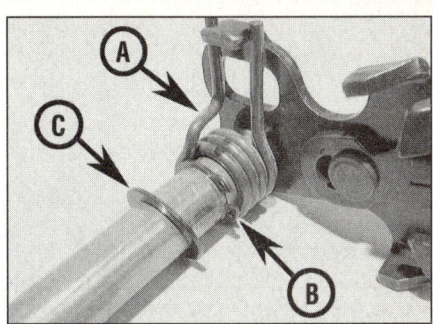

20.10a Make sure the centralising spring (A), circlip (B) and washer (C) are correctly installed

end of the drum and remove it for safekeeping if required. On installation, locate the pin in the cut-out in the back of the cam. Apply a suitable non-permanent thread locking compound to the cam bolt and tighten it to the torque setting specified at the beginning of the Chapter.

7 Inspect the shaft centralising spring and the stopper arm return spring for fatigue, wear or damage. If any is found, they must be replaced with new ones. Also check that the centralising spring locating pin in the crankcase is securely tightened. If it is loose, remove it and apply a non-permanent thread locking compound to its threads, then tighten it securely.

8 Check the gearchange shaft for straightness and damage to the splines. If the shaft is bent you can attempt to straighten it, but if the splines are damaged the shaft must be replaced with a new one. Also check the condition of the shaft oil seal in the left-hand

20.10b Locate the selector arm as shown

side of the crankcase. If it is damaged, deteriorated or shows signs of leakage it must be replaced with a new one. Unscrew the bolt securing the seal retainer plate and remove the plate. Lever out the old seal with a screwdriver and drive the new one squarely into place, with its lip facing inward, using a seal driver or suitable socket. Fit the retainer plate and tighten its bolt securely.

Installation

9 If removed, fit the bolt through the stopper arm, then fit the washer onto the bolt and locate the spring onto the arm (see illustration). Install the arm, locating the roller onto the neutral detent on the selector drum and making sure the spring ends are positioned correctly (see illustration). Tighten the bolt securely. Check that the arm and spring ends are correctly positioned (see illustration 20.5).

10 Check that the shaft centralising spring is properly positioned and slide the washer onto the shaft if removed (see illustration). Apply some grease to the lips of the gearchange shaft oil seal in the left-hand side of the crankcase. Slide the shaft into place and push it all the way through the case until the splined end comes out the other side (see illustration 20.4). Locate the selector arm pawls onto the pins on the selector drum and the centralising spring ends onto each side of the locating pin (see illustration).

11 Install the clutch (see Section 16).

12 Slide the gearchange lever linkage arm onto the shaft, on VTR models aligning the

punchmark on the shaft with the slit in the arm (see illustration 20.2), and on XL models aligning the two punchmarks. Install the pinchbolt and tighten it securely.

21 Timing rotor and primary drive gear – removal and installation

Note: *The timing rotor and primary drive gear can be removed with the engine in the frame. If the engine has been removed, ignore the steps which don't apply.*

Removal

1 Remove the clutch (see Section 16). During the removal procedure, slacken the primary drive gear bolt in the end of the crankshaft as described in Step 5 of Section 16 (see illustration 16.5). Alternatively, a holding tool the same as the one used for slackening the clutch nut can be used to hold the primary drive gear (see illustration). There is no need to remove the oil pump drive and driven sprockets and chain.

2 Remove the bolt and its washer, then slide the timing rotor and primary drive gear off the end of the crankshaft (see illustration).

3 Refer to Section 16, Step 16, and check the primary drive and driven gears.

Installation

4 Slide the primary drive gear onto the end of the crankshaft, aligning the wide splines (see illustration). Fit the timing

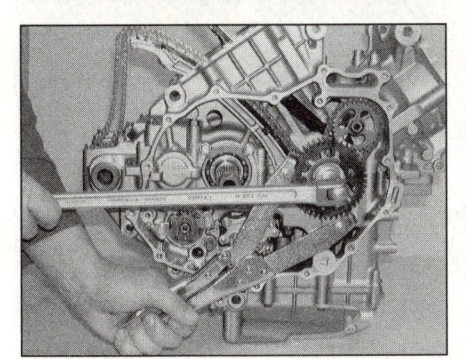

21.1 A holding tool can be used as shown when slackening the primary drive gear bolt

21.2 Unscrew the bolt and remove the timing rotor and primary drive gear

21.4a Align the wide spline on the crankshaft with that in the gear (arrowed) . . .

2•46 Engine, clutch and transmission

21.4b . . . and do the same for the timing rotor (arrowed)

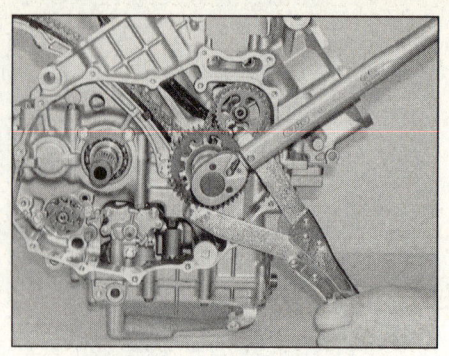

21.5 Tighten the primary drive gear bolt using either a holding tool . . .

21.6 . . . or the locking method shown after installing the clutch housing

rotor in the same way **(see illustration)**.

5 Apply some engine oil to the threads and the underside of the head on the bolt. Install the bolt with its washer **(see illustration 21.2)** and tighten it as much as possible at this stage, unless the holding tool is used in which case the bolt can be tightened to the specified torque setting **(see illustration)**.

6 Install the clutch (see Section 16). During the installation procedure, and if not already done, tighten the primary drive gear bolt to its specified torque setting using the same method to lock the gears as used on removal, noting that the locking method will need to be applied in the opposite direction **(see illustration)**.

22 Crankcase halves – separation and reassembly

Note: *To separate the crankcase halves, the engine must be removed from the frame (Section 5).*

Separation

1 To access the pistons, connecting rods, crankshaft, bearings, and transmission shafts, the crankcase must be split into two parts. The selector drum and forks can be removed and installed with the crankcases joined.

2 Before the crankcases can be separated the following components must be removed:
a) Oil cooler (VTR models) (Section 7).
b) Valve covers (Section 8).
c) Camshafts (Section 10).
d) Cylinder heads (Section 12) – see Note below.
e) Alternator/starter clutch (Chapter 9).
f) Clutch (Section 16).
g) Cam chains and blades (Section 11).
h) Gearchange mechanism (Section 20) – see Note below.
i) Oil sump (Section 18).
j) Oil pump (Section 19).
k) Starter motor (Chapter 9).

Note: *If the crankcases are being separated to inspect the crankshaft without removing it, to remove the crankshaft without removing the connecting rods and pistons, or to inspect or remove the transmission shafts, the cylinder heads can remain in situ. However, if removal of the connecting rod assemblies is intended, full disassembly of the top-end is necessary. The gearchange mechanism can also remain in situ unless the selector drum and forks are being removed.*

3 Unscrew the two 6 mm, nine 8 mm and one 10 mm upper crankcase bolts **(see illustration)**. Unscrew the bolts evenly, a little at a time and in a criss-cross sequence until they are finger-tight, then remove them. On VTR Y models onward (see *Frame and engine numbers* at the start of the manual) and all XL models note the sealing washer fitted to the forward 8 mm bolt on the left-hand side. **Note:** *As each bolt is removed, store it in its relative position in a cardboard template of the crankcase halves. This will ensure all bolts are installed in the correct location on reassembly.*

4 Turn the engine upside down.

5 Unscrew the two 6 mm and the six 8 mm lower crankcase bolts, followed by the eight 10 mm bolts **(see illustration)**. Unscrew the bolts evenly, a little at a time and in a criss-cross sequence until they are finger-tight, then remove them. **Note:** *As each bolt is removed, store it in its relative position in a cardboard template of the crankcase halves. This will ensure all bolts are installed in the correct location on reassembly.*

6 Carefully lift the lower crankcase half off the upper half, using a soft-faced hammer to tap around the joint to initially separate the halves

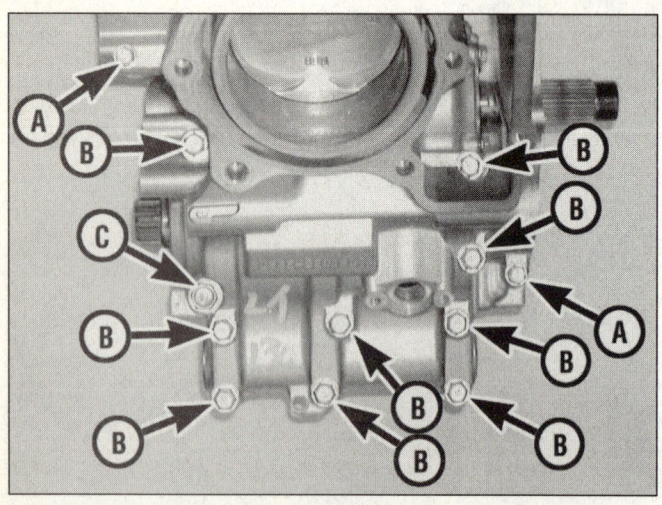

22.3 Upper crankcase 6 mm bolts (A), 8 mm bolts (B) and 10 mm bolt (C)

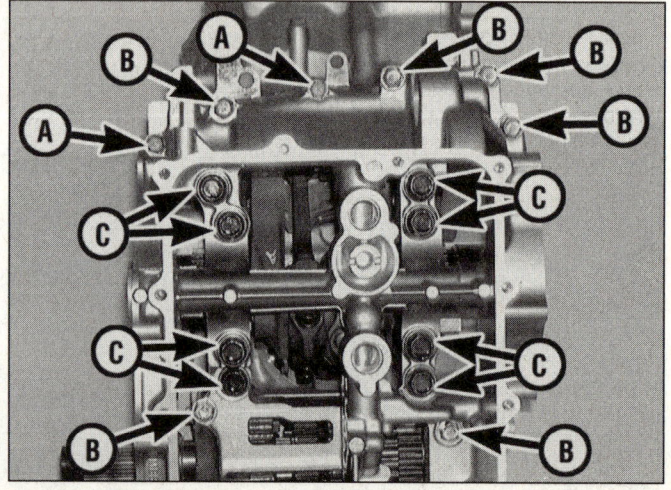

22.5 Lower crankcase 6 mm bolts (A), 8 mm bolts (B) and 10 mm bolts (C)

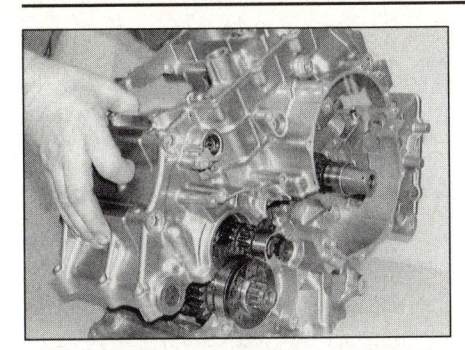

Engine, clutch and transmission 2•47

22.6 Carefully separate the crankcase halves

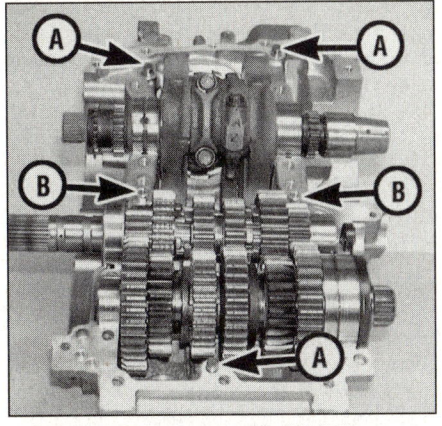

22.7 Remove the dowels (A) if they are loose, and the oil orifices (B)

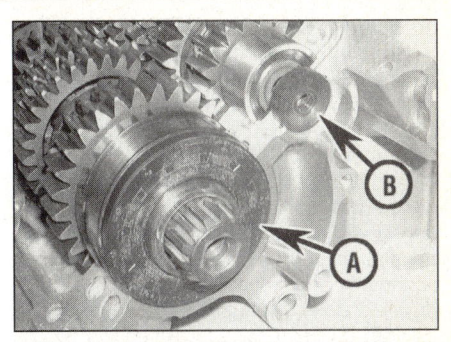

22.10 Check the output shaft seal (A) and the pushrod seal (B)

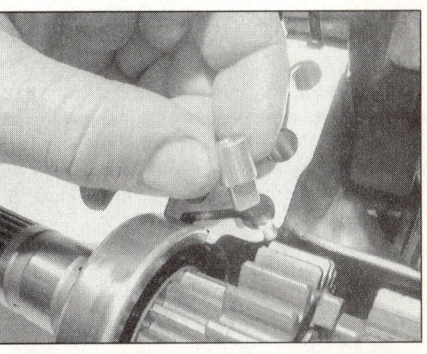

22.12 Install the oil orifices as shown

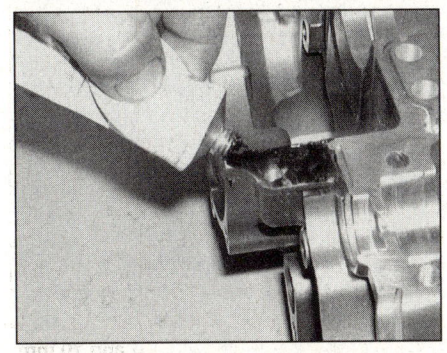

22.13a Apply sealant to one crankcase half ...

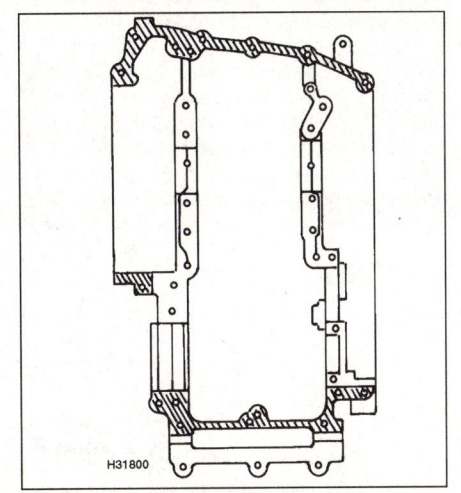

22.13b ... applying it to the shaded areas only

22.16 Tighten the bolts as described to the specified torque

if necessary **(see illustration)**. *Note: If the halves do not separate easily, make sure all fasteners have been removed. Do not try and separate the crankcase mating surfaces by levering against the crankcase mating surfaces as they are easily scored and will leak oil in the future if damaged.* The lower crankcase half will come away with the gearchange mechanism (if not already removed) and the selector drum and forks, leaving the crankshaft and transmission shafts in the upper crankcase half.

7 Remove the three locating dowels from the crankcase if they are loose (they could be in either crankcase half), and the two oil orifices, noting how they fit **(see illustration)**.

8 Refer to Sections 23 to 31 for the removal and installation of the components housed within the crankcases. *Note: The transmission shafts are not secured in position in the upper crankcase half.*

Reassembly

9 Remove all traces of sealant from the crankcase mating surfaces.

10 Ensure that all components and their bearings are in place in the upper and lower crankcase halves. If the transmission shafts have not been removed, check the condition of the output shaft oil seal on the left-hand end of the shaft and the clutch pushrod oil seal on the left-hand end of the input shaft and replace them if they are damaged or deteriorated **(see illustration)**.

11 Generously lubricate the crankshaft and transmission shafts, particularly around the bearings, with clean engine oil, then use a rag soaked in high flash-point solvent to wipe over the mating surfaces of both crankcase halves to remove all traces of oil.

12 If removed, install the three locating dowels and the two oil orifices in the upper crankcase half **(see illustration 22.7)**. Make sure the orifices are installed the correct way round **(see illustration)**.

13 Apply a small amount of suitable sealant to the indicated outer mating surfaces of one crankcase half **(see illustrations)**.

Caution: Do not apply an excessive amount of sealant as it will ooze out when the case halves are assembled and may obstruct oil passages. Do not apply the sealant on or too close to any of the bearing inserts or surfaces.

14 Check again that all components are in position, particularly that the bearing shells are still correctly located in the lower crankcase half. Carefully install the lower crankcase half down onto the upper crankcase half, making sure each selector fork locates correctly in the groove in its pinion, and the dowels all locate correctly into the lower crankcase half **(see illustration 22.6)**.

15 Check that the lower crankcase half is correctly seated. *Note: The crankcase halves should fit together without being forced.* If the casings are not correctly seated, remove the lower crankcase half and investigate the problem. Do not attempt to pull them together using the crankcase bolts, as the casing will crack and be ruined.

16 Clean the threads of the eight 10 mm lower crankcase bolts. Apply some oil to the threads and the underside of the heads of the bolts and insert them in their original locations **(see illustration 22.5)**. Secure all bolts finger-tight at first, then tighten them evenly and a little at a time in a criss-cross sequence to the torque setting specified at the beginning of the Chapter **(see illustration)**.

17 Clean the threads of the six 8 mm and two 6 mm lower crankcase bolts and insert them in their original locations **(see illustration 22.5)**. Secure all bolts finger-tight at first, then tighten them evenly and a little at a time in a criss-cross sequence to the torque settings specified at the beginning of the Chapter.

2•48 Engine, clutch and transmission

18 Turn the engine over. Clean the threads of the two 6 mm, nine 8 mm and one 10 mm upper crankcase bolts and insert them in their original locations (see illustration 22.3). On VTR Y models onward and all XL models do not forget the sealing washer fitted to the forward 8 mm bolt on the left-hand side, and use a new one if the old one is damaged or deformed. Secure all bolts finger-tight at first, then tighten them evenly a little at a time in a criss-cross sequence to the torque settings specified at the beginning of the Chapter.
19 With all crankcase fasteners tightened, check that the crankshaft and transmission shafts rotate smoothly and easily. Check that the transmission shafts rotate freely and independently in neutral, then rotate the selector drum by hand and select each gear in turn whilst rotating the input shaft. Check that all gears can be selected and that the shafts rotate freely in every gear. If there are any signs of undue stiffness, tight or rough spots, or of any other problem, the fault must be rectified before proceeding further.
20 Install all other removed assemblies in the reverse of the sequence given in Step 2.

23 Crankcase halves and cylinder bores – inspection and servicing

Crankcase halves

1 After the crankcases have been separated, remove the crankshaft, connecting rods and pistons, transmission shafts, selector drum and forks, neutral switch and oil pressure switch, referring to the relevant Sections of this Chapter and to Chapter 9 for the oil pressure and neutral switches. On XL-3 models onward remove the piston oil jet from the bottom of each cylinder.
2 The crankcases should be cleaned thoroughly with new solvent and dried with compressed air. All oil passages should be blown out with compressed air.
3 All traces of old gasket sealant should be removed from the mating surfaces. Minor damage to the surfaces can be cleaned up with a fine sharpening stone or grindstone.
Caution: Be very careful not to nick or gouge the crankcase mating surfaces or oil leaks will result. Check both crankcase halves very carefully for cracks and other damage.
4 Small cracks or holes in aluminium castings may be repaired with an epoxy resin adhesive as a temporary measure. Permanent repairs can only be effected by argon-arc welding, and only a specialist in this process is in a position to advise on the economy or practical aspect of such a repair. If any damage is found that can't be repaired, replace the crankcase halves as a set.
5 Damaged threads can be economically reclaimed by using a diamond section wire insert, of the Heli-Coil type, which is easily fitted after drilling and re-tapping the affected thread.

6 Sheared studs or screws can usually be removed with screw extractors, which consist of a tapered, left-hand thread screw of very hard steel. These are inserted into a pre-drilled hole in the stud, and usually succeed in dislodging the most stubborn stud or screw.

HAYNES HiNT *Refer to Tools and Workshop Tips for details of installing a thread insert and using screw extractors.*

7 Install all components and assemblies, referring to the relevant Sections of this Chapter and to Chapter 9, before reassembling the crankcase halves. On XL-3 models onward fit the piston oil jet into the bottom of each cylinder.

Cylinder bores

8 Do not attempt to separate the cylinder liners from the cylinder block.
9 Check the cylinder walls carefully for scratches and score marks.
10 Using a precision straight-edge and a feeler gauge set to the warpage limit listed in the Specifications at the beginning of the Chapter, check the block gasket mating surface for warpage. Refer to *Tools and Workshop Tips* in the Reference section for details of how to use the straight-edge. If warpage is excessive the crankcases must be replaced with new ones.
11 Using telescoping gauges and a micrometer (see *Tools and Workshop Tips*), check the dimensions of each cylinder to assess the amount of wear, taper and ovality. Measure near the top (but below the level of the top piston ring at TDC), centre and bottom (but above the level of the oil ring at BDC) of the bore, both parallel to and across the crankshaft axis **(see illustration)**. Compare the results to the specifications at the beginning of the Chapter. If the cylinders are worn, oval or tapered beyond the service limit the they can be rebored, two oversizes (+0.25 and +0.50) of pistons and rings and available.
12 If the precision measuring tools are not available, take the crankcases to a Honda dealer or specialist motorcycle repair shop for assessment and advice.
13 If the cylinder bores are in good condition and the piston-to-bore clearance is within specifications (see Section 26), the cylinders should be honed (de-glazed). To perform this operation you will need the proper size flexible hone with fine stones, or a bottle-brush type

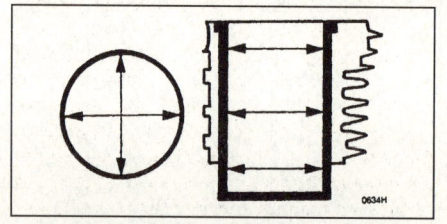

23.11 Measure the cylinder bore in the directions shown with a telescoping gauge, then measure the gauge with a micrometer

hone, plenty of light oil or honing oil, some clean rags and an electric drill motor.
14 Hold the block sideways (so that the bores are horizontal rather than vertical) in a vice with soft jaws or cushioned with wooden blocks. Mount the hone in the drill motor, compress the stones and insert the hone into the cylinder. Thoroughly lubricate the cylinder, then turn on the drill and move the hone up and down in the cylinder at a pace which produces a fine cross-hatch pattern on the cylinder wall with the lines intersecting at an angle of approximately 60∞. Be sure to use plenty of lubricant and do not take off any more material than is necessary to produce the desired effect. Do not withdraw the hone from the cylinder while it is still turning. Switch off the drill and continue to move it up and down in the cylinder until it has stopped turning, then compress the stones and withdraw the hone. Wipe the oil from the cylinder and repeat the procedure on the other cylinder. Remember, do not take too much material from the cylinder wall.
15 Wash the bores thoroughly with warm soapy water to remove all traces of the abrasive grit produced during the honing operation. Be sure to run a brush through the stud holes and flush them with running water. On XL-3 models onward flush the piston oil jet with solvent and blow through the passage with compressed air. After rinsing, dry the cylinders thoroughly and apply a thin coat of light, rust-preventative oil to all machined surfaces.
16 If you do not have the equipment or desire to perform the honing operation, take the crankcase to a Honda dealer or specialist motorcycle repair shop.

24 Main and connecting rod bearings – general information

1 Even though main and connecting rod bearings are generally replaced with new ones during the engine overhaul, the old bearings should be retained for close examination as they may reveal valuable information about the condition of the engine.
2 Bearing failure occurs mainly because of lack of lubrication, the presence of dirt or other foreign particles, overloading the engine, and/or corrosion. Regardless of the cause of bearing failure, it must be corrected before the engine is reassembled to prevent it from happening again.
3 When examining the connecting rod bearings, remove them from the connecting rods and caps and lay them out on a clean surface in the same general position as their location on the crankshaft journals. This will enable you to match any noted bearing problems with the corresponding crankshaft journal.
4 Dirt and other foreign particles get into the engine in a variety of ways. It may be left in the engine during assembly or it may pass through filters or breathers. It may get into the oil and from there into the bearings. Metal chips from machining operations and normal engine wear

Engine, clutch and transmission 2•49

25.2 Measure the connecting rod side clearance using a feeler gauge

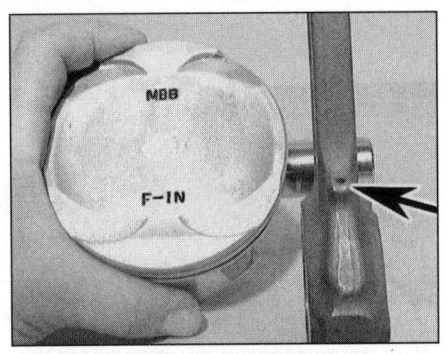

25.3 Note the various markings as described, and the oil hole (arrowed)

25.5 Withdraw the piston and connecting rod assembly from the top of the cylinder

are often present. Abrasives are sometimes left in engine components after reconditioning operations, especially when parts are not thoroughly cleaned using the proper cleaning methods. Whatever the source, these foreign objects often end up embedded in the soft bearing material and are easily recognised. Large particles will not embed in the bearing and will score or gouge the bearing and journal. The best prevention for this cause of bearing failure is to clean all parts thoroughly and keep everything spotlessly clean during engine reassembly. Frequent and regular oil and filter changes are also recommended.

5 Lack of lubrication or lubrication breakdown has a number of interrelated causes. Excessive heat (which thins the oil), overloading (which squeezes the oil from the bearing face) and oil leakage or throw off (from excessive bearing clearances, worn oil pump or high engine speeds) all contribute to lubrication breakdown. Blocked oil passages will also starve a bearing and destroy it. When lack of lubrication is the cause of bearing failure, the bearing material is wiped or extruded from the steel backing of the bearing. Temperatures may increase to the point where the steel backing and the journal turn blue from overheating.

HAYNES HINT *Refer to Tools and Workshop Tips for bearing fault finding.*

6 Riding habits can have a definite effect on bearing life. Full throttle low speed operation, or labouring the engine, puts very high loads on bearings, which tend to squeeze out the oil film. These loads cause the bearings to flex, which produces fine cracks in the bearing face (fatigue failure). Eventually the bearing material will loosen in pieces and tear away from the steel backing. Short trip riding leads to corrosion of bearings, as insufficient engine heat is produced to drive off the condensed water and corrosive gases produced. These products collect in the engine oil, forming acid and sludge. As the oil is carried to the engine bearings, the acid attacks and corrodes the bearing material.

7 Incorrect bearing installation during engine assembly will lead to bearing failure as well. Tight fitting bearings which leave insufficient bearing oil clearances result in oil starvation.

Dirt or foreign particles trapped behind a bearing insert result in high spots on the bearing which lead to failure.

8 To avoid bearing problems, clean all parts thoroughly before reassembly, double check all bearing clearance measurements and lubricate the new bearings with clean engine oil during installation.

25 Connecting rods – removal, inspection and installation

Note 1: To remove the connecting rods the engine must be removed from the frame and the crankcases separated.

Note 2: The connecting rod bolts must be discarded and new ones used on installation – it is best to obtain the bolts in advance. The old bolts can, however, be used for the oil clearance check.

Removal

1 Remove the engine from the frame (see Section 5) and separate the crankcase halves (see Section 22).
2 Before removing the rods from the crankshaft, measure the side clearance with a feeler gauge as shown **(see illustration)**. If the clearance is greater than the service limit listed in this Chapter's Specifications, replace the rods with new ones. If the clearance is still excessive, replace the crankshaft with a new one.
3 Using paint or a felt marker pen, mark the relevant cylinder identity on each connecting rod and cap. Mark across the cap-to-connecting rod join and note which side of the rod faces the front of the engine to ensure that the cap and rod are fitted the correct way around on reassembly. Note that the number already across the rod and cap indicates rod size grade. On the front cylinder, the piston is marked F-IN and this mark faces the intake side of the cylinder, the connecting rod is marked MBBF, and the oil hole in the big-end of the connecting rod should face the back of the engine **(see illustration)**. For the rear cylinder, the piston is marked R-IN and this mark faces the intake side of the cylinder, the connecting rod is marked MBBR, and the oil hole in the big-end of the connecting rod should face the back of the engine.
4 Remove the crankshaft (see Section 28).

5 Push each piston/connecting rod assembly up and remove it from the top of the bore making sure the connecting rod does not mark the cylinder bore walls **(see illustration)**. Keep the rod, cap, bolts, and (if they are to be reused) the bearing shells together in their correct positions to ensure correct installation.

HAYNES HINT *To ease removal of the pistons, carefully remove any ridge of carbon built up on the top of each cylinder bore using a scraper. If there is a pronounced wear ridge, remove it using a ridge reamer.*

Caution: *Do not try to remove the piston/connecting rod from the bottom of the cylinder bore. The piston will not pass the crankcase main bearing webs. If the piston is pulled right to the bottom of the bore the oil control ring will expand and lock the piston in position. If this happens it is likely the ring will be broken.*

6 Immediately install the relevant bearing shells (if removed), bearing cap, and bolts on each piston/connecting rod assembly so that they are all kept together as a matched set.
7 Remove the pistons from the connecting rods if required (see Section 26).

Inspection

8 Check the connecting rods for cracks and other obvious damage.
9 Apply clean engine oil to the connecting rod pin, insert it into the connecting rod small-end and check for any freeplay between the two **(see illustration)**. Measure the pin external diameter

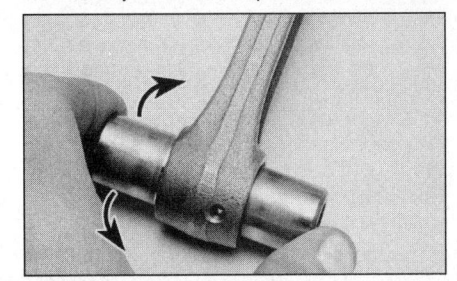

25.9a Slip the piston pin into the rod's small-end and rock it back and forth to check for looseness

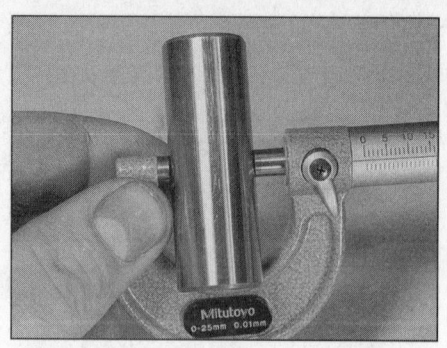

25.9b Measure the external diameter of the pin ...

25.9c ... and the internal diameter of the connecting rod small-end

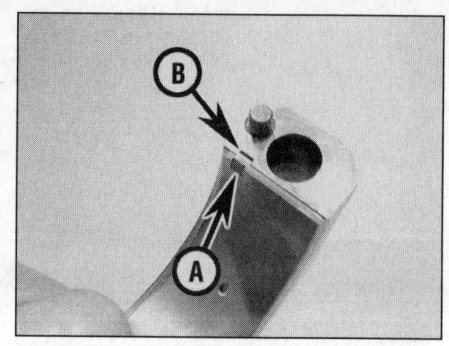

25.14 Make sure the tab (A) locates in the notch (B)

and the small-end bore diameter, then calculate the difference to obtain the small-end-to-piston pin clearance **(see illustrations)**. Compare the result to the Specifications at the beginning of the Chapter. If the clearance is greater than specified, renew the components that are worn beyond their specified limits.

10 Refer to Section 24 and examine the connecting rod bearing shells. If they are scored, badly scuffed or appear to have seized, new shells must be installed. Always replace the shells in the connecting rods as a set. If they are badly damaged, check the corresponding crankpin. Evidence of extreme heat, such as discoloration, indicates that lubrication failure has occurred. Be sure to thoroughly check the oil pump and pressure regulator as well as all oil holes and passages before reassembling the engine.

11 Have the rods checked for twist and bend by a Honda dealer if you are in doubt about their straightness.

Oil clearance check

12 Whether new bearing shells are being fitted or the original ones are being re-used, the connecting rod bearing oil clearance should be checked prior to reassembly. Check the clearance on one rod at a time.

13 Clean the backs of the bearing shells and the bearing locations in both the connecting rod and cap.

14 Press the bearing shells into their locations, ensuring that the tab on each shell engages the notch in the connecting rod/cap **(see illustration)**. Make sure the bearings are fitted in the correct locations and take care not to touch any shell's bearing surface with your fingers. Lay the crankshaft in the upper crankcase half, making sure it is the correct way round and that all the main bearing shells are installed (see Section 28).

15 Cut a length of the appropriate size Plastigauge (it should be slightly shorter than the width of the crankpin). Place a strand of Plastigauge on the (cleaned) crankpin journal and fit the (clean) connecting rod, shells and cap **(see illustration 28.25)**. Make sure the cap is fitted the correct way around so the previously made markings align, and that the rod is facing the right way (see Step 3). Apply some clean oil to the threads and under the heads of the old connecting rod bolts **(see illustration 28.26a)**. Install the bolts and tighten them evenly, in two or three stages, to the torque setting specified at the beginning of the Chapter, then tighten them by a further 120° using a degree disc, all the time ensuring that the connecting rod does not rotate on the crankshaft **(see illustrations 28.26b and 28.26c)**. It is highly advisable to have an assistant to hold the crankshaft down in the crankcase while tightening the bolts as it could jump out.

> **HAYNES HiNT** *If a degree disc is not available, the angle can be determined by using the points on the connecting rod cap nut. There are six points on the nut, so the angle between each point is 60°. Select one point as a reference and mark it with paint or a marker. Now select the second point clockwise from it and mark its position on the connecting rod cap. Tighten the nut – when the mark on the first point aligns with the mark made on the connecting rod cap, it will have turned through 120°.*

16 Slacken the cap bolts and remove the connecting rod, again taking great care not to rotate the rod or crankshaft. Compare the width of the crushed Plastigauge on the crankpin to the scale printed on the Plastigauge envelope to obtain the connecting rod big-end bearing oil clearance **(see illustration 28.16)**. Compare the reading to the Specifications at the beginning of the Chapter.

25.21a Crankpin journal size letters (arrowed)

17 On completion carefully scrape away all traces of the Plastigauge material from the crankpin and bearing shells using a fingernail or other object which is unlikely to score the shells.

18 If the clearance is within the range listed in this Chapter's Specifications and the bearings are in perfect condition, they can be reused. If the clearance is beyond the service limit, replace the bearing shells with new ones (see Steps 21 and 22). Check the oil clearance once again (the new shells may be thick enough to bring bearing clearance within the specified range). Always replace all of the shells at the same time.

19 If the clearance is still greater than the service limit listed in this Chapter's Specifications, the crankpin is worn and the crankshaft should be replaced with a new one.

20 Repeat the oil clearance check for the other connecting rod.

Bearing shell selection

21 Replacement bearing shells for the big-end bearings are supplied on a selected fit basis. Code letters and numbers stamped on various components are used to identify the correct replacement bearings. The crankpin journal size letters are stamped on the crankshaft webs and will be either an A, a B or a C **(see illustration)**. Each letter is adjacent to the crankpin journal it represents. The connecting rod size code number is marked on the flat face of the connecting rod and cap and will be either a 1, a 2 or a 3 **(see illustration)**.

25.21b Connecting rod size number

Engine, clutch and transmission 2•51

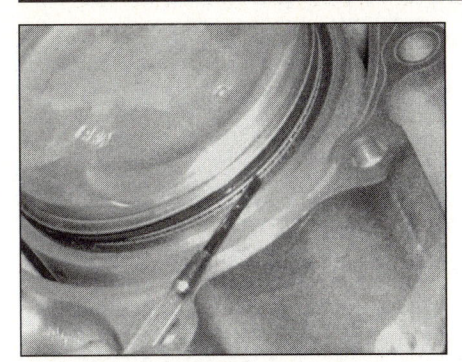

25.25a Carefully feed each ring into the bore

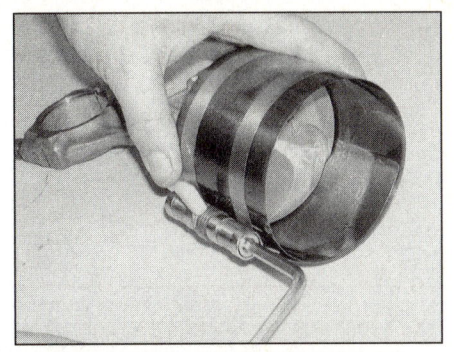

25.25b Clamp the rings in position by tightening the bands on the compressor . . .

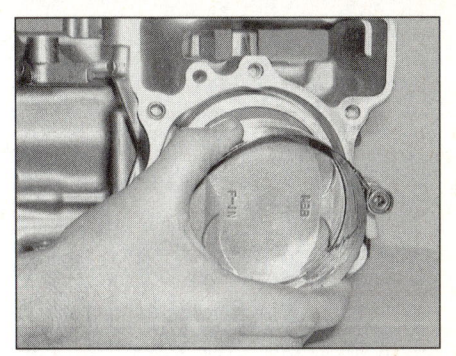

25.25c . . . then push the piston into its bore

22 A range of bearing shells is available. To select the correct bearing shell colour code for a particular big-end, using the table below cross-refer the crankpin journal size letter (stamped on the web) with the connecting rod size number (stamped on the rod). For example, if the crankpin size is B, and the connecting rod size is 3, then the bearing required is black. The colour is marked on the side of the shell. **Note:** *Replacement shells for the front cylinder bearing are marked by a single colour mark, while replacement shells for the rear cylinder bearing are marked by a double colour mark. Be sure to fit the correct shells on the relevant bearing.*

Crankpin size	Connecting Rod size		
	1	2	3
A	Yellow	Green	Brown
B	Green	Brown	Black
C	Brown	Black	Blue

Installation

23 Fit the pistons onto the connecting rods (see Section 26).
24 Clean the backs of the bearing shells and the bearing cut-outs in both cap and rod. If new shells are being fitted, ensure that all traces of the protective grease are cleaned off using paraffin (kerosene). Wipe the shells, cap and rod dry with a clean lint free cloth. Install the bearing shells in the connecting rods and caps (see **Note** in Step 22), aligning the notch in the bearing with the groove in the rod or cap **(see illustration 25.14)**. Lubricate the shells with molybdenum disulphide oil (a 50/50 mixture of molybdenum disulphide grease and clean engine oil).
25 Lubricate the pistons, rings and cylinder bore with clean engine oil. Insert the piston/connecting rod assembly into the top of its bore, taking care not to allow the connecting rod to mark the bore. Make sure the IN mark on the piston crown is on the intake side of the bore and the connecting rod is the right way round (see Step 3), then carefully compress and feed each piston ring into the bore until the piston crown is flush with the top of the bore **(see illustration)**. If available, a piston ring compressor makes installation a lot easier **(see illustrations)**.
26 Install the crankshaft (see Section 28).
27 Reassemble the crankcase halves (see Section 22).

26 Pistons – removal, inspection and installation

Note: *To remove the pistons the engine must be removed from the frame and the crankcase halves separated.*

Removal

1 Remove the connecting rods (see Section 25).
2 Before removing the piston from the connecting rod, use a sharp scriber or felt marker pen to write the cylinder identity on the crown of each piston (or on the inside of the skirt if the piston is dirty and going to be cleaned). On the front cylinder the piston should already be marked F-IN and on the rear cylinder marked R-IN, though these marks are likely to be invisible until the piston is cleaned.
3 Carefully prise out the circlip on one side of the piston using needle-nose pliers or a small flat-bladed screwdriver inserted into the notch **(see illustration)**. Push the piston pin out from the other side to free the piston from the connecting rod **(see illustration)**. Remove the

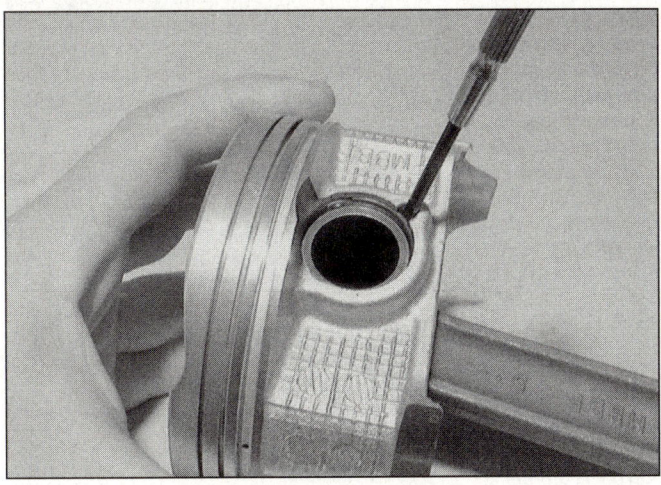

26.3a Prise out the circlip . . .

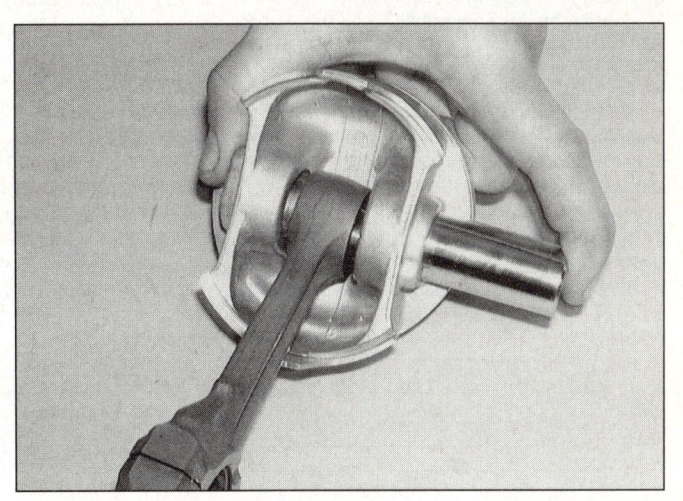

26.3b . . . then push out the pin and remove the piston

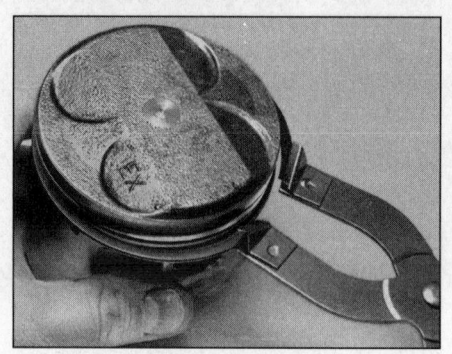

2•52 Engine, clutch and transmission

26.5 Removing the piston rings using a ring removal and installation tool

26.11 Measure the piston ring-to-groove clearance with a feeler gauge

26.12 Measure the piston diameter with a micrometer at the specified distance from the bottom of the skirt

other circlip and discard them, as new ones must be used. When the piston has been removed, install its pin back into its bore so that related parts do not get mixed up.

> **HAYNES HiNT** *If a piston pin is a tight fit in the piston bosses, soak a rag in boiling water then wring it out and wrap it around the piston – this will expand the alloy piston sufficiently to release its grip on the pin. If the piston pin is particularly stubborn, extract it using a drawbolt tool, but be careful to protect the piston's working surfaces.*

Inspection

4 Before the inspection process can be carried out, the pistons must be cleaned and the old piston rings removed.
5 Using your thumbs or a piston ring removal and installation tool, carefully remove the rings from the pistons **(see illustration)**. Do not nick or gouge the pistons in the process. Carefully note which way up each ring fits and in which groove as they must be installed in their original positions if being re-used. The upper surface of each ring is marked with a letter at one end. The top ring is identified by the letter R, and the second (middle) ring by the letters RN.
6 Scrape all traces of carbon from the tops of the pistons. A hand-held wire brush or a piece of fine emery cloth can be used once most of the deposits have been scraped away. **Do not**, under any circumstances, use a wire brush mounted in a drill motor to remove deposits from the pistons; the piston material is soft and will be eroded away by the wire brush.
7 Use a piston ring groove cleaning tool to remove any carbon deposits from the ring grooves. If a tool is not available, a piece broken off an old ring will do the job. Be very careful to remove only the carbon deposits. Do not remove any metal and do not nick or gouge the sides of the ring grooves.
8 Once the deposits have been removed, clean the pistons with solvent and dry them thoroughly. If the identification previously marked on the piston is cleaned off, be sure to re-mark it with the correct identity. Make sure the oil return holes below the oil ring groove are clear.
9 Carefully inspect each piston for cracks around the skirt, at the pin bosses and at the ring lands. Normal piston wear appears as even, vertical wear on the thrust surfaces of the piston and slight looseness of the top ring in its groove. If the skirt is scored or scuffed, the engine may have been suffering from overheating and/or abnormal combustion, which caused excessively high operating temperatures. The oil pump should be checked thoroughly. Also check that the circlip grooves are not damaged.
10 A hole in the piston crown, an extreme to be sure, is an indication that abnormal combustion (pre-ignition) was occurring. Burned areas at the edge of the piston crown are usually evidence of spark knock (detonation). If any of the above problems exist, the causes must be corrected or the damage will occur again.
11 Measure the piston ring-to-groove clearance by laying each piston ring in its groove and slipping a feeler gauge in beside it **(see illustration)**. Make sure you have the correct ring for the groove (see Step 5). Check the clearance at three or four locations around the groove. If the clearance is greater than specified, renew both the piston and rings as a set. If new rings are being used, measure the clearance using the new rings. If the clearance is greater than that specified, the piston is worn and must be replaced with a new one.
12 Check the piston-to-bore clearance by measuring the bore (see Section 23) and the piston diameter. Make sure each piston is matched to its correct cylinder. Measure the piston 20.0 mm up from the bottom of the skirt and at 90° to the piston pin axis **(see illustration)**. Subtract the piston diameter from the bore diameter to obtain the clearance. If it is greater than the specified figure, the piston must be replaced with a new one (assuming the bore itself is within limits).
13 Apply clean engine oil to the piston pin, insert it into the piston and check for any freeplay between the two **(see illustration)**. Measure the pin external diameter **(see illustration 25.9b)**, and the pin bore in the piston **(see illustration)**. Calculate the difference to obtain the piston pin-to-piston pin bore clearance. Compare the result with the Specifications at the beginning of the Chapter. If the clearance is greater than specified, replace the components that are worn beyond their specified limits. If not already done (see Section 25), repeat the measurements between the pin and the connecting rod small-end **(see illustration 25.9c)**.

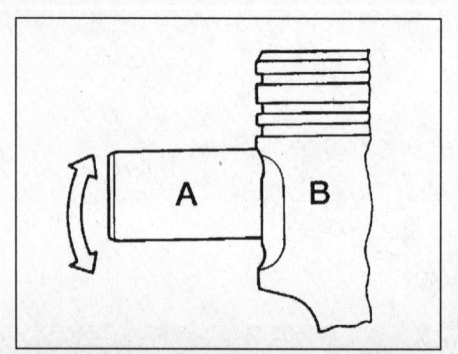

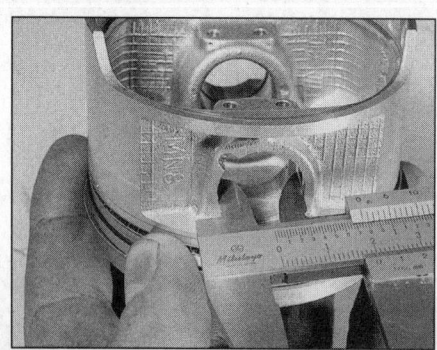

Installation

14 Inspect and install the piston rings (see Section 27).

26.13a Slip the pin (A) into the piston (B) and try to rock it back and forth. If it's loose, replace the piston and pin

26.13b Measure the internal diameter of the bore in the piston

Engine, clutch and transmission 2•53

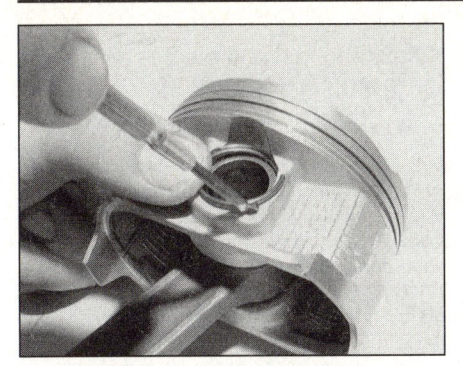

26.17 Do not over-compress the circlip when fitting it into the piston

27.3 Measuring piston ring installed end gap

27.5 Ring end gap can be enlarged by clamping a file in a vice and filing the ring ends

15 Lubricate the piston pin, the piston pin bore and the connecting rod small-end bore with molybdenum disulphide oil (a 50/50 mixture of molybdenum disulphide grease and clean engine oil).

16 When installing the pistons onto the connecting rods, refer to Section 25, Step 3, to identify their correct location and which way round they fit.

17 Install a *new* circlip in one side of the piston (do not re-use old circlips). Line up the piston on its correct connecting rod, and insert the piston pin from the other side **(see illustration 26.3b)**. Secure the pin with the other *new* circlip. When installing the circlips, compress them only just enough to fit them in the piston, and make sure they are properly seated in their grooves with the open end away from the removal notch **(see illustration)**.

18 Install the connecting rods (see Section 25) and reassemble the crankcase halves (see Section 22).

27 Piston rings –
inspection and installation

1 It is good practice to renew the piston rings when an engine is being overhauled. Before installing the new rings, the end gaps must be checked with the rings installed in the bore.

2 Lay out the pistons and the new ring sets so the rings will be matched with the same piston and bore during the end gap measurement procedure and engine assembly.

3 To measure the installed ring end gap, insert the top ring into the top of the bore and square it up with the bore walls by pushing it in with the top of the piston. The ring should be about 20 mm below the top edge of the bore. To measure the end gap, slip a feeler gauge between the ends of the ring and compare the measurement to the Specifications at the beginning of the Chapter **(see illustration)**.

4 If the gap is larger or smaller than specified, double check to make sure that you have the correct rings before proceeding.

5 If the gap is too small, it must be enlarged or the ring ends may come in contact with each other during engine operation, which can cause serious damage. The end gap can be increased by filing the ring ends very carefully with a fine file. When performing this operation, file only from the outside in **(see illustration)**.

6 Excess end gap is not critical unless it exceeds the service limit. Again, double-check to make sure you have the correct rings for your engine and check that the bore is not worn.

7 Repeat the procedure for each ring that will be installed in the bore. Remember to keep the rings, pistons and bores matched up.

8 Once the ring end gaps have been checked/ corrected, the rings can be installed on the pistons.

9 The oil control ring (lowest on the piston) is installed first. It is composed of three separate components, namely the expander and the upper and lower side rails. Slip the expander into the groove, then install the lower side rail **(see illustrations)**. Do not use a piston ring installation tool on the oil ring side rails as they may be damaged. Instead, place one end of the side rail into the groove between the expander and the ring land. Hold it firmly in place and slide a finger around the piston while pushing the rail into the groove. Next, install the upper side rail in the same manner. Make sure the ends of the expander do not overlap.

10 After the three oil ring components have been installed, check to make sure that both the upper and lower side rails can be turned smoothly in the ring groove.

11 The upper surface of each compression ring is marked with a mark or letter at one end. The top ring is identified by the letter R, and the second (middle) ring by the letters RN **(see illustration)**. Install the second (middle) ring next. Make sure that the identification mark or letter near the end gap is facing up. Fit the ring into the middle groove in the

27.9a Install the oil ring expander in its groove . . .

27.9b . . . and fit the side rails each side of it. The oil ring must be installed by hand

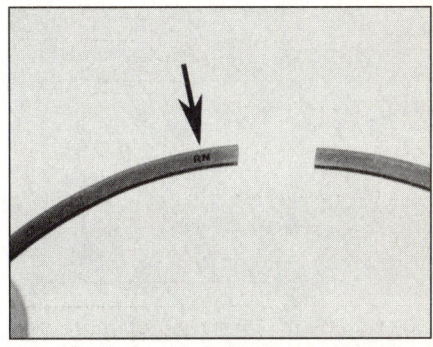

27.11a Note the identification letters on the end of the ring

2•54 Engine, clutch and transmission

27.11b Install the middle ring ...

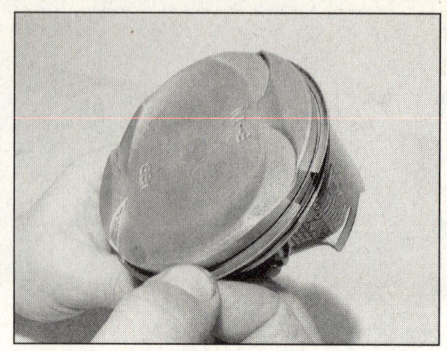

27.12 ... and the top ring as described

piston **(see illustration)**. Do not expand the ring any more than is necessary to slide it into place. To avoid breaking the ring, use a piston ring installation tool.

12 Finally, install the top ring in the same manner into the top groove in the piston **(see illustration)**. Make sure the identification letter near the end gap is facing up.

13 Once the rings are correctly installed, check they move freely without snagging and stagger their end gaps as shown **(see illustration)**.

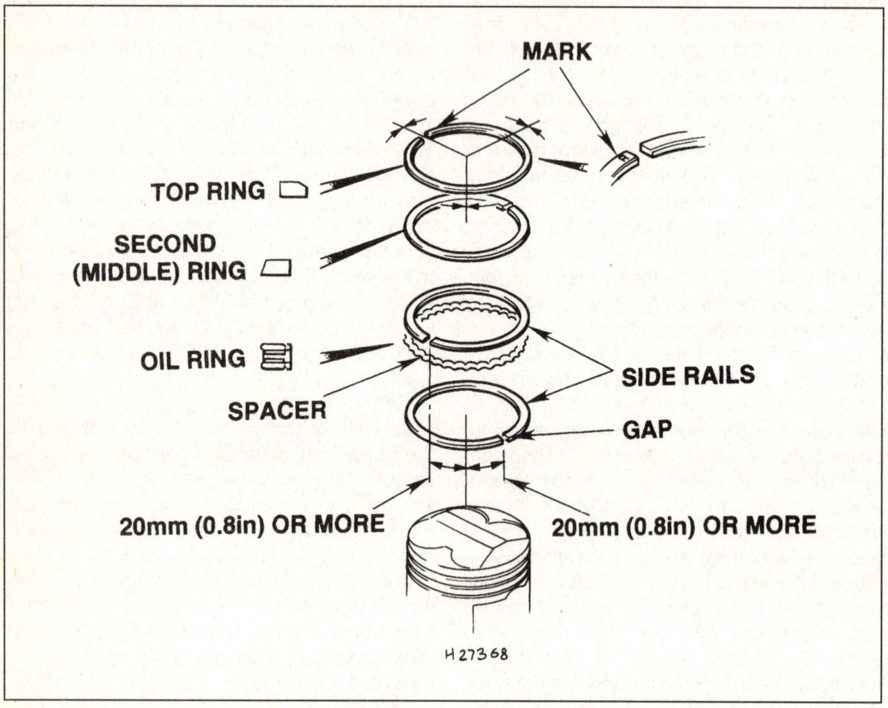

27.13 Stagger the ring end gaps as shown

28 Crankshaft and main bearings – removal, inspection and installation

Note 1: *To remove the crankshaft the engine must be removed from the frame and the crankcase halves separated.*

Note 2: *The connecting rod bolts must be discarded and new ones used on installation – it is best to obtain the bolts in advance. The old bolts can, however, be used for the oil clearance check.*

Removal

1 Remove the engine from the frame (see Section 5) and separate the crankcase halves (see Section 22).

2 Unscrew the connecting rod cap bolts and separate the caps from the crankpin **(see illustrations)**.

Note: *If no work is to be carried out on the piston/connecting rod assemblies there is no need to remove them from the bores, but push them up to the top of the bores so that the bottom ends are clear of the crankshaft.*

3 Lift the crankshaft out of the upper crankcase half, taking care not to dislodge the main bearing shells **(see illustration)**.

4 The main bearing shells can be removed from the crankcase halves by pushing their centres to the side, then lifting them out **(see illustration)**. Keep the shells in order.

Inspection

5 Clean the crankshaft with solvent, using a rifle-cleaning brush to scrub out the oil

28.2a Unscrew the bolts (arrowed) ...

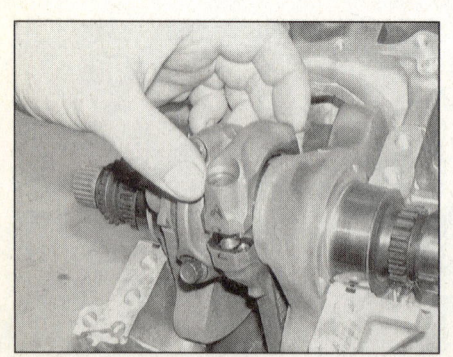

28.2b ... and remove the connecting rod caps

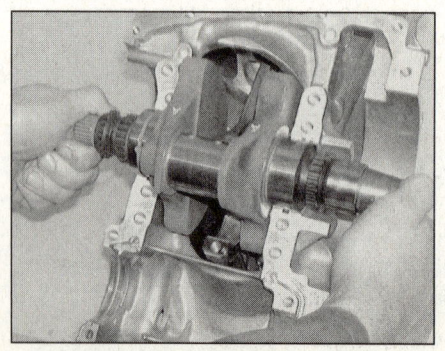

28.3 Lift the crankshaft out of the crankcase ...

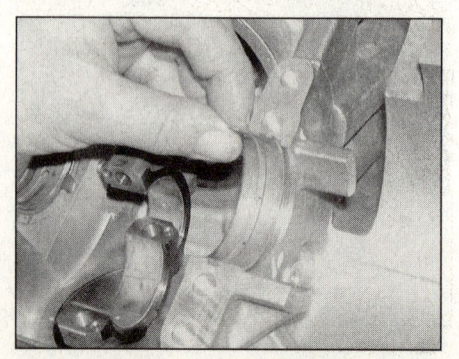

28.4 ... and remove the shells if required

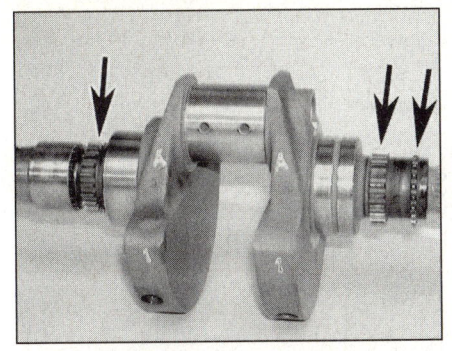

Engine, clutch and transmission 2•55

28.5 Check the teeth of the sprockets (arrowed) for wear and damage

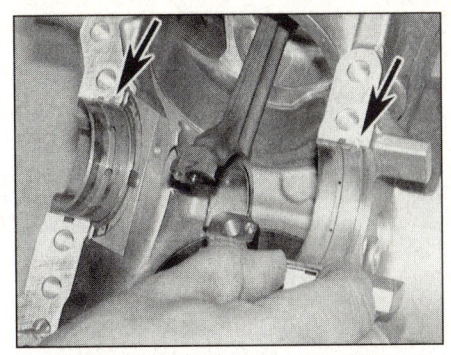

28.11 Fit the shells, locating the tabs in the notches (arrowed)

28.13 Lay a strip of Plastigauge on each journal parallel to the crankshaft centreline

passages. If available, blow the crank dry with compressed air, and also blow through the oil passages. Check the cam chain and water pump drive chain sprockets for wear or damage **(see illustration)**. If any of the teeth are excessively worn, chipped or broken, the crankshaft must be replaced with a new one. If wear or damage is found, also inspect the sprockets on the camshafts and the cam chains (see Sections 10 and 11).

6 Refer to Section 24 and examine the main bearing shells. If they are scored, badly scuffed or appear to have been seized, new bearings must be installed. Always replace the main bearings as a set. If they are badly damaged, check the corresponding crankshaft journals. Evidence of extreme heat, such as discoloration, indicates that lubrication failure has occurred. Be sure to thoroughly check the oil pump and pressure regulator as well as all oil holes and passages before reassembling the engine.

7 The crankshaft journals should be given a close visual examination, paying particular attention where damaged bearings have been discovered. If the journals are scored or pitted in any way a new crankshaft will be required. Note that undersizes are not available, precluding the option of re-grinding the crankshaft.

8 Place the crankshaft on V-blocks and check the runout at the main bearing journals using a dial gauge. Compare the reading with the maximum specified at the beginning of the Chapter. If the runout exceeds the limit, the crankshaft must be replaced.

Oil clearance check

9 Whether new bearing shells are being fitted or the original ones are being re-used, the main bearing oil clearance should be checked before the engine is reassembled. Main bearing oil clearance is measured with a product known as Plastigauge.

10 Clean the backs of the bearing shells and the bearing housings in both crankcase halves.

11 Press the bearing shells into their cut-outs, ensuring that the tab on each shell engages in the notch in the crankcase **(see illustration)**. Make sure the bearings are fitted in the correct locations and take care not to touch any shell's bearing surface with your fingers.

12 Ensure the shells and crankshaft are clean and dry. Lay the crankshaft in position in the upper crankcase **(see illustration 28.3)**. Install the crankcase dowels if removed.

13 Cut two lengths of the appropriate size Plastigauge (they should be slightly shorter than the width of the crankshaft journals). Place a strand of Plastigauge on each (cleaned) journal, avoiding the oil hole **(see illustration)**. Make sure the crankshaft is not rotated.

14 Carefully install the lower crankcase half on to the upper half **(see illustration 22.6)**. Check that the lower crankcase half is correctly seated. **Note:** *Do not tighten the crankcase bolts if the casing is not correctly seated.* Apply some oil to the threads and under the heads of the lower crankcase 10 mm bolts. Install them in their original locations and tighten them evenly a little at a time in a criss-cross sequence to the torque setting specified at the beginning of the Chapter **(see illustration 22.5)**. Make sure that the crankshaft is not rotated as the bolts are tightened.

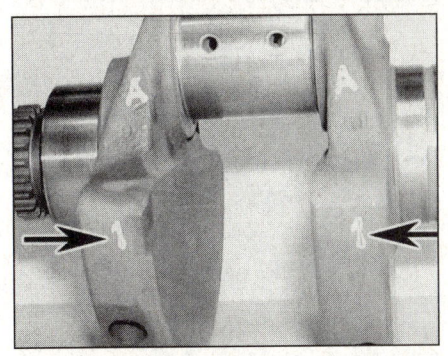

15 Slacken each bolt evenly a little at a time in a criss-cross sequence until they are all finger-tight, then remove the bolts. Carefully lift off the lower crankcase half, making sure the Plastigauge is not disturbed.

16 Compare the width of the crushed Plastigauge on each crankshaft journal to the scale printed on the Plastigauge envelope to obtain the main bearing oil clearance **(see illustration)**. Compare the reading with the Specifications at the beginning of the Chapter.

17 On completion carefully scrape away all traces of the Plastigauge material from the crankshaft journal and bearing shells; use a fingernail or other object which is unlikely to score them.

18 If the oil clearance falls into the specified range, no bearing shell replacement is required (provided they are in good condition). If the clearance is beyond the service limit, refer to the marks on the case and the marks on the crankshaft and select new bearing shells (see Steps 20 and 21). Install the new shells and check the oil clearance once again (the new shells may bring bearing clearance within the specified range). Always replace all of the shells at the same time.

19 If the clearance is still greater than the service limit listed in this Chapter's Specifications (even with replacement shells), the crankshaft journal is worn and the crankshaft should be replaced with a new one.

Main bearing shell selection

20 Replacement bearing shells for the main bearings are supplied on a selected fit basis. Code letters and numbers stamped on various components are used to identify the correct replacement bearings. The crankshaft main bearing journal size numbers are stamped on the crankshaft webs and will be either a 1, a 2 or a 3 **(see illustration)**. Each number is adjacent to the journal it represents. The

28.16 Measure the width of the crushed Plastigauge (be sure to use the correct scale – metric and imperial are included)

28.20 Main bearing journal size numbers (arrowed)

2•56 Engine, clutch and transmission

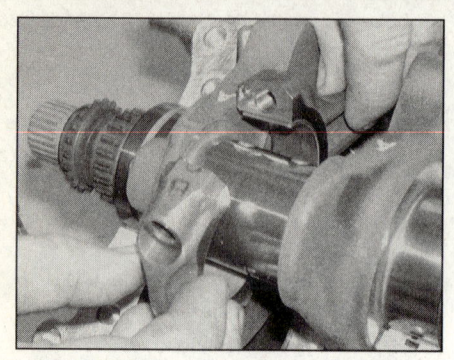

28.25 Pull the connecting rod onto the crankpin and fit the cap

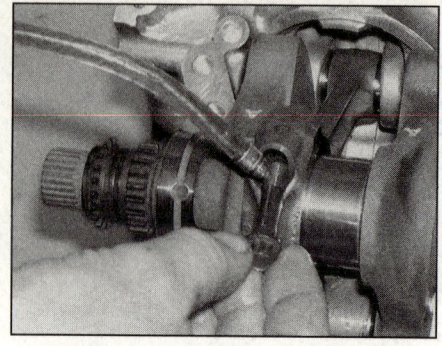

28.26a Oil the bolts as described . . .

28.26b . . . and tighten them first to the specified torque . . .

corresponding main bearing housing size letters are stamped into the upper crankcase half on the outside of the left-hand bearing housing and will be either an A, a B or a C. The left-hand letter corresponds to the left-hand journal, the right-hand letter to the right-hand journal.

21 A range of bearing shells is available. To select the correct bearing for a particular journal, using the table below cross-refer the main bearing journal size number (stamped on the crank web) with the main bearing housing size letter (stamped on the crankcase) to determine the colour code of the bearing required. For example, if the journal code is 2, and the housing code is A, then the bearing required is Green. The colour is marked on the side of the shell. **Note:** *Replacement shells for the right-hand bearing have a large oil hole, while replacement shells for the left-hand bearing have small oil holes. Be sure to fit the correct shells on the relevant bearing.*

Journal code	Main bearing housing code		
	A	B	C
1	Yellow	Green	Brown
2	Green	Brown	Black
3	Brown	Black	Blue

Installation

22 Clean the backs of the bearing shells and the bearing cut-outs in both crankcase halves. If new shells are being fitted, ensure that all traces of the protective grease are cleaned off using paraffin (kerosene). Wipe the shells and crankcase halves dry with a lint-free cloth. Make sure all the oil passages and holes are clear, and blow them through with compressed air if it is available.

23 Press the bearing shells into their locations (see **Note** in Step 21). Make sure the tab on each shell engages in the notch in the casing **(see illustration 28.11)**. Make sure the bearings are fitted in the correct locations and take care not to touch any shell's bearing surface with your fingers. Lubricate each shell with molybdenum disulphide oil (a 50/50 mixture of molybdenum disulphide grease and clean engine oil).

24 Lower the crankshaft into position in the upper crankcase, making sure all bearings remain in place **(see illustration 28.3)**.

25 Lubricate the crankpin with molybdenum disulphide oil (a 50/50 mixture of molybdenum disulphide grease and clean engine oil). Pull the connecting rod onto the crankpin and fit the connecting rod cap with its shell onto the rod **(see illustration)**. Make sure the cap is fitted the correct way around so the connecting rod and bearing cap size marking is correctly aligned.

26 Apply some clean oil to the threads and under the heads of the new connecting rod bolts **(see illustration)**. Install the bolts and tighten them evenly, in two or three stages, to the torque setting specified at the beginning of the Chapter, then tighten them by a further 120° using a degree disc **(see illustrations)**. It is highly advisable to have an assistant to hold the crankshaft down in the crankcase while tightening the bolts as it could jump out.

27 Check that the crankshaft is free to rotate easily, then install the other connecting rod in the same way. Check to make sure that all components have been returned to their original locations using the marks made on disassembly.

28 Check that the rods rotate smoothly and freely on the crankpin. If there are any signs of roughness or tightness, remove the rods and re-check the bearing clearance. Sometimes tapping the bottom of the connecting rod cap will relieve tightness, but if in doubt, recheck the clearances.

29 Reassemble the crankcase halves (see Section 22).

> **HAYNES HINT**
> *If a degree disc is not available, the angle can be determined by using the points on the connecting rod cap nut. There are six points on the nut, so the angle between each point is 60°. Select one point as a reference and mark it with paint or a marker. Now select the second point clockwise from it and mark its position on the connecting rod cap. Tighten the nut – when the mark on the first point aligns with the mark made on the connecting rod cap, it will have turned through 120°.*

28.26c . . . and then to the specified angle

29.1 Remove the pushrod oil seal, noting how it locates

29 Transmission shafts and bearings – removal and installation

Note: *To remove the transmission shafts the engine must be removed from the frame and the crankcases separated. If the engine has already been removed, ignore the steps which do not apply.*

Removal

1 Remove the engine from the frame (see Section 5) and separate the crankcase halves (see Section 22). Remove the clutch pushrod oil seal **(see illustration)**.

2 Unscrew the two bolts securing the transmission input shaft bearing retainer plate

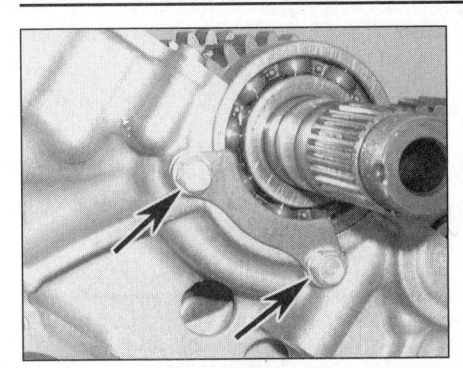

Engine, clutch and transmission 2•57

29.2 Unscrew the bolts (arrowed) and remove the plate

29.3a Remove the input shaft...

29.3b ...and the output shaft

to the right-hand side of the crankcase and remove the plate **(see illustration)**.
3 Lift the input shaft and output shaft out of the casing, noting their relative positions and how they fit together **(see illustrations)**. If they are stuck, use a soft-faced hammer and gently tap on the ends of the shafts to free them. Remove the needle bearing dowels – if they are not in their holes in the crankcase, remove them from the bearings themselves on the shafts. If necessary, the input shaft and output shaft can be disassembled and inspected for wear or damage (see Section 30).
4 Referring to *Tools and Workshop Tips* (Section 5) in the Reference Section, check the bearings on the transmission shafts. Replace the bearings if necessary, noting that the output shaft left-hand bearing is not available separately from the shaft. Also check the condition of the output shaft oil seal and clutch pushrod oil seal and renew them if worn or damaged.

Installation

5 Install the needle bearing dowels into their holes in the crankcase **(see illustration)**.
6 Lubricate the left-hand end of the output shaft with clean oil and slide the output shaft oil seal on, using a new one if necessary **(see illustration)**. Smear the seal lips with oil.
7 Lower the output shaft into position in the upper crankcase **(see illustration 29.3b)**, making sure the ring retainer on the ball

bearing engages correctly with the groove in the bearing housing, the locating pin sits in the cut-out in the crankcase, and the hole in the needle bearing engages correctly with the dowel **(see illustration)**. Also ensure that the oil seal lip locates in the crankcase groove.
8 Lower the input shaft into position in the upper crankcase, making sure the hole in the needle bearing engages correctly with the dowel **(see illustration 29.3a)**.
9 Make sure both transmission shafts are correctly seated and their related pinions are correctly engaged **(see illustration)**. Fit the clutch pushrod oil seal into its seat, using a new one if necessary, making sure the lip seats in the groove **(see illustration 29.1)**.

29.5 Fit the bearing dowels into their holes (arrowed)

Caution: If the bearing half-ring retainer or dowel are not correctly engaged with their bearings, the crankcase halves will not seat correctly.
10 Fit the input shaft bearing retainer plate onto the right-hand side of the crankcase, then apply a non-permanent thread locking compound to its bolts and tighten them securely **(see illustration 29.2)**.
11 Position the gears in the neutral position and check the shafts are free to rotate easily and independently (i.e. the input shaft can turn whilst the output shaft is held stationary) before proceeding further.
12 Reassemble the crankcase halves (see Section 22).

29.6 Lubricate the end of the shaft and fit the oil seal

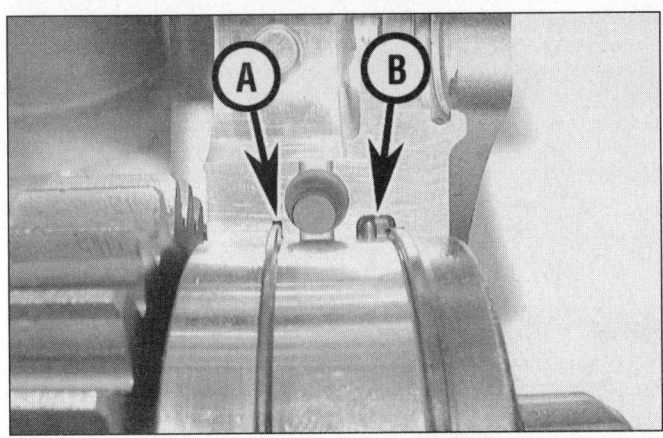

29.7 Make sure the ring retainer (A) and the bearing pin (B) locate correctly as shown

29.9 Make sure the shafts are correctly installed and engaged as shown

2•58 Engine, clutch and transmission

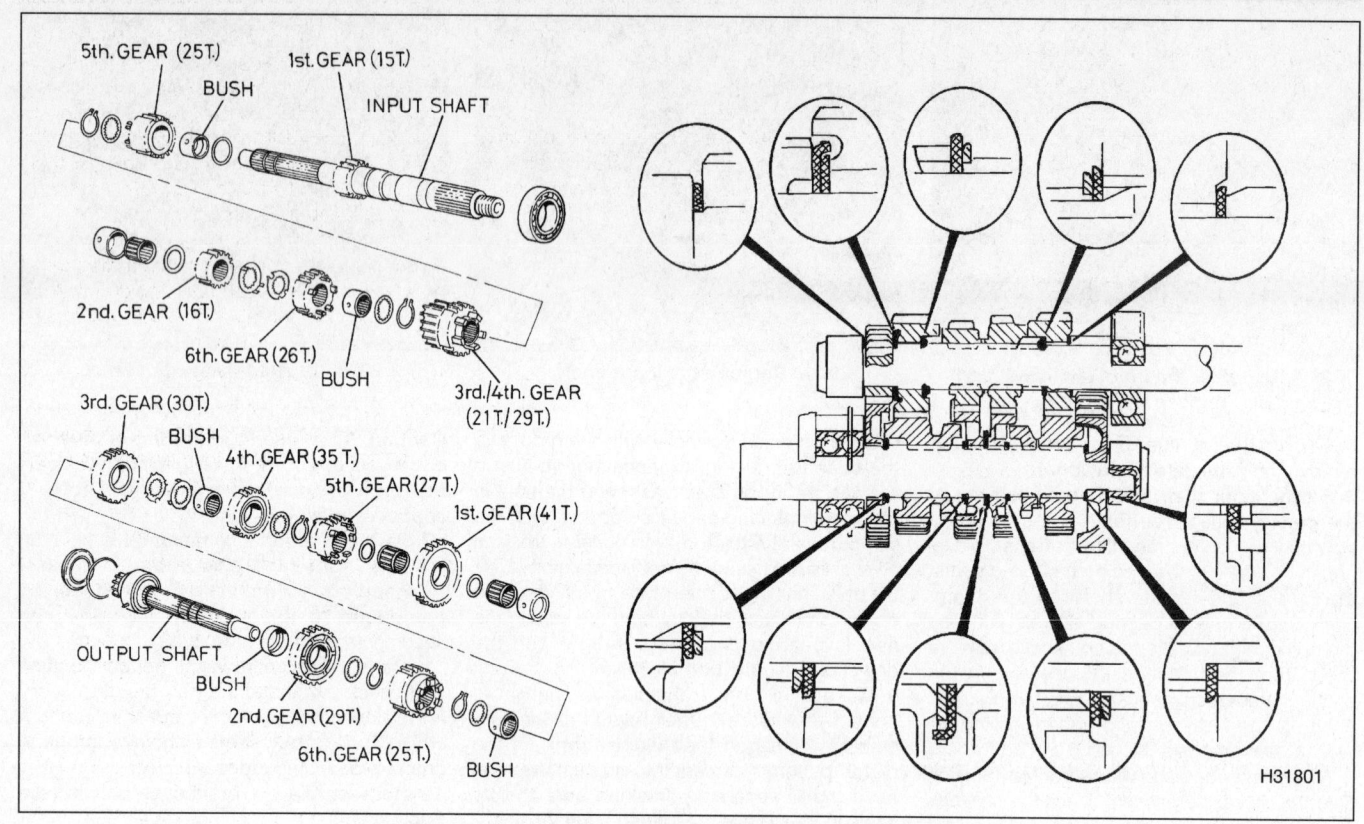

30.1a Transmission assembly components – VTR models

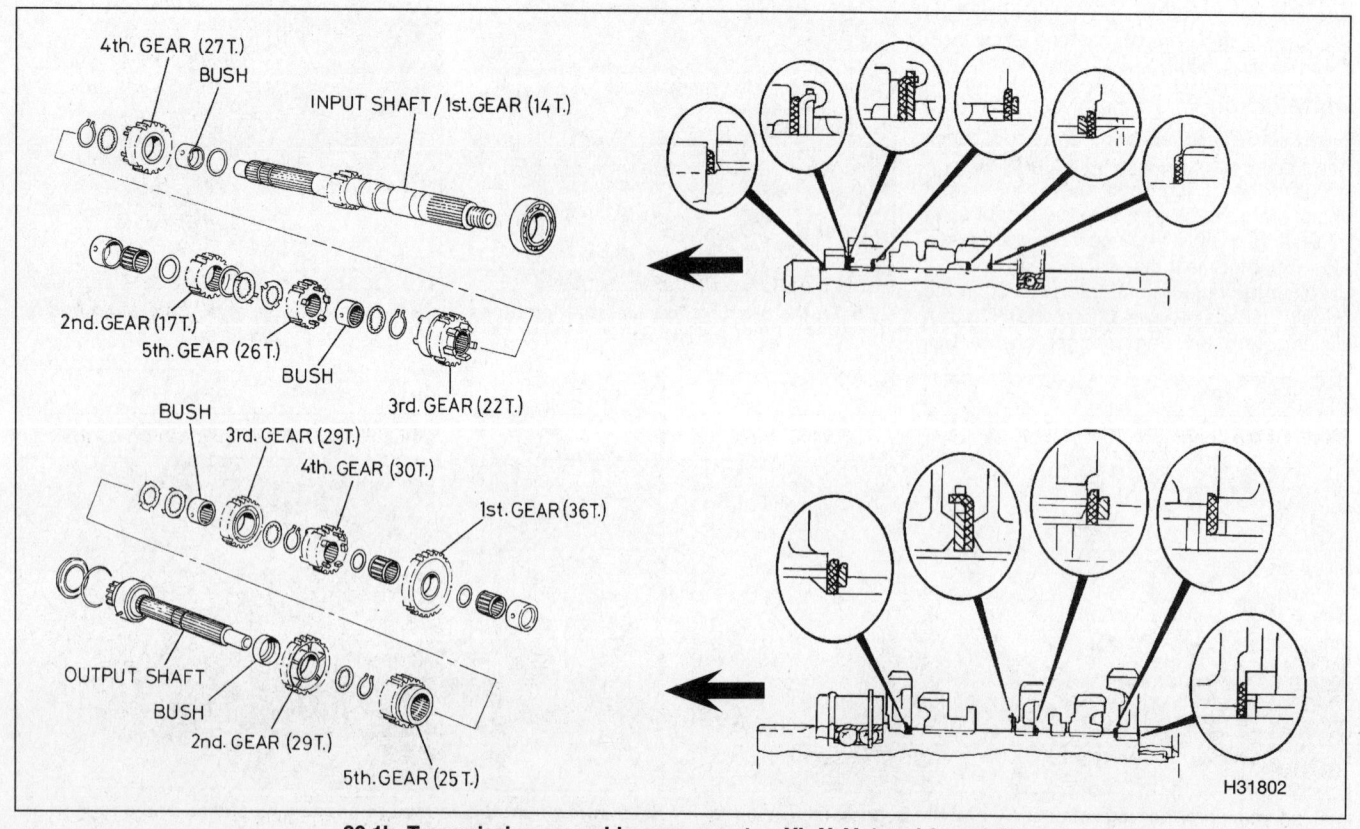

30.1b Transmission assembly components – XL-X, Y, 1 and 2 models

Engine, clutch and transmission 2•59

30 Transmission shafts – disassembly, inspection and reassembly

1 Remove the transmission shafts from the crankcase (see Section 29). Always disassemble the transmission shafts separately to avoid mixing up the components **(see illustrations)**.

VTR models and XL-3 models onward – six speed transmission
Input shaft disassembly

> **HAYNES HiNT** *When disassembling the transmission shafts, place the parts on a long rod or thread a wire through them to keep them in order and facing the proper direction.*

2 Slide the needle bearing cage and bearing off the left-hand end of the shaft, followed by the thrust washer and the 2nd gear pinion **(see illustrations 30.20d, 30.20c, 30.20b and 30.20a)**.
3 Slide the tabbed lockwasher off the shaft, then turn the slotted splined washer to offset the splines and slide it off the shaft, noting how they fit together **(see illustrations 30.19c and 30.19a)**. Slide the sixth gear pinion and its bush off the shaft, followed by the splined washer **(see illustrations 30.18c, 30.18b and 30.18a)**.
4 Remove the circlip securing the combined 3rd/4th gear pinion, then slide the pinion off the shaft **(see illustrations 30.17b and 30.17a)**.
5 Remove the circlip securing the 5th gear pinion, then slide the splined washer, the pinion and its bush, and the thrust washer off the shaft **(see illustrations 30.16e, 30.16d, 30.16c, 30.16b and 30.16a)**. The 1st gear pinion is integral with the shaft **(see illustration 30.15)**.
6 If required, remove the caged ball bearing from the right-hand end of the shaft, referring to *Tools and Workshop Tips* in the Reference Section **(see illustration 30.15)**.

Input shaft inspection

7 Wash all of the components in clean solvent and dry them off.
8 Check the gear teeth for cracking, chipping, pitting and other obvious wear or damage. Any pinion that is damaged as such must be replaced.
9 Inspect the dogs and the dog holes in the gears for cracks, chips, and excessive wear especially in the form of rounded edges. Make sure mating gears engage properly. Replace the paired gears as a set if necessary.
10 Check for signs of scoring or bluing on the pinions, bushes and shaft. This could be caused by overheating due to inadequate lubrication. Check that all the oil holes and passages are clear. Replace any damaged pinions or bushes.
11 Check that each pinion moves freely on the shaft or bush but without undue freeplay. Check that each bush moves freely on the shaft but without undue freeplay. If the necessary equipment is available the individual components can be measured and the results compared with the Specifications at the beginning of this Chapter.
12 The shaft is unlikely to sustain damage unless the engine has seized, placing an unusually high loading on the transmission, or the machine has covered a very high mileage. Check the surface of the shaft, especially where a pinion turns on it, and replace the shaft if it has scored or picked up, or if there are any cracks. Damage of any kind can only be cured by replacement.
13 Check the washers and circlips and replace any that are bent or appear weakened or worn. Use new ones if in any doubt. Note that it is good practice to renew all circlips when overhauling gearshafts.

Input shaft reassembly

14 During reassembly, apply molybdenum disulphide oil (a 50/50 mixture of molybdenum disulphide grease and clean engine oil) to the mating surfaces of the shaft, pinions and bushes. When installing the circlips, do not expand their ends any further than is necessary. Install the stamped circlips and washers so that their chamfered side faces the pinion it secures **(see illustration 30.1)**.
15 If removed, fit the caged ball bearing onto the right-hand end of the shaft, referring to *Tools and Workshop Tips* in the Reference Section **(see illustration)**.
16 Slide the thrust washer onto the left-hand end of the shaft, followed by the 5th gear pinion bush, aligning the oil hole in the bush with the hole in the shaft **(see illustrations)**. Fit the 5th gear pinion with its dogs facing away from the integral 1st gear **(see illustration)**. Slide the splined washer onto the shaft, then fit the circlip, making sure that it locates correctly in the groove in the shaft **(see illustrations)**.

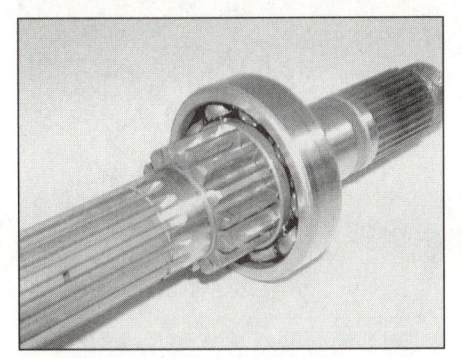

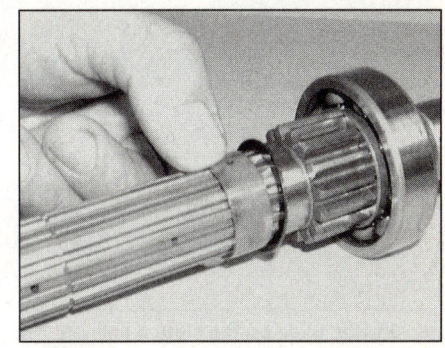

30.15 Fit the bearing onto the shaft as shown

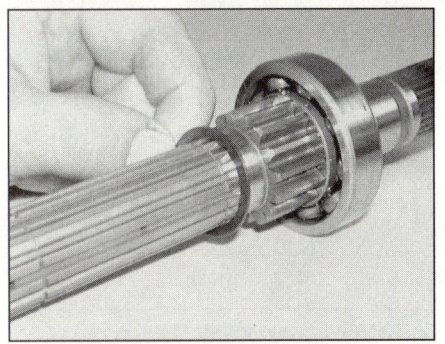

30.16a Slide the thrust washer . . .

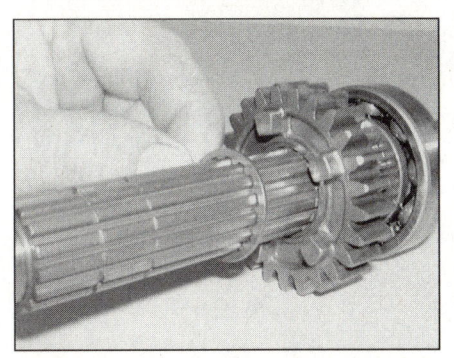

30.16b . . . the 5th gear pinion bush . . .

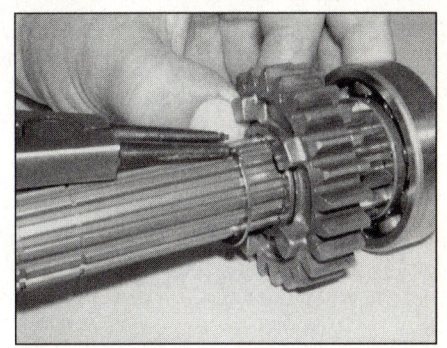

30.16c . . . the 5th gear pinion . . .

30.16d . . . and the spline washer onto the shaft . . .

30.16e . . . and secure them with the circlip, making sure it locates properly in its groove

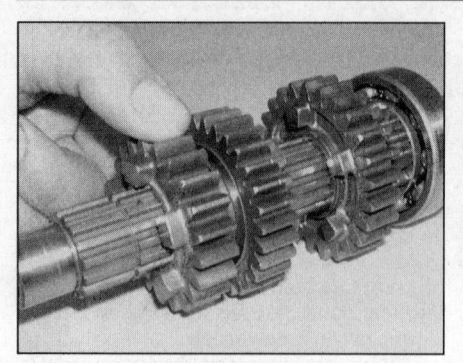

2•60 Engine, clutch and transmission

30.17a Slide the combined 3rd/4th gear pinion onto the shaft . . .

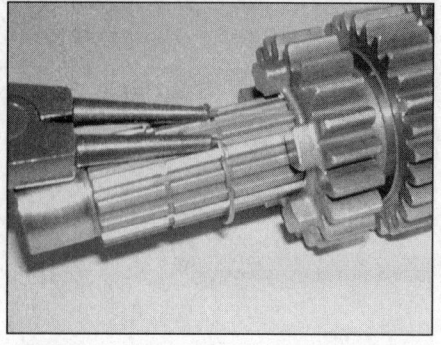

30.17b . . . and secure it with the circlip

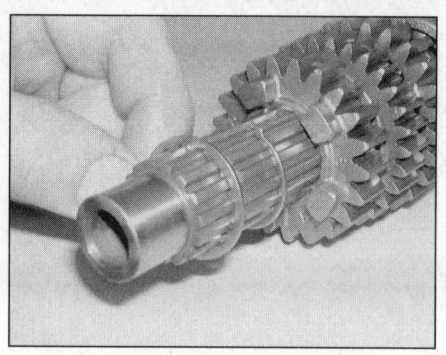

30.18a Slide the spline washer . . .

17 Slide the combined 3rd/4th gear pinion onto the shaft with the larger 4th gear pinion facing the 5th gear pinion **(see illustration)**.

Fit the circlip, making sure it is locates correctly in its groove in the shaft **(see illustration)**.

18 Slide the splined washer onto the shaft, followed by the 6th gear pinion bush, aligning the oil hole in the bush with the hole in the shaft, and the 6th gear pinion, making sure its dogs face the 3rd/4th gear pinion **(see illustrations)**.

19 Slide the slotted splined washer onto the shaft and locate it in its groove, then turn it in the groove so that the splines on the washer align the splines of the shaft and secure the washer in the groove **(see illustrations)**. Slide the tabbed lockwasher onto the shaft, so that the tabs locate into the slots in the outer rim of the splined washer **(see illustrations)**.

20 Slide the 2nd gear pinion and the thrust washer onto the end of the shaft, then fit the needle roller bearing and its cage over the end of the shaft **(see illustrations)**.

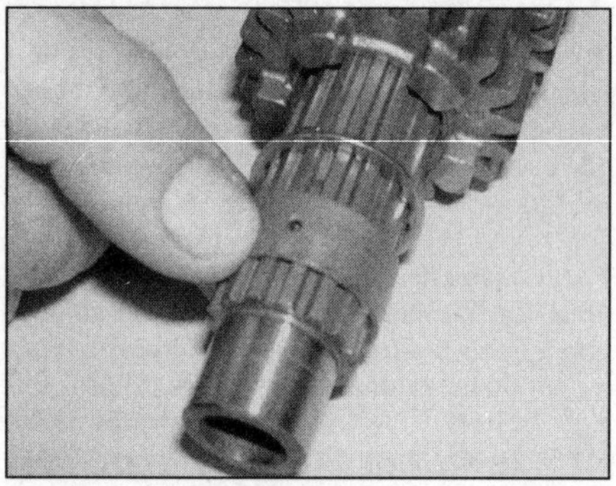

30.18b . . . the 6th gear pinion bush . . .

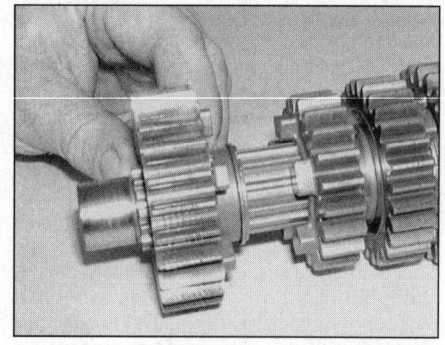

30.18c . . . and the 6th gear pinion onto the shaft

30.19a Slide on the slotted splined washer . . .

30.19b . . . and locate it as shown . . .

30.19c . . . then slide on the tabbed lockwasher . . .

30.19d . . . and locate it as shown

30.20a Slide the 2nd gear pinion . . .

30.20b . . . the thrust washer . . .

Engine, clutch and transmission 2•61

30.20c ... the needle bearing ...

30.20d ... and the bearing cage onto the shaft

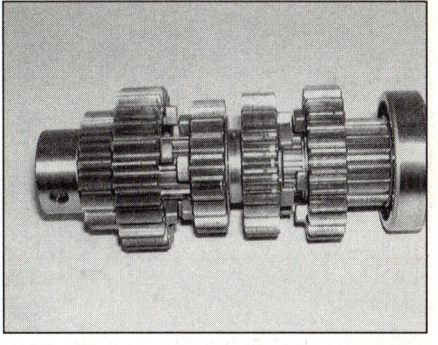

30.21 The complete assembly should be as shown

21 Check that all components have been correctly installed **(see illustration)**.

Output shaft disassembly

22 Slide the needle bearing cage and bearing off the right-hand end of the shaft **(see illustration 30.37d)**.
23 Slide the thrust washer off the shaft, followed by the 1st gear pinion and its needle roller bearing, the thrust washer and the 5th gear pinion **(see illustrations 30.37c, 30.37b, 30.37a, 30.36b and 30.36a)**.
24 Remove the circlip securing the 4th gear pinion, then slide the splined washer, the pinion and its splined bush off the shaft **(see illustrations 30.35d, 30.35c, 30.35b and 30.35a)**.
25 Slide the tabbed lockwasher off the shaft, then turn the slotted splined washer to offset the splines and slide it off the shaft, noting how they fit together **(see illustrations 30.34c, 30.34b and 30.34a)**.
26 Slide the 3rd gear pinion and its splined bush, followed by the splined washer, off the shaft **(see illustrations 30.33c, 30.33b and 30.33a)**.
27 Remove the circlip securing the 6th gear pinion, then slide the pinion off the shaft **(see illustrations 30.32b and 30.32a)**.
28 Remove the circlip securing the 2nd gear pinion, then slide the splined washer, the pinion and its bush off the shaft **(see illustrations 30.31e, 30.31c, 30.31b and 30.31a)**.

Output shaft inspection

29 Refer to Steps 7 to 13 above.

Output shaft reassembly

30 During reassembly, apply engine oil to the mating surfaces of the shaft, pinions and bushes. When installing the circlips, do not expand the ends any further than is necessary. Install the stamped circlips and washers so that their chamfered side faces the pinion it secures **(see illustration 30.1a)**.
31 Slide the 2nd gear pinion bush onto the shaft, aligning the oil hole in the bush with the hole in the shaft, then slide on the 2nd gear pinion and the splined washer, then fit the circlip, making sure it is locates correctly in its groove in the shaft **(see illustrations)**.
32 Slide the 6th gear pinion with its selector fork groove facing away from the 2nd gear

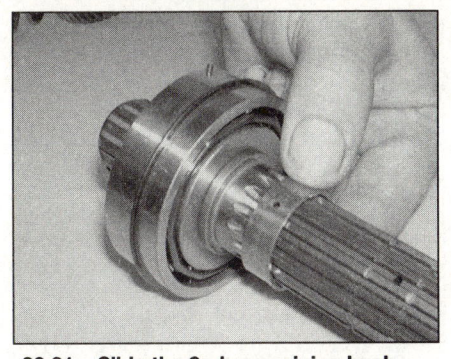

30.31a Slide the 2nd gear pinion bush ...

30.31b ... the 2nd gear pinion ...

30.31c ... and the spline washer onto the shaft ...

30.31d ... and secure them with the circlip ...

30.31e ... making sure it locates in the groove

30.32a Slide the 6th gear pinion onto the shaft ...

2•62 Engine, clutch and transmission

30.32b . . . and secure it with the circlip

30.33a Slide the spline washer . . .

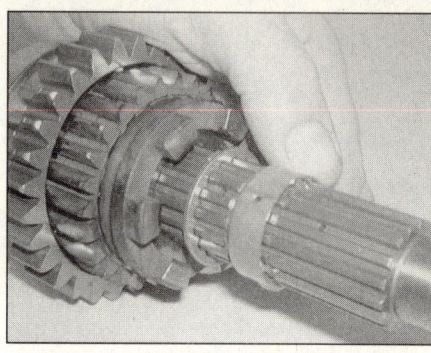

30.33b . . . the 3rd gear pinion bush . . .

pinion, then fit the circlip, making sure it is locates correctly in its groove in the shaft **(see illustrations)**.

33 Slide the splined washer and the 3rd gear pinion bush onto the shaft, making sure the oil hole in the bush aligns with the hole in the shaft, then slide on the 3rd gear pinion **(see illustrations)**.

34 Slide the slotted splined washer onto the shaft and locate it in its groove, then turn it in the groove so that the splines on the washer align with the splines of the shaft and secure the washer in the groove **(see illustrations)**. Slide the lockwasher onto the shaft, so that the tabs on the lockwasher locate into the slots in the outer rim of the spline washer **(see illustration)**.

35 Slide the 4th gear pinion bush onto the shaft, making sure the oil hole in the bush aligns with the hole in the shaft, followed by the 4th gear pinion and the splined washer, then fit the circlip, making sure it is locates correctly in its groove in the shaft **(see illustrations)**.

36 Slide the 5th gear pinion onto the shaft

30.33c . . . and the 3rd gear pinion onto the shaft

30.34a Slide the slotted spline washer onto the shaft . . .

30.34b . . . and locate it as shown

30.34c Slide the lockwasher onto the shaft and locate it as shown

30.35a Slide the 4th gear pinion bush . . .

30.35b . . . the 4th gear pinion . . .

30.35c . . . and the spline washer onto the shaft . . .

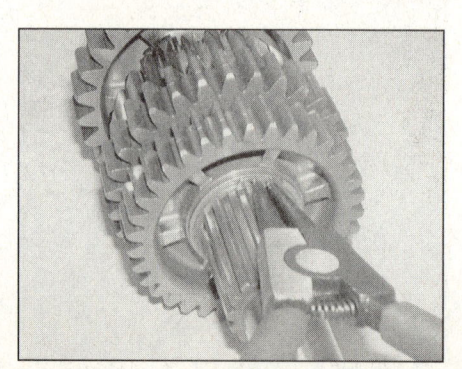

30.35d . . . and secure them with the circlip

30.36a Slide the 5th gear pinion . . .

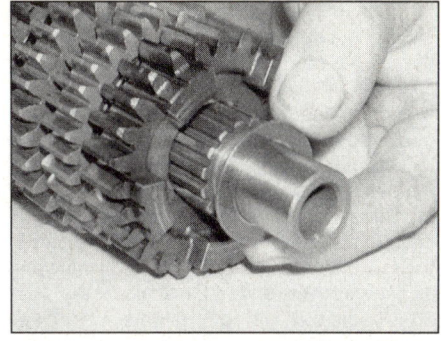

30.36b . . . and the thrust washer onto the shaft

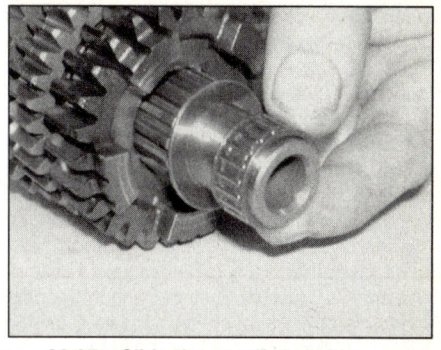

30.37a Slide the needle bearing . . .

with its selector fork groove facing the 4th gear pinion, followed by the thrust washer **(see illustrations)**.

37 Slide the 1st gear pinion needle roller bearing onto the shaft, followed by the 1st gear pinion and the thrust washer, then fit the needle roller bearing and its cage over the end of the shaft **(see illustrations)**.

38 Check that all components have been correctly installed **(see illustration)**.

XL-X, Y, 1 and 2 models – five speed transmission

Input shaft disassembly

HAYNES HiNT *When disassembling the transmission shafts, place the parts on a long rod or thread a wire through them to keep them in order and facing the proper direction.*

39 Slide the needle bearing cage and bearing off the left-hand end of the shaft, followed by the thrust washer, the 2nd gear pinion and the thrust washer.

40 Slide the tabbed lockwasher off the shaft, then turn the slotted splined washer to offset

30.37b . . . the 1st gear pinion . . .

the splines and slide it off the shaft, noting how they fit together.

41 Slide the 5th gear pinion and its bush off the shaft.

42 Remove the circlip securing the 3rd gear pinion, then slide the pinion and the splined washer off the shaft. Note which way round the pinion fits.

43 Remove the circlip securing the 4th gear pinion, then slide the splined washer, the pinion and its bush, and the thrust washer off the shaft.

44 The 1st gear pinion is integral with the shaft.

30.37c . . . and the thrust washer onto the shaft . . .

45 If required, remove the caged ball bearing from the right-hand end of the shaft, referring to *Tools and Workshop Tips* in the Reference Section.

Input shaft inspection

46 Wash all of the components in clean solvent and dry them off.

47 Check the gear teeth for cracking, chipping, pitting and other obvious wear or damage. Any pinion that is damaged as such must be replaced.

48 Inspect the dogs and the dog holes in the

30.37d . . . then fit the bearing onto the end of the shaft

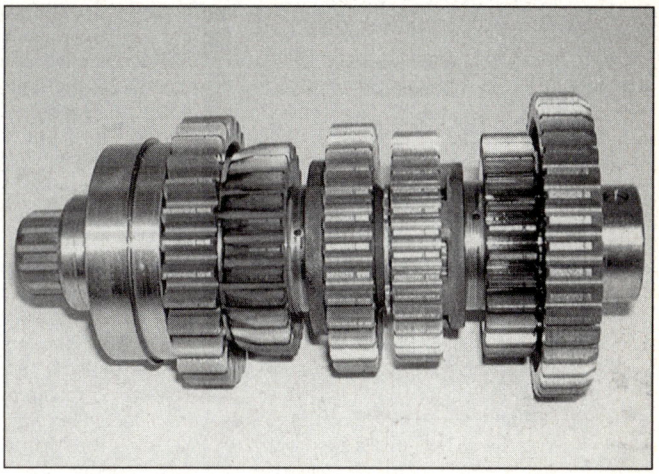

30.38 The assembled shaft should be as shown

2•64 Engine, clutch and transmission

gears for cracks, chips, and excessive wear especially in the form of rounded edges. Make sure mating gears engage properly. Replace the paired gears as a set if necessary.

49 Check for signs of scoring or bluing on the pinions, bushes and shaft. This could be caused by overheating due to inadequate lubrication. Check that all the oil holes and passages are clear. Replace any damaged pinions or bushes.

50 Check that each pinion moves freely on the shaft or bush but without undue freeplay. Check that each bush moves freely on the shaft but without undue freeplay. If the necessary equipment is available the individual components can be measured and the results compared with the Specifications at the beginning of this Chapter.

51 The shaft is unlikely to sustain damage unless the engine has seized, placing an unusually high loading on the transmission, or the machine has covered a very high mileage. Check the surface of the shaft, especially where a pinion turns on it, and replace the shaft if it has scored or picked up, or if there are any cracks. Damage of any kind can only be cured by replacement.

52 Check the washers and circlips and replace any that are bent or appear weakened or worn. Use new ones if in any doubt. Note that it is good practice to renew all circlips when overhauling gearshafts.

Input shaft reassembly

53 During reassembly, apply molybdenum disulphide oil (a 50/50 mixture of molybdenum disulphide grease and clean engine oil) to the mating surfaces of the shaft, pinions and bushes. When installing the circlips, do not expand their ends any further than is necessary. Install the stamped circlips and washers so that their chamfered side faces the pinion it secures.

54 If removed, fit the caged ball bearing onto the right-hand end of the shaft, referring to *Tools and Workshop Tips* in the Reference Section.

55 Slide the thrust washer onto the left-hand end of the shaft, followed by the 4th gear pinion bush, aligning the oil hole in the bush with the hole in the shaft. Fit the 4th gear pinion with its dogs facing away from the integral 1st gear. Slide the splined washer onto the shaft, then fit the circlip, making sure that it locates correctly in the groove in the shaft.

56 Slide the 3rd gear pinion onto the shaft with the pinion dogs facing the 4th gear pinion. Slide the splined washer onto the shaft, then fit the circlip, making sure it locates correctly in its groove in the shaft.

57 Slide the 5th gear pinion bush onto the shaft, aligning the oil hole in the bush with the hole in the shaft. Fit the 5th gear pinion onto the bush with its dogs facing the 3rd gear pinion.

58 Slide the slotted splined washer onto the shaft and locate it in its groove, then turn it in the groove so that the splines on the washer align the splines of the shaft and secure the washer in the groove. Slide the lockwasher onto the shaft, so that the tabs on the lockwasher locate into the slots in the outer rim of the splined washer.

59 Slide the thrust washer, the 2nd gear pinion and the thrust washer onto the end of the shaft, then fit the needle roller bearing and its cage over the end of the shaft.

60 Check that all components have been correctly installed.

Output shaft disassembly

61 Slide the needle bearing cage and bearing off the right-hand end of the shaft.

62 Slide the thrust washer off the shaft, followed by the 1st gear pinion and its needle roller bearing, the thrust washer and the 4th gear pinion.

63 Remove the circlip securing the 3rd gear pinion, then slide the splined washer, the pinion and its splined bush off the shaft.

64 Slide the tabbed lockwasher off the shaft, then turn the slotted splined washer to offset the splines and slide it off the shaft, noting how they fit together.

65 Slide the 5th gear pinion off the shaft.

66 Remove the circlip securing the 2nd gear pinion, then slide the splined washer, the pinion and its bush off the shaft.

Output shaft inspection

67 Refer to Steps 46 to 52 above.

Output shaft reassembly

68 During reassembly, apply engine oil to the mating surfaces of the shaft, pinions and bushes. When installing the circlips, do not expand the ends any further than is necessary. Install the stamped circlips and washers so that their chamfered side faces the pinion it secures.

69 Slide the 2nd gear pinion bush onto the shaft, aligning the oil hole in the bush with the hole in the shaft, then slide on the 2nd gear pinion and the splined washer, then fit the circlip, making sure it locates correctly in its groove in the shaft.

70 Slide the 5th gear pinion onto the shaft with its selector fork groove facing away from the 2nd gear pinion.

71 Slide the slotted splined washer onto the shaft and locate it in its groove, then turn it in the groove so that the splines on the washer align with the splines of the shaft and secure the washer in the groove. Slide the lockwasher onto the shaft, so that the tabs on the lockwasher locate into the slots in the outer rim of the spline washer.

72 Slide the 3rd gear pinion bush onto the shaft, making sure the oil hole in the bush aligns with the hole in the shaft, followed by the 3rd gear pinion and the splined washer, then fit the circlip, making sure it is locates correctly in its groove in the shaft.

73 Slide the 4th gear pinion onto the shaft with its selector fork groove facing the 3rd gear pinion, followed by the thrust washer.

74 Slide the 1st gear pinion needle roller bearing onto the shaft, followed by the 1st gear pinion and the thrust washer, then fit the needle roller bearing and its cage over the end of the shaft.

75 Check that all components have been correctly installed.

31 Selector drum and forks – removal, inspection and installation

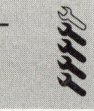

Note: *The selector drum and forks can be removed and installed with the crankcases joined and the engine in the frame. Having said that, it is much easier if the engine is removed so that you don't have to work upside down. If the crankcases are being separated anyway, remove the selector drum and forks afterwards as it is slightly easier.*

Removal

1 The selector drum and forks are located in the lower crankcase half. If required, remove the engine (see Section 5) and, again if required, separate the crankcase halves (see Section 22). Otherwise, just remove the sump (see Section 18) and the oil pump (see Section 19).

2 If not already done, remove the gearchange mechanism (see Section 20).

3 Before removing the selector forks, note that each fork carries an identification letter. The right-hand fork has an RL, the centre fork a C, and the left-hand fork an L (though on the models stripped down, the left fork was also marked RL – the left and right forks are identical and interchangeable, though it is best to keep them in their original location) **(see illustration)**. These letters face the right-hand side of the engine. If no letters are visible, mark them yourself using a felt pen.

4 Unscrew the bolts securing the selector drum bearing retainer plates and remove

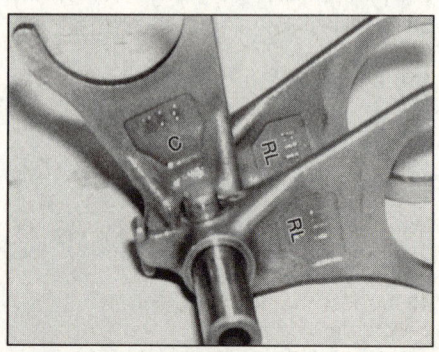

31.3 Each fork is lettered to identify its position on the shaft

Engine, clutch and transmission 2•65

31.4 Unscrew the bolts (arrowed) and remove the plates

31.6a Withdraw the shaft and displace the forks from the selector drum . . .

31.6b . . . then remove the selector drum

the plates, noting how they fit **(see illustration)**.

5 If the crankcases have been separated, support the selector forks and withdraw the shaft from the casing, then remove the forks. Withdraw the selector drum from the right-hand side of the engine.

6 If the crankcases have not been separated, withdraw the selector fork shaft from the casing, then pivot each fork out of its track in the selector drum **(see illustration)**. Withdraw the selector drum from the right-hand side of the engine **(see illustration)**. Remove the selelctor forks, noting how they locate in the groove in their pinion **(see illustrations 31.15c, 31.15b and 31.15a)**.

7 Once removed from the case, slide the forks back onto the shaft in their correct order and way round **(see illustration 31.3)**.

Inspection

8 Inspect the selector forks for any signs of wear or damage, especially around the fork ends where they engage with the groove in the pinion. Check that each fork fits correctly in its pinion groove. Check closely to see if the forks are bent. If the forks are in any way damaged they must be replaced.

9 Measure the thickness of the fork ends and compare the readings with the Specifications. Replace the forks with new ones if they are worn beyond their specifications.

10 Check that the forks fit correctly on their shaft. They should move freely with a light fit but no appreciable freeplay. Measure the internal diameter of the fork bores and the corresponding diameter of the fork shaft. Replace the forks and/or shaft with new ones if they are worn beyond their specifications. Check that the fork shaft holes in the casing are neither worn nor damaged.

11 Check the selector fork shaft for trueness by rolling it along a flat surface. A bent rod will cause difficulty in selecting gears and make the gearshift action heavy. Replace the shaft with a new one if it is bent.

12 Inspect the selector drum grooves and selector fork guide pins for signs of wear or damage. If either component shows signs of wear or damage the fork(s) and drum must be replaced with new ones.

13 Check that the selector drum bearing rotates freely and has no sign of freeplay between it and the casing. To fit a new bearing, remove the selector drum cam by unscrewing the bolt in its centre. Note the locating pin in the end of the drum and remove it for safekeeping if required. Remove the old bearing and fit a new one (see *Tools and Workshop Tips* in the Reference Section if necessary). Install the selector drum cam, locating the pin in the cut-out in the back of the cam. Apply a suitable non-permanent thread locking compound to the cam bolt and tighten it to the torque setting specified at the beginning of the Chapter.

Installation

14 If the crankcases have been separated, slide the selector drum into position in the crankcase. Make sure the drum end locates into its bore in the casing, and position it so that the neutral contact is against the neutral switch. Lubricate the selector fork shaft with clean engine oil and slide it into the crankcase, through each fork in turn, and into its bore, locating the guide pin on the end of each fork into its groove in the drum.

15 If the crankcases have not been separated, install the selector forks, locating each in the groove of its pinion, making sure they are fitted in the correct order and way round (see Step 3) **(see illustrations)**. Position they forks so they will not get in the way of the selector drum when sliding it in. Slide the selector drum into position in the crankcase, making sure the drum end locates into its bore in the casing **(see illustration)**. Position the drum so that the neutral contact is against the neutral

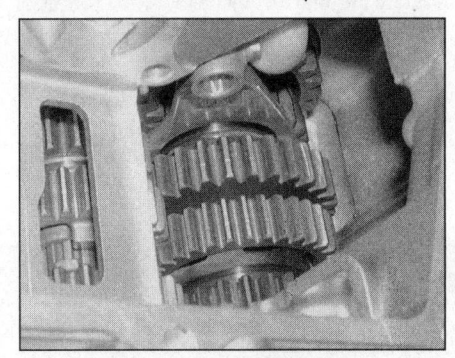

31.15a Install each fork in turn . . .

31.15b . . . making sure each locates correctly . . .

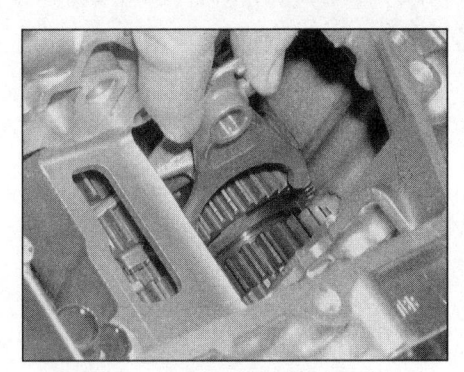

31.15c . . . in the groove in its pinion

31.15d Slide the drum into the crankcase, locating its end into the bore (arrowed)

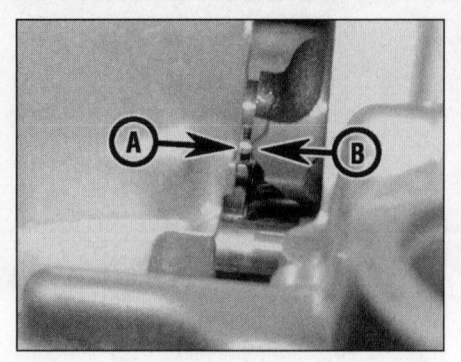

2•66 Engine, clutch and transmission

31.15e Position the drum so the neutral contact (A) is against the neutral switch contact (B)

31.15g ... locating the guide pins in the drum grooves

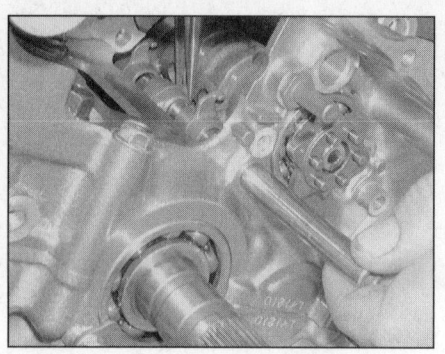

31.15f Slide the shaft through each fork in turn ...

Install the plates, locating them as shown, and tighten the bolts securely (see illustration 31.4).

17 Install any remaining components according to your removal procedure.

32 Initial start-up after overhaul

1 Make sure the engine oil and coolant levels are correct (see *Daily (pre-ride) checks*). Make sure there is fuel in the tank.
2 Turn the engine kill switch to the ON position and shift the gearbox into neutral. Turn the ignition ON and set the choke enough to encourage the bike to start, but not so much as to allow it to race.
3 Start the engine and allow it to run at a moderately fast idle until it reaches operating temperature.

⚠ **Warning: If the oil pressure warning light doesn't go off, or it comes on while the engine is running, stop the engine immediately.**

switch **(see illustration)**. Lubricate the selector fork shaft with clean engine oil and slide it into the crankcase, through each fork in turn, and into its bore, locating the guide pin on the end of each fork into its groove in the drum **(see illustrations)**.

16 Clean the threads of the selector drum retainer plate bolts, then apply a suitable non-permanent thread locking compound.

4 Check carefully for oil and coolant leaks and make sure the transmission and controls, especially the brakes, function properly before road testing the machine. Refer to Section 33 for the recommended running-in procedure.
5 Upon completion of the road test, and after the engine has cooled down completely, recheck the valve clearances (see Chapter 1) and check the engine oil and coolant levels (see *Daily (pre-ride) checks*).

33 Recommended running-in procedure

1 Treat the machine gently for the first few miles to make sure oil has circulated throughout the engine and any new parts installed have started to seat.
2 Even greater care is necessary if new pistons/rings or a new crankcase have been fitted, and the bike will have to be run in as when new. This means greater use of the transmission and a restraining hand on the throttle until at least 600 miles (1000 km) have been covered. There's no point in keeping to any set speed limit – the main idea is to keep from labouring the engine and to gradually increase performance up to the 600 mile (1000 km) mark. Experience is the best guide, since it's easy to tell when an engine is running freely. The following maximum engine speed limitations (see table), which Honda provide for new motorcycles, can be used as a guide.
3 If a lubrication failure is suspected, stop the engine immediately and try to find the cause. If an engine is run without oil, even for a short period of time, severe damage will occur.

Recommended running-in speeds

Up to 600 miles (1000 km)	4000 rpm max	Vary throttle position/speed
600 to 1000 miles (1000 to 1600 km)	6000 rpm max	Vary throttle position/speed. Use full throttle for short bursts
Over 1000 miles (1600 km)	9500 rpm max	Do not exceed tachometer red line

Chapter 3
Cooling system

Contents

Coolant hoses – removal and installation.................... 9
Coolant level check .... see *Daily (pre-ride) checks*
Coolant reservoir – removal and installation 3
Coolant temperature gauge and thermosensor – check and
   replacement 5
Cooling fan and fan switch or relay – check and replacement 4
Cooling system – checks .... see Chapter 1
Cooling system – draining, flushing and refilling .... see Chapter 1
General information 1
Radiator pressure cap – check........................... 2
Radiators – removal and installation 7
Thermostat and housing – removal, check and installation....... 6
Water pump – check, removal and installation 8

Degrees of difficulty

| Easy, suitable for novice with little experience | Fairly easy, suitable for beginner with some experience | Fairly difficult, suitable for competent DIY mechanic | Difficult, suitable for experienced DIY mechanic | Very difficult, suitable for expert DIY or professional |

Specifications

Coolant
Mixture type and capacity .... see Chapter 1

Radiator
Cap valve opening pressure............................... 16 to 20 psi (1.1 to 1.4 bar)

Coolant temperature thermosensor
Resistance
  @ 80°C .... 47 to 57 ohms
  @ 120°C .... 14 to 18 ohms

Thermostat
VTR models
  Opening temperature..................................... 73 to 77°C
  Fully open... 90°C
  Valve lift... 8 mm (min)
XL models
  Opening temperature..................................... 75 to 82°C
  Fully open... 82°C
  Valve lift... 8 mm (min)

Torque settings
Fan switch
  VTR models .... 18 Nm
  XL models... 17 Nm
Coolant temperature thermosensor
  VTR models .... 12 Nm
  XL models... 9 Nm

3•2 Cooling system

1 General information

The cooling system uses a water/antifreeze coolant to carry away excess energy in the form of heat. The cylinders are surrounded by a water jacket from which the heated coolant is circulated by thermo-syphonic action in conjunction with a water pump, which is driven by chain and sprocket off the right-hand end of the crankshaft. The hot coolant passes upwards to the thermostat and through to the left-hand radiator. The coolant then flows across the core of the radiator, then via two hoses to the right-hand radiator, to the water pump and back to the engine where the cycle is repeated.

A thermostat is fitted in the system to prevent the coolant flowing through the radiators when the engine is cold, therefore accelerating the rate at which the engine reaches normal operating temperature. A coolant temperature thermosensor mounted in the thermostat housing transmits information to the temperature gauge on the instrument panel. A cooling fan is fitted to the rear of the right-hand radiator to aid cooling in extreme conditions. On all VTR models and XL1000V-X to V-6 models a thermostatically-controlled switch fitted to the side of the right-hand radiator triggers the operation of the fan motor. On XL1000V-7 models onward, fan motor operation is controlled by a fan relay using information provided by the ECT sensor and ECU.

The complete cooling system is partially sealed and pressurised, the pressure being controlled by a valve contained in the spring-loaded radiator cap. By pressurising the coolant the boiling point is raised, preventing premature boiling in adverse conditions. The overflow pipe from the system is connected to a reservoir into which excess coolant is expelled under pressure. The discharged coolant automatically returns to the radiator when the engine cools.

Warning: *Do not remove the pressure cap from the radiator when the engine is hot. Scalding hot coolant and steam may be blown out under pressure, which could cause serious injury. When the engine has cooled, place a thick rag, like a towel over the pressure cap; slowly rotate the cap anti-clockwise to the first stop. This procedure allows any residual pressure to escape. When the steam has stopped escaping, press down on the cap while turning it anti-clockwise and remove it.*

Warning: *Do not allow antifreeze to come in contact with your skin or painted surfaces of the motorcycle. Rinse off any spills immediately with plenty of water. Antifreeze is highly toxic if ingested. Never leave antifreeze lying around in an open container or in puddles on the floor; children and pets are attracted by its sweet smell and may drink it. Check with the local authorities about disposing of used antifreeze. Many communities will have collection centres which will see that antifreeze is disposed of safely.*

Caution: *At all times use the specified type of antifreeze, and always mix it with distilled water in the correct proportion. The antifreeze contains corrosion inhibitors which are essential to avoid damage to the cooling system. A lack of these inhibitors could lead to a build-up of corrosion which would block the coolant passages, resulting in overheating and severe engine damage. Distilled water must be used as opposed to tap water to avoid a build-up of scale which would also block the passages.*

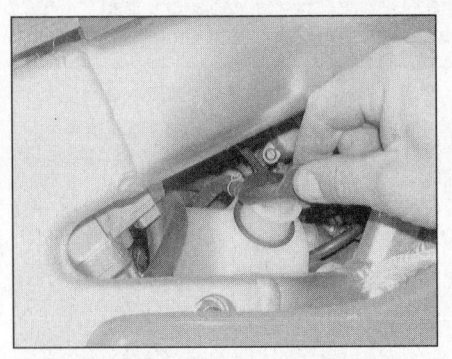

2 Radiator pressure cap – check

1 If problems such as overheating or loss of coolant occur, check the entire system as described in Chapter 1. The radiator cap opening pressure should be checked by a Honda dealer with the special tester required to do the job. If the cap is defective, replace it with a new one.

3 Coolant reservoir – removal and installation

Warning: *The engine must be completely cool before carrying out this procedure.*

Removal

1 On VTR models, the coolant reservoir is located on the right-hand side between the engine cylinders. Remove the fairing to access it (see Chapter 8). Note how the reservoir is located and how the various hoses and cables are routed around it before removing it.

2 On XL models, the coolant reservoir is located on the right-hand side below the fuel tank. Remove the right-hand fairing side panel and the belly-pan (see Chapter 8, Section 4).

3 Place a suitable container underneath the reservoir. Remove the reservoir cap **(see illustrations)**. Detach the reservoir hose from the radiator filler neck, then position it below the level of the reservoir and allow it to drain into the container **(see illustrations)**.

4 On VTR models, unscrew the reservoir mounting bolt and manoeuvre the reservoir out from the right-hand side, noting how the lug at the back locates in the hole on the inside of the left-hand lower frame rail **(see illustrations)**.

5 On XL models, displace the right-hand

3.3a On VTR models, remove the cap . . .

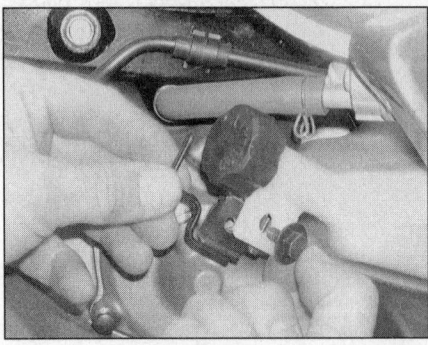

3.3b . . . on XL models, unscrew the bolt and remove the clamp, then unscrew the cap

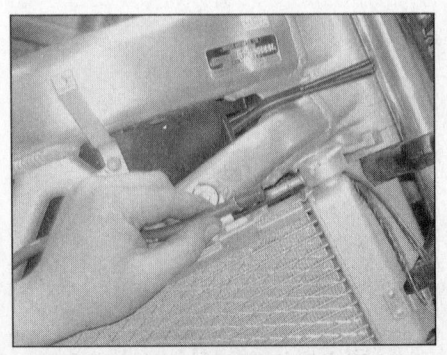

3.3c Detach the hose from the filler neck . . .

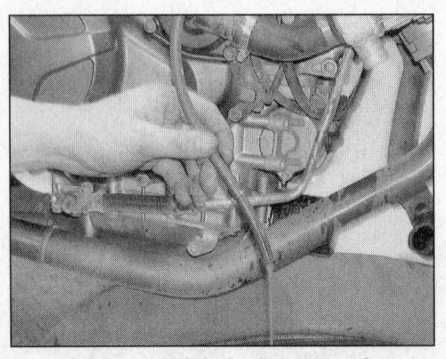

3.3d . . . and drain the reservoir

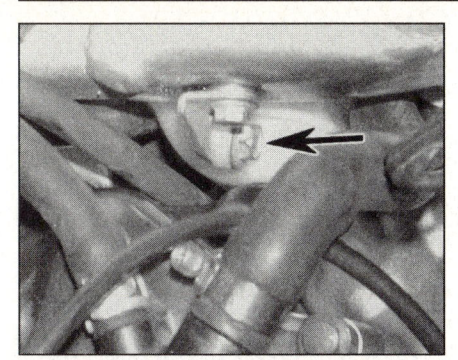

Cooling system 3•3

3.4a Unscrew the bolt (arrowed) . . .

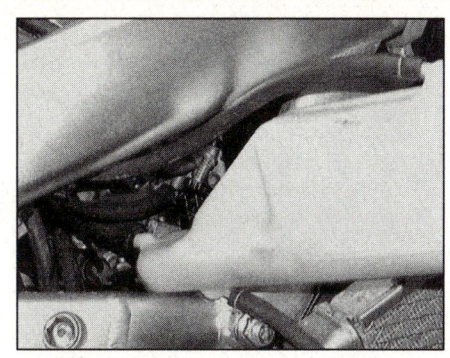

3.4b . . . and remove the reservoir

3.5 Reservoir mounting bolt (arrowed) – XL models

radiator by unscrewing its mounting bolts (see Section 7) – this should provide enough clearance to remove the reservoir, though it will depend on the exact length and condition of the radiator hoses. Otherwise, drain the coolant (see Chapter 1) and remove the radiator. Unscrew the reservoir mounting bolt and manoeuvre the reservoir up and out from between the frame and the radiator, noting how the lug on the bottom locates in the hole in the mounting bracket **(see illustration)**.

Installation

6 Installation is the reverse of removal. On completion refill the reservoir as described in *Daily (pre-ride) checks*.

4 Cooling fan and fan switch or relay – check and replacement

Cooling fan
Check

1 If the engine is overheating and the cooling fan isn't coming on, first check the cooling fan circuit fuse (see Chapter 9) and then the fan switch or relay as described according to model below.
2 If the fan does not come on (and the fan switch or relay is good), the fault lies in either the cooling fan motor or the relevant wiring. Test the wiring and connections as described in Chapter 9. Disconnect the fan wiring connector (see Step 3) and check for battery voltage at the black/blue wire terminal on the loom side of the connector.
3 To test the cooling fan motor, on VTR models remove the fairing, and on XL models remove the right-hand fairing side panel (see Chapter 8). Disconnect the fan wiring connector on the right-hand radiator **(see illustration)**. Using a 12 volt battery and two jumper wires with suitable connectors, connect the battery positive (+ve) lead to the black/blue wire terminal on the fan side of the wiring connector, and the battery negative (–ve) lead to the green wire terminal on XL-7 models onward, and to the fan switch wiring connector on all other models. Once connected the fan should operate. If it does not, and the wiring is all good, then the fan is faulty.

Replacement

⚠ **Warning: The engine must be completely cool before carrying out this procedure.**

4 Remove the right-hand radiator (see Section 7).
5 On all except XL-7 models onward disconnect the wiring connector from the fan switch. Free all the wiring from any clamps **(see illustration)**.
6 Unscrew the three bolts securing the fan shroud and fan assembly to the radiator, noting that the one bolt also secures the earth (ground) cable **(see illustration 4.5)**.
7 Unscrew the fan blade nut and remove the blade. Unscrew the three bolts on the front of the fan motor securing it to the shroud and separate them.
8 Installation is the reverse of removal. Apply a suitable non-permanent thread locking compound the fan blade nut. Do not forget to attach the earth (ground) cable to the radiator.
9 Install the radiator (see Section 7).

Cooling fan switch – all VTR models and XL-X to XL-6 models
Check

10 If the engine is overheating and the cooling fan isn't coming on, first check the cooling fan circuit fuse (see Chapter 9). If the fuse is blown, check the fan circuit for a short to earth (see the wiring diagrams at the end of this book).
11 If the fuse is good, on VTR models remove the fairing, and on XL models remove the right-hand fairing side panel (see Chapter 8, Section 4). Disconnect the wiring connector from the fan switch on the right-hand radiator **(see illustrations)**. Using a jumper wire if necessary, connect the wire to earth (ground).

4.3 Disconnect the cooling fan wiring connector (arrowed) – VTR models

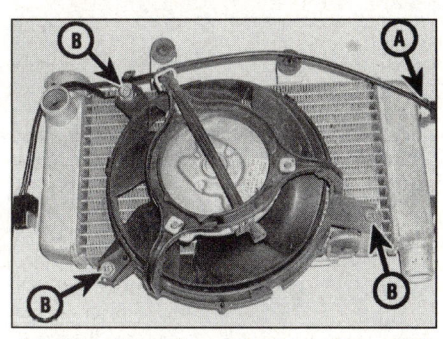

4.5 Disconnect the wiring from the switch (A), then unscrew the bolts (B) noting the earth lead

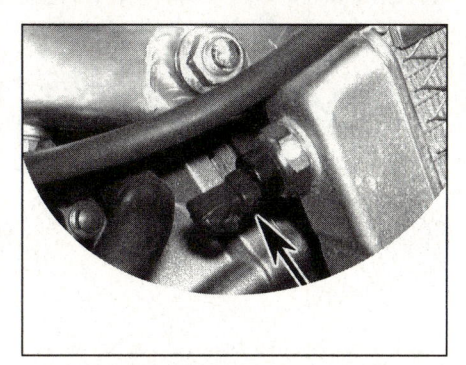

4.11a Fan switch wiring connector (arrowed) – VTR models

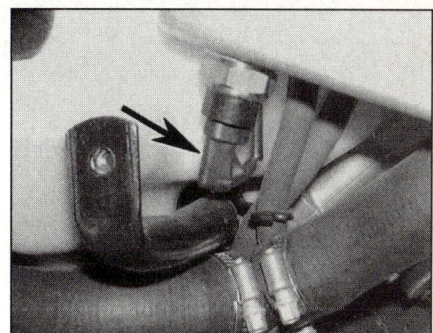

4.11b Fan switch wiring connector (arrowed) – XL models

3•4 Cooling system

The fan should come on. If it does, the fan switch is defective and must be replaced with a new one. If it does not come on, test the fan (see Step 3).

12 If the fan is on the whole time, disconnect the wiring connector. The fan should stop. If it does, the switch is defective and must be replaced. If it doesn't, check the wiring between the switch and the fan, and the fan itself.

13 If the fan works but is suspected of cutting in at the wrong temperature, a more comprehensive test of the switch can be made as follows. Unfortunately Honda do not provide any figures for the test, but those given provide a general guide.

14 Remove the switch (see Steps 17 to 20). Fill a small heatproof container with coolant and place it on a stove. Connect the positive (+ve) probe of an ohmmeter to the terminal of the switch and the negative (–ve) probe to the switch body, and using some wire or other support suspend the switch in the coolant so that just the sensing portion and the threads are submerged (see illustration 5.9). Also place a thermometer capable of reading temperatures up to 110°C in the coolant so that its bulb is close to the switch. **Note:** *None of the components should be allowed to directly touch the container.*

15 Initially the ohmmeter reading should be very high indicating that the switch is open (OFF). Heat the coolant, stirring it gently.

⚠️ **Warning: This must be done very carefully to avoid the risk of personal injury.**

16 When the temperature reaches around 98 to 102°C the meter reading should drop to around zero ohms, indicating that the switch has closed (ON). Now turn the heat off. As the temperature falls below 93 to 97°C the meter reading should show infinite (very high) resistance, indicating that the switch has opened (OFF). If the meter readings obtained are different, or they are obtained at different temperatures, then the switch is faulty and must be replaced with a new one.

Replacement

⚠️ **Warning: The engine must be completely cool before carrying out this procedure.**

17 Drain the cooling system (see Chapter 1).
18 Disconnect the wiring connector from the fan switch on the right-hand radiator (see illustration 4.11a or 4.11b). Unscrew the switch and withdraw it from the radiator. Discard the O-ring as a new one must be used.
19 Install the switch using a new O-ring and tighten it to the torque setting specified at the beginning of the Chapter. Take care not to overtighten the switch as the radiator could be damaged.
20 Reconnect the switch wiring and refill the cooling system (see Chapter 1).

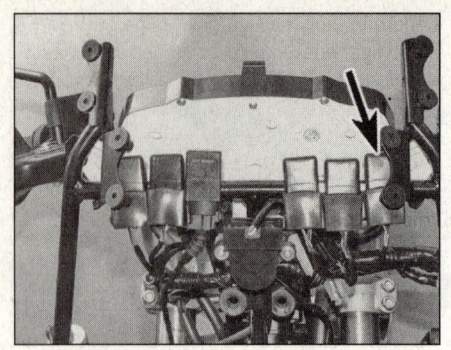

4.22 Cooling fan relay (arrowed)

Cooling fan relay – XL-7 models onward

Check

21 If the engine is overheating and the cooling fan isn't coming on, first check the cooling fan fuse (see Chapter 9). If the fuse is blown, check the fan circuit for a short to earth (see the wiring diagrams at the end of Chapter 9).
22 If the fuse is good, remove the fairing (see Chapter 8). Displace the relay from its mount and disconnect the wiring connector (see illustration). Using a jumper wire short between the blue/orange and black/blue wire terminals on the loom side of the connector with the ignition ON – the fan should come on. If it does check the relay as follows.
23 Set a multimeter to the ohms x 1 scale and connect it between the blue/orange and black/blue wire terminals. There should be no continuity (infinite resistance). Using a fully-charged 12 volt battery and two insulated jumper wires, connect the positive (+) terminal of the battery to the black/white wire terminal on the relay, and the negative (–) terminal to the green/blue wire terminal. At this point the relay should be heard to click and the multimeter read 0 ohms (continuity). If this is the case the relay is proved good. If the relay does not click when battery voltage is applied and still indicates no continuity (infinite resistance) across its terminals, it is faulty and must be replaced with a new one.
24 If the relay is good, check for battery voltage at the blue/orange wire in the wiring connector with the ignition switch ON. If there

5.2a Disconnect the wiring connector (arrowed) from the thermosensor . . .

is no voltage, check the wiring between the relay and the fusebox for continuity, referring to the relevant wiring diagram at the end of Chapter 9. If voltage is present, check that there is continuity to the fan wiring connector in the black/blue wire. If there is no continuity, check the wiring between the relay, the fan wiring connector, the fan then back to the connector and in the green wire to earth. If all is good check the green/blue and black/white wires between the relay and the ECU (electronic control unit) for continuity.
25 If the fan is on the whole time, pull the relay off its connector. The fan should stop. If it does, the relay is defective and must be replaced with a new one.
26 If the fan works but is suspected of cutting in at the wrong temperature, check the ECT sensor (see Section 4 and Chapter 4B, Section 5).

Removal and installation

27 Remove the fairing (see Chapter 8).
28 Displace the relay from its mount, then disconnect the wiring connector (see illustration 4.22).
29 Installation is the reverse of removal.

5 Coolant temperature gauge and thermosensor – check and replacement

Coolant temperature gauge

Check – VTR-V to VTR-Y models and all XL models

1 The circuit consists of the thermosensor (ECT sensor on XL1000V-7 models onward) mounted in the bottom of the thermostat housing and the gauge assembly mounted in the instrument cluster. If the system malfunctions check first that the battery is fully charged and that the fuses are all good.
2 If the gauge is not working, on XL models remove the fuel tank (see Chapter 4A). Disconnect the wiring connector from the sensor and turn the ignition switch ON (see illustrations). The temperature gauge should show 'C'. Now earth the wiring connector terminal on the engine using an auxiliary wire between them (on XL-7 models onward it is

5.2b . . . or on XL-7 models onward from the ECT sensor (arrowed)

Cooling system 3•5

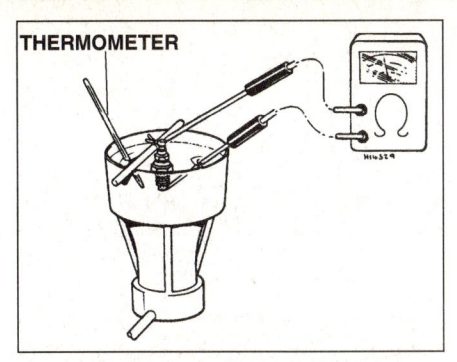

5.13 Temperature gauge thermosensor testing set-up

the green/blue wire terminal). The gauge should show 'H'. If the gauge behaves as described, it is proven good, however the sensor is proven defective and must be replaced with a new one.
Caution: Do not earth the wire for any longer than is necessary to take the reading, or the gauge may be damaged.
3 If the gauge movement is still faulty, or if it does not move at all, the fault lies in the wiring or the gauge itself. Remove the fairing (see Chapter 8).
4 Check for continuity in the green/blue wire between the temperature thermosensor and its temperature gauge terminal on the back of the instrument cluster. If there is no continuity, locate the break in the wire and repair it or replace it with a new one.
5 If continuity is present, check for battery voltage between the black/brown (+ve) and green/black (–ve) wire terminals. If voltage is present, replace the gauge with a new one (see Chapter 9, Section 16). Otherwise check the wiring for the cause of the lack of power, referring to the *Wiring Diagrams* at the end of Chapter 9.

Check – VTR-1 to VTR-6 models

6 The circuit consists of the sensor mounted in the thermostat housing and the display which is part of the instrument cluster LCD unit. If the system malfunctions check the instrument cluster fuse (see Chapter 9). When the ignition is first switched on all the digital display segments and modes should come on temporarily – this serves as an indication that the LCD is functioning correctly.
7 Under normal operating conditions, when the coolant temperature is below 34°C the display will show '- -'. When the temperature is between 35°C and 132°C the display will show the actual temperature. Once the temperature reaches 122°C the actual temperature figure will start to flash and a red line will appear under the figure. If this occurs stop the engine and check the coolant level in the reservoir (see *Pre-ride checks*). If the temperature goes above 132°C the display will continue to show that temperature.
8 If the display is not working at all, check the instrument cluster (see Chapter 9). If the wiring is good, then either the printed circuit board (PCB) or the LCD display unit could be faulty.
9 If the display as a whole works but the coolant function doesn't or is thought to be inaccurate, check the sensor (see below). If the sensor is good check the wiring between the sensor and the instrument cluster for continuity. If the wiring is good the display is faulty.
Caution: Do not leave the ignition switched on for any longer than is necessary to take the reading, or the gauge may be damaged.

Replacement

10 See Chapter 9, Section 16.

Temperature gauge thermosensor

Check

11 Drain the cooling system (see Chapter 1). The thermosensor is mounted in the bottom of the thermostat housing.
12 Disconnect the thermosensor wiring connector **(see illustration 5.2)**. Using a continuity tester, check for continuity between the thermosensor body and earth (ground). There should be continuity. If there is no continuity, check that the thermostat earth connector is secure and the wire is good.
13 Remove the thermosensor (see Steps 12 to 15 below). Fill a small heatproof container with coolant and place it on a stove. Using an ohmmeter, connect the positive (+ve) probe of the meter to the terminal on the thermosensor, and the negative (–ve) probe to the body of the thermosensor. Using some wire or other support suspend the thermosensor in the coolant so that just the sensing head and the threads are submerged, with the head a minimum of 40 mm above the bottom of the container. Also place a thermometer capable of reading temperatures up to 110°C in the water so that its bulb is close to the thermosensor **(see illustration)**. **Note:** *None of the components should be allowed to directly touch the container.*
14 Leave the thermosensor to stand in the coolant for three minutes, then begin to heat the coolant, stirring it gently.

> **Warning:** *This must be done very carefully to avoid the risk of personal injury.*

15 When the temperature reaches around 80°C the meter should read between 47 and 57 ohms. When the temperature reaches around 120°C the meter should read between 14 and 18 ohms. If the meter readings obtained are different by a margin of 10% or more, then the thermosensor is faulty and must be replaced with a new one.

Replacement

> **Warning:** *The engine must be completely cool before carrying out this procedure.*

16 Drain the cooling system (see Chapter 1). The thermosensor mounted in the bottom of the thermostat housing.
17 Disconnect the thermosensor wiring connector **(see illustration 5.2)**. Unscrew the thermosensor and remove it from the thermostat housing.
18 Apply a smear of sealant to the threads of the new thermosensor, making sure none gets on the head. Install it in the thermostat housing and tighten it to the torque setting specified at the beginning of the Chapter. Connect the thermosensor wiring.
19 Refill the cooling system (see Chapter 1).

6 Thermostat and housing – removal, check and installation

Removal

Note: *The complete thermostat housing can be removed without removing the thermostat itself – ignore the points in Step 3 relating to cover and thermostat removal.*

> **Warning:** *The engine must be completely cool before carrying out this procedure.*

1 The thermostat is automatic in operation and should give many years service without requiring attention. In the event of a failure, the valve will probably jam open, in which case the engine will take much longer than normal to warm up. Conversely, if the valve jams shut, the coolant will be unable to circulate and the engine will overheat. Neither condition is acceptable, and the fault must be investigated promptly.
2 Drain the cooling system (see Chapter 1). Remove the fuel tank (see Chapter 4). The thermostat housing is between the engine cylinders on the left-hand side.
3 To remove the thermostat, slacken the clamp securing the hose to the housing cover and detach the hose **(see illustration)**. Unscrew the two bolts securing the cover and separate it from the housing, noting the earth wire secured by the outer bolt. Withdraw the thermostat,

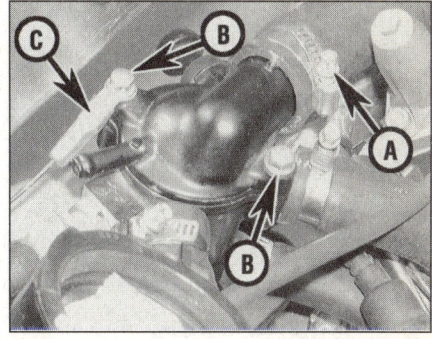

6.3a Slacken the clamp (A) and detach the hose, then unscrew the cover bolts (B), noting the earth wire (C)

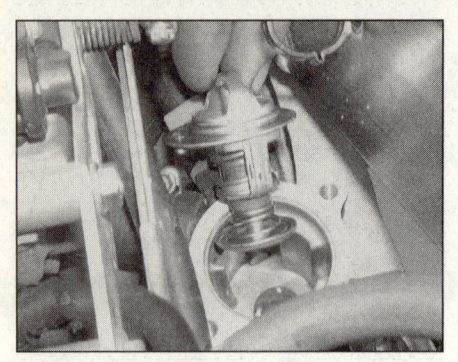

3•6 Cooling system

6.3b Withdraw the thermostat from the housing

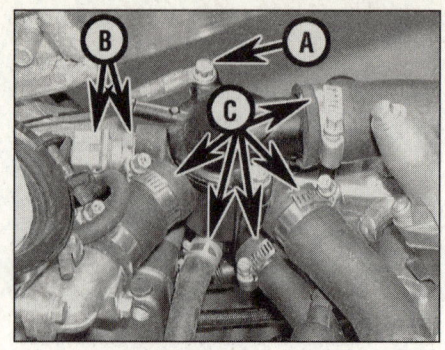

6.4 Unscrew the bolt (A) and detach the wire, disconnect the wiring connectors (B), detach the hoses (C)

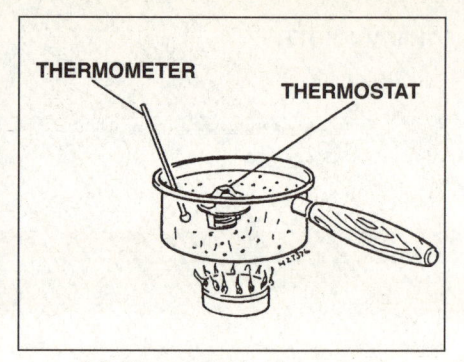

6.6 Thermostat testing set-up

noting how it fits **(see illustration)**. Discard the cover O-ring as a new one must be used.

4 To remove the thermostat housing, unscrew the cover bolt securing the earth wire and detach the wire, then reinstall the bolt **(see illustration)**. Disconnect the temperature gauge thermosensor and ECT sensor wiring connectors. Slacken the clamps securing the hoses to the cover and housing and detach the hoses, then remove the housing.

Check

5 Examine the thermostat visually before carrying out the test. If it remains in the open position at room temperature, it should be replaced.

6 Suspend the thermostat by a piece of wire in a container of cold water. Place a thermometer in the water so that the bulb is close to the thermostat **(see illustration)**. Heat the water, noting the temperature when the thermostat opens, and compare the result with the Specifications given at the beginning of the Chapter. Also check the amount the valve opens after it has been heated for a few minutes and compare the measurement to the Specifications. If the readings obtained differ from those given, the thermostat is faulty and must be replaced with a new one.

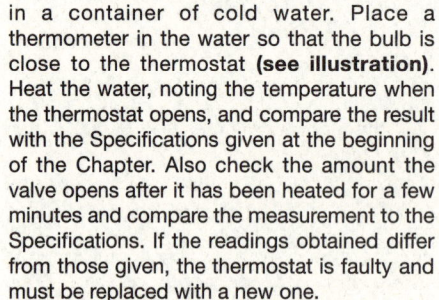

7 In the event of thermostat failure, as an emergency measure only, it can be removed and the machine used without it. **Note:** *Take care when starting the engine from cold as it will take much longer than usual to warm up.* Ensure that a new unit is installed as soon as possible.

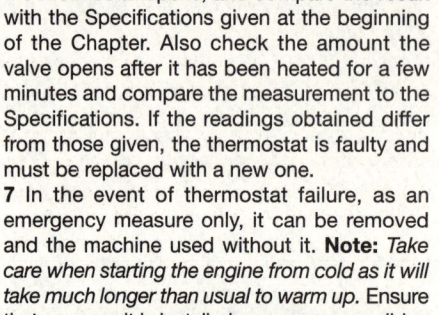

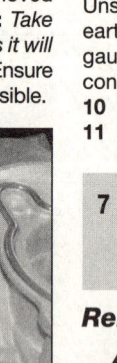

Installation

8 To install the thermostat, locate it in its housing with the hole facing rearwards **(see illustration)**. Fit a new O-ring onto the cover, using a dab of grease to keep it in place if required **(see illustration)**. Fit the cover onto the housing, then install the two bolts, not forgetting to connect the earth wire with the outer bolt, and tighten them securely **(see illustration 6.3a)**. Attach the hose and tighten the clamp.

9 To install the thermostat housing, attach the hoses to their unions on the cover and housing and tighten the clamps **(see illustration 6.4)**. Unscrew the outer cover bolt and secure the earth wire with it. Connect the temperature gauge thermosensor and ECT sensor wiring connectors.

10 Refill the cooling system (see Chapter 1).
11 Install the fuel tank (see Chapter 4).

7 Radiators – removal and installation

Removal

⚠️ **Warning: The engine must be completely cool before carrying out this procedure.**

1 Drain the cooling system (see Chapter 1).
2 If removing the right-hand radiator, disconnect the fan connector **(see illustration 4.3)**. Also detach the reservoir hose from the filler neck **(see illustration 3.3c)**.
3 Slacken the clamps securing the hoses to the radiator and detach them, noting which fits where **(see illustrations)**.
4 Unscrew the two bolts and remove the washers securing the radiator, then lift (VTR models) or draw back (XL models) the radiator slightly to free the grommet on the bottom or front from the lug in the mounting bracket and remove it **(see illustrations)**. Note the arrangement of the collars and rubber grommets.
5 If necessary, remove the cooling fan and its switch from the right-hand radiator (see Section 4).
6 Remove the stone guard from the upper

6.8a Install the thermostat with the hole at the back

6.8b Fit a new O-ring into the groove in the cover

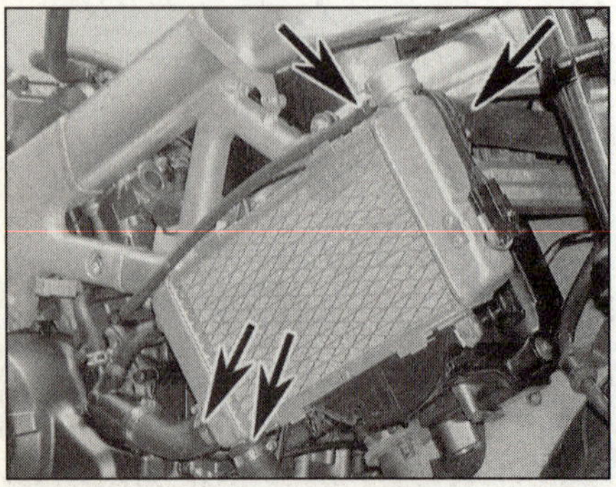

7.3a Right-hand radiator hoses (arrowed) – VTR models

7.3b Left-hand radiator hoses (arrowed) – VTR models

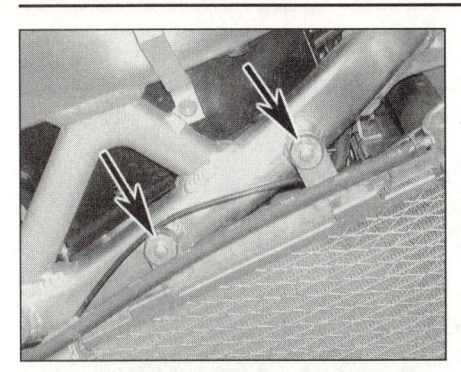

Cooling system 3•7

7.4a Right-hand radiator mounting bolts (arrowed) – VTR models

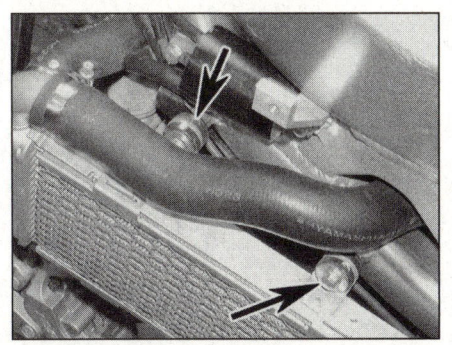

7.4b Left-hand radiator mounting bolts (arrowed) – VTR models

7.4c Right-hand radiator mounting bolts (arrowed) – XL models

radiator. Check the stone guard and the radiator for signs of damage and clear any dirt or debris that might obstruct air flow and inhibit cooling. If the radiator fins are badly damaged or broken the radiator must be replaced with a new one. Also check the rubber mounting grommets, and renew them if necessary.

Installation

7 Installation is the reverse of removal, noting the following.
 a) *Make sure the rubber grommets fit correctly onto the locating lugs.*
 b) *Make sure the collars and washers are correctly installed with the mounting bolts – the collars fit into the grommets from the inside.*
 c) *On the right-hand radiator, make sure that the fan wiring, and the reservoir hose, are correctly connected.*
 d) *Ensure the coolant hoses are in good condition (see Chapter 1), and are securely retained by their clamps, using new ones if necessary.*
 e) *On completion refill the cooling system as described in Chapter 1.*

8 Water pump – check, removal and installation

Check

1 The water pump is located on the lower right-hand side of the engine. Visually check the area around the pump for signs of leakage.
2 To prevent leakage of water from the cooling system to the lubrication system and vice versa, two seals are fitted on the pump shaft. On the front of the pump housing there is also a drain hose **(see illustration)**. If either seal fails, the drain allows the coolant or oil to escape and prevents them mixing.
3 The seal on the water pump side is of the mechanical type which bears on the rear face of the impeller. The second seal, which is mounted behind the mechanical seal is of the normal feathered lip type. If on inspection the drain hose shows signs of coolant leakage, remove the pump and replace the mechanical seal with a new one. If it is oil that is leaking, replace the oil seal with a new one. If the leakage is white and with the texture of emulsion, replace both seals with new ones.

Removal

4 Drain the coolant (see Chapter 1). On XL models, unscrew the bolt securing the coolant reservoir and displace it for access **(see illustration 3.5)**.
5 Slacken the clamps securing the coolant hoses to the pump cover and detach the hoses, noting which fits where **(see illustration)**. Also detach the drain hose from the front of the cover **(see illustration 8.2)**.
6 Unscrew the bolts securing the pump cover and remove the cover **(see illustration)**. Note the position of the shorter bolt. Discard the cover O-ring as a new one must be used. Remove the dowels if they are loose.
7 Trace the pulse generator coil wiring from the front of the clutch cover and disconnect it at the connector. On VTR models the connector is located under the left-hand side of the frame **(see illustration)**. On XL models

7.4d On XL models, draw the radiator back to free the grommet from the lug (arrowed)

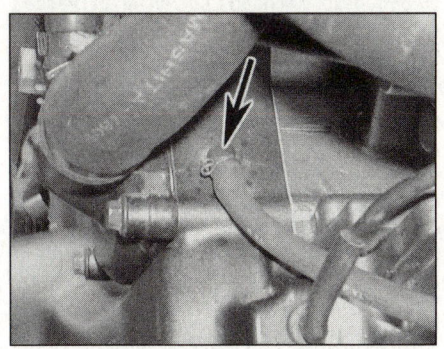

8.2 Check the drain hose (arrowed) for leakage

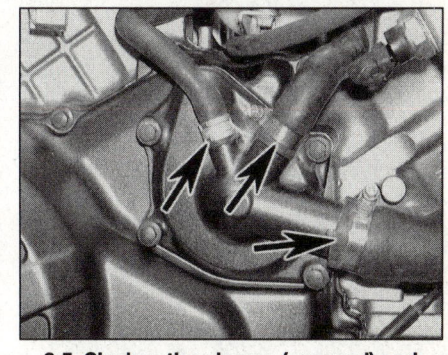

8.5 Slacken the clamps (arrowed) and detach the hoses from the cover

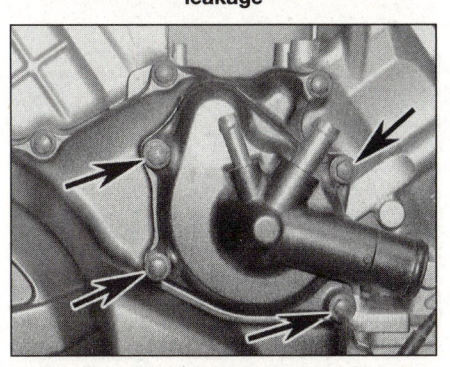

8.6 Unscrew the bolts (arrowed) and remove the cover

8.7a Pulse generator coil wiring connector (arrowed) – VTR models

3•8 Cooling system

8.7b Pulse generator coil wiring connector – XL models

8.8 Unscrew the clutch cover bolts (arrowed) and remove the cover

8.9 Remove the sprocket and disengage the chain

the connector is housed inside the rubber boot on the left-hand side – raise or remove the fuel tank to access it, unless you have small hands **(see illustration)**.

8 Unscrew the bolts securing the clutch cover and remove the cover **(see illustration)**. Discard the gasket as a new one must be used. Remove the dowels if they are loose.

9 To access the pump drive chain and driven sprocket, remove the primary drive gear and timing rotor (see Chapter 2). Slide the sprocket out of its bore in the engine and disengage the chain from the crankshaft **(see illustration)**.

10 Wiggle the water pump impeller back-and-forth and in-and-out **(see illustration)**. If there is excessive movement, determine whether it is the bearing, the seals, the impeller or the housing causing the problem and renew the faulty component(s) **(see illustration)**. Also check for corrosion or a build-up of scale in the pump body and clean or replace the pump as necessary. Check the drive chain and drive and driven sprockets for wear and damage. The drive sprocket is integral with the crankshaft.

11 The pump shaft/impeller is an interference fit in the housing. If either the shaft/impeller or the bearings and seals are being renewed, the shaft/impeller will need to be driven or pressed out.

Seal and bearing replacement

12 Drive or press the impeller out of the housing. To replace the bearing, tap it out from the inside of the housing using a bearing driver or suitable socket, or draw it out from the outside using a slide-hammer – refer to *Tools and Workshop Tips* in the Reference Section for information on bearing replacement methods.

13 To replace the oil seal, first remove the bearing (see above). Tap the seal out from the outside of the housing using a bearing driver or suitable socket, noting which way round the seal fits. Discard it as a new one must be fitted.

14 To replace the mechanical seal, tap the seal out from the inside of the housing using a bearing driver or suitable socket, noting which way round the seal fits. Discard it as a new one must be fitted.

15 Press or carefully drive the new mechanical seal into the front of the housing, making sure it is the correct way round, using a suitable-sized socket or seal driver **(see illustration)**.

16 Apply a smear of grease to the lips of the new oil seal. Press or carefully drive the new oil seal into the inside of the housing, making sure it is the correct way round **(see illustration 8.15)**.

17 Press or drive the new bearing into the rear of the pump body using a suitable-sized socket or bearing driver, making sure the markings on the bearing face out of the housing. Drive the bearing in until it is properly seated.

Installation

18 Press or drive the shaft/impeller into the housing, using a suitable socket to support the inner race of the bearing as you do.

19 If removed, apply some molybdenum disulphide oil (a 50/50 mixture of molybdenum

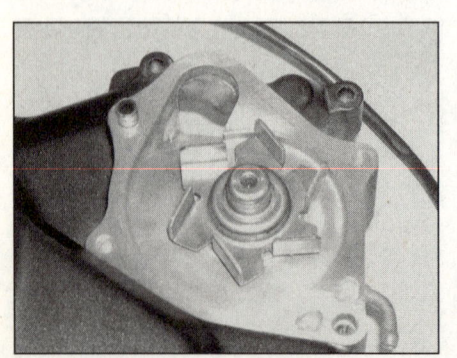

8.10a Check the impeller . . .

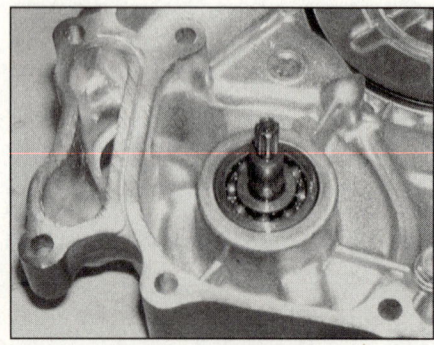

8.10b . . . and the bearing

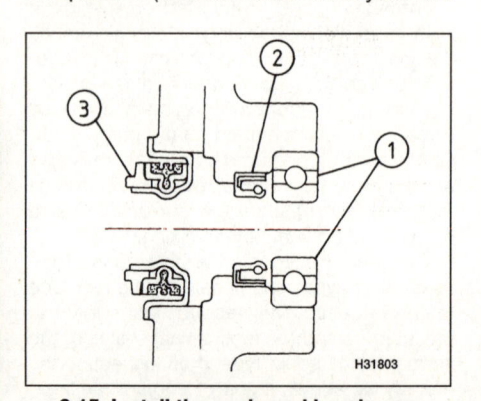

8.15 Install the seals and bearing as shown

1 Bearing   2 Oil seal   3 Mechanical seal

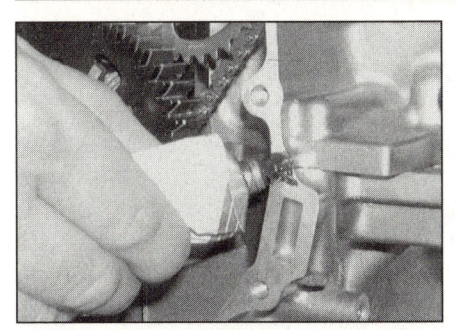

Cooling system 3•9

8.20a Apply a sealant to the crankcase joints

8.20b Fit the dowels (arrowed) and a new gasket ...

8.20c ... then install the cover, locating the shaft (A) in the sprocket (B)

disulphide grease and engine oil) to the water pump driven sprocket shaft and to the centre of the sprocket where the pump shaft locates. Fit the chain around the driven sprocket, then engage it with the drive sprocket on the crankshaft and locate the driven sprocket shaft into the crankcase **(see illustration 8.9)**. Install the primary drive gear and timing rotor (see Chapter 2).

20 Apply a smear of suitable sealant to the crankcase joints **(see illustration)**. Fit the clutch cover dowels into the crankcase, if removed, then fit a new gasket **(see illustration)**. Install the cover, making sure the water pump shaft locates into the centre of the driven sprocket **(see illustration)**.

21 Connect the pulse generator coil wiring connector **(see illustration 8.7a or 8.7b)**.

22 Fit a new O-ring into its groove in the pump **(see illustration)**. Fit the dowels into the cover if removed.

23 Fit the cover onto the pump and install the bolts – the short bolt is for the bottom left hole **(see illustration)**.

24 Attach the coolant hoses to the pump cover and secure them with their clamps **(see illustration 8.5)**. Attach the drain hose to the front of the housing **(see illustration 8.2)**.

25 On XL models, install the reservoir mounting bolt **(see illustration 3.5)**. Refill the cooling system (see Chapter 1).

9 Coolant hoses – removal and installation

Removal

1 Before removing a hose, drain the coolant (see Chapter 1).

2 Use a screwdriver to slacken the larger-bore hose clamps, then slide them back along the hose and clear of the union spigot. The smaller-bore hoses are secured by spring clamps which can be expanded by squeezing their ears together with pliers.

Caution: The radiator unions are fragile. Do not use excessive force when attempting to remove the hoses.

3 If a hose proves stubborn, release it by rotating it on its union before working it off. If all else fails, cut the hose with a sharp knife then slit it at each union so that it can be peeled off in two pieces. Whilst this means

replacing the hose, it is preferable to buying a new radiator.

4 The water pipe outlet unions from the cylinder heads can be removed by unscrewing their bolts **(see illustration)**. If the unions are removed, the O-rings must be replaced with new ones.

Installation

5 Slide the clips onto the hose and then work it on to its respective union.

6 Rotate the hose on its unions to settle it in position before sliding the clamps into place and tightening them securely.

> **HAYNES HiNT** *If the hose is difficult to push on its union, it can be softened by soaking it in very hot water, or alternatively a little soapy water can be used as a lubricant.*

7 If the outlet unions from the cylinder heads have been removed, fit a new O-ring, then install the union and tighten the mounting bolts securely.

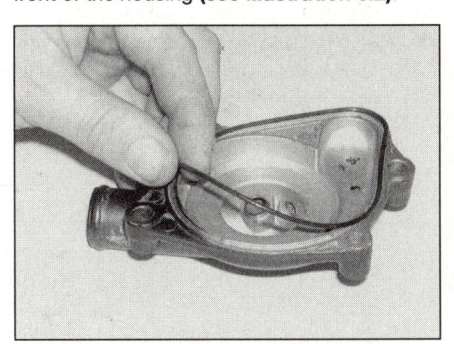

8.22 Install the cover using a new O-ring ...

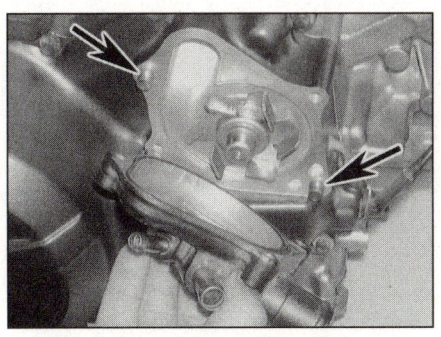

8.23 ... and not forgetting the dowels (arrowed)

9.4 Water pipe union bolts (arrowed)

Chapter 4A
Fuel and exhaust systems – carburettor models

Contents

Air filter housing – removal and installation	4
Air filter – replacement	see Chapter 1
Carburettor overhaul – general information	6
Carburettors – synchronisation	see Chapter 1
Carburettors – disassembly, cleaning and inspection	8
Carburettors – reassembly and float height check	10
Carburettors – removal and installation	7
Carburettors – separation and joining	9
Choke cable – removal and installation	12
Evaporative emission control (EVAP) system components (California models)	17
Exhaust system – removal and installation	13
Fuel hoses – check and replacement	see Chapter 1
Fuel pump and relay – check, removal and installation (XL models)	14
Fuel system – check	see Chapter 1
Fuel tank – cleaning and repair	3
Fuel tank and fuel tap – removal and installation	2
Fuel warning light/gauge and sensor – check and replacement	15
General information and precautions	1
Idle fuel/air mixture adjustment – general information	5
Idle speed – check	see Chapter 1
Pulse secondary air injection (PAIR) system components	16
Throttle and choke cables – check and adjustment	see Chapter 1
Throttle cables – removal and installation	11

Degrees of difficulty

| Easy, suitable for novice with little experience | Fairly easy, suitable for beginner with some experience | Fairly difficult, suitable for competent DIY mechanic | Difficult, suitable for experienced DIY mechanic | Very difficult, suitable for expert DIY or professional |

Specifications

Fuel
Grade . . . . Unleaded, minimum 91 RON (Research Octane Number)
Fuel tank capacity (including reserve)
   VTR models . . . . 16.0 litres
   XL models. . . . . 25.0 litres

Carburettors
Type CV
Model
   UK VTR-V VPT0B
   UK VTR-W to VTR-Y. VPT0G
   UK VTR-1 and VTR-2 . . . . VPT3A
   UK VTR-3 onward. VPT3E
   US VTR 49-state models VPT2A
   US VTR California models VPT1A
   XL-X to XL-2 . . . . VPJ0A
Pilot screw setting (turns out). . . . . see Text (and see **Note** on page 4•2)
Float height
   VTR models . . . . 16.1 to 17.1 mm
   XL models. . . . . 13.2 to 14.2 mm
Idle speed. . . . . see Chapter 1

4A•2 Fuel and exhaust systems – carburettor models

Carburettor jet sizes
Pilot jet
    VTR-V models. 45
    VTR-W, X and Y models 48
    VTR-1, 2, 3 models. 45
    XL models. 42
Main jet
    VTR models
        Front cylinder carburettor . . . . 175* (see **Note** below)
        Rear cylinder carburettor . . . . 178* (see **Note** below)
    XL models
        Front cylinder carburettor 168
        Rear cylinder carburettor 170
Jet needle
    UK VTR-V, W, X and Y models
        Front cylinder carburettor A1UD
        Rear cylinder carburettor A1UC
    UK VTR-1 to 6 and all US VTR models
        Front cylinder carburettor A1UF
        Rear cylinder carburettor A1UE
    XL models
        Front cylinder carburettor B51C
        Rear cylinder carburettor B51B

__Note:__ For US models that will be used continuously above an altitude of 2000m, the main jet sizes should be 172 for the front and 175 for the rear. The pilot screws should also be set 1/2 turn in from their standard position

Fuel pump (XL models)
Minimum flow rate . . . . 700 cc per min

Torque settings
Front cylinder exhaust downpipe nuts . . . . 12 Nm
Rear cylinder exhaust header pipe nuts . . . . 12 Nm
Exhaust system clamp bolts
    VTR models and XL-X, Y, 1 and 2 models . . . . 26 Nm
    XL-3 models onward
        Downpipe-to-silencer clamp bolts . . . . 26 Nm
        Downpipe-to-rear header pipe clamp bolt . . . . 21 Nm
PAIR system check valve bolts . . . . 5 Nm

1 General information and precautions

General information

The fuel system consists of the fuel tank, fuel tap(s) with integral filter(s), carburettors, fuel hoses and control cables. XL models also have a fuel pump and in-line filter.

On VTR models, the fuel tap is automatic and opens by vacuum when the engine is turning. On XL models, the fuel taps are operated manually.

All models have a low fuel level warning light in the instrument cluster which is triggered by a sensor inside the fuel tank.

The carburettors used on all models are CV types. There is a carburettor for each cylinder. For cold starting, on VTR models a choke knob is mounted on the lower frame rail on the left-hand side. On XL models, a choke lever is mounted with the clutch lever bracket on the handlebar.

Air is drawn into the carburettors via an air filter which is housed under the fuel tank.

The exhaust system is a two-into-two design.

Many of the fuel system service procedures are considered routine maintenance items and for that reason are included in Chapter 1.

Precautions

Warning: Petrol (gasoline) is extremely flammable, so take extra precautions when you work on any part of the fuel system. Don't smoke or allow open flames or bare light bulbs near the work area, and don't work in a garage where a natural gas-type appliance is present. If you spill any fuel on your skin, rinse it off immediately with soap and water. When you perform any kind of work on the fuel system, wear safety glasses and have a fire extinguisher suitable for a class B type fire (flammable liquids) on hand.

Always perform service procedures in a well-ventilated area to prevent a build-up of fumes.

Never work in a building containing a gas appliance with a pilot light, or any other form of naked flame. Ensure that there are no naked light bulbs or any sources of flame or sparks nearby.

Do not smoke (or allow anyone else to smoke) while in the vicinity of petrol (gasoline) or of components containing it. Remember the possible presence of vapour from these sources and move well clear before smoking.

Check all electrical equipment belonging to the house, garage or workshop where work is being undertaken (see the *Safety first!* section of this manual). Remember that certain electrical appliances such as drills, cutters, etc. create sparks in the normal course of operation and must not be used near petrol (gasoline) or any component containing it. Again, remember the possible presence of fumes before using electrical equipment.

Always mop up any spilt fuel and safely dispose of the rag used.

Any stored fuel that is drained off during servicing work must be kept in sealed containers that are suitable for holding petrol (gasoline), and clearly marked as such; the containers themselves should be kept in a safe place.

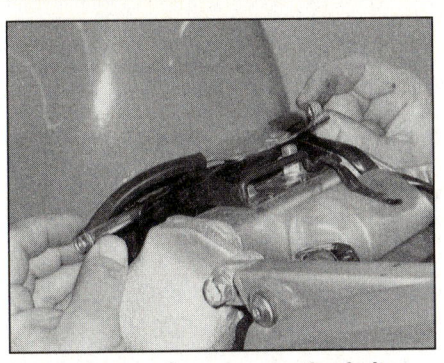

Fuel and exhaust systems – carburettor models 4A•3

2.1a Remove the rear mounting bolt . . .

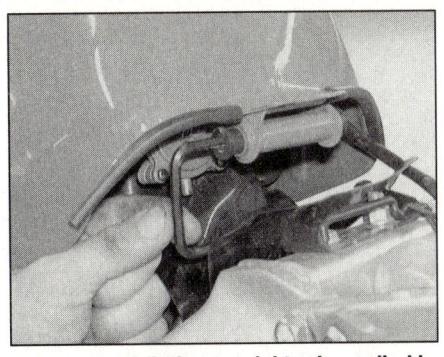

2.1b . . . and fit the special tool supplied in the toolkit – VTR models

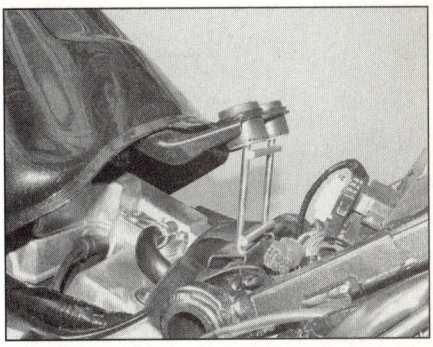

2.1c Tank shown in raised position using tool supplied (XL-7 model shown)

Note that this last point applies equally to the fuel tank if it is removed from the machine; also remember to keep its filler cap closed at all times.

Read the *Safety first!* section of this manual carefully before starting work.

2 Fuel tank and fuel tap – removal and installation

⚠ **Warning: Refer to the precautions given in Section 1 before starting work.**

Fuel tank

Removal

1 Make sure the fuel cap is secure. Remove the seat (see Chapter 8). The rear of the fuel tank can be raised to access the rear cylinder spark plug, or on XL models the wiring connectors in the boot on the left-hand side. To raise the tank, remove the rear mounting bolt(s) **(see illustration 2.2f or 2.3c)**. On XL models also remove the bolts securing each fairing side panel to the tank, and where applicable the cockpit trim panel bolts. Lift the rear of the tank and fit the special tool supplied in the toolkit **(see illustrations)**.

2 On VTR models, disconnect the fuel level sensor wiring connector **(see illustration)**. Unscrew the two bolts securing the front of the tank to the frame **(see illustration)**. Raise the front of the tank. On V, W, X and Y models turn the fuel tap OFF using a suitable spanner **(see illustration)**. Disconnect the fuel hoses and vacuum hose from the tap **(see illustrations)**. Also disconnect the breather and drain hoses from their unions, noting which fits where. Unscrew and remove the tank rear mounting bolt, then carefully lift the tank off the frame **(see illustration)**.

3 On XL models, turn the fuel taps OFF, then disconnect the fuel hoses from the taps **(see**

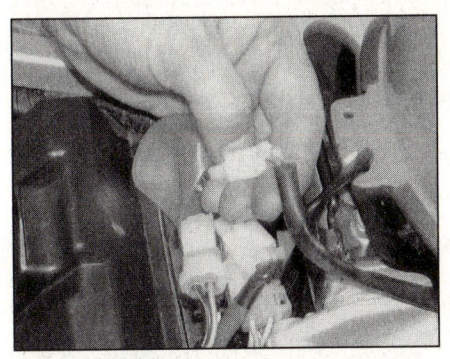

2.2a Disconnect the wiring connector

2.2b Unscrew the bolts (arrowed) and raise the tank

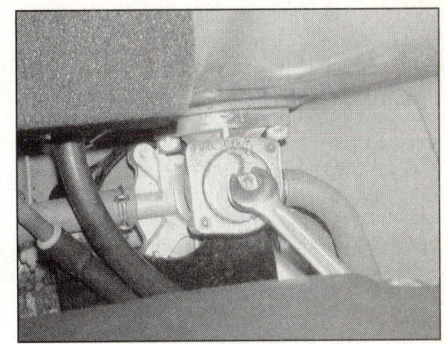

2.2c On V, W, X and Y models turn the fuel tap OFF

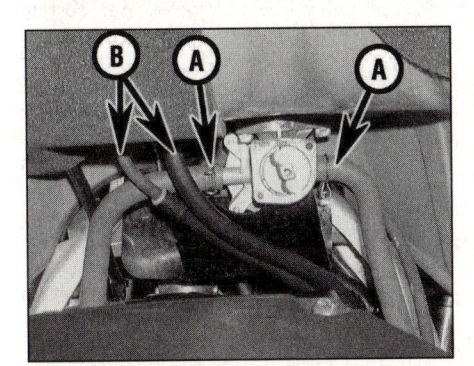

2.2d Disconnect the fuel hoses (A) and the drain and breather hoses (B) . . .

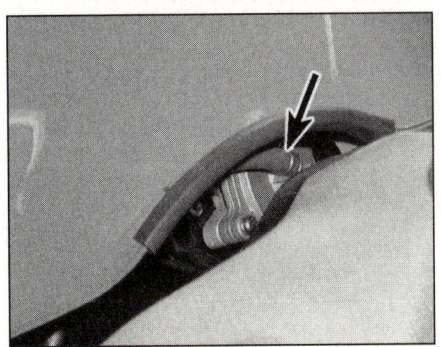

2.2e . . . and the vacuum hose (arrowed)

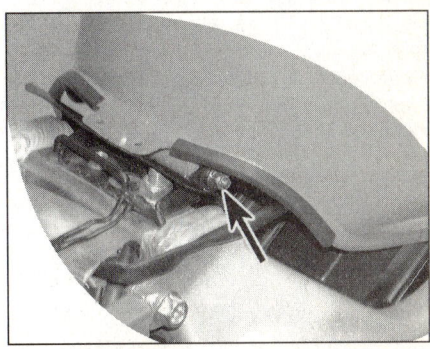

2.2f Unscrew the nut (arrowed) and withdraw the rear mounting bolt

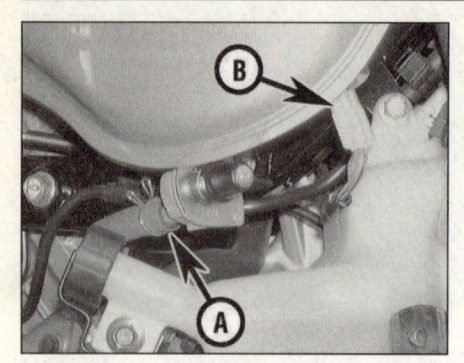

4A•4 Fuel and exhaust systems – carburettor models

2.3a Turn each tap OFF, then disconnect the fuel hose (A) from each tap and disconnect the wiring connectors (B)

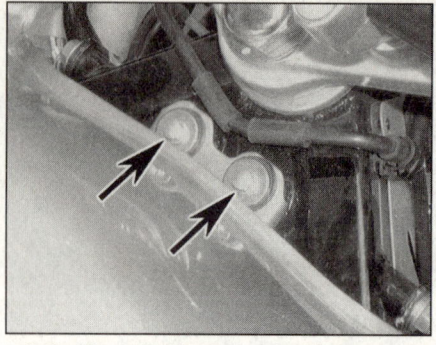

2.3b Unscrew the front mounting bolts (arrowed) . . .

2.3c . . . and the rear mounting bolts (arrowed)

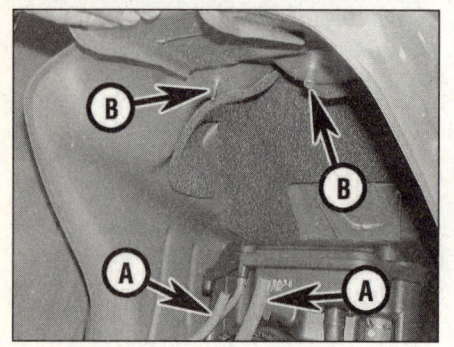

2.3d On XL-X, Y, 1 and 2 models raise the rear of the tank and disconnect the hoses (A) from their unions (B)

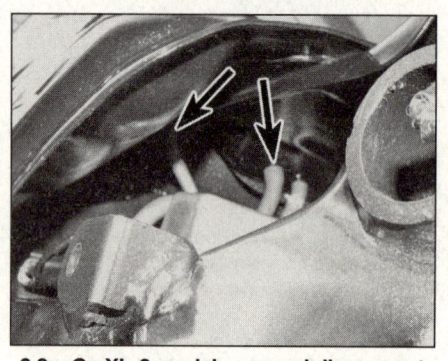

2.3e On XL-3 models onward disconnect the breather and drain hoses (arrowed) from the tank . . .

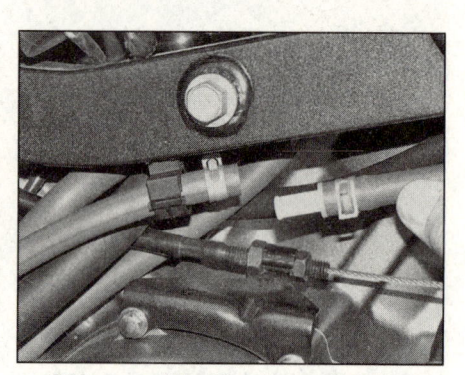

2.3f . . . and the bleed hose from the union

illustration). Disconnect the fuel level sensor wiring connectors. Unscrew and remove the front and rear tank mounting bolts, noting the arrangement of the washers and/or collars (according to model) **(see illustrations)**. Also remove the bolts securing each fairing side panel to the tank, and where applicable the cockpit trim panel bolts. Raise the rear of the tank, then disconnect the breather and drain hoses from their unions, noting which fits where **(see illustrations)**. On XL-3 models onward also disconnect the air bleed hose at the joint under the frame on the left-hand side **(see illustration)**. Carefully lift the tank off the frame.

4 Inspect the tank mounting rubbers for signs of damage or deterioration and replace them if necessary.

Installation

5 Installation is the reverse of removal. Check that the tank mounting rubbers are fitted and in good condition. Make sure all the hoses are securely connected. Start the engine and check that there is no sign of fuel leakage. On VTR models, do not forget to turn the fuel tap ON before installing the front mounting bolts **(see illustration 2.2c)**.

Fuel tap

Removal

6 The tap should not be removed unnecessarily from the tank to prevent the possibility of damaging the O-ring or the filter.
7 On VTR models, the fuel tap is automatic, operated by a vacuum created when the engine is turned over. If it is faulty, it can be disassembled and inspected. The most likely problem is a hole or split in the diaphragm. Before removing and dismantling the tap, check that the vacuum hose is securely attached at both ends, and that there are no splits or cracks in the hose. If in doubt, attach a spare hose to the vacuum union on the tap and apply a vacuum to the hose. If fuel does not flow through the tap (on V, W, X and Y models make sure it is turned ON), remove it and disassemble it to check the diaphragm. No individual components are available for the tap (except the filter), so if it is faulty an new one must be installed.

8 Remove the fuel tank as described above. Connect a drain hose to the fuel hose union and insert its end in a container suitable and large enough for storing the petrol. On VTR-V, W, X and Y models, turn the fuel tap to the ON position, then on all VTR models attach a suitable hose to the vacuum union and apply a vacuum to allow the tank to drain. On XL models, turn the fuel tap to the ON position and allow the tank to drain.

9 On VTR-V, W, X and Y models, unscrew the two bolts securing the tap and withdraw it from the tank, taking care not to damage the filter **(see illustration)**. On all other VTR models release the fuel hose clamp and detach the hose, then unscrew the bolts securing the tap and remove it. On XL models, and on VTR-1 to 6 models to remove the fuel union and filter, unscrew the nut securing the tap/union and withdraw it from the tank, taking care not to damage the filter **(see illustration)**.

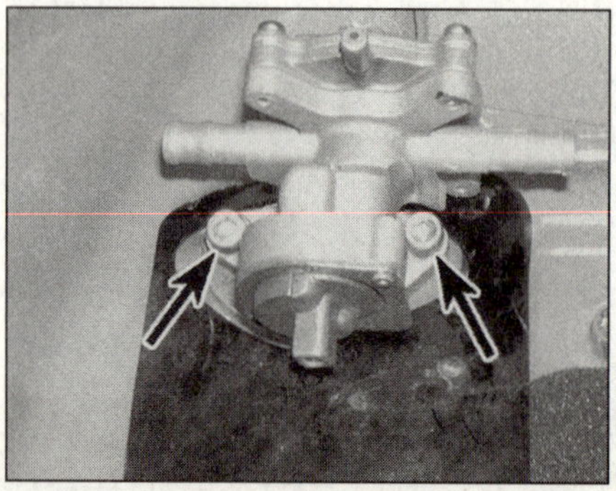

2.9a Fuel tap mounting bolts (arrowed) – VTR models

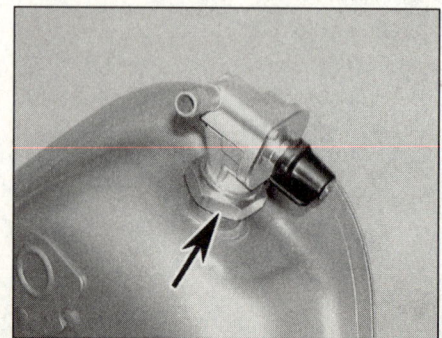

2.9b Fuel tap nut (arrowed) – XL models

Fuel and exhaust systems – carburettor models 4A•5

4.3 Undo the screws (arrowed) and remove the ducts

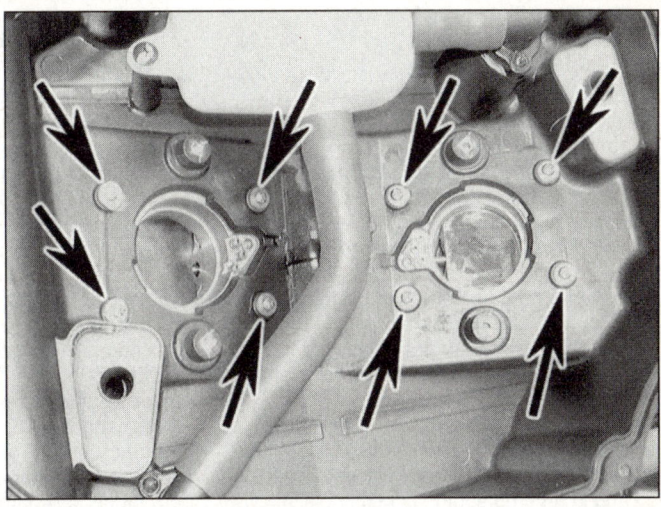

4.4a Undo the screws ...

Check the condition of the O-ring. If it is in good condition it can be re-used, though it is better to use a new one. If it is in any way deteriorated or damaged it must be replaced with a new one.

10 If the fuel tap has been leaking, tightening the assembly screws may help. Slacken all the screws a little first, then tighten them evenly a little at a time to ensure the cover seats properly on the tap body. If leakage persists, the tap should be replaced with a new one, however nothing is lost by dismantling it for further inspection. Unscrew the screws and disassemble the tap, noting how the components fit. Inspect all components for wear or damage. No individual components are available for the tap (except the filter), so if it is faulty a new one must be installed.

11 Clean the gauze filter to remove all traces of dirt and fuel sediment. Check the gauze for holes. If any are found, replace the filter with a new one.

Installation

12 Install the fuel tap into the tank, using a new O-ring if required, and tighten the bolts or nut securely **(see illustration 2.9a or 2.9b)**.
13 Install the fuel tank (see above).

3 Fuel tank – cleaning and repair

1 All repairs to the fuel tank should be carried out by a professional who has experience in this critical and potentially dangerous work. Even after cleaning and flushing of the fuel system, explosive fumes can remain and ignite during repair of the tank.

2 If the fuel tank is removed from the bike, it should not be placed in an area where sparks or open flames could ignite the fumes coming out of the tank. Be especially careful inside garages where a natural gas-type appliance is located, because the pilot light could cause an explosion.

4 Air filter housing – removal and installation

Removal

1 Remove the fuel tank (see Section 2), and the air filter (see Chapter 1).
2 Release the clamps securing the front and rear cylinder air and breather hoses to the housing and detach the hoses, noting which fits where. Where fitted, detach the PAIR control valve vacuum hose and air supply hose from the filter housing, then release the valve from its holder which is screwed to the underside. On XL models, also disconnect the vacuum hose from the rear of the housing.
3 Undo the screws securing the air intake ducts to the air filter housing and remove the ducts, noting how they fit **(see illustration)**.
4 Undo the screws securing the filter housing to the carburettors **(see illustration)**. Lift the housing up off the carburettors and remove it **(see illustration)**.

Installation

5 Installation is the reverse of removal. Check the condition of the carburettor O-rings and use new ones if they are in any way damaged or deteriorated **(see illustration)**. Check the condition of the various hoses and their clamps and use new ones if they are in any way damaged or deteriorated. On VTR models, the longer air intake duct is for the rear carburettor. When installing the ducts, align the triangle mark on the duct with that on the housing **(see illustration)**.

4.4b ... and lift the housing off the carburettors

4.5a Use a new O-ring if necessary

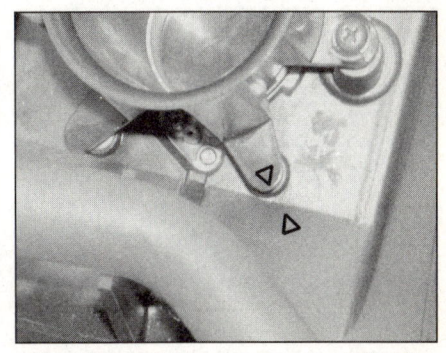

4.5b Align the triangles when installing the ducts

4A•6 Fuel and exhaust systems – carburettor models

5 Idle fuel/air mixture adjustment – general information

1 Due to the increased emphasis on controlling exhaust emissions, certain governmental regulations have been formulated which directly affect the carburation of this machine. The pilot screws can be adjusted, but the use of an exhaust gas analyser and an auxiliary tachometer capable of accurately displaying changes of 50 rpm is the only certain way to adjust the idle fuel/air mixture and be sure the machine doesn't exceed the emissions regulations.

2 The pilot screws are set to their correct position by the manufacturer and should not be adjusted or removed unless it is necessary to do so during a carburettor overhaul. If the screws are to be removed, record the pilot screw's current setting by turning the screw it in until it seats lightly, counting the number of turns necessary to achieve this, then fully unscrew it. On installation, the screw is simply backed out the number of turns you've recorded.

3 If the engine runs extremely rough at idle or continually stalls, and if a carburettor overhaul does not cure the problem, take the motorcycle to a Honda dealer equipped with an exhaust gas analyser. They will be able to properly adjust the idle fuel/air mixture to achieve a smooth idle and restore low speed performance.

6 Carburettor overhaul – general information

1 Poor engine performance, hesitation, hard starting, stalling, flooding and backfiring are all signs that major carburettor maintenance may be required.

2 Keep in mind that many so-called carburettor problems are really not carburettor problems at all, but mechanical problems within the engine or ignition system malfunctions. Try to establish for certain that the carburettors are in need of maintenance before beginning a major overhaul.

3 Check the fuel tap and filter, the fuel and vacuum hoses, the intake manifold joint clamps, the air filter, the ignition system, the spark plugs and carburettor synchronisation before assuming that a carburettor overhaul is required.

4 Most carburettor problems are caused by dirt particles, varnish and other deposits which build up in and block the fuel and air passages. Also, in time, gaskets and O-rings shrink or deteriorate and cause fuel and air leaks which lead to poor performance.

5 When overhauling the carburettors, disassemble them completely and clean the parts thoroughly with a carburettor cleaning solvent and dry them with filtered, unlubricated compressed air. Blow through the fuel and air passages with compressed air to force out any dirt that may have been loosened but not removed by the solvent. Once the cleaning process is complete, reassemble the carburettor using new gaskets and O-rings.

6 Before disassembling the carburettors, make sure you have all necessary O-rings and other parts, some carburettor cleaner, a supply of clean rags, some means of blowing out the carburettor passages, and a clean place to work. It is recommended that only one carburettor be overhauled at a time to avoid mixing up parts.

7 Carburettors – removal and installation

⚠️ **Warning:** *Refer to the precautions given in Section 1 before starting work.*

Removal

1 Drain the coolant (see Chapter 1). Remove the fuel tank and the air filter housing (see Sections 2 and 4).

2 Detach the throttle cables from the carburettors (see Section 11, Step 3 or 4, according to model). If access is too restricted, detach them after the carburettors have been lifted off the cylinder head intakes.

3 Disconnect the throttle position sensor wiring connector **(see illustration)**.

4 Release the coolant inlet hose clamp and detach the hose from the rear carburettor **(see illustration)**. The outlet hose from the front carburettor is only accessible after the carburettors have been lifted off – either detach it then, or detach it now from its union on the water pump cover.

5 On XL models, release the idle speed adjuster from its holder and feed it through to the base of the carburettors **(see illustration)**.

6 Fully slacken the upper clamps on the cylinder head intake rubbers, accessing the front one on VTR models as shown **(see illustrations)**. Ease the carburettors up off the intakes, noting that they are quite a tight fit **(see illustration)**. On California VTR models, detach the No. 5 and No. 11 hoses from the

7.3 Disconnect the throttle position sensor wiring connector

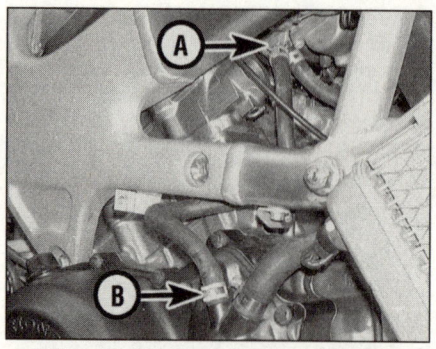

7.4 Detach the rear carburettor hose (A), and the front hose from either the water pump cover (B), or from the carburettor after it has been displaced

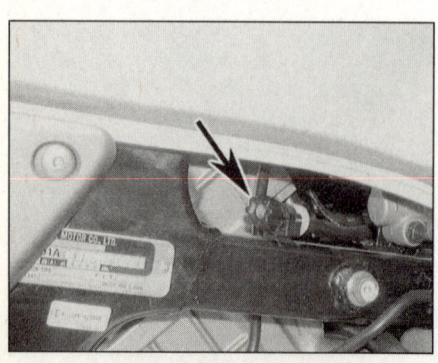

7.5 Release the idle speed adjuster (arrowed) from its holder

7.6a Slacken the front clamp screw . . .

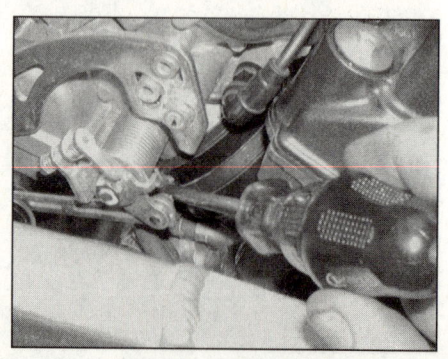

7.6b . . . and the rear clamp screw . . .

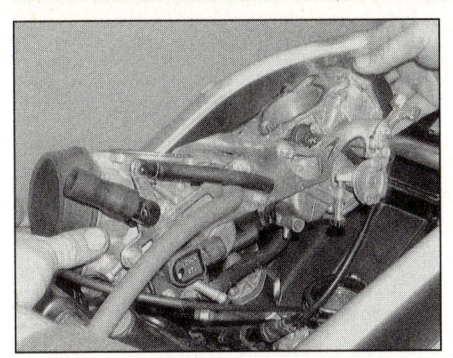

Fuel and exhaust systems – carburettor models 4A•7

7.6c . . . and displace the carburettors

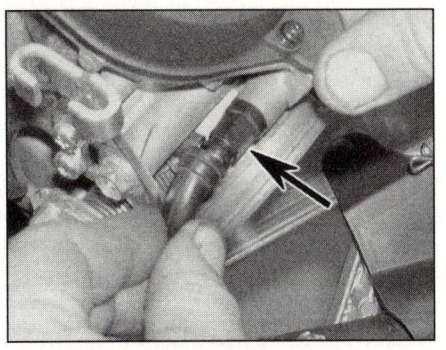

7.7a Pull back the boot and unscrew the nut (arrowed) . . .

7.7b . . . and withdraw each choke plunger

carburettors, and the No. 10 and No. 4 hoses from the EVAP control valve. **Note:** *Keep the carburettors upright to prevent fuel spillage from the float chambers and the possibility of the piston diaphragms being damaged.*
Caution: *Stuff clean rag into each cylinder head intake after removing the carburettors to prevent anything from falling in.*

7 Pull the rubber boot back off each choke plunger assembly **(see illustration)**. Unscrew each plunger nut and draw the assemblies out of the carburettors **(see illustration)**. Remove the carburettors.

8 Place a suitable container below the float chambers, then slacken the drain screw on each chamber in turn and drain all the fuel from the carburettors **(see illustration)**. Discard the drain screw O-rings as new ones must be used. Once all the fuel has been drained, fit the new O-rings and tighten the drain screws securely.

9 If necessary, slacken the clamps securing the intake rubbers to the cylinder head and remove the rubbers, noting which way up and round they fit.

Installation

10 Installation is the reverse of removal, noting the following.
 a) Check for cracks or splits in the cylinder head intake rubbers and the various hoses, and replace them with new ones if necessary.
 b) If removed, make sure the intake rubbers are installed with the CARB UP marking facing out (towards the carburettor), and align the slotted tab on the side with the projection on the head.
 c) Make sure the carburettors are fully engaged with the intake rubbers and the clamps are securely tightened.
 d) Make sure all hoses are correctly routed and secured and not trapped or kinked.
 e) Refer to Section 11 for installation of the throttle cables. Check the operation of the cables and adjust them as necessary (see Chapter 1).
 f) Check idle speed and carburettor synchronisation and adjust as necessary (see Chapter 1).
 g) Fill the cooling system (see Chapter 1).

8 Carburettors – disassembly, cleaning and inspection

⚠️ **Warning:** *Refer to the precautions given in Section 1 before starting work.*

Disassembly

1 Remove the carburettors from the machine as described in the previous Section **(see illustration)**. **Note:** *Do not separate the carburettors unless absolutely necessary; each carburettor can be dismantled sufficiently for*

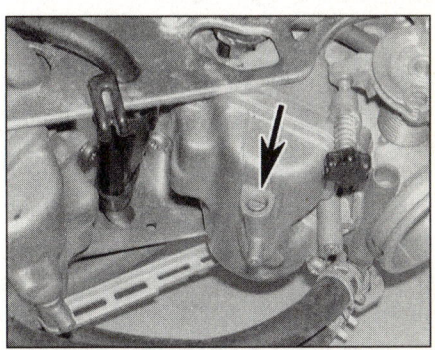

7.8 Carburettor drain screw (arrowed)

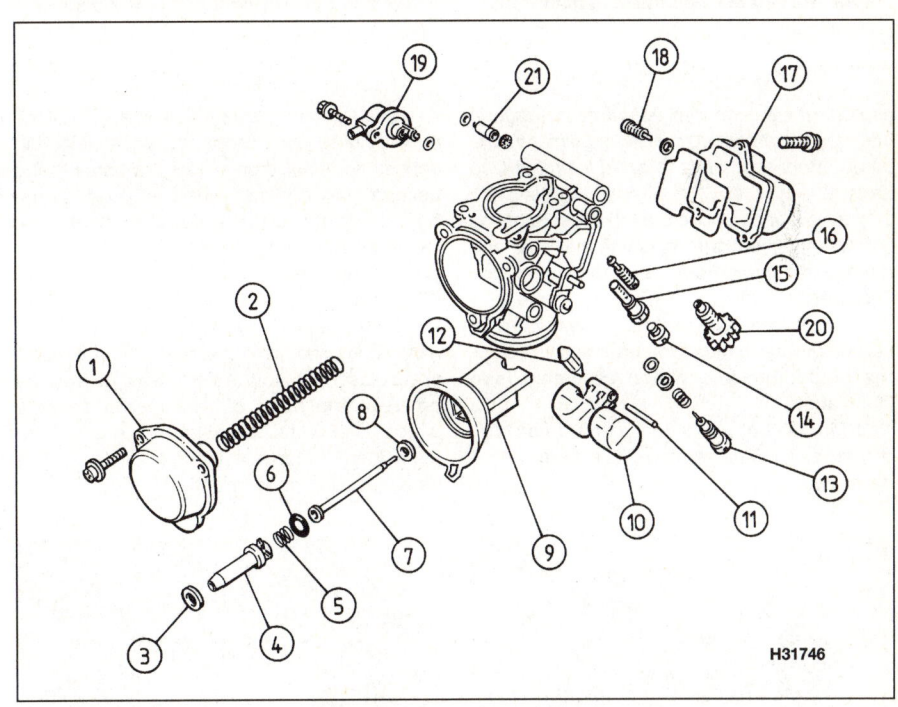

8.1 Carburettor components

1 Top cover	8 Washer	15 Needle jet holder
2 Spring	9 Diaphragm/piston	16 Pilot jet
3 Washer	10 Float	17 Float chamber
4 Holder	11 Float pin	18 Drain screw
5 Spring	12 Float needle valve	19 Air cut-off valve
6 O-ring	13 Pilot screw	20 Idle speed adjuster
7 Jet needle	14 Main jet	21 Union

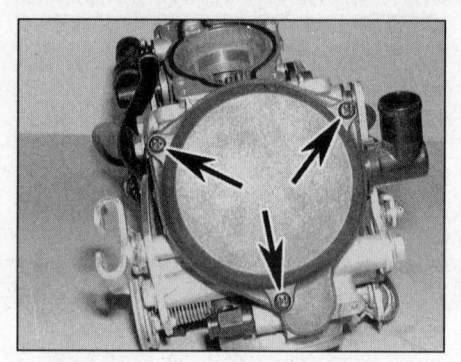

4A•8 Fuel and exhaust systems – carburettor models

8.2a Undo the screws (arrowed) . . .

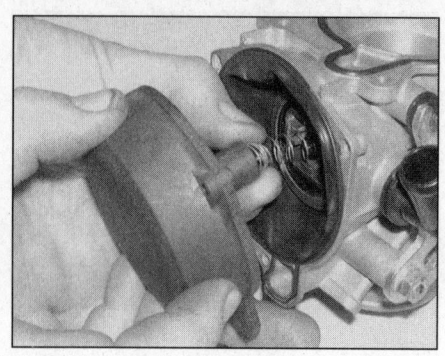

8.2b . . . and remove the cover and spring

8.3 Peel the diaphragm off the carburettor and withdraw the diaphragm and piston assembly

8.4a Thread the bolt into the holder . . .

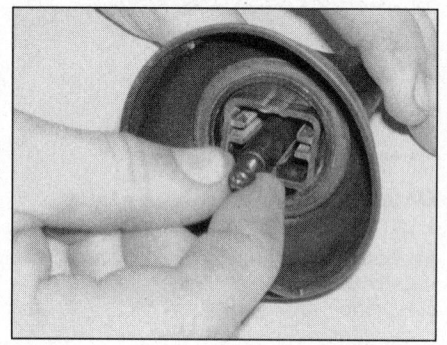

8.4b . . . and draw it out of the piston

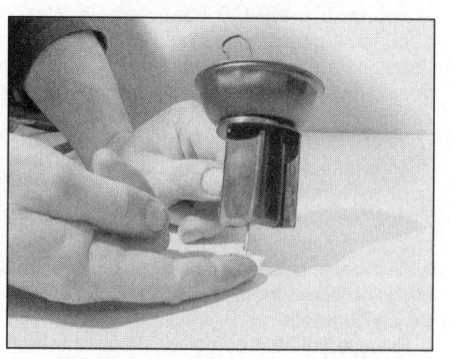

8.4c Push the needle up from the bottom and withdraw it from the top

all normal cleaning and adjustments while in place on the mounting brackets. Dismantle the carburettors separately to avoid interchanging parts.

2 Unscrew and remove the top cover retaining screws (see illustration). Lift off the cover and remove the spring from inside the piston (see illustration).

3 Carefully peel the diaphragm away from its sealing groove in the carburettor and withdraw the diaphragm and piston assembly (see illustration).
Caution: Do not use a sharp instrument to displace the diaphragm as it is easily damaged.

4 Thread a 4 mm screw into the top of the needle holder (one of the top cover retaining screws is ideal), then grasp the screw head using a pair of pliers and carefully draw the holder out of the piston (see illustrations). Push the needle up from the bottom of the piston and withdraw it from the top (see illustration). Note the spring in the base of the needle holder and the washer on its shaft – the spring should stay in place, but take care not to lose it. Also note the washer that fits between the head of the needle and the piston. Check the condition of the O-ring on the holder and replace it with a new one if it is damaged, deformed or deteriorated.

5 Remove the screws securing the float chamber to the base of the carburettor and remove it (see illustration). Remove the rubber gasket and discard it as a new one must be used.

6 Using a pair of thin-nose pliers, carefully withdraw the float pin (see illustration). If necessary, displace the pin using a small punch or a nail. Remove the float, then slide the float needle valve off, noting how it fits (see illustrations 10.4b and 10.4a).

7 Unscrew and remove the main jet from the base of the needle jet holder (see illustration).

8.5 Remove the screws (arrowed) and lift off the chamber

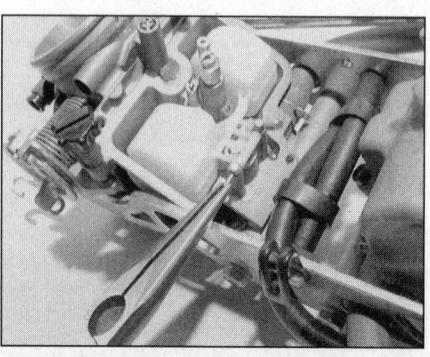

8.6 Withdraw the float pin and remove the float assembly

8.7 Remove the main jet (arrowed) . . .

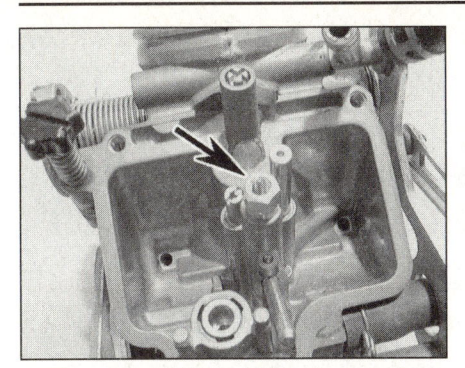

Fuel and exhaust systems – carburettor models 4A•9

8.8 ... the needle jet holder (arrowed) ...

8.9 ... and the pilot jet (arrowed)

8.10 If required, remove the pilot screw (arrowed) along with its O-ring, washer and spring

8 Unscrew and remove the needle jet holder **(see illustration)**.
9 Unscrew and remove the pilot jet **(see illustration)**.
10 The pilot screw can be removed if required, but note that its setting will be disturbed **(see Haynes Hint)**. Unscrew and remove the pilot screw along with its spring, washer and O-ring **(see illustration)**. Discard the O-ring as a new one must be used.

> **HAYNES HINT**
> *To record the pilot screw's current setting, turn the screw in until it seats lightly, counting the number of turns necessary to achieve this, then fully unscrew it. On installation, the screw is simply backed out the number of turns you've recorded.*

Cleaning

Caution: Use only a petroleum-based solvent for carburettor cleaning. Don't use caustic cleaners.

11 Submerge the metal components in the solvent for approximately thirty minutes (or longer, if the directions recommend it).
12 After the carburettor has soaked long enough for the cleaner to loosen and dissolve most of the varnish and other deposits, use a nylon-bristled brush to remove the stubborn deposits. Rinse it again, then dry it with compressed air.
13 Use a jet of compressed air to blow out all of the fuel and air passages in the main and upper body, not forgetting the air jets in the carburettor intake.

Caution: Never clean the jets or passages with a piece of wire or a drill bit, as they will be enlarged, causing the fuel and air metering rates to be upset.

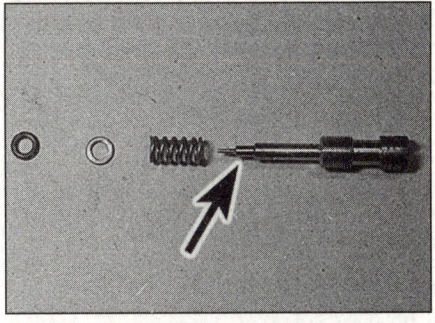

Inspection

14 Inspect the needle on the end of the choke plunger and the spring **(see illustration)**. Renew any component that is worn, damaged or bent.
15 If removed from the carburettor, check the tapered portion of the pilot screw and the spring and O-ring for wear or damage **(see illustration)**. Replace them with new ones if necessary.
16 Check the carburettor body, float chamber and top cover for cracks, distorted sealing surfaces and other damage. If any defects are found, replace the faulty component, although replacement of the entire carburettor will probably be necessary (check with a Honda dealer on the availability of separate components).
17 Check the piston diaphragm for splits, holes and general deterioration. Holding it up to a light will help to reveal problems of this nature.
18 Insert the piston in the carburettor body and check that it moves up-and-down smoothly. Check the surface of the piston for wear. If it's worn excessively or doesn't move smoothly in the guide, renew the components as necessary.
19 Check the jet needle for straightness by rolling it on a flat surface such as a piece of glass. Replace it with a new one if it's bent or if the tip is worn.
20 Check the tip of the float needle valve and the valve seat **(see illustrations)**. If either has grooves or scratches in it, or is in any way worn, they should be renewed as a set. Gently push down on the rod on the top of the needle valve then release it – if it doesn't spring back, replace the valve with a new one.
21 Operate the throttle shaft to make sure the throttle butterfly valve opens and closes smoothly. If it doesn't, cleaning the throttle linkage may help. Otherwise, replace the carburettor with a new one.
22 Check the float for damage. This will usually be apparent by the presence of fuel inside the float. If the float is damaged, it must be replaced with a new one.
23 To check the air cut-off valves, the carburettors must be separated (see Section 9). Remove the screw securing the cut-off valve and separate it from the carburettor **(see illustration)**.

8.14 Check the choke plunger assembly as described

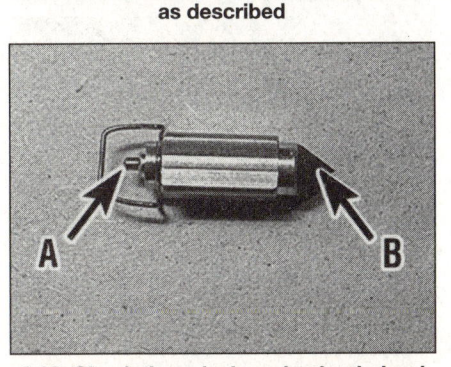

8.15 Check the tapered portion of the pilot screw (arrowed) for wear

8.20 Check the valve's spring loaded rod (A) and tip (B) for wear or damage

8.23 Air cut-off valve mounting screw (arrowed)

4A•10 Fuel and exhaust systems – carburettor models

Remove the O-rings and joint piece. Check the condition of the O-rings and discard them if they are damaged, deformed or deteriorated. To check the valve, apply a vacuum to the hose attached to the valve cover. With the vacuum applied, air should not be able to flow between the ports in the valve. With no vacuum applied, air should be able to flow. If the valve does not behave as described, replace it with a new one.

9 Carburettors – separation and joining

Warning: Refer to the precautions given in Section 1 before proceeding

Separation

1 The carburettors do not need to be separated for normal overhaul. If you need to separate them (to replace a carburettor body, for example), refer to the following procedure.
2 Remove the carburettors from the machine (see Section 7). Mark the body of each carburettor with its cylinder location to ensure that it is positioned correctly on reassembly **(see illustration)**.
3 Make a careful note or sketch of the layout and routing of the various hoses attached to and between the carburettors, and on California VTR models the EVAP control valve **(see illustration)**. Detach the hoses and remove them, and on California models remove the control valve.
4 Make a careful note of the arrangement of the various washers on each end of the throttle linkage bar. Remove the split pin and outer washers from each end of the throttle linkage bar and remove the bar and the inner washer, noting how it fits **(see illustrations)**.
5 Undo the screws securing the throttle cable bracket to the front carburettor and remove the bracket, noting how it fits **(see illustration)**.
6 Unscrew the nuts and withdraw the bolts securing the carburettor mounting plates **(see illustration)**. Remove the plates, noting how they locate onto the carburettors, and separate the carburettors. Remove the mounting plate dowels if they are loose – there are four on each side – two for each bolt.

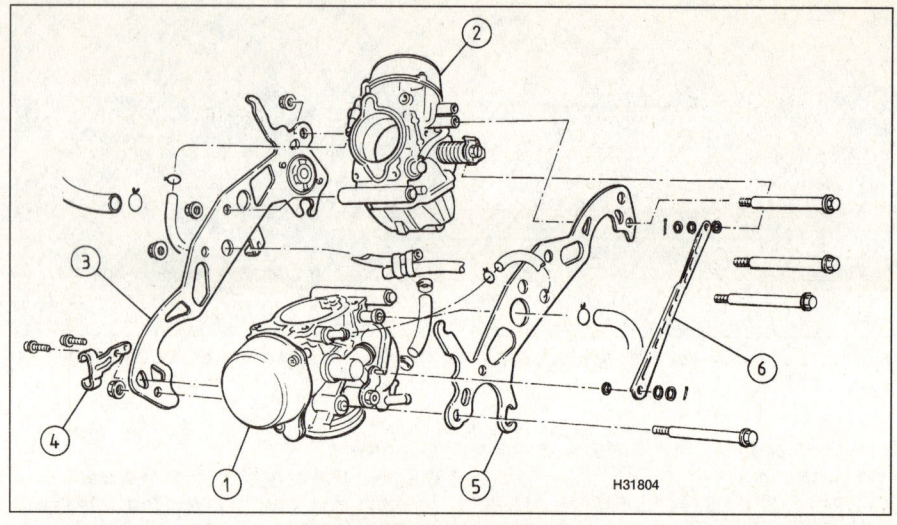

9.2 Carburettor assembly

| 1 Front carburettor | 3 Right mounting plate | 5 Left mounting plate |
| 2 Rear carburettor | 4 Throttle cable bracket | 6 Throttle linkage bar |

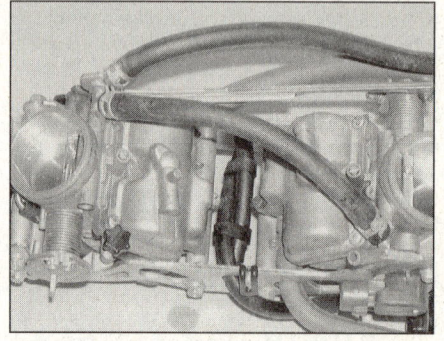

9.3 Note the routing of the various hoses before detaching them

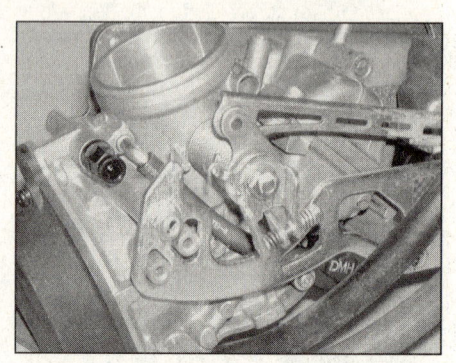

9.4a Note the arrangement of the throttle linkage . . .

7 If required, remove the various hose joints and unions from the carburettors, noting where they fit. Discard their O-rings as new ones should be used.
8 Do not remove the throttle position sensor from the mounting plate unless it is known to be faulty, in which case refer to Chapter 5.

Joining

9 If removed, fit new O-rings onto the various hose joints and unions the fuel and vent fittings. Fit them into their holes, making sure they seat properly.
10 Fit the mounting plate dowels into the carburettors if removed.
11 Locate the left-hand mounting plate onto the front carburettor and the right-hand mounting plate onto the rear carburettor, making sure they locate correctly onto the dowels. On VTR models, make sure the pin on the inside of the throttle position sensor locates between the tabs on the end of the

9.4b . . . on each end before removing it

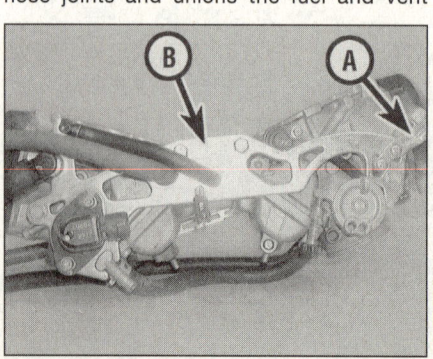

9.5 Throttle cable bracket (A), right-hand mounting plate (B) . . .

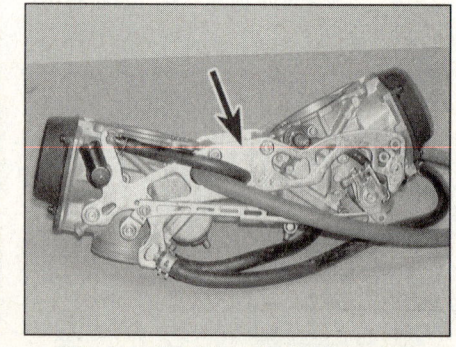

9.6 . . . and left-hand mounting plate (arrowed)

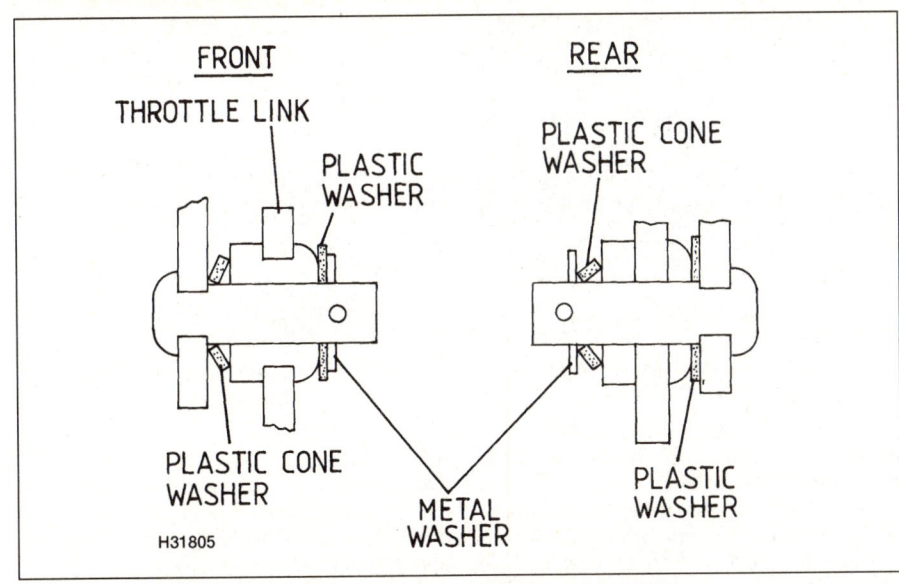

Fuel and exhaust systems – carburettor models 4A•11

FRONT — THROTTLE LINK, PLASTIC WASHER, PLASTIC CONE WASHER, METAL WASHER

REAR — PLASTIC CONE WASHER, PLASTIC WASHER

H31805

9.14 Throttle linkage washer arrangement

throttle shaft. On XL models, make sure the flat end of the throttle shaft locates into the slot in the throttle position sensor.
12 Join the carburettors together, making sure the mounting plates locate correctly onto the dowels **(see illustrations 9.5 and 9.6)**. Install the four mounting bolts and tighten the nuts securely.
13 Install the throttle cable bracket.
14 Install the throttle linkage bar, making sure it is correctly set up at each end with the various washers positioned as shown **(see illustrations and illustrations 9.4a and 9.4b)**.
15 Fit the various hoses onto and between the carburettors, making sure they are correctly routed through and around the mounting plates, and are pushed fully onto their unions **(see illustration 9.3)**. On California VTR models also install the EVAP control valve.
16 Install the carburettors (see Section 7) and check carburettor synchronisation and idle speed (see Chapter 1). Make sure the throttle linkage operates smoothly and returns quickly under spring pressure. Also check that the choke plungers operate smoothly.

10 Carburettors – reassembly and float height check

⚠️ **Warning:** *Refer to the precautions given in Section 1 before proceeding.*

Note: *When reassembling the carburettors, be sure to use new O-rings and seals. Do not overtighten the carburettor jets and screws as they are easily damaged.*

1 Install the pilot screw (if removed) along with its spring, washer and O-ring, turning it in until it seats lightly **(see illustration 8.10)**. Now, turn the screw out the number of turns previously recorded on disassembly.
2 Install the pilot jet **(see illustration)**.
3 Install the needle jet holder **(see illustration)**. Screw the main jet into the end of the needle jet holder **(see illustration)**.
4 Slide the float needle valve onto the float, then position the float assembly in the carburettor and install the pin, making sure it is secure **(see illustrations)**.
5 To check the float height, hold the carburettor so the float hangs down, then tilt it back until the needle valve is just seated, but

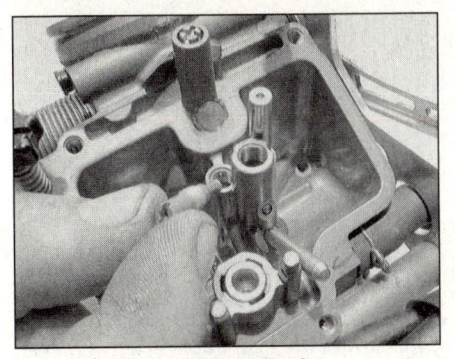

10.2 Install the pilot jet . . .

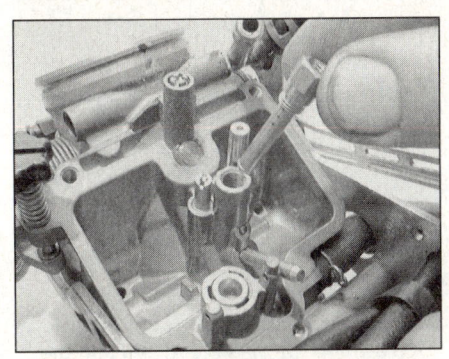

10.3a . . . the needle jet holder . . .

10.3b . . . and the main jet

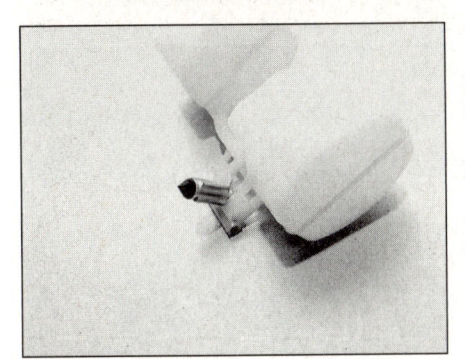

10.4a Fit the needle valve into the holder . . .

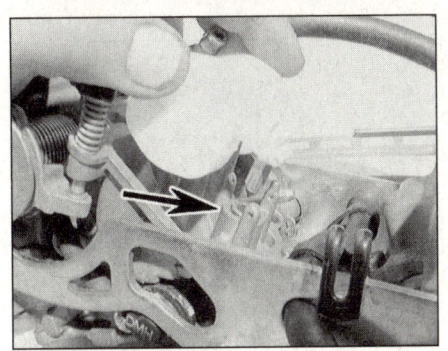

10.4b . . . then fit the float assembly, making sure the valve enters the seat (arrowed) . . .

10.4c . . . and secure it with the pin

4A•12 Fuel and exhaust systems – carburettor models

10.6 Fit a new gasket (arrowed) and install the float chamber

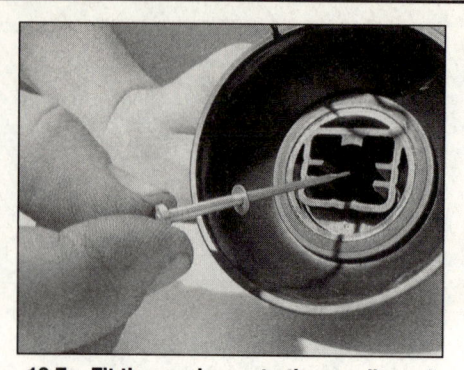

10.7a Fit the washer onto the needle and the needle into the piston

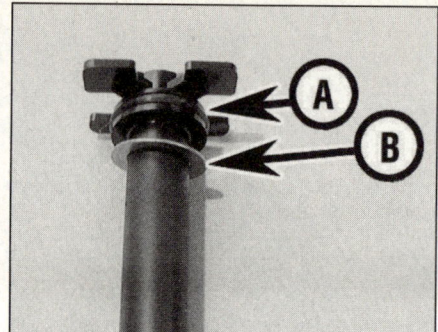

10.7b Fit a new O-ring (A) and the washer (B)

not so far that the needle's spring-loaded tip is compressed. Measure the distance between the gasket face (with the gasket removed) and the bottom of the float with an accurate ruler. The correct setting should be as given in the Specifications at the beginning of the Chapter. If it is incorrect, replace the float and needle valve with new ones – the float height is not adjustable.

6 With the float height checked, fit a new rubber gasket onto the float chamber, making sure it is seated properly in its groove, and install the chamber onto the carburettor **(see illustration)**.

7 Fit the washer onto the needle and insert the needle into the piston **(see illustration)**. Fit a new O-ring into the groove in the needle holder and smear it with oil, and fit the washer onto the shaft if removed **(see illustration)**. Check that the spring is in the base of the needle holder, or install it if removed **(see illustration)**. Align the tabs on the holder with the slots in the piston and insert the holder, pushing it down until the O-ring is felt to locate in its groove **(see illustration)**. Remove the bolt used on removal from the holder, if not already done.

8 Turn the diaphragm inside out so that its rim faces down **(see illustration)**. Insert the piston assembly into the carburettor, ensuring the needle is correctly aligned with the needle jet **(see illustration)**. Align the loop on the diaphragm rim with its groove in the carburettor body, then press the diaphragm outer edge into its groove, making sure it is correctly seated **(see illustration)**. Keep the diaphragm inside out.

9 Fit the spring into the bore in the centre of the top cover, using a pencil as shown to prevent it pinging out to the side **(see illustration)**. Hold the end of the spring and fit the top cover onto the carburettor, making sure the bottom of the spring locates over the raised section on the inside of the piston, and the protrusion on the cover aligns with the loop on the diaphragm, and while doing this keep a finger on the bottom of the piston to

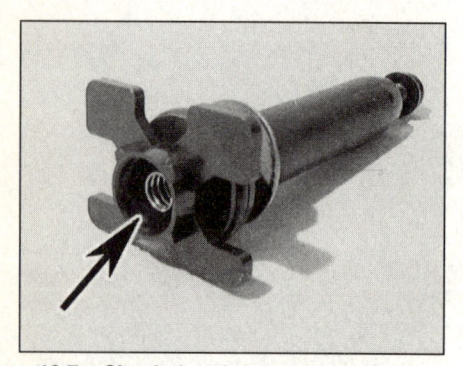

10.7c Check that the spring is installed (arrowed)

10.7d Align the holder and fit it into the piston

10.8a Turn the diaphragm inside out as shown . . .

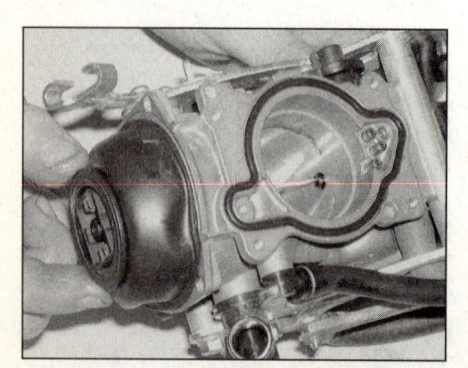

10.8b . . . then install the piston . . .

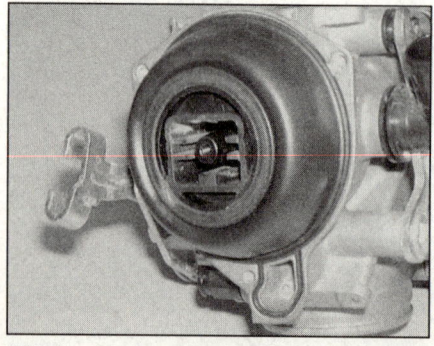

10.8c . . . and press the diaphragm rim into the groove

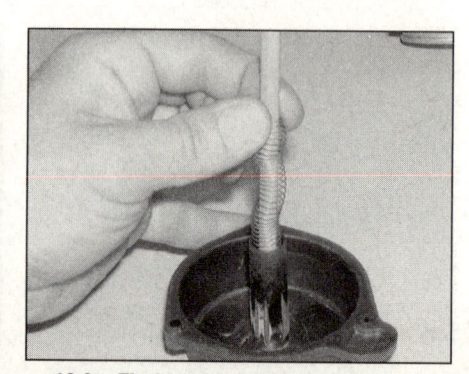

10.9a Fit the spring into the cover . . .

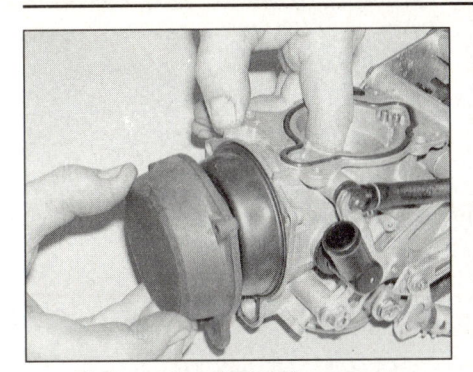

Fuel and exhaust systems – carburettor models 4A•13

10.9b . . . then install the cover as described

keep it raised so the diaphragm stays inside out – this prevents the rim popping out of the groove **(see illustration)**. Make sure the diaphragm rim stays seated in its groove and does not get pinched by the cover, then install the cover screws and tighten them securely.

10 Install the carburettors (see Section 7).

11 Throttle cables – removal and installation

Warning: Refer to the precautions given in Section 1 before proceeding.

Removal

1 Remove the fuel tank and the air filter housing (see Sections 2 and 4). Mark each cable according to its location.
2 Slacken the opening (top) cable adjuster locknut, then unscrew the adjuster until the captive nut is free, then slip the adjuster out of the bracket and detach the cable nipple from the carburettors **(see illustrations)**. Now unscrew the closing (bottom) cable adjuster until the captive nut is free, then slip the adjuster out of the bracket and detach the cable nipple from the carburettors **(see illustration)**. Withdraw the cables from the machine noting the correct routing of each cable.
3 On VTR models, slacken the cable elbow nuts at the throttle pulley housing, then remove the housing screws and lift off the top half **(see illustrations)**. Detach the cable nipples from the pulley **(see illustration)**. Detach the lower housing half from the handlebar, then fully unscrew the closing (rear) cable elbow nut and remove the cable from the housing **(see illustration)**. Thread the

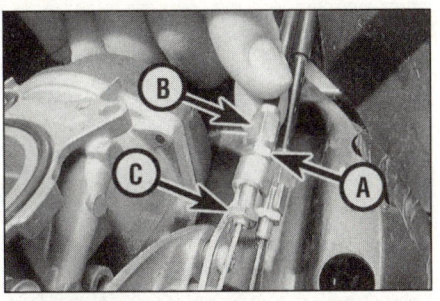

11.2a Slacken the locknut (A), then unscrew the adjuster (B) until the captive nut (C) is free of its lug, then slip the cable out of the bracket . . .

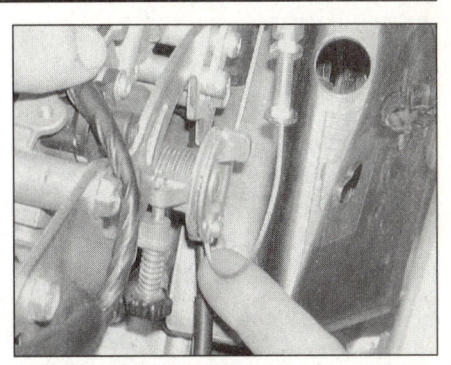

11.2b . . . and detach the cable end from the carburettor

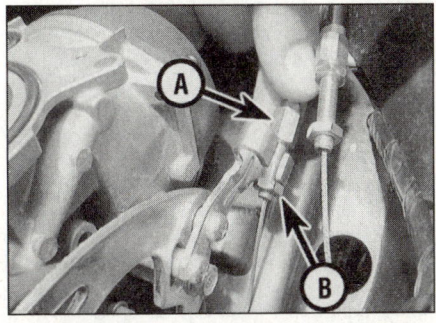

11.2c Unscrew the adjuster (A) until the captive nut (B) is clear of its lug, then slip the cable out of the bracket . . .

11.2d . . . and detach the cable end from the carburettor

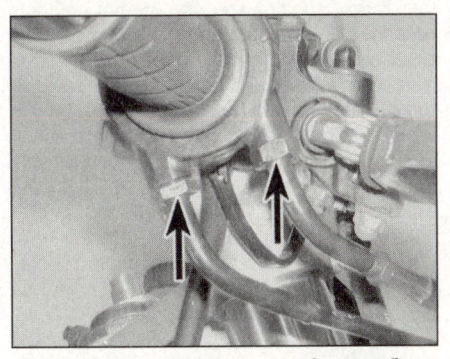

11.3a Slacken the elbow nuts (arrowed) . . .

11.3b . . . and remove the screws . . .

11.3c . . . then lift off the housing . . .

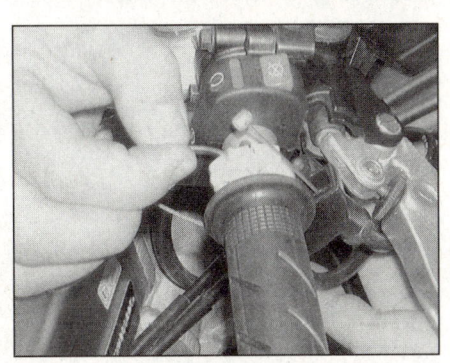

11.3d . . . and detach the cable ends from the pulley

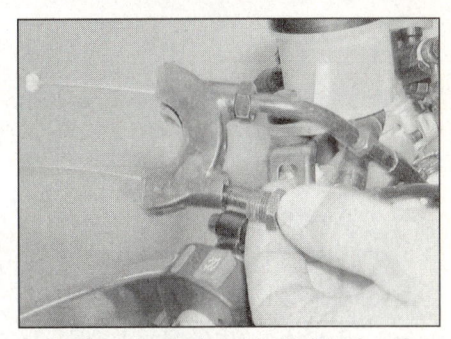

11.3e Remove the lower half of the housing, unscrew the decelerator cable elbow nut and withdraw the cable from the housing . . .

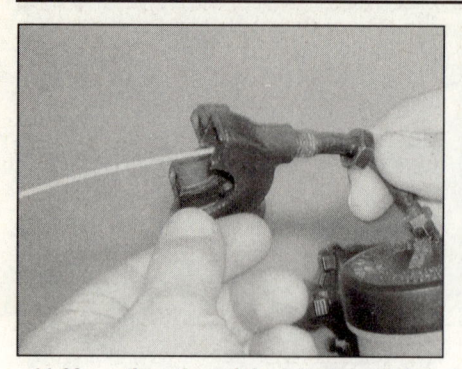

4A•14 Fuel and exhaust systems – carburettor models

11.3f ... then thread the housing off the accelerator cable elbow

11.5a Thread the housing onto the cable ...

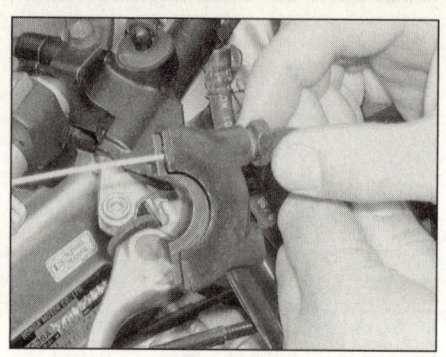

11.5b ... then thread on the nut

housing off the opening (front) cable elbow and withdraw the cable **(see illustration)**. Mark each cable to ensure it is connected correctly on installation.

4 On XL models, pull the rubber boot back off the throttle housing on the handlebar. Undo the throttle housing screws and remove the front half – unless an angled screwdriver is available you may have to remove the handguard. Remove the cable guide and displace the cables from the housing, noting how they fit, then detach the cable nipples from the pulley. Mark each cable to ensure it is connected correctly on installation.

Installation

5 On VTR models, fit the opening cable elbow into the front socket of the lower half of the throttle pulley housing and thread the housing onto it as far as it will go without becoming tight on the bottom of the threads – the elbow must stay loose so that it aligns itself – then thread the nut onto the adjuster, again not so that it is tight **(see illustrations)**. Fit the closing cable into the rear socket and tighten the nut finger-tight **(see illustration 11.3e)**. Fit the lower half of the housing onto the handlebar, then lubricate the cable nipples with multi-purpose grease and install them into the throttle pulley **(see illustration 11.3d)**. Fit the top half of the housing onto the handlebar, making sure the pin locates in the hole in the top of the handlebar, then install the screws and tighten them securely **(see illustrations 11.3c and 11.3b)**. Now tighten both cable elbow nuts **(see illustration 11.3a)**.

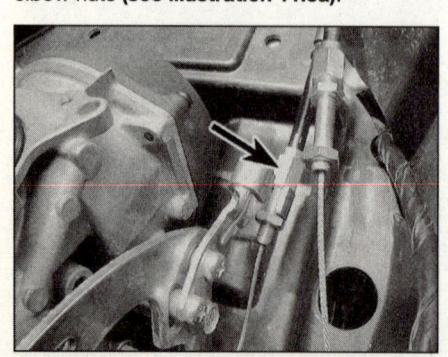

6 On XL models, lubricate the cable nipples with multi-purpose grease and install them into the throttle pulley at the handlebar. Fit the cables into the housing, making sure they locate correctly. Install the cable guide, then join the housing halves and tighten the screws, aligning the housing mating surfaces with the punchmark on the handlebar. Fit the rubber boot. If removed, install the handguard.

7 Feed the cables through to the carburettors, making sure they are correctly routed. The cables must not interfere with any other component and should not be kinked or bent sharply.

8 Lubricate the closing cable nipple with multi-purpose grease and fit it into the lower socket on the carburettor throttle cam **(see illustration 11.2d)**. Fit the cable adjuster into the lower bracket, locating the nut against the lug so that it is captive **(see illustration 11.2c)**, then thread the adjuster into the nut until it is tight **(see illustration)**. Lubricate the opening cable nipple with multi-purpose grease and fit it into the upper socket on the carburettor throttle cam **(see illustration 11.2b)**. Fit the opening cable adjuster into the upper bracket, locating the nut against the lug so that it is captive, then thread the top nut down the adjuster, but do not yet tighten it **(see illustration 11.2a)**. Thread the adjuster in or out until the specified amount of cable freeplay is obtained (see Chapter 1). Tighten the locknut against the bracket.

9 Operate the throttle to check that it opens and closes freely.

10 Check and adjust the throttle cable freeplay if required (see Chapter 1). Turn the handlebars back and forth to make sure the cable doesn't cause the steering to bind.

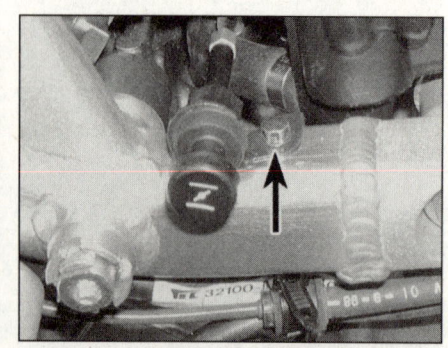

11 Install the air filter housing and the fuel tank (see Sections 4 and 2).

12 Start the engine and check that the idle speed does not rise as the handlebars are turned. If it does, the throttle cable is routed incorrectly. Correct the problem before riding the motorcycle.

12 Choke cable – removal and installation

Removal

1 Remove the fuel tank and the air filter housing (see Sections 2 and 4).
2 Refer to Section 7 and displace the carburettors, then detach the choke plungers as described.
3 On VTR models, unscrew the bolt securing the choke knob to the left-hand lower frame rail **(see illustration)**. Withdraw the cable, noting its routing.
4 On XL models, refer to Chapter 6, Section 5, and follow the procedure for clutch lever removal, which incorporates the choke lever. Displace the choke lever and free the cable end from it, then slip the cable out of its holder. Withdraw the cable from the machine noting its routing.

Installation

5 Installation is the reverse of removal. Make sure the cable is correctly routed – it must not interfere with any other component and should not be kinked or bent sharply. Check the operation of the cable (see Chapter 1, Section 11).

13 Exhaust system – removal and installation

⚠ **Warning:** *If the engine has been running the exhaust system will be very hot. Allow the system to cool before carrying out any work.*

11.8 Tighten the adjuster (arrowed) onto the bracket

12.3 Unscrew the bolt (arrowed) and remove the cable

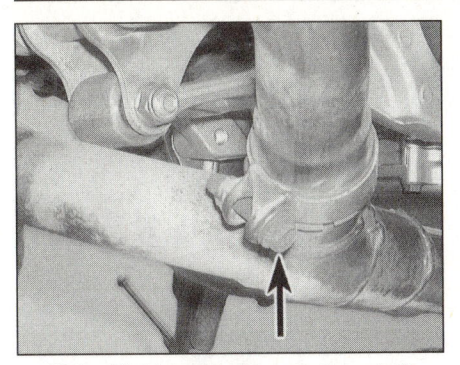

Fuel and exhaust systems – carburettor models 4A•15

13.2a Right-hand silencer clamp bolt (arrowed)

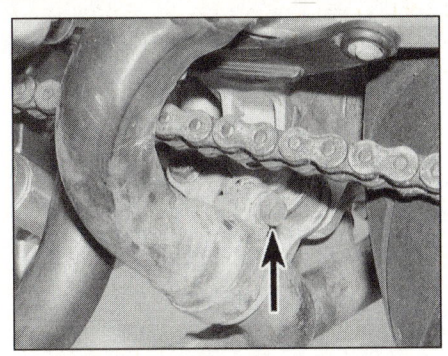

13.2b Left-hand silencer clamp bolt (arrowed)

13.3a Silencer upper mounting bolt (arrowed) – VTR models

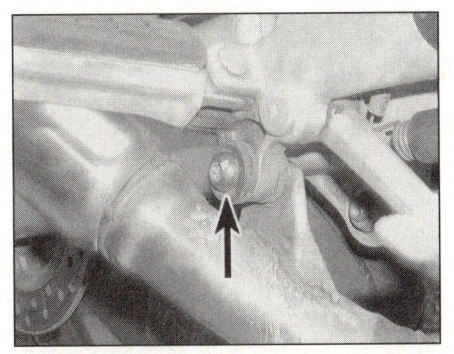

13.3b Silencer lower mounting bolt (arrowed) – VTR models

13.3c Silencer mounting bolts (arrowed) – XL models

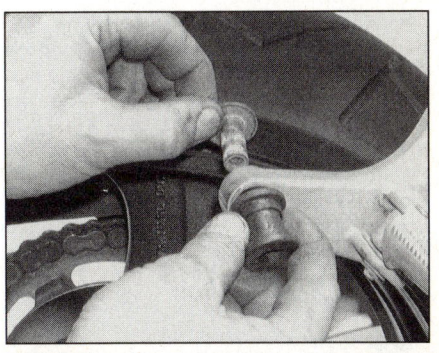

13.3d Note the arrangement of the collars and rubber mounts for the silencers

Note: The exhaust system can be removed as a complete assembly (with the exception of the rear cylinder header pipe), but it can be tricky and requires two people.

Removal

Silencers

1 On XL models, remove the seat cowling (see Chapter 8). If required remove the oxygen sensor, or alternatively just disconnect the wiring connector and feed the wiring back to the sensor (see Chapter 4B, Section 5).
2 Slacken the clamp bolt securing the silencer in the downpipe assembly **(see illustrations)**.
3 Unscrew the two silencer mounting bolts, then draw the silencer back out of the downpipe assembly and remove it **(see illustrations)**. Note the arrangement of the washers, collars

> **HAYNES HiNT**
> Exhaust system clamp bolts tend to become corroded and seized. It is advisable to spray them with a penetrating fluid before attempting to slacken them.

and rubbers on the silencer mountings **(see illustration)**. Fit new rubbers if the old ones are damaged, deformed or deteriorated. Check the condition of the sealing ring between the silencer and downpipe assembly and replace it with a new one if it is damaged or deformed **(see illustration 13.9b)**. Honda recommend always using a new one, but they can be difficult to remove, and unless they are damaged they are re-usable. It is too easy to damage a new one trying to install it to make it

worthwhile destroying a good one that is already installed.
4 On XL models, you can separate the heat shields from the silencers by unscrewing the bolts that secure them – note the collars and rubber bushes.

Downpipe assembly

5 Remove the belly pan (see Chapter 8, Section 4).
6 Remove the silencers (see above).
7 Slacken the clamp bolt securing the rear cylinder header pipe in the downpipe assembly **(see illustration)**. Unscrew the two nuts securing the downpipe to the front cylinder head, then remove the downpipe assembly **(see illustration)**. Remove the gasket from the port in the cylinder head and discard it as a new one must be used **(see illustration)**.

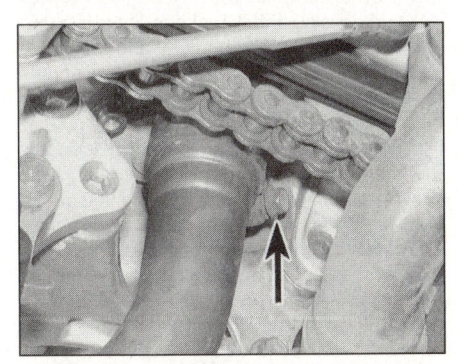

13.7a Rear cylinder header pipe clamp bolt (arrowed) . . .

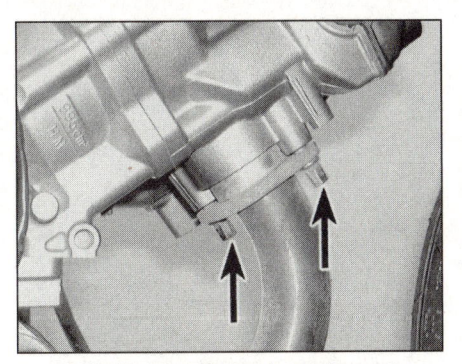

13.7b Front cylinder downpipe nuts (arrowed)

13.7c Remove the old gasket from the head

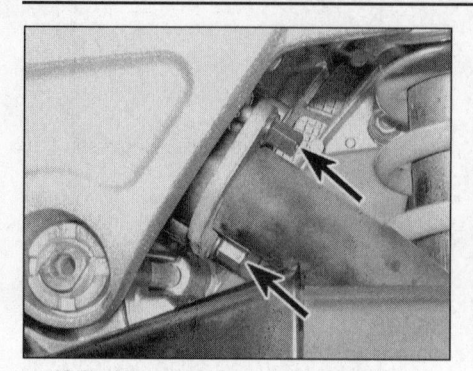

4A•16 Fuel and exhaust systems – carburettor models

13.8a Unscrew the nuts (arrowed) . . .

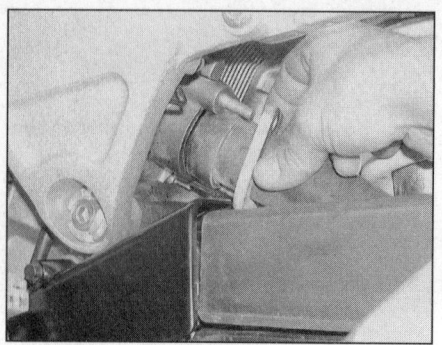

13.8b . . . and remove the rear cylinder downpipe

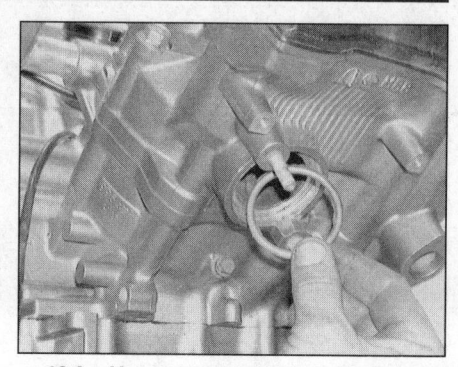

13.9a Use a new gasket in each head port . . .

Check the condition of the sealing ring between the rear cylinder header pipe and the downpipe assembly and replace it with a new one if necessary, bearing in mind the information in Step 3 above.

8 Unscrew the two nuts securing the header pipe to the rear cylinder head and remove the pipe **(see illustrations)**. Remove the gasket from the port in the cylinder head and discard it as a new one must be used **(see illustration 13.7c)**.

Installation

9 Installation is the reverse of removal, noting the following:
a) Use new gaskets in each cylinder head port *(see illustration)*.
b) Use new sealing rings between the rear cylinder header pipe and the downpipe assembly, and between the silencers and the downpipe assembly if required, bearing in mind the information in Step 3 above *(see illustration)*.
c) Leave all fasteners loose until the entire system has been installed, making alignment of the various sections easier. Tighten the silencer mountings last.
d) Apply some copper grease to the clamp bolts to prevent them from seizing up.
e) Tighten the front downpipe and rear header pipe nuts and the clamp bolts to the torque setting specified at the beginning of the Chapter.
f) Run the engine and check the system for leaks.

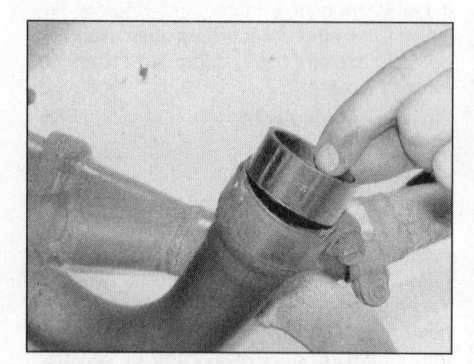

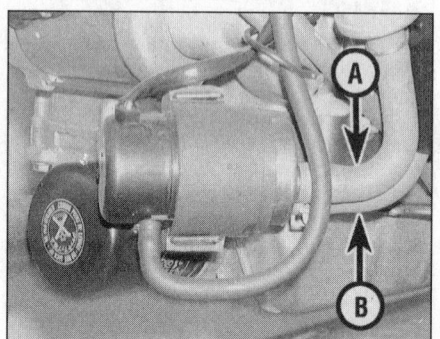

13.9b . . . and new sealing rings if the old ones are damaged or deteriorated

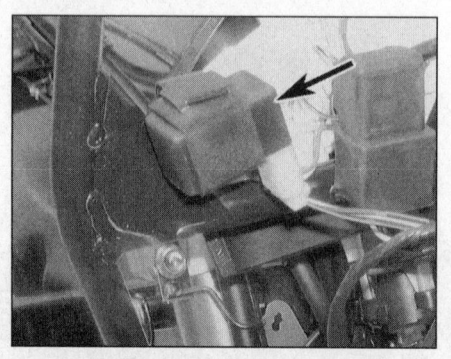

14.1a Fuel pump assembly – inlet hose (A), outlet hose (B)

14.1b Fuel cut-off relay (arrowed)

14.5 Fuel pump wiring connector

14 Fuel pump and relay – check, removal and installation (XL models)

> **Warning:** Refer to the precautions given in Section 1 before starting work.

Check

1 The fuel pump is mounted at the front of the engine on the left-hand side **(see illustration)** – remove the belly-pan to access it (see Chapter 8, Section 4). The relay is mounted on the right-hand side of the fairing bracket in front of the instrument cluster **(see illustration)** – remove the fairing to access it (see Chapter 8).
2 The fuel pump is controlled through the fuel cut-off relay so that it runs whenever the ignition is switched ON and the ignition is operative (i.e. only when the engine is turning over). As soon as the ignition is killed, the relay will cut off the fuel pump's electrical supply (so that there is no risk of fuel being sprayed out under pressure in the event of an accident).
3 It should be possible to hear or feel the fuel pump running whenever the engine is turning over – either place your ear close beside the pump or feel it with your fingertips. If you can't hear or feel anything, check the circuit fuse (see Chapter 9). If the fuse is good, check the pump and relay for loose or corroded connections or physical damage and rectify as necessary.
4 Check for full battery voltage at the relay's black/white terminal with the ignition switch ON. If there is no battery voltage, there is a fault in the circuit between the relay and the fuse – turn off the ignition, then trace and rectify the fault as outlined in Chapter 9; refer to the wiring diagrams at the end of that Chapter.
5 If battery voltage was present, disconnect the wiring connectors from the relay and ignition control module, and trace the wiring from the pump and disconnect it at the black 2-pin wiring connector **(see illustration)** – remove the seat to access the ICU connector (see Chapter 8), and either raise or remove the fuel tank to access the fuel pump wiring connector (unless you have small hands) (see Section 2). Using an ohmmeter, check for continuity between the blue/yellow wire on the

Fuel and exhaust systems – carburettor models 4A•17

relay's wire connector and the blue/yellow wire on the control module's wire connector. Check for continuity between the black/blue wire on the relay's wire connector and the black/blue wire on the fuel pump's wire connector. Continuity should be indicated in all tests; if not, trace and rectify the fault as described in Chapter 9. Reconnect all wire connectors.

6 If the pump still does not work, trace the wiring from the pump and disconnect it at the black 2-pin wiring connector (see Step 5) **(see illustration 14.5)**. Using a fully charged 12 volt battery and two insulated jumper wires, connect the positive (+ve) terminal of the battery to the pump's black/blue terminal, and the negative (–ve) terminal of the battery to the pump's green terminal. The pump should operate. If the pump does not operate it must be replaced.

7 If the pump works, check for battery voltage at the black/blue terminal on the supply side of the connector. If there is no voltage, check the wiring as above. If all the relevant wiring and connectors are good, then the relay is at fault. The only definitive test of the relay is to substitute one that is known to be good. If substitution does not cure the problem, bear in mind that the ignition control module could be faulty.

8 If the pump operates but is thought to be delivering an insufficient amount of fuel, first check that all fuel hoses are in good condition and not pinched or trapped. Check that the in-line filter, the filters in the fuel tank and the fuel delivery hoses are not blocked.

9 The fuel pump's output can be checked as follows: make sure the ignition switch is OFF.

10 Release the clamp securing the fuel outlet hose to the outlet union on the fuel pump and detach the hose, being prepared to catch any residual fuel **(see illustration 14.1a)**. Connect an auxiliary hose of the same internal diameter to the union. Place the end into a graduated beaker suitable for holding petrol (gasoline).

11 Disconnect the fuel cut-off relay wiring connector. Using a short length of insulated jumper wire, connect across the black/white and the black/blue wire terminals of the connector.

12 Turn the ignition switch ON and let fuel flow from the pump into the beaker for 5 seconds, then switch the ignition OFF.

13 Measure the amount of fuel that has flowed into the beaker, then multiply that amount by 12 to determine the fuel pump flow rate per minute. The minimum flow rate required is 700 cc per minute. If the flow rate recorded is below this, then the fuel pump must be replaced with a new one.

Removal

14 Make sure the ignition is switched OFF.
15 The fuel pump is mounted at the front of the engine on the left-hand side **(see illustration 14.1a)** – remove the belly-pan to access it (see Chapter 8, Section 4). Trace the wiring from the pump and disconnect it at the black 2-pin wiring connector – either raise or remove the fuel tank to access it, unless you have small hands (see Section 2) **(see illustration 14.5)**. Make a note or sketch of which fuel hose fits where as an aid to installation. Using a rag to mop up any spilled fuel, disconnect the two fuel hoses from the front of the fuel pump, and the hose from the underside of the pump body **(see illustration 14.1a)**. Displace the pump from its mounting and remove it.

16 The relay is mounted on the right-hand side of the fairing bracket in front of the instrument cluster **(see illustration 14.1b)** – remove the fairing to access it (see Chapter 8). Disconnect the relay wiring connector and remove the relay from its mounting.

Installation

17 Installation is a reverse of the removal procedure. Make sure the fuel hoses are correctly and securely fitted to the pump – the hose from the in-line filter attaches to the union marked INLET; the hose to the carburettors attaches to the other union **(see illustration 14.1a)**. Start the engine and check carefully that there are no leaks at the pipe connections.

15 Fuel warning light/gauge and sensor – check and replacement

Check

VTR-V, W, X and Y models and all XL models

1 The circuit consists of the sensor mounted in the fuel tank and the warning light mounted in the instrument panel. If the system malfunctions check first that the battery is fully charged and that the bulb and fuses are good (see Chapter 9).

2 If the warning light is permanently on, on VTR models remove the seat (see Chapter 8), then trace the wiring from the sensor in the fuel tank and disconnect it at the white 2-pin wiring connector **(see illustration 2.2a)**. On XL models remove the right-hand fairing side panel (see Chapter 8), then disconnect the wiring connectors from the switch, which is on the right-hand side of the tank **(see illustration 2.3a)**. Turn the ignition switch ON. If the warning light does not come on, replace the sensor with a new one. If it comes on, check for a short circuit to earth in the brown/black wire between the sensor and the light.

3 If the warning light does not come on at all, on VTR models remove the seat (see Chapter 8), then trace the wiring from the sensor in the fuel tank and disconnect it at the white 2-pin wiring connector **(see illustration 2.2a)**. On XL models remove the right-hand fairing side panel (see Chapter 8), then disconnect the wiring connectors from the switch, which is on the right-hand side of the tank **(see illustration 2.3a)**. Using an insulated jumper wire, connect between the two sensor wires. Turn the ignition switch ON. If the warning comes on, replace the sensor with a new one. If it does not come on, check the wiring between the sensor and the light for continuity, referring to the *Wiring Diagrams* at the end of Chapter 9.

4 On VTR models, if the wiring is good, displace the instrument cluster (see Chapter 9), and check for battery voltage between the black/brown (+ve) and green(–ve) wire terminals on the back of the instrument cluster with the ignition ON. If no voltage is present, check the wiring and connectors, referring to the *Wiring Diagrams* at the end of Chapter 9.

VTR-1 to 6 models

5 The circuit consists of the sensor in the fuel tank, and the LCD gauge, which is part of the instrument cluster printed circuit board. If the system malfunctions first check that the fuses are good (see Chapter 9).

6 If the fuel gauge display does not function as it should, disconnect the sensor wiring connector. Turn the ignition ON – segment E on the gauge should be blinking. Now connect between the terminals in the loom side of the connector using an auxiliary jumper wire – all segments on the gauge should come on. If both results are good the gauge is working correctly – go to Step 7 and check the sensor. If the gauge does not do as described check the wiring and connectors between the fuel tank and the instrument cluster for continuity using the wiring diagrams at the end of Chapter 9. Also check for continuity to earth (ground) in the green and green/black wires. If continuity (zero resistance) is not present, locate the break or short in the wire or faulty connector and repair or replace as required.

7 To check the sensor remove it from the tank (Steps 9 and 10). Connect an ohmmeter between the wire terminals in the connector. Check the resistance reading with the sensor float arm in the empty and full positions – there should be 80 to 90 ohms in the empty position and 4 to 10 ohms in the full position. If the readings differ from those specified replace the sensor with a new one.

Replacement

8 See Chapter 9, Section 17, for replacement of the warning light bulb.
9 To replace the sensor, remove the fuel tank and drain it (see Section 2).
10 On VTR models, free the wiring from the tank. Unscrew the nuts securing the sensor and draw it out of the tank **(see illustration)**.

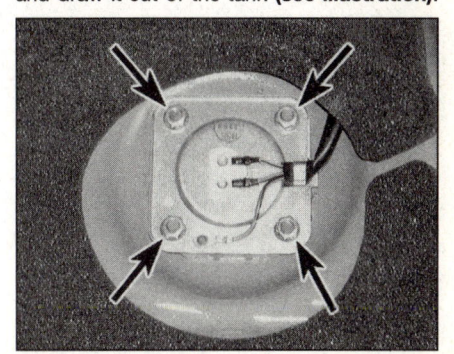

15.10 Fuel level sensor nuts (arrowed) – VTR models

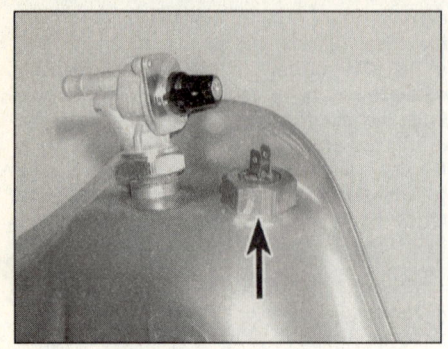

4A•18 Fuel and exhaust systems – carburettor models

15.11 Fuel level sensor (arrowed) – XL models

Discard the O-ring. Fit a new O-ring onto the sensor and install it in the tank. Tighten the nuts securely.

11 On XL models, unscrew the sensor and draw it out of the tank **(see illustration)**. Discard the sealing washer. Fit a new sealing washer onto the sensor then install it in the tank and tighten it securely.

12 Install the tank (see Section 2), and check carefully for leaks before using the bike.

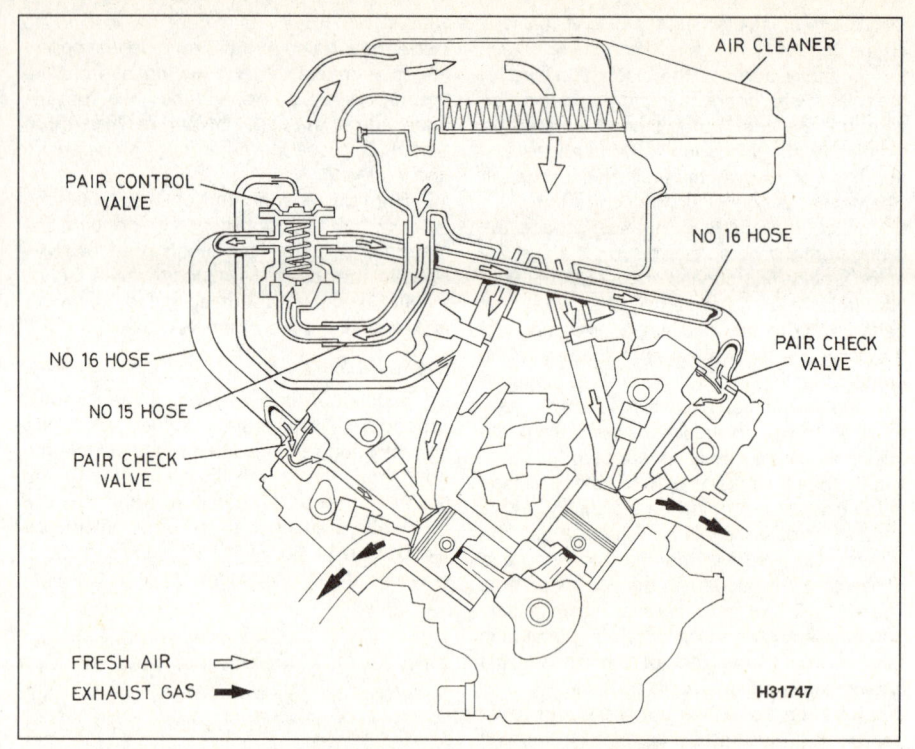

16 Pulse secondary air injection (PAIR) system components

General information

1 To reduce the amount of unburned hydrocarbons released in the exhaust gases, a pulse secondary air (PAIR) system is fitted to all models except some European market VTR-V, W, X and Y models. The system consists of the control valve (mounted under the air filter housing), the check valves (fitted to the front and rear cylinder valve covers) and the hoses linking them **(see illustrations)**. The control valve is controlled by engine vacuum on VTR models and XL-X, Y, 1 and 2 models, and electronically by the ECU on XL-3 models onward.

2 Under certain operating conditions, the vacuum or a signal from the ECU (according to model) opens up the PAIR control valve which then allows filtered air to be drawn through the check valves and cylinder head passages and into the exhaust ports. The air mixes with the exhaust gases, causing any unburned particles of fuel in the mixture to be burnt in the exhaust port/pipes. This process changes a considerable amount of hydrocarbons and carbon monoxide into relatively harmless carbon dioxide and water. The check valves in the valve covers are fitted to prevent the flow of exhaust gases back up the cylinder head passages and into the air filter housing.

Testing

Control valve

3 Remove the valve from the motorcycle (see below).

4 On VTR models and XL-X, Y, 1 and 2 models check the operation of the control valve by blowing through the lower (air filter housing) hose union; air should flow freely through the upper (check valve) hose unions. Apply a vacuum to the vacuum hose; no air should now flow through the valve if it is functioning correctly. Renew the valve if faulty.

5 On XL-3 models onward check the operation of the control valve by blowing through the air filter housing hose union; no air should flow through the check valve hose unions **(see illustration)**. Now connect battery voltage (12 volts) across the valve wiring connector terminals and repeat the check; air should now flow freely through the valve if it is functioning correctly. Check the resistance of the control valve solenoid by connecting an ohmmeter between its connector terminals and compare the reading obtained to that given in the Specifications. Replace the valve with a new one if faulty.

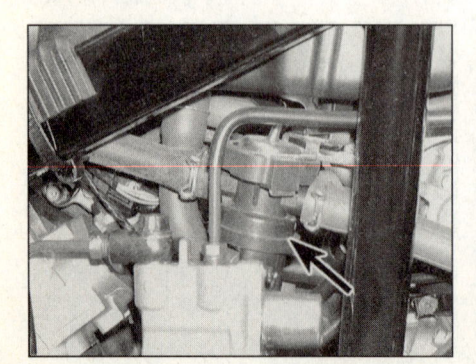

16.1a Pulse secondary air (PAIR) system

16.1b PAIR system control valve (arrowed) – XL-X, Y, 1 and 2 models

16.1c PAIR system control valve (arrowed) – XL-3 models onward

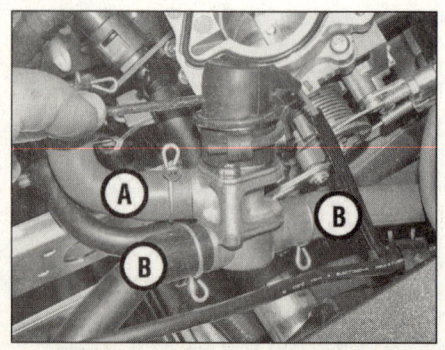

16.5 Air filter hose (A), check valve hoses (B)

Fuel and exhaust systems – carburettor models 4A•19

Check valves

6 Disconnect the check valve hoses from the control valve (see below).
7 Check each valve by blowing and sucking on the hose end. Air should flow through the hose only when blown down the hose and not when sucked back up. If this is not the case the check valve is faulty, but before buying new components it is worth disassembling the valve (see below) and checking whether the problem is caused by a build-up of carbon deposits, which can be scraped off and cleaned up.

Removal and installation
Control valve

8 Remove the air filter housing (see Section 4).
9 Release the clamps and detach the hoses from the valve, noting which fits where **(see illustration 16.1b or c)**. On XL-3 models onward disconnect the wiring connector **(see illustration)**. Remove the valve.
10 Installation is the reverse of removal.

Check valves

11 On VTR models, to access the front cylinder valve cover remove the fairing (see Chapter 8). Unscrew the two oil cooler mounting bolts, noting the collars, and displace the cooler forward. There is no need to detach the pipes. Also remove the bolts securing the cooler mounting bracket to the frame and remove the bracket.

16.9 PAIR control valve wiring connector (arrowed)

12 On XL models, to access the front cylinder valve cover remove the fairing side panels (see Chapter 8). Also remove the trim clips securing the heat shield above the valve cover and remove the shield. To release the trim clips unscrew the centre of the clip, then pull the body of the clip out.
13 On all models, to access the rear cylinder valve cover remove the fuel tank (see Section 2).
14 To remove either valve, first release the clamp and detach the air hose from its union. Unscrew the bolts securing the check valve cover and remove the cover. Remove the reed valve assembly components, noting which way around they are fitted.
15 Installation is the reverse of removal. Make sure the reed valve assembly components are correctly fitted. Apply a suitable non-permanent thread locking compound to the cover bolts and tighten them to the specified torque.

17 Evaporative emission control (EVAP) system components (California models)

General information

1 To minimise the escape into the atmosphere of fuel vapour from the tank and carburettors, an evaporative emissions control system is fitted to all California models **(see illustration)**. The fuel tank filler cap is sealed and a charcoal canister is mounted on the front of the engine. The canister collects the fuel vapours generated when the motorcycle is parked and stores them until they can be cleared from the canister, via the control valves, into the throttle body inlet tracts to be burned by the engine during normal combustion. The system control valves are opened and closed by the vacuum created in the inlet tracts when the engine is running. Vapour from the fuel tank is controlled by the purge control valve, while vapour from the carburettors is controlled by the CAV (carburettor air vent) valve.
2 The valves should be tested if there is a problem starting the engine when it is hot.

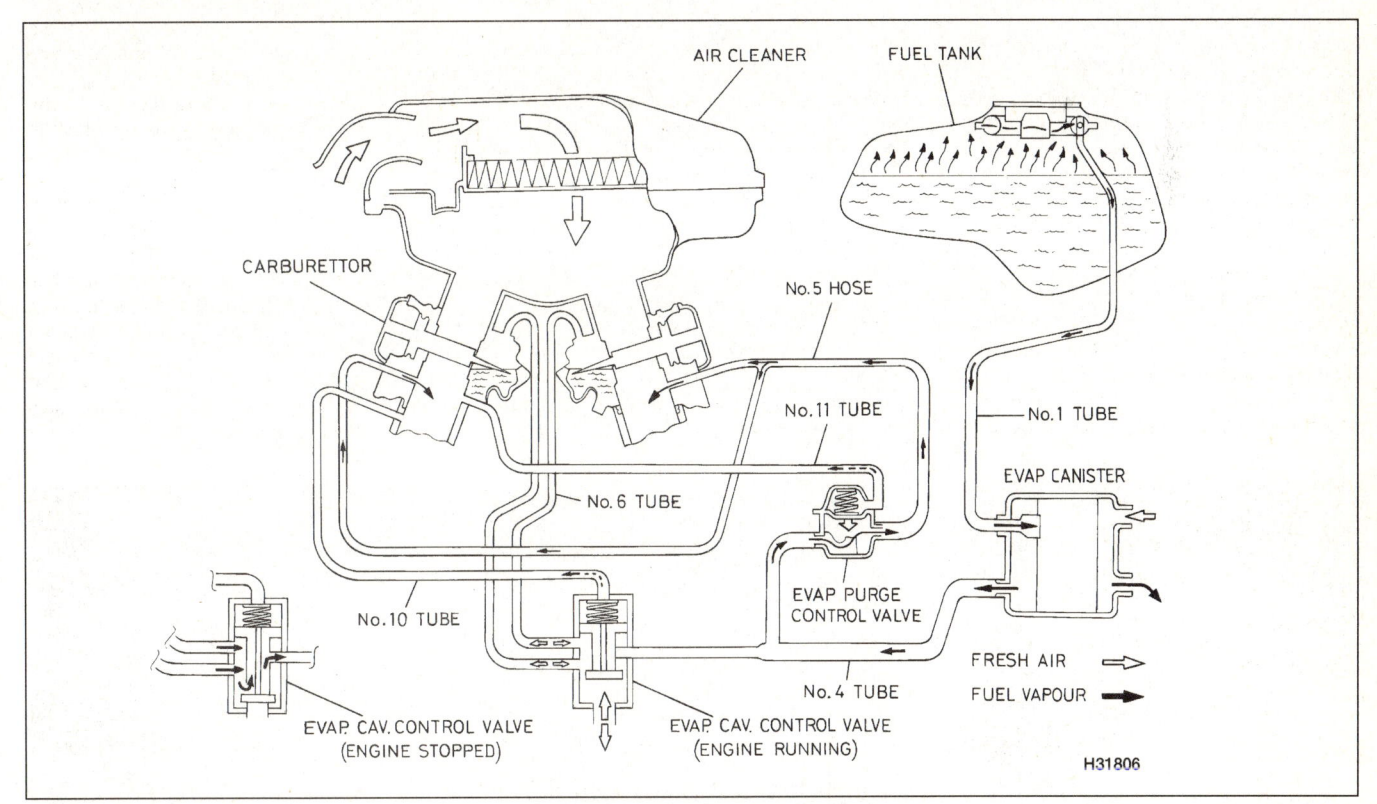

17.1 Evaporative emission control (EVAP) system

Testing

Control valves

3 Remove the relevant valve from the motorcycle (see below).
4 Check the operation of the purge control valve by blowing through the inlet (canister hose) union; air should flow freely through the valve and out the outlet hose union. Connect an auxiliary hose to the vacuum hose union and apply a vacuum; no air should now flow through the valve if it is functioning correctly. Also check that the valve is able to hold the vacuum once it is applied. Renew the valve if faulty.
5 Check the operation of the CAV control valve by blowing through the outlet (canister hose) union; air should flow freely through the valve and out the inlet (carburettor vent) unions. Connect an auxiliary hose to the vacuum hose union and apply a vacuum; air should now only flow in and out of the inlet (carburettor vent) unions if it is functioning correctly. Also check that the valve is able to hold the vacuum once it is applied. Renew the valve if faulty.

Charcoal canister

6 No testing of the canister is possible, if it is thought to be faulty it must be renewed.

Removal and installation

Control valves

7 To replace the purge control valve, remove the air filter housing (see Section 4). The CAV valve is above the canister on the front of the engine and is accessible.
8 Disconnect the vacuum hoses from the valve, noting which fits where, then release the valve from its mounting.
9 Installation is the reverse of removal.

Charcoal canister

10 Disconnect the hoses from the canister, noting their correct fitted locations.
11 Unscrew the mounting bolts and remove the canister from the front of the engine, taking care not to lose the collars and spacer from the mounting rubbers.
12 Installation is the reverse of removal.

Chapter 4B
Fuel system – fuel injection models

Contents

Air filter	see Chapter 1	Fuel system hoses	11
Air filter housing and air intake system	2	Fuel tank	see Chapter 4A
Catalytic converter	12	Fuel warning light and sensor	see Chapter 4A
Engine control unit (ECU)	5	General information and precautions	1
Evaporative emission control (EVAP) system	see Chapter 4A	Idle speed check	see Chapter 1
Exhaust system	see Chapter 4A	Ignition system and immobiliser	see Chapter 5
Fast idle cable (XL-3 to 6 models)	7	Intake air control valve (XL-7 models onward)	8
Fuel injection system description	3	Pulse secondary air (PAIR) system	see Chapter 4A
Fuel injection system fault diagnosis	4	Starter valves (XL-3 to 6 models)	7
Fuel injection system components	5	Throttle bodies	6
Fuel pump	10	Throttle cable check and adjustment	see Chapter 1
Fuel pressure check	9	Throttle cables	see Chapter 4A
Fuel system check	see Chapter 1		

Degrees of difficulty

Easy, suitable for novice with little experience	Fairly easy, suitable for beginner with some experience	Fairly difficult, suitable for competent DIY mechanic	Difficult, suitable for experienced DIY mechanic	Very difficult, suitable for expert DIY or professional

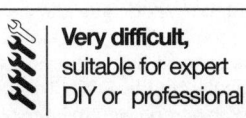

Specifications

Fuel
Grade .... Unleaded. Minimum 91 RON (Research Octane Number) for Europe. 91 RON for Mexico and Brazil. Minimum pump octane number 90 for the US
Fuel tank capacity (including reserve) .... 25.0 litres
Reserve volume (after light comes on) .... approx. 4.0 litres

Fuel injection system
Throttle body model
   XL-3 model GQ45A
   XL-4 to 6 models GQ46A
   XL-7 model onwards GQ46B
Idle speed .... 1200 ± 100 rpm
Starter valve synchronisation – max. difference between bodies ..... 20 mm Hg
Manifold absolute pressure at idle .... 200 to 250 mm Hg
Fuel pressure at specified idle speed .... 46 to 53 psi (3.2 to 3.7 Bar)
Minimum fuel flow rate .... 270 cc every 10 seconds

4B•2 Fuel system – fuel injection models

Fuel injection system test data

Note: *All values given are only accurate at 20°C (68°F)*

Air intake system control valve resistance	28 to 32 ohms @ 20°C
Camshaft position (CMP) sensor minimum peak voltage output	0.7 volt
Engine coolant temperature (ECT) sensor resistance	
XL-3 to 6 models	2.0 to 3.0 K-ohms
XL-7 model onwards	2.3 to 2.6 K-ohms
Fuel injector resistance	
XL-3 to 6 models	13.4 to 14.2 ohms
XL-7 model onwards	10.5 to 14.5 ohms
Ignition pulse generator minimum peak voltage output	0.7 volt
Intake air control valve (IACV) resistance – XL-7 model onwards	99 to 121 ohms @ 25°C
Intake air temperature (IAT) sensor resistance	1 to 4 K-ohms
Oxygen sensor heater resistance	10 to 40 ohms

Emission control

PAIR system control valve resistance	20 to 24 ohms @ 20°C

Torque settings

Engine coolant temperature (ECT) sensor	23 Nm
Fuel injector holder bolts	
XL-3 to 6 models	5.4 Nm
XL-7 model onwards	5.1 Nm
Fuel rail and delivery pipe bolts (XL-3 to 6 models)	5.4 Nm
Fuel delivery pipe banjo bolt to fuel pump (XL-3 to 6 models)	22 Nm
Oxygen sensor	44 Nm

1 General information and precautions

General information

The fuel supply system consists of the fuel tank with internal strainers and level sensor, an external fuel pump, the fuel hoses and rails, the injectors, the throttle bodies, the throttle cables, and on XL-3 to 6 models the idle speed adjuster and fast idle cable for cold starting. From the XL-7 model, idle speed and fast idle speed for cold starting is set automatically by the ECU. The fuel pump is switched on and off with the engine via a relay. The injection system, known as PGM-FI, supplies fuel and air to the engine via 42 mm throttle bodies. There is one injector per cylinder. The injectors are operated by the Engine Control Unit (ECU) using the information obtained from the various sensors it monitors – refer to Section 4 for more information on the operation of the fuel injection system.

All models have a low fuel warning light incorporated in the instrument cluster, actuated by a level sensor inside the fuel tank. The warning light comes on when there is approximately 4.0 litres of fuel left.

Many of the fuel system service procedures are considered routine maintenance items and for that reason are covered in Chapter 1.

Note: *Individual engine management system components can be checked but not repaired. If system troubles occur, and the faulty component can be isolated, the only cure for the problem in most cases is to replace the part with a new one. Keep in mind that most electronic parts, once purchased, cannot be returned. To avoid unnecessary expense, make very sure the faulty component has been positively identified before buying a new part.*

Precautions

Warning: *Petrol (gasoline) is extremely flammable, so take extra precautions when you work on any part of the fuel system. Always remove the battery (see Chapter 9). Don't smoke or allow open flames or bare light bulbs near the work area, and don't work in a garage where a natural gas-type appliance is present. If you spill any fuel on your skin, rinse it off immediately with soap and water. When you perform any kind of work on the fuel system, wear safety glasses and have a fire extinguisher suitable for a class B type fire (flammable liquids) on hand.*

Some residual pressure will remain in the fuel feed hose and fuel rails after the motorcycle has been used. Before disconnecting any fuel hose, ensure the ignition is switched OFF and make sure you have plenty of clean rag and a suitable container for catching and storing the fuel. It is vital that no dirt or debris is allowed to enter any part of the system while a fuel hose is disconnected. Any foreign matter in the fuel system components could result in injector damage or malfunction. Ensure the ignition is switched OFF before disconnecting or reconnecting any fuel injection system wiring connector. If a connector is disconnected or reconnected with the ignition switched ON, the engine control unit (ECU) may be damaged.

Always perform service procedures in a well-ventilated area to prevent a build-up of fumes.

Never work in a building containing a gas appliance with a pilot light, or any other form of naked flame. Ensure that there are no naked light bulbs or any sources of flame or sparks nearby.

Do not smoke (or allow anyone else to smoke) while in the vicinity of petrol (gasoline) or of components containing it. Remember the possible presence of vapour from these sources and move well clear before smoking.

Check all electrical equipment belonging to the house, garage or workshop where work is being undertaken (see the *Safety first!* section of this manual). Remember that certain electrical appliances such as drills, cutters etc, create sparks in the normal course of operation and must not be used near petrol (gasoline) or any component containing it. Again, remember the possible presence of fumes before using electrical equipment.

Always mop up any spilt fuel and safely dispose of the rag used.

Any stored fuel that is drained off during servicing work must be kept in sealed containers that are suitable for holding petrol (gasoline), and clearly marked as such; the containers themselves should be kept in a safe place. Note that this last point applies equally to the fuel tank if it is removed from the machine; also remember to keep its filler cap closed at all times.

Read the *Safety first!* section of this manual carefully before starting work.

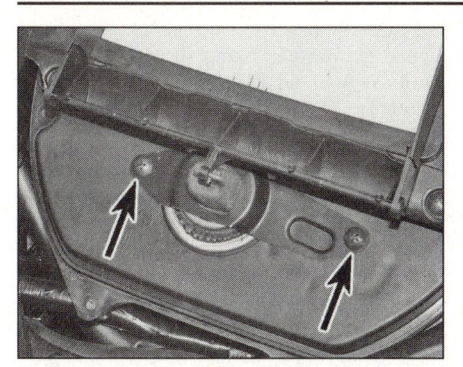

Fuel system – fuel injection models 4B•3

2.3a Undo the screws (arrowed), swivel the plate ...

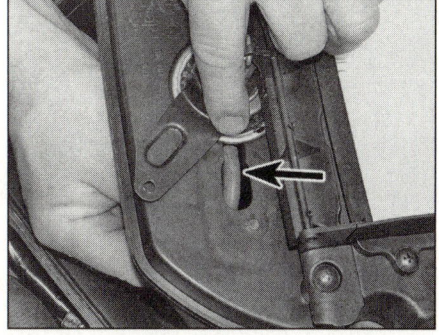

2.3b ... then lift the holder and disconnect the hose (arrowed)

2.4a Detach the front cylinder hose (arrowed) ...

2.4b ... and the rear cylinder hose

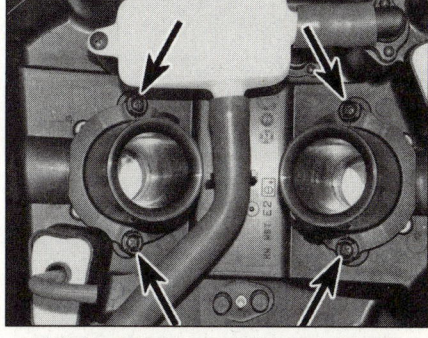

2.5 Undo the screws (arrowed) and remove the funnels

2.6 Undo the screws (arrowed) and lift the housing ...

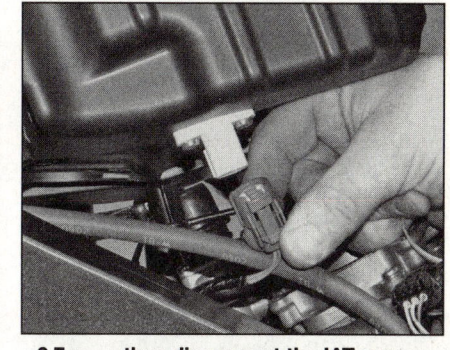

2.7a ... then disconnect the IAT sensor wiring connector ...

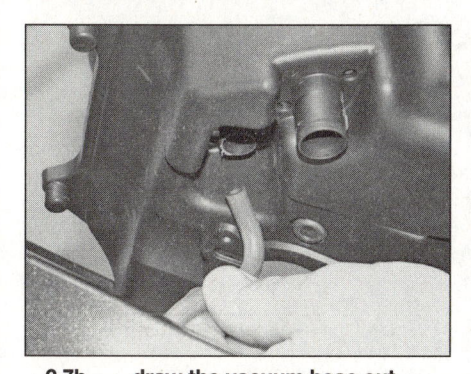

2.7b ... draw the vacuum hose out ...

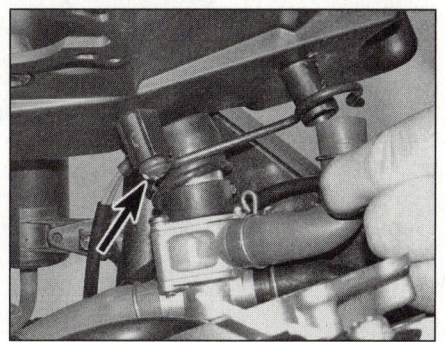

2.7c ... detach the PAIR hose and undo the PAIR valve screw (arrowed)

2.8 Make sure the seals are in good condition and correctly located

2 Air filter housing and air intake system

Air filter housing

Removal

1 Remove the fuel tank (see Chapter 4A).
2 Remove the air filter (see Chapter 1).
3 Undo the diaphragm valve set plate screws and move the plate round to expose the vacuum hose (see illustration). Lift the air filter holder and disconnect the vacuum hose from the diaphragm valve, then remove the holder (see illustration).
4 Release the clamps securing the front and rear cylinder breather hoses to the housing and detach the hoses (see illustrations).
5 Undo the air funnel screws and remove the funnels, noting which fits where (see illustration).
6 Undo the screws securing the filter housing to the intake ducts (see illustration).
7 Displace the housing up off the throttle bodies then disconnect the IAT sensor wiring connector and draw the vacuum hose out (see illustrations). Detach the PAIR system air hose, then undo the PAIR control valve screw and detach the valve (see illustration). Remove the air filter housing. Cover the throttle bodies with a clean rag.

Installation

8 Installation is the reverse of removal. Check the condition of the throttle body seals and fit new ones if necessary (see illustration). Make sure each seal is seated correctly in its groove.

Check the condition of the PAIR and crankcase breather hoses and their clamps and use new ones if they are in any way damaged or

4B•4 Fuel system – fuel injection models

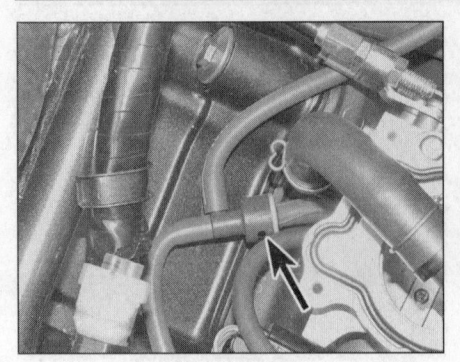

2.12a Air intake system one way valve (arrowed) . . .

2.12b . . . vacuum chamber . . .

2.12c . . . control valve (arrowed) . . .

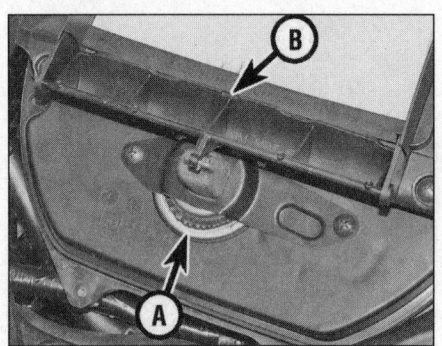

2.12d . . . diaphragm valve (A) and air flap (B)

deteriorated. Make sure the IAT sensor wiring connector is securely connected.
9 Make sure the vacuum hose is securely connected at each end.

Air intake system
Check
10 Support the bike on its centrestand (see Chapter 7). Remove the air filter (see Chapter 1). Make sure the transmission is in neutral. Disconnect the neutral switch wiring connector (see Chapter 9).
11 Start the engine and check the operation of the air flap – below 5000 rpm the flap should be closed, and above 5000 rpm the flap should be open. If it doesn't function as described check the components as follows.
12 First check that the vacuum hoses between the front cylinder throttle body, the one-way valve, the vacuum chamber, the control valve and the diaphragm valve are all in good condition and securely fitted at each end **(see illustrations)** – remove the air filter housing to access the one-way valve. If a hose is split, the system will not work as it relies on vacuum. Check that the control valve wiring connector is secure, that the terminals and wiring are good, and that there is continuity in the wiring between the valve and the ECU. Check the vacuum chamber and diaphragm valve for damage.
13 Make sure the air flap can open and close manually. If not undo the holder screws, detach the actuating rod and remove the flap. Check that the rod moves in and out of the diaphragm valve. If not replace the valve with a new one.
14 Remove the control valve (Step 18). Check the operation of the valve by blowing through the union A; no air should flow through the valve and out of union B **(see illustration)**. Now apply battery voltage (12 volts) to the valve wiring terminals and repeat the check; air should now flow freely through the valve if it is functioning correctly.
15 Check the resistance of the control valve windings by connecting an ohmmeter between its connector terminals and compare the reading obtained to that given in the Specifications. Replace the valve with a new one if faulty.
16 Check the operation of the one-way valve by blowing through the union A; air should flow through the valve and out of unions B and C **(see illustration)**. Now blow through union B; air should not flow through the valve and out of unions A and C if it is functioning correctly.
17 Check the operation of the diaphragm valve by applying a vacuum to its hose union to see whether the air flap moves **(see illustration 2.3b)** – a specified vacuum at which the valve should actuate is not given, so start with a small one and gradually increase it. If the valve does not move the diaphragm may be split.

Removal
18 To remove the control valve, remove the left-hand fairing side panel (see Chapter 8) and the fuel tank (see Chapter 4A). Disconnect the wiring connector, then detach the vacuum hoses, noting which fits where **(see illustration 2.12c)**. Undo the screw and remove the valve.
19 To remove the vacuum chamber, remove the fuel tank (see Chapter 4A). Detach the vacuum hose **(see illustration 2.12b)**. Undo the screw and remove the valve.

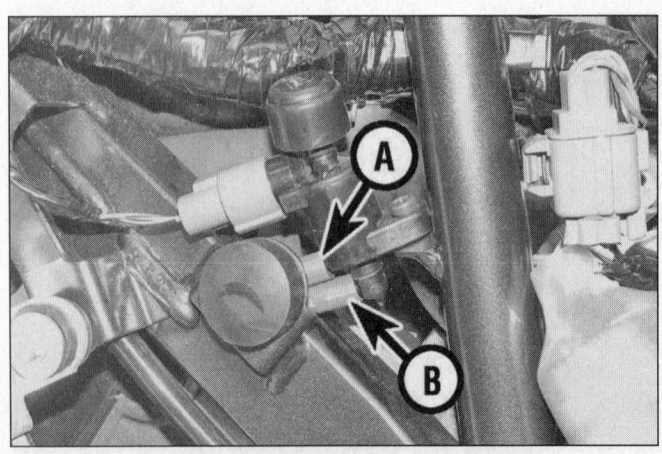

2.14 Control valve union identification

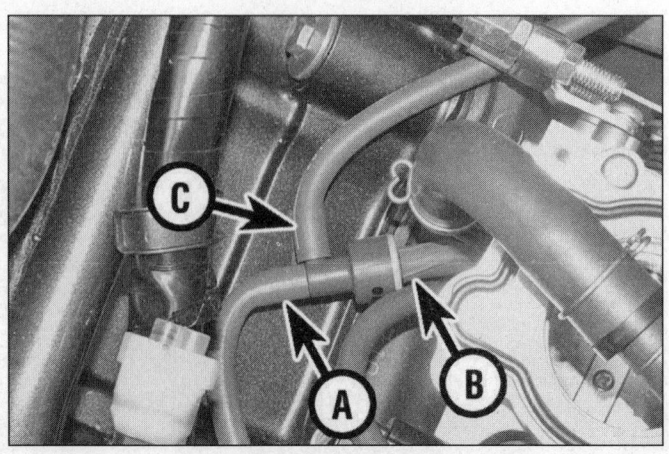

2.16 One-way valve union identification

Fuel system – fuel injection models 4B•5

2.21a Displace the valve and detach the rod ...

2.21b ... remove the plate ...

2.21c ... and disconnect the hose

20 To remove the one-way valve remove the air filter housing. Detach the vacuum hoses, noting which fits where, and remove the valve **(see illustration 2.12a)**.
21 To remove the diaphragm valve remove the fuel tank (see Chapter 4A). Undo the diaphragm valve set plate screws **(see illustration 2.3a)**. Displace the valve and detach the rod from the air flap, then remove the set plate and detach the vacuum hose **(see illustrations)**.

Installation

22 Installation is the reverse of removal. Make sure the vacuum hoses are securely connected at each end.

3 Fuel injection system description

1 All models are equipped with Honda's programmed fuel injection (PGM-FI) system. It is controlled by a management system with an engine control unit (ECU) that operates both the injection and ignition systems.
2 The engine control unit (ECU) monitors signals from the following sensors.
- Throttle position (TP) sensor – informs the ECU of the throttle position, and the rate of throttle opening or closing.
- Engine coolant temperature (ECT) sensor – informs the ECU of engine temperature. It also actuates the temperature gauge (see Chapter 3).
- Manifold absolute pressure (MAP) sensor – informs the ECU of the engine load by monitoring the pressure in the throttle body inlet tracts.
- Intake air temperature (IAT) sensor – informs the ECU of the temperature of the air entering the throttle body.
- Camshaft position (CMP) sensor – informs the ECU of engine speed and camshaft position.
- Ignition pulse generator – informs the ECU of engine speed and crankshaft position.
- Speed sensor – informs the ECU of the speed of the motorcycle (see Chapter 8).
- Lean angle sensor – stops the engine if the bike falls over.
- Oxygen sensor (on models with catalytic converter) – informs the ECU of the oxygen content of the exhaust gases. The sensor

is fitted on XL-3 to 6 Germany models and to all European XL-7 models onwards.
3 All the information from the sensors is analysed by the ECU, and from that it determines the appropriate ignition and fuelling requirements of the engine. The ECU controls each fuel injector by varying its pulse width – the length of time the injector is held open – to provide more or less fuel, as appropriate for cold starting, warm up, idle, cruising, and acceleration. Due to the layout of the engine, the fuelling needs for each cylinder are slightly different and the ECU is programmed to compensate for this; the injection system is fully sequential, with each injector receiving its own signal from the ECU.
4 Cold starting and warm up idle speeds are controlled by a conventional fast idle lever actuating on starter valves in the throttle bodies via cable and linkage on XL-3 to 6 models, and automatically by the ECU and a fast idle control valve (known as IACV or intake air control valve, and not to be confused with the air intake system in the air filter housing which also has a control valve) on XL-7 models onward.
5 If there is an abnormality in any of the readings obtained from any sensor, the ECU enters its back-up mode. In this event, the ECU ignores the abnormal sensor signal, and assumes a pre-programmed value which will allow the engine to continue running (albeit at reduced efficiency). If the ECU enters this back-up mode, or when any faults occur, the fuel injection system (FI) warning light in the instrument cluster will come on or flash (depending on the situation), and the relevant fault code will be stored in the ECU memory. The fault can be identified using the fault codes which can be accessed using the self-diagnosis function (see Section 4). However if there are certain faults detected in the injectors or the cam position sensor or ignition pulse generator, the back-up mode becomes ineffective and the ECU will not allow the engine to run at all. Note that many European models have an immobiliser system (HISS – Honda Ignition Security System) which will not allow the engine to be started unless the correct key is used. A fault in this system should not be confused with a fuel injection system fault. The immobiliser system has its own fault diagnosis function (see Chapter 5).

4 Fuel injection system fault diagnosis

1 If the fuel injection system (FI) warning light on the instrument cluster comes on when the motorcycle is running, a fault has occurred in the fuel injection/ignition system. The engine control unit (ECU) will store the relevant fault code in its memory and this code can be read as follows using the self-diagnostic mode of the ECU. While the engine is running above 5000 rpm and the motorcycle is being ridden, the light will come on and stay on. When the motorcycle is on its sidestand and the engine is off or running below 5000 rpm, the light will flash, the pattern of the flashes indicating the code for the fault the ECU has identified.
2 If the engine can be started, place the motorcycle on its sidestand then start the engine and allow it to idle. Whilst the engine is idling, observe the FI warning light on the instrument cluster.
3 If the engine cannot be started, place the motorcycle on its sidestand. With the kill switch in the run position turn the engine over on the starter motor for more then ten seconds and observe the FI warning light on the instrument cluster.
4 Alternatively, and to check for any stored fault codes even though the warning lights have not illuminated, remove the seat (see Chapter 8) to gain access to the fuel injection system data link connector (DLC), which is a capped 4-pin connector coming out of the wiring loom **(see illustration)**. Ensure the

4.4 DLC connector (arrowed)

ignition is switched OFF then remove the cap and fit the Honda DLC short connector (Part No. 070PZ-ZY30100, available at reasonable cost from your dealer). Make sure the kill switch is in the RUN position then turn the ignition ON and observe the warning light. If there are no stored fault codes, the light will come on and stay on. If there are stored fault codes, the light will flash.

5 The light emits long (1.3 second) and short (0.5 second) flashes to give out the fault code. A long flash is used to indicate the first digit of a double digit fault code (i.e. 10 and above). If a single digit fault code is being displayed (i.e. 0 – 9), there will be a number of short flashes equivalent to the code being displayed. For example, two long (1.3 sec) flashes followed by three short (0.5 sec) flashes indicates the fault code number 23. If there is more than one fault code, there will be a gap before the other codes are revealed (the codes will be revealed in order, starting with the lowest and finishing with the highest). Once all codes have been revealed, the ECU will continuously run through the code(s) stored in its memory, revealing each one in turn with a short gap between them. The fault codes are shown in the table.

Fault code (No. of flashes)	Symptoms	Possible causes
0 – no code (warning light off)	Engine does not start	● Blown fuse (main, engine stop, PGM-FI or fuel pump) ● Faulty power supply to electronic control unit (ECU) ● Short circuit in ECU output voltage (yellow/red) wire ● Faulty engine stop relay or wiring ● Faulty engine stop switch/open circuit on switch earth (ground) wire ● Faulty ignition switch ● Faulty lean angle sensor or wiring ● Faulty electronic control unit (ECU)
0 – no code (warning light off)	Engine runs normally	● Open or short circuit in warning light wiring ● Faulty electronic control unit (ECU)
0 – no code (warning light constantly on)	Engine runs normally	● Short circuit in data link connector or wiring ● Faulty electronic control unit (ECU)
1	Engine runs normally	Faulty manifold absolute pressure (MAP) sensor or wiring
2	Engine runs normally	Faulty manifold absolute pressure (MAP) sensor or vacuum hose
7	Engine difficult to start at low temperatures	Faulty engine coolant temperature (ECT) sensor or wiring
8	Poor throttle response	Faulty throttle position (TP) sensor or wiring
9	Engine runs normally	Faulty intake air temperature (IAT) sensor or wiring
11	Engine operates normally	Faulty speed sensor or wiring
12	Engine does not start	Faulty No. 1 (rear cylinder) injector or wiring
13	Engine does not start	Faulty No. 2 (front cylinder) injector or wiring
18	Engine does not start	Faulty camshaft position (CMP) sensor or wiring
19	Engine does not start	Faulty ignition pulse generator or wiring
The following code is only applicable to XL-3 to 6 models		
33	Engine operates normally	Faulty EPROM in ECU
The following code is only applicable to XL-7 models onward		
29	Engine hard to start, stalls, rough idle	Faulty intake air control valve (IACV) or wiring
The following codes are only applicable to models with catalytic converter		
21	Engine operates normally	Faulty oxygen sensor or wiring
23	Engine operates normally	Faulty oxygen sensor or wiring, or faulty oxygen sensor heating element

Once all the codes have been revealed, switch off the ignition and (where necessary) remove the tool from the data link connector. Identify the fault using the table above, then refer below for checking procedures.

6 Once the fault has been identified and corrected, it will be necessary to reset the system by removing the fault code from the ECU memory. To do this, ensure the ignition is switched OFF then fit the Honda DLC short connector (see Step 4). Make sure the kill switch is in the RUN position, then turn the ignition switch ON. Disconnect the tool from the DLC. When the tool is disconnected the light should come on for about five seconds, during which time the tool must be reconnected. The light should start to flash when it is reconnected, indicating that all fault codes have been erased. However if the light flashes twenty times the memory has not been erased and the procedure must be repeated. Turn off the ignition then remove the tool. Check the FI warning light (in some cases it may be necessary to repeat the erasing procedure more than once) then install the seat.

7 While some of the sensors can be checked using home equipment, there are others which

Fuel system – fuel injection models 4B•7

can only be tested using the Honda diagnostic system (HDS) tester which can be plugged into the system. If a fault appears, use the diagnostic function and fault code system described above to work out which component is faulty. First ensure that the relevant system wiring connectors are securely connected and free of corrosion – poor connections are the cause of the majority of problems. Also check the wiring itself for any obvious faults or breaks, and use a continuity tester to check the wiring between the component, its connectors and the ECU, referring to the wiring diagrams and electrical system fault finding section in Chapter 9. Next refer to Section 5 to see if there are any other specific checks that can be made on that particular component. If this fails to reveal the cause of the problem, the motorcycle should be taken to a suitably-equipped Honda dealer for testing. They will have the tester which should locate the fault quickly and simply.

8 Also ensure that the fault is not due to poor maintenance – i.e. check that the air filter element is clean, that the spark plugs are in good condition, that the valve clearances are correctly adjusted, the cylinder compression pressures are correct, and the ignition timing is correct (refer to Chapters 1, 2 and 5). It is also worth removing the sensor(s) in question (see Section 5) and checking that the sensing tip or head is clean and not obstructed by anything. Where there is a vacuum hose to a sensor, make sure it is securely connected at both ends and has no cracks or splits.

5 Fuel injection and engine management system components

Caution: *Ensure the ignition is switched OFF before disconnecting/reconnecting any fuel injection system wiring connector. If a connector is disconnected/reconnected with the ignition switched ON the engine control unit (ECU) could be damaged.*

Manifold absolute pressure (MAP) sensor

Check

1 The MAP sensor is mounted on the throttle bodies. The sensor can only be checked using the Honda diagnostic test pin box. However you can remove the fuel tank (see Chapter 4A) and make sure that the vacuum hoses to it are securely fixed at both ends, and have no cracks or splits **(see illustration)**. If the necessary equipment is available, connect a vacuum gauge into one of the hoses between the throttle bodies and the MAP sensor using an auxiliary three-way joint and hose, and with the engine idling check that the manifold absolute pressure is as Specified at the beginning of the Chapter. If not, replace all the vacuum hoses with new ones. If the pressure is out of specification with new or good hoses, check for leaks between the air filter housing, the throttle bodies and the cylinder head.

2 The sensor power supply can be checked as follows. Remove the fuel tank (see Chapter 4A). Disconnect the wiring connector from the sensor **(see illustration 5.1)**. Connect the positive (+) lead of a voltmeter to the light green/yellow wire terminal of the sensor wiring connector, then connect the negative (–) lead to the green/orange terminal. Turn the ignition switch ON and set the kill switch to RUN and check that a voltage of 4.75 to 5.25 volts is present on XL-3 to 6 models, and 2.7 to 3.1 volts on XL-7 models onward. If it is the MAP sensor is faulty. If there is no voltage, check for continuity in each wire to the ECU. Similarly check the same voltage is present between yellow/red terminal and the wire terminals of the connector and a good earth (ground). If it is check for continuity to earth in the light green/yellow wire – if there is continuity repair the wire; if there isn't the MAP sensor is faulty. If the voltage isn't present, check for continuity in the yellow/red wire between the sensor and the ECU. If there is continuity the ECU is faulty.

Removal and installation

3 Remove the air filter housing (see Section 2).
4 Disconnect the wiring connector and detach the vacuum hose from the sensor **(see illustration 5.1)**. Undo the screw and remove the sensor.
5 Installation is the reverse of removal.

Engine coolant temperature (ECT) sensor

Check

6 Remove the air filter housing (see Section 2).
7 Disconnect the wiring connector from the sensor **(see illustration)**. With the engine cold, connect an ohmmeter between the terminals on the sensor and measure its resistance. Compare the reading obtained to that given in the Specifications, noting that the specified value is valid at 20°C (68°F). If the resistance reading differs greatly from that specified, the sensor is probably faulty.

8 If the sensor appears to be functioning correctly, check its power supply. Connect the positive (+) lead of a voltmeter to the pink/white wire terminal in the sensor wiring connector, then connect the negative (–) lead to a good earth. Turn the ignition switch ON and check that a voltage of 4.75 to 5.25 volts is present. If it isn't, there is a fault in the pink/white wire or the ECU. If voltage was present, now connect the negative lead to the green/orange terminal of the connector and check that the same voltage is present. If it isn't, there is a fault in the green/orange wire or the ECU. If there is voltage, the ECU is probably faulty.

Removal and installation

Warning: *The engine must be completely cool before carrying out this procedure.*

9 Drain the cooling system (see Chapter 1). Remove the air filter housing (see Section 2).
10 Disconnect the sensor wiring connector **(see illustration 5.7)**. Unscrew and remove the sensor. Discard the sealing washer.
11 Fit a new sealing washer onto the sensor. Install the sensor and tighten it to the torque setting specified at the beginning of the Chapter. Connect the wiring **(see illustration 5.7)**.
12 Install the air filter housing (see Section 2). Refill the cooling system (see Chapter 1).

Throttle position (TP) sensor

Check

13 The throttle sensor operation can only be checked using the Honda diagnostic system tester. Its power supply can be checked as follows. Remove the fuel tank (see Chapter 4A). Disconnect the wiring connector from the sensor **(see illustration)**. Connect the positive (+) lead of a voltmeter to the yellow/red terminal of the sensor wiring connector, then connect the negative (–) lead to a good earth. Turn the ignition switch ON and check that a

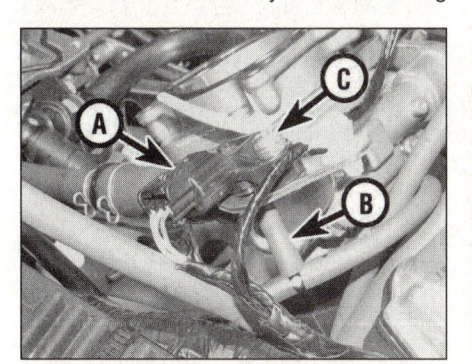

5.1 MAP sensor wiring connector (A), vacuum hose (B) and screw (C)

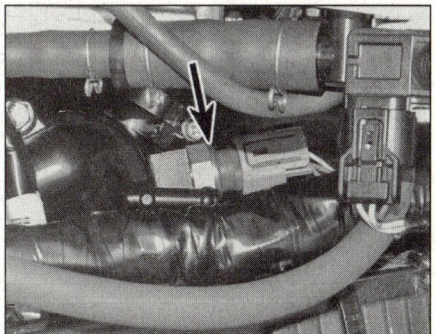

5.7 ECT sensor (arrowed)

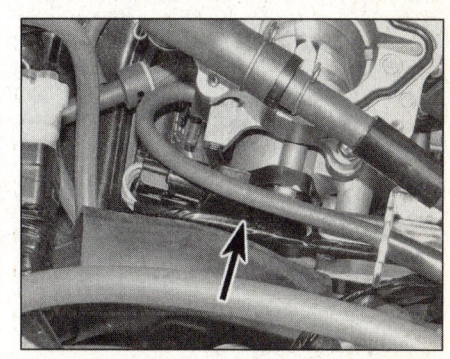

5.13 Throttle position sensor (arrowed)

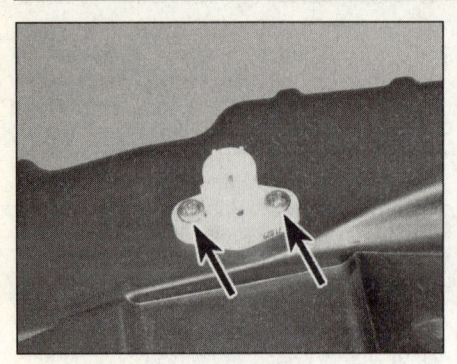

4B•8 Fuel system – fuel injection models

5.19 Undo the screws (arrowed) and remove the sensor

5.24a Fuel injector wiring connector (arrowed) – XL-3 to 6 models

5.24b Fuel injector wiring connector (arrowed) – XL-7 models onward

voltage of 4.75 to 5.25 volts is present. If it isn't, there is a fault in the yellow/red wire or the ECU. If voltage was present, now connect the negative lead to the green/orange wire terminal of the connector and check that the same voltage is present. If it isn't, there is a fault in the green/orange wire or the ECU. If there is voltage, check for continuity to earth in the red/yellow wire. If there is, trace the fault in the wire and repair it. If there isn't, and the sensor is proven good by the Honda tester, then the ECU is faulty.

Removal and installation

14 The throttle sensor is an integral part of the throttle body assembly and is not available separately. If the sensor is faulty, a complete new throttle body assembly will have to be installed, though it is worth checking with your Honda parts specialist whether anything can be done to avoid this.

Intake air temperature (IAT) sensor

Check

15 Remove the fuel tank (see Chapter 4A). The sensor is mounted in the air filter housing. Disconnect its wiring connector (see illustration 2.7a).
16 Connect an ohmmeter across the sensor terminals and measure its resistance. Compare the reading obtained to that given in the Specifications noting that the specified value is valid at 20°C (68°F). If the resistance reading

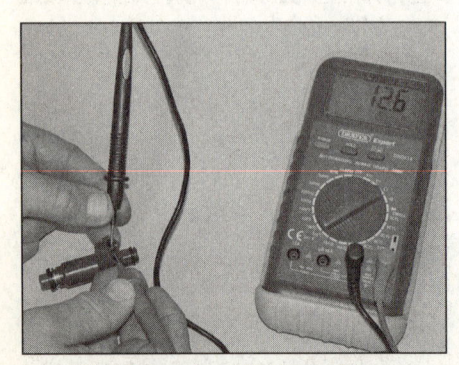

differs greatly from that specified, the sensor is probably faulty.
17 If the sensor appears to be functioning correctly, check its power supply. Connect the positive (+) lead of a voltmeter to the grey/blue terminal of the sensor wiring connector, then connect the negative (–) lead to a good earth. Turn the ignition switch ON and check that a voltage of 4.75 to 5.25 volts is present. If it isn't, there is a fault in the grey/blue wire or the ECU. If voltage was present, now connect the negative lead to the green/orange terminal of the connector and check that the same voltage is present. If it isn't, there is a fault in the green/orange wire or the ECU. If there is voltage, the ECU is probably faulty.

Removal and installation

18 Remove air filter housing (see Section 2).
19 Undo the screws securing the sensor and remove it (see illustration).
20 Installation is the reverse of removal.

Speed sensor

21 See Chapter 9, Section 16.

Fuel rail and injectors

⚠️ **Warning: Refer to the precautions given in Section 1 before starting work.**

Check

22 If the engine runs, raise the fuel tank (see Chapter 4A). Start the engine and allow it to

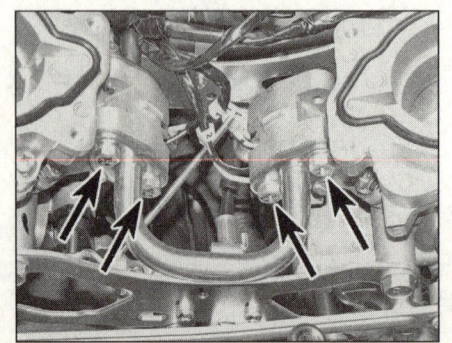

5.24c Measuring injector resistance (injector removed for clarity)

5.28 Unscrew the bolts (arrowed) and remove the fuel rail

idle. You can check the operation of each injector in the throttle bodies using a mechanic's stethoscope or sounding rod; an injector will emit a 'clicking' noise when functioning. If any injector is silent, either the injector or its wiring harness is faulty.
23 If the engine does not run, remove the air filter housing (see Section 2).
24 Disconnect the wiring connector from the injector (see illustrations). Connect an ohmmeter between the terminals and measure the resistance (see illustration). Compare the reading to that given in the Specifications. Also check that there is no continuity to earth on the black/white wire terminal on the injector. If the resistance of any injector differs greatly from that specified, or there is continuity to earth, a new injector should be installed. Also check for battery voltage at the black/white wire terminal in the wiring connector with the ignition ON and the kill switch set to RUN. If there is no voltage, check the wiring. Check for continuity in the other wire in the connector – there should be no continuity to earth, and there should be continuity to the wire terminal in the ECU wiring connector.

Removal – XL-3 to 6 models

25 Remove the air filter housing (Section 2). For best access remove the throttle bodies (see Section 6).
26 Disconnect the wiring connector from each injector, noting which fits where (see illustration 5.24a), and from the TP sensor (see illustration 5.13). Release the wiring from the fuel delivery pipe and remove the sub-harness (see illustration 6.4). If the throttle bodies have not been removed unscrew the delivery pipe bolts and detach the pipe. Discard the O-ring.
27 Undo the vacuum hose guide screw, then detach the hose from each throttle body and from the MAP sensor and remove it (see illustration 5.1).
28 Have some rag to hand to catch residual fuel. Unscrew the fuel rail bolts then remove the fuel rail and O-rings (see illustration). Discard the O-rings as new ones must be used.
29 Unscrew the injector holder bolts (see

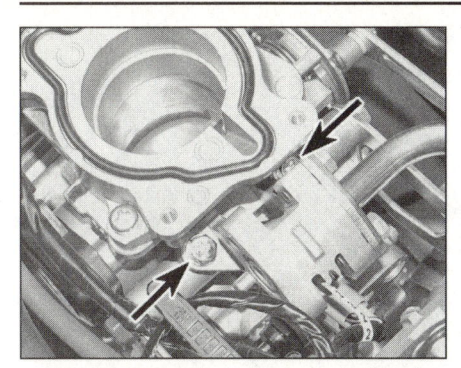

Fuel system – fuel injection models 4B•9

5.29 Unscrew the bolts (arrowed) and remove the holder

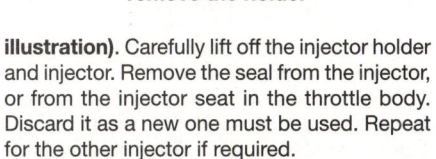

5.31a Pull the rubber surround out ...

5.31b ... then press the tabs in and pull the hose off

illustration). Carefully lift off the injector holder and injector. Remove the seal from the injector, or from the injector seat in the throttle body. Discard it as a new one must be used. Repeat for the other injector if required.

30 If required remove the injector from the holder. Note the positions of the O-ring and rubber cushion on the injector; the O-ring must be replaced with a new one, but the cushion can be reused as long as it is not damaged, deformed or deteriorated. Repeat for the other injector if required.

Removal – XL-7 model onwards

31 Remove the air filter housing (Section 2). For best access remove the throttle bodies (see Section 6). If you don't remove the throttle bodies, and if you are removing the front cylinder injector or the distribution hose, release the rubber surround from the fuel supply hose joint, then depress the tabs and draw the hose off its union **(see illustrations)** – have some rag to hand to catch residual fuel.

32 Taking care to catch residual fuel, unscrew the fuel distribution hose bolts then detach the hose from the injector **(see illustrations)**. Disconnect the injector wiring connector and remove the injector **(see illustrations)**. Discard the injector O-ring and seal as new ones must be used. Repeat for the other injector if required.

Installation – XL-3 to 6 models

33 If the injector has been removed from its rail, slide the cushion onto the top of the injector (using a new one if necessary), then fit a new O-ring lubricated with clean engine oil into the groove. Ease the injector into the holder taking care not to damage the O-ring. Repeat for the other injector if required.

34 Fit a new seal onto the bottom of the injector. Fit the injector and holder, making sure the injector enters its seat and the seal stays in place and locates correctly. Fit the holder bolts and tighten them to the torque setting specified at the beginning of the Chapter **(see illustration 5.29)**. Repeat for the other injector if required.

35 Fit a new O-ring into the groove in each injector holder. Fit the fuel rail and tighten the bolts to the torque setting specified at the beginning of the chapter **(see illustration 5.28)**.

36 Refit the vacuum hose and secure it with its guide. Make sure the hose is fully pushed onto each union.

37 If the throttle bodies are in situ fit a new O-ring into the groove in the fuel delivery pipe and smear it with oil. Fit the pipe and tighten the bolts to the torque setting specified at the beginning of the chapter **(see illustration 6.4)**. Refit the wiring sub-harness and connect the injector and TP sensor wiring connectors – the brown connector is for the No. 1 (rear cylinder) injector, and the grey connector is for the No. 2 (front cylinder) injector **(see illustration 5.24a)**.

38 Install the throttle bodies if removed (see Section 6). Install the air filter housing and fuel tank (Section 2 and Chapter 4A). Run the engine and check that the fuel system is working correctly before taking the machine out on the road.

Installation – XL-7 model onwards

39 Fit a new O-ring lubricated with clean engine oil into the groove in the top of the injector a new seal onto the bottom of the injector. Ease the injector into the throttle body making sure the seal stays in place and locates correctly **(see illustration 5.32d)**. Repeat for the other injector if required.

40 Connect the injector wiring connector – the brown connector is for the No. 1 (rear cylinder) injector, and the grey connector is for the No. 2 (front cylinder) injector **(see illustration 5.32c)**.

41 Fit the distribution hose onto the injector, aligning the tab with the groove and making sure the O-ring locates correctly **(see illustration 5.32b)**. Fit the bolts and tighten them to the torque setting specified at the beginning of the Chapter **(see illustration 5.32a)**. Repeat for the other injector if required.

5.32a Unscrew the bolts (arrowed) ...

5.32b ... and detach the hose

5.32c Disconnect the wiring connector ...

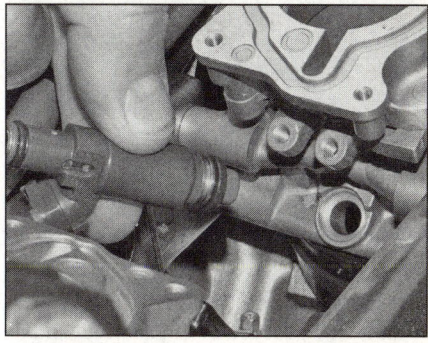

5.32d ... and remove the injector

4B•10 Fuel system – fuel injection models

5.44 CMP sensor wiring connector (arrowed)

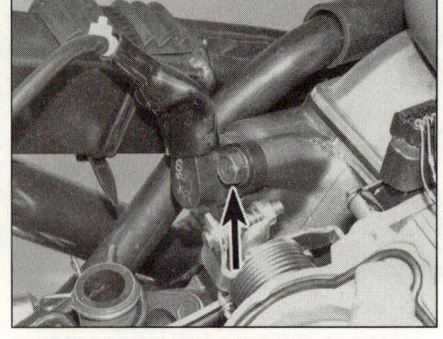

5.50 Unscrew the bolt (arrowed) and remove the sensor

5.55 The sensor wiring connector is inside the boot (arrowed)

42 Install the throttle bodies if removed (see Section 6). If not connect the fuel supply hose to its union, making sure the tabs on the lock engage in the slots, then refit the rubber surround so it prevents the tabs from being inadvertently depressed **(see illustration 5.31b and a)**. Install the air filter housing and fuel tank (Section 2 and Chapter 4A). Run the engine and check that the fuel system is working correctly before taking the machine out on the road.

Camshaft position (CMP) sensor

Check

43 Remove the air filter housing (see Section 2).
44 Disconnect the sensor wiring connector **(see illustration)**. Perform the following check(s).
45 Using an ohmmeter check for continuity first between the grey wire terminal on the sensor side of the connector and earth (ground) and then between the white/yellow wire terminal and earth. If there is continuity in either case the camshaft position sensor is faulty. Measure the resistance of the sensor by connecting the meter, set to the ohms x 100 scale, to the terminals. Honda do not specify a value but if it is zero or infinity the sensor is faulty.
46 Connect the positive (+) lead of a voltmeter and peak voltage adapter arrangement* to the grey terminal on the sensor side of the cam position sensor connector and the negative (–) lead to the white/yellow terminal of the connector. Turn the engine over on the starter motor and note the voltage reading obtained. If this reading is below the specified minimum, the sensor is faulty.*Note: *Honda specify their own peak voltage adapter (Pt. No. 07HGJ-0020100) with an aftermarket digital multimeter having an impedance of 10 M-ohm/ DCV minimum for this test.*
47 If the sensor functions correctly then the fault must be in the wiring harness or the ECU, and can be located by a Honda dealer with the test pin box.

Removal and installation

48 Remove the air filter housing (see Section 2).
49 Disconnect the sensor wiring connector **(see illustration 5.44)**.
50 Unscrew the bolt and draw the sensor out of the head **(see illustration)**. Discard the O-ring.
51 Clean the sensor tip and fit a new O-ring smeared with oil into the groove in the sensor body. Fit the sensor into the cylinder head and secure it with the bolt **(see illustration 5.50)**.
52 Reconnect the wiring connector **(see illustration 5.44)**. Install the air filter housing (see Section 2).

Ignition pulse generator

53 See Chapter 5, Section 4.

Oxygen sensor

Check

54 Apart from the wiring checks that are outlined in Section 4, the operation of the oxygen sensor can only be checked using the Honda diagnostic test pin box.
55 To check the sensor heater, raise the fuel tank (see Chapter 4A). Disconnect the sensor 4-pin wiring connector **(see illustration)**. Connect an ohmmeter between the two white wire terminals on the sensor side of the connector and check that the resistance is between 10 and 40 ohms. Also check that there is no continuity to earth (ground) in each white wire. If the resistance is not as specified or if there is continuity to earth, replace the sensor with a new one. Otherwise check for battery voltage between the black/white (+) wire terminal and earth with the ignition ON. If there is no voltage, check the wiring, using the wiring diagrams at the end of Chapter 9. Also check for continuity in the black/green wire to the ECU wiring connector – if there is no continuity locate the break and repair the wire. Otherwise have the sensor and its circuit tested by a Honda dealer equipped with the diagnostic tester.

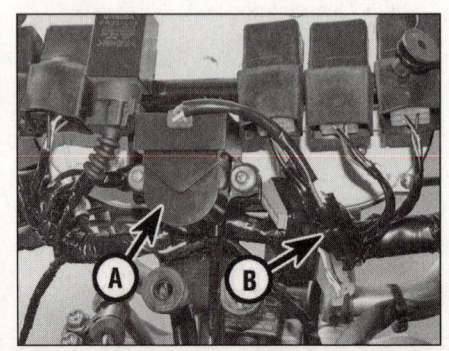

Removal and installation

Note: *The oxygen sensor is delicate and will not work if it is dropped or knocked, or if any cleaning materials are used on it. Ensure the exhaust system is cold before proceeding.*
56 Raise the fuel tank (see Chapter 4A).
57 Trace the wiring from the sensor in the exhaust and disconnect it at the 4-pin connector **(see illustration 5.55)**. Release the wiring from any clamp(s) and note its routing.
58 Unscrew the shield bolts and remove the shield, then unscrew and remove the sensor **(see illustration)**.
59 Installation is the reverse of removal. Tighten the sensor to the torque setting specified at the beginning of the Chapter.

Lean angle sensor

Check

60 Position the motorcycle on its centrestand stand so it is level. Remove the fairing (see Chapter 7).
61 With the ignition switch ON and the kill switch set to run, connect the negative (–) lead of a voltmeter to the green wire terminal of the lean angle sensor connector (with the connector still connected) **(see illustration)**.

5.58 Unscrew the bolts (arrowed) and remove the shield to access the sensor

5.61 Lean angle sensor (A) and its wiring connector (B)

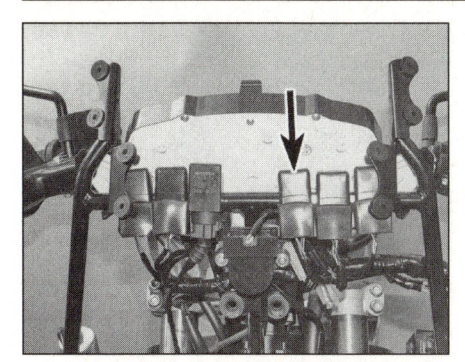

Fuel system – fuel injection models 4B•11

5.70 Engine stop relay (arrowed)

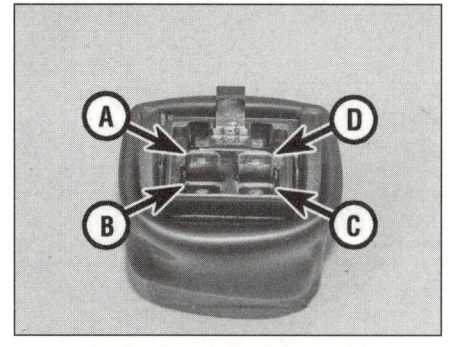

5.73 Fuel cut-off relay terminal identification

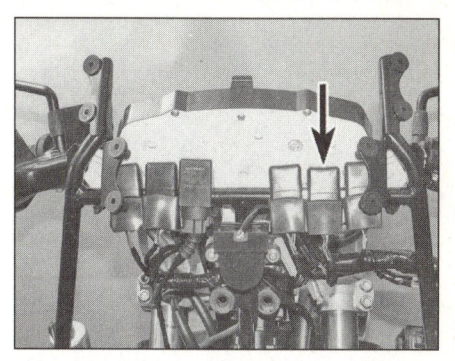

5.74 Fuel cut-off relay (arrowed)

Connect the voltmeter positive (+) lead first to the white/black or white wire terminal (depending on which side of the connector you are connecting to) and check that battery voltage (approximately 12 volts) is present, then connect it to the red/orange or red/white wire terminal and check that between 0 to 1 volt is present. Turn the ignition OFF. If there is no voltage check the green wire for continuity to earth – there should be continuity. If battery voltage was not present also check the white/black wire and connectors between the sensor, the fusebox and the switch housing, referring to the wiring diagrams at the end of Chapter 9. Otherwise check the red/orange wire to the engine stop relay, then check the relay itself.

62 Undo the sensor mounting screws and displace the sensor. Hold the sensor horizontal. Set the kill switch to RUN and switch the ignition ON; the engine stop relay (next to the sensor) should click, indicating the power supply is closed (on) **(see illustration 5.70)**. Slowly tilt the sensor to the left whilst listening to the engine stop relay; once the sensor reaches an angle of approximately 60° the relay should be heard to click, indicating the power supply is open (off). Switch the ignition OFF and return the sensor to the horizontal, then switch the ignition back ON again (engine stop relay should click again) and tilt the sensor to the right. The engine stop relay should be heard to click again once the sensor reaches an angle of around 60°.

63 If the relay does not click when the lean angle sensor is tilted the sensor is faulty. If the relay does not click at all it could be faulty.

Removal and installation

64 Remove the fairing (see Chapter 8).
65 Disconnect the lean angle sensor wiring connector **(see illustration 5.61)**. Undo the screws and remove the sensor. Note the collars in the mounting grommets.
66 Installation is the reverse of removal. Make sure the collars are in place and the sensor is fitted with its UP mark facing upwards and with the wiring to the front **(see illustration 5.61)**.

Engine stop relay

Check

67 Remove the relay (see below).
68 Connect an ohmmeter between the black/white and white/black wire terminals on the relay. Using a 12 volt battery and auxiliary wires, connect the battery positive (+) terminal to the red/orange wire terminal on the relay and the negative (–) terminal to the black wire terminal and note the meter reading obtained. If the relay is operating correctly there should be continuity (zero resistance) when the battery is connected and no continuity (infinite resistance) when the battery is disconnected. If this is not the case, replace the relay with a new one.

Removal and installation

69 Remove the fairing (see Chapter 8).

5.75a Displace the relay . . .

5.75b . . . then pull back the rubber cover and disconnect the wiring connector

70 Displace the relay from its mount and disconnect the wiring connector **(see illustration)**.
71 Installation is the reverse of removal.

Fuel cut-off relay

Check

72 Remove the relay (see below).
73 Connect an ohmmeter between the A and B terminals on the relay **(see illustration)**. Using a 12 volt battery and auxiliary wires, connect the battery positive (+) terminal to the C terminal on the relay and the negative (–) terminal to the D terminal and note the meter reading obtained. If the relay is operating correctly there should be continuity (zero resistance) when the battery is connected and no continuity (infinite resistance) when the battery is disconnected. If this is not the case, replace the relay with a new one.

Removal and installation

74 Remove the fairing (see Chapter 8) **(see illustration 5.70)**.
75 Displace the relay box from its mount and disconnect the wiring connector **(see illustrations)**.
76 Installation is the reverse of removal.

Engine control unit (ECU)

Check

77 The engine control unit (ECU) itself can not be checked, but a process of elimination of other possible faulty components can point to it being faulty. The best thing to do is to substitute it with one known to be good and see whether the problem is solved. Otherwise the only thing you can do is to check all the wiring and connectors between all components in the system and the ECU. Alternatively take the bike to a dealer with the test harness.

Removal and installation

78 Make sure the ignition is OFF.
79 Remove the left-hand fairing side panel (see Chapter 8).
80 Release the strap and displace the ECU

4B•12 Fuel system – fuel injection models

5.80 ECU (arrowed) – on models with ABS do not confuse it with the ABS control unit that is mounted outside of the ECU

then disconnect the wiring connectors **(see illustration)**.
81 Installation is the reverse of removal.

6 Throttle bodies

⚠️ *Warning: Refer to the precautions given in Section 1 before starting work.*

Removal

1 Remove the air filter housing (Section 2). Have some rag to hand to catch residual fuel.
2 On XL-3 to 6 models release the idle speed adjuster from its holder **(see illustration)**.

6.2 Release the idle speed adjuster (arrowed)

3 Release the throttle body sub-harness wiring connector and disconnect it **(see illustration)**. Disconnect the MAP sensor wiring connector **(see illustration 5.1)**. On XL-7 models onward disconnect the IACV wiring connector **(see illustration)**.
4 On XL-3 to 6 models release the wiring from the fuel delivery pipe, then unscrew the bolts and detach the pipe **(see illustration)**. Remove and discard the O-ring as a new one must be used.
5 On XL-7 models onward, release the rubber surround from the fuel supply hose joint, then depress the tabs and draw the hose off its union **(see illustrations 5.31a and b)**. Free the hose from the clamp.
6 Unscrew the throttle cable bracket screws and detach the cable ends from the pulley **(see illustration)**.

6.3a Throttle body sub-harness wiring connector (arrowed)

Caution: Do not snap the throttle cam/valves from fully open to fully closed once the cables have been disconnected because this can lead to engine idle speed problems.

7 Disconnect the air intake system vacuum hose from the throttle bodies **(see illustration)**.
8 Fully slacken the upper clamps on the cylinder head intake adapters using a long screwdriver, noting their orientation **(see illustration)**. Ease the throttle body assembly up out of the rubbers, noting that it may be quite a tight fit, and remove it. On XL-3 to 6 models free the fast idle cable end from the linkage **(see illustration)**.

Caution: Tape over or stuff clean rag into each cylinder head intake after removing the throttle body assembly to prevent anything from falling in.

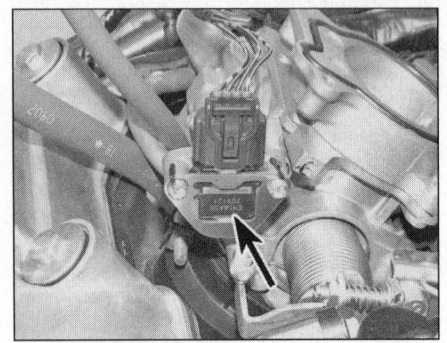

6.3b IACV wiring connector (arrowed)

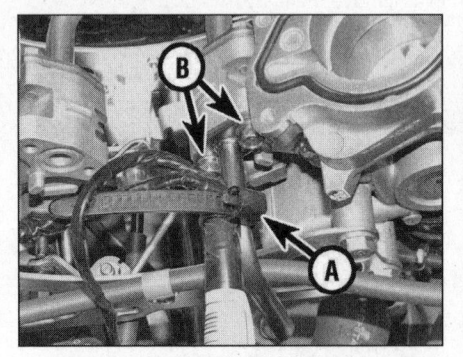

6.4 Release the wiring tie (A) then unscrew the pipe bolts (B)

6.6 Undo the screws (arrowed) then detach the cable ends

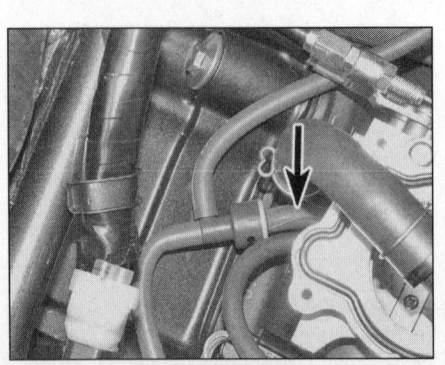

6.7 Detach the vacuum hose (arrowed)

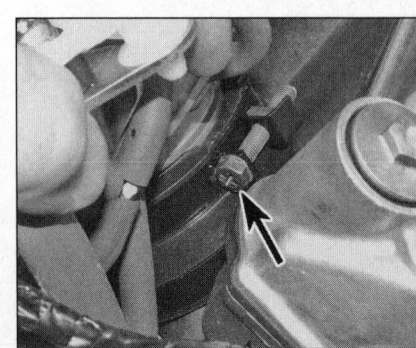

6.8a Slacken the clamp screw (arrowed) on each intake adapter

6.8b On XL-3 to 6 models detach the fast idle cable (arrowed)

Fuel system – fuel injection models 4B•13

9 If you are going to fit new throttle bodies, remove the joint piece from each intake by undoing its screws **(see illustration)** – on XL-7 models onward first remove the IACV and its hoses and unions (Section 8). Remove the O-rings and discard them. Fit the joint pieces to the new throttle bodies using new O-rings.

10 If the intake adapters on the cylinder heads show signs of cracking or deterioration new ones must be fitted. Note their orientation and how the clamps locate and are orientated before slackening the clamps and removing them. On installation make sure that the adapter marked FR is on the front cylinder head with its arrow pointing to the front and that marked RR is on the rear with its arrow to the rear. Also check the throttle body vacuum hoses for signs of damage or deterioration and replace any suspect hoses with new ones.

Caution: The throttle body assembly must be treated as a sealed unit. With the exception of the intake joint pieces, NEVER loosen any of the white-painted nuts/bolts/screws on the assembly as these are pre-set at the factory to ensure correct synchronisation of the throttle valves. The only components on the assembly which are serviceable are the starter valves (see Section 7) and the various vacuum hoses.

Caution: NEVER use a solvent-based cleaner to clean the throttle body components. The throttle bores are covered with a molybdenum coating which could be removed by the cleaner.

Installation

11 Remove the tape/plugs from the intakes. Make sure the intake adapter clamp screws are correctly orientated as noted on removal **(see illustration 6.8a)**. Lubricate the inside of the rubbers with a light smear of engine oil to aid installation.

12 On XL-3 to 6 models connect the fast idle cable to the linkage **(see illustration 6.8b)**. Position the throttle body assembly on the intakes and push them down until they are fully engaged. Lightly tighten the clamps **(see illustration 6.8a)**.

13 Connect the vacuum hose to its union on the throttle body assembly **(see illustration 6.7)**.

14 Connect the throttle cable ends to the pulley, then fit the bracket and tighten the screws **(see illustration 6.6)**.

15 On XL-3 to 6 models fit a new O-ring into the groove in the fuel delivery pipe and smear it with oil. Fit the pipe and tighten the bolts to the torque setting specified at the beginning of the chapter **(see illustration 6.4)**. Secure the wiring in the tie.

16 On XL-7 models onwards connect the fuel supply hose to its union, making sure the tabs on the lock engage in the slots, then refit the rubber surround so it prevents the tabs from being inadvertently depressed. **(see illustrations 5.31b and a)**.

6.9 Each joint piece is secured by two screws (arrowed)

17 Connect the throttle body sub-harness and MAP sensor wiring connectors, and on XL-7 models onward the IACV wiring connector, making sure they are secure **(see illustrations 6.3a, 5.1 and 6.3b)**.

18 On XL-3 to 6 models fit the idle speed adjuster into its holder **(see illustration 6.2)**.

19 Install the air filter housing (Section 2).

7 Starter valves and fast idle cable – XL-3 to 6 models

⚠️ *Warning: Refer to the precautions given in Section 1 before starting work.*

Note: If the starter valves are removed they will have to be synchronized using vacuum gauges after installation to ensure accurate set-up. Do not alter the setting of the synchronization nuts to ensure minimal adjustment on installation – note that the No. 1 (rear cylinder throttle body) valve is the base valve, and the nut is pre-set and locked at the factory and must not be disturbed.

Starter valves

Removal

1 Remove the air filter housing (Section 2). For better access also remove the throttle bodies (see Section 6).

2 For best access remove the fuel rail and injectors (see Section 5).

3 Unscrew the starter valve base nut, then turn the starter valve linkage and remove the valve, noting how the linkage arm locates **(see illustration)**. Repeat for the other starter valve.

4 Check all components for wear and damage and replace with new ones as necessary.

Installation

5 Clean the starter valves and throttle body passages using compressed air only. Do not use a throttle body/injector cleaner or any other solvent.

Caution: NEVER use a solvent-based cleaner to clean the throttle body components. The throttle bores are covered with a molybdenum coating which could be removed by the cleaner.

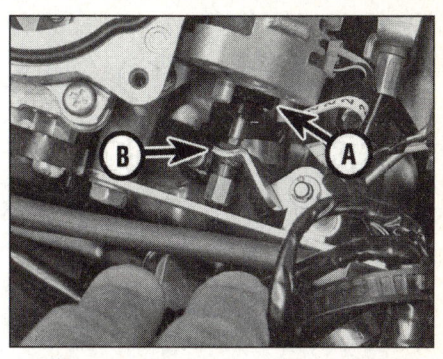

7.3 Unscrew the base nut (A) and free the valve from the linkage arm (B)

6 Fit each starter valve into its original location (the one with the adjuster nut on its outer end goes into the front cylinder throttle body), engaging it with the linkage arm, and tighten the valve base nut **(see illustration 7.3)**. Check that each valve moves smoothly and easily in its bore by turning the linkage, and that it closes fully under spring pressure.

7 Check the operation of the starter valve linkage before continuing; it should move smoothly and easily, drawing both valves out simultaneously, and return to the fully closed position under pressure of the return springs. If the No. 2 (front cylinder throttle body) valve is obviously out of synchronization with the No. 1 (base) valve (i.e. it starts to move before or after it) turn the adjuster nut as required to approximate the setting **(see illustration 7.18)**.

8 If removed install the fuel injectors and rail (see Section 5), then install the throttle body assembly (Section 6). Install the air filter housing (Section 2). On completion check the starter valve synchronisation (see below).

Fast idle cable

9 Remove the clutch lever (see Chapter 6) – its pivot bolt secures the choke lever. Detach the cable from the lever.

10 Refer to Section 6 and displace the throttle bodies, then free the fast idle cable end from the linkage. Withdraw the cable, noting its routing.

11 Installation is the reverse of removal.

Starter valve synchronisation

⚠️ *Warning: Do not allow exhaust gases to build up in the work area; either perform the check outside or use an exhaust gas extraction system.*

Note: Honda do not specify this as a service item, and say that it need only be carried out if the starter valves have been removed from the throttle body assembly. The procedure does not alter the setting of the throttle valves themselves (these are pre-set at the factory and fixed), but only the starter valves, which control the idle speed when the engine is cold and warming up. However on high mileage machines the linkage could wear and produce uneven idling when cold and warming up. If

4B•14 Fuel system – fuel injection models

7.15 Detach the air hose (arrowed) from each valve cover

7.18 Adjust the No. 2 starter valve by turning the adjuster nut (arrowed)

this is the case, then the synchronisation procedure should be carried out.

12 Starter valve synchronisation is simply the process of adjusting the No. 2 (front cylinder throttle body) valve so it passes the same amount of fuel/air mixture to the front cylinder as the No. 1 (rear cylinder throttle body) valve (which is the base valve and cannot be adjusted) passes to the rear cylinder on cold start and warm-up. This is done by measuring the vacuum produced in each intake duct. Starter valves that are out of synchronisation will result in uneven idling when cold starting and warming the engine. Before synchronising the starter valves, make sure the valve clearances are properly set (see Chapter 1).

13 To properly synchronise the starter valves, you will need a pair of vacuum gauges to indicate engine vacuum. The equipment used must have the necessary hoses and adapters to connect to the MAP sensor vacuum hoses on the throttle body. *Note: Because of the nature of the synchronisation procedure and the need for special instruments, most owners leave the task to a Honda dealer.*

14 Start the engine and warm it up to normal temperature, then stop it. Raise the fuel tank (see Chapter 4A). Detach the vacuum hoses from the side arms of the three-way T-joint to the MAP sensor **(see illustration 5.1)**. Start the engine and run it at more than 2000 rpm for more than five seconds to register a MAP sensor fault code in the ECU – this means the ECU will give it a pre-set value and allows the vacuum hoses to be connected to the gauges.

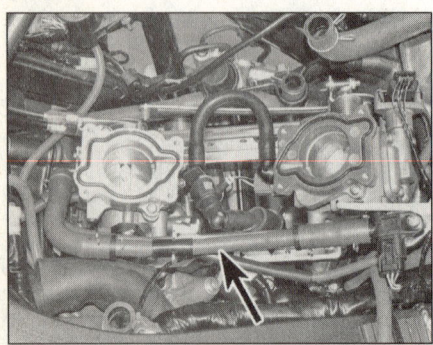

15 Remove the fuel tank (see Chapter 4A). Detach the air hose from the PAIR system reed valve cover union on each valve cover and fit a blanking cap onto each union **(see illustration)**.

16 Connect the gauge hoses to the vacuum hoses using suitable adapters, making sure the No. 1 gauge goes to the No. 1 throttle body. Make sure everything is a good fit because any air leaks will result in false readings.

17 Install the fuel tank in the raised position. Start the engine and adjust the idle speed (see Chapter 1). If using vacuum gauges fitted with damping adjustment, set this so that the needle flutter is just eliminated but so that they can still respond to small changes in pressure.

18 The vacuum reading for the No. 2 (front) cylinder should be the same as the No. 1 cylinder, or at least within the maximum difference specified at the beginning of the Chapter. The No. 1 cylinder starter valve is the base to which the No. 2 is matched, and cannot itself be adjusted. If the vacuum readings vary, adjust the No. 2 starter valve as required by turning the synchronisation nut on the end of the valve using a long screwdriver inserted from the left-hand side, until the reading is the same as No. 1 **(see illustration)**. *Note: Do not press hard on the nut whilst adjusting it, otherwise a false reading will be obtained.*

19 When the adjustment is complete, recheck the vacuum readings, then check and adjust the idle speed (see Chapter 1). Stop the engine.

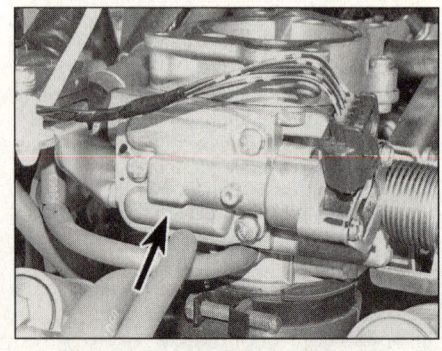

20 Remove the air filter housing. Disconnect the vacuum gauges and the hose adapters. Fit the vacuum hoses on to the MAP sensor three-way joint **(see illustration 5.1)**. Fit the PAIR system hoses back onto the unions on the reed valve covers and secure them with the clamps **(see illustration 7.15)**. Install the air filter housing, and the fuel tank. Check and adjust idle speed again. Refer to Section 4 and reset the ECU.

8 Intake air control valve (IACV) – XL-7 models onward

⚠️ *Warning: Refer to the precautions given in Section 1 before starting work.*

Check

1 Remove the fuel tank (see Chapter 4A). The control valve is mounted on the top of the rear cylinder throttle body. First make sure the wiring connector is secure **(see illustration 6.3b)**. Check that the system hoses linking the throttle bodies are secure and in good condition **(see illustration)**. Also make sure the valve and valve cover are not loose **(see illustration)**.

2 Turn the ignition ON and check that the valve makes a beeping sound. If no sound is heard turn the ignition OFF then remove the fuel tank (see Chapter 4A). Remove the valve (see below), leaving the wiring connected. Turn the ignition ON and visually check the movement of the valve.

3 If there is no movement, turn the ignition OFF, then disconnect the wiring connector from the valve. Also disconnect the ECU black wiring connector (see Section 5).

4 First make sure there is continuity in each wire between its terminal in the loom side of the control valve connector and the corresponding terminal in the ECU connector – if there isn't locate the break in the wire and repair it.

5 The control valve's internal circuitry can be checked by measuring the resistance between the two outer pins on the valve's connector (which connect to the black/orange and black/yellow wires), then the resistance between the two inner pins (which connect to the black/blue and black/red wires). The value in each case should agree with the figure in the Specifications at the beginning of this Chapter.

Removal

6 Remove the fuel tank (see Chapter 4A).
7 Disconnect the wiring connector from the valve **(see illustration 6.3b)**. Undo the valve screws, then remove the plate and withdraw the valve. Check the valve for wear and damage.
8 If required undo the valve cover screws and remove the cover **(see illustration 8.1b)**. Cover the opening with clean cloth. Check the

8.1a Intake air control valve link hoses (arrowed)

8.1b Intake air control valve cover (arrowed)

Fuel system – fuel injection models 4B•15

9.2 Slacken the bolt (arrowed) initially to release pressure, then unscrew it

10.3 The fuel pump wiring connector is inside the rubber boot (arrowed)

10.8 Release the clamps and detach the hoses (arrowed)

condition of the O-ring – Honda specify to use a new one whatever its condition.

Installation

9 Fit the new O-ring into the groove in the valve cover. Fit the cover and tighten the screws, making sure the O-ring stays in place **(see illustration 8.1b)**.
10 Turn the valve fully clockwise, then slide it into the cover, aligning the groove in the valve with the tab on the top of the cover. Fit the plate and tighten the screws **(see illustration 6.3b)**.
11 Connect the wiring connector).
12 Install the fuel tank (see Chapter 4A).

9 Fuel pressure check

⚠ **Warning: Refer to the precautions given in Section 1 before starting work.**

Note: *A pressure gauge is required for this check. Honda specify the use of their gauge (Pt. No. 07406-004000 3) along with a special banjo bolt and two sealing washers for the gauge to thread onto (Pt Nos. 90008-PP46-E02, 90428-PD6-003 and 90430-PD6-003). If a different gauge is used an adapter may be needed, either so it can thread onto the special banjo bolt, or that can be used in place of the special bolt. A gauge with a male end of the correct thread size and length could be used in place of the special bolt without an adapter. Two new sealing washers for the supply hose banjo bolt are also required.*

1 Remove the seat and the belly-pan, and disconnect the battery negative (–) terminal (see Chapters 8 and 9).
2 Place some rag around the fuel delivery pipe banjo bolt in the bottom of the fuel pump, and place a suitable container for holding fuel under the pump. Slacken the bolt until fuel comes out, but do not fully unscrew it until all residual fuel pressure is released **(see illustration)**. Unscrew the bolt with its sealing washer and catch any remaining fuel.
3 Fit a sealing washer onto the special banjo bolt then fit it through the delivery pipe union, thread it into the pump and tighten it. Thread the gauge into the banjo bolt using the second sealing washer and tighten it. Mop up any spilt fuel.
4 Connect the battery negative (–) lead then start the engine and allow it to idle at the specified speed. Note the pressure present in the fuel system by reading the gauge, then turn the engine off. Compare the reading obtained to that given in the Specifications.
5 If the fuel pressure is higher than specified, the fuel pump is faulty and must be replaced with a new one.
6 If the fuel pressure is lower than specified, likely causes are.
● Leaking fuel hose union.
● Blocked fuel strainer(s).
● Faulty fuel pump.
If necessary remove the fuel pump and clean the strainer. If the filter is blocked or the pressure regulator is faulty a new pump assembly must be installed (Section 10) – individual components are not available.
7 On completion, disconnect the battery negative (–) lead again. Remove the fuel gauge assembly, being prepared to catch the residual fuel. Fit a new sealing washer on each side of the delivery pipe union and fit the original banjo bolt through, tightening it to the torque setting specified at the beginning of the Chapter.
8 Reconnect the battery then start the engine and check that there is no sign of fuel leakage. If all is well, install the belly-pan and seat (see Chapter 8).

10 Fuel pump

⚠ **Warning: Refer to the precautions given in Section 1 before starting work.**

Check

1 The fuel pump is located under the front of the engine. The fuel pump runs for a few seconds when the ignition is switched ON to pressurise the fuel system, and then cuts out until the engine is started. Check that it does this. If the pump is thought to be faulty, first check the main and fuel pump fuses (see Chapter 9). If they are OK proceed as follows.
2 Raise the fuel tank (see Chapter 4A).
3 Ensure the ignition is switched OFF then disconnect the fuel pump wiring connector **(see illustration)**. Connect the positive (+) lead of a voltmeter to the brown wire terminal on the loom side of the connector and the negative (–) lead to the green wire terminal. Switch the ignition ON whilst noting the reading obtained on the meter.
4 If battery voltage is present for a few seconds, the fuel pump circuit is operating correctly and the fuel pump itself is faulty and must be replaced with a new one.
5 If no reading is obtained, check the fuel pump circuit wiring for continuity and make sure all the connectors are free from corrosion and are securely connected. Repair/replace the wiring as necessary and clean the connectors using electrical contact cleaner. If this fails to reveal the fault, check the following components.
● Engine stop switch (see Chapter 9).
● Fuel cut-off relay (see Section 5).
● Engine stop relay (see Section 5).
● Lean angle sensor (see Section 5).
● Engine control unit (ECU) (see Section 5).

Removal

6 Remove the seat and the belly-pan, and disconnect the battery negative (–) terminal (see Chapters 8 and 9). Turn the fuel taps OFF. Raise the fuel tank (see Chapter 4A).
7 Disconnect the fuel pump wiring connector **(see illustration 10.3)**. Place some rag around the fuel delivery pipe banjo bolt in the bottom of the fuel pump, and place a suitable container for holding fuel under the pump. Slacken the bolt until fuel comes out, but do not fully unscrew it until all residual fuel pressure is released **(see illustration 9.2)**. Unscrew the bolt and catch any remaining fuel. Discard the sealing washers on each side of the delivery pipe union and obtain new ones.
8 Release the clamps and detach the hoses from the top of the pump, noting which fits where, again being prepared with rag and container to catch residual fuel **(see illustration)**.

4B•16 Fuel system – fuel injection models

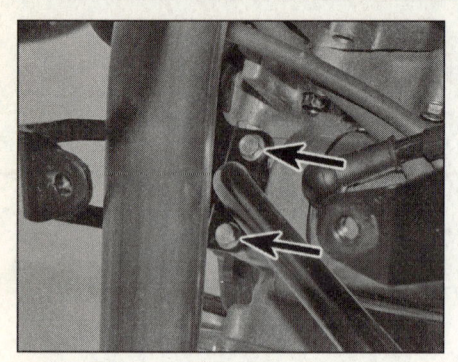

10.9a Unscrew the starter motor bolts (arrowed) . . .

10.9b . . . and the pump bracket bolts (arrowed)

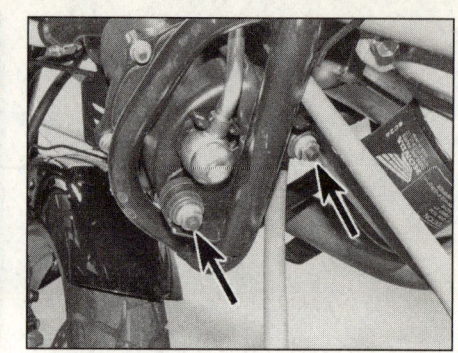

10.9c Unscrew the nuts to separate the pump from its bracket

9 Unscrew the starter motor mounting bolts **(see illustration)**. Unscrew the fuel pump mounting bracket bolts and carefully remove the pump assembly **(see illustration)**. Drain the pump of fuel by up-ending it into the container so the fuel come out of the top hose unions. If required unscrew the nuts and separate the pump from its bracket **(see illustration)**. Note the collars in the rubber grommets. The pump comes as a complete assembly and no individual components are available.

Installation

10 Installation is the reverse of removal. Make sure the pump mounting grommets are in good condition and the collars are fitted in them. Use new sealing washers on each side of the delivery pipe union. Make sure the hose clamps are secure. Check for leakage after starting the engine.

11 Fuel system hoses

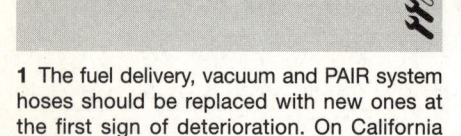

1 The fuel delivery, vacuum and PAIR system hoses should be replaced with new ones at the first sign of deterioration. On California models, also replace the EVAP emission control system hoses.
2 Remove the fuel tank and the air filter housing (see Sections 2 and 3).
3 Before detaching a hose, note any clamp that secures it and its routing between the components. Disconnect the vacuum hoses from the throttle bodies, the MAP sensor, air intake control valve and vacuum chamber, referring to the relevant Sections where necessary. Disconnect the PAIR system hoses from the control valve and reed valves, noting the routing of each one and how it is secured (see Chapter 4A). On California models refer to Chapter 4A for the EVAP system. **Note:** *It is advisable to make a sketch of the hoses before removing them to ensure they are correctly installed.* Make sure each new hose is correctly routed, not kinked or pinched, and fully pushed onto its union. Use new clamps if necessary where fitted.
4 The fuel supply hoses run from the fuel taps on the tank to the top of the fuel pump and the delivery pipe runs from the bottom of the pump to the throttle bodies. Refer to the relevant Section of this Chapter when detaching the hoses from the tank, pump or throttle bodies.
5 Use a new O-ring and sealing washers when fitting the new delivery pipe between the pump and throttle bodies. Tighten the union bolts to the torque settings specified at the beginning of the chapter. Run the engine and check that the fuel system is working correctly before taking the machine out on the road.

12 Catalytic converter

Note: *A catalytic converter is fitted as standard on XL-3 to 6 Germany models and all XL-7 onward European models, and may be available as standard or as an optional extra in some other markets.*

General information

1 A catalytic converter is incorporated in the exhaust system to minimise the level of exhaust pollutants released into the atmosphere.
2 The catalytic converter consists of a canister containing a fine mesh impregnated with a catalyst material, over which the hot exhaust gases pass. The catalyst speeds up the oxidation of harmful carbon monoxide, unburned hydrocarbons and soot, effectively reducing the quantity of harmful products released into the atmosphere via the exhaust gases.
3 The catalytic converter is of the closed-loop type with exhaust gas oxygen content information being fed back to the fuel injection system engine control unit (ECU) by the oxygen sensor.
4 The oxygen sensor contains a heating element which is controlled by the ECU. When the engine is cold, the ECU switches on the heating element which warms the exhaust gases as they pass over the sensor. This brings the catalytic converter quickly up to its normal operating temperature and decreases the level of exhaust pollutants emitted whilst the engine warms up. Once the engine is sufficiently warmed up, the ECU switches off the heating element.
5 Refer to Chapter 4A for exhaust system removal and installation, and Section 5 for oxygen sensor removal and installation information.

Precautions

6 The catalytic converter is a reliable and simple device which needs no maintenance in itself, but there are some facts of which an owner should be aware if the converter is to function properly for its full service life.

- DO NOT use leaded or lead replacement petrol (gasoline) – the additives will coat the precious metals, reducing their converting efficiency and will eventually destroy the catalytic converter.
- Always keep the ignition and fuel systems well-maintained in accordance with the manufacturer's schedule – if the fuel/air mixture is suspected of being incorrect have it checked on an exhaust gas analyser.
- If the engine develops a misfire, do not ride the bike at all (or at least as little as possible) until the fault is cured.
- DO NOT use fuel or engine oil additives – these may contain substances harmful to the catalytic converter.
- DO NOT continue to use the bike if the engine burns oil to the extent of leaving a visible trail of blue smoke.
- Remember that the catalytic converter and oxygen sensor are FRAGILE – do not strike them with tools during servicing work.

Chapter 5
Ignition system

Contents

Clutch switch – check and replacement . . . . see Chapter 9	Ignition HT coils – check, removal and installation 3
ECU (fuel injection models) – check, removal and installation. . . . . .see Chapter 4B	Ignition pulse generator – check, removal and installation 4
	Ignition system – check 2
Engine coolant temperature (ECT) sensor – check, adjustment and replacement. 8	Ignition timing – general information and check 6
	Immobiliser system 9
General information 1	Neutral switch – check and replacement. . . . . see Chapter 9
Ignition (main) switch – check, removal and installation . see Chapter 9	Sidestand switch – check and replacement. . . . . see Chapter 9
Ignition control unit (carburettor models) – check, removal and installation 5	Spark plugs – gap check and replacement . . . . see Chapter 1
	Throttle position sensor – check, adjustment and replacement . . . 7

Degrees of difficulty

Easy, suitable for novice with little experience	Fairly easy, suitable for beginner with some experience	Fairly difficult, suitable for competent DIY mechanic	Difficult, suitable for experienced DIY mechanic	Very difficult, suitable for expert DIY or professional

Specifications

General information
Spark plugs . . . . See Chapter 1

Ignition timing
At idle . . . . 15° BTDC (F mark)

Ignition HT coils
Primary winding resistance
   VTR models . . . . 0.4 to 0.8 ohms @ 20°C
   XL models. . . . . 3.2 ohms @ 20°C
Secondary winding resistance
   VTR models
      With plug cap . . . . 17.0 to 19.0 k ohms @ 20°C
      Without plug cap . . . . 12.0 to 14.0 k ohms @ 20°C
   XL models
      With plug cap . . . . 18.0 to 20.0 k ohms @ 20°C
      Without plug cap . . . . 13.0 to 15.0 k ohms @ 20°C
Plug cap resistance . . . . approx. 5 k ohms
Initial voltage (see text). . . . . Battery voltage (approximately 12 volts)
Minimum peak voltage (see text) . . . . 100 volts

Ignition pulse generator
Resistance . . . . 600 to 620 ohms @ 20°C
Minimum peak voltage (see text) . . . . 0.7 volts

5•2 Ignition system

Throttle position sensor
Resistance .... 4 to 6 k ohms @ 20°C
Input voltage (see text).. 4.7 to 5.3 volts

Engine coolant temperature sensor
Resistance
 @ 20°C .... 2 to 3 k ohms
 @ 80°C .... 200 to 400 k ohms

Torque settings
Ignition coil mounting bolts
 VTR models .... 10 Nm
 XL models... 12 Nm
Pulse generator bolts .... 12 Nm
Timing inspection cap .... 10 Nm
Engine coolant temperature sensor .... 23 Nm

1 General information

All models are fitted with a fully-transistorised electronic ignition system which, due to its lack of mechanical parts, is totally maintenance-free. The system comprises a rotor, pulse generator coil, ignition control unit, converter unit (VTR models) and ignition HT coils (refer to the wiring diagrams at the end of Chapter 9 for details).

The ignition triggers, which are on the right-hand end of the crankshaft, magnetically operate the pulse generator coil as the crankshaft rotates. The pulse generator coil sends a signal to the ignition control unit which then supplies the ignition HT coils with the power necessary to produce a spark at the plugs. A throttle position sensor and an engine coolant temperature sensor also supply the control unit with information that is used in determining the optimum firing point for all conditions. The system incorporates an electronic advance system controlled by the signals from the pulse generator coil and the sensors.

The system uses two HT coils, one for each cylinder. On VTR models, the front cylinder coil is mounted on the left-hand side of the frame above the front cylinder, the rear cylinder coil is mounted on the right-hand side of the rear sub-frame behind the seat cowl. On XL models, the front cylinder coil is mounted behind the heat shield above the front cylinder, the rear cylinder coil is mounted on the left-hand side of the rear sub-frame behind the side cover.

The system incorporates a safety interlock circuit which will cut the ignition if the sidestand is extended whilst the engine is running and in gear, or if a gear is selected whilst the engine is running and the sidestand is down. It also prevents the engine from being started if the sidestand is down and the engine is in gear unless the clutch lever is pulled in.

Because of their nature, the individual ignition system components can be checked but not repaired. If ignition system troubles occur, and the faulty component can be isolated, the only cure for the problem is to replace the part with a new one. Keep in mind that most electrical parts, once purchased, cannot be returned. To avoid unnecessary expense, make very sure the faulty component has been positively identified before buying a replacement part.

Note that there is no provision for adjusting the ignition timing on these models.

Many models are fitted with an immobiliser system (HISS – Honda Ignition Security System) which will not allow the engine to be started unless the correct key is used. The immobiliser system has its own fault diagnosis function.

Note: *Individual engine management system components can be checked but not repaired. If system troubles occur, and the faulty component can be isolated, the only cure for the problem in most cases is to replace the part with a new one. Keep in mind that most electronic parts, once purchased, cannot be returned. To avoid unnecessary expense, make very sure the faulty component has been positively identified before buying a new part.*

2 Ignition system – check

Warning: *The energy levels in electronic systems can be very high. On no account should the ignition be switched on whilst the plugs or plug caps are being held. Shocks from the HT circuit can be most unpleasant. Secondly, it is vital that the engine is not turned over or run with any of the plug caps removed, and that the plugs are soundly earthed (grounded) when the system is checked for sparking. The ignition system components can be seriously damaged if the HT circuit becomes isolated.*

1 As no means of adjustment is available, any failure of the system can be traced to failure of a system component or a simple wiring fault. Of the two possibilities, the latter is by far the most likely. In the event of failure, check the system in a logical fashion, as described below.

2 Disconnect the HT leads from the spark plugs – to access the rear cylinder spark plug, raise the rear of the fuel tank (see Chapter 4). Connect each lead to a spare spark plug that is known to be good and lay the plug on the engine with the threads contacting the engine **(see illustration)**. If necessary, hold the spark plug with an insulated tool.

Warning: *Do not remove either of the spark plugs from the engine to perform this check – atomised fuel being pumped out of the open spark plug hole could ignite, causing severe injury. Make sure the plugs are securely held against the engine – if they are not earthed when the engine is turned over, the ignition control unit could be damaged.*

3 Having observed the above precautions, check that the kill switch is in the RUN position and the transmission is in neutral, then turn the ignition switch ON and turn the engine over on the starter motor. If the system is in good condition a regular, fat blue spark should

2.2 Earth (ground) the spark plug and operate the starter - bright blue sparks should be visible

Ignition system 5•3

TOOL TiP

A simple spark gap testing tool can be made from a block of wood, a large alligator clip and two nails, one of which is fashioned so that a spark plug cap or bare HT lead end can be connected to its end. Make sure the gap between the two nail ends is the same as specified

2.5 Connect the tester as shown - when the starter is operated sparks should jump between the nails

be evident at each plug electrode. If the spark appears thin or yellowish, or is non-existent, further investigation will be necessary. Turn the ignition OFF.

4 The ignition system must be able to produce a spark which is capable of jumping a particular size gap. Honda do not provide a specification, but a healthy system should produce a spark capable of jumping at least 6 mm. A simple testing tool can be made to test the minimum gap across which the spark will jump **(see Tool Tip)**, or alternatively it is possible to buy an ignition spark gap tester tool and some of these tools are adjustable to alter the spark gap.

5 Connect one of the spark plug HT leads from one coil to the protruding electrode on the test tool, and clip the tool to a good earth (ground) on the engine or frame **(see illustration)**. Check that the kill switch is in the RUN position, turn the ignition switch ON and turn the engine over on the starter motor. If the system is in good condition a regular, fat blue spark should be seen to jump the gap between the nail ends. Repeat the test for the other coil. If the test results are good the entire ignition system can be considered good. If the spark appears thin or yellowish, or is non-existent, further investigation will be necessary.

6 Ignition faults can be divided into two categories, namely those where the ignition system has failed completely, and those which are due to a partial failure. The likely faults are listed below, starting with the most probable source of failure. Work through the list systematically, referring to the subsequent sections for full details of the necessary checks and tests. **Note:** *Before checking the following items ensure that the battery is fully charged and that all fuses are in good condition.*

a) Loose, corroded or damaged wiring connections, broken or shorted wiring between any of the component parts of the ignition system (see Chapter 9).
b) Faulty HT lead or spark plug cap, faulty spark plug, dirty, worn or corroded plug electrodes, or incorrect gap between electrodes.
c) Faulty ignition (main) switch or engine kill switch (see Chapter 9).
d) Faulty neutral, clutch or sidestand switch (see Chapter 9).
e) Faulty pulse generator coil or damaged trigger rotor.
f) Faulty ignition HT coil(s).
g) Faulty ignition control unit or converter unit (VTR models).

7 If the above checks don't reveal the cause of the problem, have the ignition system tested by a Honda dealer.

3 Ignition HT coils – check, removal and installation

Check

1 In order to determine conclusively that the ignition coils are defective, they must be tested by a Honda dealer equipped with a peak voltage tester.

2 However, you can check the coils visually (for loose or damaged terminals, cracks and other damage) and measure the primary and secondary coil resistance using any multimeter, or you can test them by using the Honda specified equipment and test procedures covered in Steps 8 to 10. If the coils and terminals are undamaged, and if the test readings are as specified at the beginning of the Chapter, they are probably capable of proper operation.

3 Remove the seat (see Chapter 8). Disconnect the battery negative (–ve) lead.

4 On VTR models, remove the fairing to access the front cylinder coil, and the seat to access the rear cylinder coil (see Chapter 8) **(see illustrations)**. Trace the primary circuit wiring from the coil and disconnect it at the connector **(see illustrations)**. Also disconnect the HT lead from the spark plug.

5 To access the front coil wiring connector(s),

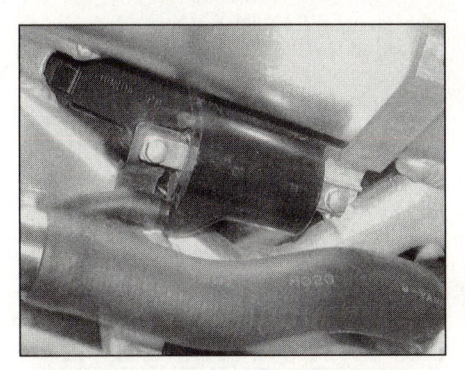

3.4a Front cylinder coil - VTR models

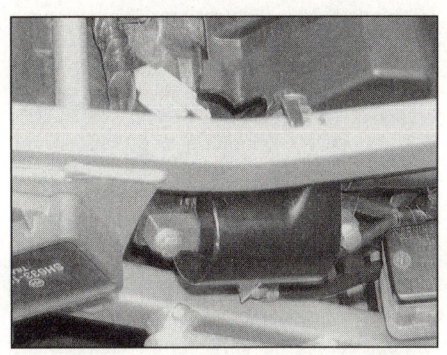

3.4b Rear cylinder coil - VTR models

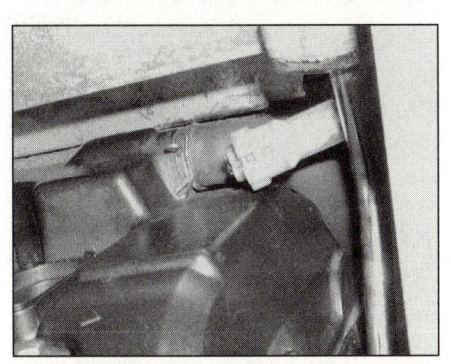

3.4c Front cylinder coil primary circuit connector - VTR models

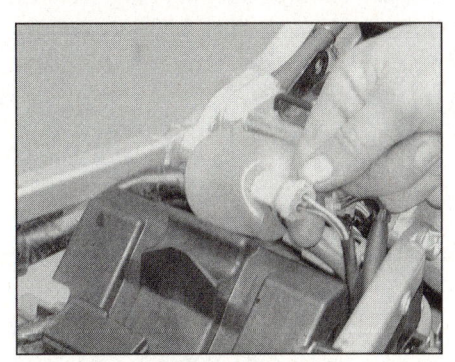

3.4d Rear cylinder coil primary circuit connector - VTR models

5•4 Ignition system

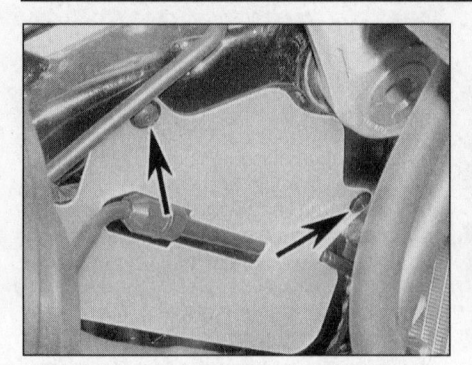

3.5a Release the trim clips (arrowed) and remove the shield on XL-X, Y, 1 and 2 models

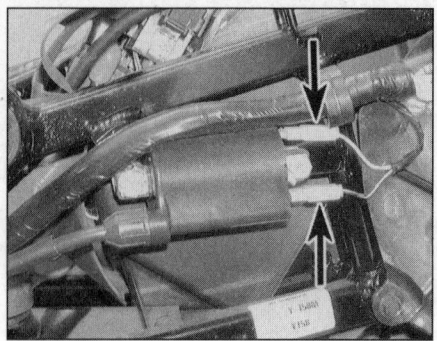

3.5b Rear cylinder coil and its primary circuit connectors (arrowed) – XL-X, Y, 1 and 2 models

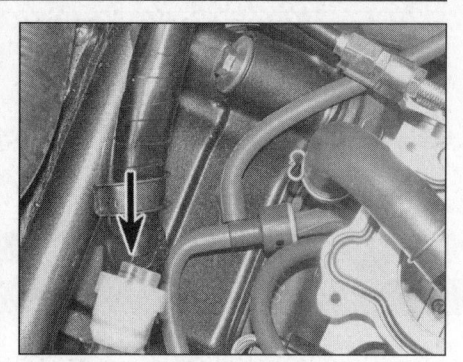

3.5c Front cylinder coil wiring connector (arrowed) – XL-3 models onward

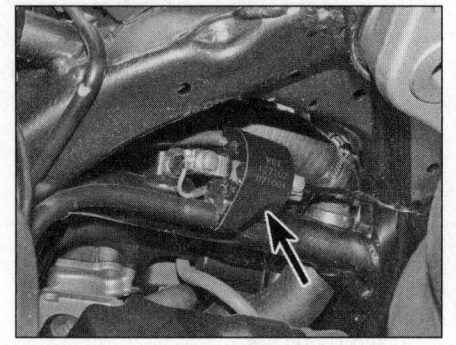

3.5d Front cylinder coil (arrowed) – XL-3 models onward

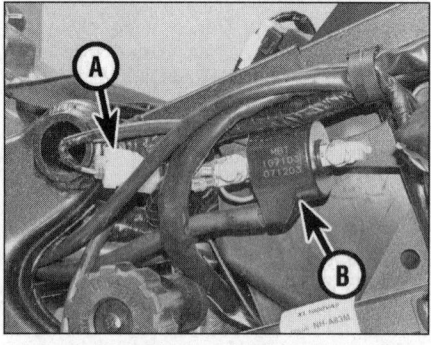

3.5e Rear cylinder coil (B) and its wiring connector (A) – XL-3 models onward

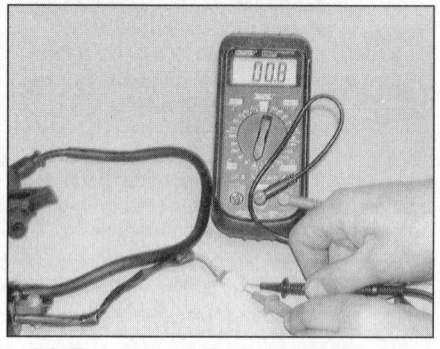

3.6 To test the coil primary resistance, connect the multimeter leads between the primary circuit terminals

on XL-X, Y, 1 and 2 models, remove the heat shield above the front cylinder **(see illustration)**, and on XL-3 models onward remove the air filter housing (see Chapter 4B). To access the rear coil wiring connector(s) remove the left-hand side cover (see Chapter 8). On XL-X, Y, 1 and 2 models disconnect the wiring connectors from the coil **(see illustrations)**. On XL-3 models onward disconnect the coil wiring connector **(see illustrations)**. On all models disconnect the HT lead from the spark plug. Mark the locations of all wires and leads before disconnecting them.

6 Set the meter to the ohms x 1 scale and measure the resistance between the primary circuit terminals on the coil side of the connector (VTR models) or on the coil itself (XL models) **(see illustration)**. This will give a resistance reading of the primary windings of the coil and should be consistent with the value given in the Specifications at the beginning of the Chapter.

7 To check the condition of the secondary windings, set the meter to the k ohm scale. Connect one meter probe to the spark plug cap and the other probe to the negative primary circuit terminal (green wire terminal on VTR models, black/white wire terminal on XL models) **(see illustration)**. If the reading obtained is not within the range shown in the Specifications, on VTR models unscrew the cap from the end of the HT lead, and on XL models remove lead from the coil by unscrewing the retainer, and repeat the measurement **(see illustration)**. If the reading is now as specified for the coil only, replace the spark plug caps on VTR models and the leads/caps on XL models with new ones. If the reading is still outside the specified range, it is likely that the coil is defective. To confirm this, the coil must be tested as described below using the specified equipment, or by a Honda dealer. To confirm that a lead or cap is faulty, measure its resistance and compare the reading to the Specifications **(see illustration)**.

8 Honda specify their own Imrie diagnostic tester (model 625), or the peak voltage adapter (Pt. No. 07HGJ-0020100) with an aftermarket digital multimeter having an impedance of

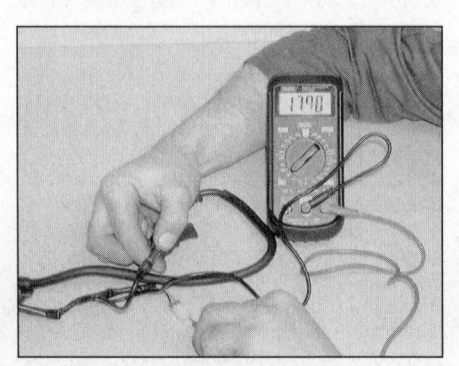

3.7a To test the coil secondary resistance, connect the multimeter leads as described

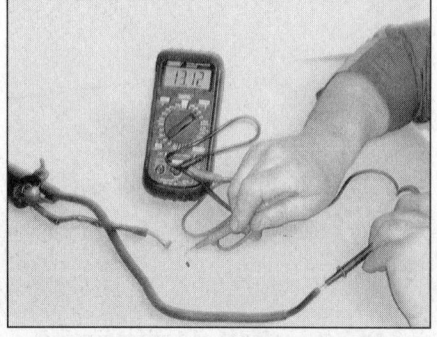

3.7b To eliminate a faulty cap or lead, remove it/them and check the coil again

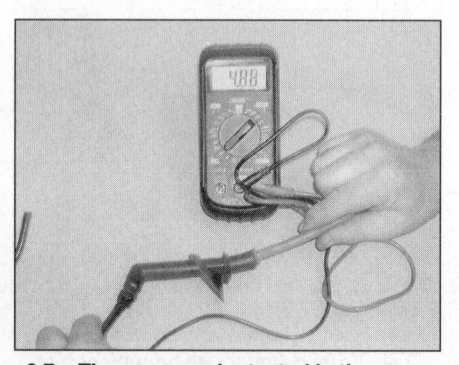

3.7c The caps can be tested in the same way

10 M ohm/DCV minimum, for a complete test. If this equipment is available, connect the positive (+ve) lead of the voltmeter and peak voltage adapter arrangement to the blue/yellow (front coil) or yellow/blue (rear coil) terminal of the connector (VTR) or coil (XL) with the wiring connector still securely connected, and connect the negative (–ve) lead to a suitable earth (ground) point.

9 Check that the kill switch is in the RUN position and the transmission is in neutral, then turn the ignition switch ON. Note the initial voltage reading on the meter, then turn the engine over on the starter motor and note the ignition coil peak voltage reading on the meter. Once both readings have been noted, turn the ignition switch off and disconnect the meter.

10 If the initial voltage reading is not as expected or the peak voltage readings are lower than the specified minimum then a fault is present in the ignition system circuit (see Section 2); note that the peak voltage readings for each coil can be different but each one must exceed the specified minimum.

11 If the initial and peak voltage readings are as specified and the plug does not spark, then the ignition HT coil, HT lead or plug cap are faulty (the plug caps and leads are available separately). In order to determine conclusively that an ignition coil is defective, it should be tested by a Honda dealer. If the coil is confirmed to be faulty, it must be renewed; the coil is a sealed unit and cannot therefore be repaired.

Removal

12 On VTR models, the front cylinder coil is mounted on the left-hand side of the frame above the front cylinder, the rear cylinder coil is mounted on the right-hand side of the rear sub-frame behind the seat cowl **(see illustrations 3.4a and 3.4b)**. Remove the fairing to access the front cylinder coil, and the seat to access the rear cylinder coil (see Chapter 8). Trace the primary circuit wiring from the coil and disconnect it at the connector **(see illustrations 3.4c and 3.4d)**. Also disconnect the HT lead from the spark plug.

13 On XL models, the front cylinder coil is mounted behind the heat shield above the front cylinder – remove the heat shield to access it **(see illustration 5.5a)**, and on XL-3 models onward remove the air filter housing to access the wiring connector (see Chapter 4B). The rear cylinder coil is mounted on the left-hand side of the rear sub-frame – remove the left-hand side cover to access it (see Chapter 8). On XL-X, Y, 1 and 2 models disconnect the wiring connectors from the coil **(see illustration 5.5b)**. On XL-3 models onward disconnect the coil wiring connector **(see illustrations 5.5c and d)**. On all models disconnect the HT lead from the spark plug. Mark the locations of all wires and leads before disconnecting them.

14 Unscrew the two bolts securing each coil, noting any spacers, and remove the coils. Note the routing of the HT leads.

Installation

15 Installation is the reverse of removal. Tighten the coil mounting bolts to the torque setting specified at the beginning of the Chapter. Make sure the wiring connectors and HT leads are securely connected.

4 Ignition pulse generator – check, removal and installation

Check

1 Remove the seat (see Chapter 8) and disconnect the battery negative (–ve) lead.
2 On VTR models remove the fairing (see Chapter 8). On XL models raise or remove the fuel tank (see Chapter 4A).
3 Trace the pulse generator coil wiring from the front of the clutch cover and disconnect it at the connector. On VTR models the connector is located under the left-hand side of the frame **(see illustration)**. On XL models the connector is housed inside the rubber boot on the left-hand side **(see illustration)**. Using a multimeter set to the K-ohms scale, measure the resistance between the white/yellow and yellow terminals on the pulse generator side of the connector **(see illustration)**.

4 Compare the reading obtained with that given in the Specifications at the beginning of this Chapter. The pulse generator must be replaced with a new one if the reading obtained differs greatly from that given, particularly if the meter indicates a short circuit (no measurable resistance) or an open circuit (infinite, or very high resistance).

5 If the pulse generator is thought to be faulty, first check that this is not due to a damaged or broken wire from the coil to the connector; pinched or broken wires can usually be repaired. If the readings obtained are as specified, check for continuity between the wiring connector on the loom side and the ignition control unit wiring connector.

6 Honda specify their own Imrie diagnostic tester (model 625), or the peak voltage adapter (Pt. No. 07HGJ-0020100) with an aftermarket digital multimeter having an impedance of 10 M ohm/DCV minimum, for a complete test. If this equipment is available, connect the positive lead of the voltmeter and peak voltage adapter to the yellow wire terminal of the connector, and connect the negative lead to the white/yellow wire terminal.

7 Turn the engine over on the starter motor and note the voltage reading obtained. If this reading is below the specified minimum, the ignition pulse generator is faulty.

Removal

8 Remove the seat (see Chapter 8) and disconnect the battery negative (–ve) lead.
9 On VTR models remove the fairing (see Chapter 8). On XL models raise the fuel tank (see Chapter 4).
10 Trace the pulse generator wiring from the front of the clutch cover and disconnect it at the connector. On VTR models the connector is located under the left-hand side of the frame **(see illustration 4.3a)**. On XL models the connector is housed inside the rubber boot on the left-hand side **(see illustration 4.3b)**.
11 Remove the water pump cover and water pump housing, which is integral with the clutch cover, that houses the pulse generator coil (see Chapter 3).
12 Unscrew the bolts securing the pulse

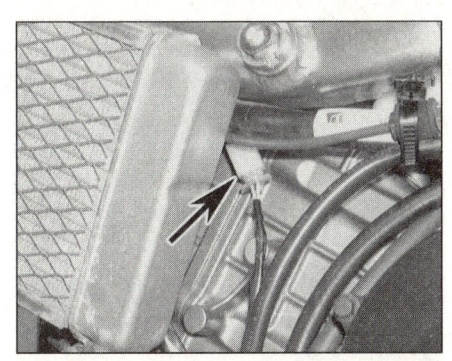

4.3a Pulse generator coil wiring connector (arrowed) – VTR models

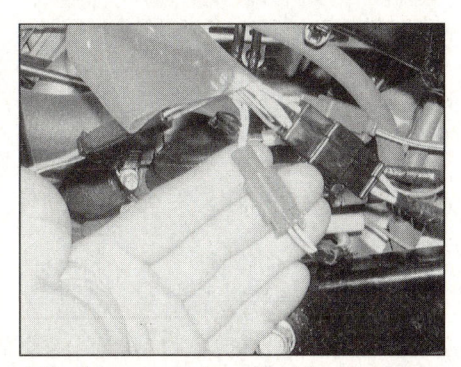

4.3b Pulse generator coil wiring connector – XL models

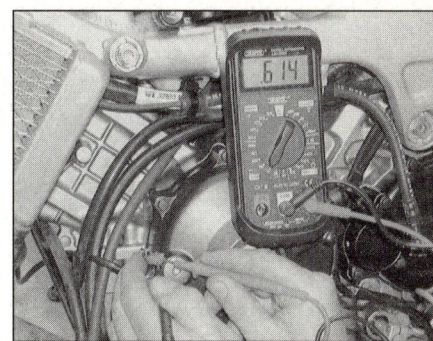

4.3c Testing the coil resistance

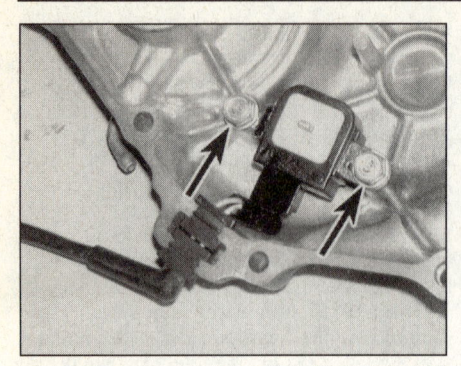

5•6 Ignition system

4.12 Pulse generator coil bolts (arrowed)

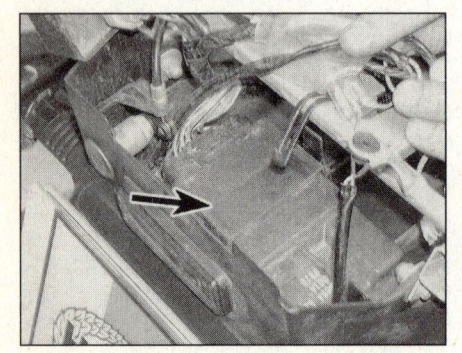

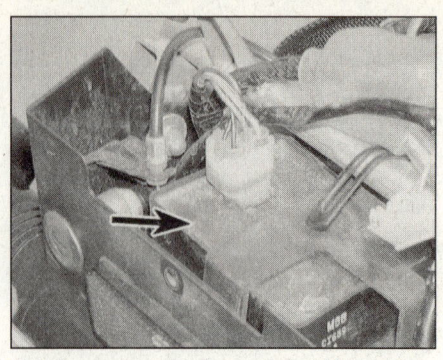

5.4 Converter unit (arrowed) - VTR models

5.5a Ignition control unit (arrowed) - VTR models

5.5b Ignition control unit (arrowed) - XL models

generator to the cover **(see illustration)**. Remove the rubber wiring grommet from its recess, then remove the pulse generator.

13 Examine the triggers on the rotor for signs of damage and replace it with a new one if necessary (see Chapter 2).

Installation

14 Install the pulse generator in the crankcase cover and tighten the bolts to the torque setting specified at the beginning of the Chapter – on XL-X, Y, 1 and 2 models Honda recommend using a thread-locking compound **(see illustration 4.12)**. Apply a suitable sealant to the wiring grommet and fit it into its recess.

15 Install the water pump cover and water pump housing (see Chapter 3).

16 Connect the pulse generator coil wiring connector **(see illustration 4.3a or b)**.

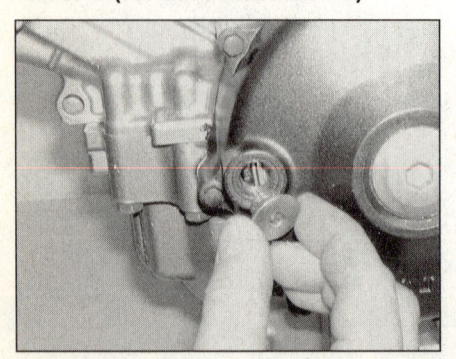

17 On VTR models install the fairing (see Chapter 8). On XL models lower the fuel tank (see Chapter 4).

18 Reconnect the battery negative (–ve) lead and install the seat (see Chapter 8).

5 Ignition control unit (carburettor models) – check, removal and installation

Check

1 If the tests shown in the preceding Sections have failed to isolate the cause of an ignition fault, it is possible that the ignition control unit (or its converter unit, where fitted) is faulty. No test details are available with which the unit(s) can be tested on home workshop equipment. Take the machine to a Honda dealer for testing.

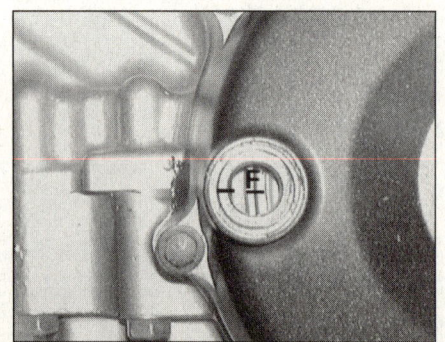

6.4 Remove the timing inspection cap

6.5 F mark and static timing mark

Removal

2 Remove the seat (see Chapter 8) and disconnect the battery negative (–ve) lead.
3 The control unit is mounted on the rear mudguard at the back, ahead of the taillight unit. On VTR models, remove the seat cowling (see Chapter 8, Section 4). On XL models, it should not be necessary to remove the seat cowling, but doing so maximises clearance.
4 Where fitted, disconnect the converter unit wiring connector and remove the unit if required, or just displace it to access the ignition control unit **(see illustration)**.
5 Lift the ignition control unit with its rubber sleeve off the sleeve's mounting lugs, then disconnect the wiring connector and remove the unit **(see illustrations)**.

Installation

6 Installation is the reverse of removal. Make sure the wiring connector is correctly and securely connected.

6 Ignition timing – general information and check

General information

1 Since no provision exists for adjusting the ignition timing and since no component is subject to mechanical wear, there is no need for regular checks; only if investigating a fault such as a loss of power or a misfire, should the ignition timing be checked.
2 The ignition timing is checked dynamically (engine running) using a stroboscopic lamp. The inexpensive neon lamps should be adequate in theory, but in practice may produce a pulse of such low intensity that the timing mark remains indistinct. If possible, one of the more precise xenon tube lamps should be used, powered by an external source of the appropriate voltage. **Note:** *Do not use the machine's own battery as an incorrect reading may result from stray impulses within the machine's electrical system.*

Check

3 Warm the engine up to normal operating temperature then stop it.
4 Unscrew the timing inspection cap from the left-hand crankcase cover **(see illustration)**. Discard the O-ring as a new one must be used.
5 The timing mark on the rotor which indicates the firing point at idle speed for the No. 1 cylinder is an F mark **(see illustration)**. The static timing mark with which these should align is the index line on the crankcase cover.

HAYNES HINT *The timing marks can be highlighted with white paint to make them more visible under the stroboscope light.*

Ignition system 5•7

6 Connect the timing light to the front cylinder HT lead as described in the manufacturer's instructions.
7 Start the engine and aim the light at the static timing mark.
8 With the machine idling, the timing mark F should align with the static timing mark.
9 Slowly increase the engine speed whilst observing the timing mark. The timing mark should start to move anti-clockwise at approximately 1500 rpm, increasing in relation to the engine speed until it reaches full advance (no identification mark).
10 As already stated, there is no means of adjustment of the ignition timing on these machines. If the ignition timing is incorrect, or suspected of being incorrect, one of the ignition system components is at fault, and the system must be tested as described in the preceding Sections of this Chapter.
11 When the check is complete, Install the timing inspection cap using a new O-ring, and smear it and the cap threads with grease **(see illustration 6.4)**. Tighten the cap to the torque settings specified at the beginning of the Chapter.

7 Throttle position sensor – check, adjustment and replacement

Note: *This procedure applies to carburettor-engined models. Refer to Chapter 4B, Section 5 for fuel injection models.*

1 The throttle position sensor (TPS) is mounted on the right-hand side of the rear cylinder carburettor and is keyed to the throttle shaft. The sensor provides the ignition control unit with information on throttle position and rate of opening or closing.

Check

2 Raise the fuel tank (see Chapter 4).
3 Make sure the ignition is switched OFF, then disconnect the sensor's wiring connector **(see illustration)**. Start the engine and increase the speed to 3500 rpm or above, then hold the throttle steady and reconnect the sensor wiring connector. The engine speed should increase.
4 Disconnect the sensor's wiring connector. Using an ohmmeter or multimeter set to the k ohms range, measure the sensor resistance by connecting the meter probes between the yellow/black and green/black (VTR models) or yellow/red and blue (XL models) wire terminals on the sensor. The meter reading should be as specified at the beginning of the Chapter.
5 Now measure the resistance range by connecting the meter probes between the red/yellow and green/black (VTR models) or yellow/blue and blue (XL models) wire terminals on the sensor, and slowly opening the throttle from fully closed to fully open and back to fully closed. The resistance should

increase as the throttle is opened, and decrease as the throttle is closed.
6 Turn the ignition switch ON and set the kill switch in the RUN position. Using a voltmeter, check the input voltage to the sensor by connecting the positive (+ve) probe to the yellow/black (VTR) or yellow/red (XL) wire terminal on the sensor connector, and the negative (–ve) probe to the green/black (VTR) or blue (XL) wire terminal. The voltage should be as specified at the beginning of the Chapter.
7 If the readings were as specified, using a multimeter set to resistance or a continuity tester, check for continuity between the terminals on the wiring loom side of the sensor wiring connector and the corresponding terminals on the ignition control unit connector, referring to the *Wiring Diagrams* at the end of Chapter 9 (first disconnect the ICU connector). There should be continuity between each terminal. If not, this is probably due to a damaged or broken wire between the connectors; pinched or broken wires can usually be repaired. Also check the connectors for loose or corroded terminals, and check the sensor itself for cracks and other damage. If the wiring and connectors are good, check the adjustment of the sensor as described below.
8 If the sensor is suspected of being faulty, take it to a Honda dealer for further testing. If it is confirmed to be faulty, it must be replaced with a new one; the sensor is a sealed unit and cannot therefore be repaired. If the sensor is good, have the ignition control unit checked by the dealer.

Replacement

9 Remove the carburettors (see Chapter 4). The throttle position sensor is mounted on the right-hand side of the rear cylinder carburettor **(see illustration)**.
10 On VTR models, the sensor is secured by shear-head bolts, which obviously cannot be undone using conventional tools. It may be possible to grip the outer edges sufficiently to turn them using pipe wrench pliers or something similar, otherwise the heads will have to be drilled off. Alternatively, cut a slot in the top of the bolts using a junior hacksaw or

Dremel, and then use a screwdriver in the normal way. Remove the sensor, noting how it keys onto the end of the throttle shaft. Obtain new shear-head bolts from a Honda dealer.
11 On XL models, the sensor is secured by Torx screws. Undo the screws and remove the sensor, noting how it keys onto the end of the throttle shaft.
12 On VTR models, install the sensor, locating the pin on the inside of the sensor between the tabs on the throttle shaft and lightly tighten the bolts. Using an ohmmeter set the ohms x 100 scale, connect the probes between the bottom two terminals on the sensor. Adjust the position of the sensor until the meter reading is between 490 and 510 ohms, then tighten the bolts until the heads shear off.
13 On XL models, install the sensor, locating the tab on the throttle shaft in the cut-outs on the inside of the sensor. Apply a suitable non-permanent thread locking compound to the Torx screw threads and lightly tighten them. Using an ohmmeter set the ohms x 100 scale, connect the probes between the bottom two terminals on the sensor. Adjust the position of the sensor until the meter reading is between 490 and 510 ohms, then tighten the screws securely.

8 Engine coolant temperature (ECT) sensor – check, adjustment and replacement

Note: *This procedure applies to carburettor-engined models. Refer to Chapter 4B, Section 5 for fuel injection models.*

Check

1 Remove the fuel tank (see Chapter 4). Drain the cooling system (see Chapter 1). The sensor is threaded into the thermostat housing.
2 Remove the sensor (see Step 7 below). Fill a small heatproof container with water and place it on a stove. Using an ohmmeter set to the k ohms scale, connect the probes of the meter to the terminals on the sender. Using some wire or other support suspend the sender in the coolant so that just the sensing portion and the threads are submerged. Also

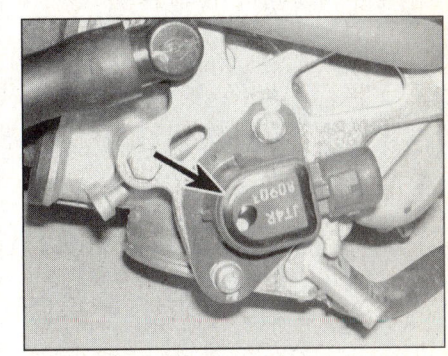

7.2 Disconnect the throttle position sensor wiring connector

7.9 Throttle position sensor (arrowed)

5•8 Ignition system

place a thermometer capable of reading temperatures up to 110°C in the water so that its bulb is close to the sender **(see illustration 5.9 in Chapter 3)**. **Note:** *None of the components should be allowed to directly touch the container.*

3 Heat the coolant, stirring it gently.

> **Warning:** *This must be done very carefully to avoid the risk of personal injury.*

4 When the temperature reaches around 20°C the meter should read between 2 and 3 k ohms. When the temperature reaches around 80°C the meter should read between 200 and 400 k ohms. If the meter readings obtained are different, or they are obtained at different temperatures, then the sensor is faulty and must be replaced with a new one.

5 If the readings were as specified, using a multimeter set to resistance or a continuity tester, check for continuity between the terminals on the wiring loom side of the sensor wiring connector and the corresponding terminals on the ignition control unit connector, referring to the *Wiring Diagrams* at the end of Chapter 9 (first disconnect the ICU connector). There should be continuity between each terminal. If not, this is probably due to a damaged or broken wire between the connectors; pinched or broken wires can usually be repaired. Also check the connectors for loose or corroded terminals, and check the sensor itself for cracks and other damage.

Replacement

> **Warning:** *The engine must be completely cool before carrying out this procedure.*

6 Remove the fuel tank (see Chapter 4). Drain the cooling system (see Chapter 1). The sensor is threaded into the thermostat housing.

7 Disconnect the sensor wiring connector **(see illustration)**. Unscrew the sensor and remove it from the thermostat housing. Discard the sealing washer.

8 Install the sensor using a new sealing washer and tighten it to the torque setting specified at the beginning of the Chapter. Connect the sensor wiring.

9 Refill the cooling system (see Chapter 1).

10 Install the fuel tank (see Chapter 4).

9 Immobiliser system

General information

1 An immobiliser system (known as HISS – Honda Ignition Security System) is fitted as standard to models in some markets from 2001-on as an anti-theft device. The system will only allow the machine to be started if the correct registered key is used to turn the ignition ON. The system consists of a transponder which is part of the ignition key, a

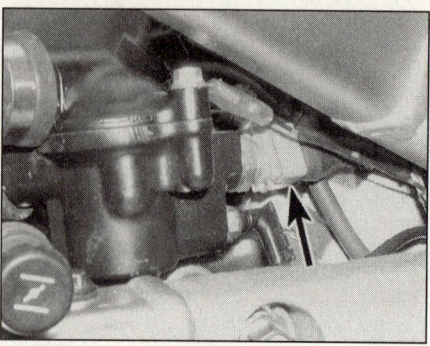

8.7 Engine coolant temperature sensor (arrowed)

receiver which is fitted around the ignition switch, and the ignition control unit (ICU– carburettor models) or engine control unit (ECU – XL models with fuel injection).

2 When the ignition is switched ON, the ICU/ECU sends power through the receiver to the transponder. The transponder sends a coded signal back through the receiver to the ICU/ECU. If the signal sent by the transponder matches the signal stored in the ICU/ECU memory, the immobiliser indicator light in the instrument cluster comes on for two seconds, then goes out, and the ICU/ECU allows the engine to be started. If the key code signal is not recognised, or if there is a fault in the system, the indicator light stays on. If the light stays on, refer to the fault diagnosis and troubleshooting sections below. Likewise if the light does not come on at all.

3 The ICU/ECU can store the codes for up to four registered keys. They keys should be kept separately (i.e. not on the same key-ring) as the proximity of another key to the one being used in the switch can lead to the signal from it being jammed, and the bike will not start. The key has a built-in transponder which can be damaged if the key is dropped or knocked, gets too hot, is too close to a magnetic object, or is submerged in water for too long. If all the keys are lost, the ICU/ECU must be replaced with a new one, so always make sure you have at least one spare key. If a new key is obtained, it must be registered into the system before the bike can be started with the key.

Key registration procedure

With the original ignition switch

Note: *To do this you will need the Honda special tool (Part No. 07XMZ-MBW0100 or 0101 according to model – ask your dealer) which is a wiring loom adapter that connects to a battery and plugs into the loom side of the ignition pulse generator wiring connector. If this tool is not available, registration must be carried out at a Honda dealer with the special tool.*

4 Obtain a new key from a Honda dealer, and have it cut to match the original key.

5 On VTR models remove the fairing (see Chapter 8). On XL models raise the fuel tank (see Chapter 4A). Trace the ignition pulse generator wiring from the front of the clutch cover and disconnect it at the 2-pin wiring connector **(see illustration 4.3a or b)**. Connect the special tool wiring connector to the loom side of the connector, then connect the red coloured clip of the tool to the battery positive (+) terminal and the green coloured clip to the battery negative (–) terminal.

6 Turn the ignition switch ON using your original key. The immobiliser indicator light should come on and stay on – if it starts to flash after ten seconds, then there is a fault in the system, which will have gone into fault diagnosis mode, and the pattern of the flashes it emits should be matched with the fault code (see below). Now disconnect the red clip from the battery positive terminal and leave it disconnected for at least two seconds, then reconnect it. The indicator should now come on for two seconds, then begin to flash repeatedly four times. This indicates that the system is in registration mode. At this point the registrations of all keys except the one in the switch will have been cancelled, so if you have another spare apart from the new one you want to register, this will also have to be registered.

7 Turn the ignition OFF and remove the key, placing it well away from the receiver.

8 Insert the new key into the switch and turn it ON. The indicator should now come on for four seconds, then begin to flash repeatedly four times. This indicates that the system has registered the new key. Turn the ignition OFF and remove the key.

9 To register any other spare keys that will have been cancelled, repeat Steps 7 and 8. Up to four keys can be registered.

10 On completion turn the ignition OFF, then remove the special tool and reconnect the ignition pulse generator wiring connector. Now turn the ignition ON using any of the registered keys to return the system to normal mode.

11 Check that all registered keys can start the motorcycle.

With a new ignition switch

Note: *To do this you will need the Honda special tool (Part No. 07XMZ-MBW0100 or 0101 according to model – ask your dealer) which is a wiring loom adapter that connects to a battery and plugs into the loom side of the ignition pulse generator wiring connector. If this tool is not available, registration must be carried out at a Honda dealer with the special tool.*

12 Obtain a new switch and two (or more if you want) new keys.

13 Remove the faulty switch (see Chapter 9), but retain the HISS receiver to fit with the new switch.

14 On VTR models remove the fairing (see Chapter 8). On XL models raise the fuel tank (see Chapter 4A). Trace the ignition pulse generator wiring from the front of the clutch cover and disconnect it at the 2-pin wiring connector **(see illustration 4.3a or b)**.

Ignition system

Connect the special tool wiring connector to the loom side of the connector, then connect the red coloured clip of the tool to the battery positive (+) terminal and the green coloured clip to the battery negative (–) terminal.

15 Place one of the original registered keys for the faulty switch next to the receiver.

16 Connect the new ignition switch to its connector in the wiring loom, but keep it away from the receiver. Turn the new switch ON with one of the new keys. The immobiliser indicator light should come on and stay on, which means the ICU/ECU recognises the old key that is next to the receiver – if it starts to flash after ten seconds, then there is a fault in the system, which will have gone into fault diagnosis, and the pattern of the flashes it emits should be matched with the fault code (see below). Now disconnect the red clip from the battery positive terminal and leave it disconnected for at least two seconds, then reconnect it. The indicator should now come on for two seconds, then begin to flash repeatedly four times. This indicates that the system is in registration mode. At this point the registrations of all keys except the one near the receiver will have been cancelled.

17 Turn the ignition OFF and remove the new key.

18 Install the new ignition switch, then fit the receiver onto it (see Chapter 9).

19 Insert the new key into the switch and turn it ON. The indicator should now come on for four seconds, then begin to flash repeatedly four times. This indicates that the system has registered the new key. If the indicator starts to flash after ten seconds, then there is a fault in the system, which will have gone into fault diagnosis mode, and the pattern of the flashes it emits should be matched with the fault code (see below). Turn the ignition OFF and disconnect the red clip of the special tool from the battery positive terminal.

20 Turn the ignition ON using the newly registered key. The indicator light should come on for two seconds, then go off.

21 Turn the ignition OFF and reconnect the red clip to the battery positive terminal.

22 Turn the ignition ON using the newly registered key. The indicator light should come on and stay on. Now disconnect the red clip from the battery positive terminal and leave it disconnected for at least two seconds, then reconnect it. The indicator should now come on for two seconds, then begin to flash repeatedly four times. This indicates that the system is in registration mode. At this point the registrations of all old keys (for the faulty switch) are cancelled.

23 Turn the ignition OFF and remove the key, placing it well away from the receiver.

24 Insert the second new unregistered key and turn the ignition ON. The indicator should now come on for four seconds, then begin to flash repeatedly four times. This indicates that the system has registered the second new key. Turn the ignition OFF and remove the key.

25 To register any other new spare keys, repeat Steps 23 and 24. Up to four keys can be registered.

26 On completion turn the ignition OFF, then remove the special tool and reconnect the ignition pulse generator wiring connector. Now turn the ignition ON using any of the registered keys to return the system to normal mode.

27 Check that all newly registered keys can start the motorcycle.

With a new ICU/ECU

28 Obtain a new ICU/ECU along with two (or more if you want) new keys. Install the new ICU/ECU (see Section 5 for carburettor models or Chapter 4B for fuel injection models). Have the keys cut to match the original key for your ignition switch.

29 Insert a new key into the switch and turn it ON. The indicator should now come on for two seconds, then begin to flash repeatedly four times. This indicates that the system has registered the new key. If the indicator stays on for ten seconds then starts to flash, then there is a fault in the system, which will have gone into fault diagnosis mode, and the pattern of the flashes it emits should be matched with the fault code (see below).

30 Turn the ignition OFF and remove the key.

31 Insert the second new key and turn the ignition ON. The indicator should now come on for two seconds, then begin to flash repeatedly four times. This indicates that the system has registered the second new key.

32 Turn the ignition OFF and remove the key.

33 The new ICU/ECU must have two new keys registered (or it will not enter normal mode) and will only register two keys at this stage. If you have a third key that you want to register, refer to Steps 4 to 10 to register it, noting that you will need the special tool mentioned therein.

34 Check that both newly registered keys can start the motorcycle.

Fault diagnosis

Note: *To do this you will need the Honda special tool (Part No. 07XMZ-MBW0100 or 0101 according to model – ask your dealer) which is a wiring loom adapter that connects to a battery and plugs into the loom side of the ignition pulse generator wiring connector. If this tool is not available, registration must be carried at a Honda dealer with the special tool.*

35 There are two fault diagnosis modes, one for if there is a fault during normal use, and one for a fault that occurs when registering a new key. Make sure you refer to the correct table below when matching the fault code pattern.

36 If the indicator light has come on and stayed on during normal use, on VTR models remove the fairing (see Chapter 8). On XL models raise the fuel tank (see Chapter 4A). Trace the ignition pulse generator wiring from the front of the clutch cover and disconnect it at the 2-pin wiring connector (see illustration 4.3a or b). Connect the special tool wiring connector to the loom side of the connector, then connect the red coloured clip of the tool to the battery positive (+) terminal and the green coloured clip to the battery negative (–) terminal.

37 Turn the ignition switch ON. The indicator light in the instrument cluster will come on for ten seconds, then start to flash. This means it has entered diagnostic mode, and the pattern of the flashes indicates the fault that has occurred. The pattern repeats continuously. Match the pattern with the fault codes below, making sure you refer to the relevant table. If the indicator stays on after ten seconds and does not flash, then there is no fault logged in the system.

If fault is indicated during normal use		
Flash pattern	**Fault**	**Solution**
Two short, one long, one short	Faulty ICU/ECU	Install new ICU/ECU
Two short, two long	Faulty receiver or wiring	Follow Troubleshooting procedure below
One long, three short	Signal jammed by other key	Place other key well away from receiver
One long, two short, one long	Signal jammed by other key	Place other key well away from receiver

If fault is indicated during key registration		
Flash pattern	**Fault**	**Solution**
One short, one long, one short, one long	Key already registered	Use a new or cancelled key
Two short, two long	Faulty receiver or wiring	Follow Troubleshooting procedure below
One short, one long, two short	Key already registered on old ICU/ECU	Use a new key

5•10 Ignition system

Troubleshooting procedure

Indicator light does not come on when ignition switched ON

38 Check the fuses (see Chapter 9).
39 If the fuses are good, make sure the engine is in neutral then turn the ignition ON and check whether the oil pressure and neutral warning lights come on.
40 If the lights have not come on, access the instrument cluster wiring connector, then pull the rubber boot off but leave it connected (see Chapter 9). Using a voltmeter, connect the positive (+) probe to the black/brown wire terminal on the loom side of the instrument cluster connector and the negative (–) probe to the green wire terminal on the loom side of the connector. With the ignition ON there should be battery voltage. If voltage is present, the instrument cluster is faulty (see Chapter 9). If there is no voltage, check for continuity in the wiring, referring to the wiring diagrams at the end of Chapter 9. The green wire goes to earth (ground).
41 If the lights have come on, see Section 5 for carburettor models or Chapter 4B for fuel injection models to access the ICU/ECU and disconnect the wiring connector. Using a voltmeter, connect the positive (+) probe to the white/red (VTR models) or blue/orange (XL models) wire terminal on the loom side of the connector and the negative (–) probe to earth (ground). Turn the ignition ON – there should be battery voltage.
42 If there was no voltage, using a voltmeter, connect the positive (+) probe to the white/red (VTR models) or blue/orange (XL models) wire terminal on the instrument cluster connector and the negative (–) probe to earth. Turn the ignition ON – there should be no voltage for two seconds, then there should be battery voltage. If there is no voltage after two seconds, check for continuity in the white/red or blue/orange wire, and also in the green wire to earth, referring to the wiring diagrams at the end of Chapter 9. If voltage is present, the instrument cluster is faulty (see Chapter 9).
43 If there is voltage in Step 41, disconnect the ICU/ECU wiring connector. Using a voltmeter, connect the positive (+) probe to the black/white wire terminal on the loom side of the connector and the negative (–) probe to earth (ground). Turn the ignition ON – there should be battery voltage. If there is no voltage, check for continuity in the black/white wire referring to the wiring diagrams at the end of Chapter 9. If voltage is present, check that there is continuity to earth (ground) in the green wire. If the wire is good, check the ICU/ECU connector for loose, damaged or corroded terminals. If the connector is good, then the ICU/ECU could be faulty, and should be checked by a Honda dealer.

Indicator light stays on when ignition switched ON

44 Check that none of the other registered keys are close to the receiver. If they are, remove them and try the ignition again.
45 Turn the ignition ON with a spare key and check the indicator light, which should come on for two seconds, then go out. If it does, the first key is faulty. If it doesn't, perform the fault diagnosis procedure described above. If a fault code is displayed, use the appropriate table to determine the fault and the solution.
46 If no fault code is displayed, or the system does not go into fault diagnosis mode, see Section 5 for carburettor models or Chapter 4B for fuel injection models to access the ICU/ECU and disconnect the wiring connector. Using a voltmeter, connect the positive (+) probe to the white/red (VTR models) or blue/orange (XL models) wire terminal on the loom side of the connector and the negative (–) probe to earth (ground). Turn the ignition ON – there should be battery voltage. If there is no voltage, check for continuity in the white/red or blue/orange wire between the ICU/ECU and the indicator light.
47 If there is voltage, check for continuity in the yellow and white/yellow wires between the ICU/ECU and the ignition pulse generator coil, referring to the wiring diagrams at the end of Chapter 9. If there is no continuity, trace the fault and repair or replace the wiring as necessary. If there is continuity, the ICU/ECU could be faulty and should be taken to a Honda dealer for assessment.

Fault code indicated by flash pattern

48 If the 'two short, two long' flash pattern has been indicated during the fault diagnosis procedure, trace the wiring from the receiver on the ignition switch and disconnect it at the 4-pin connector. Using a voltmeter, connect the positive (+) probe to the yellow/red wire terminal on the loom side of the receiver connector and the negative (–) probe to earth (ground). Turn the ignition ON – there should be approximately 5 volts present. If there is no voltage, check for continuity in the yellow/red wire between the ICU/ECU and the receiver, and repair or replace the wiring if there is no continuity.
49 If there is 5 volts present, check for continuity to earth (ground) in the green/orange (VTR and XL-3 models onward) or green/black (XL-1 and 2 models) wire on the loom side of the connector, and repair or replace the wiring if there is no continuity.
50 If the wiring is good, using a voltmeter, connect the positive (+) probe to the pink wire terminal on the loom side of the receiver connector and the negative (–) probe to earth (ground). Turn the ignition ON – there should be approximately 5 volts present. If there is, the receiver is faulty.
51 If there is no voltage, check for continuity in the orange/blue and pink wires between the ICU/ECU and the receiver, and repair or replace the wiring if there is no continuity between the connectors, or if there is continuity in either to earth (ground). If the wiring is good, the receiver is faulty.

Replacement

52 To replace the receiver, trace the wiring from the receiver on the ignition switch and disconnect it at the 4-pin connector. Feed the wiring back to the receiver, freeing it from any ties and noting its routing. Undo the screws and remove the receiver, noting how it fits. If you don't have the correct tools to easily access the screws, removing the fairing will help (see Chapter 8), otherwise follow the procedure for removing the top yoke in the ignition switch replacement Section in Chapter 9.
53 To replace the ICU/ECU see Section 5 for carburettor models or Chapter 4B for fuel injection models.

Chapter 6
Frame, suspension and final drive

Contents

Drive chain – removal, cleaning and installation	15
Drive chain and sprockets – check, adjustment and lubrication	see Chapter 1
Footrests, brake pedal and gearchange lever – removal and installation	3
Forks – disassembly, inspection and reassembly	7
Forks – oil change	see Chapter 1
Forks – removal and installation	6
Frame – inspection and repair	2
General information	1
Handlebar switches – check	see Chapter 9
Handlebar switches – removal and installation	see Chapter 9
Handlebars and levers – removal and installation	5
Rear shock absorber – removal, inspection and installation	10
Rear sprocket coupling/rubber dampers – check and replacement	17
Rear suspension linkage – removal, inspection and installation	11
Sidestand – check	see Chapter 1
Sidestand – lubrication	see Chapter 1
Sidestand – removal and installation	4
Sidestand switch – check and replacement	see Chapter 9
Sprockets – check and replacement	16
Steering head bearings – freeplay check and adjustment	see Chapter 1
Steering head bearings – inspection and replacement	9
Steering head bearings – lubrication	see Chapter 1
Steering stem – removal and installation	8
Suspension – adjustments	12
Suspension – check	see Chapter 1
Swingarm – inspection and bearing replacement	14
Swingarm – removal and installation	13
Swingarm and suspension linkage bearings – lubrication	see Chapter 1

Degrees of difficulty

Easy, suitable for novice with little experience	Fairly easy, suitable for beginner with some experience	Fairly difficult, suitable for competent DIY mechanic	Difficult, suitable for experienced DIY mechanic	Very difficult, suitable for expert DIY or professional

Specifications

Front forks

Fork oil type	Pro-Honda SS8 suspension fluid or 10W fork oil
Fork oil capacity	
VTR models	448 ± 2.5 cc
XL-X, Y, 1 and 2 models	529 ± 2.5 cc
XL-3 models onward without ABS	531 ± 2.5 cc
XL-4 models onward with ABS	
Right-hand fork	538 ± 2.5 cc
Left-hand fork	511 ± 2.5 cc
Fork oil level*	
VTR models	130 mm
XL-X, Y, 1 and 2 models	114 mm
XL-3 models onward without ABS	112 mm
XL-4 models onward with ABS	
Right-hand fork	103 mm
Left-hand fork	114 mm
Fork spring free length (min)	
VTR models	
Standard	309.9 mm
Service limit	303.7 mm
XL-X, Y, 1 and 2 models	
Standard	428.8 mm
Service limit	420.2 mm
XL-3 models onward without ABS	
Standard	422.6 mm
Service limit	414.1 mm
XL-4 models onward with ABS	
Standard	485.4 mm
Service limit	475.7 mm
Fork tube runout limit	0.2 mm

*Oil level is measured from the top of the tube with the fork spring removed and the leg fully compressed.

Frame, suspension and final drive

Final drive
Drive chain slack and lubricant	See Chapter 1
Drive chain	
VTR models	
Type	DID 50ZVM or RK 50LFOZ2
Length	102 links
XL models	
Type	DID 525HV or RK 525ROZ1
Length	112 links
Joining link pin projection from side plate (unstaked)	
DID type chain	1.30 to 1.50 mm
RK type chain	1.20 to 1.40 mm
Joining link staked ends diameter	
DID type chain	5.50 to 5.80 mm
RK type chain	5.45 to 5.85 mm
Sprocket sizes	
Front (engine) sprocket	
VTR models	16T
XL models	16T
Rear (wheel) sprocket	
VTR models	41T
XL models	47T

Torque settings
Rear master cylinder mounting bolts	
VTR models	10 Nm
XL models	12 Nm
Footrest bracket bolt (XL models)	
X, Y, 1 and 2 models	35 Nm
3 models onward	40 Nm
Swingarm pivot bolt nut	93 Nm
Sidestand pivot bolt	10 Nm
Sidestand pivot bolt nut	29 Nm
Handlebar end-weight screws	10 Nm
Front brake master cylinder clamp bolts	12 Nm
Clutch master cylinder clamp bolts (VTR models)	12 Nm
Handlebar holder clamp bolts (XL models)	27 Nm
Handlebar holder nuts (XL models)	27 Nm
Bottom yoke fork clamp bolts	
VTR models	49 Nm
XL models	27 Nm
Top yoke fork clamp bolts	
VTR models	23 Nm
XL models	22 Nm
Fork top bolt	
VTR models	23 Nm
XL models	22 Nm
Fork damper rod bolt	20 Nm
Steering head bearing adjuster nut (see text)	25 Nm
Steering stem nut	103 Nm
Shock absorber mounting bolt nuts	
VTR models	44 Nm
XL models	
Upper	59 Nm
Lower	44 Nm
Suspension linkage bolt nuts	
VTR models	44 Nm
XL models	
Linkage arm to linkage plate	44 Nm
Linkage arm to bracket	59 Nm
Linkage plate to swingarm	88 Nm
Front sprocket bolt	54 Nm
Rear sprocket nuts	108 Nm

Frame, suspension and final drive 6•3

3.1a Front footrest pivot pin (arrowed)

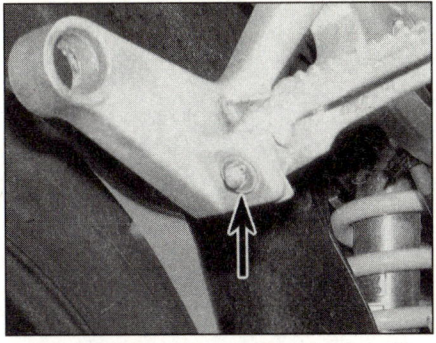

3.1b Rear footrest pivot pin (arrowed)

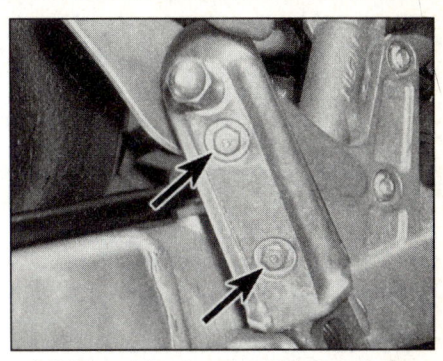

3.2 The rubber is secured by two bolts (arrowed)

1 General information

The VTR models use an aluminium trellis type frame. The XL models use a box-section steel trellis type frame.

Front suspension is by a pair of oil-damped telescopic forks. On VTR models, the forks have a cartridge damper and are adjustable for spring pre-load and rebound damping. Standard XL models (non-ABS) have a conventional damper and are not adjustable, but on models with ABS the left-hand fork is fitted with a cartridge damper.

At the rear, an alloy swingarm acts on a single shock absorber via a three-way linkage. The swingarm is mounted onto the back of the engine. On VTR models, the shock absorber is adjustable for spring preload and rebound damping. On standard XL models, the shock absorber is adjustable for spring pre-load, and on models with ABS it is also adjustable for rebound damping.

The drive to the rear wheel is by chain and sprockets.

2 Frame – inspection and repair

1 The frame should not require attention unless accident damage has occurred. In most cases, frame replacement is the only satisfactory remedy for such damage. A few frame specialists have the jigs and other equipment necessary for straightening the frame to the required standard of accuracy, but even then there is no simple way of assessing to what extent the frame may have been over-stressed.

2 After the machine has accumulated a lot of miles, the frame should be examined closely for signs of cracking or splitting at the welded joints. Loose engine mount bolts can cause ovaling or fracturing of the mounting tabs. Minor damage can often be repaired by welding, depending on the extent and nature of the damage.

3 Remember that a frame which is out of alignment will cause handling problems. If misalignment is suspected as the result of an accident, it will be necessary to strip the machine completely so the frame can be thoroughly checked.

3 Footrests, brake pedal and gearchange lever – removal and installation

Footrests

Removal

1 Remove the split pin and washer from the bottom of the footrest pivot pin, then withdraw the pivot pin and remove the footrest (see illustrations). On the front footrests, note the fitting of the return spring. On the rear footrests, note the fitting of the detent plate, ball and spring, and take care that they do not spring out when removing the footrest.

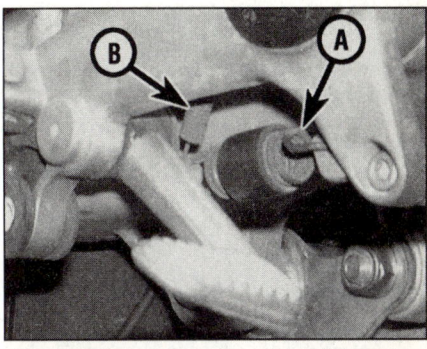

3.4a Brake pedal return spring (A), brake light switch spring (B) – VTR models

2 The rider's footrest rubbers can be renewed if required – they are secured to the footrest by two bolts on the underside (see illustration).

Installation

3 Installation is the reverse of removal.

Brake pedal

Removal

4 Unhook the brake pedal return spring from the hook on the bracket and the brake light switch spring from the hook on the pedal (see illustrations). On VTR models, slacken the rear brake master cylinder mounting bolts (see illustration).

5 Unscrew the bolt securing the footrest bracket to the engine and the bolt securing the footrest bracket to the silencer (see illustrations). On VTR models, note the spacer between the bracket and the engine.

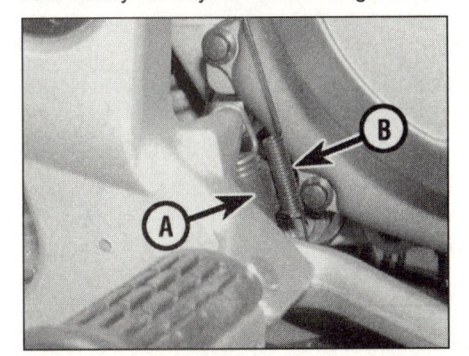

3.4b Brake pedal return spring (A), brake light switch spring (B) – XL models

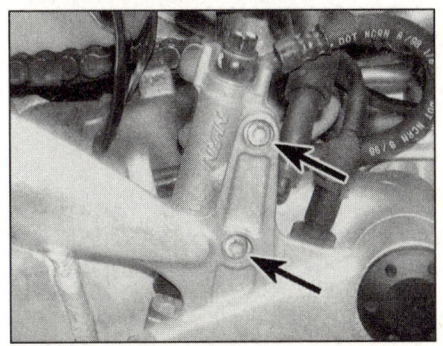

3.4c Master cylinder mounting bolts (arrowed)

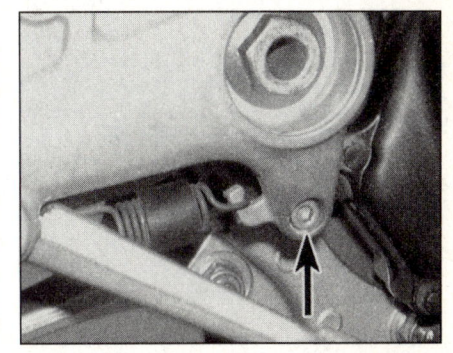

3.5a Footrest bracket to engine bolt (arrowed) – VTR models

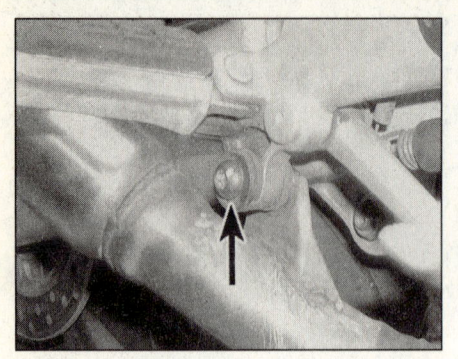

6•4 Frame, suspension and final drive

3.5b Footrest bracket to silencer bolt (arrowed) – VTR models

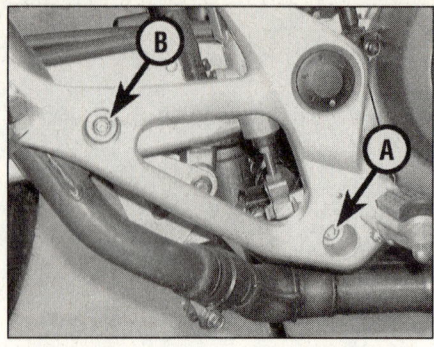

3.5c Footrest bracket-to-engine bolt (A), bracket-to-silencer bolt (B) – XL models

3.6a Remove the pivot covers, then unscrew the nut on the left-hand end of the pivot bolt

6 Remove the swingarm pivot covers and unscrew the nut on the left-hand end of the pivot bolt **(see illustration)**. Draw the right-hand footrest bracket away from the engine until the silencer mounting lug clears the silencer pipe, then pivot it anti-clockwise until the inside of the brake pedal pivot is accessible **(see illustration)**. Do not draw the footrest away any more than is necessary to provide the necessary clearance.

7 Remove the circlip and washer securing the brake pedal on its pivot **(see illustration)**. On VTR models, unscrew the rear brake master cylinder mounting bolts and draw the pedal and master cylinder off the bracket. On XL models, if there is enough clearance to remove the clevis from the master cylinder pushrod without displacing the master cylinder, then do so **(see illustration)**. Otherwise unscrew the bolts and displace it.

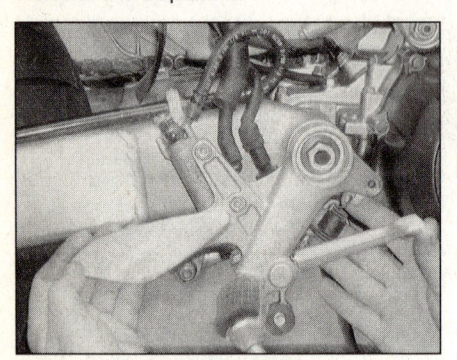

8 Remove the split pin from the clevis pin securing the brake pedal to the master cylinder pushrod **(see illustration 3.7a or 3.7b)**. Remove the clevis pin and separate the pedal from the pushrod. On XL models, if not done as above, now slide the pedal off its pivot.

Installation

9 Installation is the reverse of removal, noting the following:
a) Apply molybdenum disulphide oil to the brake pedal pivot.
b) Use a new split pin on the clevis pin securing the brake pedal to the master cylinder pushrod.
c) Tighten the master cylinder mounting bolts to the torque setting specified at the beginning of the Chapter.
d) Tighten the footrest bracket bolt before the swingarm pivot bolt/nut. Tighten the swingarm bolt/nut, and on XL models the footrest bracket bolt, to the specified torque settings. On VTR models tighten the footrest bolt securely, and do not omit the spacer **(see illustration)**.
e) Check the operation of the rear brake light switch (see Chapter 1).

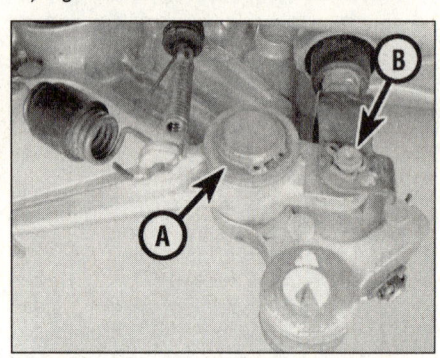

Gearchange lever

Removal

10 Slacken the gearchange lever linkage rod locknuts, then unscrew the rod and separate it from the lever and the arm (the rod is reverse-threaded on one end and so will simultaneously unscrew from both lever and arm when turned in the one direction) **(see illustrations)**. Note how far the rod is

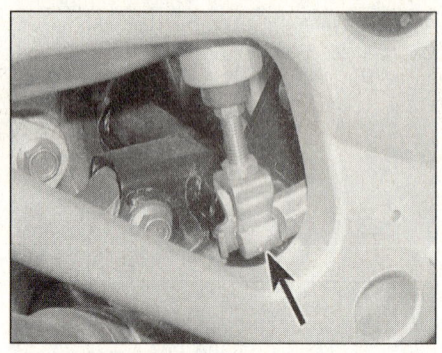

3.6b Draw the footrest bracket out and pivot it as shown

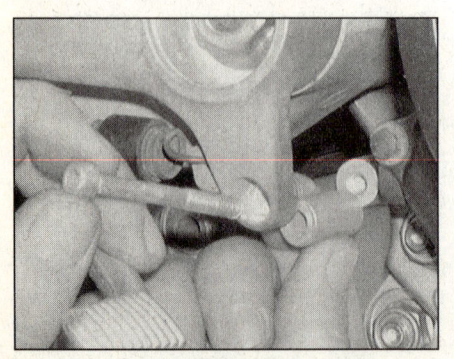

3.7a Brake pedal retaining circlip (A), master cylinder pushrod clevis pin (B)

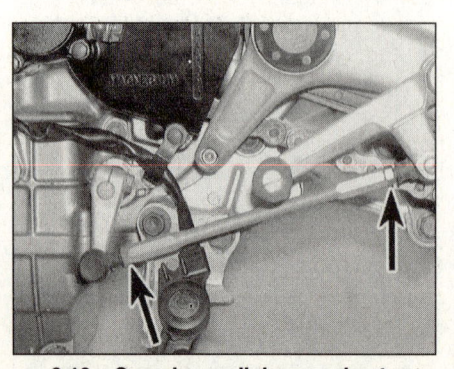

3.7b On XL models, remove the clevis pin (arrowed) if clearance allows

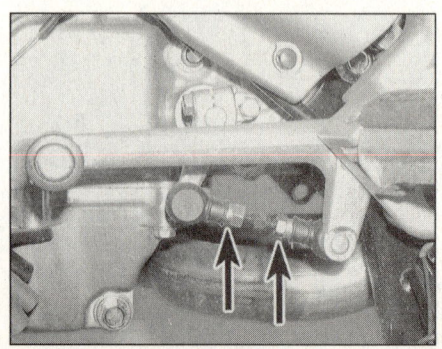

3.9 Do not forget the spacer

3.10a Gearchange linkage rod nuts (arrowed) – VTR models

3.10b Gearchange linkage rod nuts (arrowed) – XL models

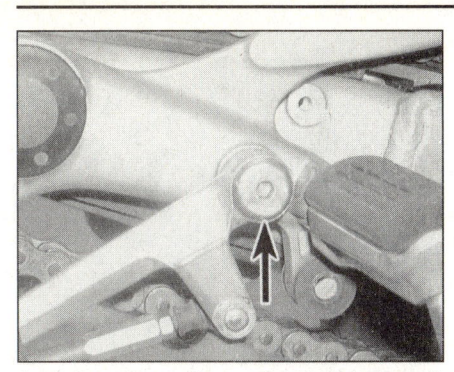

Frame, suspension and final drive 6•5

3.11 Gearchange lever pivot bolt (arrowed) – VTR models

5.1a Disconnect the wiring connectors (arrowed)

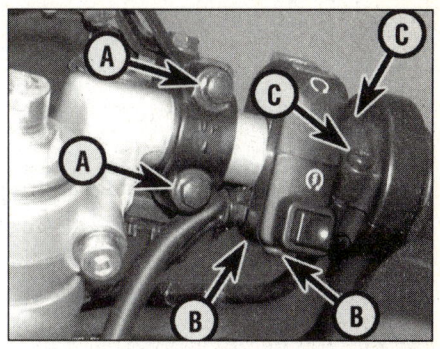

5.1b Master cylinder clamp bolts (A), handlebar switch screws (B), throttle housing screws (C)

threaded into the lever and arm as this determines the height of the lever relative to the footrest.

11 On VTR models, unscrew the lever pivot bolt and remove the bolt, the lever and the washer **(see illustration)**.

12 On XL models, unscrew the bolt securing the left-hand footrest bracket to the engine and the bolt securing the footrest bracket to the silencer. Remove the swingarm pivot covers and unscrew the nut on the left-hand end of the pivot bolt. Remove the footrest bracket. Unscrew the lever pivot bolt and remove the bolt, the lever and the washer.

Installation

13 Installation is the reverse of removal, noting the following:
a) Apply molybdenum disulphide oil to the gear lever pivot.
b) On XL models, tighten the footrest bracket bolt before the swingarm pivot bolt/nut, and tighten them to the torque settings specified at the beginning of this Chapter. On VTR models tighten the footrest bolt securely.
c) Adjust the gear lever height as required by screwing the linkage rod in or out of the lever and arm. Tighten the locknuts securely.

4 Sidestand – removal and installation

1 The sidestand is attached to a bracket on the frame. Springs anchored to the stand ensures that it is held in the retracted or extended position.
2 Support the bike using an auxiliary stand. Remove the sidestand switch (see Chapter 9).
3 Unhook the stand springs, then unscrew the nut on the inside of the pivot bolt. Unscrew the pivot bolt and remove the stand.
4 On installation apply grease to the pivot bolt shank and tighten the bolt and nut to the torque settings specified at the beginning of the Chapter. Reconnect the sidestand springs and check that they hold the stand securely up when not in use – an accident is almost certain to occur if the stand extends while the machine is in motion.
5 Check the operation of the sidestand switch (see Chapter 1).

5 Handlebars and levers – removal and installation

VTR models

Right handlebar removal

Note: *The handlebar can be displaced from the top yoke without having to remove the individual assemblies from them – follow Steps 4 and 5 only.*

1 Disconnect the wires from the brake light switch **(see illustration)**. Unscrew the two master cylinder assembly clamp bolts and position the assembly clear of the handlebar, making sure no strain is placed on the hydraulic hose **(see illustration)**. Keep the master cylinder reservoir upright to prevent possible fluid leakage.
2 Unscrew the two handlebar switch screws and free the switch from the handlebar **(see illustration 5.1b)**. Unscrew the two throttle cable housing screws and lift the top of the housing off.
3 Unscrew the handlebar end-weight retaining screw, then remove the weight from the end of the handlebar **(see illustration 5.8)**.

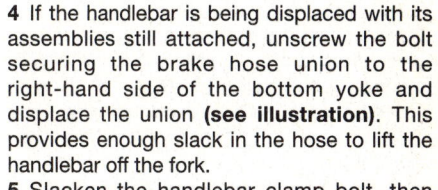

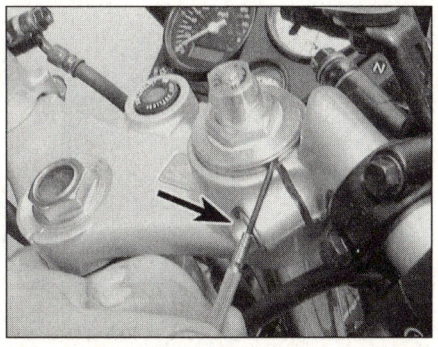

5.5a Slacken the clamp bolt (arrowed) and remove the circlip . . .

4 If the handlebar is being displaced with its assemblies still attached, unscrew the bolt securing the brake hose union to the right-hand side of the bottom yoke and displace the union **(see illustration)**. This provides enough slack in the hose to lift the handlebar off the fork.
5 Slacken the handlebar clamp bolt, then prise the circlip from the top of the fork using a small screwdriver inserted in the slit in the clamp **(see illustration)**. Ease the handlebar up and off the fork **(see illustration)**. Slide the throttle twistgrip and cable housing assembly off the handlebar.

Left handlebar removal

Note: *The handlebar can be displaced from the top yoke without having to remove the*

5.4 Unscrew the bolt (arrowed) and displace the union

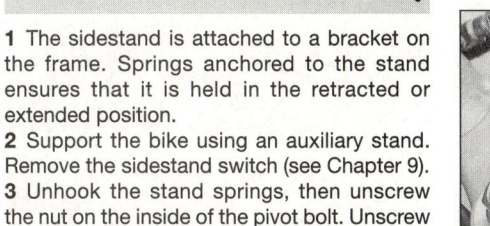

5.5b . . . then slide the handlebar up off the fork

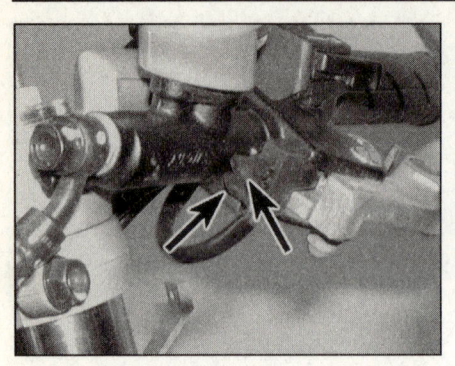

6•6 Frame, suspension and final drive

5.6a Disconnect the wiring connectors (arrowed)

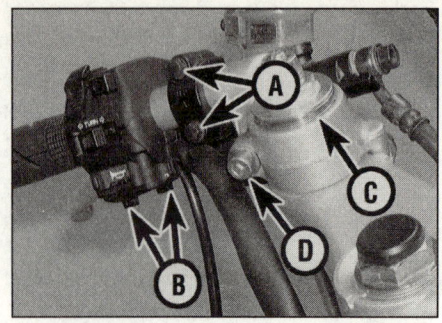

5.6b Master cylinder clamp bolts (A), handlebar switch screws (B), circlip (C), handlebar clamp bolt (D)

5.8 Handlebar end-weight screw (arrowed)

individual assemblies from them – follow Step 9 only.

6 Disconnect the wires from the clutch switch **(see illustration)**. Unscrew the two master cylinder assembly clamp bolts and position the assembly clear of the handlebar, making sure no strain is placed on the hydraulic hose **(see illustration)**. Keep the master cylinder reservoir upright to prevent possible fluid leakage.

7 Unscrew the two handlebar switch screws and free the switch from the handlebar **(see illustration 5.6b)**.

8 If required, unscrew the handlebar end-weight retaining screw, then remove the weight from the end of the handlebar and slide off the grip **(see illustration)**. If the grip has been glued on, you will probably have to slit it with a knife to remove it.

9 Slacken the handlebar clamp bolt, then prise the circlip from the top of the fork using a small screwdriver inserted in the slit in the clamp **(see illustrations 5.6b and 5.5a)**. Ease the handlebar up and off the fork **(see illustration)**.

Installation

10 Installation is the reverse of removal, noting the following.
a) When installing the right handlebar, apply some grease to it and slide the throttle twistgrip and cable housing assembly on before fitting the handlebar onto the fork.
b) When fitting the handlebars onto the forks, locate the lug on the bottom of each handlebar in the slot in the yoke, so that the handlebars are set in the correct position **(see illustration)**.
c) Fit the circlip into its groove before tightening the handlebar clamp bolt **(see illustration)**. Refer to the Specifications at the beginning of the Chapter and tighten the clamp bolts to the specified torque setting.
d) Make sure the front brake and clutch master cylinder assembly clamps are installed with the UP mark facing up, and with the clamp mating surfaces aligned with the punchmark on the top of the handlebar. Tighten the master cylinder clamp bolts to the specified torque setting, tightening the top bolt first.
e) Make sure the pin in the lower half of each switch housing and in the top of the throttle cable housing locates in its hole in the handlebar. Tighten the front housing screw first, then the rear.
f) When installing the handlebar end-weights, align the boss with the groove on the inner weight inside the handlebar. Use new end-weight retaining screws and tighten them to the specified torque setting. If new grips are being fitted, secure them using a suitable adhesive.
g) Do not forget to reconnect the front brake light switch and clutch switch wiring connectors **(see illustrations 5.1a and 5.6a)**.

Front brake lever removal

11 Undo the lever pivot screw locknut, then undo the pivot screw and remove the lever **(see illustration)**.

Clutch lever removal

12 Undo the lever pivot screw locknut, then undo the pivot screw and remove the lever **(see illustration)**. Note how the pushrod end locates into the hole in the swivel-piece.

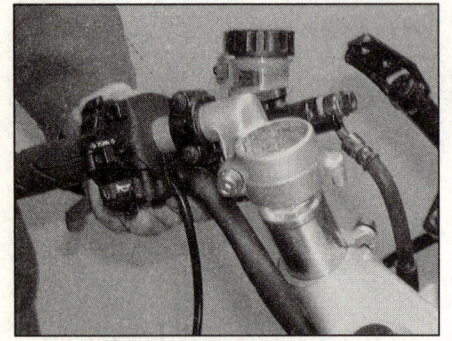

5.9 Slide the handlebar up off the fork

5.10a Locate the lug in the slit in the yoke (arrowed)

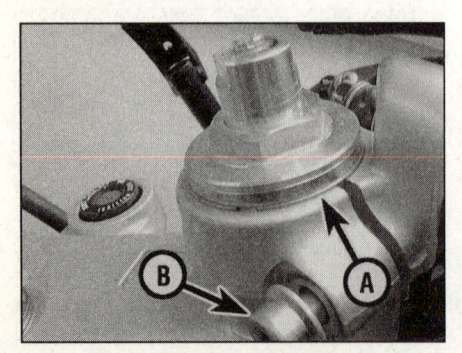

5.10b Locate the circlip (A) before tightening the clamp bolt (B)

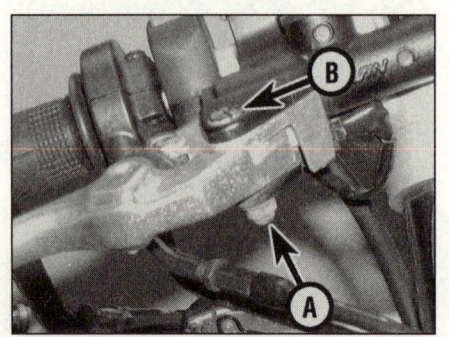

5.11 Undo the nut (A), then undo the pivot screw (B) and remove the lever

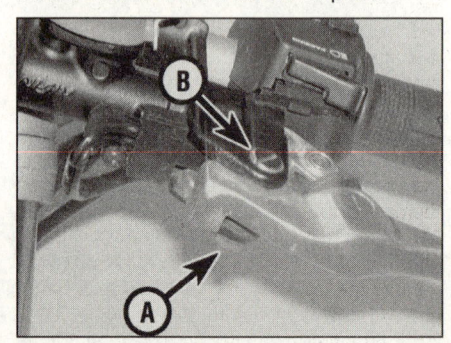

5.12 Undo the nut (A), then undo the pivot screw (B) and remove the lever

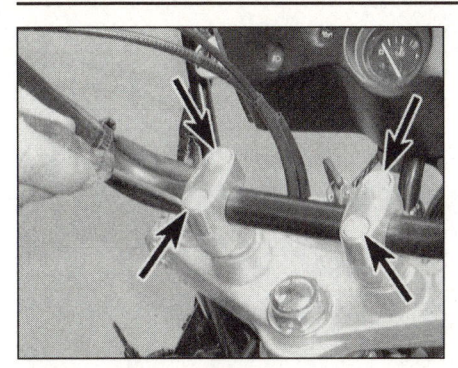

Frame, suspension and final drive 6•7

5.21 Prise off the caps and unscrew the clamp bolts (arrowed)

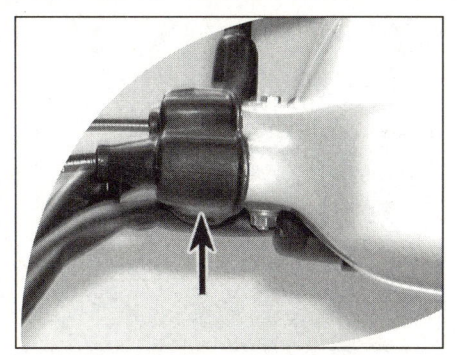

5.26a Pull back the rubber boot (arrowed) . . .

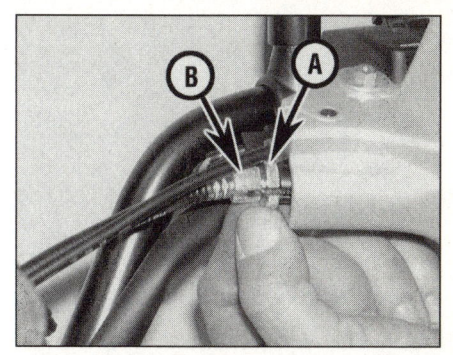

5.26b . . . then slacken the lockring (A) and thread the adjuster (B) fully in

Installation

13 Installation is the reverse of removal. Apply grease to the pivot bolt shafts the contact areas between the lever and its bracket. Apply a spray lubricant such as WD-40, or a dry-film Teflon lubricant to the lever span adjuster mechanism.

XL models

Handlebar removal

Note: *The handlebars can be displaced from the top yoke without having to remove the individual assemblies from them – follow Steps 4 and 5 only.*

14 Remove the rear view mirrors (see Chapter 8). Also remove the handguards (see below under lever removal).

15 Disconnect the wires from the brake light switch. Unscrew the two master cylinder assembly clamp bolts and position it clear of the handlebar, making sure no strain is placed on the hydraulic hose. Keep the master cylinder reservoir upright to prevent possible fluid leakage.

16 Disconnect the wires from the clutch switch. Unscrew the two clutch lever assembly clamp bolts and position it clear of the handlebar.

17 Unscrew the handlebar switch screws and free the switches from the handlebar.

18 Refer to Chapter 4, Section 11, Step 4, and detach the throttle cables.

19 Unscrew the right handlebar end-weight retaining screw, then remove the weight from the end of the handlebar and slide the throttle twistgrip off the end. If required, unscrew the left handlebar end-weight retaining screw, then remove the weight from the end of the handlebar and slide off the grip. If the grip has been glued on, you will probably have to slit it with a knife to remove it.

20 If the handlebar holders are being removed from the top yoke, slacken the nuts securing them on the underside of the yoke now.

21 Prise the caps out of the handlebar holder clamp bolts, then unscrew the bolts and remove the clamp(s) and the handlebars **(see illustration)**.

22 If required, unscrew the nuts and remove the washers on the handlebar holders, then draw them out of the top yoke. Check the condition of the rubber bushes in the top yoke and replace them with new ones if they are damaged or deteriorated.

Installation

23 Installation is the reverse of removal, noting the following.

a) If removed, tighten the handlebar holder nuts after the handlebars are installed, and tighten them to the torque setting specified at the beginning of the Chapter.
b) Align the punchmark on the back of the handlebar with the mating surfaces of the right handlebar holder and clamp. Fit the individual handlebar clamps on XL-X, Y, 1 and 2 models with the punch mark at the front, and the one-piece clamp on all other models with the punch marks at the front, and tighten the front bolts first, then the rear, to the specified torque setting.
c) Apply some grease to the throttle twistgrip section of the handlebar.
d) Make sure the front brake master cylinder assembly clamp is installed with the UP mark facing up, and with the clamp mating surfaces aligned with the punchmark on the top of the handlebar. Tighten the master cylinder clamp bolts to the specified torque setting, tightening the top bolt first.
e) Align the clutch lever assembly clamp mating surfaces with the punchmark on the back of the handlebar, and tighten the front bolt before the rear bolt.
f) Make sure the pin in the lower half of each switch housing locates in its hole in the handlebar.. Tighten the front housing screw first, then the rear.
g) Align the throttle cable housing half mating surfaces with the punchmark on the handlebar.
h) When installing the handlebar end-weights, align the boss with the groove on the inner weight inside the handlebar. Use new end-weight retaining screws and tighten them to the specified torque setting. If new grips are being fitted, secure them using a suitable adhesive.
i) Do not forget to reconnect the front brake light switch and clutch switch wiring connectors.

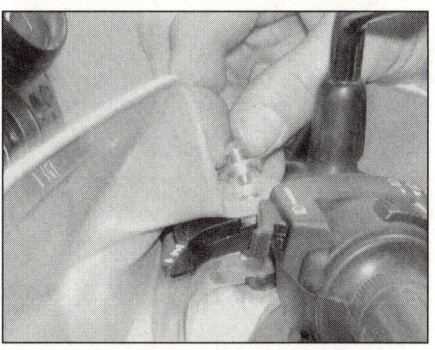

Front brake lever removal

24 Unscrew the nut and remove the collar on the underside of the handguard, then unscrew the bolt and remove the collar on the top and remove the guard **(see illustrations 5.26a and 5.26b)**.

25 Unscrew the pivot bolt and remove the lever **(see illustration 5.28)**.

Clutch lever removal

26 Pull the rubber boot off the clutch cable adjuster **(see illustration)**. Slacken the adjuster lockring and thread the adjuster fully into the bracket to provide maximum freeplay in the cable **(see illustration)**.

27 Unscrew the nut and remove the collar on the underside of the handguard, then unscrew the bolt and remove the collar on the top and remove the guard **(see illustrations)**.

5.27a Unscrew the nut and bolt and remove the collars . . .

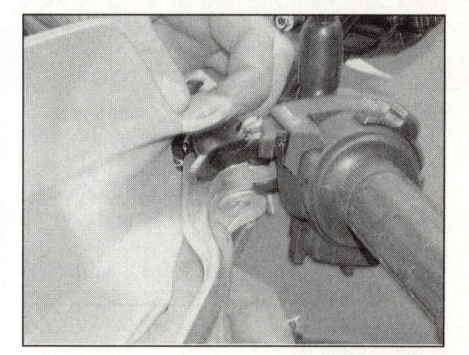

5.27b . . . then remove the guard

6•8 Frame, suspension and final drive

5.28 Unscrew the pivot bolt (arrowed) and remove the lever

6.1a Front brake hose holder bolt (arrowed) – VTR models

6.1b Front brake hose holder bolt (arrowed) – XL models

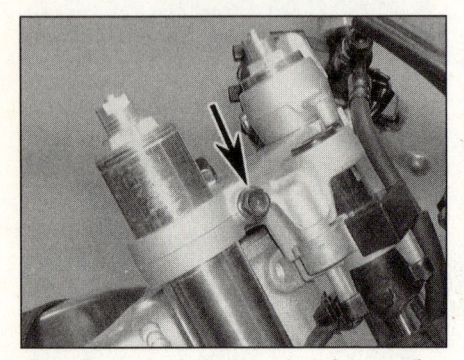

6.5a Top yoke fork clamp bolt (arrowed) – VTR models

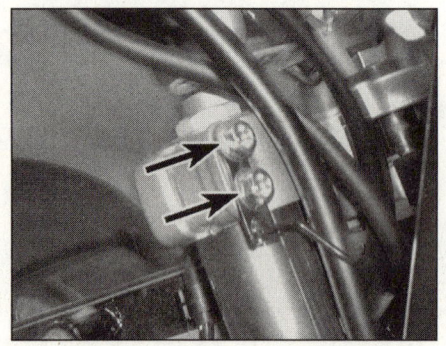

6.5b Top yoke fork clamp bolts (arrowed) – XL models. Note the hose guide secured by the bolts on the right-hand side

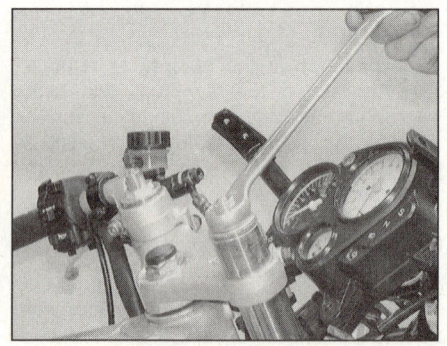

6.5c Slacken the top bolt now if the forks are being overhauled

28 Unscrew the pivot bolt and washer and remove the choke lever and the clutch lever, detaching the cable nipples as you do **(see illustration)**. Note the wave washer between the choke lever and the lever plate. Remove the plate from the lever bracket if required, noting how it fits.

Installation

29 Installation is the reverse of removal. Apply grease to the pivot bolt shafts and the contact areas between the lever and its bracket, and to the cable nipples. Adjust the clutch cable freeplay (see Chapter 1).

6 Forks – removal and installation

Removal

Caution: Although not strictly necessary, before removing the forks it is recommended that the fairing and fairing panels are removed (see Chapter 8). This will prevent accidental damage to the paintwork.

1 Remove the front wheel (see Chapter 7). Unscrew the bolt securing the front brake hose holder to the fork and displace it **(see illustrations)**.

2 Remove the front mudguard (see Chapter 8).

3 On VTR models, displace the handlebars and tie them up using cable ties, making sure no strain is placed on the master cylinder hoses (see Section 5).
4 On XL models, if removing the left-hand fork, displace the brake caliper/secondary master cylinder assembly (see Chapter 7).
5 Slacken the fork clamp bolt(s) in the top yoke **(see illustrations)**. If the forks are to be disassembled, or if the fork oil is being changed, slacken the fork top bolts at this stage **(see illustration)**. On XL models, note the amount of protrusion of the forks above the top yoke.
6 Slacken the fork clamp bolt(s) in the bottom yoke, and remove the forks by twisting them and pulling them downwards **(see illustrations)**.

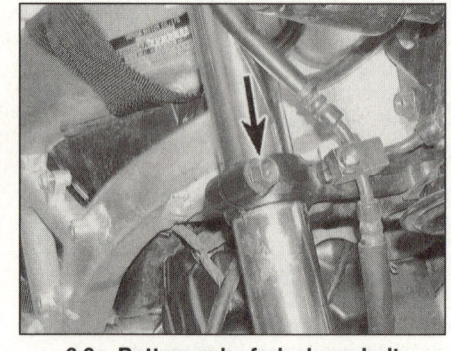

6.6a Bottom yoke fork clamp bolt (arrowed) – VTR models

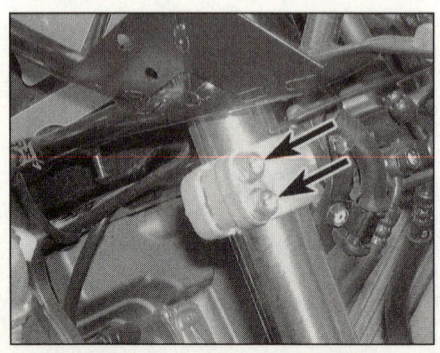

6.6b Bottom yoke fork clamp bolts (arrowed) – XL models

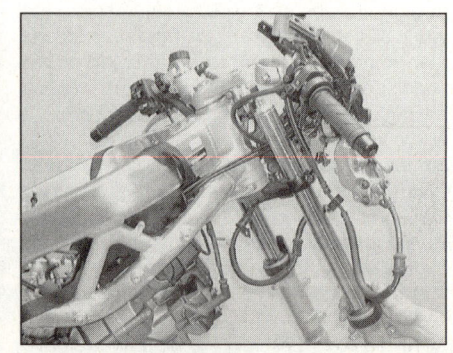

6.6c Draw the fork down and out of the yokes

Frame, suspension and final drive 6•9

6.8a Fit the handlebar onto the fork...

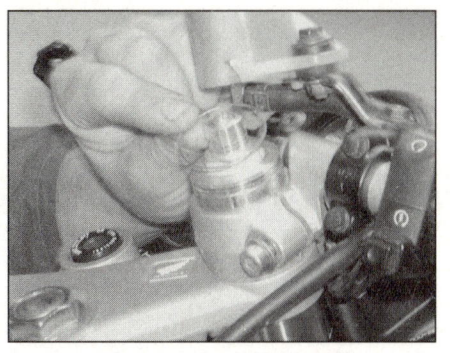

6.8b ...then fit the circlip

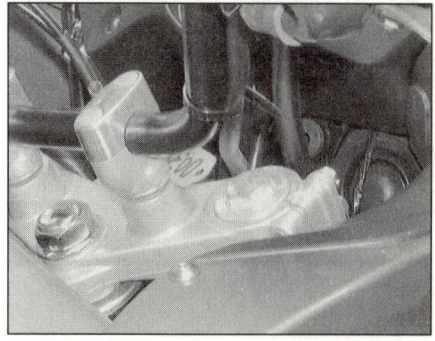

6.9 Set the fork height as shown

HAYNES HiNT: *If the fork legs are seized in the yokes, spray the area with penetrating oil and allow time for it to soak in before trying again.*

Installation

7 Remove all traces of corrosion from the fork tubes and the yokes. Slide the forks up through the bottom yoke and into the top yoke, making sure all cables, hoses and wiring are routed on the correct side of the fork **(see illustration 6.6c)**.

8 On VTR models, slide the fork higher in the top yoke than necessary and fit the handlebar onto it, locating the lug on the handlebar clamp into the slot in the top yoke **(see illustration and illustration 5.10a)**. Install the snap ring, making sure it locates in its groove in the fork **(see illustration)**, then draw the fork back down until the circlip sits on top of the handlebar clamp, but not so far that the ring is slightly below the level of the top of the clamp or it will be pinched by the handlebar clamp when it is tightened **(see illustration 5.10b)**.

9 On XL models, make sure the amount of protrusion of the fork tube above the top yoke is as noted on removal and equal on both sides – as standard the top of the fork tube should sit flush with the top of the yoke so that it is only the top bolt itself that protrudes **(see illustration)**.

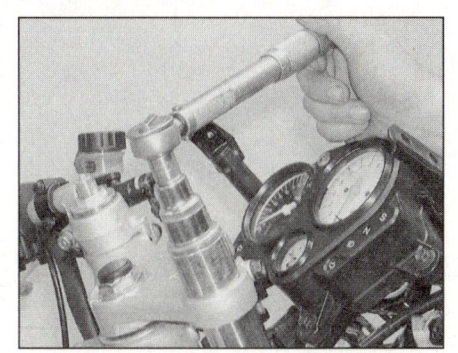

6.10 If necessary and not already done, tighten the fork top bolt to the specified torque

10 Tighten the fork clamp bolts in the bottom yoke to the torque setting specified at the beginning of the Chapter **(see illustration 6.6a or 6.6b)**. If the forks have been dismantled or if the fork oil has been changed, now tighten the fork top bolts to the specified torque setting **(see illustration)**. Now tighten the fork clamp bolts in the top yoke, and on VTR models the handlebar clamp bolts **(see illustration 6.5a or 6.5b)**.

11 Install the front wheel (see Chapter 7), and the front mudguard (see Chapter 8). Fit the brake hose holder(s) on to the fork(s) **(see illustration 6.1a or 6.1b)**. On XL models, install the left-hand brake caliper/secondary master cylinder assembly.

12 Check the operation of the front forks and brakes before taking the machine out on the road.

7 Forks – disassembly, inspection and reassembly

XL models

Disassembly

1 Remove the forks (see Section 6). Always dismantle the fork legs separately to avoid interchanging parts and thus causing an accelerated rate of wear. Store all components in separate, clearly marked containers **(see illustration)**.

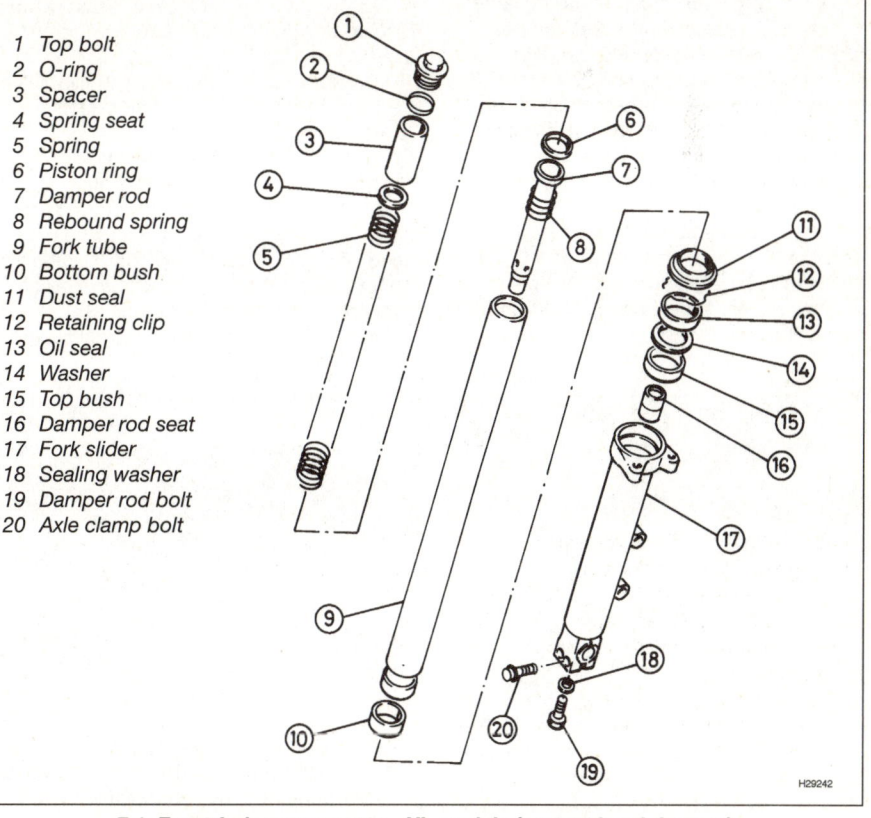

1 Top bolt
2 O-ring
3 Spacer
4 Spring seat
5 Spring
6 Piston ring
7 Damper rod
8 Rebound spring
9 Fork tube
10 Bottom bush
11 Dust seal
12 Retaining clip
13 Oil seal
14 Washer
15 Top bush
16 Damper rod seat
17 Fork slider
18 Sealing washer
19 Damper rod bolt
20 Axle clamp bolt

7.1 Front fork components – XL models (conventional damper)

6•10 Frame, suspension and final drive

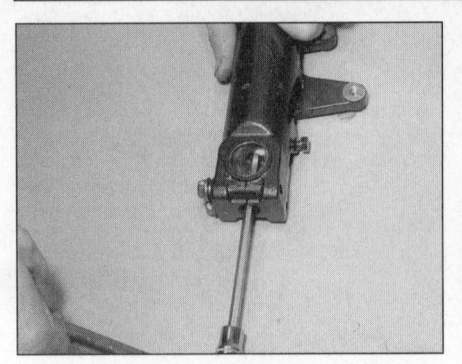

7.2 Slacken the damper rod bolt

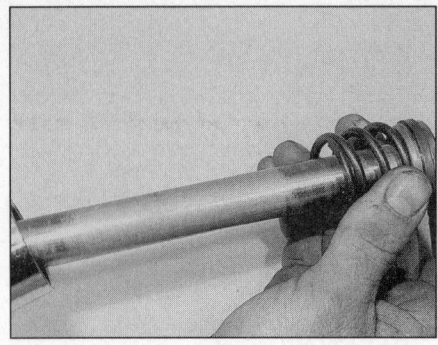

7.8 Withdraw the damper rod and rebound spring from the tube

7.9 Prise out the dust seal using a flat-bladed screwdriver

2 Before dismantling the fork, slacken the damper rod bolt at this stage. Compress the fork tube in the slider so that the spring exerts maximum pressure on the damper rod head, then have an assistant slacken the damper rod bolt in the base of the fork slider **(see illustration)**. If an assistant is not available, clamp the brake caliper mounting lugs in a soft-jawed vice to support the fork. If the bolt won't unscrew use an air impact wrench.

3 Unscrew the fork top bolt from the top of the fork tube.

4 On models with ABS, when dismantling the left-hand fork, to remove the top bolt from the damper rod, counter-hold the locknut on the base of the top bolt with a spanner and unscrew the top bolt **(see illustration 7.34)**.

⚠️ **Warning: The fork spring is pressing on the fork top bolt with considerable pressure. Unscrew the bolt very carefully, keeping a downward pressure on it and release it slowly as it is likely to spring clear. It is advisable to wear some form of eye and face protection when carrying out this operation.**

5 Slide the fork tube down into the slider and withdraw the spacer (not fitted on left fork on ABS models), spring seat and the spring from the tube **(see illustrations 7.26b, 7.26a and 7.56)**.

6 Invert the fork leg over a suitable container and pump the fork vigorously to expel as much fork oil as possible. On ABS models, when working on the left-hand fork, also pump the damper cartridge rod.

7 Remove the previously slackened damper rod bolt and its copper sealing washer from the bottom of the slider **(see illustration 7.2)**. Discard the sealing washer as a new one must be used on reassembly.

8 Invert the fork and withdraw the damper rod from inside the fork tube **(see illustration)**. Remove the rebound spring from the damper rod (not separate on left fork of ABS models).

9 Carefully prise out the dust seal from the top of the slider to gain access to the oil seal retaining clip **(see illustration)**. Discard the dust seal as a new one must be used.

10 Carefully remove the retaining clip, taking care not to scratch the surface of the tube **(see illustration)**.

11 To separate the tube from the slider it is necessary to displace the top bush and oil seal. The bottom bush should not pass through the top bush, and this can be used to good effect. Push the tube gently inwards until it stops against the damper rod seat. Take care not to do this forcibly or the seat may be damaged. Then pull the tube sharply outwards until the bottom bush strikes the top bush. Repeat this operation until the top bush and seal are tapped out of the slider **(see illustration)**.

12 With the tube removed, slide off the oil seal and its washer, noting which way up they fit **(see illustration)**. Discard the oil seal as a new one must be used. The top bush can then also be slid off its upper end.

Caution: Do not remove the bottom bush from the tube unless it is to be replaced.

13 Tip the damper rod seat out of the slider, noting which way up it fits.

Inspection

14 Clean all parts in solvent and blow them dry with compressed air, if available. Check the fork tube for score marks, scratches, flaking of the chrome finish and excessive or abnormal wear. Look for dents in the tube and replace the tube in both forks if any are found. Check the fork seal seat for nicks, gouges and scratches. If damage is evident, leaks will occur. Also check the oil seal washer for damage or distortion and replace it if necessary.

15 Check the fork tube for runout using V-blocks and a dial gauge, or have it done at a dealer service department or other repair shop

7.10 Prise out the retaining clip using a flat-bladed screwdriver

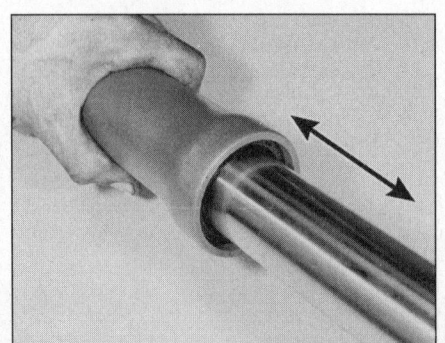

7.11 To separate the inner and outer fork tubes, pull them apart firmly several times – the slide hammer effect will pull the tubes apart

7.12 The oil seal (1), washer (2), top bush (3) and bottom bush (4) will come out with the fork tube

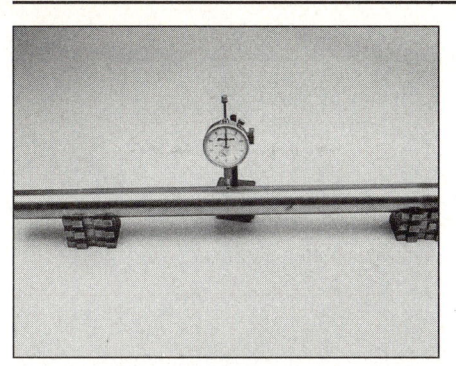

Frame, suspension and final drive 6•11

7.15 Check the fork tube for runout using V-blocks and a dial gauge

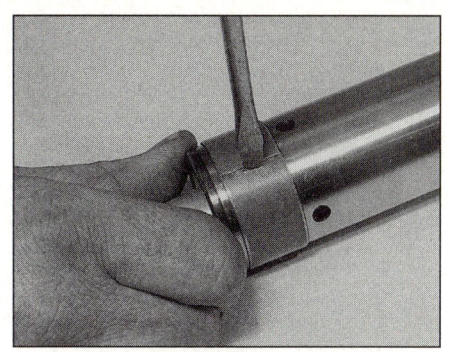

7.17 Prise off the bottom bush using a flat-bladed screwdriver

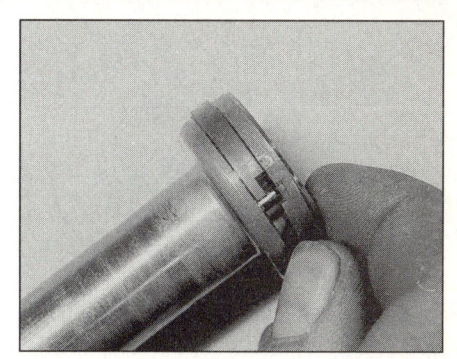

7.18 Replace the damper rod piston ring if it is worn or damaged

(see illustration). If the amount of runout exceeds the service limit specified, the tube should be replaced.

> ⚠ **Warning:** *If the tube is bent or exceeds the runout limit, it should not be straightened; replace it with a new one.*

16 Check the spring for cracks and other damage. Measure the spring free length and compare the measurement with the Specifications at the beginning of the Chapter. If it is defective or sagged below the service limit, replace the springs in both forks with new ones. Never replace only one spring. Also check the rebound spring.

17 Examine the working surfaces of the two bushes; if worn or scuffed they must be replaced. To remove the bottom bush from the fork tube, prise it apart at the slit using a flat-bladed screwdriver and slide it off **(see illustration)**. Make sure the new one seats properly.

18 Check the damper rod and its piston ring for damage and wear, and replace them if necessary **(see illustration)**. Do not remove the ring from the piston unless it is being replaced. Check the cartridge damper fitted to the left-hand fork of ABS models for damage.

Reassembly

19 If removed, install the piston ring into the groove in the damper rod head **(see illustration 7.18)**, then slide the rebound spring onto the rod **(see illustration)**. Insert the damper rod into the fork tube and slide it into place so that it projects fully from the bottom of the tube, then install the seat on the bottom of the damper rod **(see illustration)**.

20 Oil the fork tube and bottom bush with the specified fork oil and insert the assembly into the slider **(see illustration)**. Fit a new copper sealing washer onto the damper rod bolt and apply a few drops of a suitable non-permanent thread locking compound, then install the bolt into the bottom of the slider **(see illustration)**. Tighten the bolt to the specified torque setting. If the damper rod rotates inside the tube, temporarily install the fork spring and top bolt (see Steps 26 and 27) and compress the fork to hold the damper rod.

21 Push the fork tube fully into the slider, then oil the top bush and slide it down over the

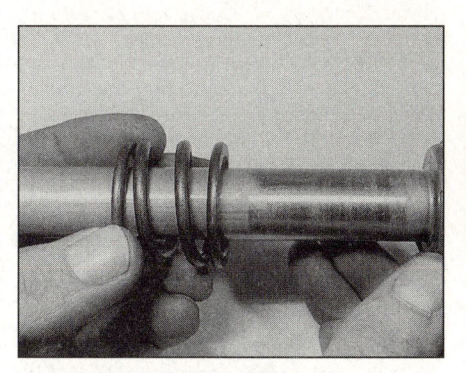

7.19a Slide the rebound spring onto the damper rod

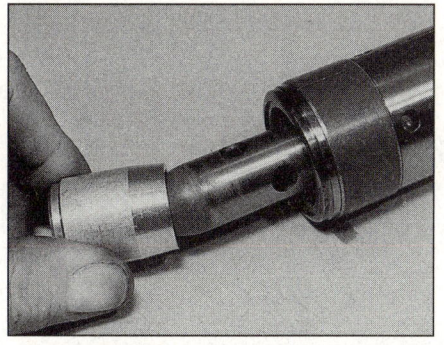

7.19b Fit the seat to the bottom of the rod

7.20a Slide the tube into the slider

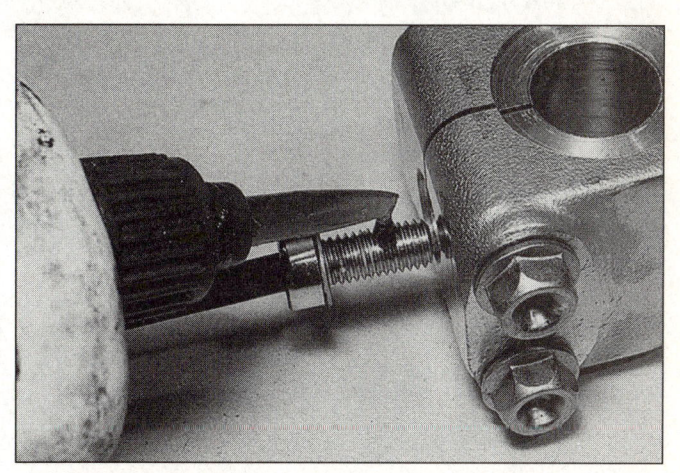

7.20b Apply a thread locking compound to the damper rod bolt and use a new sealing washer

6•12 Frame, suspension and final drive

7.21a Install the top bush . . .

7.21b . . . followed by the washer

7.22 Make sure the oil seal is the correct way up

tube **(see illustration)**. Press the bush squarely into its recess in the slider as far as possible, then install the oil seal washer **(see illustration)**. Either use the Honda service tool (Pt. Nos. 07947-KA50100 and 07947-KA40200) or a suitable piece of tubing to tap the bush fully into place; the tubing must be slightly larger in diameter than the fork tube and slightly smaller in diameter than the bush recess in the slider. Take care not to scratch the fork tube during this operation; it is best to make sure that the fork tube is pushed fully into the slider so that any accidental scratching is confined to the area above the oil seal.

22 When the bush is seated fully and squarely in its recess in the slider (remove the washer to check, wipe the recess clean, then reinstall the washer), install the new oil seal. Smear the seal's lips with fork oil and slide it over the tube so that its markings face upwards and drive the seal into place as described in Step

21 until the retaining clip groove is visible above the seal **(see illustration)**.
23 Once the seal is correctly seated, fit the retaining clip, making sure it is correctly located in its groove **(see illustration)**.

HAYNES HiNT *Place the old oil seal on top of the new one to protect it when driving the seal into place.*

24 Lubricate the lips of the new dust seal then slide it down the fork tube and press it into position **(see illustration)**.
25 Slowly pour in the specified quantity of fork oil and pump the fork at least ten times to distribute it evenly **(see illustration)**. On the left-hand fork of ABS models, also pump the damper rod gently. Fully compress the fork tube into the slider and measure the fork oil level from the top of the tube **(see illustration)**.

Add or subtract oil until it is at the level specified at the beginning of this chapter.
26 On conventional forks (i.e. all except the left-hand fork on ABS models) pull the fork tube out of the slider as far as possible then install the spring with its closer-spaced coils at the bottom **(see illustration 7.56)**, followed by the spring seat and the spacer **(see illustrations)**. Fit a new O-ring smeared with fork oil onto the fork top bolt and thread the bolt into the top of the fork tube. Keep the fork tube fully extended whilst pressing on the spring. Screw the top bolt carefully into the tube making sure it is not cross-threaded. *Note: The top bolt can be tightened to the specified torque setting at this stage if the tube is held between the padded jaws of a vice, but do not risk distorting the tube by doing so. A better method is to tighten the top bolt when the fork has been installed in the bike and is securely held in the bottom yoke.*

7.23 Install the retaining clip . . .

7.24 . . . followed by the dust seal . . .

7.25a Pour the oil into the top of the tube

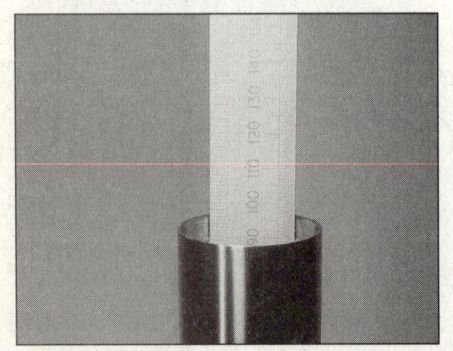

7.25b Measure the oil level with the fork held vertical

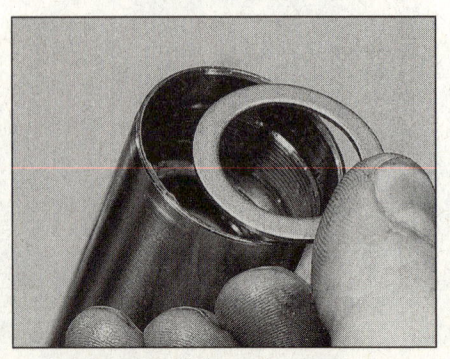

7.26a Install the spring seat . . .

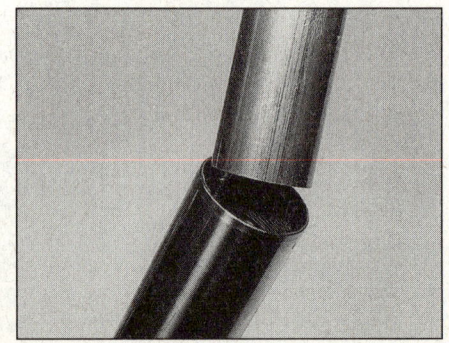

7.26b . . . followed by the spacer

Frame, suspension and final drive 6•13

Tool Tip

Use a ratchet-type tool when installing the fork top bolt. This makes it unnecessary to remove the tool from the bolt whilst threading it in making it easier to maintain a downward pressure on the spring

⚠️ **Warning:** *It will be necessary to compress the spring by pressing it down using the top bolt to engage the threads of the top bolt with the fork tube. This is a potentially dangerous operation and should be performed with care, using an assistant if necessary. Wipe off any excess oil before starting to prevent the possibility of slipping.*

27 On models with ABS, when rebuilding the left-hand fork, pull the fork tube and damper rod out of the slider as far as possible then install the spring with its closer-spaced coils at the bottom **(see illustration 7.56)**, followed by the spring seat. Keep the damper rod held above the level of the spring. Thread the locknut to the bottom of the threads on the rod. Thread the top bolt onto the rod, then counter-hold the locknut and tighten the top bolt securely against it **(see illustration 7.34)**. Fit a new O-ring smeared with fork oil onto the fork top bolt and thread the bolt carefully into the top of the tube making sure it is not cross-threaded. **Note:** *The top bolt can be tightened to the specified torque setting at this stage if the tube is held between the padded jaws of a vice, but do not risk distorting the tube by doing so. A better method is to tighten the top bolt when the fork has been installed in the bike and is securely held in the bottom yoke.*
28 Install the forks (see Section 6).
29 Check the operation of the forks before taking the bike on the road.

VTR models

Disassembly

30 Remove the forks (see Section 6). Always dismantle the fork legs separately to avoid interchanging parts and thus causing an accelerated rate of wear. Store all components in separate, clearly marked containers **(see illustration)**.
31 Before dismantling the fork, it is advised that the damper rod bolt be slackened at this stage. Compress the fork tube in the slider so that the spring exerts maximum pressure on the damper rod head, then have an assistant slacken the damper rod bolt in the base of the fork slider **(see illustration)**.
32 If the fork top bolt was not slackened with the fork *in situ*, carefully clamp the fork tube in a vice equipped with soft jaws, taking care not to overtighten or score its surface, and slacken the top bolt **(see illustration 6.5c)**.
33 Unscrew the fork top bolt from the top of the fork tube **(see illustration)**. The bolt will remain threaded on the pre-load adjuster.
34 Carefully clamp the fork slider in a vice and slide the fork tube down into the slider a little way (wrap a rag around the top of the tube to minimise oil spillage) while, with the aid of an assistant if necessary, keeping the damper rod fully extended. Note the amount of protrusion of the pre-load adjuster above the top of the top bolt – there are lines to indicate this. Counter-hold the nut on the base

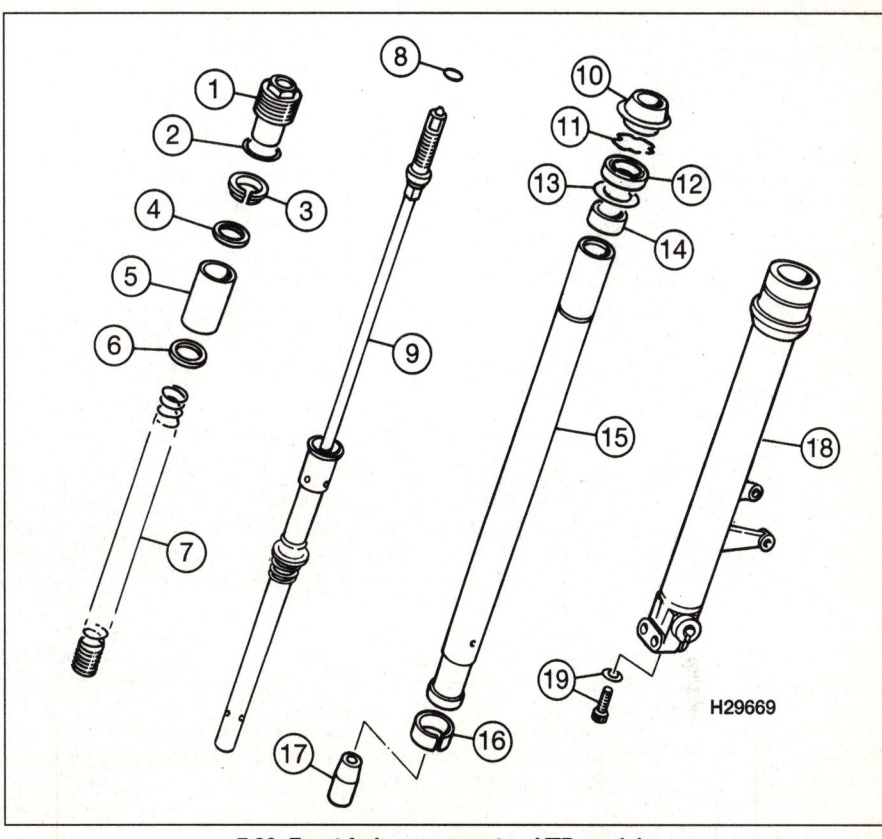

7.30 Front fork components – VTR models

1 Top bolt	8 O-ring	15 Fork tube
2 O-ring	9 Damper rod	16 Bottom bush
3 Slotted spring collar	10 Dust seal	17 Damper rod seat
4 Washer	11 Retaining clip	18 Fork slider
5 Spacer	12 Oil seal	19 Damper rod bolt and sealing washer
6 Spring seat	13 Washer	
7 Spring	14 Top bush	

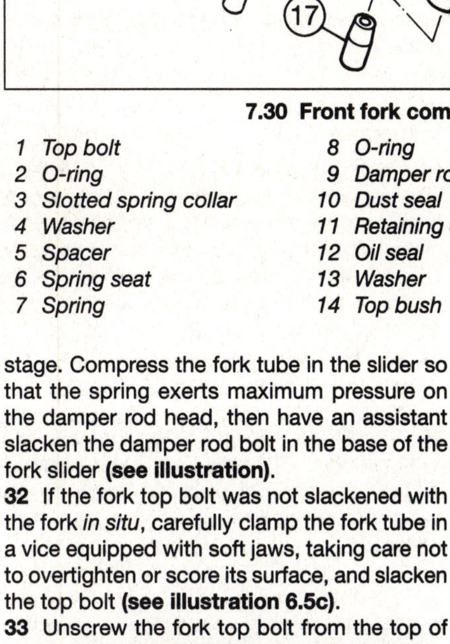

7.31 Slacken the damper rod bolt

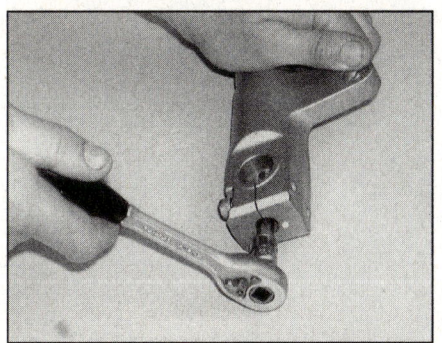

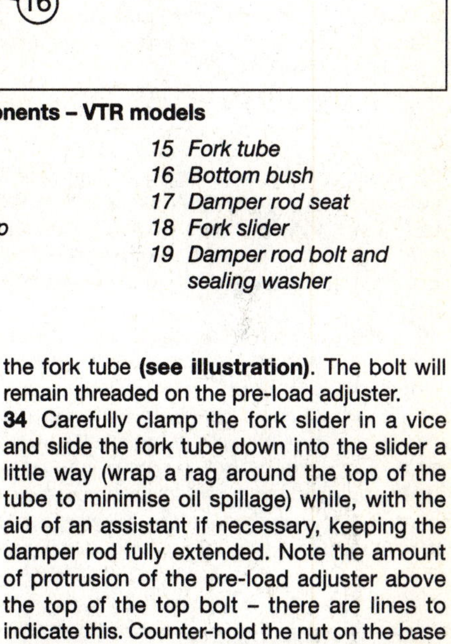

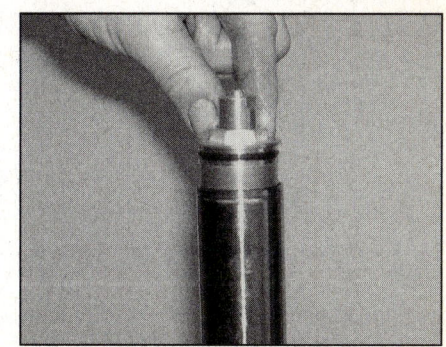

7.33 Unscrew the top bolt . . .

6•14 Frame, suspension and final drive

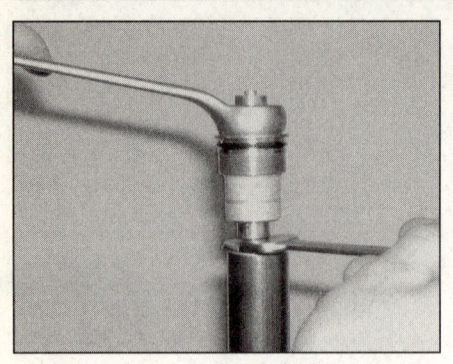

7.34 . . . then counter-hold the nut and thread the top bolt off the adjuster

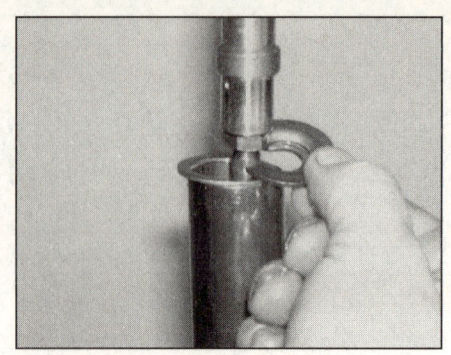

7.35a Remove the slotted spring collar . . .

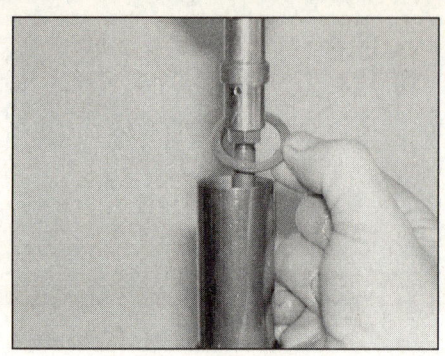

7.35b . . . the washer . . .

of the pre-load adjuster and thread the fork top bolt off the damper rod **(see illustration)**.
35 Remove the slotted spring collar by slipping it out to the side **(see illustration)**, then remove the washer, the spacer, the spring seat and the spring **(see illustrations)**.
36 Invert the fork leg over a suitable container and pump the fork and damper rod vigorously to expel as much fork oil as possible.
37 Remove the previously slackened damper rod bolt and its copper sealing washer from the bottom of the slider **(see illustration 7.31)**. Discard the sealing washer as a new one must be used on reassembly.
38 Invert the fork and withdraw the damper rod from inside the fork tube **(see illustration 7.49a)**.
39 Remove the fork protector, noting how it fits. Carefully prise out the dust seal from the top of the slider to gain access to the oil seal retaining clip **(see illustration 7.9)**. Discard the dust seal as a new one must be used.
40 Carefully remove the retaining clip, taking care not to scratch the surface of the tube **(see illustration 7.10)**.
41 To separate the tube from the slider it is necessary to displace the top bush and oil seal. The bottom bush should not pass through the top bush, and this can be used to good effect. Push the tube gently inwards until it stops against the damper rod seat. Take care not to do this forcibly or the seat may be damaged. Then pull the tube sharply outwards until the bottom bush strikes the top bush. Repeat this operation until the top bush and seal are tapped out of the slider **(see illustration 7.11)**.
42 With the tube removed, slide off the oil seal, washer and top bush, noting which way up they fit **(see illustration 7.12)**. Discard the oil seal as a new one must be used.
Caution: Do not remove the bottom bush from the tube unless it is to be replaced.
43 Tip the damper rod seat out of the slider, noting which way up it fits.

Inspection

44 Clean all parts in solvent and blow them dry with compressed air, if available. Check the fork tube for score marks, scratches, flaking of the chrome finish and excessive or abnormal wear. Look for dents in the tube and replace the tube in both forks if any are found. Check the fork seal seat for nicks, gouges and scratches. If damage is evident, leaks will occur. Also check the oil seal washer for damage or distortion and replace it if necessary.
45 Check the fork tube for runout using V-blocks and a dial gauge **(see illustration 7.15)**. If the amount of runout exceeds the service limit specified, the tube should be replaced.

⚠ *Warning: If the tube is bent or exceeds the runout limit, it should not be straightened; replace it with a new one.*

46 Check the spring for cracks and other damage. Measure the spring free length and compare the measurement to the Specifications at the beginning of the Chapter. If it is defective or sagged below the service limit, replace the springs in both forks with new ones. Never replace only one spring.
47 Examine the working surfaces of the two bushes; if worn or scuffed they must be replaced. To remove the bottom bush from the fork tube, prise it apart at the slit using a flat-bladed screwdriver and slide it off **(see illustration 7.17)**. Make sure the new one seats properly.
48 Check the damper rod assembly for damage and wear, and replace it if necessary. Holding the outside of the damper, pump the rod in and out of the damper. If the rod does not move smoothly in the damper it must be replaced.

Reassembly

49 Insert the damper rod into the fork tube and slide it into place so that it projects fully from the bottom of the tube, then install the

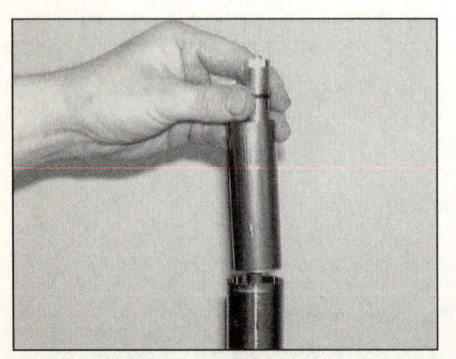

7.35c . . . the spacer . . .

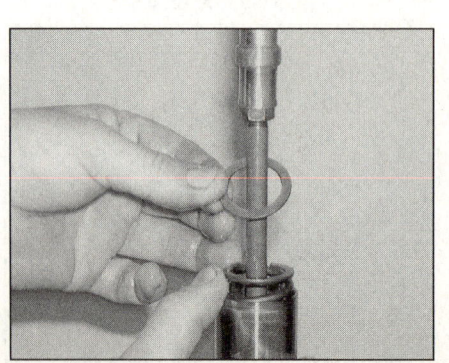

7.35d . . . the spring seat . . .

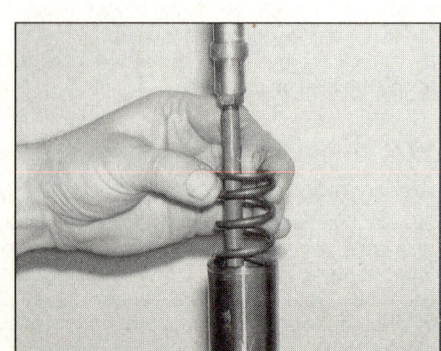

7.35e . . . and the spring

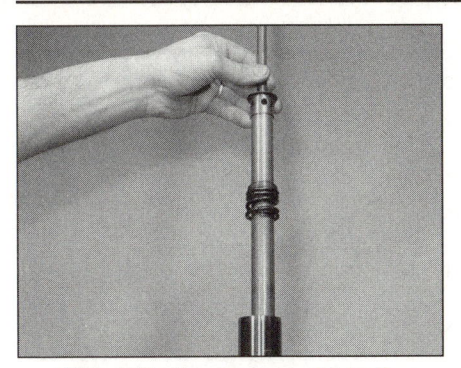

Frame, suspension and final drive 6•15

7.49a Slide the damper rod into the tube . . .

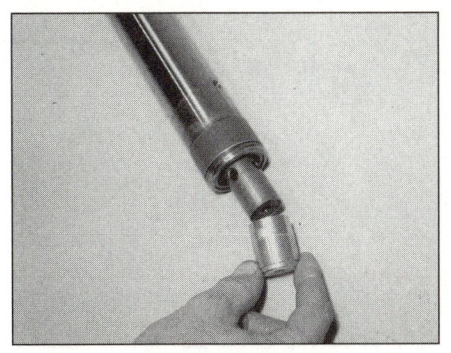

7.49b . . . and fit the seat onto the bottom of the rod

seat on the bottom of the damper rod **(see illustrations)**.
50 Oil the fork tube and bottom bush with the specified fork oil and insert the assembly into the slider **(see illustration 7.20a)**. Fit a new copper sealing washer onto the damper rod bolt and apply a few drops of a suitable non-permanent thread locking compound, then install the bolt into the bottom of the slider **(see illustration 7.20b)**. Tighten the bolt to the specified torque setting. If the damper rod rotates inside the tube, wait until the fork is fully reassembled before tightening the bolt.
51 Push the fork tube fully into the slider, then oil the top bush and slide it down over the tube **(see illustration 7.21a)**. Press the bush squarely into its recess in the slider as far as possible, then install the oil seal washer with its flat side facing up **(see illustration 7.21b)**. Either use the Honda service tool (Pt. Nos. 07947-KA50100 and 07947-KF00100) or a suitable piece of tubing to tap the bush fully into place; the tubing must be slightly larger in diameter than the fork tube and slightly smaller in diameter than the bush recess in the slider. Take care not to scratch the fork tube during this operation; it is best to make sure that the fork tube is pushed fully into the slider so that any accidental scratching is confined to the area above the oil seal.
52 When the bush is seated fully and squarely in its recess in the slider (remove the washer to check, wipe the recess clean, then reinstall the washer), install the new oil seal **(see illustration 7.22)**. Smear the seal's lips with fork oil and slide it over the tube so that its markings face upwards and drive the seal into place as described in Step 51 until the retaining clip groove is visible above the seal.

> **HAYNES HiNT** *Place the old oil seal on top of the new one to protect it when driving the seal into place.*

53 Once the seal is correctly seated, fit the retaining clip, making sure it is correctly located in its groove **(see illustration 7.23)**.
54 Lubricate the lips of the new dust seal then slide it down the fork tube and press it into position **(see illustration 7.24)**.
55 Slowly pour in the specified quantity of the specified grade of fork oil and pump the fork and damper rod at least ten times each to distribute it evenly **(see illustration 7.25a)**; the oil level should also be measured and adjustment made by adding or subtracting oil. Fully compress the fork tube and damper rod into the slider and measure the fork oil level from the top of the tube **(see illustration 7.25b)**. Add or subtract fork oil until it is at the level specified at the beginning of the Chapter.
56 Clamp the slider in a vice via the brake caliper mounting lugs, taking care not to overtighten and damage them. Pull the fork tube and damper rod out of the slider as far as possible then install the spring with its closer-wound coils at the bottom **(see illustration)**. Install the spring seat, the spacer and the washer **(see illustrations 7.35d, 7.35c and 7.35b)**.
57 Slide the slotted spring collar into position between the washer and the nut on the base of the pre-load adjuster **(see illustration 7.35a)**.
58 Fit new O-rings onto the pre-load adjuster and fork top bolt **(see illustration)**. Thread the top bolt onto the pre-load adjuster, using a spanner on the nut on the base of the adjuster to prevent the it from turning, and set it so that the amount of protrusion of the adjuster above the top of the top bolt is roughly as noted on removal **(see illustration 7.34)**.
59 Withdraw the tube fully from the slider and carefully screw the top bolt into the tube making sure it is not cross-threaded **(see illustration 7.33)**. **Note:** *The top bolt can be tightened to the specified torque setting at this stage if the tube is held between the padded jaws of a vice, but do not risk distorting the tube by doing so. A better method is to tighten the top bolt when the fork leg has been installed and is securely held in the triple clamps.*

> **TOOL TiP** *Use a ratchet-type tool when installing the fork top bolt. This makes it unnecessary to remove the tool from the bolt whilst threading it in making it easier to maintain a downward pressure on the spring.*

60 If the damper rod bolt requires tightening (see Step 50), clamp the fork slider between the padded jaws of a vice and have an assistant compress the tube into the slider so that maximum spring pressure is placed on the damper rod head – tighten the damper rod bolt to the specified torque setting **(see illustration 7.31)**.
61 If removed, fit the fork protector onto the top of the slider.
62 Install the forks (see Section 6). Set the spring pre-load adjuster as required (see Section 11).

8 Steering stem – removal and installation

Removal
1 Remove the fuel tank (see Chapter 4A) and the fairing (see Chapter 8). This will prevent the possibility of damage should a tool slip. Also remove the front forks (see Section 6).
2 On VTR models, unscrew the bolts securing the front brake hose union and hose guide to

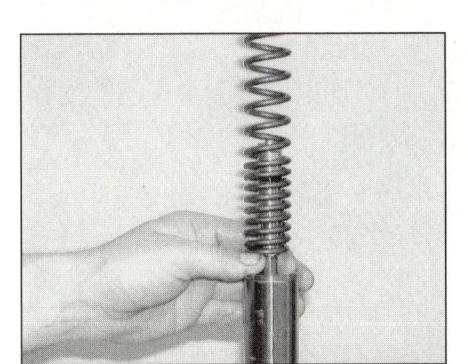

7.56 Install the spring with its closer wound coils at the bottom

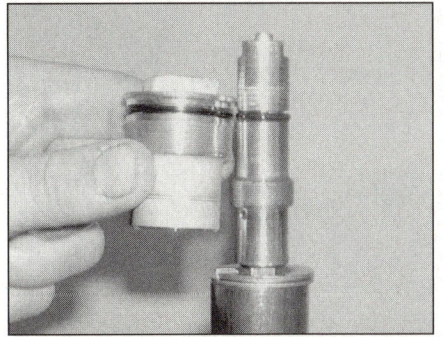

7.58 Fit new O-rings onto the top bolt and adjuster

6•16 Frame, suspension and final drive

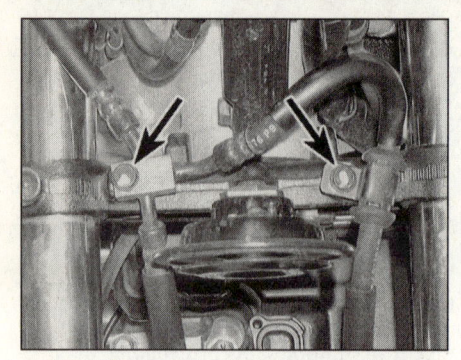

8.2a Remove the bolts (arrowed) and detach the brake hose union and clamp

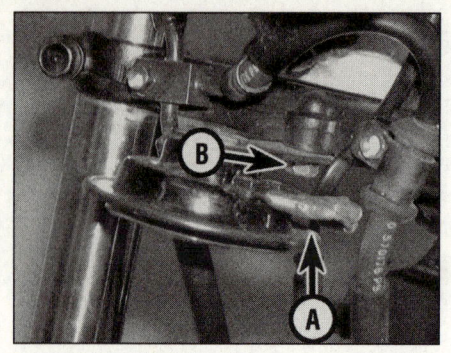

8.2b Disconnect the wiring connectors (A), then unscrew the bolt (B) and remove the horn

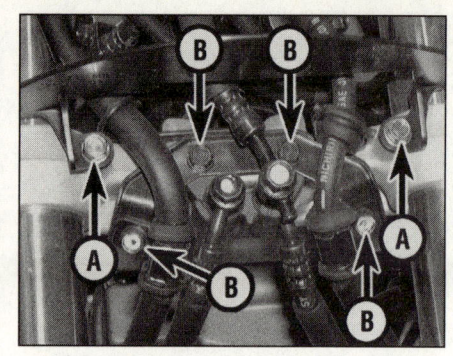

8.3 Unscrew the bolts (A) and remove the shield, then unscrew the bolts (B) and displace the bracket

the bottom yoke **(see illustration)**. Disconnect the horn wiring connectors, then unscrew the mounting bolt and remove the horn **(see illustration)**. Take care not to strain or knock the brake hoses when removing the steering stem.

3 On XL models, displace the handlebars (see Section 5). Unscrew the two bolts securing the shield to the bottom yoke and remove it **(see illustration)**. Unscrew the bolts securing the front brake hose and delay valve bracket to the bottom yoke. Take care not to strain or knock the brake hoses when removing the steering stem.

4 If the top yoke is being removed from the bike rather than just being displaced, trace the wiring from the ignition switch and disconnect it at the connector. On VTR models, the connector is inside the rubber boot on the right-hand side of the instrument cluster **(see illustration)**. On XL models, the connector is inside the rubber boot above the left-hand radiator **(see illustration)** – remove the left-hand fairing side panel to access it (see Chapter 8).

5 On VTR models, prise the cap off the steering stem nut **(see illustration 8.15b)**, then unscrew and remove the nut **(see illustration)**. On XL models, unscrew the steering stem nut and remove it along with its washer. Lift the top yoke up off the steering stem and position it clear, using a rag to protect the tank or other components **(see illustration)**.

6 Bend down the tabs on the steering stem lockwasher to release it from the locknut, then unscrew and remove the locknut using either a suitable C-spanner or a drift located in one of the notches **(see illustration)**. Remove the lockwasher, bending up the remaining tabs to release it from the adjuster nut if necessary **(see illustration)**. Inspect the tabs for cracks or signs of fatigue. If there are any, discard the lockwasher and use a new one; otherwise the old one can be re-used.

7 Supporting the bottom yoke, unscrew the adjuster nut using either a C-spanner, a peg-spanner or socket, or a drift located in

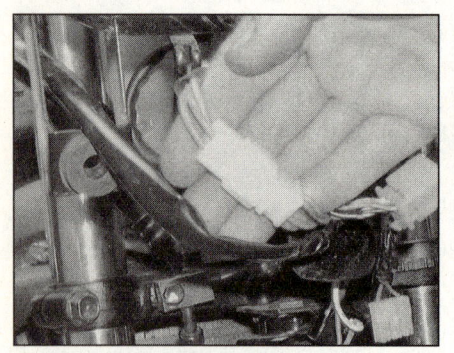

8.4a Ignition switch wiring connector – VTR models

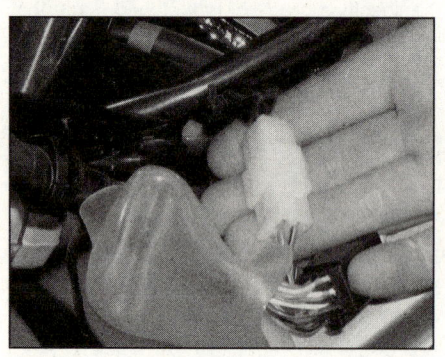

8.4b Ignition switch wiring connector – XL models

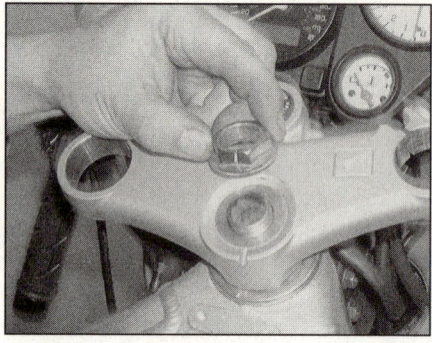

8.5a Unscrew the steering stem nut . . .

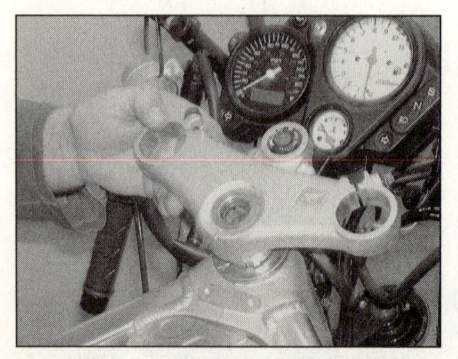

8.5b . . . and remove the top yoke

8.6a Unscrew the locknut . . .

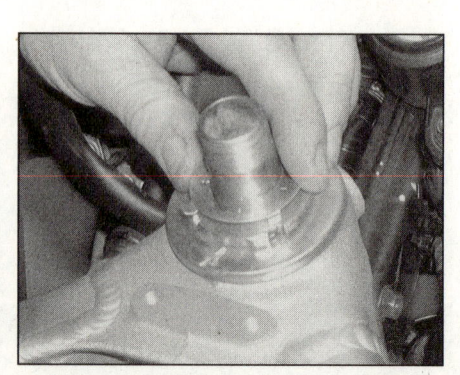

8.6b . . . and remove the lockwasher

Frame, suspension and final drive 6•17

8.7 A socket such as this is ideal for unscrewing the adjuster nut

8.8 Draw the bottom yoke/steering stem out of the steering head

8.10 Fit the lower bearing onto the steering stem

one of the notches **(see illustration)**. Remove the adjuster nut and the bearing cover from the steering stem **(see illustrations 8.11d and 8.11c)**.

8 Gently lower the bottom yoke and steering stem out of the frame **(see illustration)**.

9 Remove the inner race and bearing from the top of the steering head **(see illustrations 8.11b and 8.11a)**. Remove the bearing from the base of the steering stem. Remove all traces of old grease from the bearings and races and check them for wear or damage as described in Section 9. **Note:** *Do not attempt to remove the races from the steering head or the steering stem unless they are to be replaced with new ones.*

Installation

10 Smear a liberal quantity grease onto the bearing races – on VTR models Honda recommend molybdenum disulphide grease, on XL models multi-purpose grease. Also work some grease well into both the upper and lower bearings. Fit the lower bearing onto the steering stem **(see illustration)**.

11 Carefully lift the steering stem/bottom yoke up through the steering head **(see illustration 8.8)**. Fit the upper bearing and the inner race into the top of the steering head, then install the bearing cover **(see illustrations)**. Apply some clean engine oil to the adjuster nut and thread the nut on the steering stem **(see illustration)**.

12 If the correct tools are available **(see illustration 8.7)**, tighten the adjuster nut to the torque setting specified at the beginning of the Chapter, then turn the steering stem through its full lock four or five times and re-tighten the adjuster nut to the specified setting. Ensure that the steering stem is able to move freely from lock to lock following adjustment – if necessary reset the bearing adjustment as described in Chapter 1.

13 If the correct tools are not available, tighten the nut using a C-spanner or drift so that bearing play is eliminated, but the steering stem is able to move freely from lock to lock – refer to the procedure in Chapter 1 for details. **Caution: Take great care not to apply excessive pressure because this will cause premature failure of the bearings.**

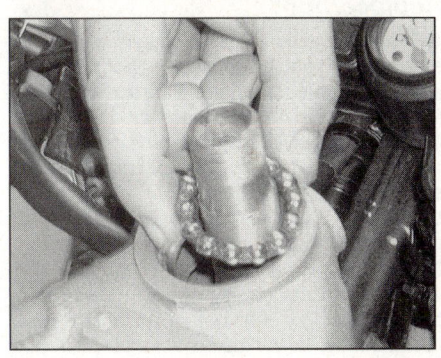

8.11a Fit the upper bearing . . .

14 When the bearings are correctly adjusted, install the lockwasher, using a new one if the tabs are weakened or cracked, onto the adjuster nut and fit two tabs into the slots in the adjuster nut **(see illustration 8.6b)**. Install the locknut and tighten it finger-tight, then tighten it further (to a maximum of 90°) until the remaining tabs on the lockwasher align with the slots in the locknut **(see illustration 8.6a)**. Hold the adjuster nut to prevent it from moving if necessary. Secure the locknut in position by bending up the lockwasher tabs into its notches **(see illustration)**.

15 Fit the top yoke onto the steering stem **(see illustration 8.5b)**, then install the washer (XL models) and steering stem nut and tighten it finger-tight **(see illustration 8.5a)**. Temporarily install one of the forks to align the

8.11b . . . its inner race . . .

8.11c . . . the bearing cover . . .

8.11d . . . and the adjuster nut

8.14 Bend the lockwasher tabs up into the notches in the lockwasher

6•18 Frame, suspension and final drive

8.15a Tighten the steering stem nut to the specified torque

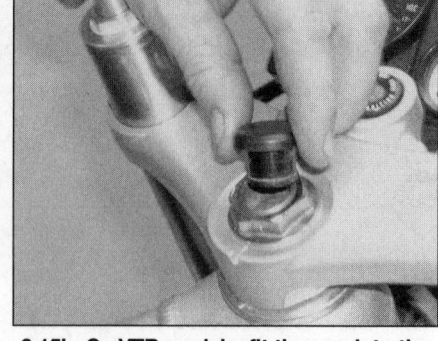

8.15b On VTR models, fit the cap into the nut

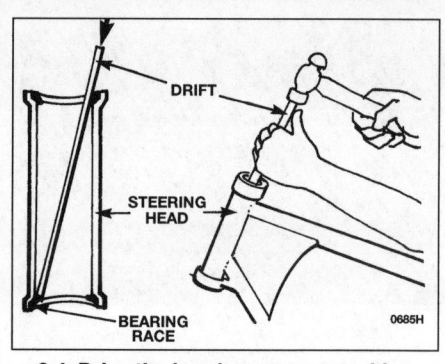

9.4 Drive the bearing races out with a brass drift as shown

top and bottom yokes, and secure it by tightening the bottom yoke clamp bolt(s) only. Now tighten the steering stem nut to the torque setting specified at the beginning of the Chapter **(see illustration)**. On VTR models, fit the steering stem nut cap **(see illustration)**.

16 Install the remaining components in a reverse of the removal procedure, referring to the relevant Sections or Chapters, and to the torque settings specified at the beginning of the Chapter.

17 Carry out a check of the steering head bearing freeplay as described in Chapter 1, and if necessary re-adjust.

9 Steering head bearings – inspection and replacement

Inspection

1 Remove the steering stem (see Section 8).

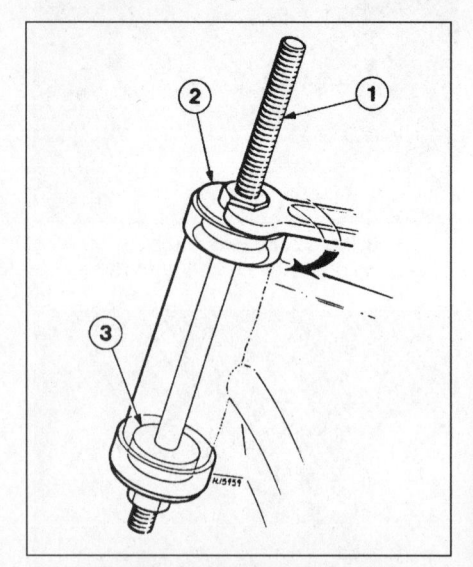

9.6 Drawbolt arrangement for fitting steering stem bearing races
1 Long bolt or threaded bar
2 Thick washer
3 Guide for lower race

2 Remove all traces of old grease from the bearings and races and check them for wear or damage.

3 The outer races should be polished and free from indentations. Inspect the bearing rollers for signs of wear, damage or discoloration, and examine the bearing roller retainer cage for signs of cracks or splits. Spin the bearing balls by hand. They should spin freely and smoothly. If there are any signs of wear on any of the above components both upper and lower bearing assemblies must be renewed as a set. Only remove the outer races in the steering head and the lower bearing inner race on the steering stem if they need to be replaced – do not re-use them once they have been removed.

Replacement

4 The outer races are an interference fit in the steering head and can be tapped from position with a suitable drift **(see illustration)**. Tap firmly and evenly around each race to ensure that it is driven out squarely. It may prove advantageous to curve the end of the drift slightly to improve access.

5 Alternatively, the races can be removed using a slide-hammer type bearing extractor; these can often be hired from tool shops.

6 The new outer races can be pressed into the head using a drawbolt arrangement **(see illustration)**, or by using a large diameter tubular drift. Ensure that the drawbolt washer or drift (as applicable) bears only on the outer

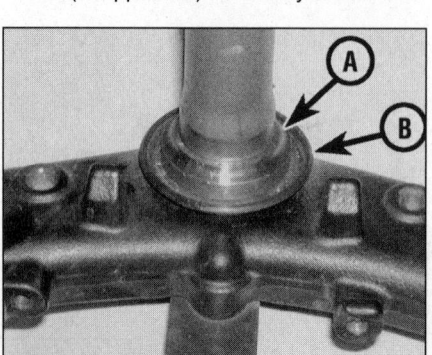

9.7a Lower bearing inner race (A) and dust seal (B)

edge of the race and does not contact the working surface. Alternatively, have the races installed by a Honda dealer equipped with the bearing race installing tools.

> **HAYNES HiNT** *Installation of new bearing outer races is made much easier if the races are left overnight in the freezer. This causes them to contract slightly making them a looser fit. Alternatively, use a freeze spray.*

7 The lower bearing inner race should only be removed from the steering stem if a new one is being fitted. To remove the race from the steering stem, use two screwdrivers placed on opposite sides of the race to work it free, using blocks of wood to improve leverage and protect the yoke, or tap under it using a cold chisel **(see illustration)**. If the race is firmly in place it will be necessary to use a puller **(see illustration)**, or in extreme circumstances to split the race using an angle grinder. Take the steering stem to a Honda dealer if required.

8 Remove the dust seal from the bottom of the stem and replace it with a new one **(see illustration 9.7a)**. Smear the new one with grease.

9 Fit the new lower race onto the steering

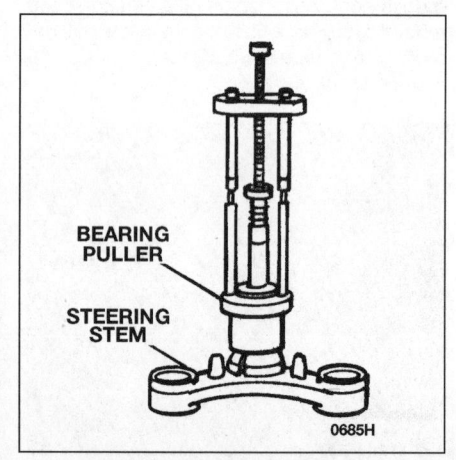

9.7b Remove the lower bearing inner race using a puller if necessary

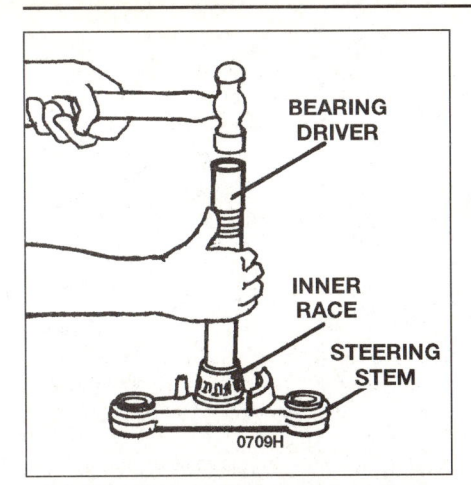

Frame, suspension and final drive 6•19

9.9 Drive the new inner race on using a suitable bearing driver or a length of pipe that bears only against its inner edge and not against the working surface

stem. A length of tubing with an internal diameter slightly larger than the steering stem will be needed to tap the new race into position (see illustration).
10 Install the steering stem (see Section 8).

10 Rear shock absorber – removal, inspection and installation

Warning: Do not attempt to disassemble this shock absorber. It is nitrogen-charged under high pressure. Improper disassembly could result in serious injury. Instead, take the shock to a dealer service department with the proper equipment to do the job.

Removal

1 Support the motorcycle securely in an upright position using an auxiliary stand. Position a support under the rear wheel so that it does not drop when the shock absorber is removed, but also making sure that the weight of the machine is off the rear suspension so that the shock is not compressed.

10.2 Undo the screw (A) and remove the knob, ball and spring, then unscrew the bolt (B)

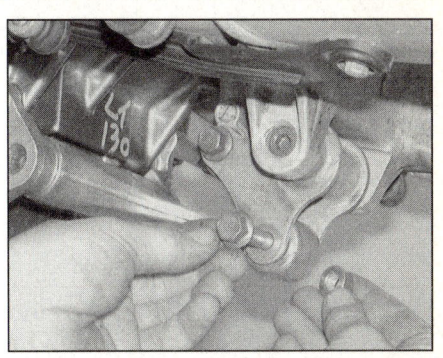

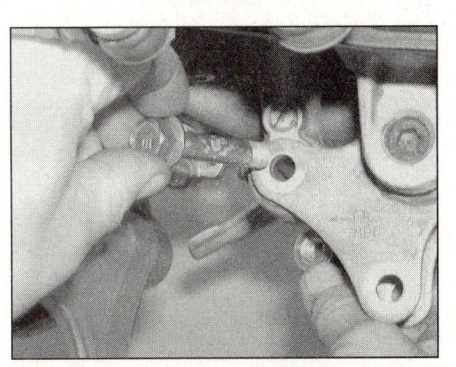

10.5a Remove the shock absorber lower mounting bolt

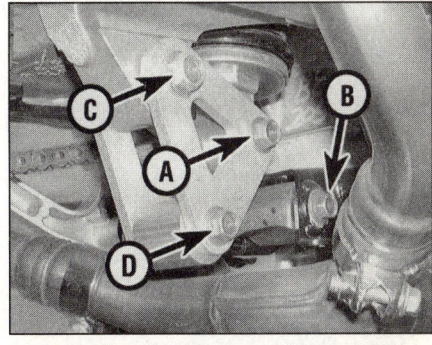

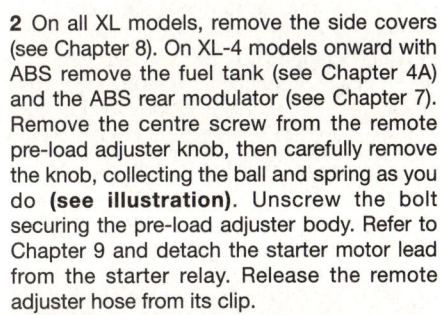

2 On all XL models, remove the side covers (see Chapter 8). On XL-4 models onward with ABS remove the fuel tank (see Chapter 4A) and the ABS rear modulator (see Chapter 7). Remove the centre screw from the remote pre-load adjuster knob, then carefully remove the knob, collecting the ball and spring as you do (see illustration). Unscrew the bolt securing the pre-load adjuster body. Refer to Chapter 9 and detach the starter motor lead from the starter relay. Release the remote adjuster hose from its clip.
3 On VTR models, remove the fuel tank and the exhaust system (see Chapter 4A).
4 On VTR models and XL-4 models onward with ABS unscrew the nut and withdraw the bolt securing the suspension linkage arm to the linkage plates (see illustration).

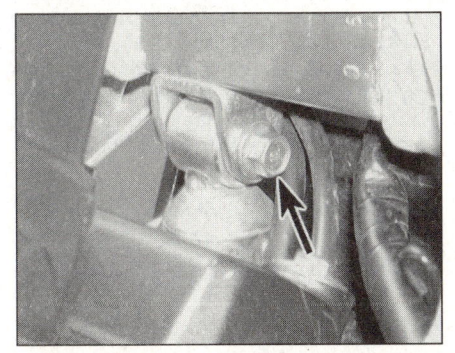

10.5c Remove the upper mounting bolt (arrowed) . . .

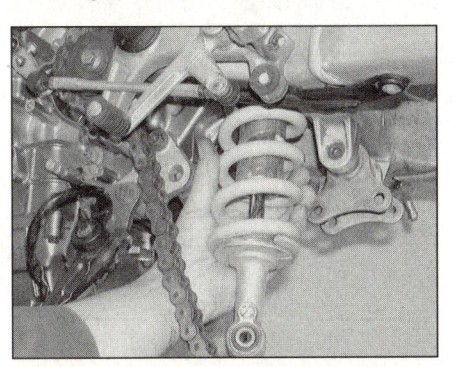

10.4 Remove the linkage arm-to-linkage plates bolt and swing the arm down

10.5b Shock lower mounting bolt (A), linkage arm-to-bracket bolt (B), linkage plates-to-swingarm bolt (C), linkage arm-to-plates bolt (D)

5 Unscrew the nut and withdraw the bolt securing the bottom of the shock absorber to the linkage plates (see illustrations). Unscrew the nut on the shock absorber upper mounting bolt. Support the shock absorber, then withdraw the bolt and manoeuvre the shock out of the bottom of the frame on VTR models and XL-4 models onward with ABS, and out the side on all other XL models (see illustrations).

Inspection

6 Inspect the shock absorber for obvious physical damage and the coil spring for looseness, cracks or signs of fatigue.
7 Inspect the damper rod for signs of bending, pitting and oil leakage (see illustration).

10.5d . . . and remove the shock absorber – VTR models

10.7 Look for pitting and oil leakage on the rod (arrowed)

6•20 Frame, suspension and final drive

11.4 Remove the linkage plates-to-swingarm bolt and remove the plates

11.5 Remove the linkage arm-to-bracket bolt and remove the arm

8 Inspect the pivot hardware at the top and bottom of the shock for wear or damage.
9 Check that there is not an excessive amount of freeplay between the spacer and the needle bearing in the lower mounting. Withdraw the spacer. Check the condition of the grease seals and replace them with new ones if they are damaged, deformed or deteriorated. Lever out the old ones using a flat-bladed screwdriver and press the new ones squarely into place.
10 With the dust seals removed, check the condition of the bearing and replace it with a new one if necessary. Refer to *Tools and Workshop Tips* in the Reference Section for more information on bearing checks and replacement methods.
11 With the exception of the lower pivot hardware, individual components are not available for the shock absorber. If it is worn or damaged, it must be replaced with a new one.

Installation

12 Installation is the reverse of removal. Apply grease to the shock absorber and linkage arm/plate pivot points – on VTR models Honda recommend molybdenum disulphide grease, on XL models multi-purpose grease. Install the bolts and nuts finger-tight only until all components are in position, then

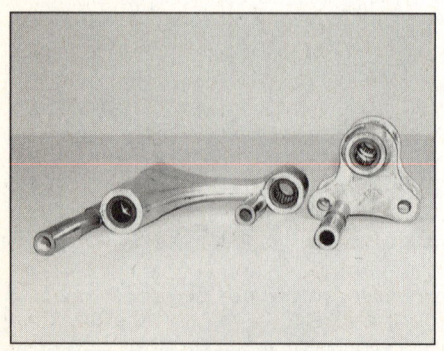

11.6 Suspension linkage components – VTR models

tighten the nuts to the torque settings specified at the beginning of the Chapter. On XL models without ABS, the pre-load adjuster faces the right-hand side and on models with ABS it faces the left.

11 Rear suspension linkage – removal, inspection and installation

Removal

1 Support the motorcycle securely in an upright position using an auxiliary stand. Position a support under the rear wheel so that it does not drop when the shock absorber lower mounting bolt is removed, but also making sure that the weight of the machine is off the rear suspension so that the shock is not compressed.
2 For best clearance, remove the exhaust system (see Chapter 4).
3 Unscrew the nut and withdraw the bolt securing the linkage arm to the linkage plates **(see illustration 10.3 or 10.4b)**.
4 Unscrew the nuts and withdraw the bolts securing the linkage plates to the shock absorber **(see illustration 10.4a)** and the swingarm and remove the plates, noting which way round they fit **(see illustration)**.
5 Unscrew the nut and withdraw bolt securing the linkage arm to the bracket and remove the arm, noting which way round it fits **(see illustration)**.

Inspection

6 Withdraw all the spacers from the linkage arm, plates (VTR models) and swingarm (XL models), noting their different sizes, then lever out the grease seals **(see illustration)**. Thoroughly clean all components, removing all traces of dirt, corrosion and grease.
7 Inspect all components closely, looking for obvious signs of wear such as heavy scoring, or for damage such as cracks or distortion. Slip each spacer back into its bearing and check that there is not an excessive amount of freeplay between the two components. Renew any components as required.
8 Check the condition of the needle roller bearings. Refer to *Tools and Workshop Tip* in the Reference section for more information on bearings. On XL models, if the linkage plate bearings in the swingarm need to be renewed, remove the swingarm (see Section 13).
9 Worn bearings can be drifted out of their bores, but note that removal will destroy them; new bearings should be obtained before work commences. The new bearings should be pressed or drawn into their bores rather than driven into position. In the absence of a press, a suitable drawbolt tool can be made up as described in *Tools and Workshop Tips* in the Reference section. Set the bearings centrally in their bores.
10 Check the condition of the grease seals arm and renew them if they are damaged, deformed or deteriorated. Lubricate the needle bearings, spacers and seals with grease – on VTR models Honda recommend molybdenum disulphide grease, on XL models multi-purpose grease.
11 Press the seals squarely into place. Install the spacers.

Installation

12 Installation is the reverse of removal. Apply grease to the pivot points – on VTR models Honda recommend molybdenum disulphide grease, on XL models multi-purpose grease. Install the bolts and nuts finger-tight only until all components are in position, then tighten the nuts to the torque settings specified at the beginning of the Chapter.

12 Suspension – adjustments

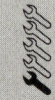

Front forks

1 On VTR models, the front forks are adjustable for spring pre-load and rebound

Frame, suspension and final drive 6•21

12.1a Spring pre-load adjuster (arrowed) – VTR models

12.1b Rebound damping adjuster (arrowed) – VTR models

damping. Spring pre-load is adjusted using a suitable spanner on the adjuster flats **(see illustration)**. Turn it clockwise to increase pre-load and anti-clockwise to decrease it. The amount of pre-load is indicated by grooves on the adjuster. The standard position is with the 4th groove aligned with the top of the hex on the fork bolt. Always make sure both adjusters are set equally. Damping is adjusted using a screwdriver in the slot in the top of the damper rod protruding from the pre-load adjuster **(see illustration)**. Turn it clockwise to increase damping and anti-clockwise to decrease it. To set the standard position, turn the adjuster fully clockwise until it stops, then turn it anti-clockwise approximately one full turn until the punchmark on the adjuster aligns with the reference mark on the directional arrow.

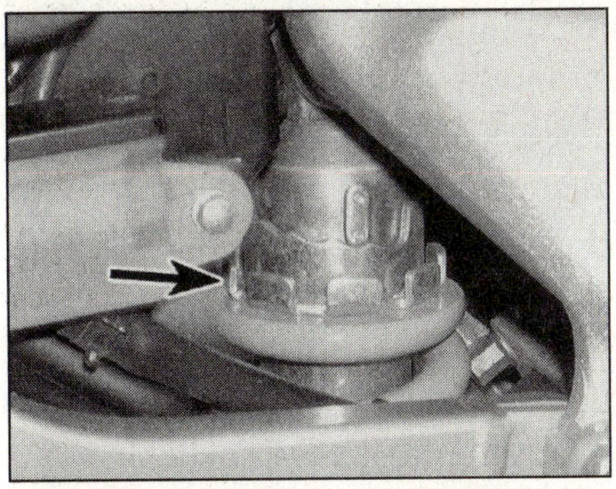

2 On XL models, the front forks are not adjustable.

Rear shock absorber

3 On VTR models, the shock absorber is adjustable for spring pre-load and rebound damping. Spring pre-load is adjusted using a suitable C-spanner (one is provided in the toolkit) to turn the spring seat on the top of the shock absorber **(see illustrations)**. There are seven positions. Position 1 is the softest setting, position 2 the standard, and position 7 the hardest. Align the setting required with the adjustment stopper. To increase the pre-load, turn the spring seat anti-clockwise. To decrease the pre-load, turn the spring seat clockwise. Damping adjustment is made by turning the adjuster on the bottom of the shock absorber using a flat-bladed screwdriver **(see illustration)**. To increase the damping, turn the adjuster clockwise. To decrease the damping, turn the adjuster anti-clockwise. To set the standard position, turn the adjuster clockwise until it stops, then turn it anti clockwise 1 turn until the punch mark on the adjuster aligns with the index mark on the shock absorber.

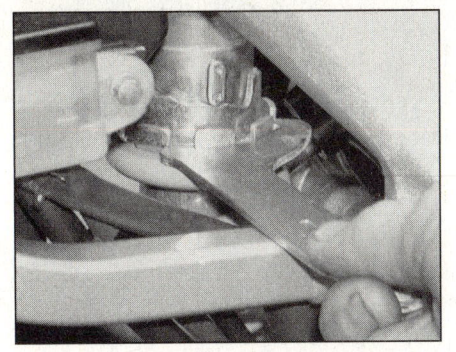

4 On XL models, the shock absorber is adjustable for spring pre-load. Pre-load adjustment is made by turning the adjuster on the right-hand side of the shock absorber on models without ABS **(see illustration)**, and on the left on models with ABS **(see illustration 10.2)**. Turn the adjuster clockwise to increase preload and anti-clockwise to decrease it. To set the standard position, turn the adjuster anti-clockwise until it stops, then turn it clockwise the specified number of clicks:

XL-X, Y, 1 and 2 models – 12 clicks
XL-3 to 6 models without ABS – 4 clicks
XL-4 to 6 models with ABS – 20 clicks
XL-7 models onward without ABS – 2 clicks
XL-7 models onward with ABS – 18 clicks

5 On XL models with ABS the rear shock absorber is also adjustable for rebound damping. Damping adjustment is made by turning the adjuster on the bottom of the shock absorber using a flat-bladed screwdriver. To increase the damping, turn the adjuster clockwise. To decrease the damping, turn the adjuster anti-clockwise. To set the standard position, turn the adjuster clockwise until it stops, then turn it anti clockwise approximately 2 1/2 turns until the punch mark on the adjuster aligns with the index mark on the shock absorber.

12.3a Spring pre-load adjuster (arrowed) – VTR models

12.3b Adjust the spring using the tool supplied

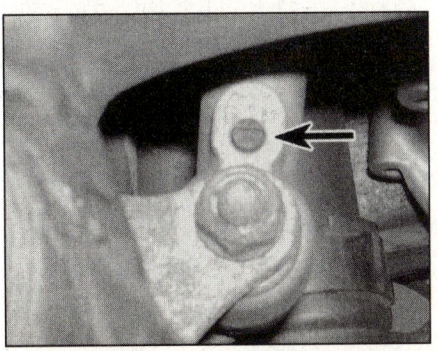

12.3c Rebound damping adjuster (arrowed) – VTR models

12.4 Spring pre-load adjuster – XL models without ABS

6•22 Frame, suspension and final drive

13.2a Brake hose clamps (arrowed) – VTR models

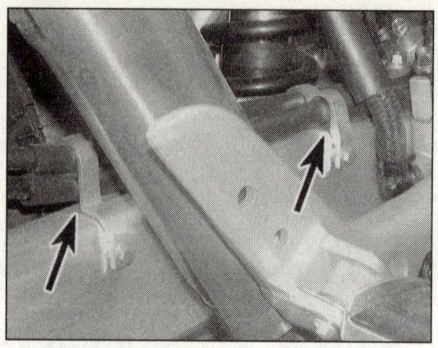

13.2b Brake hose clamps – XL models

13.2c Detach the caliper assembly from the swingarm and tie it to the frame – VTR models

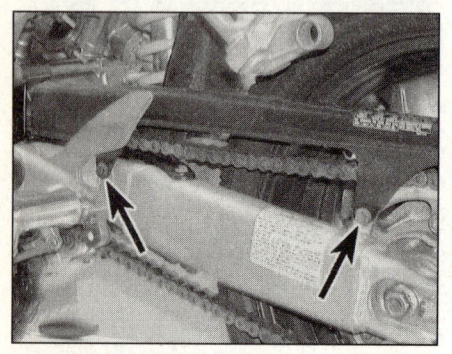

13.3 Unscrew the bolts (arrowed) and remove the chain guard – VTR models

13.4 Unscrew the nut (arrowed), withdraw the bolt and detach the linkage plates from the swingarm

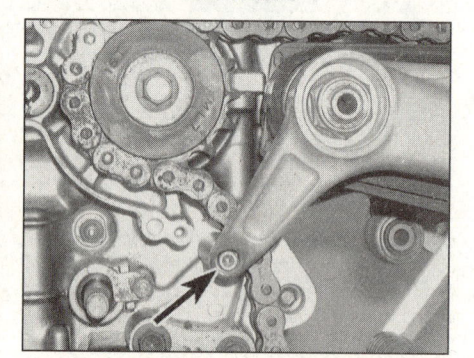

13.5a Slacken or remove the footrest bracket-to-engine bolt (arrowed) . . .

13 Swingarm – removal and installation

Removal

1 Remove the rear wheel (see Chapter 7). On VTR models, remove the silencers (see Chapter 4).

2 Release the rear brake hose(s) and wiring on ABS models from the clamps on the swingarm – remove the clamps if necessary **(see illustrations)**. Remove the rear brake caliper and bracket assembly, noting that there is no need to disconnect the brake hose(s), and tie it to the frame, making sure no strain is placed on the hose(s) **(see illustration)**.

3 Unscrew the bolts securing the chain guard to the swingarm and remove the guard, noting how it locates **(see illustration)**.

4 Unscrew the nut and withdraw the bolt securing the linkage plates to the swingarm **(see illustration or illustration 10.4b)**.

5 Slacken or remove the bolts securing the footrest brackets to the engine – the brackets can remain loosely in position with the bolts slackened, or the brackets can be left to dangle with the bolts removed **(see illustration)**. On VTR models, note the collar fitted between the right-hand footrest bracket and the engine **(see illustration)**. On XL models, also slacken or remove the bolt securing each silencer to the footrest brackets **(see illustration)**.

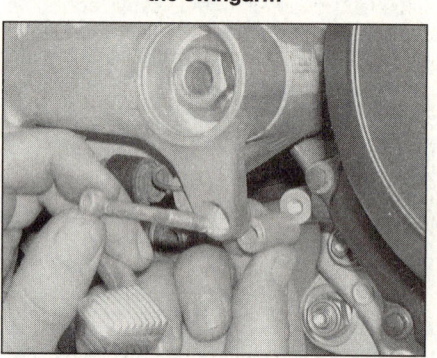

13.5b . . . noting the collar on the right-hand side on VTR models

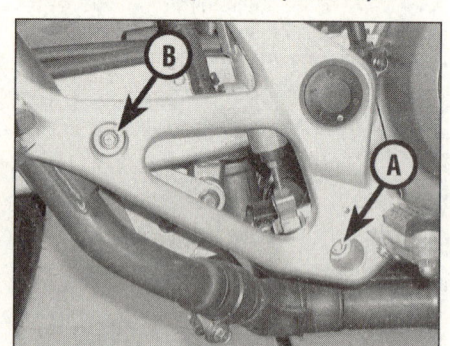

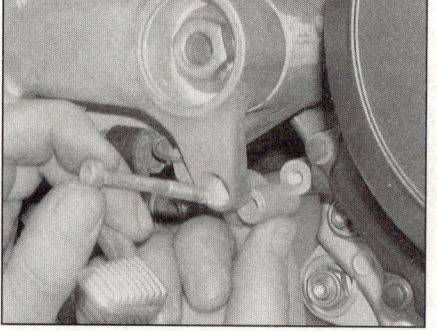

6 Remove the swingarm pivot caps **(see illustration)**. Unscrew the nut on the left-hand end of the swingarm pivot bolt (see

13.6a Remove the pivot caps . . .

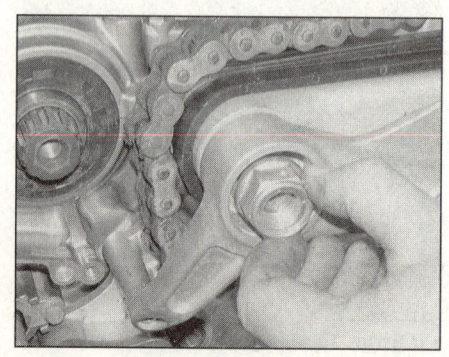

13.5c Footrest bracket-to-engine bolt (A), bracket-to-silencer bolt (B) – XL models

illustration). If the footrest brackets are not being left in place, draw the left-hand bracket off the end of the pivot bolt and rest it on the

13.6b . . . then unscrew the pivot bolt nut

Frame, suspension and final drive 6•23

13.6c Remove the left-hand footrest bracket if required

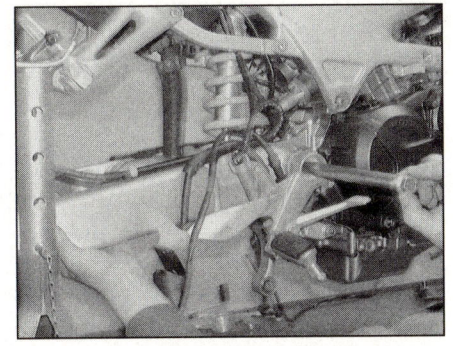

13.7 Withdraw the pivot bolt and remove the swingarm

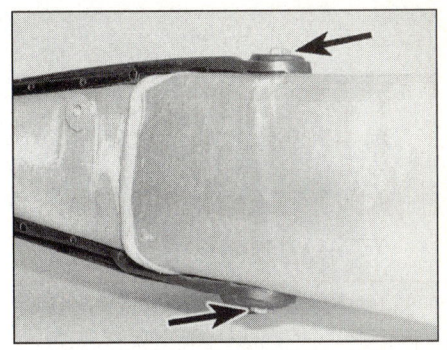

13.8 Chain slider bolts (arrowed) – VTR models

ground – if you want to remove it completely, unscrew the gearchange linkage arm pinchbolt and slide the arm off the shaft, noting its alignment **(see illustration)**.

7 Support the swingarm, then withdraw the pivot bolt and remove the swingarm **(see illustration)**. Support the right-hand footrest bracket assembly so that the brake hoses aren't strained.

8 Remove the chain slider from the swingarm if necessary **(see illustration)**. If it is badly worn or damaged, it should be replaced with a new one – there are some wear limit lines on the front.

9 Inspect all pivot components for wear or damage as described in Section 14.

Installation

10 If removed, apply a suitable non-permanent thread locking compound to the chain slider mounting bolts or screws and install the slider **(see illustration 13.8)**. On VTR models, Honda recommend using new bolts.

11 Lubricate the grease seals, bearings, collars, and the pivot bolt with grease – on VTR models Honda recommend molybdenum disulphide grease, on XL models multi-purpose grease. Similarly lubricate the suspension linkage plate-to-swingarm pivot components.

12 Offer up the swingarm and have an assistant hold it in place. Make sure the drive chain is looped over the front of the swingarm. Slide the pivot bolt through the right-hand footrest bracket, the swingarm, the swingarm mount in the engine and the left-hand footrest bracket **(see illustration)**. Thread the pivot bolt nut finger-tight onto the left-hand end of the bolt **(see illustration 13.6b)**.

13 Install the footrest mounting bolts if they were removed, not forgetting the spacer for the right-hand footrest on VTR models **(see illustrations 13.5a, 13.5b or 13.5c)**. Tighten the bolts securely on VTR models, and to the torque setting specified at the beginning of the Chapter on XL models. On XL models, also install (if removed) and tighten the silencer mounting bolts **(see illustration 13.5c)**.

14 Tighten the pivot bolt nut to the specified torque setting **(see illustration)**. Fit the pivot caps **(see illustration)**.

15 Align the rear suspension linkage plates with the swingarm, then install the bolt and tighten the nut to the specified torque setting **(see illustration 13.4 or illustration 10.4b)**.

16 Install the chain guard, making sure it locates correctly over the tab on the swingarm, and tighten the bolts securely **(see illustration and illustration 13.3)**.

17 Locate the rear brake caliper and bracket assembly onto the swingarm **(see illustration 13.2c)**. Secure the brake hose(s) (and sensor wiring on ABS models) in the clamps **(see illustrations 13.2a or b)**.

18 Install the rear wheel (see Chapter 7).

19 Check and adjust the drive chain slack (see Chapter 1). Check the operation of the rear suspension before taking the machine on the road.

14 Swingarm – inspection and bearing replacement

Inspection

1 Remove the swingarm (see Section 13).

2 Thoroughly clean all components, removing all traces of dirt, corrosion and grease.

3 Inspect all components closely, looking for obvious signs of wear such as heavy scoring, and cracks or distortion due to accident damage. Any damaged or worn component must be replaced.

4 Check the swingarm pivot bolt for straightness by rolling it on a flat surface such as a piece of plate glass (first wipe off all old

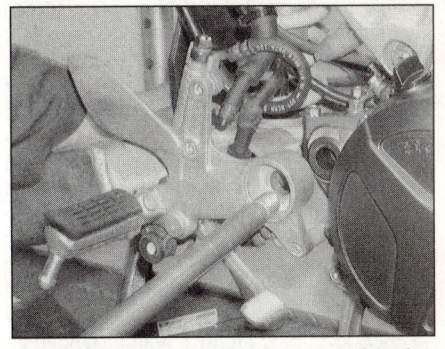

13.12 Offer up the swingarm and slide the pivot bolt through as described

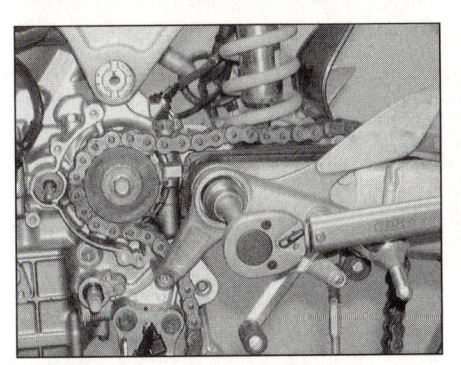

13.14a Tighten the pivot bolt nut to the specified torque . . .

13.14b . . . then install the pivot caps

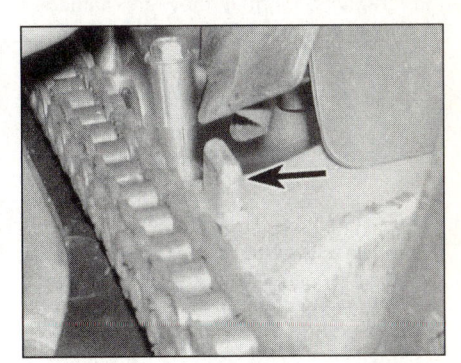

13.16 Make sure the chain guard locates correctly over the tab (arrowed)

6•24 Frame, suspension and final drive

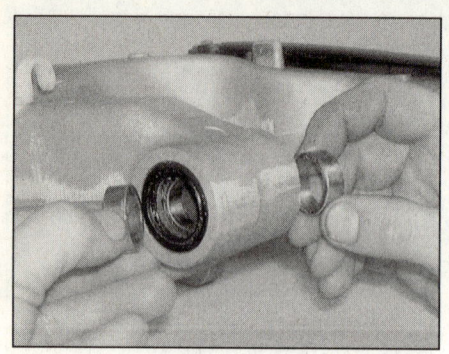

14.5a Remove the collars from the right-hand pivot . . .

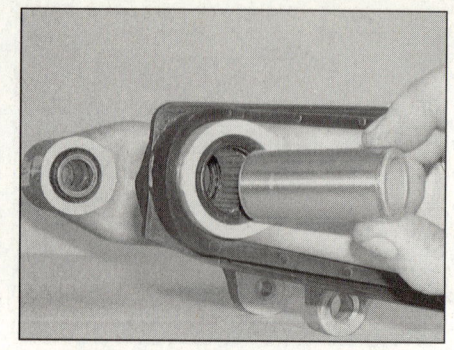

14.5b . . . and the spacer from the left-hand pivot – VTR models

15.6 Loop the chain around the font sprocket and swingarm

grease and remove any corrosion using fine emery cloth). If the equipment is available, place the pivot bolt in V-blocks and measure the runout using a dial gauge. If the pivot bolt is bent, replace it; Honda do not specify a runout limit.

Bearing replacement

5 Remove the collar from each side of the right-hand pivot and withdraw the spacer from the left-hand pivot **(see illustrations)**. Lever out the grease seal on each side of each pivot. Remove the circlip from the outside of the right-hand pivot.
6 Refer to *Tools and Workshop Tips* in the Reference section and check the bearings – there are two caged ball bearings in the right hand pivot with a spacer between them, and a needle bearing in the left-hand pivot. Clean them and inspect them for wear or damage. If the bearings do not run smoothly and freely or if there is excessive freeplay, they must be replaced with new ones – refer to the Reference Section for removal and installation methods. The needle bearing in the left-hand side of the swingarm should be replaced with a new one if it is removed – they cannot be re-used.
7 Do not forget to install the bearing spacer between the caged ball bearings in the right-hand pivot. When installing the new needle bearing, lubricate it with molybdenum disulphide grease and set it centrally in the pivot. Check the condition of the grease seals and replace them if they are damaged, deformed or deteriorated.

15 Drive chain – removal, cleaning and installation

Removal

Note: *The original equipment drive chain fitted to these models has a staked-type master (joining) link which can be disassembled using either Honda service tool, Pt. No. 07HMH-MR10103 for UK models, or 07HMH-MR1010B for US models, or one of several commercially-available drive chain cutting/staking tools. Such chains can be recognised by the master link side plate's identification marks (and usually its different colour), as well as by the staked ends of the link's two pins which look as if they have been deeply centre-punched, instead of peened over as with all the other pins.*

⚠ **Warning: NEVER install a drive chain which uses a clip-type master (split) link. Use ONLY the correct service tools to secure the staked-type of master link – if you do not have access to such tools, have the chain replaced by a dealer service department or bike repair shop to be sure of having it securely installed.**

1 Locate the joining link in a suitable position to work on by rotating the back wheel. Slacken the drive chain as described in Chapter 1.
2 Unscrew the bolts securing the chain guard to the swingarm and remove the guard, noting how it locates **(see illustration 13.3)**.
3 Remove the front sprocket cover (see Section 16).
4 Split the chain at the joining link using the chain cutter, following carefully the manufacturer's operating instructions (see also Chain section in *Tools and Workshop Tips* in the Reference Section). Remove the chain from the bike, noting its routing around the swingarm.

Cleaning

5 Soak the chain in kerosene (paraffin) for approximately five or six minutes, then clean it using a soft brush.

Caution: Don't use gasoline (petrol), solvent or other cleaning fluids which might damage its internal sealing properties. Don't use high-pressure water. Remove the chain, wipe it off, then blow dry it with compressed air immediately. The entire process shouldn't take longer than ten minutes – if it does, the O-rings in the chain rollers could be damaged.

Installation

⚠ **Warning: NEVER install a drive chain which uses a clip-type master (split) link. If you do not have access to a chain riveting tool, have the chain fitted by a dealer service department.**

6 Install the drive chain around the swingarm and front sprocket, leaving the two ends in a convenient position to work on **(see illustration)**.
7 Refer to the Chain section in *Tools and Workshop Tips* in the Reference Section. Install the new joining link from the inside with the four O-rings correctly located between the link plate and side plate. Install the new side plate with its identification marks facing out. Measure the amount that the joining link pins project from the side plate and check they are within the measurements specified at the beginning of the Chapter. Stake the new link using the drive chain cutting/staking tool, following carefully the instructions of both the chain manufacturer and the tool manufacturer. DO NOT re-use old joining link components.
8 After staking, check the joining link and staking for any signs of cracking. If there is any evidence of cracking, the joining link, O-rings and side plate must be replaced. Measure the diameter of the staked ends in two directions and check that it is evenly staked and within the measurements specified at the beginning of the Chapter.
9 Install the sprocket cover (see Section 16).
10 Install the chain guard, making sure it locates correctly over the tab on the swingarm, and tighten the bolts securely **(see illustrations 13.16 and 13.3)**.
11 On completion, adjust and lubricate the chain following the procedures described in Chapter 1.

Caution: Use only the recommended lubricant.

16 Sprockets – check and replacement

Check

1 On VTR models, displace the clutch release cylinder (see Chapter 2) – there is no need to disconnect the hose. Unscrew the bolts securing the front sprocket cover, noting the wiring clamp, and position the cover aside **(see**

Frame, suspension and final drive 6•25

16.1a Sprocket cover bolts (arrowed) – VTR models

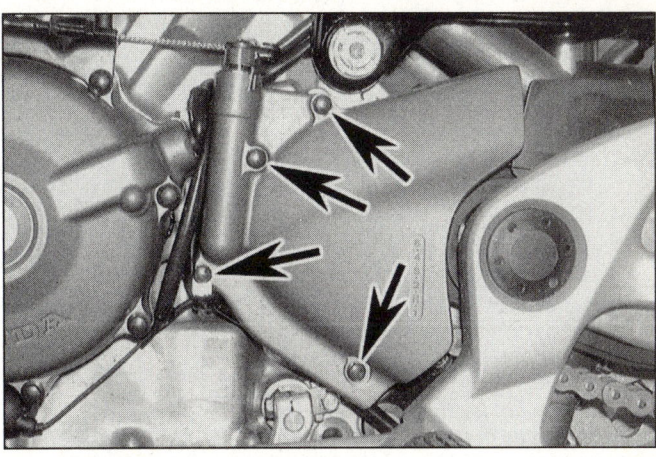

16.1b Sprocket cover bolts (arrowed) – XL models

illustrations). On XL models detach the clutch cable from the release lever. Remove the dowels and the guide plate if they are loose, noting that you will probably need a new gasket for between the plate and the cover.

2 Slacken the drive chain as described in Chapter 1.

3 Check the wear pattern on both sprockets (see Chapter 1, Section 1). If the sprocket teeth are worn excessively, replace the chain and both sprockets as a set. Whenever the sprockets are inspected, the drive chain should be inspected also (see Chapter 1). If you are renewing the chain, renew the sprockets as well.

4 Adjust and lubricate the chain following the procedures described in Chapter 1.

Caution: Use only the recommended lubricant.

Replacement

Front sprocket

5 On VTR models, displace the clutch release cylinder (see Chapter 2) – there is no need to disconnect the hose. Unscrew the bolts securing the front sprocket cover, noting the wiring clamp, and position the cover aside **(see illustration 16.1a or 16.1b)**. On XL models detach the clutch cable from the release lever. Remove the dowels and the guide plate if they are loose, noting that you will probably need a new gasket for between the plate and the cover.

Slacken the drive chain as described in Chapter 1.

7 Have an assistant apply the rear brake, then unscrew the sprocket bolt and remove the washer.

8 Slide the sprocket and chain off the shaft and slip the sprocket out of the chain **(see illustration)**.

9 Engage the new sprocket with the chain and slide it on the shaft. Take up the slack in the chain.

10 Install the sprocket bolt with its washer and tighten it to the torque setting specified at the beginning of the Chapter, using the method employed on removal to prevent the sprocket from turning **(see illustrations)**.

11 Fit the dowels and guide plate if removed, using a new gasket between the plate and the cover **(see illustration)**. Install the sprocket cover, on XL models attaching the clutch cable to the release lever as you do **(see illustration 16.1a or 16.1b)**. On VTR models, install the clutch release cylinder (see Chapter 2). Adjust and lubricate the chain following the procedures described in Chapter 1.

Rear sprocket

12 Remove the rear wheel (see Chapter 7).
13 Unscrew the nuts securing the sprocket to the hub assembly **(see illustration)**. Remove the sprocket, noting which way round it fits.

16.8 Draw the sprocket off the shaft and disengage the chain

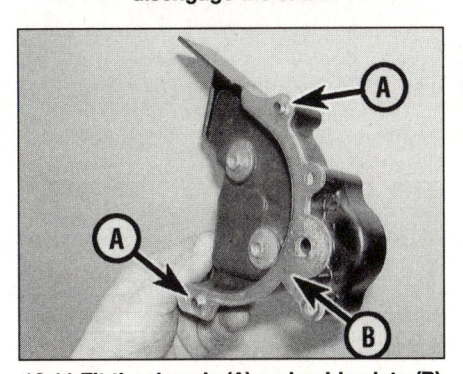

16.10a Install the bolt with its washer . . .

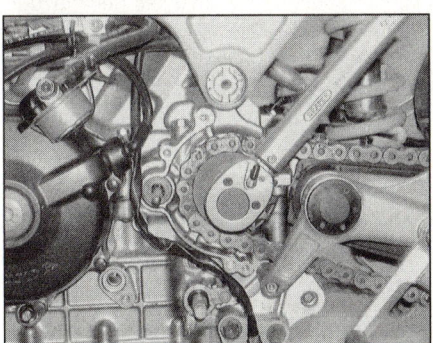

16.10b . . . and tighten it to the specified torque

16.11 Fit the dowels (A) and guide plate (B)

16.13 Rear sprocket nuts (arrowed)

6•26 Frame, suspension and final drive

14 Install the sprocket onto the hub with the stamped mark facing out. Tighten the nuts evenly and in a criss-cross sequence to the torque setting specified at the beginning of the Chapter.
15 Install the rear wheel (see Chapter 7).

17 Rear sprocket coupling/ rubber dampers – check and replacement

1 Remove the rear wheel (see Chapter 7).
Caution: Do not lay the wheel down on the disc as it could become warped. Lay the wheel on wooden blocks so that the disc is off the ground.
2 Lift the sprocket coupling away from the wheel leaving the rubber dampers in position in the wheel **(see illustration)**. Note the spacer inside the coupling – it should be a tight fit but remove it if it is likely to drop out. Check the coupling for cracks or any obvious signs of damage. Also check the sprocket studs for wear or damage.
3 Lift the rubber damper segments from the wheel and check them for cracks, hardening and general deterioration **(see illustration)**. Renew the rubber dampers as a set if necessary.
4 Check the condition of the hub O-ring and replace it with a new one if it is damaged, deformed or deteriorated **(see illustration 17.3)**.
5 Checking and replacement procedures for the sprocket coupling bearing are described in Chapter 7.
6 Installation is the reverse of removal. Make sure the spacer is still correctly installed in the coupling, or install it if it was removed.
7 Install the rear wheel (see Chapter 7).

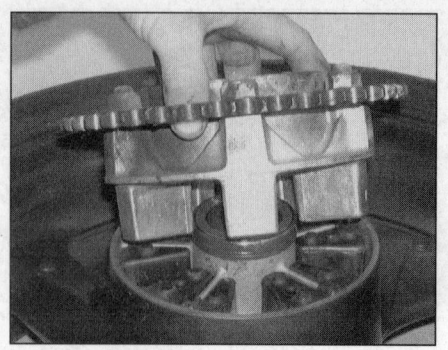

17.2 Lift the sprocket coupling out of the wheel

17.3 Check the rubber dampers and the O-ring (arrowed)

Chapter 7
Brakes, wheels and tyres

Contents

ABS (Anti-lock Brake System) – operation and fault finding	17
ABS (Anti-lock Brake System) – system checks	18
ABS (Anti-lock Brake System) – component removal and installation	19
Brake discs (front and rear) – inspection, removal and installation	4
Brake fluid level check	see *Daily (pre-ride) checks*
Brake hoses, pipes and unions – inspection and replacement	9
Brake light switches – check and replacement	see Chapter 9
Brake pads – replacement	2
Brake pads – wear check	see Chapter 1
Brake system – bleeding	10
Brake system – check	see Chapter 1
Dual combined braking system components (XL models) – removal, overhaul and installation	6
Front brake calipers – removal, overhaul and installation	3
Front brake master cylinder – removal, overhaul and installation	5
Front wheel – removal and installation	13
General information	1
Rear brake caliper – removal, overhaul and installation	7
Rear brake master cylinder – removal, overhaul and installation	8
Rear wheel – removal and installation	14
Tyres – general information and fitting	16
Tyres – pressure, tread depth and condition	see *Daily (pre-ride) checks*
Wheel bearings – check	see Chapter 1
Wheel bearings – removal, inspection and installation	15
Wheels – alignment check	12
Wheels – general check	see Chapter 1
Wheels – inspection and repair	11

Degrees of difficulty

Easy, suitable for novice with little experience	**Fairly easy,** suitable for beginner with some experience	**Fairly difficult,** suitable for competent DIY mechanic	**Difficult,** suitable for experienced DIY mechanic	**Very difficult,** suitable for expert DIY or professional

Specifications

Brakes

Brake fluid type	DOT 4	
Front caliper bore ID	**Standard**	**Service limit**
VTR models		
Upper bore	30.230 to 30.280 mm	30.29 mm
Lower bore	27.000 to 27.050 mm	27.06 mm
XL models		
Right-hand caliper – upper bore	27.000 to 27.050 mm	27.06 mm
Right-hand caliper – middle bore	22.650 to 22.700 mm	22.71 mm
Right-hand caliper – lower bore	27.000 to 27.050 mm	27.06 mm
Left-hand caliper – upper bore	25.400 to 25.450 mm	25.46 mm
Left-hand caliper – middle bore	22.650 to 22.700 mm	22.71 mm
Left-hand caliper – lower bore	25.400 to 25.450 mm	25.46 mm
Front caliper piston OD		
VTR models		
Upper bore	30.148 to 30.198 mm	30.14 mm
Lower bore	26.918 to 26.968 mm	26.91 mm
XL models		
Right-hand caliper – upper bore	26.935 to 26.968 mm	26.91 mm
Right-hand caliper – middle bore	22.585 to 22.618 mm	22.56 mm
Right-hand caliper – lower bore	26.935 to 26.968 mm	26.91 mm
Left-hand caliper – upper bore	25.335 to 25.368 mm	25.31 mm
Left-hand caliper – middle bore	22.585 to 22.618 mm	22.56 mm
Left-hand caliper – lower bore	25.335 to 25.368 mm	25.31 mm
Front disc minimum thickness – all models	4.4 to 4.6 mm	3.5 mm
Disc maximum runout	0.3 mm	
Front master cylinder bore ID		
VTR models	14.000 to 14.043 mm	14.055 mm
XL models	12.700 to 12.743 mm	12.755 mm

Brakes (continued)

	Standard	Service limit
Front master cylinder piston OD		
VTR models	13.957 to 13.984 mm	13.945 mm
XL models	12.657 to 12.684 mm	12.645 mm
Secondary master cylinder bore ID – XL models	12.700 to 12.743 mm	12.755 mm
Secondary master piston OD – XL models	12.657 to 12.684 mm	12.645 mm
Rear caliper bore ID		
VTR models	38.180 to 38.230 mm	38.240 mm
XL models		
Front bore	22.650 to 22.700 mm	22.71 mm
Middle bore	27.000 to 27.050 mm	27.06 mm
Rear bore	22.650 to 22.700 mm	22.71 mm
Rear caliper piston OD		
VTR models	38.098 to 38.148 mm	38.09 mm
XL models		
Front bore	22.585 to 22.618 mm	22.56 mm
Middle bore	26.935 to 26.968 mm	26.91 mm
Rear bore	22.585 to 22.618 mm	22.56 mm
Rear disc minimum thickness – all models	4.8 to 5.2 mm	4.0 mm
Disc maximum runout	0.3 mm	
Rear master cylinder bore ID		
VTR models	14.000 to 14.043 mm	14.055 mm
XL models	17.460 to 17.503 mm	17.515 mm
Rear master cylinder piston OD		
VTR models	13.957 to 13.984 mm	13.945 mm
XL models	17.417 to 17.444 mm	17.405 mm

ABS

Wheel speed sensor air gap . . . . 0.2 to 1.2 mm

Wheels

Maximum wheel runout (front and rear)
   Axial (side-to-side) . . . . 2.0 mm
   Radial (out-of-round) . . . . 2.0 mm
Maximum axle runout (front and rear) . . . . 0.20 mm

Tyres

Tyre pressures . . . . see *Daily (pre-ride)* checks

Tyre sizes*	Front	Rear
VTR models	120/70-ZR17 58W	180/55-ZR17 73W
XL models	110/80-R19 59H	150/70-R17 69H

*Refer to the owners handbook or the tyre information label on the swingarm for approved tyre brands.

Torque settings

Brake pad retaining pins . . . . 18 Nm
Front brake caliper mounting bolts
   VTR models . . . . 30 Nm
   XL models . . . . 31 Nm
Rear brake caliper mounting bolts/slider pin (VTR models) . . . . 23 Nm
Brake caliper joining bolts
   VTR models . . . . 32 Nm
   XL models . . . . 32 Nm
Brake hose banjo bolts
   VTR models . . . . 34 Nm
   XL models . . . . 35 Nm
Brake disc bolts
   Front . . . . 20 Nm
   Rear . . . . 42 Nm
Front master cylinder clamp bolts . . . . 12 Nm
Brake pipe joint nuts . . . . 17 Nm
Delay valve mounting bolts . . . . 12 Nm
Proportional control valve mounting bolts . . . . 12 Nm
Brake caliper bleed valves . . . . 6 Nm
Front axle bolt . . . . 59 Nm
Front axle clamp bolts . . . . 22 Nm
Rear axle nut . . . . 93 Nm
ABS front wheel pulser ring . . . . 7 Nm
ABS rear wheel pulser ring . . . . 9 Nm
ABS modulator hose banjo bolts . . . . 34 Nm

Brakes, wheels and tyres 7•3

1 General information

All models covered in this manual are fitted with cast alloy wheels designed for tubeless tyres only. Both front and rear brakes are hydraulically-operated disc brakes.

On VTR models, the front brakes have twin opposed piston caliper and the rear brake has a single piston sliding caliper. On XL models, both front and rear brakes have triple piston sliding calipers.

XL models are fitted with the dual combined braking system (Dual-CBS) which applies both front and rear brakes even if only either the front brake lever or rear brake pedal is applied. Operating the front brake lever activates each front brake caliper and a proportion of the rear caliper, the amount depending upon how hard the front brake lever is applied. The left front caliper is hinged and linked to the rear caliper via a secondary master cylinder and a proportional control valve. When the braking force is sufficient, the left caliper operates the secondary master cylinder and the rear brake is applied. Operating the rear brake pedal activates the rear brake caliper and a proportion of each front caliper equally. A delay valve in the rear pedal system provides progressive braking, enhancing control on rough or slippery surfaces.

XL1000VA models (XL-VA4 onwards) are fitted with an anti-lock braking system (ABS) that prevents the wheels locking up under heavy braking. Refer to Section 17 for a full description of the system.

Caution: *Disc brake components rarely require disassembly. Do not disassemble components unless absolutely necessary. If a hydraulic brake line is loosened, the entire system must be disassembled, drained, cleaned and then properly filled and bled upon reassembly. Do not use solvents on internal brake components. Solvents will cause the seals to swell and distort. Use only clean brake fluid or denatured alcohol for cleaning. Use care when working with brake fluid as it can injure your eyes and it will damage painted surfaces and plastic parts.*

2 Brake pads – replacement

⚠️ **Warning:** *The dust created by the brake system may contain asbestos, which is harmful to your health. Never blow it out with compressed air and don't inhale any of it. An approved filtering mask should be worn when working on the brakes.*

VTR models

Front

Note: *Honda recommend using new caliper bolts when the old ones are removed. This is because the bolts are pre-treated with a locking compound. It is possible, however, to clean up the old bolts and reinstall them using a suitable non-permanent thread locking compound that is commercially available.*

1 Unscrew the pad retaining pin plug, then slacken the pad retaining pin (see illustrations). Unscrew the caliper mounting bolts and slide the caliper off the disc (see illustrations).

2 To allow for the increased friction material thickness of new pads, push the pistons as far back into the caliper as possible using a piece of wood, a metal bar or a screwdriver inserted between the old pads, using a rag to protect the caliper body (see illustration). It may be necessary to remove the master cylinder reservoir cover and diaphragm and siphon out some fluid (see *Daily (pre-ride) checks*). If the pistons are difficult to push back, attach a length of clear hose to the bleed valve and place the open end in a suitable container, then open the valve and try again. Take great care not to draw any air into the system. If in doubt, bleed the brakes afterwards (see Section 10).

2.1a Unscrew the plug . . .

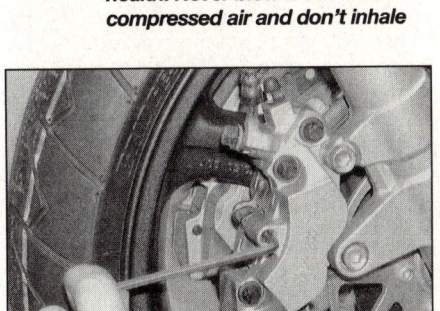

2.1b . . . and slacken the retaining pin

2.1c Unscrew the caliper mounting bolts (arrowed) . . .

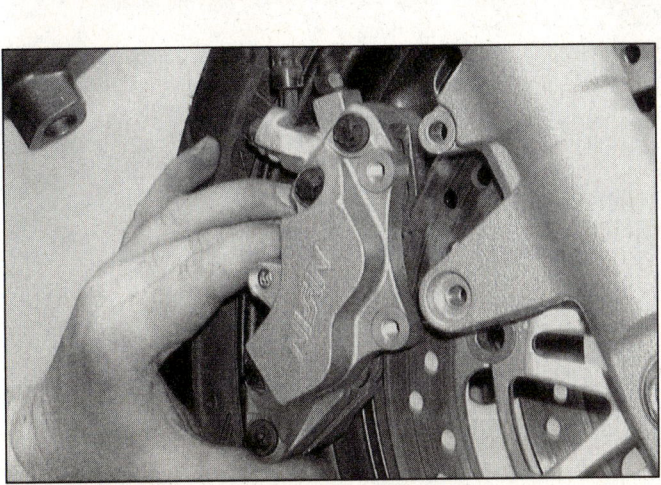

2.1d . . . and slide the caliper off the disc

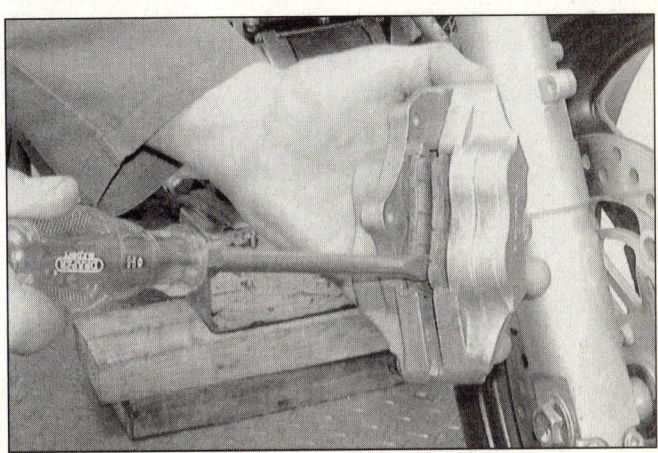

2.2 Press the pistons back into the caliper to allow for the new pads

7•4 Brakes, wheels and tyres

2.3a Remove the retaining pin . . .

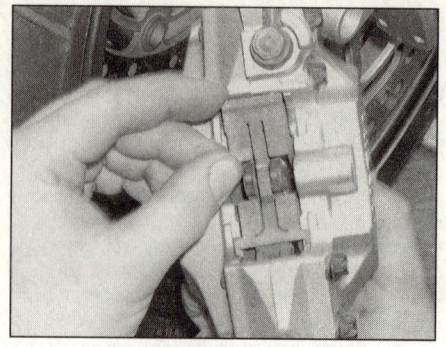

2.3b . . . and the pad spring, noting how it fits . . .

2.3c . . . then lift the pads out of the caliper

3 Unscrew the pad retaining pin, then lift off the pad spring, noting how it fits, and remove the pads **(see illustrations)**.
4 Inspect the surface of each pad for contamination and check whether the friction material has worn beyond its service limit (see Chapter 1, Section 3). If either pad is worn to or beyond the service limit, is fouled with oil or grease, or is heavily scored or damaged by dirt and debris, both sets of pads must be renewed as a set. Note that it is not possible to degrease the friction material; if the pads are contaminated in any way new ones must be fitted.
5 If the pads are in good condition clean them carefully, using a fine wire brush which is completely free of oil and grease to remove all traces of road dirt and corrosion. Using a pointed instrument, clean out the grooves in the friction material and dig out any embedded particles of foreign matter. Any areas of glazing may be removed using a fine flat file. Spray with a dedicated brake cleaner to remove any dust.
6 Check the condition of the brake disc (see Section 4).
7 Remove all traces of corrosion from the pad pin and check that it is not bent or damaged. Note that the original pads come with a shim and a lining that sits between the shim and the back of the pad – check they are properly fitted **(see illustration)**. Smear the pin, the back of the pads and the leading and trailing edges of the backing material with copper-based grease, making sure that none gets on the friction material.

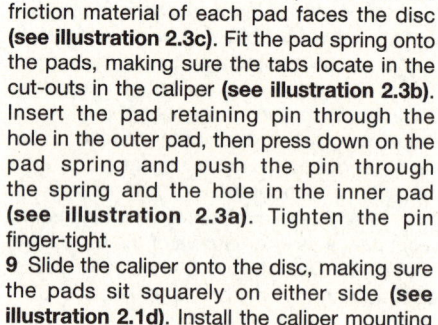

8 Insert the pads into the caliper so that the friction material of each pad faces the disc **(see illustration 2.3c)**. Fit the pad spring onto the pads, making sure the tabs locate in the cut-outs in the caliper **(see illustration 2.3b)**. Insert the pad retaining pin through the hole in the outer pad, then press down on the pad spring and push the pin through the spring and the hole in the inner pad **(see illustration 2.3a)**. Tighten the pin finger-tight.
9 Slide the caliper onto the disc, making sure the pads sit squarely on either side **(see illustration 2.1d)**. Install the caliper mounting bolts, using new ones if required (see **Note** above), and tighten them to the torque setting specified at the beginning of the Chapter **(see illustrations)**. Now tighten the pad retaining pin to the specified torque, then install the plug **(see illustration)**.
10 Top up the master cylinder reservoir if necessary (see *Daily (pre-ride) checks*).
11 Operate the brake lever several times to bring the pads into contact with the disc. Check the operation of the brake before riding the motorcycle.

Rear

12 To allow for the increased friction material thickness of new pads, push the brake caliper against the disc so that the piston is forced back into the caliper **(see illustration)**. It may be necessary to remove the master cylinder reservoir cover and diaphragm and siphon out some fluid. If the pistons are difficult to push

2.7 Check that the shim and lining are properly fitted

2.9a Install the caliper . . .

2.9b . . . and tighten the bolts to the specified torque

2.9c Also tighten the retaining pin to the specified torque

2.12 Push the caliper against the disc to force the piston back

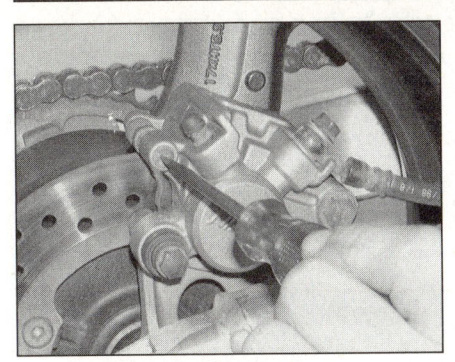

Brakes, wheels and tyres 7•5

2.13a Unscrew the plug . . .

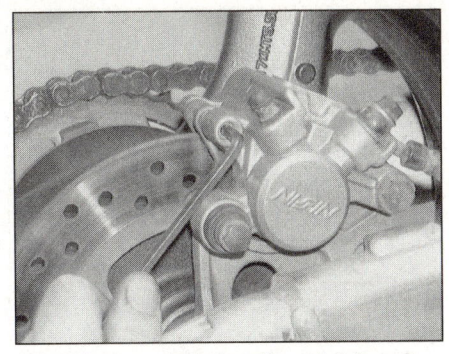

2.13b . . . and slacken the retaining pin

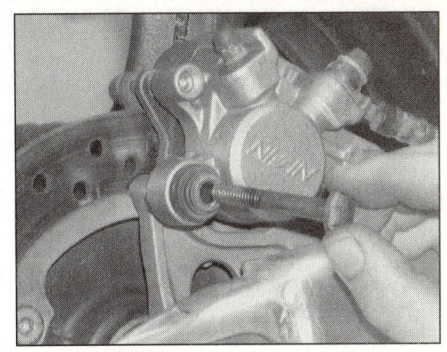

2.13c Remove the rear bolt . . .

back, attach a length of clear hose to the bleed valve and place the open end in a suitable container, then open the valve and try again. Take great care not to draw any air into the system. If in doubt, bleed the brakes afterwards (see Section 10).

13 Unscrew the pad retaining pin plug, then slacken the pad retaining pin **(see illustrations)**. Unscrew the caliper rear mounting bolt/slider pin and pivot the back of the caliper up off the disc **(see illustrations)**.

14 Unscrew the pad retaining pin, then remove the pads, noting how they fit. Note the pad spring in the top of caliper and the pad guide on the caliper bracket and remove them if required for cleaning or replacement, noting how they fit.

15 Refer to Steps 4, 5, 6 and 7 above.

16 Fit the pads into the caliper so that the friction material of each pad faces the disc, then insert the pad pin and tighten it finger-tight. Pivot the caliper down onto the disc while keeping the pads held in position, making sure the front ends of the pads locate correctly against the guide on the caliper bracket as you do **(see illustration 2.13d)**. Install the caliper rear mounting bolt/slider pin **(see illustration 2.13c)** and tighten it and the pad pin to the torque settings specified at the beginning of the Chapter **(see illustration)**. Install the pad pin plug **(see illustration 2.13a)**.

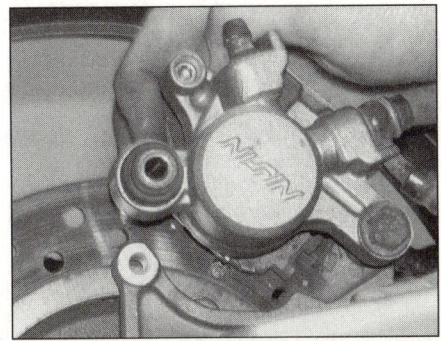

2.13d . . . and pivot the caliper up

2.16 Tighten the rear mounting bolt/slider pin to the specified torque

17 Top up the master cylinder reservoir if necessary (see *Daily (pre-ride) checks*).

18 Operate the brake lever several times to bring the pads into contact with the disc. Check the operation of the brake before riding the motorcycle.

XL models

Front and rear

19 To allow for the increased friction material thickness of new pads, push the brake caliper against the disc so that the piston is forced back into the caliper **(see illustration 2.12)**. It may be necessary to remove the master cylinder reservoir cover and diaphragm and

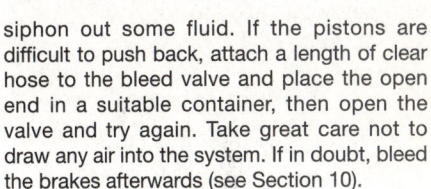

siphon out some fluid. If the pistons are difficult to push back, attach a length of clear hose to the bleed valve and place the open end in a suitable container, then open the valve and try again. Take great care not to draw any air into the system. If in doubt, bleed the brakes afterwards (see Section 10).

20 Unscrew the pad retaining pin plug and the pad retaining pin, then remove the pads **(see illustrations)**. Note how the pad spring is fitted and remove it if required.

21 Refer to Steps 4, 5, 6 and 7 above.

22 Make sure the pad spring is correctly positioned in the caliper. Insert the pads into the caliper so that the friction material faces the disc, then press the pads against the

2.20a Unscrew the plug . . .

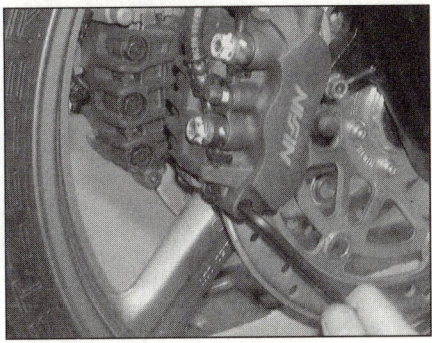

2.20b . . . and the retaining pin . . .

20.20c . . . and remove the pads

7•6 Brakes, wheels and tyres

2.22a Press the pads against the spring and insert the retaining pin

2.22b Make sure the pads locate correctly in the pad guide

3.1a Brake hose guide bolt (arrowed) – VTR models

spring and slide the pad retaining pin through **(see illustration)**. Make sure the pin passes through the hole in each pad, and the pads locate correctly **(see illustration)**. Tighten the pad retaining pin to the torque setting specified at the beginning of the Chapter. Install the pad pin plug **(see illustration 2.20a)**.
23 Top up the master cylinder reservoir if necessary (see *Daily (pre-ride) checks*).
24 Operate the brake lever or pedal several times to bring the pads into contact with the disc. Check the operation of the brake before riding the motorcycle.

3 Front brake calipers – removal, overhaul and installation

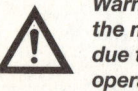

⚠️ **Warning:** *If a caliper indicates the need for an overhaul (usually due to leaking fluid or sticky operation), all old brake fluid should be flushed from the system. Also, the dust created by the brake system may contain asbestos, which is harmful to your health. Never blow it out with compressed air and don't inhale any of it. An approved filtering mask should be worn when working on the brakes. Do not, under any circumstances, use petroleum-based solvents to clean brake parts. Use clean brake fluid, brake cleaner or denatured alcohol only.*
Note: *Honda recommend using new caliper mounting bolts and body joining bolts when the old ones are removed. This is because the bolts are pre-treated with a locking compound. It is possible, however, to clean up the old bolts and reinstall them using a suitable non-permanent thread locking compound that is commercially available.*

Removal

1 If the calipers are just being displaced and not completely removed or overhauled, do not disconnect the brake hose(s), but unscrew the bolt securing the hose guide to the front fork **(see illustrations)**. If the calipers are being completely removed or overhauled, remove the brake hose banjo bolt(s) and detach the hose(s), noting the alignment with the caliper, and on XL models which hose fits where **(see illustrations)**. Plug the hose end(s) or wrap a plastic bag tightly around to minimise fluid loss and prevent dirt entering the system. Discard the sealing washers as new ones must be used on installation. **Note:** *If you are planning to overhaul the caliper and don't have a source of compressed air to blow out the pistons, just loosen the banjo bolt at this stage and retighten it lightly. The bike's hydraulic system can then be used to force the pistons out of the body once the pads have been removed. Disconnect the hose once the pistons have been sufficiently displaced.* On models with ABS, if removing the right-hand caliper free the wheel speed sensor wiring from its three clamps and detach the sensor from the caliper bracket **(see illustrations 19.2a and b)**.
2 On VTR models, if the calipers are being overhauled, remove the brake pads (see Section 2). If not, unscrew the caliper mounting bolts and slide the caliper off the disc **(see illustrations 2.1c and 2.1d)**.
3 On XL models, if the calipers are being overhauled, remove the brake pads (see Section 2). Unscrew the caliper bracket mounting bolts and slide the caliper assembly off the disc **(see illustrations and 2.1c)**. When removing the left-hand caliper, note how the lower mounting bolt acts as the pivot for the caliper to activate the secondary master

3.1b Brake hose guide bolt (arrowed) – XL models

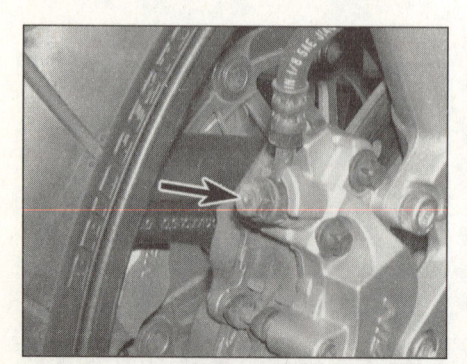

3.1c Brake hose banjo bolt (arrowed) – VTR models

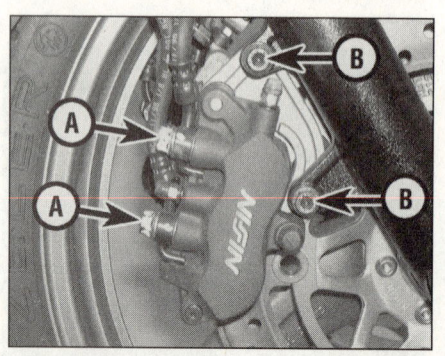

3.3a Brake hose banjo bolts (A), caliper mounting bolts (B) – XL models, right-hand caliper

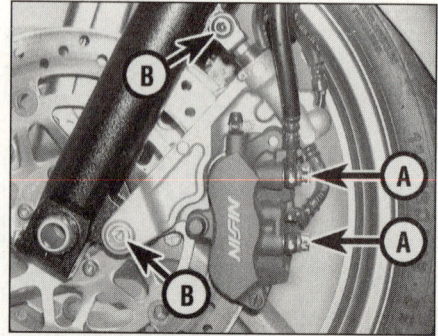

3.3b Brake hose banjo bolts (A), caliper mounting bolts (B) – XL models, left-hand caliper

Brakes, wheels and tyres 7•7

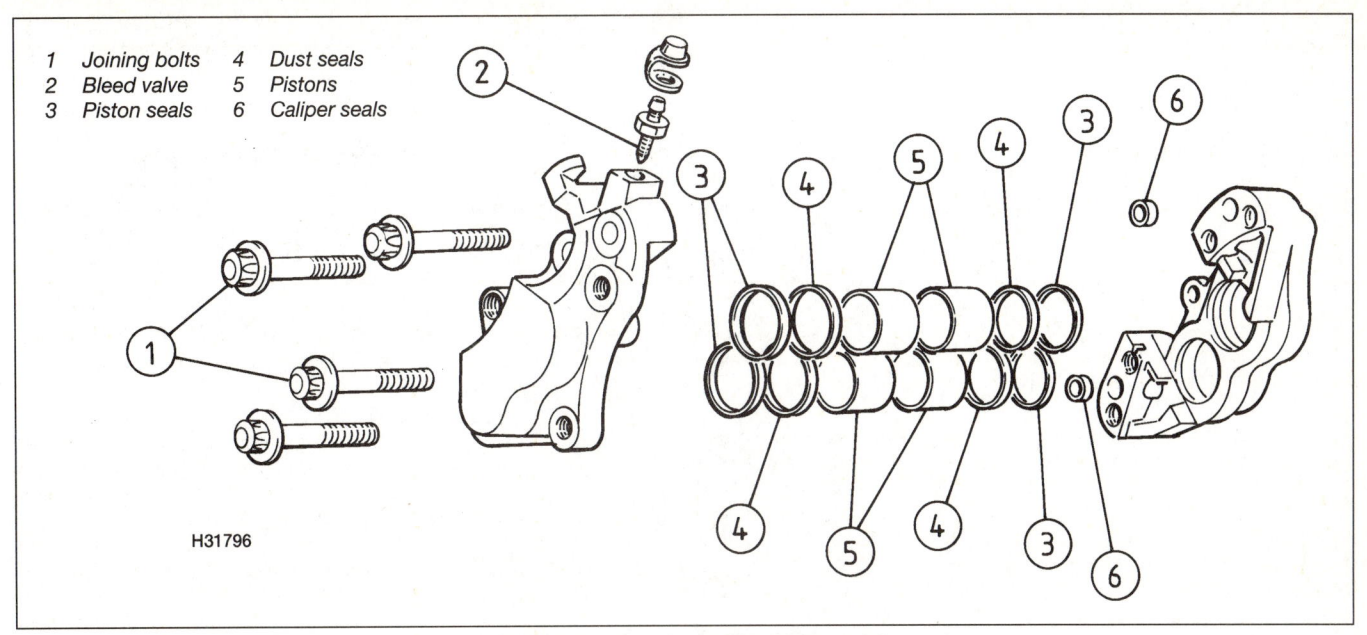

1 Joining bolts
2 Bleed valve
3 Piston seals
4 Dust seals
5 Pistons
6 Caliper seals

H31796

3.4a Front caliper assembly – VTR models

cylinder, and that the upper mounting bolt secures the secondary master cylinder pushrod. Separate the caliper from the bracket by sliding them apart, noting how they locate **(see illustration 3.4b and 3.4c)**. If required, remove the pad spring from the caliper and the guide from the bracket, noting how they fit.

Overhaul

4 Clean the exterior of the caliper with denatured alcohol or brake system cleaner **(see illustrations)**.

⚠ *Warning: Never place your fingers in front of the pistons in an attempt to catch or protect them when applying compressed air, as serious injury could result.*

5 On VTR models, displace the pistons as far as possible from the caliper body, either by pumping them out by operating the front brake lever, or by forcing them out using compressed air. If the compressed air method is used, place a piece of cardboard between the pistons to act as a cushion, then use compressed air directed into the fluid inlet to force the pistons out of the body. Use only low pressure to ease the pistons out and make sure both pistons are displaced at the same time. If the air pressure is too high and the pistons are forced out, the caliper and/or

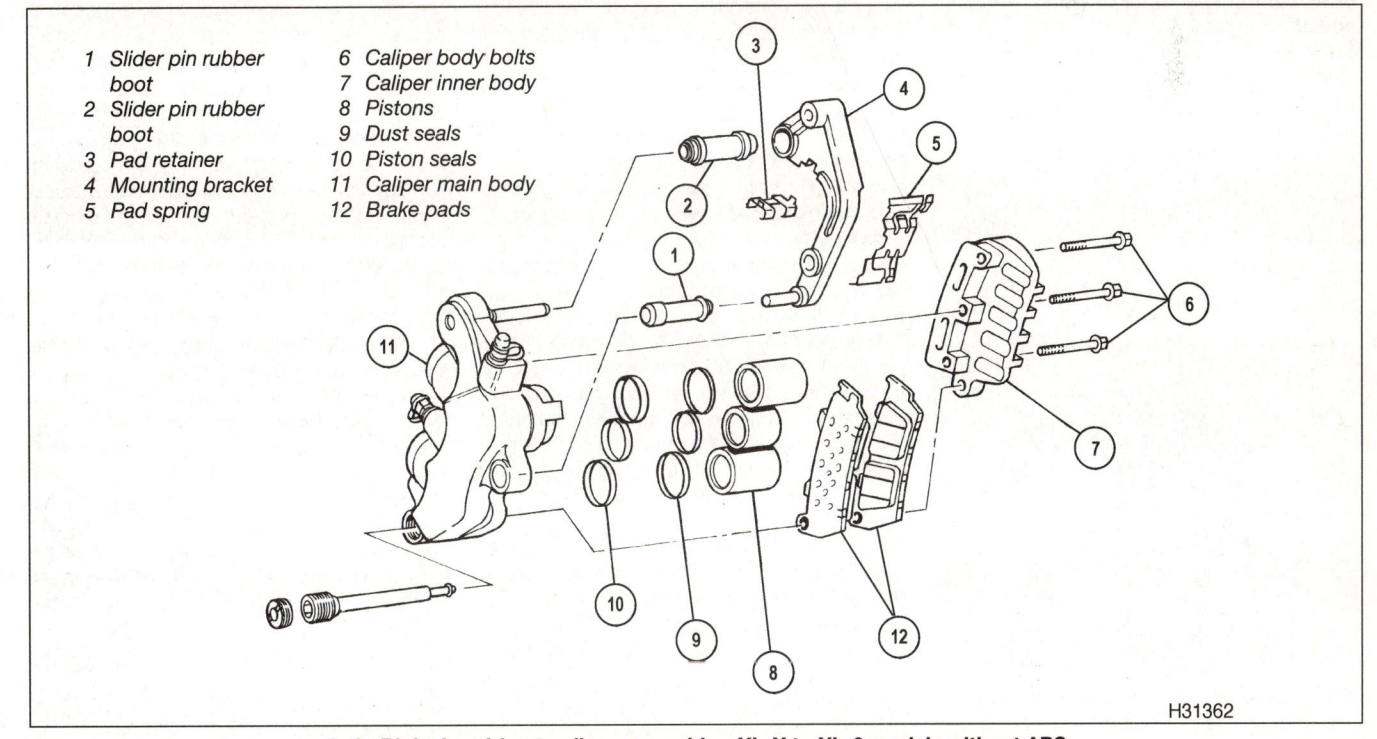

1 Slider pin rubber boot
2 Slider pin rubber boot
3 Pad retainer
4 Mounting bracket
5 Pad spring
6 Caliper body bolts
7 Caliper inner body
8 Pistons
9 Dust seals
10 Piston seals
11 Caliper main body
12 Brake pads

H31362

3.4b Right-hand front caliper assembly – XL-X to XL-6 models without ABS

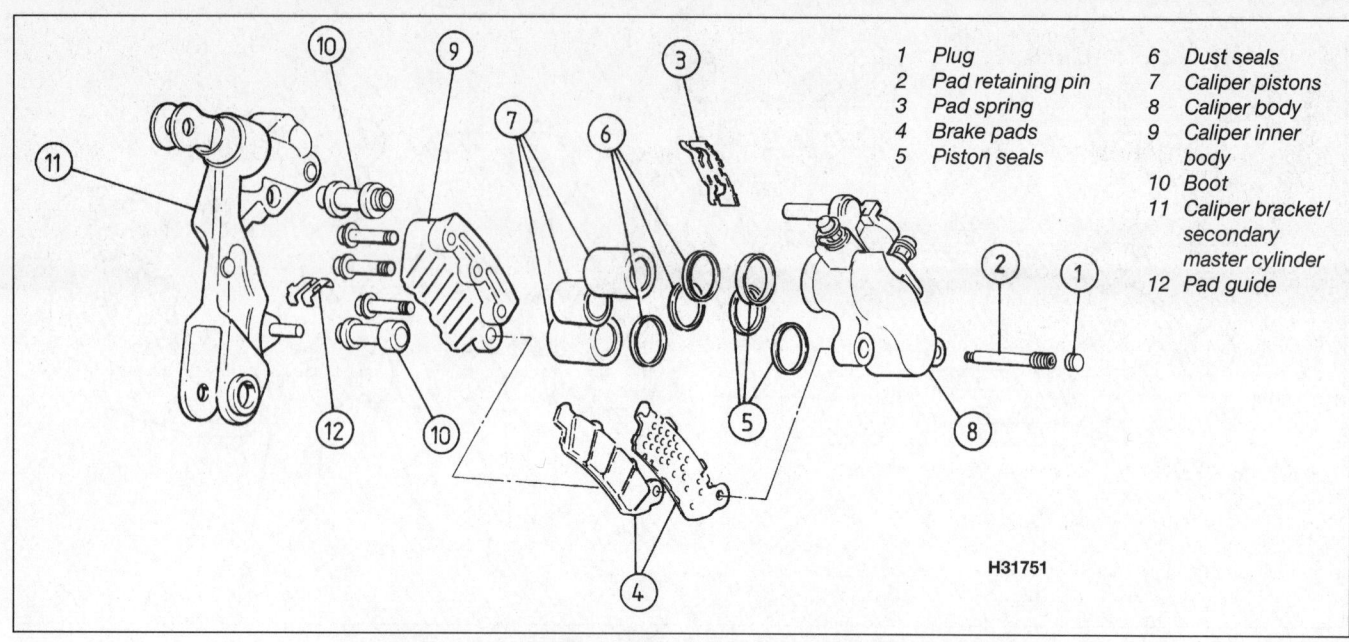

3.4c Left-hand front caliper assembly – XL-X to XL-6 models without ABS

1 Plug
2 Pad retaining pin
3 Pad spring
4 Brake pads
5 Piston seals
6 Dust seals
7 Caliper pistons
8 Caliper body
9 Caliper inner body
10 Boot
11 Caliper bracket/ secondary master cylinder
12 Pad guide

pistons may be damaged. Unscrew the caliper body joining bolts and separate the caliper halves. Mark each piston head and caliper body with a felt marker to ensure that the pistons can be matched to their original bores on reassembly, then remove the pistons. Remove the caliper seals from either half of the caliper body and discard them as new ones must be used.

Caution: Do not try to remove the pistons by levering them out, or by using pliers or any other grips.

6 On XL-X to XL-6 models without ABS unscrew the joining bolts securing the caliper inner body to the main body and separate them. On all models, remove the pistons from the caliper body, either by pumping them out by operating the front brake lever until the pistons are displaced (be prepared for a shower of fluid), or by forcing them out using compressed air. Mark each piston head and caliper body with a felt marker to ensure that the pistons can be matched to their original bores on reassembly. If the compressed air method is used, hold a wad of rag over the pistons to act as a cushion, then use compressed air directed into the fluid inlet to force the pistons out of the body. Use only low pressure and make sure the pistons are displaced at the same time.

7 Using a wooden or plastic tool, remove the dust seals from the caliper bores (see illustration). Discard them as new ones must be used on installation. If a metal tool is being used, take great care not to damage the caliper bores.

8 Remove and discard the piston seals in the same way.

9 Clean the pistons and bores with clean brake fluid of the specified type.

Caution: Do not, under any circumstances, use a petroleum-based solvent to clean brake parts.

10 Inspect the caliper bores and pistons for signs of corrosion, nicks and burrs and loss of plating. If surface defects are present, the caliper assembly must be renewed. If the necessary measuring equipment is available, compare the dimensions of the caliper bores and piston diameters with those specified at the beginning of the Chapter, and install a new caliper if necessary. If the caliper is in bad shape the master cylinder should also be checked.

11 Lubricate the new piston seals with clean brake fluid and install them in their grooves in the caliper bores. Note that different sizes of bore and piston are used (see Specifications), and care must therefore be taken to ensure that the correct size seals are fitted to the correct bores. The same applies when fitting the new dust seals and pistons.

12 Lubricate the new dust seals with clean brake fluid (VTR models) or silicone grease (XL models) and install them in their grooves in the caliper bores.

13 Lubricate the pistons with clean brake fluid and install them closed-end first into the caliper bores. Using your thumbs, push the pistons all the way in, making sure they enter the bore squarely.

14 On VTR models, lubricate the new caliper seals with clean brake fluid and install them in one half of the caliper body and join the body halves together. Apply a suitable non-permanent thread locking compound to the caliper body joining bolts, using new ones if required (see **Note**) and tighten them to the torque setting specified at the beginning of the Chapter (note that they can be fully tightened after the calipers have been installed if required, to prevent having to hold the calipers by hand – just tighten them as much as possible before installing them).

15 On XL models, check that the caliper body is able to slide freely on the slider pins. Clean off all traces of corrosion and hardened grease. Apply a smear of copper or silicone based grease to the slider pins and reassemble the two components. Renew the rubber boots if they are damaged, deformed or deteriorated. On XL-X to XL-6 models without ABS install the caliper inner body, then apply a suitable non-permanent thread locking compound to the joining bolts, using new ones if required (see **Note**) and tighten then to the torque setting specified at the beginning of this Chapter.

Installation

16 On VTR models, if the calipers have been overhauled, install the brake pads (see Section 2). If not, slide the caliper onto the disc,

3.7 Remove the dust seal with a plastic or wooden tool (a pencil works well) to avoid damage to the bore and seal groove

Brakes, wheels and tyres 7•9

4.2 Set up a dial gauge with the probe contacting the brake disc, then rotate the wheel to check for runout

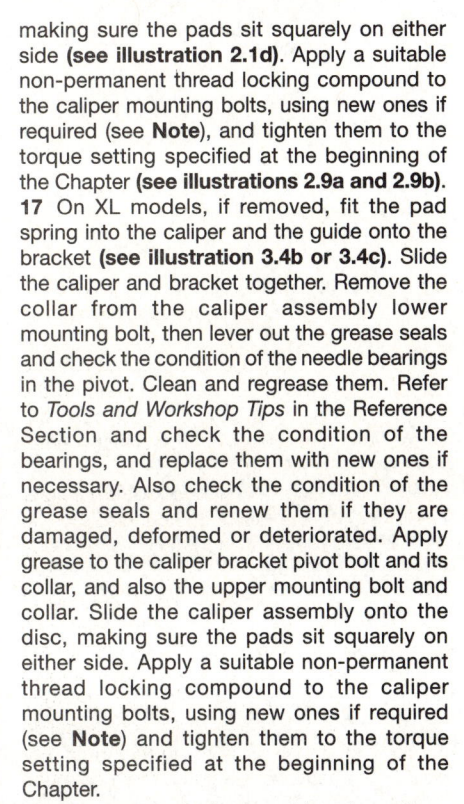

4.3a The minimum disc thickness is marked on each disc

4.3b Using a micrometer to measure disc thickness

making sure the pads sit squarely on either side (see illustration 2.1d). Apply a suitable non-permanent thread locking compound to the caliper mounting bolts, using new ones if required (see **Note**), and tighten them to the torque setting specified at the beginning of the Chapter (see illustrations 2.9a and 2.9b).
17 On XL models, if removed, fit the pad spring into the caliper and the guide onto the bracket (see illustration 3.4b or 3.4c). Slide the caliper and bracket together. Remove the collar from the caliper assembly lower mounting bolt, then lever out the grease seals and check the condition of the needle bearings in the pivot. Clean and regrease them. Refer to *Tools and Workshop Tips* in the Reference Section and check the condition of the bearings, and replace them with new ones if necessary. Also check the condition of the grease seals and renew them if they are damaged, deformed or deteriorated. Apply grease to the caliper bracket pivot bolt and its collar, and also the upper mounting bolt and collar. Slide the caliper assembly onto the disc, making sure the pads sit squarely on either side. Apply a suitable non-permanent thread locking compound to the caliper mounting bolts, using new ones if required (see **Note**) and tighten them to the torque setting specified at the beginning of the Chapter.
18 Connect the brake hose(s) to the caliper, using new sealing washers on each side of the fitting. Align the hose(s) as noted on removal

(see illustration 3.1c, 3.1d or 3.1e). Tighten the banjo bolt(s) to the torque setting specified at the beginning of this Chapter. On the right-hand caliper of ABS equipped models, install the wheel speed sensor and its wiring clamps (see Section 19).
19 Fill the master cylinder reservoir with DOT 4 brake fluid (see *Daily (pre-ride) checks*) and bleed the hydraulic system as described in Section 10.
20 Check for leaks and thoroughly test the operation of the brake before riding the motorcycle on the road.

4 Brake discs (front and rear) – inspection, removal and installation

Note: *Honda recommend using new disc mounting bolts when the old ones are removed. This is because the bolts are pre-treated with a locking compound. It is possible, however, to clean up the old bolts and reinstall them using a suitable non-permanent thread locking compound that is commercially available.*

Inspection

1 Visually inspect the surface of the disc for score marks and other damage. Light scratches are normal after use and won't affect brake operation, but deep grooves and heavy score marks will reduce braking efficiency and accelerate pad wear. If a disc is badly grooved it must be machined or replaced.
2 To check disc runout, position the bike on an auxiliary stand and support it so that the wheel is raised off the ground. Mount a dial gauge to a fork leg or on the swingarm, according to wheel, with the plunger on the gauge touching the surface of the disc about 10 mm (1/2 in) from the outer edge (see illustration). Rotate the wheel and watch the indicator needle, comparing the reading with the limit listed in the Specifications at the beginning of the Chapter. If the runout is greater than the service limit, check the wheel bearings for play (see Chapter 1). If the bearings are worn, replace them with new ones (see Section 15) and repeat this check. If the disc runout is still excessive, it will have to be replaced with a new one, although machining by an engineer may be possible.
3 The disc must not be machined or allowed to wear down to a thickness less than the service limit as listed in this Chapter's Specifications and as marked on the disc itself (see illustration). Check the thickness of the disc using a micrometer (see illustration). If the thickness of the disc is less than the service limit, it must be replaced with a new one.

Removal

Note: *Refer to Section 19 for details of pulser ring removal and installation on ABS equipped models.*
4 Remove the wheel (see Section 13 or 14). **Caution: *Do not lay the wheel down and allow it to rest on the disc – the disc could become warped. Set the wheel on wood blocks so the disc doesn't support the weight of the wheel.***
5 Mark the relationship of the disc to the wheel, so it can be installed in the same position. Unscrew the disc retaining bolts, loosening them a little at a time in a criss-cross pattern to avoid distorting the disc, then remove the disc from the wheel (see illustrations).

4.5a Front disc bolts (arrowed) – VTR models

4.5b Rear disc bolts (arrowed) – XL models

7•10 Brakes, wheels and tyres

Installation

6 Install the disc on the wheel, making sure the directional arrow is on the outside and pointing in the direction of normal (i.e. forward) rotation. Align the previously applied matchmarks (if you're reinstalling the original disc).

7 Apply a suitable non-permanent thread locking compound to the bolts, using new ones if required (see **Note**) and tighten them evenly in a criss-cross pattern to the torque setting specified at the beginning of the Chapter. Clean off all grease from the brake disc(s) using acetone or brake system cleaner. If a new brake disc has been installed, remove any protective coating from its working surfaces.

8 Install the wheel (see Section 13 or 14).

9 Operate the brake lever or pedal several times to bring the pads into contact with the disc. Check the operation of the brakes carefully before riding the bike.

5 Front brake master cylinder
– removal, overhaul and installation

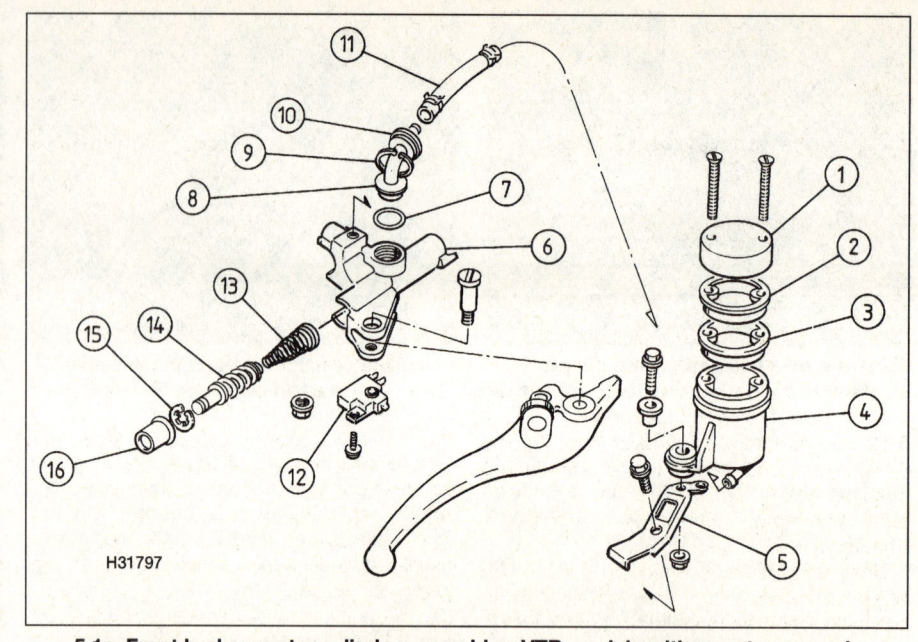

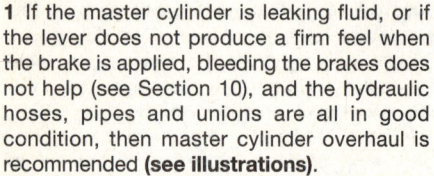

1 If the master cylinder is leaking fluid, or if the lever does not produce a firm feel when the brake is applied, bleeding the brakes does not help (see Section 10), and the hydraulic hoses, pipes and unions are all in good condition, then master cylinder overhaul is recommended **(see illustrations)**.

2 Before disassembling the master cylinder, read through the entire procedure and make sure that you have the correct rebuild kit. Also, you will need some new DOT 4 brake fluid, some clean rags and internal circlip pliers.

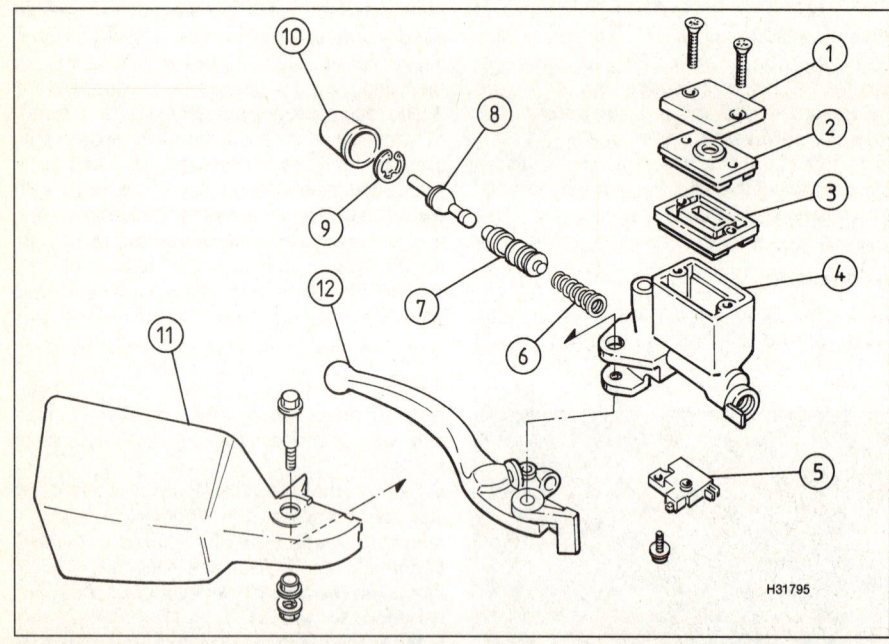

5.1a Front brake master cylinder assembly – VTR models with remote reservoir

1 Reservoir cap	7 O-ring	12 Brake light switch
2 Diaphragm plate	8 Hose union	13 Spring
3 Diaphragm	9 Circlip	14 Piston
4 Reservoir	10 Rubber cap	15 Circlip
5 Stay	11 Reservoir hose	16 Boot
6 Master cylinder		

Note: *To prevent damage to the paint from spilled brake fluid, always cover the fuel tank when working on the master cylinder.*

Caution: *Disassembly, overhaul and reassembly of the brake master cylinder must be done in a spotlessly clean work area to avoid contamination and possible failure of the brake hydraulic system components.*

Removal

Note: *If the master cylinder is being displaced from the handlebar and not being removed completely or overhauled, follow Steps 4 and 7 only.*

3 Loosen, but do not remove, the screws holding the reservoir cap or cover in place.

4 Disconnect the electrical connectors from the brake light switch **(see illustration)**.

5.1b Front brake master cylinder assembly – all XL models and VTR-5 and 6 models

1 Reservoir cover	5 Brake light switch	9 Circlip
2 Diaphragm plate	6 Spring	10 Boot
3 Diaphragm	7 Piston	11 Hand guard
4 Front master cylinder body	8 Pushrod	12 Brake lever assembly

5.4 Disconnect the brake light switch wiring connectors

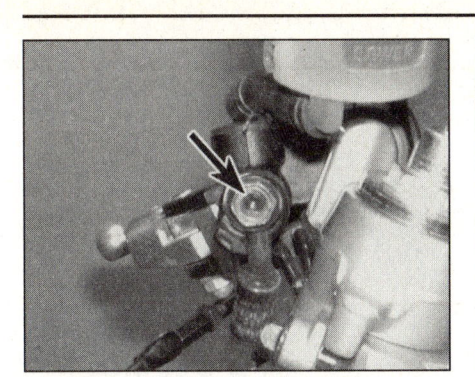

Brakes, wheels and tyres 7•11

5.6 Note the alignment of the hose before removing the banjo bolt (arrowed)

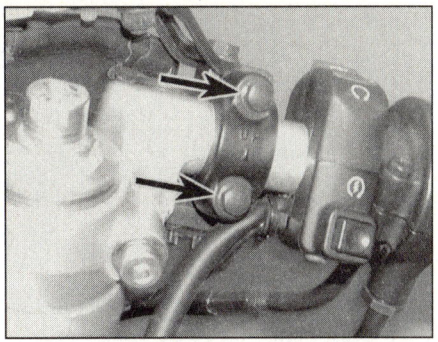

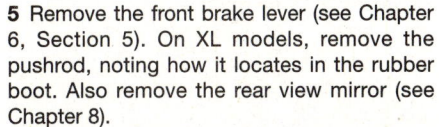

5.7 Unscrew the clamp bolts (arrowed) and remove the master cylinder assembly

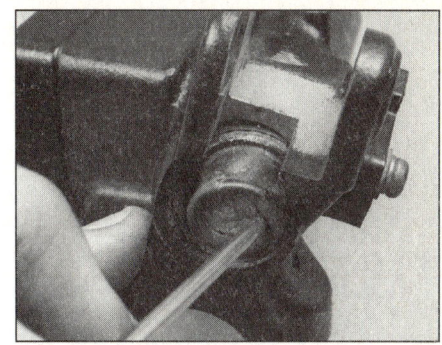

5.10 Remove the rubber boot from the end of the master cylinder piston . . .

5 Remove the front brake lever (see Chapter 6, Section 5). On XL models, remove the pushrod, noting how it locates in the rubber boot. Also remove the rear view mirror (see Chapter 8).

6 Unscrew the brake hose banjo bolt and separate the hose from the master cylinder, noting its alignment **(see illustration)**. Discard the two sealing washers as they must be replaced with new ones. Wrap the end of the hose in a clean rag and suspend it in an upright position or bend it down carefully and place the open end in a clean container. The objective is to prevent excessive loss of brake fluid, fluid spills and system contamination.

7 Unscrew the master cylinder clamp bolts, then lift the master cylinder and reservoir away from the handlebar, noting how the top mating surfaces of the clamp align with the punch mark on the top of the handlebar **(see illustration)**.

Caution: Do not tip the master cylinder upside down or brake fluid will run out.

8 Remove the reservoir cap or cover, diaphragm plate and rubber diaphragm, and on VTR-5 and 6 models the float. Drain the brake fluid from the reservoir into a suitable container. Wipe any remaining fluid out of the reservoir with a clean rag. On VTR models with a remote reservoir, unscrew the bolt securing the reservoir bracket to the master cylinder **(see illustration 5.24)**. Release the clamp securing the reservoir hose to the union on the master cylinder, then detach the hose and remove the reservoir.

9 Remove the brake light switch (see Chapter 9).

Overhaul

10 Carefully remove the dust boot from the end of the piston **(see illustration)**.

11 Using circlip pliers, remove the circlip and slide out the piston assembly and the spring, noting how they fit. Lay the parts out in order as you remove them to prevent confusion during reassembly **(see illustration)**.

12 On VTR models with a remote reservoir, remove the fluid reservoir hose union rubber cap, then remove the circlip and detach the union from the master cylinder. Discard the O-ring as a new one must be used. Inspect the reservoir hose for cracks or splits and replace it with a new one if necessary.

13 Clean all parts with clean brake fluid or denatured alcohol. If compressed air is available, use it to dry the parts thoroughly (make sure it's filtered and unlubricated).

Caution: Do not, under any circumstances, use a petroleum-based solvent to clean brake parts.

14 Check the master cylinder bore for corrosion, scratches, nicks and score marks. If the necessary measuring equipment is available, compare the dimensions of the piston and bore with those given in the Specifications Section of this Chapter. If damage or wear is evident, the master cylinder must be replaced with a new one. If the master cylinder is in poor condition, then the caliper(s) should be checked as well. Check that the fluid inlet and outlet ports in the master cylinder are clear.

15 The dust boot, circlip, piston, seal cup and spring are included in the rebuild kit. Use all of the new parts, regardless of the apparent condition of the old ones and fit them according to the layout of the old ones.

16 Install the spring in the master cylinder so that its tapered end faces the piston.

17 Lubricate the piston assembly with clean brake fluid and fit it into the master cylinder, making sure it is the correct way round. Make sure the lips on the cup do not turn inside out when they are slipped into the bore. Depress the piston and install the new circlip, making sure that it locates in the groove in the master cylinder **(see illustration 5.11)**.

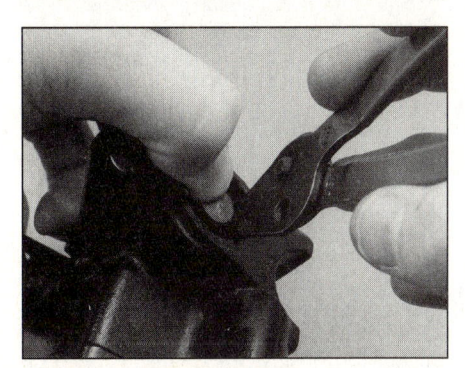

18 Install the rubber dust boot, making sure the lip is seated correctly in the groove in the master cylinder **(see illustration 5.10)**. On VTR models, also make sure it locates in the groove around the end of the piston.

19 On VTR models with a remote reservoir, fit a new O-ring onto the reservoir hose union, then press the union into the master cylinder and secure it with the circlip. Fit the rubber cap over the circlip.

20 Inspect the reservoir rubber diaphragm and renew it if it is damaged or deteriorated.

Installation

21 Install the brake light switch (see Chapter 9).

22 Attach the master cylinder to the handlebar and fit the clamp with its UP mark facing up **(see illustration 5.7)**. Align the top mating surfaces of the clamp with the punch mark on the top of the handlebar, then tighten the top bolt first, then the bottom bolt to the torque setting specified at the beginning of the Chapter.

23 Connect the brake hose to the master cylinder, using new sealing washers on each side of the union, and aligning the hose as noted on removal **(see illustration 5.6)**. Tighten the banjo bolt to the torque setting specified at the beginning of the Chapter.

24 On VTR models with a remote reservoir, mount the reservoir onto the master cylinder and tighten the bracket bolt securely **(see**

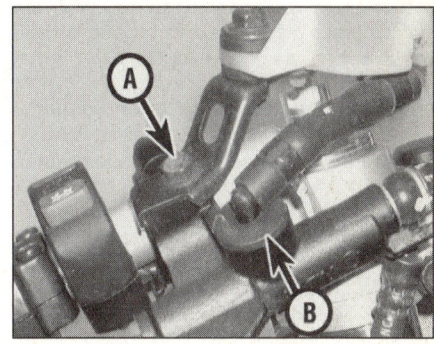

5.11 . . . then depress the piston and remove the circlip using a pair of internal circlip pliers

5.24 Reservoir bracket bolt (A) and hose union (B)

7•12 Brakes, wheels and tyres

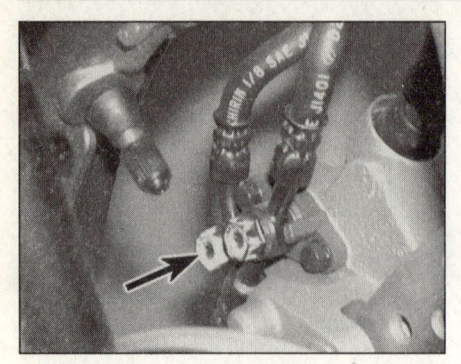

6.3 Secondary master cylinder hose banjo bolts (arrowed) – XL models, left-hand caliper

1 Pushrod
2 Piston assembly
3 Spring
4 Caliper mounting bracket

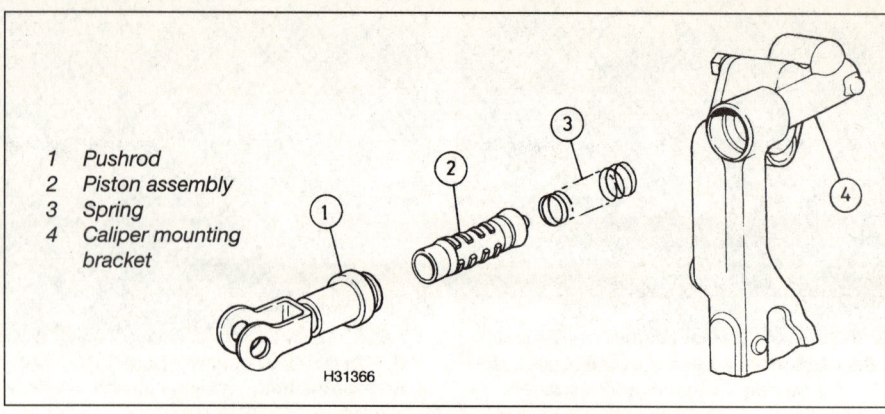

6.4 Secondary master cylinder assembly – XL models

illustration). Connect the reservoir hose to the union and secure it with the clamp.

25 On XL models, smear the pushrod ends with silicone grease. Install the pushrod, locating the rubber boot around the groove in the middle. Also install the rear view mirror (see Chapter 8).

26 Install the brake lever (see Chapter 6).

27 Connect the brake light switch wiring (see illustration 5.4).

28 Fill the fluid reservoir with new DOT 4 brake fluid as described in *Daily (pre-ride) checks*. Refer to Section 10 of this Chapter and bleed the air from the system.

29 Fit the rubber diaphragm, making sure it is correctly seated, the diaphragm plate and the cover or cap onto the reservoir.

30 Check the operation of the front brake before riding the motorcycle.

6 Dual combined braking system components (XL models) – removal, overhaul and installation

Secondary master cylinder

Removal

1 Before disassembling the master cylinder, read through the entire procedure and make sure that you have the correct rebuild kit. Also, you will need some new DOT 4 brake fluid, some clean rags and internal circlip pliers.
Note: *To prevent damage to the paint from spilled brake fluid, always cover the fuel tank when working on the master cylinder.*
Caution: *Disassembly, overhaul and reassembly of the brake master cylinder must be done in a spotlessly clean work area to avoid contamination and possible failure of the brake hydraulic system components.*

2 Remove the left-hand front brake caliper assembly and slide the caliper off the bracket (see Section 3). The secondary master cylinder is integral with the caliper bracket (see illustration 3.4c).

3 Unscrew the brake hose banjo bolts, noting their alignment and which fits where, and separate the hoses from the caliper bracket (see illustration). Plug the hose ends or wrap a plastic bag tightly around them to minimise fluid loss and prevent dirt entering the system. Discard the sealing washers as new ones must be used on installation.

Overhaul

4 Dislodge the rubber dust boot from the master cylinder to reveal the pushrod retaining circlip (see illustration).

5 Depress the pushrod and, using circlip pliers, release the circlip. Slide out the pushrod, piston assembly and spring. If they are difficult to remove, apply low pressure compressed air to the fluid outlet. Lay the parts out in the proper order to prevent confusion during reassembly.

6 Clean all of the parts with clean brake fluid or denatured alcohol. If compressed air is available, use it to dry the parts thoroughly (make sure it's filtered and unlubricated).
Caution: *Do not, under any circumstances, use a petroleum-based solvent to clean brake parts.*

7 Check the master cylinder bore for corrosion, scratches, nicks and score marks. If the necessary measuring equipment is available, compare the dimensions of the piston and bore with those given in the Specifications Section of this Chapter. If damage is evident, the master cylinder must be replaced with a new one. If the master cylinder is in poor condition, then the caliper should be checked as well.

8 The dust boot, circlip, piston assembly and spring are included in the rebuild kit. Use all of the new parts, regardless of the apparent condition of the old ones. If the cup and seal are not already on the piston, fit them according to the layout of the old ones.

9 Install the spring in the master cylinder so that its tapered end faces the piston.

10 Lubricate the piston assembly with clean hydraulic fluid and install it into the master cylinder, making sure it is the correct way round. Make sure the lips on the cup and seal do not turn inside out when the piston is slipped into the bore.

11 Apply some silicone grease to the contact area between the pushrod and piston. Install the pushrod and depress it, then secure it with the circlip, making sure it is properly seated in the groove.

12 Locate the rubber dust boot in the groove.

13 Withdraw the spacer from the pivot in the bottom of the caliper bracket. Thoroughly clean all components, removing all traces of dirt, corrosion and old grease. Lubricate the collar and the pivot bolt with grease and install the spacer.

Installation

14 Connect the brake hoses to the caliper bracket, using new sealing washers on each side of the banjo unions (see illustration 6.3). Ensure that the hoses are positioned so that they butt against the lugs. Tighten the banjo bolts to the specified torque setting.

15 Install the caliper assembly (see Section 3).

16 Bleed the system following the procedure in Section 10.

17 Check the operation of the brakes carefully before riding the motorcycle.

Delay valve and proportional control valve

Removal

18 The delay valve is mounted on the bottom yoke. Unscrew the two bolts securing the shield to the bottom yoke and remove it (see illustration). Unscrew the two brake hose banjo bolts, noting the alignment of the hoses

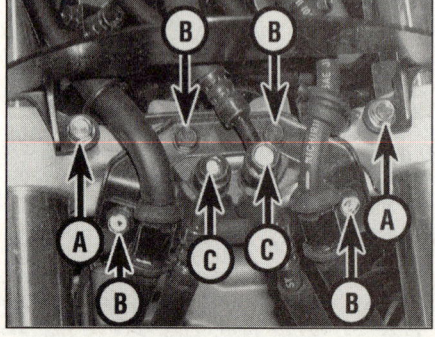

6.18 Shield bolts (A), delay valve bolts (B), banjo bolts (C)

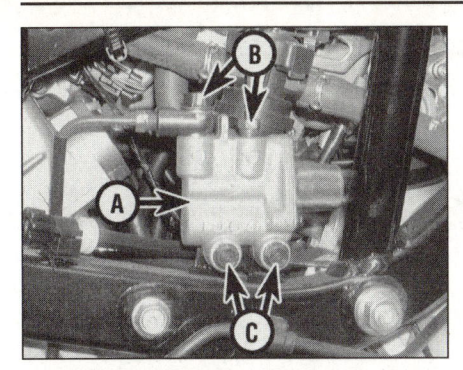

Brakes, wheels and tyres 7•13

6.19 Delay valve (A), pipe banjo bolt and nut (B), mounting bolts (C)

7.1a Brake hose banjo bolt (arrowed) – VTR models

7.1b Brake hose banjo bolts (arrowed) – XL models

on the valve and which fits where, and separate the hoses from the valve. Plug the hose ends or wrap a plastic bag tightly around them to minimise fluid loss and prevent dirt entering the system. Discard the sealing washers as new ones must be used on installation. Unscrew the bolts securing the front brake hose guide plate and delay valve to the bottom yoke, then draw the valve out from behind the plate and remove it.

19 The proportional control valve is mounted on the frame on the right-hand side **(see illustration)**. Remove the fuel tank for access (see Chapter 4). Unscrew the rear pipe union banjo bolt and the front pipe joint nut and separate the pipes from the valve. Plug the pipe ends or wrap a plastic bag tightly around them to minimise fluid loss and prevent dirt entering the system. Discard the union sealing washers as new ones must be used on installation. Unscrew the two bolts securing the valve and remove the valve.

Overhaul

20 Neither the delay valve nor the proportional control valve can be dismantled for overhaul, and no component parts are available. If either valve fails, it must be replaced with a new one.

Installation

21 Installation is the reverse of removal. Use new sealing washers on each side of the banjo bolt unions. Tighten the banjo bolts, the pipe joint nut and the valve mounting bolts to the torque settings specified at the beginning of the Chapter. Bleed the hydraulic system as described in Section 10.

7 Rear brake caliper – removal, overhaul and installation

⚠️ **Warning:** *If a caliper indicates the need for an overhaul (usually due to leaking fluid or sticky operation), all old brake fluid should be flushed from the system. Also,*

the dust created by the brake system may contain asbestos, which is harmful to your health. Never blow it out with compressed air and don't inhale any of it. An approved filtering mask should be worn when working on the brakes. Do not, under any circumstances, use petroleum-based solvents to clean brake parts. Use clean brake fluid, brake cleaner or denatured alcohol only.

Note: *Honda recommend using new caliper mounting bolts and body joining bolts (XL models) when the old ones are removed. This is because the bolts are pre-treated with a locking compound. It is possible, however, to clean up the old bolts and reinstall them using a suitable non-permanent thread locking compound that is commercially available.*

Removal

1 If the calipers are just being displaced and not completely removed or overhauled, do not disconnect the brake hose(s). If the calipers are being completely removed or overhauled, remove the brake hose banjo bolt(s) and detach the hose(s), noting the alignment with the caliper, and on XL models which hose fits where **(see illustrations)**. Plug the hose end(s) or wrap a plastic bag tightly around to minimise fluid loss and prevent dirt entering the system. Discard the sealing washers as new ones must be used on installation. **Note:** *If you are planning to*

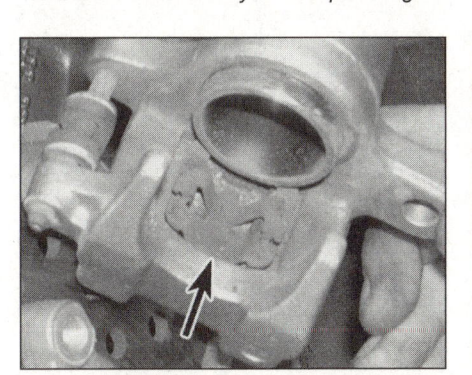

7.2a Remove the pad spring (arrowed) from the caliper . . .

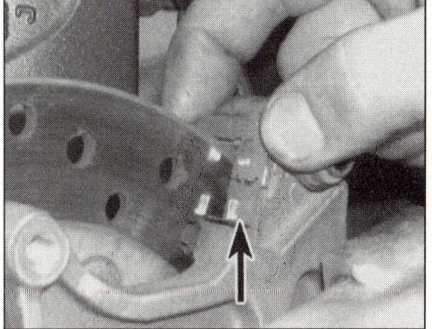

overhaul the caliper and don't have a source of compressed air to blow out the piston(s), just loosen the banjo bolt(s) at this stage and retighten it/them lightly. The bike's hydraulic system can then be used to force the piston(s) out of the body once the pads have been removed. Disconnect the hose(s) once the piston(s) have been sufficiently displaced. On models with ABS, disconnect wheel speed sensor from the caliper bracket **(see illustration 19.10b)**.

2 On VTR models, if the caliper is being overhauled, remove the brake pads (see Section 2). If not, unscrew the caliper rear mounting bolt/slide pin and pivot the back of the caliper up off the disc **(see illustrations 2.13c and 2.13d)**. Slide the caliper out of the front mounting in the caliper bracket. If required, remove the pad spring from the caliper and the guide from the bracket, noting how they fit **(see illustrations)**.

3 On XL models, if the caliper is being overhauled, remove the brake pads (see Section 2). Remove the rear wheel (see Section 14). Detach the caliper bracket from the swingarm, noting how it fits. Separate the caliper from the bracket by sliding them apart, noting how they locate **(see illustration 7.4b)**. If required, remove the pad spring from the caliper and the guide from the bracket, noting how they fit.

Overhaul

4 Clean the exterior of the caliper with

7.2b . . . and the pad guide (arrowed) from the bracket

7•14 Brakes, wheels and tyres

denatured alcohol or brake system cleaner **(see illustrations)**.

5 On XL models, unscrew the bolts securing the caliper inner body to the main body and separate them.

Warning: Never place your fingers in front of the pistons in an attempt to catch or protect them when applying compressed air, as serious injury could result.

6 Remove the piston(s) from the caliper body, either by pumping it/them out by operating the brake pedal, or by using compressed air. On XL models, mark each piston head and caliper bore with a felt marker to ensure that the pistons can be matched to their original bores on reassembly. If the compressed air method is used, place a wad of rag between the pistons and the caliper to act as a cushion, then use compressed air directed into the fluid inlet to force the pistons out of the body. Use only low pressure to ease the pistons out and make sure both pistons are displaced at the same time. If the air pressure is too high and the pistons are forced out, the caliper and/or pistons may be damaged.

7 Using a wooden or plastic tool, remove the dust seals from the caliper bores **(see illustration 3.7)**. Discard them as new ones must be used on installation. If a metal tool is being used, take great care not to damage the caliper bores.

8 Remove and discard the piston seals in the same way.

9 Clean the pistons and bores with denatured alcohol, clean brake fluid or brake system cleaner. If compressed air is available, use it to dry the parts thoroughly (make sure it's filtered and unlubricated).

Caution: Do not, under any circumstances, use a petroleum-based solvent to clean brake parts.

10 Inspect the caliper bores and pistons for signs of corrosion, nicks and burrs and loss of plating. If surface defects are present, the caliper assembly must be replaced. If the necessary measuring equipment is available, compare the dimensions of the pistons and bores with those given in the Specifications

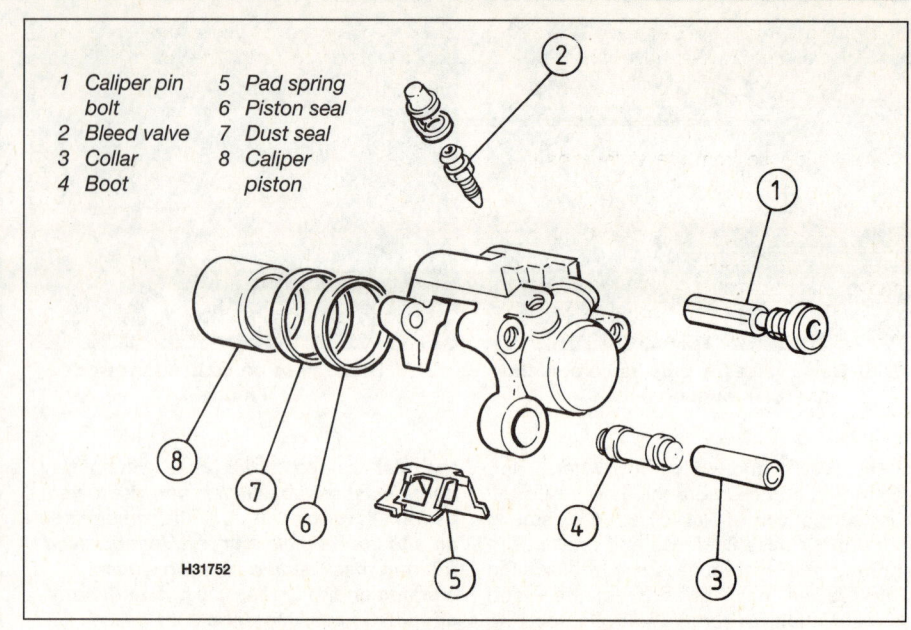

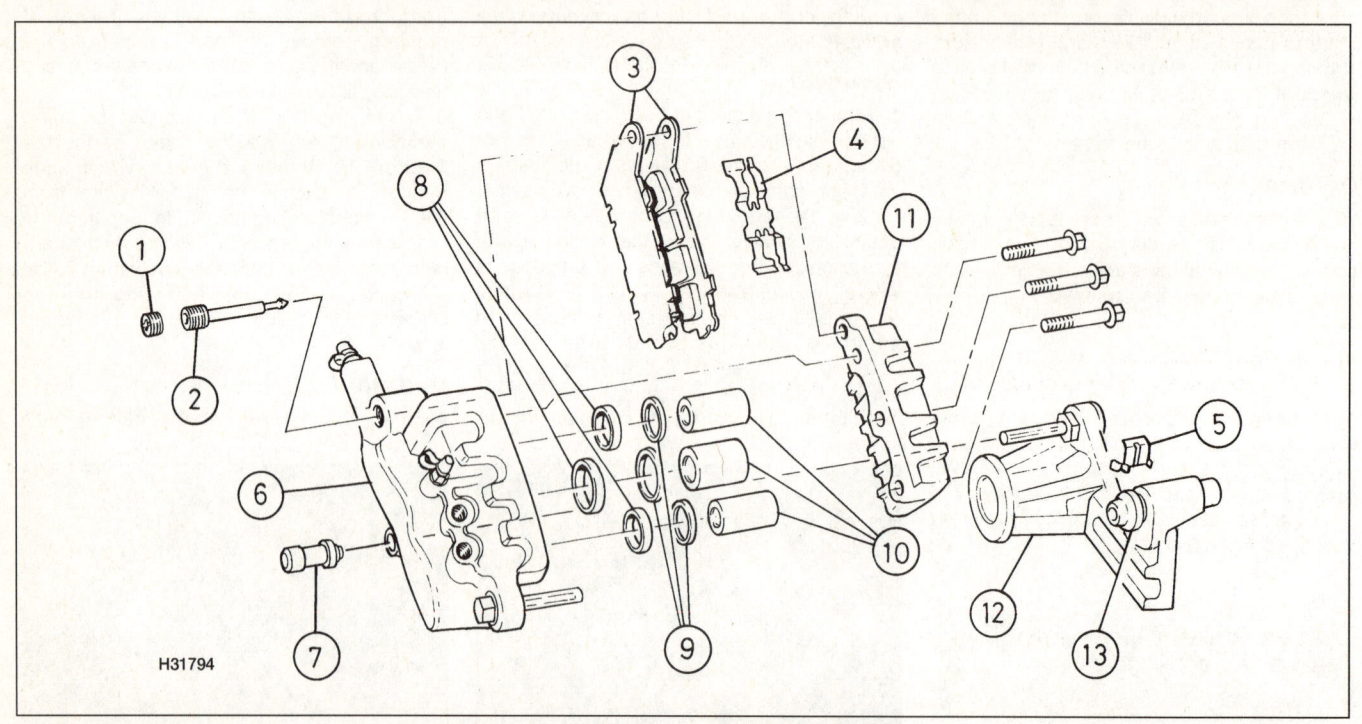

1 Caliper pin bolt
2 Bleed valve
3 Collar
4 Boot
5 Pad spring
6 Piston seal
7 Dust seal
8 Caliper piston

7.4a Rear brake caliper assembly – VTR models

7.4b Rear brake caliper assembly – XL models

1 Plug
2 Pad retaining pin
3 Brake pads
4 Pad spring
5 Pad guide
6 Caliper body
7 Boot
8 Piston seals
9 Dust seals
10 Caliper pistons
11 Caliper inner body
12 Caliper bracket
13 Boot

Brakes, wheels and tyres 7•15

Section of this Chapter, replacing any component that is worn beyond the service limit. If the caliper is in bad shape the master cylinder should also be checked.

11 Clean off all traces of corrosion and hardened grease from the slider pins in the caliper and bracket, and from the collar inside the rubber boot in the caliper on VTR models. Check the condition of the rubber boos for the sliders and replace them with new ones if they are damaged, deformed or deteriorated. Apply a smear of copper or silicone based grease to the slider pins and boots. Slide the caliper onto the bracket and check that it slides freely on the pins. Separate the caliper and bracket again.

12 Lubricate the new piston seals with clean brake fluid and install them in their grooves in the caliper bores. On XL models note that different sizes of bore and piston are used (see *Specifications*), and care must therefore be taken to ensure that the correct size seals are fitted to the correct bores. The same applies when fitting the new dust seals and pistons.

13 Lubricate the new dust seals with clean brake fluid (VTR models) or silicone grease (XL models) and install them in their grooves in the caliper bores.

14 Lubricate the pistons with clean brake fluid and install them closed-end first into the caliper bores. Using your thumbs, push the pistons all the way in, making sure they enter the bore squarely.

15 On XL models, install the caliper inner body, then apply a suitable non-permanent thread locking compound to the joining bolts, using new ones if required (see **Note**) and tighten them to the torque setting specified at the beginning of the Chapter.

Installation

16 On VTR models, make sure that the pad spring and pad guide are correctly fitted, then slide the caliper onto the bracket **(see illustrations 7.2a and 7.2b)**. Install the brake pads if removed (see Section 2). If not, pivot the caliper down onto the disc while keeping the pads held in position, making sure the front ends of the pads locate correctly against the guide on the caliper bracket as you do **(see illustration 2.13d)**. Install the caliper rear mounting bolt/slider pin and tighten it to the torque settings specified at the beginning of the Chapter **(see illustrations 2.13c and 2.16)**.

17 On XL models, make sure that the pad spring and pad guide are correctly fitted, then slide the caliper onto the bracket. Locate the bracket onto the inside of the swingarm. Install the rear wheel (see Section 14). If removed, install the brake pads (see Section 2). On ABS equipped models install the wheel speed sensor as described in Section 19).

18 Connect the brake hose(s) to the caliper, using new sealing washers on each side of the fitting. Align the hose(s) as noted on removal **(see illustration 7.1a or 7.1b)**. Tighten the banjo bolt(s) to the torque setting specified at the beginning of the Chapter.

19 Fill the master cylinder reservoir with DOT 4 brake fluid (see *Daily (pre-ride) checks*) and bleed the hydraulic system as described in Section 10.

20 Check for leaks and thoroughly test the operation of the brake before riding the motorcycle.

8 Rear brake master cylinder – removal, overhaul and installation

1 If the master cylinder is leaking fluid, or if the lever does not produce a firm feel when the brake is applied, and bleeding the brakes does not help (see Section 10), and the hydraulic hoses, pipes and unions are all in good condition, then master cylinder overhaul is recommended.

2 Before disassembling the master cylinder, read through the entire procedure and make sure that you have the correct rebuild kit. Also, you will need some new DOT 4 brake fluid, some clean rags and internal circlip pliers. **Note:** *To prevent damage to the paint from spilled brake fluid, always cover the surrounding components when working on the master cylinder.*

Caution: Disassembly, overhaul and reassembly of the brake master cylinder must be done in a spotlessly clean work area to avoid contamination and possible failure of the brake hydraulic system components.

Removal

3 On XL models, remove the right-hand side cover (see Chapter 8, Section 4). Unscrew the bolt securing the reservoir, and on VTR models manoeuvre it out from behind the frame section **(see illustrations)**. Undo the two reservoir cover screws or cap and remove the cover or cap, the diaphragm plate and diaphragm and pour the fluid into a container. Separate the fluid reservoir hose from the elbow on the master cylinder by releasing the hose clamp **(see illustration)**.

4 Unscrew the brake hose banjo bolt and separate the brake hose, and on XL models the brake pipe, from the master cylinder, noting the alignment **(see illustrations)**.

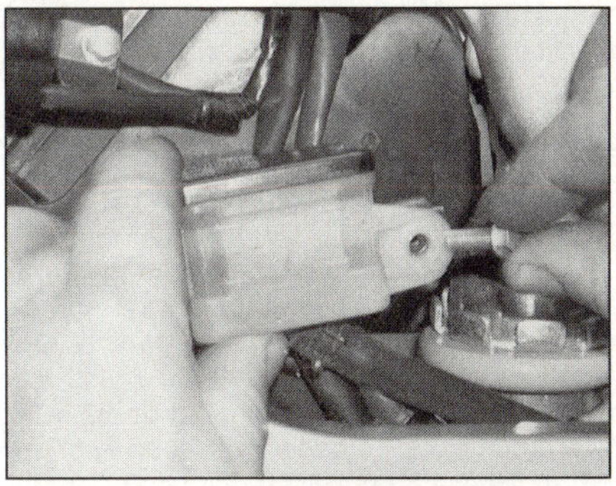

8.3a Unscrew the reservoir bolt and displace it

8.3b Reservoir mounting bolt (arrowed) – XL models

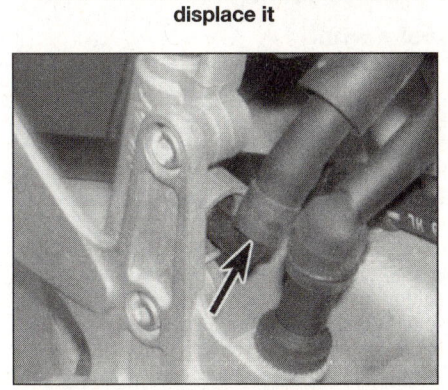

8.3c Release the clamp (arrowed) and detach the hose from the union – VTR models

8.4a Brake hose banjo bolt (arrowed) – VTR models

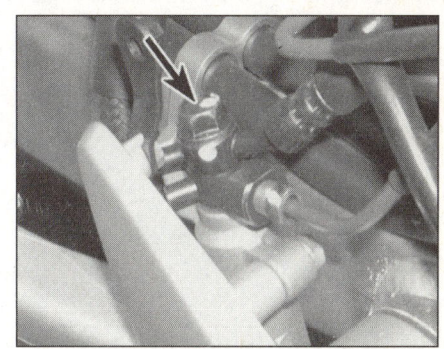

8.4b Brake hose banjo bolt (arrowed) – XL models

7•16 Brakes, wheels and tyres

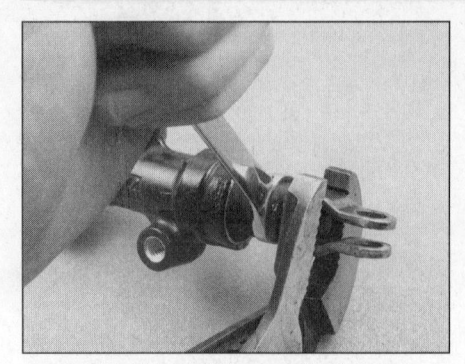

8.6 Hold the clevis and slacken the locknut

Discard the sealing washers as they must be replaced with new ones. Wrap the end of the hose and pipe (XL models) in a clean rag and suspend in an upright position, or bend down carefully and place the open end in a clean container. The objective is to prevent excessive loss of brake fluid, fluid spills and system contamination.

5 Remove the rear brake pedal (see Chapter 6, Section 3). This procedure involves displacing the master cylinder from the inside of the footrest bracket. On XL models, where there is an option in the procedure to leave the master cylinder mounted, ignore this. Instead, depending on the clearance for removal of the clevis securing the pedal to the pushrod, it may be possible to leave the pedal on its pivot and remove the master cylinder on its own.

Overhaul

6 If necessary, slacken the clevis locknut, then on VTR models drive out the spring pin securing the pushrod in the clevis, and remove the clevis from the pushrod, noting how far up it is threaded **(see illustration)**. Discard the spring pin as a new one must be used.
7 Dislodge the rubber dust boot from the base of the master cylinder to reveal the pushrod retaining circlip **(see illustration)**.
8 Depress the pushrod and, using circlip pliers, remove the circlip **(see illustration)**. Slide out the pushrod, piston assembly, primary cup and spring. If they are difficult to remove, apply low pressure compressed air to the fluid outlet. Lay the parts out in the proper

8.8 Depress the pushrod and, using circlip pliers, remove the circlip

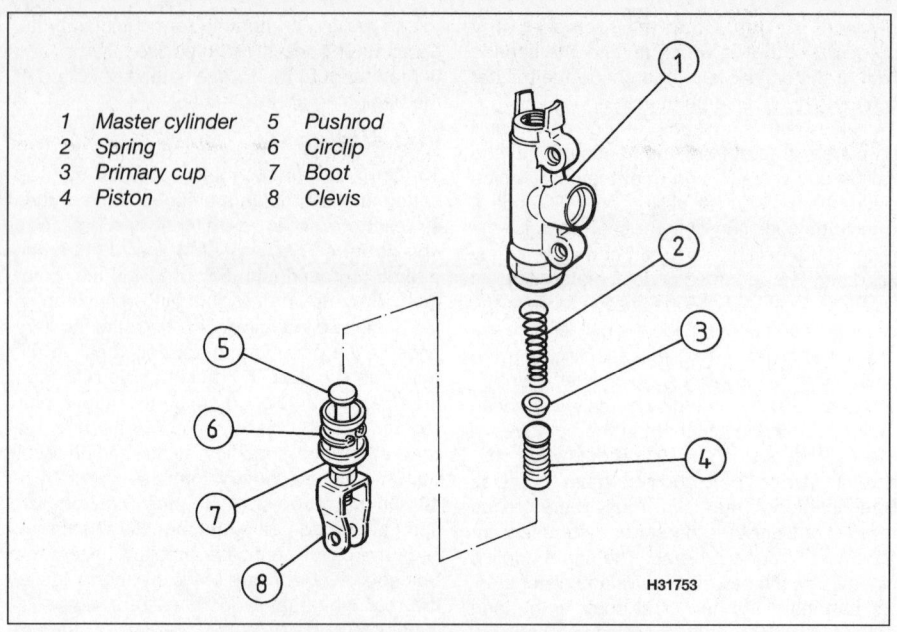

1 Master cylinder
2 Spring
3 Primary cup
4 Piston
5 Pushrod
6 Circlip
7 Boot
8 Clevis

8.7 Rear brake master cylinder assembly

order to prevent confusion during reassembly. Note how the primary cup locates on the end of the spring. On XL models, the pushrod and piston can stay as an assembly if required.
9 If required, on VTR models remove the circlip and on XL models remove the screw securing the fluid reservoir hose union and detach it from the master cylinder. Discard the O-ring as a new one must be used. Inspect the reservoir hose for cracks or splits and replace with a new one if necessary.
10 Clean all of the parts with clean brake fluid or denatured alcohol. If compressed air is available, use it to dry the parts thoroughly (make sure it's filtered and unlubricated).

Caution: Do not, under any circumstances, use a petroleum-based solvent to clean brake parts.

11 Check the master cylinder bore for corrosion, scratches, nicks and score marks. If the necessary measuring equipment is available, compare the dimensions of the piston and bore to those given in the Specifications Section of this Chapter. If damage is evident, the master cylinder must be replaced with a new one. If the master cylinder is in poor condition, then the caliper should be checked as well.
12 The dust boot, circlip, piston assembly, primary cup and spring are included in the rebuild kit. Use all of the new parts, regardless of the apparent condition of the old ones. If the seal is not on the piston, fit it according to the position of the old one.
13 Lubricate the primary cup with clean brake fluid and fit it onto the narrow end of the spring, so that the coil fits over the lug on the inside of the cup. Install the spring and cup in the master cylinder, with the cup facing out, making sure its lips do not turn inside out.
14 Lubricate the piston assembly with clean

hydraulic fluid and insert it in the master cylinder, making sure it is the correct way round. Make sure the lips on the seal do not turn inside out.
15 Install and depress the pushrod assembly, then install the new circlip, making sure it is properly seated in the groove **(see illustration 8.8)**.
16 Install the rubber dust boot, making sure it is seated properly in the groove.
17 If removed, fit a new O-ring to the fluid reservoir hose union, then install the union onto the master cylinder and secure it with its circlip (VTR models) or screw (XL models).
18 If removed, install the clevis locknut and the clevis onto the master cylinder pushrod end. Set the clevis position as noted on removal. On XL models Honda specify the distance between the eye in the clevis and the lower mounting bolt hole should be 82.5 to 84.5 mm. On VTR models press a new spring pin into the bottom of the pushrod. Tighten the clevis locknut securely against the clevis.

Installation

19 Install the master cylinder and rear brake pedal onto the footrest bracket then install the bracket, reversing the procedure for brake pedal removal as described in Chapter 6 **(see illustration 8.11)**.
20 Connect the brake hose, and on XL models the brake pipe, to the master cylinder, using new sealing washers on each side of the union. Align the hose as noted on removal and tighten the banjo bolt to the specified torque setting **(see illustration 8.4a or 8.4b)**.
21 Secure the fluid reservoir to the frame with its retaining bolt **(see illustration 8.3a or 8.3b)**. On VTR models ensure that the hose is correctly routed behind the frame section. Connect the hose to the union on the master cylinder and

Brakes, wheels and tyres 7•17

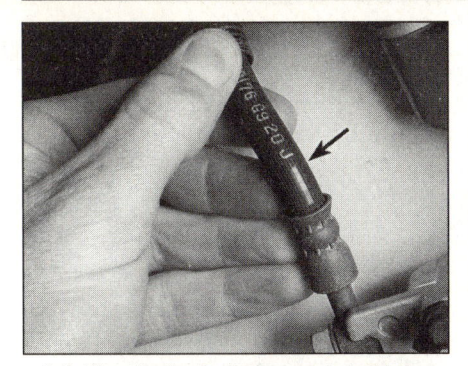

9.2 Flex the brake hoses and check for cracks, bulges and leaking fluid

9.4 Remove the banjo bolt and separate the hose from the caliper; there is a sealing washer on each side of the fitting

secure it with the clamp **(see illustration 8.3c)**. Check that the hose is secure and clamped at the reservoir end as well. If the clamps have weakened, use new ones.

22 Fill the fluid reservoir with new DOT 4 brake fluid (see *Daily (pre-ride) checks*) and bleed the system following the procedure in Section 10.

23 Check the operation of the brake carefully before riding the motorcycle.

9 Brake hoses, pipes and unions – inspection and replacement

Inspection

1 Brake hose and pipe condition should be checked regularly and the hoses replaced at the specified interval (see Chapter 1).

2 Twist and flex the rubber hoses while looking for cracks, bulges and seeping fluid **(see illustration)**. Check extra carefully around the areas where the hoses connect with the banjo fittings, as these are common areas for hose failure.

3 Inspect the metal brake pipes and the banjo union fittings connected to the brake hoses. If the fittings are rusted, scratched or cracked, replace them.

Replacement

4 The brake hoses have banjo union fittings on each end and the brake pipes have joint nuts **(see illustration)**. Cover the surrounding area with plenty of rags and unscrew the banjo bolt or joint nut at each end of the hose or pipe, noting its alignment. Free the hose or pipe from any clips or guides and remove it. Discard the sealing washers on the hose banjo unions.

5 Position the new hose or pipe, making sure it isn't twisted or otherwise strained, and abut the tab on the hose union with the lug on the component casting, where present. Otherwise align the hose or pipe as noted on removal. Install the hose banjo bolts using new sealing washers on both sides of the unions. Tighten the banjo bolts and joint nuts to the torque settings specified at the beginning of this Chapter. Make sure the hoses and pipes are correctly aligned and routed clear of all moving components.

6 Flush the old brake fluid from the system, refill with new DOT 4 brake fluid (see *Daily (pre-ride) checks*) and bleed the air from the system (see Section 10). Check the operation of the brakes carefully before riding the motorcycle.

10 Brake system – bleeding

1 Bleeding the brakes is simply the process of removing all the air bubbles from the brake fluid reservoirs, the hoses and the brake calipers. Bleeding is necessary whenever a brake system hydraulic connection is loosened, when a component or hose is replaced, or when the master cylinder or caliper is overhauled. Leaks in the system may also allow air to enter, but leaking brake fluid will reveal their presence and warn you of the need for repair.

VTR models

2 To bleed the brakes, you will need some new DOT 4 brake fluid, a length of clear vinyl or plastic tubing, a small container partially filled with clean brake fluid, some rags and a spanner to fit the brake caliper bleed valves.

3 Cover the fuel tank and other painted components to prevent damage in the event that brake fluid is spilled.

10.6a Brake caliper bleed valve (arrowed)

4 If bleeding the rear brake, unscrew the reservoir bolt, then displace the reservoir and rest it on the frame for best access.

5 Remove the reservoir cap or cover, diaphragm plate and rubber diaphragm, and on VTR-5 and 6 models the float. Slowly pump the brake lever or pedal a few times, until no air bubbles can be seen floating up from the holes in the bottom of the reservoir. Doing this bleeds the air from the master cylinder end of the line. Loosely refit the reservoir cover.

6 Pull the dust cap off the bleed valve **(see illustration)**. Attach one end of the clear vinyl or plastic tubing to the bleed valve and submerge the other end in the brake fluid in the container **(see illustration)**.

7 Remove the reservoir cap or cover and check the fluid level. Do not allow the fluid level to drop below the lower mark during the bleeding process.

8 Carefully pump the brake lever or pedal three or four times and hold it in (front) or down (rear) while opening the caliper bleed valve. When the valve is opened, brake fluid will flow out of the caliper into the clear tubing and the lever will move toward the handlebar or the pedal will move down.

9 Retighten the bleed valve, then release the brake lever or pedal gradually. Repeat the process until no air bubbles are visible in the brake fluid leaving the caliper and the lever or pedal is firm when applied. On completion, disconnect the bleeding equipment, then tighten the bleed valve to the torque setting specified at the beginning of the chapter and install the dust cap.

10 Install the float (where fitted), the diaphragm, plate and cover or cap assembly, wipe up any spilled brake fluid and check the entire system for leaks.

> **HAYNES HiNT** *If it's not possible to produce a firm feel to the lever or pedal the fluid may be aerated. Let the brake fluid in the system stabilise for a few hours and then repeat the procedure when the tiny bubbles in the system have settled out.*

10.6b To bleed the brakes, you need a spanner, a short section of clear tubing, and a clear container half-filled with brake fluid

7•18 Brakes, wheels and tyres

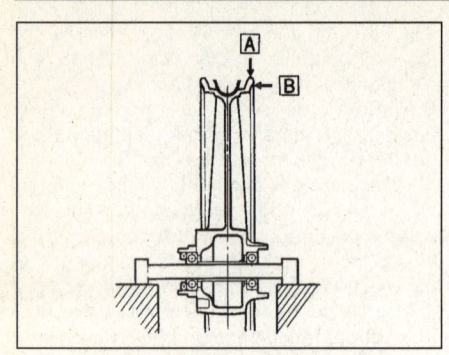

11.2 Check the wheel for radial (out-of-round) runout (A) and axial (side-to-side) runout (B)

XL models

Note: *Honda specify the use of a vacuum-type brake bleeder to simplify the bleeding process. The bleeder is connected to the bleed valve, which is then opened, and is used to draw the air/fluid through the system and out of the bleed valve. Once all the air has been removed, the bleeder is removed and the brakes are then bled in the conventional way (described below) to complete the bleeding procedure. If you find that the conventional method of bleeding fails to remove the trapped air from the system, it will be necessary to obtain a vacuum-type brake bleeder kit from a motor accessory shop or entrust the work to a Honda dealer.*

11 The principle involved in bleeding the brakes on these models is the same as on standard models, and the appropriate steps detailed above for the standard models should be followed. The difference is that the order in which the components are bled is important.

12 The brake system should be bled in the following order, using the front brake lever or rear brake pedal as instructed:

1. *Left front caliper – upper bleed valve – front brake lever*
2. *Right front caliper – upper bleed valve – front brake lever*
3. *Left front caliper – lower bleed valve – rear brake pedal*
4. *Right front caliper – lower bleed valve – rear brake pedal*
5. *Rear caliper – front bleed valve – rear brake pedal*
6. *Rear caliper – rear bleed valve – rear brake pedal*

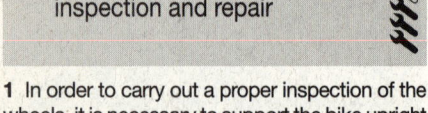

11 Wheels – inspection and repair

1 In order to carry out a proper inspection of the wheels, it is necessary to support the bike upright so that the wheel being inspected is raised off the ground. Position the motorcycle on an auxiliary stand. Clean the wheels thoroughly to remove mud and dirt that may interfere with the inspection procedure or mask defects. Make a general check of the wheels and tyres (see Chapter 1 and *Daily (pre-ride) checks*).

2 Attach a dial gauge to the fork slider or the swingarm and position its stem against the side of the rim **(see illustration)**. Spin the wheel slowly and check the axial (side-to-side) runout of the rim. In order to accurately check radial (out-of-round) runout with the dial gauge, the wheel would have to be removed from the machine, and the tyre from the wheel. With the axle clamped in a vice and the dial gauge positioned on the top of the rim, the wheel can be rotated to check the runout.

3 An easier, though slightly less accurate, method is to attach a stiff wire pointer to the fork slider or the swingarm and position the end a fraction of an inch from the wheel (where the wheel and tyre join). If the wheel is true, the distance from the pointer to the rim will be constant as the wheel is rotated. **Note:** *If wheel runout is excessive, check the wheel bearings very carefully before replacing the wheel.*

4 The wheels should also be visually inspected for cracks, flat spots on the rim and other damage. Look very closely for dents in the area where the tyre bead contacts the rim. Dents in this area may prevent complete sealing of the tyre against the rim, which leads to deflation of the tyre over a period of time. If damage is evident, or if runout in either direction is excessive, the wheel will have to be replaced with a new one. Never attempt to repair a damaged cast alloy wheel.

12 Wheels – alignment check

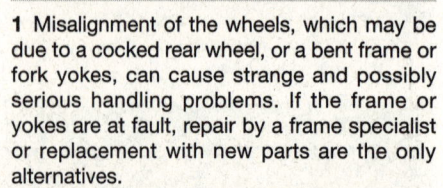

1 Misalignment of the wheels, which may be due to a cocked rear wheel, or a bent frame or fork yokes, can cause strange and possibly serious handling problems. If the frame or yokes are at fault, repair by a frame specialist or replacement with new parts are the only alternatives.

2 To check the alignment you will need an assistant, a length of string, or a perfectly straight piece of wood, and a ruler. A plumb bob or other suitable weight will also be required.

3 In order to make a proper check of the wheels it is necessary to support the bike in an upright position, using a suitable stand. Measure the width of both tyres at their widest points. Subtract the smaller measurement from the larger measurement, then divide the difference by two. The result is the amount of offset that should exist between the front and rear tyres on both sides.

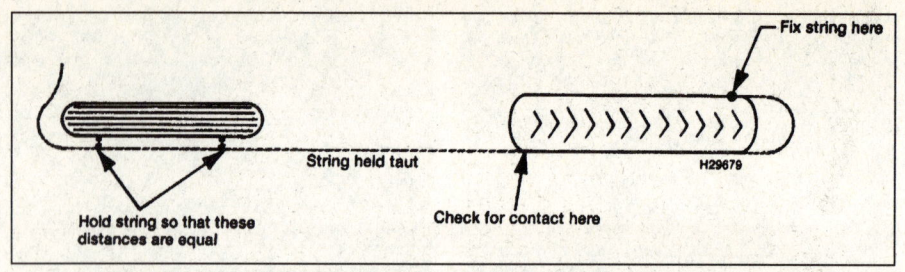

12.5 Wheel alignment check using string

4 If a string is used, have your assistant hold one end of it about halfway between the floor and the rear axle, touching the rear sidewall of the tyre.

5 Run the other end of the string forward and pull it tight so that it is roughly parallel to the floor **(see illustration)**. Slowly bring the string into contact with the front sidewall of the rear tyre, then turn the front wheel until it is parallel with the string. Measure the distance from the front tyre sidewall to the string.

6 Repeat the procedure on the other side of the motorcycle. The distance from the front tyre sidewall to the string should be equal on both sides.

7 As previously mentioned, a perfectly straight length of wood or metal bar may be substituted for the string **(see illustration)**. The procedure is the same.

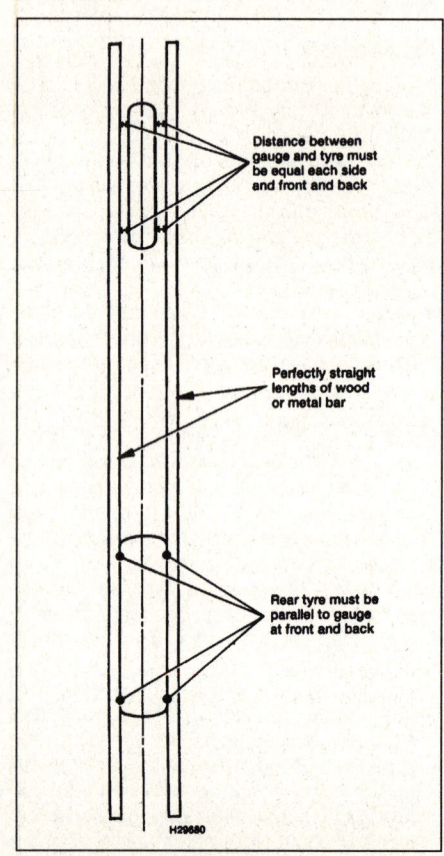

12.7 Wheel alignment check using a straight-edge

Brakes, wheels and tyres 7•19

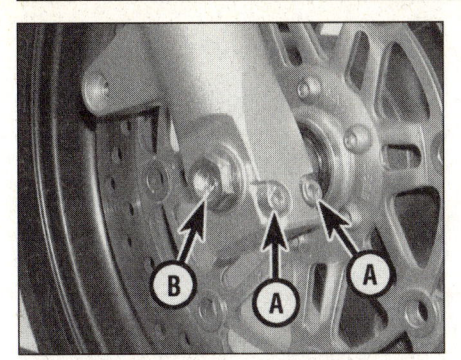

13.3 Slacken the axle clamp bolts (A), then unscrew the axle bolt (B)

13.4a Slacken the axle clamp bolts (arrowed) . . .

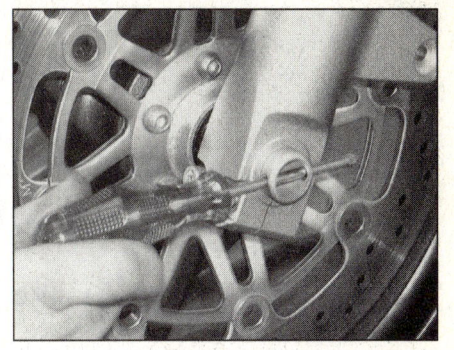

13.4b . . . then withdraw the axle

8 If the distance between the string and tyre is greater on one side, or if the rear wheel appears to be cocked, refer to Chapter 1 and check that the drive chain adjuster markings are in the same position on each side of the swingarm.
9 If the front-to-back alignment is correct, the wheels still may be out of alignment vertically.
10 Using a plumb bob, or other suitable weight, and a length of string, check the rear wheel to make sure it is vertical. To do this, hold the string against the tyre upper sidewall and allow the weight to settle just off the floor. When the string touches both the upper and lower tyre sidewalls and is perfectly straight, the wheel is vertical. If it is not, place thin spacers under one leg of the stand until it is.
11 Once the rear wheel is vertical, check the front wheel in the same manner. If both wheels are not perfectly vertical, the frame and/or major suspension components are bent.

13 Front wheel –
removal and installation

Removal

1 Position the motorcycle on an auxiliary stand and support it under the crankcase so that the front wheel is off the ground. Always make sure the motorcycle is properly supported.
2 On VTR models displace both front brake calipers, and on XL models displace the right-hand caliper (see Section 3). Support the caliper(s) with a piece of wire or a bungee cord so that no strain is placed on the hydraulic hose(s). There is no need to disconnect the hose(s) from the caliper(s). *Note: Do not operate the front brake lever, and on XL models the rear brake pedal, with the caliper(s) removed.*
3 Slacken the axle clamp bolts on the bottom of the right-hand fork, then unscrew the axle bolt from the right-hand end of the axle **(see illustration)**.
4 Slacken the axle clamp bolts on the bottom of the left-hand fork **(see illustration)**. Support the wheel, then withdraw the axle from the left-hand side, using a screwdriver inserted through the holes in the end of the axle as a lever, and carefully lower the wheel **(see illustration)**.
5 Remove the long wheel spacer from the right-hand side of the wheel and the short spacer from the left-hand side for safekeeping **(see illustrations)**.
Caution: Don't lay the wheel down and allow it to rest on a disc – the disc could become warped. Set the wheel on wood blocks so the disc doesn't support the weight of the wheel.
6 Check the axle for straightness by rolling it on a flat surface such as a piece of plate glass (first wipe off all old grease and remove any corrosion using fine emery cloth). If the equipment is available, place the axle in V-blocks and measure the runout using a dial gauge. If the axle is bent or the runout exceeds the limit specified, replace it with a new one.
7 Check the condition of the grease seals and wheel bearings (see Section 16).

Installation

8 Apply a smear of grease to the inside of the wheel spacers, and also to the outside where they fit into the wheel. Fit the long spacer into the right-hand side of the wheel and the short spacer into the left-hand side **(see illustration 13.5a and 13.5b)**. Each side of the wheel can be identified using the directional arrow cast into one of the spokes near the rim. The arrow denotes the normal direction of rotation of the wheel.
9 Manoeuvre the wheel into position, making sure the directional arrow is pointing in the normal direction of rotation. Apply a thin coat of grease to the axle.
10 Lift the wheel into place between the fork sliders, making sure the spacers remain in position, and on XL models the disc fits between the brake pads in the left-hand caliper. Slide the axle in from the left-hand side **(see illustration)**.
11 Install the axle bolt and tighten it to the torque setting specified at the beginning of

13.5a Remove the long right-hand spacer . . .

13.5b . . . and the short left-hand spacer

13.10 Slide the axle in from the left . . .

7•20 Brakes, wheels and tyres

13.11a ... then install the axle bolt ...

13.11b ... and tighten it to the specified torque

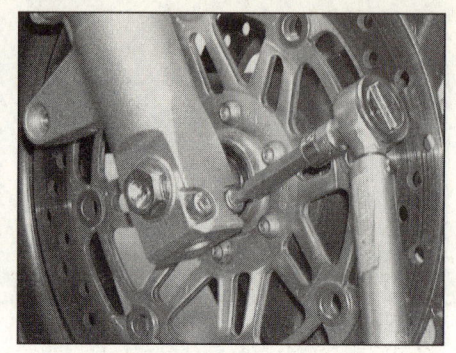

13.12 Tighten the right-hand clamp bolts to the specified torque

the Chapter **(see illustrations)**. Use a screwdriver inserted through the holes in the end of the axle to counter-hold it **(see illustration 13.4b)**.
12 Tighten the axle clamp bolts on the bottom of the right-hand fork to the specified torque setting **(see illustration)**.
13 Install the brake caliper(s) (see Section 3).
14 Apply the front brake a few times to bring the pads back into contact with the discs. Move the motorcycle off its stand, apply the front brake and pump the front forks a few times to settle all components in position.

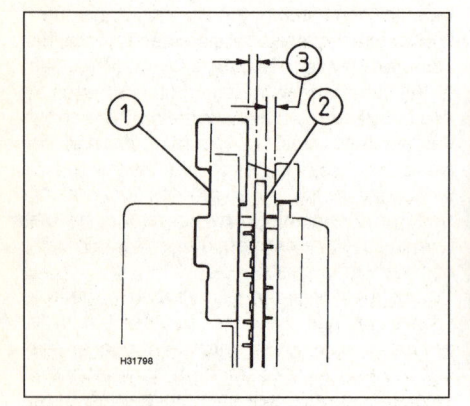

13.15 Brake caliper-to-disc clearance check – XL models
1 Caliper bracket 2 Disc 3 Clearance

Now tighten the axle clamp bolts on the bottom of the left-hand fork to the specified torque **(see illustration 13.4a)**.
15 Check for correct operation of the front brake before riding the motorcycle. On XL models, check that there is at least 0.7 mm clearance between each front brake disc and the caliper bracket – make the check using a feeler gauge **(see illustration)**. If the gauge cannot be inserted easily in all four locations, slacken the axle clamp bolts on the bottom of each fork leg and pull or push the fork leg(s) until the distance is correct. Tighten the axle clamp bolts to the specified torque. Apply the front brake to settle the components, then recheck the clearances.

14.2 Unscrew the axle nut (arrowed) and on VTR models remove the washer

14 Rear wheel – removal and installation

Removal

1 Position the motorcycle on an auxiliary stand so that the wheel is off the ground.
2 Unscrew the axle nut, and on VTR models remove the washer **(see illustration)**.
3 Support the wheel then withdraw the axle from the left-hand side and lower the wheel to the ground **(see illustration)**. Disengage the chain from the sprocket and remove the wheel from the swingarm **(see illustration)**.
4 Note how the caliper bracket locates against the swingarm, and support it so that it will not fall off. If required, displace the brake caliper bracket from the swingarm, noting how it fits, and tie it to the top of the frame, making sure no strain is placed on the hose **(see illustration)**. Do not operate the brake pedal with the wheel removed.
Caution: Do not lay the wheel down and allow it to rest on the disc or the sprocket – they could become warped. Set the wheel on wood blocks so the disc or the sprocket doesn't support the weight of the wheel.
5 If they are loose, remove the spacer from

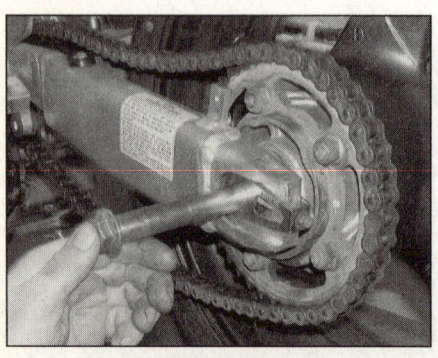

14.3a Withdraw the axle ...

14.3b ... then lower the wheel to the ground and disengage the chain

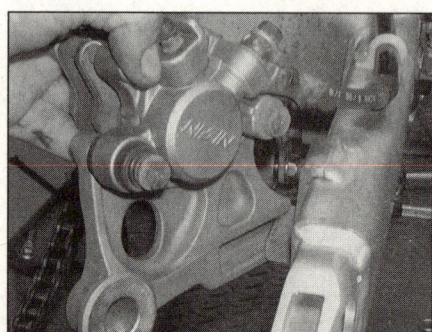

14.4 Note how the caliper bracket locates onto the swingarm

Brakes, wheels and tyres 7•21

14.5a Remove the spacer from the left-hand side . . .

14.5b . . . and from the right-hand side, noting which fits where

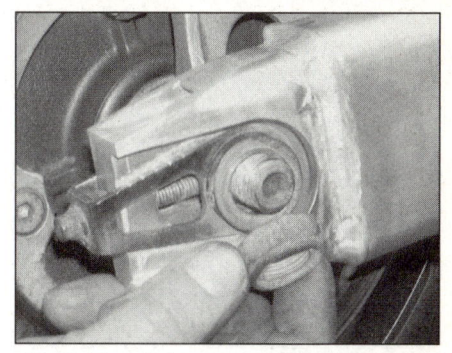

14.11a Install the nut, on VTR models not forgetting the washer . . .

each side of the wheel for safekeeping, noting which fits where **(see illustrations)**.
6 Check the axle for straightness by rolling it on a flat surface such as a piece of plate glass (if the axle is corroded, first remove the corrosion with fine emery cloth). If the equipment is available, place the axle in V-blocks and check the runout using a dial gauge. If the axle is bent or the runout exceeds the limit specified at the beginning of the Chapter, replace it with a new one.
7 Check the condition of the grease seals and wheel bearings (see Section 16).

Installation

8 Apply a thin coat of grease to the lips of each grease seal, and also to the collars and the axle. If displaced, locate the brake caliper

14.11b . . . and tighten it to the specified torque

bracket onto the swingarm **(see illustration 14.4)**.
9 If removed, fit the spacers into the wheel – on VTR models the shouldered spacer fits into the left-hand side of the wheel, and on XL models the thicker spacer fits into the left-hand side **(see illustrations 14.5a and 14.5b)**. Manoeuvre the wheel so that it is in between the ends of the swingarm and apply a thin coat of grease to the axle. Make sure the brake caliper bracket is still correctly positioned against the swingarm.
10 Engage the drive chain with the sprocket and lift the wheel into position **(see illustration 14.3b)**. Make sure the spacers and caliper bracket remain correctly in place, and that the brake disc fits squarely into the caliper with the pads positioned correctly either side of the disc. If there is not enough slack in the chain to align the wheel with the swingarm and chain adjusters, slacken the adjuster bolts and tap the ends to move them up in the swingarm.
11 Install the axle from the left, making sure it passes through the chain adjusters and the caliper bracket **(see illustration 14.3a)**. Check that everything is correctly aligned. Fit the nut, on VTR models not forgetting the washer, and tighten the nut to the torque setting specified at the beginning of the Chapter, counter-holding the axle head on the other side of the wheel to prevent it turning **(see illustrations)**.
12 Check the drive chain slack as described in Chapter 1 and adjust if necessary.
13 Operate the brake pedal several times to

bring the pads into contact with the disc. Check the operation of the rear brake carefully before riding the bike.

15 Wheel bearings – removal, inspection and installation

Front wheel bearings

Note: *Always replace the wheel bearings in pairs. Never replace the bearings individually. Avoid using a high pressure cleaner on the wheel bearing area.*

1 Remove the wheel, then remove the spacers from the wheel (see Section 13).
2 Set the wheel on blocks so as not to allow the weight to rest on the brake disc.
Caution: Don't lay the wheel down and allow it to rest on a disc – the disc could become warped.
3 Prise out the seal on each side of the wheel using a flat-bladed screwdriver, taking care not to damage the rim of the hub **(see illustration)**. Discard the seals as new ones should be used.
4 Using a metal rod (preferably a brass drift punch) inserted through the centre of the left-hand bearing, tap evenly around the inner race of the right-hand bearing to drive it from the hub **(see illustrations)**. The bearing spacer will also come out.
5 Lay the wheel on its other side so that the

15.3 Lever out the grease seal on each side

15.4a Knock out the bearings using a drift . . .

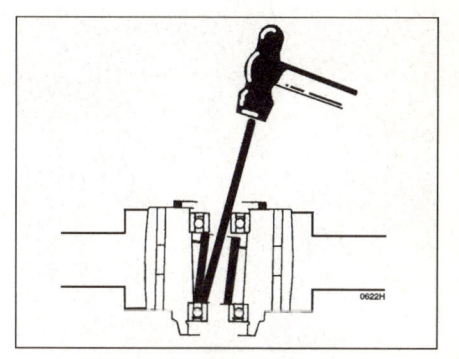

15.4b . . . locating it as shown

7•22 Brakes, wheels and tyres

15.9 A socket can be used to drive in the bearing

15.11 Fit the grease seal and tap it into place – using a piece of wood ensures the seal sits flush with the rim

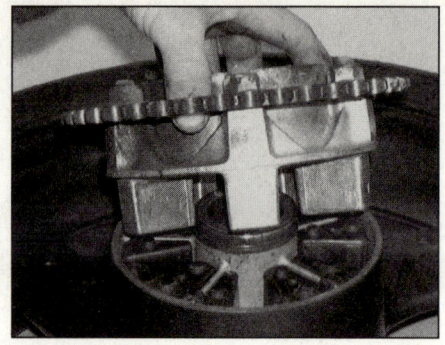

15.13 Lift the sprocket coupling out of the wheel

left-hand bearing faces down. Drive the bearing out of the wheel using the same technique as above.

6 If the bearings are of the unsealed type or are only sealed on one side, clean them with a high flash-point solvent (one which won't leave any residue) and blow them dry with compressed air (don't let the bearings spin as you dry them). Apply a few drops of oil to the bearing. **Note:** *If the bearing is sealed on both sides don't attempt to clean it.*

> **HAYNES HINT** *Refer to Tools and Workshop Tips for more information about bearings.*

7 Hold the outer race of the bearing and rotate the inner race – if the bearing doesn't turn smoothly, has rough spots or is noisy, replace it with a new one.
8 If the bearing is good and can be re-used, wash it in solvent once again and dry it, then pack the bearing with grease.
9 Thoroughly clean the hub area of the wheel. Install one bearing into its recess in the hub, with the marked or sealed side facing outwards. Using the old bearing (if new ones are being fitted), a bearing driver or a socket large enough to contact the outer race of the bearing, drive it in until it's completely seated **(see illustration)**.
10 Turn the wheel over and install the bearing

spacer. Drive the other bearing into place as described above.
11 Apply a smear of grease to the lips of the seals, then press them into the wheel. Gently drive them into place if necessary using a seal or bearing driver, a suitable socket or a flat piece of wood **(see illustration)**. As the seals sit flush with the top surface of their housing, using a piece of wood as shown will automatically set them flush without the risk of setting them too deep and having to lever them out again.
12 Clean off all grease from the brake discs using acetone or brake system cleaner then install the wheel (see Section 13).

Rear wheel bearings

13 Remove the rear wheel, then remove the spacers from the wheel (see Section 14). Lift the sprocket coupling out of the wheel, noting how it fits **(see illustration)**.
14 Set the wheel on blocks so as not to allow the weight of the wheel to rest on the brake disc.
Caution: *Do not lay the wheel down and allow it to rest on the disc or the sprocket – they could become warped.*
15 Lever out the grease seal on the right-hand side of the wheel using a flat-bladed screwdriver, taking care not to damage the rim of the hub **(see illustration)**. Discard the seal as a new one should be used.
16 Using a metal rod (preferably a brass drift

punch) inserted through the centre of one bearing, tap evenly around the inner race of the other bearing to drive it from the hub **(see illustrations 15.4a and 15.4b)**. The bearing spacer will also come out.
17 Lay the wheel on its other side so that the remaining bearing faces down. Drive the bearing out of the wheel using the same technique as above.
18 Refer to Steps 6 to 8 above and check the bearings.
19 Thoroughly clean the hub area of the wheel. First install the right-hand bearing into its recess in the hub, with the marked or sealed side facing outwards. Using the old bearing (if new ones are being fitted), a bearing driver or a socket large enough to contact the outer race of the bearing, drive it in squarely until it's completely seated.
20 Turn the wheel over and install the bearing spacer. Drive the left-hand side bearing into place as described above **(see illustration)**.
21 Check the condition of the hub O-ring and renew it if it is damaged, deformed or deteriorated **(see illustration)**.
22 Apply a smear of grease to the lips of the new grease seal, and press it into the right-hand side of the wheel, using a seal or bearing driver, a suitable socket or a flat piece of wood to drive it into place if necessary **(see illustration 15.11)**. As the seal sits flush with the top surface of their housing, using a piece of wood as shown will automatically set it

15.15 Lever out the grease seal

15.20 A socket can be used to drive in the bearing

15.21 Check the O-ring and fit a new one if necessary

Brakes, wheels and tyres 7•23

15.25 Lever out the grease seal

15.26 Drive out the spacer . . .

flush without the risk of setting it too deep and having to lever it out again.
23 Clean off all grease from the brake disc using acetone or brake system cleaner. Fit the sprocket coupling assembly onto the wheel **(see illustration 15.13)**, then install the wheel (see Section 14).

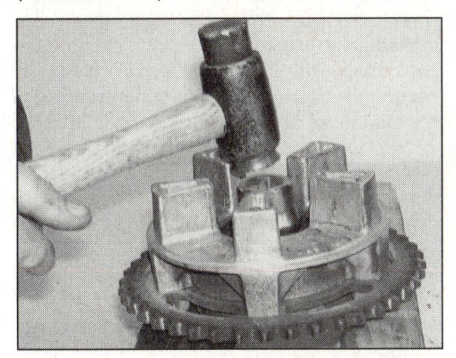

15.27 . . . then drive out the bearing

Sprocket coupling bearing

24 Remove the rear wheel (see Section 14). Lift the sprocket coupling out of the wheel, noting how it fits **(see illustration 15.13)**.
25 If not already done, remove the spacer from the outside of the sprocket coupling **(see illustration 14.5a)**. Using a flat-bladed screwdriver, lever out the grease seal from the outside of the coupling **(see illustration)**.
26 Remove the spacer from the inside of the coupling bearing, noting which way round it fits. The spacer could be a tight fit and may have to be driven out using a suitable socket or piece of tubing **(see illustration)**. Support the coupling on blocks of wood to do this.
27 Support the coupling on blocks of wood and drive the bearing out from the inside using a bearing driver or socket **(see illustration)**.
28 Refer to Steps 6 to 8 above and check the bearings.
29 Thoroughly clean the bearing recess then install the bearing into the coupling, with the marked or sealed side facing out. Using the old bearing (if a new one is being fitted), a bearing driver or a socket large enough to contact the outer race of the bearing, drive it in until it is completely seated **(see illustration)**.
30 Fit the spacer into the inside of the coupling, making sure it is the correct way round and fits squarely into the bearing. Drive it into place if it is tight, supporting the bearing on a suitable socket as you do to prevent it from being driven out at the same time **(see illustration)**.
31 Check the condition of the hub O-ring and replace it with a new one if it is damaged, deformed or deteriorated **(see illustration 15.21)**.
32 Apply a smear of grease to the lips of the new seal, and press it into the coupling, using a seal or bearing driver, a suitable socket or a flat piece of wood to drive it into place if necessary **(see illustration)**. As the seal sits flush with the

15.29 Drive in the new bearing

15.30 Support the bearing as shown when driving in the spacer

7•24 Brakes, wheels and tyres

top surface of their housing, using a piece of wood as shown will automatically set it flush without the risk of setting it too deep and having to lever it out again.
33 Check the sprocket coupling/rubber dampers (see Chapter 6).
34 Clean off all grease from the brake disc using acetone or brake system cleaner. Fit the sprocket coupling into the wheel (see illustration 15.13), then install the wheel (see Section 14).

16 Tyres –
general information and fitting

General information

1 The wheels fitted to all models are designed to take tubeless tyres only. Tyre sizes are given in the Specifications at the beginning of this chapter.
2 Refer to the *Daily (pre-ride) checks* listed at the beginning of this manual for tyre maintenance.

Fitting new tyres

3 When selecting new tyres, refer to the tyre information label on the swingarm and the tyre options listed in the owners handbook. Ensure that front and rear tyre types are compatible, the correct size and correct speed rating; if necessary seek advice from a Honda dealer or tyre fitting specialist (see illustration).
4 It is recommended that tyres are fitted by a motorcycle tyre specialist rather than attempted in the home workshop. This is particularly relevant in the case of tubeless tyres because the force required to break the seal between the wheel rim and tyre bead is substantial, and

15.32 Press or drive the seal into the coupling. Using a piece of wood as shown automatically sets the seal flush with the rim

is usually beyond the capabilities of an individual working with normal tyre levers. Additionally, the specialist will be able to balance the wheels after tyre fitting.
5 Note that punctured tubeless tyres can in some cases be repaired. Honda recommend that such repairs are carried out only by an authorised dealer.

⚠ **Warning: If a punctured tyre is repaired, Honda recommend not exceeding 50 mph (80 km/h) for the first 24 hours and not exceeding 80 mph (130km/h) thereafter.**

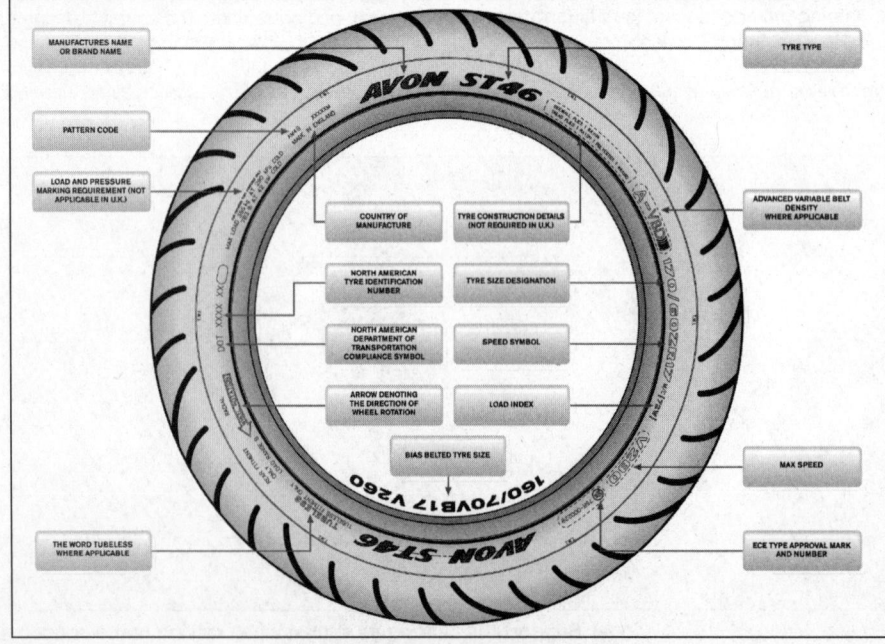

17 ABS –
operation and fault finding

1 The ABS prevents the wheels from locking up under hard braking or on uneven road surfaces. A sensor on each wheel transmits information about the speed of rotation to the ABS control unit; if the unit senses that a wheel is about to lock, it releases brake pressure to that wheel momentarily, preventing a skid.
2 The ABS is self-checking and is activated when the ignition (main) switch is turned on – the ABS indicator light in the instrument cluster will come on and will remain on until road speed increases above 6 mph (10 kph) at which point, if the ABS is normal, the light will go off. **Note:** *If the ABS indicator light does not come on initially there is a fault in the system – see Section 18.*
3 If the indicator light remains on, or starts flashing while the machine is being ridden, there is a fault in the system and the ABS function will be switched off – the brakes will still function but in normal mode.
4 If a fault is indicated, details will be stored in the control unit's memory. Access the fault code(s) as follows.
5 Remove the seat (see Chapter 8).
6 Ensure the ignition (main) switch is OFF. Open the fusebox lid and remove the No. 1 and No. 3 ABS control unit fuses (see illustration) – if either fuse has blown, perform the system checks relating to fault code 4 for the No. 1 fuse and fault code 5 for the No. 3 fuse (see Section 18). If the fuses are good, turn the ignition switch ON – the ABS indicator light should come on for 3 seconds, then go out. When the light goes out immediately (within 3 seconds) fit either of the two fuses – the indicator light will give 0.25 second flashes at 0.25 second intervals, with the number of flashes denoting the fault code.
7 Two fault codes can be stored, and they are displayed most recent first, with a five second gap between them, during which the light comes on for 3 seconds. If the light gives 2.0 second flashes at 2.0 second intervals after fitting the fuse no fault code is stored. The code or codes are repeated until the ignition is switched OFF. If two fault codes are given correct the faults relating to the first given code first.
8 Turn the ignition (main) switch OFF when the code or codes have been recorded.
9 To check the ABS components see Section 19.
10 Once the fault has been corrected, erase the fault code(s) as follows. Follow Step 6 to display the fault code(s), and while the light is

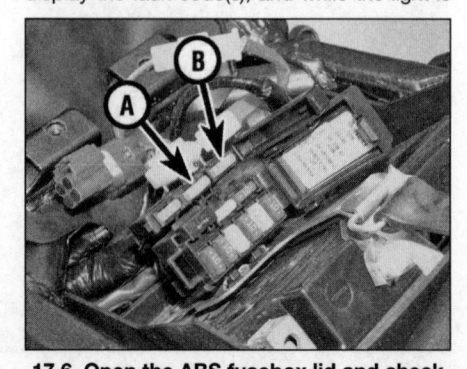

16.3 Common tyre sidewall markings

17.6 Open the ABS fusebox lid and check the modulator front (A) and rear (B) fuses

Brakes, wheels and tyres 7•25

flashing the code refit the other fuse. When the code(s) is/are erased the light will come on.
11 Turn the ignition (main) switch OFF. Install the seat (see Chapter 8). Check that the ABS is operating normally (see Step 2).
12 If necessary, repeat the reset procedure.
Note: *The ABS indicator may diagnose a fault if tyre sizes other than those specified by Honda are fitted, if the tyre pressures are incorrect, if the machine has been run continuously over bumpy roads, if the front wheel is raised whilst riding (wheelie) or if, for some reason, the machine is on an auxiliary stand with the engine running and the rear wheel turning.*

18 ABS – system checks

1 If a fault is indicated in the ABS, first check that the battery is fully charged, then check the ABS fuses (see Chapter 9).
2 Unless specified otherwise, carry-out all checks with the ignition (main) switch OFF.
3 Refer to Chapter 9, Section 2, for general electrical fault finding procedures and equipment.
4 If, after a thorough check, the source of a fault has not been identified, have the ABS control unit tested by a Honda dealer.

Fault code/flashes	Faulty component or system	Possible causes
No code displayed, but light is on – problem not detected	No voltage at instrument cluster No voltage at control unit	Blown ABS main fuse Faulty wiring or wiring connector Faulty control unit Faulty ABS indicator light
2 or 15	Front wheel speed sensor Front wheel pulser ring	Faulty wiring or wiring connector Faulty sensor Damaged pulser ring
3	Rear wheel speed sensor Rear wheel pulser ring	Faulty wiring or wiring connector Faulty sensor Damaged pulser ring
4	Front modulator motor	Blown front modulator fuse Faulty front modulator motor or crank angle sensor Faulty wiring or wiring connector
5	Rear modulator motor	Blown rear modulator fuse Faulty rear modulator motor or crank angle sensor Faulty wiring or wiring connector
6	Front modulator crank angle sensor system	Faulty front modulator crank angle sensor Faulty wiring or wiring connector
7	Rear modulator crank angle sensor system	Faulty rear modulator crank angle sensor Faulty wiring or wiring connector
8	ABS control unit – front control circuit	Blown front modulator fuse Faulty front modulator motor or crank angle sensor Faulty front wheel speed sensor Damaged front pulser ring Faulty wiring or wiring connector Faulty control unit
9	ABS control unit – rear control circuit	Blown rear modulator fuse Faulty rear modulator motor or crank angle sensor Faulty rear wheel speed sensor Damaged rear pulser ring Faulty wiring or wiring connector Faulty control unit
10	ABS control unit – front relay circuit	Blown front modulator fuse Faulty front modulator motor or crank angle sensor Faulty wiring or wiring connector Faulty control unit
11	ABS control unit – rear relay circuit	Blown rear modulator fuse Faulty rear modulator motor or crank angle sensor Faulty wiring or wiring connector Faulty control unit
12	ABS control unit – front motor driver circuit	Blown front modulator fuse Faulty front modulator motor Faulty wiring or wiring connector Faulty control unit
13	ABS control unit – rear motor driver circuit	Blown rear modulator fuse Faulty rear modulator motor Faulty wiring or wiring connector Faulty control unit
14	Power circuit	Damaged fuse Faulty wiring or wiring connector Faulty control unit

7•26 Brakes, wheels and tyres

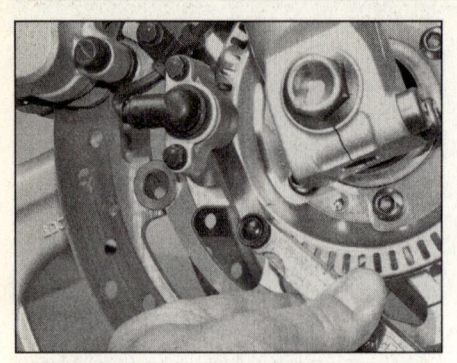

18.5 Checking the front wheel sensor air gap

18.7a ABS control unit (arrowed)

18.7b Release the heat shield . . .

Fault codes 2, 8 and 15

Note: *Before carrying out any of the checks, follow the procedure in Section 17 to reset the control unit memory, then activate the self-checking procedure. If the fault code is the result of unusual riding or conditions and the ABS is normal, the indicator light will go off. Otherwise perform the following checks.*

5 Measure the air gap between the front wheel speed sensor and the pulser ring with a feeler gauge, then compare the result with the Specification at the beginning of this Chapter **(see illustration)**. The gap is not adjustable – if it is outside the specification, check that the sensor and pulser ring fixings are tight, that the components are not damaged and that there is no dirt or anything else on the sensor tip or between the slots in the pulser ring. If any of the components are damaged they must be renewed.

6 Erase the fault code, but do not turn the ignition OFF afterwards (see Section 17). Raise the front wheel off the ground and spin the wheel in a forward direction – the ABS indicator light should start to flash. If it does, check the front wheel speed sensor wiring and connectors. If they are good it is possible the control unit has been disrupted by an extremely powerful radio wave.

7 If the light doesn't flash remove the left-hand fairing side panel (see Chapter 8). Disconnect the ABS control unit 12 pin black wiring connector **(see illustration)**. Remove the fuel tank (see Chapter 4A). Release the heat shield from the frame **(see illustration)**. Trace the wheel sensor wiring to the orange connector and disconnect it **(see illustration)**. Check for continuity first in the black/pink wire between the control unit wiring connector and the sensor wiring connector and then in the green/orange wire – there should be continuity in each wire. If not locate and repair the break.

8 If there is continuity in the wiring next check for continuity between each terminal on the sensor side of the connector and earth (ground). If there is continuity in either of the wires the sensor is faulty and must be replaced with a new one.

9 If all the checks have failed to identify the fault, replace the wheel sensor with a known good one. Connect all wiring connectors then follow the procedure in Section 17 to reset the control unit memory, then activate the self-checking procedure. If the indicator light is no longer flashing, the original sensor was faulty. If the fault code reappears have the ABS control unit checked by a Honda dealer.

Fault codes 3 and 9

Note: *Before carrying out any of the checks, follow the procedure in Section 17 to reset the control unit memory, then activate the self-checking procedure. If the fault code is the result of unusual riding or conditions and the ABS is normal, the indicator light will go off. Otherwise perform the following checks.*

Check

10 Measure the air gap between the rear wheel speed sensor and the pulser ring with a feeler gauge, then compare the result with the Specification at the beginning of this Chapter **(see illustration)**. The gap is not adjustable – if it is outside the specification, check that the sensor and pulser ring fixings are tight, that the components are not damaged and that there is no dirt or anything else on the sensor tip or between the slots in the pulser ring. If any of the components are damaged they must be renewed.

11 Erase the fault code, but do not turn the ignition OFF afterwards (see Section 17). Raise the rear wheel off the ground and spin the wheel in a forward direction – the ABS indicator light should start to flash. If it does, check the rear wheel speed sensor wiring and connectors. If they are good it is possible the control unit has been disrupted by an extremely powerful radio wave.

12 If the light doesn't flash remove the left-hand fairing side panel (see Chapter 8). Disconnect the ABS control unit 12 pin black wiring connector **(see illustration 18.7a)**. Remove the right-hand side cover (see Chapter 8). Free the wheel speed sensor wiring connector from the bracket and disconnect it **(see illustration)**. Check for continuity first in the black/orange wire between the control unit wiring connector and the sensor wiring connector and then in the blue/brown wire – there should be continuity in each wire. If not locate and repair the break.

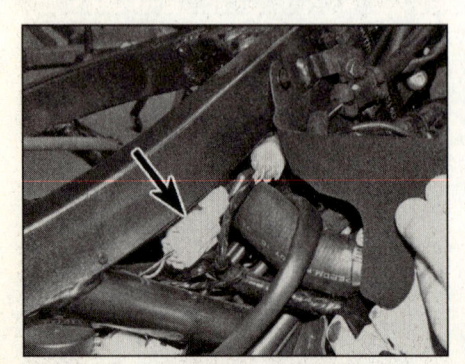

18.7c . . . and disconnect the sensor wiring connector (arrowed)

18.10 Checking the rear wheel sensor air gap

18.12 Release and disconnect the sensor wiring connector (arrowed)

Brakes, wheels and tyres 7•27

13 If there is continuity in the wiring next check for continuity between each terminal on the sensor side of the connector and earth (ground). If there is continuity in either of the wires the sensor is faulty and must be replaced with a new one.

14 If all the checks have failed to identify the fault, replace the wheel sensor with a known good one. Connect all wiring connectors then follow the procedure in Section 17 to reset the control unit memory, then activate the self-checking procedure. If the indicator light is no longer flashing, the original sensor was faulty. If the fault code reappears have the ABS control unit checked by a Honda dealer.

Fault code 4

15 Check the front modulator fuse (see Section 17, Steps 5 and 6). If the fuse has blown replace it with a new one.

16 Erase the fault code (see Section 17). Start the engine and go for a short ride so the ABS system performs its self-diagnosis. If the ABS indicator light stays off, check the front wheel speed sensor wiring and connectors. If they are OK it is possible there was a piece of fine foreign matter in the modulator or the control unit has been disrupted by an extremely powerful radio wave.

17 If the ABS indicator light flashes, remove the left-hand fairing side panel (see Chapter 8). Disconnect the ABS control unit 5 pin black wiring connector (see illustration 18.7a). Check for battery voltage between the red wire terminal on the loom side of the connector and earth (ground) – there should be voltage at all times i.e. with the ignition OFF. If there is no voltage, check for a break in the red wire between the connector and the fusebox connector, and if that wire is good check the wire between the fusebox and the battery.

18 If there is voltage, check for continuity to earth in the green/yellow wire – there should be continuity. If not locate the break in the wire and repair it.

19 Remove the right-hand fairing side panel (see Chapter 8). Disconnect the front modulator 2 pin wiring connector (see illustration). Check for continuity first in the brown/yellow wire between the ABS and modulator wiring connectors (loom side) and then in the yellow/green wire. If continuity is not shown in either or both of the wires locate the break and repair it. Next check for continuity between each terminal in the modulator connector (modulator side) and earth (ground). If there is continuity in either of the wires either repair the wire or replace the modulator with a new one.

20 If all the wiring is good remove the both front and rear modulators and interchange them (see Section 19). Reconnect the control unit wiring connector. Erase the fault code (see Section 17). Start the engine and go for a short ride so the ABS system performs its self-diagnosis. If fault code 5 is now shown the front modulator (now fitted at the rear) is faulty. If fault code 4 is again shown the modulator is OK but the ABS control unit is faulty.

Fault code 5

21 Check the rear modulator fuse (see Section 17, Steps 5 and 6). If the fuse has blown replace it with a new one.

22 Erase the fault code (see Section 17). Start the engine and go for a short ride so the ABS system performs its self-diagnosis. If the ABS indicator light stays off, check the rear wheel speed sensor wiring and connectors (see Section 19). If they are OK it is possible there was a piece of fine foreign matter in the modulator or the control unit has been disrupted by an extremely powerful radio wave.

23 If the ABS indicator light flashes, remove the left-hand fairing side panel (see Chapter 8). Disconnect the ABS control unit 5 pin brown wiring connector (see illustration 18.7a). Check for battery voltage between the black/blue wire terminal on the loom side of the connector and earth (ground) – there should be voltage at all times i.e. with the ignition OFF. If there is no voltage, check for a break in the black/blue wire between the connector and the fusebox connector, and if that wire is good check the wire between the fusebox and the battery.

24 If there is voltage, check for continuity to earth in the green/yellow wire – there should be continuity. If not locate the break in the wire and repair it.

25 Remove the right-hand side cover (see Chapter 8). Disconnect the rear modulator 2 pin wiring connector (see illustration). Check for continuity first in the brown/light green wire between the ABS and modulator wiring connectors (loom side) and then in the red/black wire. If continuity is not shown in either or both of the wires locate the break and repair it. Next check for continuity between each terminal in the modulator connector (modulator side) and earth (ground). If there is continuity in either of the wires either repair the wire or replace the modulator with a new one.

26 If all the wiring is good remove the both front and rear modulators and interchange them. Reconnect the control unit wiring connector. Erase the fault code (see Section 17). Start the engine and go for a short ride so the ABS system performs its self-diagnosis. If fault code 4 is now shown the rear modulator (now fitted at the front) is faulty. If fault code 5 is again shown the modulator is OK but the ABS control unit is faulty.

Fault code 6

27 Erase the fault code (see Section 17). Start the engine and go for a short ride so the ABS system performs its self-diagnosis. If the ABS indicator light stays off, check the front wheel speed sensor wiring and connectors. If they are OK it is possible there was a piece of fine foreign matter in the modulator or the control unit has been disrupted by an extremely powerful radio wave.

28 If the ABS indicator light still flashes, remove the right-hand fairing side panel (see Chapter 8). Disconnect the front modulator 3-pin wiring connector (see illustration 18.19). Check the voltage between the orange/green (+) wire terminal and the pink/blue (-) wire terminal on the loom side of the connector – there should be 4.5 to 5.5 volts with the ignition ON. If there is no voltage, remove the left-hand fairing side panel (see Chapter 8). Disconnect the ABS control unit 12-pin black wiring connector (see illustration 18.7a). Check for continuity first in the orange/green wire between the ABS and modulator wiring connectors (loom side) and then in the pink/blue wire. If continuity is not shown in either or both of the wires locate the break and repair it.

29 If there is the correct voltage, remove the left-hand fairing side panel (see Chapter 8). Disconnect the ABS control unit 12-pin black wiring connector (see illustration 18.7a). Check for continuity in the white/pink wire between the ABS and modulator wiring connectors (loom side) – there should be continuity. If not locate the break in the wire and repair it.

30 Next check for continuity in the white/pink wire in the modulator connector (modulator side) to earth (ground). If there is continuity either repair the wire or replace the modulator with a new one.

31 If all the wiring is good remove both front and rear modulators and interchange them. Reconnect the control unit wiring connector. Erase the fault code (see Section 17). Start the

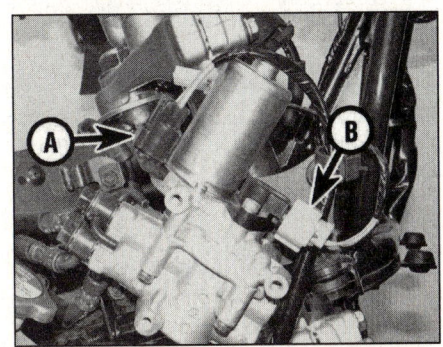

18.19 Front modulator 2-pin wiring connector (A) and 3-pin connector (B)

18.25 Rear modulator 2-pin wiring connector (arrowed)

Fault code 7

32 Erase the fault code (see Section 17). Start the engine and go for a short ride so the ABS system performs its self-diagnosis. If the ABS indicator light stays off, check the front wheel speed sensor wiring and connectors. If they are OK it is possible there was a piece of fine foreign matter in the modulator or the control unit has been disrupted by an extremely powerful radio wave.

33 If the ABS indicator light still flashes, remove the right-hand side cover (see Chapter 8). Disconnect the rear modulator 3-pin wiring connector **(see illustration)**. Check the voltage between the orange/blue (+) wire terminal and the pink/white (-) wire terminal on the loom side of the connector – there should be 4.5 to 5.5 volts with the ignition ON. If there is no voltage, remove the left-hand fairing side panel (see Chapter 8). Disconnect the ABS control unit 12-pin black wiring connector **(see illustration 18.7a)**. Check for continuity first in the orange/blue wire between the ABS and modulator wiring connectors (loom side) and then in the pink/white wire. If continuity is not shown in either or both of the wires locate the break and repair it.

34 If there is the correct voltage, remove the left-hand fairing side panel (see Chapter 8). Disconnect the ABS control unit 12-pin black wiring connector **(see illustration 18.7a)**. Check for continuity in the pink/green wire between the ABS and modulator wiring connectors (loom side) – there should be continuity. If not locate the break in the wire and repair it.

35 Next check for continuity in the pink/green wire in the modulator connector (modulator side) to earth (ground). If there is continuity either repair the wire or replace the modulator with a new one.

36 If all the wiring is good remove both front and rear modulators and interchange them. Reconnect the control unit wiring connector. Erase the fault code (see Section 17). Start the engine and go for a short ride so the ABS system performs its self-diagnosis. If fault code 7 is now shown the front modulator (now fitted at the rear) is faulty. If fault code 6 is again shown the modulator is OK but the ABS control unit is faulty.

18.33 Rear modulator 3-pin wiring connector (arrowed)

Fault code 10

37 Erase the fault code (see Section 17). Start the engine and go for a short ride so the ABS system performs its self-diagnosis. If the ABS indicator light stays off, check the front wheel speed sensor wiring and connectors. If they are OK it is possible there was a piece of fine foreign matter in the modulator or the control unit has been disrupted by an extremely powerful radio wave.

38 If the ABS indicator light still flashes fault code 10, remove both front and rear modulators and interchange them. Erase the fault code (see Section 17). Start the engine and go for a short ride so the ABS system performs its self-diagnosis. If fault code 11 is now shown the front modulator (now fitted at the rear) is faulty. If fault code 10 is again shown the modulator is OK but the ABS control unit is faulty.

39 If the ABS indicator light flashes a fault code other than 10 perform diagnosis relating to the latest code.

Fault code 11

40 Erase the fault code (see Section 17). Start the engine and go for a short ride so the ABS system performs its self-diagnosis. If the ABS indicator light stays off, check the front wheel speed sensor wiring and connectors. If they are OK it is possible there was a piece of fine foreign matter in the modulator or the control unit has been disrupted by an extremely powerful radio wave.

41 If the ABS indicator light still flashes fault code 11, remove both front and rear modulators and interchange them. Erase the fault code (see Section 17). Start the engine and go for a short ride so the ABS system performs its self-diagnosis. If fault code 10 is now shown the rear modulator (now fitted at the front) is faulty. If fault code 11 is again shown the modulator is OK but the ABS control unit is faulty.

42 If the ABS indicator light flashes a fault code other than 11 perform diagnosis relating to the latest code.

Fault codes 12 and 13

43 Erase the fault code (see Section 17). Start the engine and go for a short ride so the ABS system performs its self-diagnosis. If the ABS indicator light stays off, check the front and rear wheel speed sensor wiring and connectors. If they are OK it is possible there was a piece of fine foreign matter in the modulator or the control unit has been disrupted by an extremely powerful radio wave.

44 If the ABS indicator light still flashes fault code 12 or 13, the ABS control unit is faulty.

45 If the ABS indicator light flashes a fault code other than 12 or 13 perform diagnosis relating to the latest code.

Fault code 14

46 Check all the ABS fuses (see Chapter 9). If a fuse has blown replace it with a new one. If the fuse is good check the battery and the charging system (see Chapter 9). Also check the wiring and connectors between the fusebox and the ABS control unit **(see illustration 18.7a)** – remove the left-hand fairing side panel to access it (see Chapter 8).

47 If all is good so far erase the fault code (see Section 17). Start the engine and go for a short ride so the ABS system performs its self-diagnosis. If the ABS indicator light stays off, check the front wheel speed sensor wiring and connectors. If they are OK it is possible there was a piece of fine foreign matter in the modulator or the control unit has been disrupted by an extremely powerful radio wave.

48 If the light flashes fit a new battery, then erase the fault code (see Section 17). Start the engine and go for a short ride so the ABS system performs its self-diagnosis. If the ABS indicator light stays off, the battery was the problem. If the ABS indicator light still flashes fault code 14, the ABS control unit is faulty.

49 If the light comes on and stays on remove the left-hand fairing side panel (see Chapter 8). Disconnect the ABS control unit 5-pin brown wiring connector **(see illustration 18.7a)**. Check the voltage first between the black/blue (+) wire terminal and the green/yellow (-) wire terminal on the loom side of the connector, and then between the red (+) and green/yellow (-) wire terminal of the black 5-pin connector. Honda specifies a permanent voltage between 10 and 17 volts. If there is no voltage, check for a break in a wire. If the voltage is below the specification, check the charging system (see Chapter 9). If there is voltage the ABS control unit is faulty.

No fault code detected

50 If no code is detected but the ABS indicator light stays on, check the ABS main fuse (see Chapter 9). If a fuse has blown replace it with a new one. If the fuse is good check the wiring and connectors between the fusebox and the ABS control unit – remove the left-hand fairing side panel to access it (see Chapter 8).

51 If all is good so far remove the left-hand fairing side panel (see Chapter 8). Disconnect the ABS control unit 5-pin brown wiring connector **(see illustration 18.7a)**. Check the voltage between the red/brown (+) wire terminal and earth (ground) with the ignition ON. There should be battery voltage. If there is no voltage, check for a break in the wire.

52 If the voltage is good, reconnect the 5-pin brown wiring connector and disconnect the 5-pin black connector. Check the voltage between the blue/yellow (+) wire terminal and earth (ground) with the ignition ON. There

Brakes, wheels and tyres 7•29

should be 1 to 3 volts. If there is no voltage, check for a break in the wire between the ABS connector and the instrument cluster.
53 If the voltage is good, reconnect the 5-pin black wiring connector. Check the wiring between the control unit and each wheel speed sensor.
54 If the wiring is good erase the fault code (see Section 17). Start the engine and go for a short ride so the ABS system performs its self-diagnosis. If the ABS indicator light stays off, it is possible there was a piece of fine foreign matter in the modulator or the control unit has been disrupted by an extremely powerful radio wave.
55 If the ABS indicator light still flashes the ABS control unit is faulty.

19 ABS – component removal and installation

Front wheel sensor

1 Remove the fuel tank (see Chapter 4). Release the trim clips and remove the heat shield from the frame (see illustration 18.7b). Trace the wheel sensor wiring to the orange connector and disconnect it (see illustration 18.7c).
2 Undo the bolts securing the sensor wiring guides, and the sensor to the caliper bracket, and remove the sensor, releasing the wiring from any other clips or ties and noting its routing (see illustrations).
3 Install the new sensor and tighten the mounting bolts. Feed the wiring up to the connector, routing and securing it as noted on removal.
4 Check the air gap (see Section 18, Step 5). Install the fuel tank (see Chapter 4A).

Front pulser ring

5 Remove the front wheel (see Section 13).
6 Undo the bolts securing the ring and lift it off (see illustration).
7 Ensure there is no dirt or corrosion where the ring seats on the hub – if the ring does not

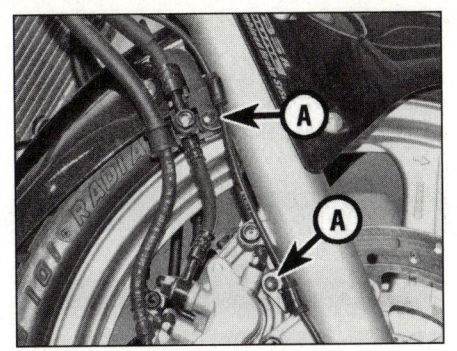

19.2a Undo the wiring guide bolts (A) . . .

sit flat when it is installed the sensor air gap will be incorrect. Clean the threads of the bolts and apply a non-permanent thread locking compound (or alternatively use new bolts from Honda which come pre-treated) and tighten them to the torque setting specified at the beginning of the Chapter.
8 Install the front wheel (see Section 13). Check the speed sensor air gap (see Section 18, Step 5).

Rear wheel sensor

9 Remove the right-hand side cover (see Chapter 8). Free the sensor wiring connector from the bracket and disconnect it (see illustration 18.12).
10 Undo the bolts securing the sensor wiring guides, and the sensor to the caliper bracket, and remove the sensor, releasing the wiring from any other clips or ties and noting its routing (see illustrations).
11 Install the new sensor and tighten the mounting bolts. Feed the wiring up to the connector, routing and securing it as noted on removal.
12 Check the air gap (see Section 18, Step 10). Install the right-hand side cover (see Chapter 8).

Rear pulser ring

13 Remove the rear wheel (see Section 14).
14 Undo the bolts securing the ring and lift it off (see illustration 19.6).

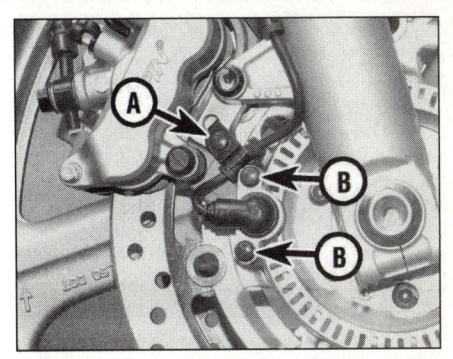

19.2b . . . and the sensor bolts (B) – XL-7 model shown

15 Ensure there is no dirt or corrosion where the ring seats on the hub – if the ring does not sit flat when it is installed the sensor air gap will be incorrect. Clean the threads of the bolts and apply a non-permanent thread locking compound (or alternatively use new bolts from Honda which come pre-treated) and tighten them to the torque setting specified at the beginning of the Chapter.
16 Install the rear wheel (see Section 14). Check the speed sensor air gap (see Section 18, Step 10).

Front modulator

Note: *Before the modulator can be removed from the bike, the brake fluid must be drained from the hydraulic system. When refilling and bleeding the ABS-equipped brake system it is essential to use a vacuum-type brake bleeder kit. Alternatively, removal and installation of the control unit should be entrusted to a Honda dealer.*

17 Remove the right-hand fairing side panel (see Chapter 8).
18 Refer to the procedure in Section 10 for changing the brake fluid – siphon the fluid out of the front and rear reservoirs and pump any residual fluid out through the brake calipers, but do not refill the system at this stage.
19 Disconnect the two wiring connectors (see illustration 18.19).
20 Cover the area around the modulator with clean rag prevent damage to paintwork in the event that brake fluid is spilled.

19.6 Small Torx bolts secure the pulser ring

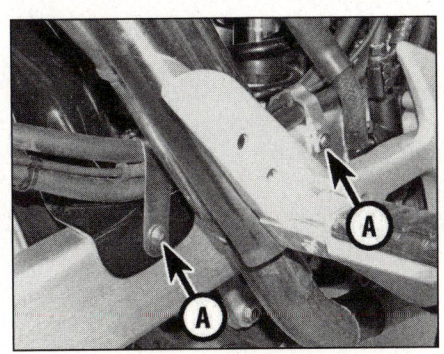

19.10a Undo the wiring guide bolts (A) . . .

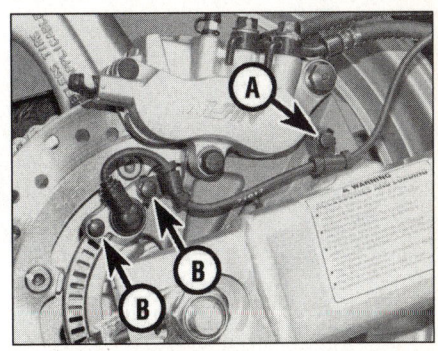

19.10b . . . and the sensor bolts (B) – XL-7 model shown

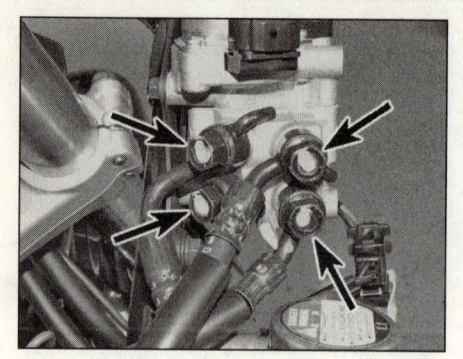

7•30 Brakes, wheels and tyres

19.21 Slacken the banjo bolts (arrowed)

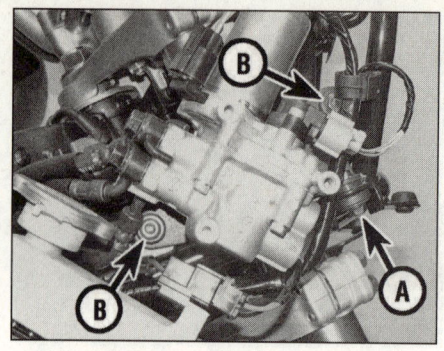

19.22 Unscrew the bolt (A) and nuts (B)

21 Slacken the four brake hose banjo bolts slightly **(see illustration)**. Make a note of which hose fits where.

22 Unscrew the modulator mounting bolt and nuts, noting the collars in the rubber grommets **(see illustration)**. Displace the modulator then unscrew the hose banjo bolts and detach the hoses, retrieving the sealing washers. New washers must be used on installation, and Honda also specify to use new banjo bolts.

23 If required, unscrew the bracket bolts and detach the modulator.

24 Installation is the reverse of removal, noting the following:
● Make sure the hoses are correctly connected with a new sealing washer on each side of each union. Fit new bolts and tighten them to the torque setting specified at the beginning of the Chapter.
● Ensure the wiring connectors are secure.
● Follow the procedure in Section 10 to refill and bleed the brake system.

Rear modulator

Note: *Before the modulator can be removed from the bike, the brake fluid must be drained from the hydraulic system. When refilling and bleeding the ABS-equipped brake system it is essential to use a vacuum-type brake bleeder kit. Alternatively, removal and installation of the control unit should be entrusted to a Honda dealer.*

25 Remove the right-hand side cover (see Chapter 8).

26 Refer to the procedure in Section 10 for changing the brake fluid – siphon the fluid out of the front and rear reservoirs and pump any residual fluid out through the brake calipers, but do not refill the system at this stage.

27 Free the rear wheel speed sensor wiring connector and wiring from the bracket **(see illustration 18.12)**. Disconnect the two modulator wiring connectors **(see illustrations 18.25 and 18.33)**.

28 Cover the area around the modulator with clean rag prevent damage to paintwork in the event that brake fluid is spilled.

29 Unscrew the modulator mounting bolts, noting the collars in the rubber grommets and the wiring clamp **(see illustration)**. Displace the modulator then unscrew the brake hose banjo bolts and detach the hoses, retrieving the sealing washers **(see illustration)**. New washers must be used on installation, and Honda also specify to use new banjo bolts. Make a note of which hose fits where. Cover the hose ends with rag and keep them upright.

30 If required, unscrew the bracket bolts and detach the modulator.

31 Installation is the reverse of removal, noting the following:
● Make sure the hoses are correctly connected with a new sealing washer on each side of each union. Fit new bolts and tighten them to the torque setting specified at the beginning of the Chapter.
● Ensure the wiring connectors are secure.
● Follow the procedure in Section 10 to refill and bleed the brake system.

ABS control unit

32 Remove the left-hand fairing side panel (see Chapter 8).

33 Release the control unit from its rubber strap then disconnect the three wiring connectors **(see illustration 18.7a)**.

34 Installation is the reverse of removal.

19.29a Unscrew the bolts (arrowed) . . .

19.29b . . . and displace the modulator to get to the banjo bolts (arrowed)

Chapter 8
Bodywork

Contents

Fairing and body panels – VTR models 4
Fairing and body panels – XL-X, Y, 1 and 2 models. 5
Fairing and body panels – XL-3 to 6 models 6
Fairing and body panels – XL-7 models onward 7
Front mudguard – removal and installation 8
General information 1
Seat – removal and installation 2
Rear view mirrors – removal and installation 3

Degrees of difficulty

Easy, suitable for novice with little experience	Fairly easy, suitable for beginner with some experience	Fairly difficult, suitable for competent DIY mechanic	Difficult, suitable for experienced DIY mechanic	Very difficult, suitable for expert DIY or professional

1 General information

This Chapter covers the procedures necessary to remove and install the body parts. Since many service and repair operations on these motorcycles require the removal of the body parts, the procedures are grouped here and referred to from other Chapters.

In the case of damage to the body parts, it is usually necessary to remove the broken component and replace it with a new (or used) one. The material that the body panels are composed of doesn't lend itself to conventional repair techniques. There are however some shops that specialise in 'plastic welding', so it may be worthwhile seeking the advice of one of these specialists before consigning an expensive component to the bin.

When attempting to remove any body panel, first study it closely, noting any fasteners and associated fittings, to be sure of returning everything to its correct place on installation. In some cases the aid of an assistant will be required when removing panels, to help avoid the risk of damage to paintwork. Once the evident fasteners have been removed, try to withdraw the panel as described but DO NOT FORCE IT – if it will not release, check that all fasteners have been removed and try again. Where a panel engages another by means of tabs, be careful not to break the tab or its mating slot or to damage the paintwork. Remember that a few moments of patience at this stage will save you a lot of money in replacing broken fairing panels!

When installing a body panel, first study it closely, noting any fasteners and associated fittings removed with it, to be sure of returning everything to its correct place. Check that all fasteners are in good condition, including all trim nuts or clips and damping/rubber mounts; any of these must be replaced if faulty before the panel is reassembled. Check also that all mounting brackets are straight and repair or replace them if necessary before attempting to install the panel. Where assistance was required to remove a panel, make sure your assistant is on hand to install it. Tighten the fasteners securely, but be careful not to overtighten any of them or the panel may break (not always immediately) due to the uneven stress.

Where quick-release fasteners are fitted, turn them 90° anti-clockwise to release them, and 90° clockwise to secure them. Where trim clips are used, to release them unscrew or pull (according to type) the centre of the clip, then

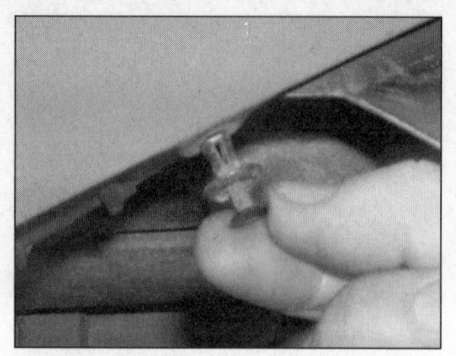

8•2 Bodywork

1.5 Unscrew the centre of the clip, then pull the body of the clip out of the panel

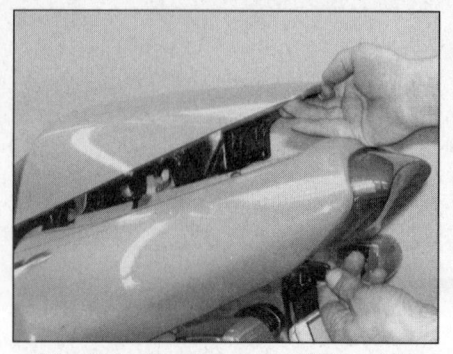

2.1a Unlocking the seat – VTR models

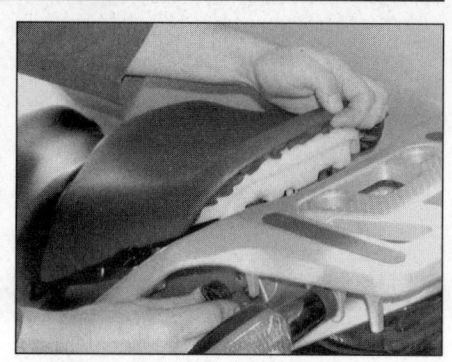

2.1b Unlocking the seat – XL models

pull the body of the clip out of the panel **(see illustration)**. When installing them, fit the body of the clip onto the panel then push the centre fully into the body. As they are made of plastic, the threads on the screw type can easily become worn and the centres may not unscrew, in which case lever the centre out of the body using a small screwdriver.

> **HAYNES HiNT** *Note that a small amount of lubricant (liquid soap or similar) applied to mounting rubber grommets will assist lugs to engage without the need for undue pressure.*

2 Seat – removal and installation

Removal

1 Insert the ignition key into the seat lock located at the back on the left-hand side and turn it clockwise to unlock the seat. Remove the seat by drawing it back and up **(see illustrations)**.

Installation

2 Installation is the reverse of removal. On VTR models, locate the tab at the front under the tank bracket and the catches at the back under the hooks on the frame **(see illustration)**. On XL models, locate the tab on the back of the

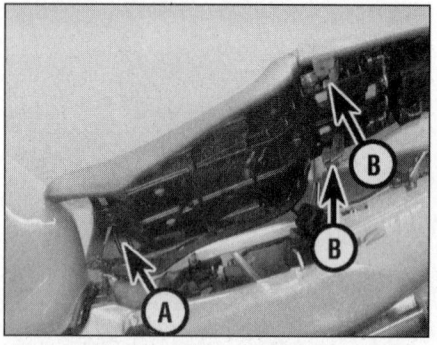

2.2a On VTR models, locate the tab (A) under the tank bracket and the catches (B) under the hooks on the frame

fuel tank in the slot in the front of the seat and the tabs in the middle under the hooks on the frame **(see illustration)**. Push the seat forward until it locates correctly, then push down on the rear to engage the latch.

3 Rear view mirrors – removal and installation

Removal

1 On VTR models, unscrew the two nuts securing each mirror and remove the mirror along with its rubber insulator pads **(see illustration)**.
2 On XL models, pull the cover up off the base of the mirror **(see illustration)**. To remove the mirror stalk leaving the mounting adapter

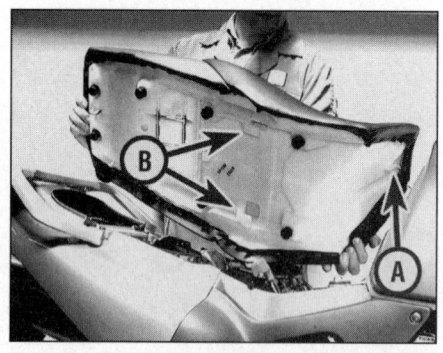

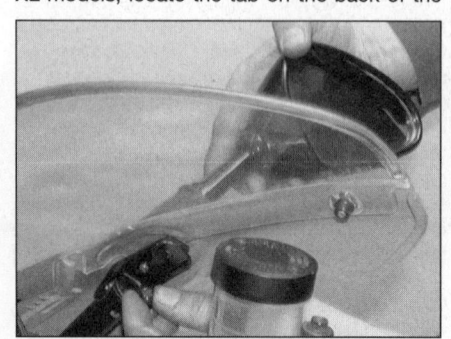

2.2b On XL models, locate the slot (A) over the tank tab and the tabs (B) under the hooks on the frame

in place, slacken the top nut then unscrew the mirror itself from the adapter. To remove the entire mirror, unscrew it using the hex on the mounting adapter.

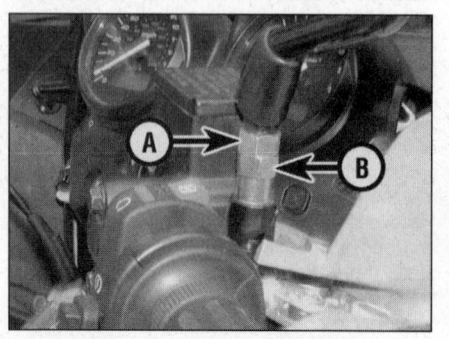

Installation

3 Installation is the reverse of removal. On XL models, to adjust the mirror position, slacken the top nut and turn the mirror until the best angle is achieved, then retighten the top nut.

4 Fairing and body panels – VTR models

Fairing removal

1 Disconnect the turn signal wiring connectors **(see illustration)**.

3.1 Unscrew the nuts on the inside and remove the mirror

3.2 Top nut (A), adapter (B)

4.1 Disconnect the turn signal wiring connectors

Bodywork 8•3

4.2 Remove the trim clip (arrowed)

4.4a Unscrew the two bolts (arrowed) on each side

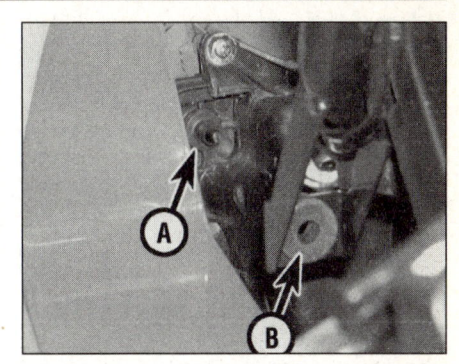

4.4b Note how the peg (A) locates in the grommet (B)

4.4c Disconnect the headlight wiring connector (arrowed) . . .

4.4d . . . and the sidelight wiring connector (arrowed) . . .

4.4e . . . and remove the fairing

2 Remove the trim clip from each side of the fairing just below the turn signal (see Section 1 for details on how to remove and install trim clips) **(see illustration)**.
3 Remove the rear view mirrors (see Section 3).
4 Unscrew the two bolts on each side of the fairing at the back **(see illustration)**. Carefully draw the fairing forward to release the pegs from the grommets on the fairing/instrument bracket **(see illustration)**. Disconnect the headlight and sidelight wiring connectors when accessible, then draw the fairing off the bike **(see illustrations)**.
5 If required, remove the headlight from the fairing (see Chapter 9).

Fairing installation

6 Installation is the reverse of removal. Make sure the wiring connectors are correctly and securely connected.

Belly-pan

7 Remove the two bolts securing the belly-pan and draw it forward **(see illustration)**.
8 Installation is the reverse of removal.

Seat cowl

9 Remove the seat (see Section 2).
10 Disconnect the taillight wiring connectors **(see illustration)**.

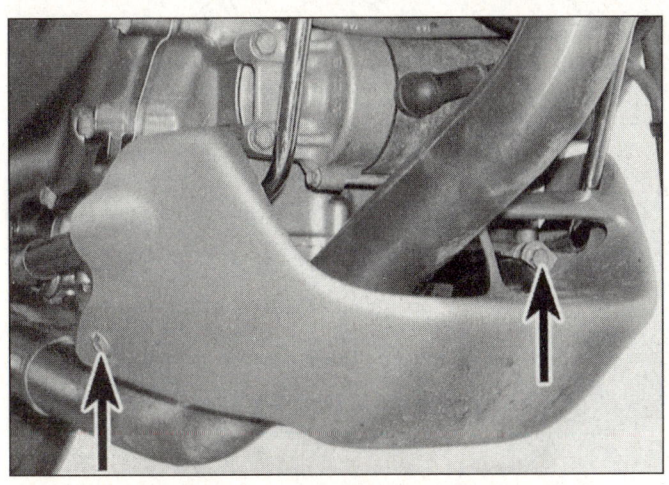

4.7 The belly-pan is secured by two bolts (arrowed)

4.10 Disconnect the taillight wiring connectors

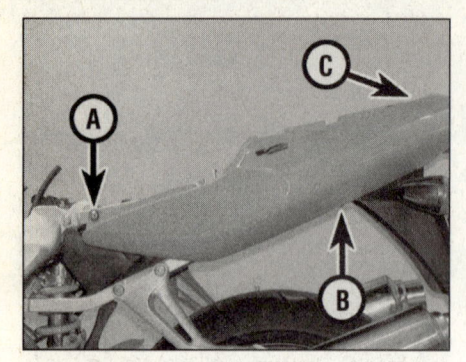

8•4 Bodywork

4.11a Remove the bolt (A), trim clip (B) and screw (C) on each side . . .

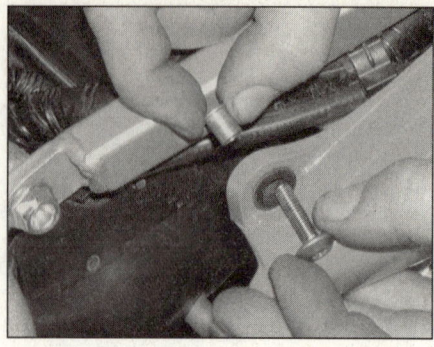

4.11b . . . noting the collar with the bolt . . .

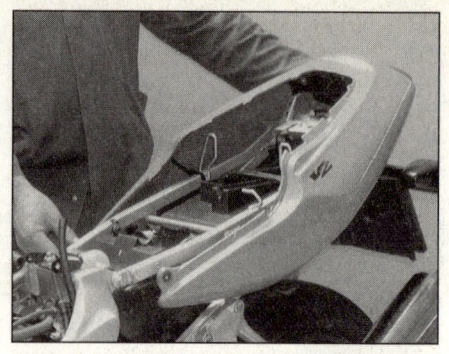

4.11c . . . and remove the seat cowl

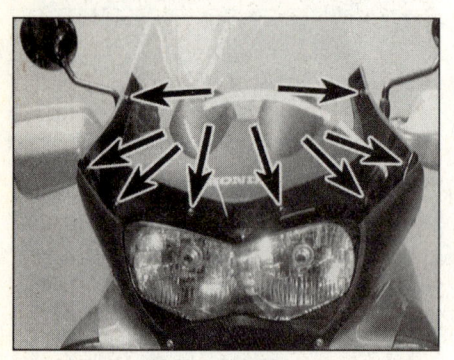

5.1 Remove the screws (arrowed) and detach the windshield

5.2 Each trim panel is secured by six fasteners (arrowed)

5.3 Disconnect the headlight wiring connector (A) and sidelight wiring connector (B)

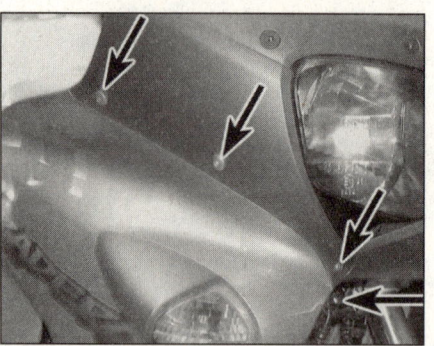

5.4a Remove the fasteners on each side (arrowed) . . .

5.4b . . . and the bolt in the middle (arrowed) . . .

5.4c . . . and remove the fairing . . .

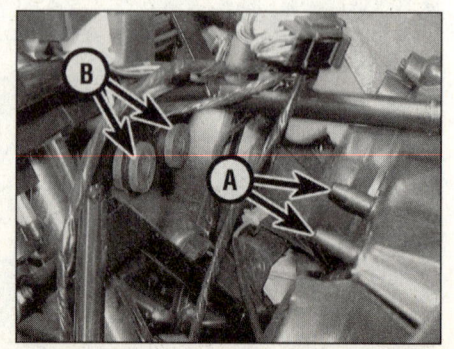

5.4d . . . noting how the pegs (A) locate in the grommets (B)

11 Remove the two bolt, two screws and two trim clips securing the seat cowl, noting which fits where, and carefully draw it back off the bike **(see illustrations)**. For details of how to remove a trim clip, see Section 1.

12 Installation is the reverse of removal.

5 Fairing and body panels – XL-X, Y, 1 and 2 models

Fairing removal

1 Remove the screws and washers securing the windshield and detach it from the fairing **(see illustration)**.

2 Remove the six fasteners securing each cockpit trim panel, noting which fits where, and remove the panels **(see illustration)**.

3 Disconnect the headlight and sidelight wiring connectors **(see illustration)**.

4 Remove all the fasteners securing the fairing to the fairing bracket and fairing side panels, noting which fits where **(see illustrations)**. Carefully draw the fairing forward and off the bike, noting how the pegs locate in the grommets **(see illustrations)**.

5 If required, remove the headlight from the fairing (see Chapter 9).

Fairing installation

6 Installation is the reverse of removal. Make sure the wiring connectors are correctly and securely connected.

Bodywork 8•5

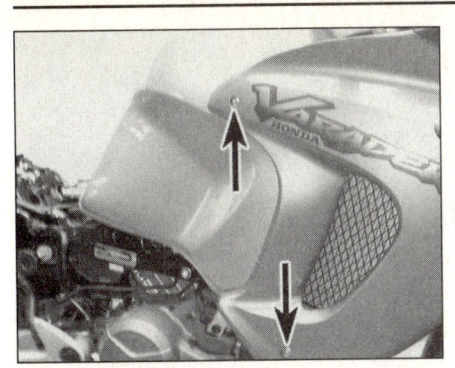

5.7 Unscrew the bolts (arrowed) securing the rear of the panel

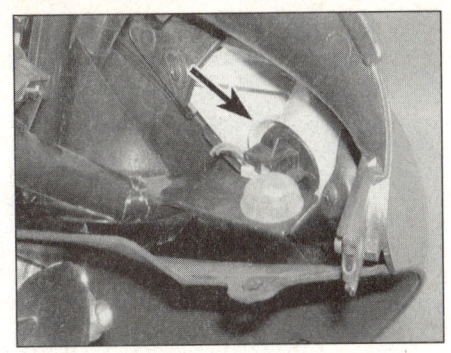

5.8 Disconnect the wiring connector (arrowed) when accessible

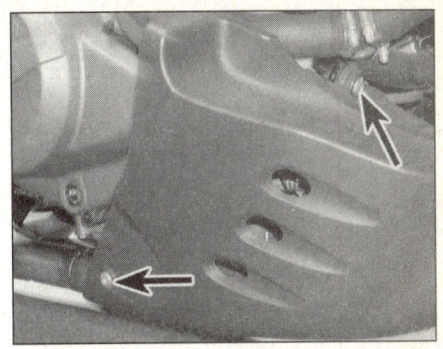

5.11 The belly-pan is secured by two bolts (arrowed) on each side

Fairing side panels

7 Remove the fasteners securing the side panel to the fairing and cockpit trim and displace the panel **(see illustration and illustrations 4.16a and 4.14)**.
8 Disconnect the turn signal wiring connector as it becomes accessible **(see illustration)**.
9 If required, release the trim clips securing each inner panel and remove the panels (see Section 1 for details on how to remove and install trim clips).
10 Installation is the reverse of removal.

Belly-pan

11 Remove the four bolts securing the belly-pan and draw it forward **(see illustration)**.
12 Installation is the reverse of removal.

Side covers

13 Remove the seat (see Section 2).
14 Remove the four bolts securing the side cover **(see illustration)**. Carefully push the lower rear section of the panel in to release it from the lower tab on the seat cowl, then draw it forwards to release it from the upper tab **(see illustration)**.
15 Installation is the reverse of removal. Make sure the tabs locate correctly.

Seat cowl

16 Remove the seat (see Section 2).
17 Disconnect the turn signal wiring connectors **(see illustration)**. Unscrew the bolts securing the luggage rack and remove the rack, taking care not to snag the wiring connectors as you draw them out **(see illustrations)**. Various different collars are

5.14a Unscrew the bolts (arrowed) . . .

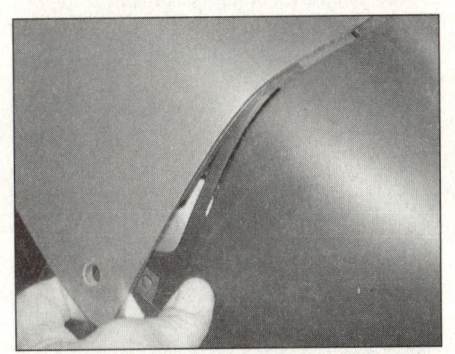

5.14b . . . and remove the panel as described

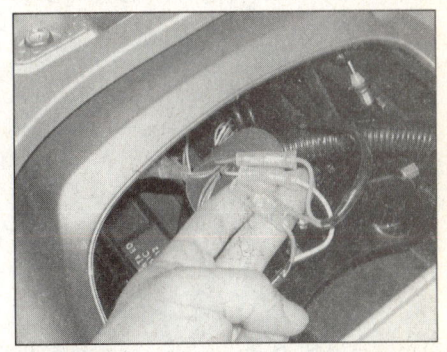

5.17a Disconnect the turn signal wiring connectors

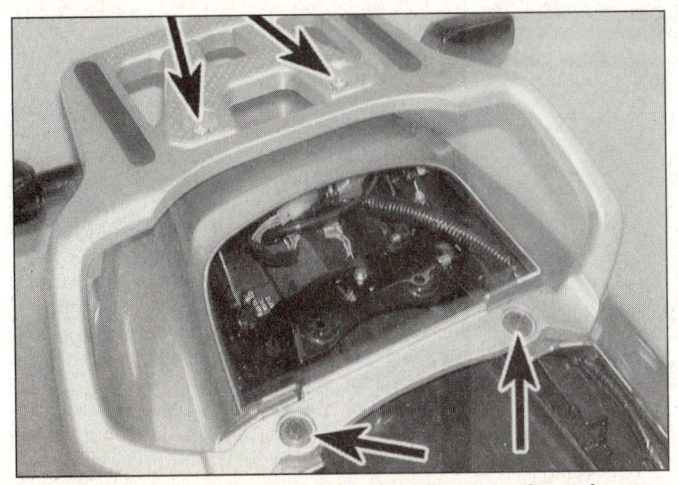

5.17b Unscrew the bolts (arrowed) and remove the rack . . .

5.17c . . . drawing the wiring out as you do

8•6 Bodywork

fitted with the bolts – note which fits where and take care not to lose any.

18 Detach the seat lock cable from the lock mechanism by sliding the outer cable sideways out of the holder and freeing the cable nipple from the arm **(see illustration)**.

19 Remove the two bolts securing the seat cowl on each side at the front **(see illustration 4.26a)**, and carefully draw it back off the bike **(see illustration)**.

20 Installation is the reverse of removal.

6 Fairing and body panels – XL-3 to 6 models

Fairing

1 Remove the windshield trim panels to access the screws **(see illustration 7.1a)**. Remove the screws and collars securing the windshield and detach it from the fairing, noting its position (there are two height settings) **(see illustration 7.1b)**.

2 Release the trim clips securing the headlight trim panel, then release the tabs and remove the panel **(see illustrations 7.2a and b)**.

3 Undo the screws and release the trim clips securing each cockpit trim panel, noting which fits where, and remove the panels **(see illustration)**.

4 Disconnect the headlight and sidelight wiring connectors **(see illustration 7.5)**.

5 Release the trim clips and undo the screws

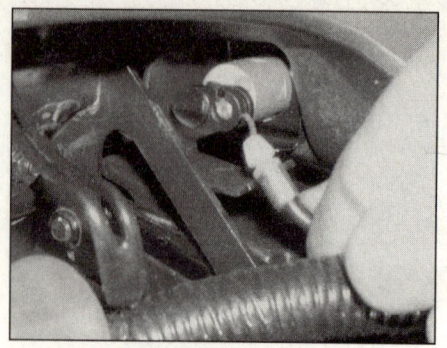

5.18 Release the seat lock cable as described . . .

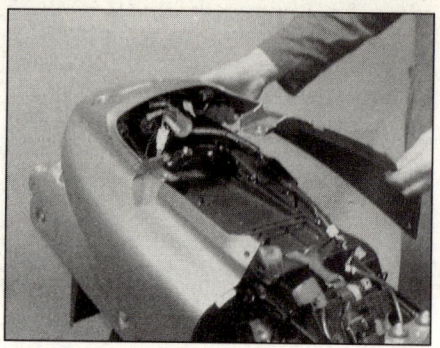

5.19 . . . Then unscrew the front bolts and remove the cowl

securing the fairing to the fairing side panels **(see illustrations 7.6a and b)**. Carefully draw the fairing forward and off the bike, noting how the pegs locate in the grommets **(see illustration 7.6c)**.

6 If required, remove the headlight from the fairing (see Chapter 9).

7 Installation is the reverse of removal. Make sure the wiring connectors are correctly and securely connected.

Fairing side panels

8 Release the trim clips securing the headlight trim panel, then release the tabs and remove the panel **(see illustrations 7.2a and b)**.

9 Remove the belly-pan (Step 14).

10 Release the inner panel trim clips and remove the panel **(see illustrations 7.11a and b)**.

11 Release the trim clip and undo the screws

securing the side panel to the fairing and cockpit trim panel **(see illustrations 7.6a and b and 6.3)**. Undo the screws securing the panel to the tank **(see illustration 7.3a)** and frame and displace the panel **(see illustrations 7.12a and b)**.

12 Disconnect the turn signal wiring connector as it becomes accessible **(see illustration 7.13)**.

13 Installation is the reverse of removal.

Belly-pan

14 Remove the six bolts securing the belly-pan and draw it forward **(see illustration)**.

15 Installation is the reverse of removal.

Side covers

16 The procedure is the same as XL-X, Y, 1 and 2 models – refer to Section 5.

Seat cowl

17 The procedure is the same as XL-X, Y, 1 and 2 models – refer to Section 5.

7 Fairing and body panels – XL-7 models onward

Fairing

1 Remove the windshield trim panels to access the screws **(see illustration)**. Remove the screws and collars securing the windshield and detach it from the fairing, noting its position (there are two height settings) **(see illustration)**.

2 Release the trim clips securing the headlight trim panel, then release the tabs and remove the panel **(see illustrations)**.

3 Unscrew the bolt securing the top of the fairing side panel to the fuel tank **(see illustration)**. Undo the screws and release the trim clips securing each cockpit trim panel, noting which fits where, then pull the fairing side panel away from the tank and remove the panel **(see illustrations)**.

4 Release the well-nut on each side and the tabs on the bottom of the instrument trim panel **(see illustration)**. Carefully pull the trim away at the top to release the tab then

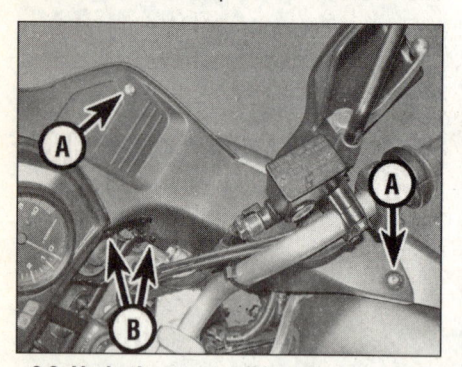

6.3 Undo the screws (A) and release the trim clips (B)

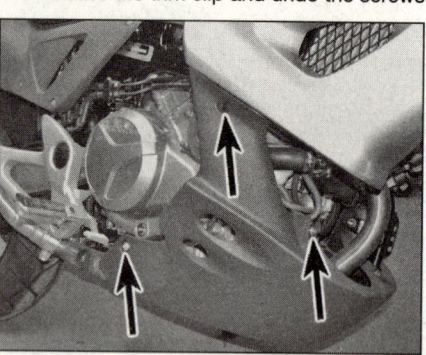

6.14 Unscrew the three bolts (arrowed) on each side

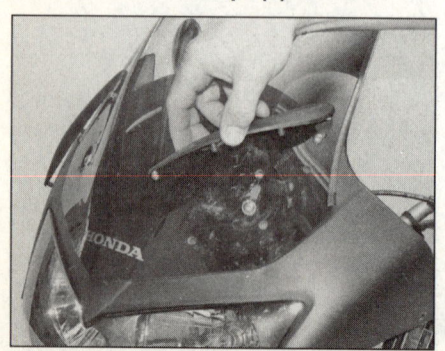

7.1a Remove the rubber trim pieces . . .

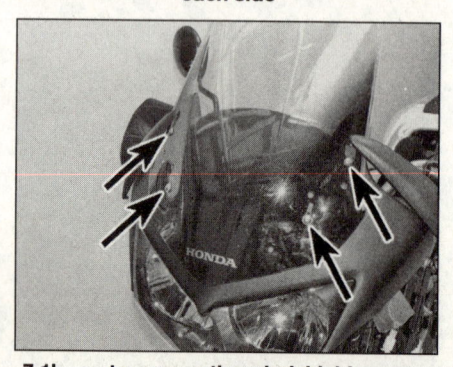

7.1b . . . to access the windshield screws (arrowed)

Bodywork 8•7

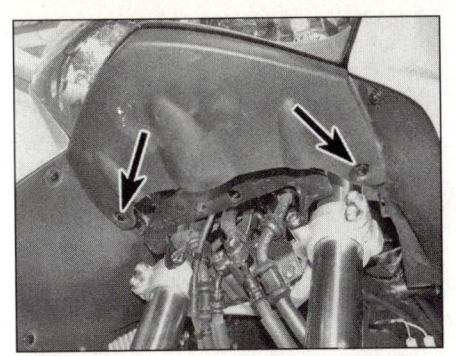

7.2a Release the trim clips (arrowed) . . .

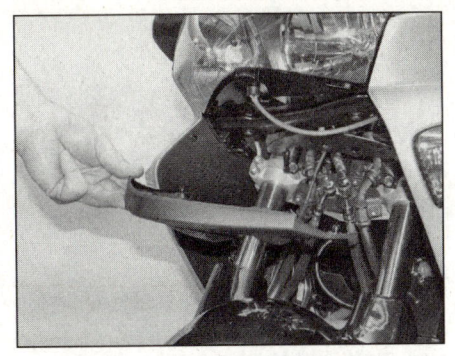

7.2b . . . and remove the panel

7.3a Unscrew the bolt (arrowed)

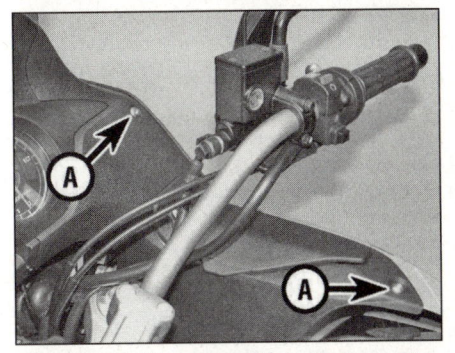

7.3b Undo the screws (A) and release the trim clips (B) . . .

7.3c . . . and remove the cockpit trim panel

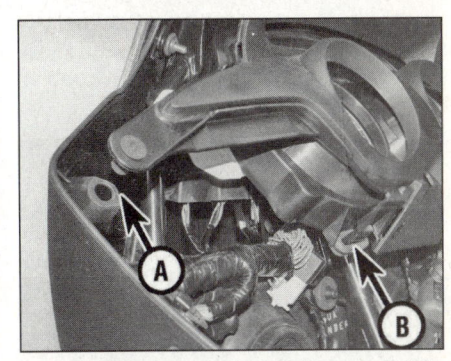

7.4a Release the well-nut (A) and tab (B) on each side . . .

lift it off the instrument cluster **(see illustrations)**.
5 Disconnect the headlight and sidelight wiring connectors **(see illustration)**.

6 Release the trim clips and undo the screws securing the fairing to the fairing side panels **(see illustrations)**. Carefully draw the fairing forward and off the bike, noting how

the pegs locate in the grommets **(see illustration)**.
7 If required, remove the headlight from the fairing (see Chapter 9).

7.4b . . . and the tab (arrowed) at the top . . .

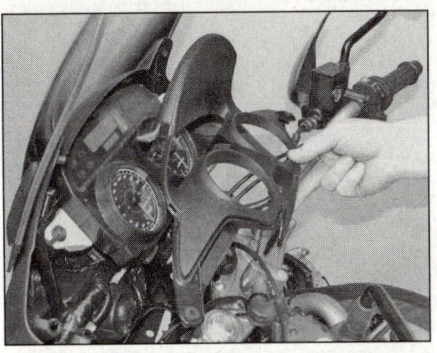

7.4c . . . and remove the instrument trim panel

7.5 Disconnect the wiring connectors

7.6a Release the trim clip (arrowed) on each side . . .

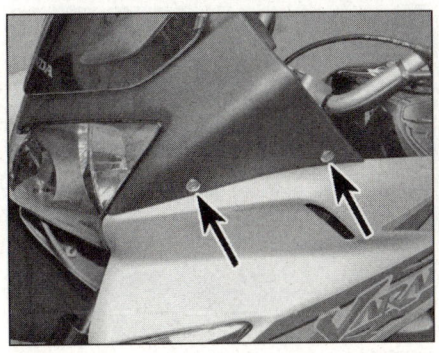

7.6b . . . and undo the screws (arrowed) on each side . . .

7.6c . . . then remove the fairing, noting how the pegs locate in the grommets

8•8 Bodywork

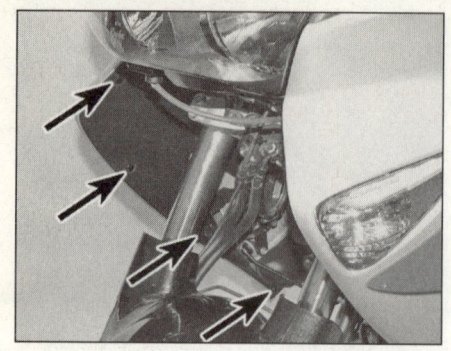

7.11a Release the trim clips (arrowed) . . .

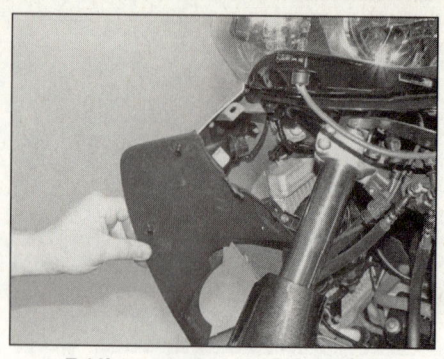

7.11b . . . and remove the panel

7.12a Undo the bottom screw (arrowed) . . .

8 Installation is the reverse of removal. Make sure the wiring connectors are correctly and securely connected.

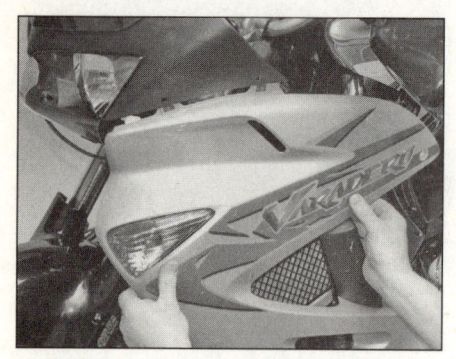

7.12b . . . then displace the panel . . .

Fairing side panels

9 Release the trim clips securing the headlight trim panel, then release the tabs and remove the panel **(see illustrations 7.2a and b)**.
10 Remove the relevant belly-pan trim panel (Step 15).
11 Release the inner panel trim clips and remove the panel **(see illustrations)**.
12 Release the trim clip and undo the screws securing the side panel to the fairing and cockpit trim panel **(see illustrations 7.6a and b and 7.3b)**. Undo the screws securing the panel to the tank **(see illustration 7.3a)** and frame and displace the panel **(see illustration)**.
13 Disconnect the turn signal wiring connector as it becomes accessible **(see illustration)**.

14 Installation is the reverse of removal.

Belly-pan

15 Release the trim clip and undo the two bolts securing each trim panel and remove them **(see illustration)**.
16 Undo the front bolts and remove the belly-pan, drawing the hoses out as you do **(see illustration)**.
17 Installation is the reverse of removal. Route the hoses through the hole **(see illustration)**.

Side covers

18 Remove the seat (Section 2).
19 Undo the two bolts, then release the tab at the back from the seat cowling and remove the cover **(see illustrations)**.

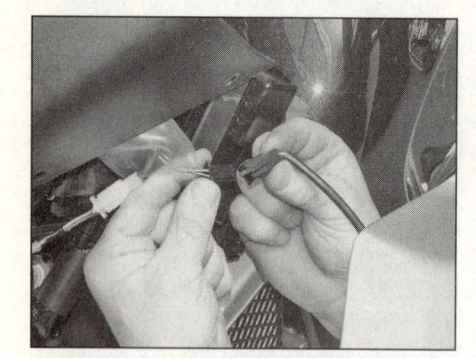

7.13 . . . and disconnect the wiring connector

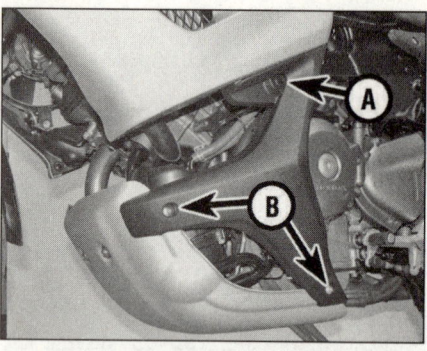

7.15 Release the trim clip (A) and undo the screws (B) to free the trim panel

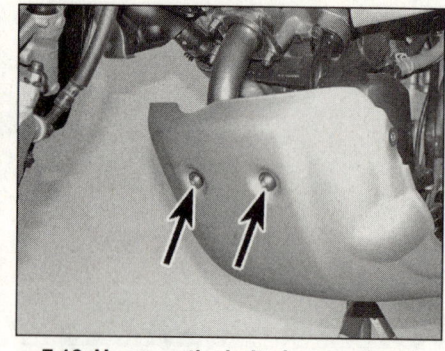

7.16 Unscrew the bolts (arrowed) and remove the belly-pan

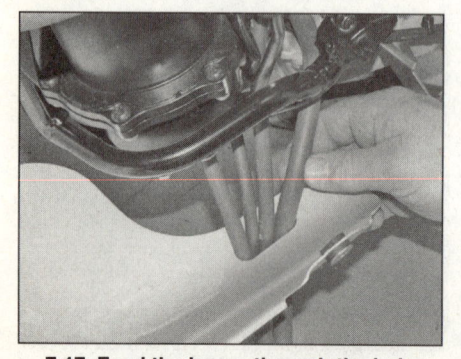

7.17 Feed the hoses through the hole

7.19a Unscrew the bolts (arrowed) . . .

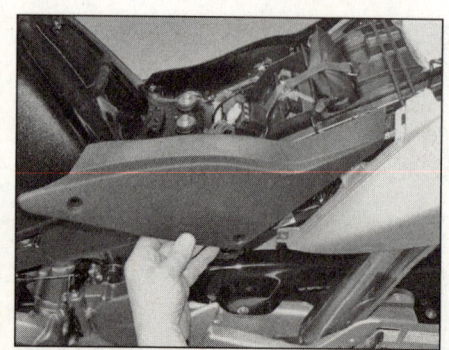

7.19b . . . and remove the cover

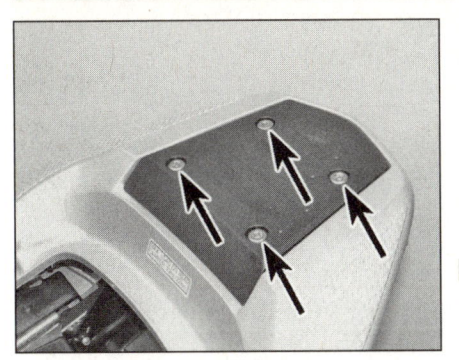

Bodywork 8•9

7.23a Unscrew the bolts (arrowed) and remove the cover

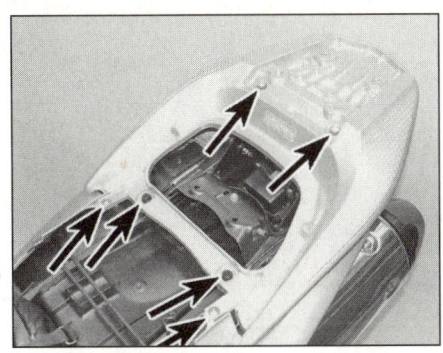

7.23b Unscrew the bolts (arrowed) . . .

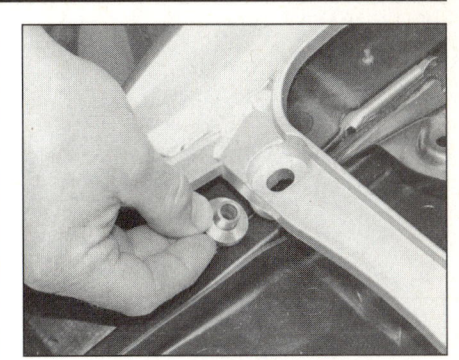

7.23c . . . noting the collars . . .

7.23d . . . and remove the rack

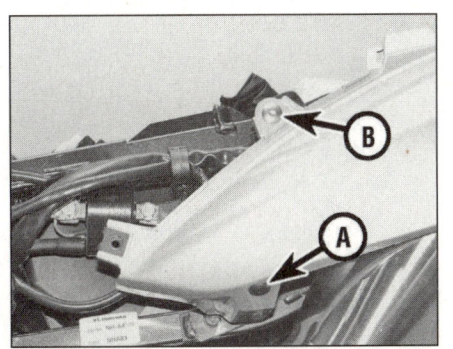

7.24a Release the trim clip (A) and undo the bolt (B)

7.24b Undo the bolts (arrowed)

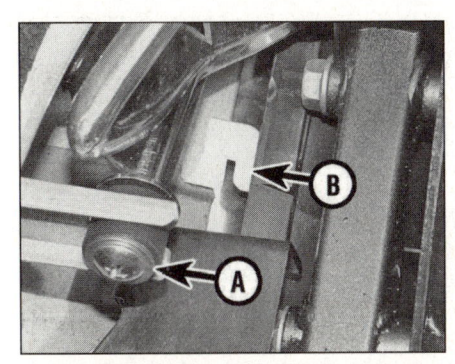

7.24c Slacken the screw (A) then release the tab (B) . . .

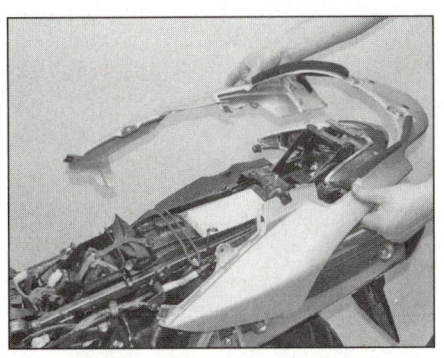

7.24d . . . and remove the cowl

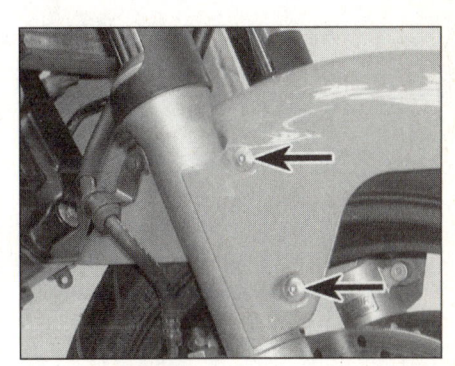

8.1 Unscrew the two bolts on each side and remove the mudguard

underside and unscrew the bolt on each front topside **(see illustration)**. Unscrew the two bolts at the back **(see illustration)**. Slacken the screws holding the side tabs in the grommets, then carefully pull the sides of the cowling away to release the tabs and hooks, and remove the cowl **(see illustrations)**.
25 Installation is the reverse of removal.

8 Front mudguard – removal and installation

Removal

VTR models

1 Unscrew the four bolts securing the mudguard to the fork sliders and remove the mudguard, noting how it fits **(see illustration)**.

XL models

2 Unscrew the six bolts securing the mudguard to its bracket and the fork sliders and remove the mudguard.
3 Unscrew the four bolts securing the bracket to the fork sliders and remove the bracket, noting how it fits.

Installation

4 Installation is the reverse of removal.

20 Installation is the reverse of removal – the short bolt goes at the front.

Seat cowl

21 Remove the seat (see Section 2).
22 Remove the side covers (Step 19).
23 Unscrew the bolts securing the luggage rack cover and remove the cover **(see illustration)**. Unscrew the bolts securing the luggage rack and remove the rack – note the collars with the rear bolts and the washers and collars on the underside with the front inner bolts **(see illustrations)**. Also note the collars for the rear bolts located in the seat cowling and remove them for safekeeping if required.
24 Release the trim clip on each front

Chapter 9
Electrical system

Contents

Alternator – check, removal and installation	32
Battery – charging	4
Battery – removal, installation, inspection and maintenance	3
Brake light switches – check and replacement	14
Brake/tail light bulb and licence plate bulb – replacement	9
Charging system – leakage and output test	31
Charging system testing – general information and precautions	30
Clutch switch – check and replacement	24
Diode – check and replacement	25
Electrical system – fault finding	2
Fuses – check and replacement	5
General information	1
Handlebar switches – check	20
Handlebar switches – removal and installation	21
Headlight aim – check and adjustment	see Chapter 1
Headlight assembly – removal and installation	8
Headlight bulb and sidelight bulb – replacement	7
Horn – check and replacement	26
Ignition (main) switch – check, removal and installation	19
Ignition system components	see Chapter 5
Instrument and warning light bulbs – replacement	17
Instrument cluster – removal and installation	15
Instruments and speed sensor – check and replacement	16
Lighting system – check	6
Neutral switch – check, removal and installation	22
Oil pressure switch – check, removal and installation	18
Regulator/rectifier – check and replacement	33
Sidestand switch – check and replacement	23
Starter motor – disassembly, inspection and reassembly	29
Starter motor – removal and installation	28
Starter relay – check and replacement	27
Tail light assembly and licence plate light – removal and installation	10
Turn signal assemblies – removal and installation	13
Turn signal bulbs – replacement	12
Turn signal circuit – check	11

Degrees of difficulty

Easy, suitable for novice with little experience	Fairly easy, suitable for beginner with some experience	Fairly difficult, suitable for competent DIY mechanic	Difficult, suitable for experienced DIY mechanic	Very difficult, suitable for expert DIY or professional

Specifications

Battery
Capacity
- VTR models .... 12 V, 10 Ah
- XL models .... 12 V, 12 Ah

Voltage
- Fully charged .... 13.0 to 13.2 V
- Uncharged .... below 12.3 V

Charging rate
- Normal .... 1.2 A for 5 to 10 hrs
- Quick
  - VTR models .... 5.0 A for 1 hr
  - XL models .... 5.0 A for 0.5 hr

Current leakage .... 0.1 mA (max)

Alternator
Stator coil resistance
- VTR models .... 0.2 to 0.5 ohms
- XL models .... 0.3 to 0.5 ohms

Output
- VTR models .... 0.280 kW @ 5000 rpm
- XL models .... 0.315 kW @ 5000 rpm

9•2 Electrical system

Regulator/rectifier
Regulated voltage output..................................... 13.5 to 15.5 V @ 5000 rpm

Starter motor
Brush length
    Standard.. 12.0 to 13.0 mm
    Service limit (min)....................................... 6.5 mm

Fuses
Main fuse (all models).. 30 A
Circuit fuses
    VTR models and XL-1, XL-2 models....................... 20A x 1, 10A x 5
    XL-3 models onward..................................... 20A x 3, 10A x 3
    XL-A4 models onward.................................... 20A x 3, 10A x 4, 30A x 2

Bulbs
Headlight
    VTR models... 60/55 W halogen
    XL models.. 60/55 W halogen x 2
Sidelight... 5 W
Brake/tail light.. 21/5 W x 2
Turn signal lights
    VTR models
        UK spec... 21 W x 4
        US spec
            Front... 32/3 cp x 2
            Rear.. 32 cp x 2
    XL models.. 21 W x 4
Instrument lights
    VTR-V, W, X and Y models................................ 1.7 W x 3
    VTR-1, 2, 3, 5 and 6 models............................. 1.4 W x 3
    XL-X, Y, 1 and 2 models................................. 1.7 W x 1, 3.4 W x 2
    XL-3 models onward..................................... LEDs
Turn signal indicator lights
    VTR-V, W, X and Y models................................ 1.7 W x 2
    VTR-1, 2, 3, 5 and 6 models............................. 1.4 W x 2
    XL-X, Y, 1 and 2 models................................. 3.4 W x 2
    XL-3 models onward..................................... LED x 2
High beam indicator light
    VTR-V, W, X and Y models................................ 1.7 W
    VTR-1, 2, 3, 5 and 6 models............................. 1.4 W
    XL-X, Y, 1 and 2 models................................. 1.7 W
    XL-3 models onward..................................... LED
Neutral indicator light
    VTR-V, W, X and Y models................................ 1.7 W
    VTR-1, 2, 3, 5 and 6 models............................. 1.4 W
    XL-X, Y, 1 and 2 models................................. 3.4 W
    XL-3 models onward..................................... LED
Oil pressure indicator light
    VTR-V, W, X and Y models................................ 1.7 W
    VTR-1, 2, 3, 5 and 6 models............................. 1.4 W
    XL-X, Y, 1 and 2 models................................. 3.4 W
    XL-3 models onward..................................... LED
Sidestand indicator light (VTR-V, W, X and Y models).......... 1.7 W
Fuel indicator light
    XL-X, Y, 1 and 2 models................................. 3.4 W
    XL-3 models onward..................................... LED
Fuel injection light (XL-3 models onward)..................... LED
Immobiliser light (where fitted).............................. LED
ABS indicator light (XL-VA4 models onward).................... LED

Torque settings
Oil pressure switch... 12 Nm
Neutral switch.. 12 Nm
Sidestand switch bolt....................................... 10 Nm
Alternator stator bolts..................................... 12 Nm
Alternator rotor bolt....................................... 157 Nm

Electrical system 9•3

1 General information

All models have a 12-volt electrical system charged by a three-phase alternator with a separate regulator/rectifier.

The regulator maintains the charging system output within the specified range to prevent overcharging, and the rectifier converts the ac (alternating current) output of the alternator to dc (direct current) to power the lights and other components, and to charge the battery. The alternator rotor is mounted on the left-hand end of the crankshaft.

The starter motor is mounted on the front of the engine. The starting system includes the motor, the battery, the relay and the various wires and switches. If the engine kill switch is in the RUN position and the ignition (main) switch is ON, the starter relay allows the starter motor to operate only if the transmission is in neutral (neutral switch on) or, if the transmission is in gear, if the clutch lever is pulled into the handlebar and the sidestand is up.

Note: *Keep in mind that electrical parts, once purchased, often cannot be returned. To avoid unnecessary expense, make very sure the faulty component has been positively identified before buying a replacement part.*

2 Electrical system – fault finding

Warning: *To prevent the risk of short circuits, the ignition (main) switch must always be OFF and the battery negative (–ve) terminal should be disconnected before any of the bike's other electrical components are disturbed. Don't forget to reconnect the terminal securely once work is finished or if battery power is needed for circuit testing.*

1 A typical electrical circuit consists of an electrical component, the switches, relays, etc. related to that component and the wiring

3.1a On VTR models, unclip the fusebox and displace it . . .

and connectors that hook the component to both the battery and the frame.

2 Before tackling any troublesome electrical circuit, first study the wiring diagram (see end of Chapter) thoroughly to get a complete picture of what makes up that individual circuit. Trouble spots, for instance, can often be narrowed down by noting if other components related to that circuit are operating properly or not. If several components or circuits fail at one time, chances are the fault lies in the fuse or earth (ground) connection, as several circuits often are routed through the same connections.

3 Electrical problems often stem from simple causes, such as loose or corroded connections or a blown fuse. Prior to any electrical fault finding, always visually check the condition of the fuse, wires and connections in the problem circuit. Intermittent failures can be especially frustrating, since you can't always duplicate the failure when it's convenient to test. In such situations, a good practice is to clean all connections in the affected circuit, whether or not they appear to be good. All of the connections and wires should also be wiggled to check for looseness which can cause intermittent failure.

4 If testing instruments are going to be utilised, use the wiring diagram to plan where you will make the necessary connections in order to accurately pinpoint the trouble spot.

5 The basic tools needed for electrical fault finding include a battery and bulb test circuit, a continuity tester, a test light, and a jumper wire. A multimeter capable of reading volts,

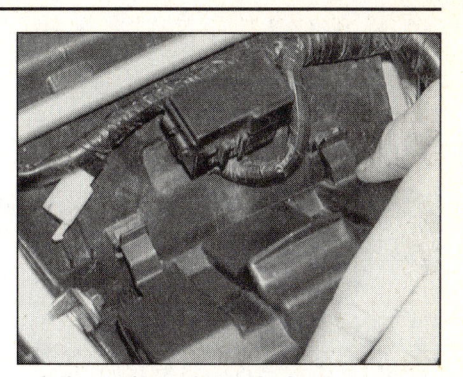

3.1b . . . then release the battery cover

ohms and amps is also very useful as an alternative to the above, and is necessary for performing more extensive tests and checks.

> **HAYNES HiNT** *Refer to Fault Finding Equipment in the Reference section for details of how to use electrical test equipment.*

3 Battery – removal, installation, inspection and maintenance

Caution: *Be extremely careful when handling or working around the battery. The electrolyte is very caustic and an explosive gas (hydrogen) is given off when the battery is charging.*

Removal and installation

1 Remove the seat (see Chapter 8). On VTR models, displace the fusebox from its mounting by releasing the clip, then release the catches on the battery cover and lift it up **(see illustrations)**. On XL models, release the battery strap.

2 Unscrew the negative (–ve) terminal bolt first and disconnect the lead from the battery **(see illustration)**. Lift up the red insulating cover to access the positive (+ve) terminal, then unscrew the bolt and disconnect the lead. Lift the battery from the bike **(see illustration)**.

3 On installation, clean the battery terminals and lead ends with a wire brush or knife and emery paper. Reconnect the leads, connecting the positive (+ve) terminal first.

> **HAYNES HiNT** *Battery corrosion can be kept to a minimum by applying a layer of petroleum jelly to the terminals after the cables have been connected. There are also dedicated sprays commercially available.*

4 Install the battery cover (VTR) or strap (XL) and the seat (see Chapter 8).

Inspection and maintenance

5 The battery fitted to the models covered in this manual is of the maintenance-free (sealed)

3.2a Disconnect the negative lead first, then the positive . . .

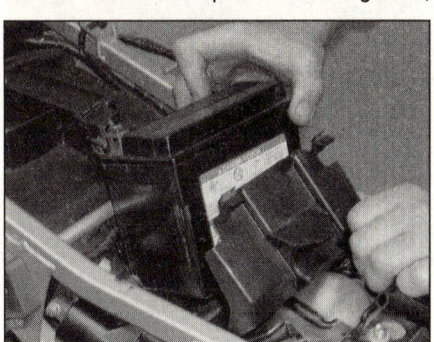

3.2b . . . and remove the battery

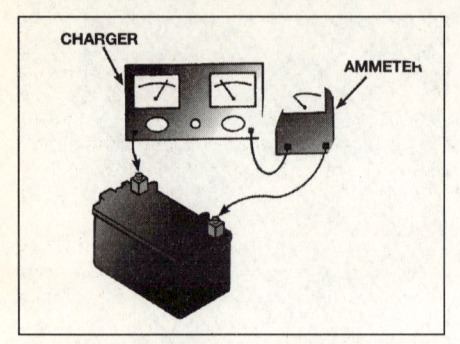

9•4 Electrical system

4.2 If the charger doesn't have ammeter built in, connect one in series as shown

DO NOT connect the ammeter between the battery terminals or it will be ruined

type, therefore requiring no regular maintenance. However, the following checks should still be regularly performed.

6 Check the battery terminals and leads for tightness and corrosion. If corrosion is evident, unscrew the terminal screws and disconnect the leads from the battery, disconnecting the negative (–ve) terminal first, and clean the terminals and lead ends with a wire brush or knife and emery paper. Reconnect the leads, connecting the negative (–ve) terminal last, and apply a thin coat of petroleum jelly to the connections to slow further corrosion.

7 Keep the battery case clean to prevent current leakage, which can discharge the battery over a period of time (especially when it sits unused). Wash the outside of the case with a solution of baking soda and water. Rinse the battery thoroughly, then dry it.

8 Look for cracks in the case and replace the battery with a new one if any are found. If acid has been spilled on the frame or battery box, neutralise it with a baking soda and water solution, dry it thoroughly, then touch up any damaged paint.

9 If the motorcycle sits unused for long periods of time, disconnect the cables from the battery terminals, negative (–ve) terminal first. Refer to Section 4 and charge the battery once every month to six weeks and leave it disconnected.

10 Check the condition of the battery by measuring the voltage present at the battery terminals. Connect the voltmeter positive (+ve) probe to the battery positive (+ve) terminal, and the negative (–ve) probe to the battery negative (–ve) terminal. When fully charged there should be more than 13.0 volts present. If the voltage falls below 12.3 volts the battery must be removed, disconnecting the negative (–ve) terminal first, and recharged as described below in Section 4.

4 Battery – charging

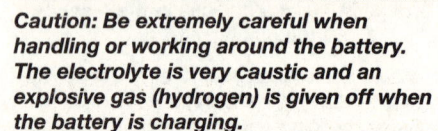

Caution: Be extremely careful when handling or working around the battery. The electrolyte is very caustic and an explosive gas (hydrogen) is given off when the battery is charging.

1 Remove the battery (see Section 3). Connect the charger to the battery, making sure that the positive (+ve) lead on the charger is connected to the positive (+ve) terminal on the battery, and the negative (–ve) lead is connected to the negative (–ve) terminal.

2 Honda recommend that the battery is charged at the rate specified at the beginning of the Chapter. Exceeding this figure can cause the battery to overheat, buckling the plates and rendering it useless. Few owners will have access to an expensive current-controlled charger, so if a normal domestic charger is used check that, after a possible initial peak, the charge rate falls to a safe level **(see illustration)**. If the battery becomes hot during charging **stop**. Further charging will cause damage. **Note:** *In emergencies the battery can be charged at a higher rate of around 5.0 amps for a period of 1 hour (VTR models) or 0.5 hour (XL models). However, this is not recommended and the low amp charge is by far the safer method of charging the battery.*

3 If the recharged battery discharges rapidly if left disconnected it is likely that an internal short caused by physical damage or sulphation has occurred. A new battery will be required. A sound item will tend to lose its charge at about 1% per day.

4 Install the battery (see Section 3).

5 If the motorcycle sits unused for long periods of time, charge the battery once every month to six weeks and leave it disconnected.

5 Fuses – check and replacement

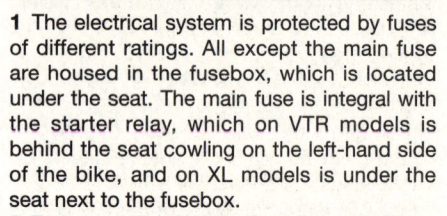

1 The electrical system is protected by fuses of different ratings. All except the main fuse are housed in the fusebox, which is located under the seat. The main fuse is integral with the starter relay, which on VTR models is behind the seat cowling on the left-hand side of the bike, and on XL models is under the seat next to the fusebox.

2 To access the fuses, remove the seat (see Chapter 8) and unclip the fusebox lid **(see illustrations)**. To access the main fuse, on VTR models remove the seat cowling (see Chapter 8), on XL models remove the seat

5.2a Unclip the lid . . .

5.2b . . . to access the fuses on VTR models

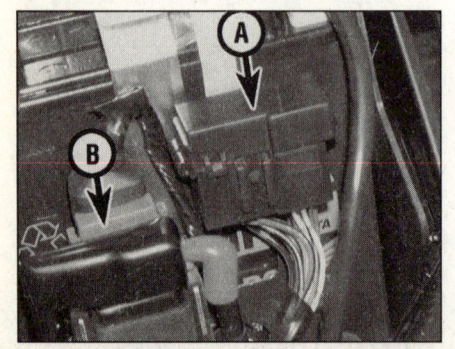

5.2c Fusebox (A), starter relay wiring connector (B) – XL models without ABS

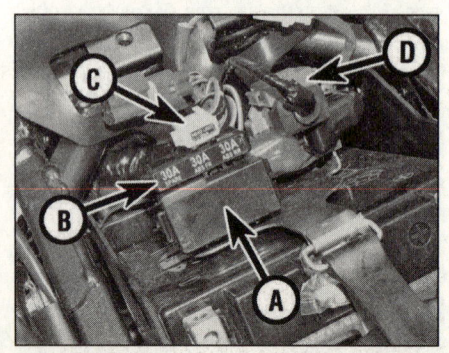

5.2d Fusebox (A), ABS modulator fuses (B), headlight fuse (C) and starter relay connector (D) – XL ABS models

5.2e Disconnect the wiring connector . . .

Electrical system 9•5

5.2f ... to access the main fuse (arrowed)

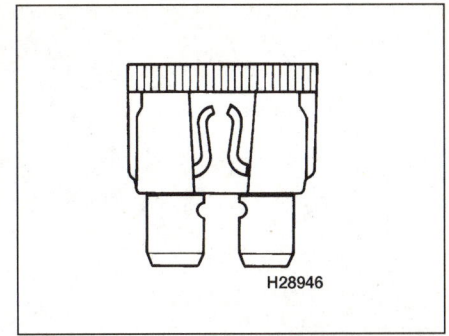

5.3 A blown fuse can be identified by a break in its element

(see Chapter 8), and disconnect the starter relay wiring connector **(see illustrations)**.

3 The fuses can be removed and checked visually. If you can't pull the fuse out with your fingertips, use a pair of suitable pliers. A blown fuse is easily identified by a break in the element **(see illustration)**. Each fuse is clearly marked with its rating and must only be replaced by a fuse of the correct rating. A spare fuse of each rating is housed in the fusebox, and a spare main fuse is housed in the bottom of the starter relay. If a spare fuse is used, always replace it so that a spare of each rating is carried on the bike at all times.

⚠ **Warning: Never put in a fuse of a higher rating or bridge the terminals with any other substitute, however temporary it may be. Serious damage may be done to the circuit, or a fire may start.**

4 If a fuse blows, be sure to check the wiring circuit very carefully for evidence of a short-circuit. Look for bare wires and chafed, melted or burned insulation. If the fuse is replaced before the cause is located, the new fuse will blow immediately.

5 Occasionally a fuse will blow or cause an open-circuit for no obvious reason. Corrosion of the fuse ends and fusebox terminals may occur and cause poor fuse contact. If this happens, remove the corrosion with a wire brush or emery paper, then spray the fuse end and terminals with electrical contact cleaner.

6 Lighting system – check

1 The battery provides power for operation of the headlight, tail light, brake light and instrument cluster lights. If none of the lights operate, always check battery voltage before proceeding. Low battery voltage indicates either a faulty battery or a defective charging system. Refer to Section 3 for battery checks and Sections 30 and 31 for charging system tests. Also, check the condition of the fuses.

Headlight

2 If the headlight fails to work, first check the fuse (see Section 5), and then the bulb (see Section 7). If they are both good, use jumper wires to connect the bulb directly to the battery terminals. If the light comes on, the problem lies in the wiring, the relay(s) (XL models), or one of the switches in the circuit. Refer to Section 20 for the switch testing procedures, and also the wiring diagrams at the end of this Chapter.

3 On XL models, if either the high beam or low beam relay is suspected of being faulty, substitute it with the other relay. Remove the fairing to access the relays – they are mounted on the fairing bracket **(see illustrations)**. If the beam in question then works, the faulty relay must be replaced with a new one. If not, check for voltage at the white/blue terminal of the headlight wiring connector for the low beam, and the blue/black terminal of the wiring connector for the high beam. If no voltage is present, check the wiring between the relays and the connectors (see the wiring diagrams at the end of the Chapter). If the wiring is good, check for voltage at the white/blue terminal of the low beam relay and the blue/black terminal of the high beam relay. If no voltage is present, check the wiring between the relays and the switches (see the wiring diagrams at the end of the Chapter). If the wiring is good, check for voltage at the black/red terminal on each relay, and at the switch. If voltage is present, and the wiring between the relay and the headlight is good, replace the relay with a new one. If no voltage is present, check the wiring between the relay or switch and the fusebox (see the wiring diagrams at the end of the Chapter).

6.3a Headlight relay (arrowed) – XL-X, Y, 1 and 2 models

Tail light

4 If the tail light fails to work, check the bulb, the bulb terminals and the wiring connectors first, then the fuse, then check for battery voltage at the brown terminal on the supply side of the tail light wiring connector. If voltage is present, check the earth (ground) circuit for an open or poor connection.

5 If no voltage is indicated, check the wiring between the tail light and the switch, then check the switch. Also check the ignition switch.

Brake light

6 If the brake light fails to work, check the bulb, the bulb terminals and the wiring connectors first, then the fuse, then check for battery voltage at the green/yellow terminal on the supply side of the tail light wiring connector, with the brake lever pulled in or the pedal depressed. If voltage is present, check the earth (ground) circuit for an open or poor connection.

7 If no voltage is indicated, check the brake light switches, then the wiring between the light and the switches.

8 See Section 14 for brake switch check and Section 9 for tail light bulb replacement.

Instrument and warning lights

9 See Section 17 for instrument and warning light bulb replacement.

Turn signals

10 See Section 11 for turn signal circuit check.

7 Headlight bulb and sidelight bulb – replacement

Note: *The headlight bulb is of the quartz-halogen type. Do not touch the bulb glass as skin acids will shorten the bulb's service life. If the bulb is accidentally touched, it should be wiped carefully when cold with a rag soaked in methylated spirit and dried before fitting.*

⚠ **Warning: Allow the bulb time to cool before removing it if the headlight has just been on.**

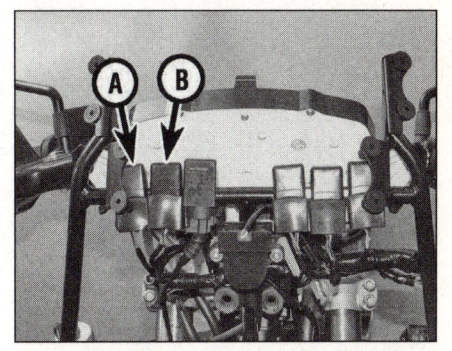

6.3b Headlight relays (arrowed – hi beam A, lo beam B) – XL-3 models onward

9•6 Electrical system

7.1a Disconnect the wiring connector . . .

7.1b . . . and remove the dust cover

Headlight

1 Disconnect the wiring connector from the back of the headlight and remove the rubber dust cover, noting how it fits **(see illustrations)**.
2 Release the bulb retaining clip, noting how it fits, then remove the bulb **(see illustrations)**.

> **HAYNES HiNT** *Always use a paper towel or dry cloth when handling new bulbs to prevent injury if the bulb should break and to increase bulb life.*

3 Fit the new bulb, bearing in mind the information in the **Note** above. Make sure the tabs on the bulb fit correctly in the slots in the bulb housing, and secure it in position with the retaining clip.
4 Install the dust cover, making sure it is correctly seated and with the TOP mark at the top, and connect the wiring connector.
5 Check the operation of the headlight.

Sidelight

VTR models

6 Undo the screws securing the sidelight lens and remove the lens **(see illustration)**.
7 Carefully pull the bulb out of the bulbholder **(see illustration)**.
8 Fit the new bulb into the bulbholder, then install the lens. Make sure the rubber seal is correctly seated and is not damaged, deformed or deteriorated, and replace it with a new one if necessary.
9 Check the operation of the sidelight.

XL models

10 Unscrew the two bolts securing the shield to the bottom yoke and remove it.
11 Pull the bulbholder out of its socket in the base of the headlight, then carefully pull the bulb out of the holder **(see illustrations)**.
12 Install the new bulb in the bulbholder, then install the bulbholder by pressing it in. Make sure the rubber cover is correctly seated.
13 Check the operation of the sidelight. Install the shield.

8 Headlight assembly – removal and installation

Removal

1 Remove the fairing (see Chapter 8).
2 Undo the four screws securing the headlight assembly to the fairing and remove the headlight, noting how it fits **(see illustrations)**.

Installation

3 Installation is the reverse of removal. Make sure all the wiring is correctly connected and secured. Check the operation of the headlight and sidelight. Check the headlight aim (see Chapter 1).

7.2a Release the clip . . .

7.2b . . . and remove the bulb

7.6 Undo the screws (arrowed) and remove the lens . . .

7.7 . . . then pull the bulb out of the holder

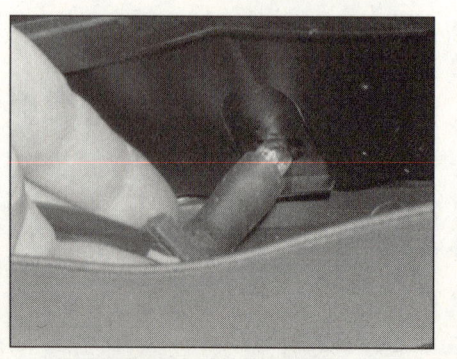

7.11a Remove the bulbholder . . .

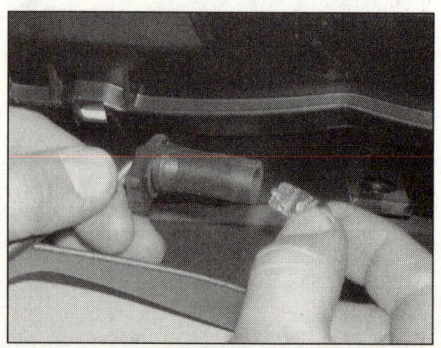

7.11b . . . and pull out the bulb (fairing shown removed for clarity)

Electrical system 9•7

8.2a Headlight mounting screws (arrowed) – VTR models

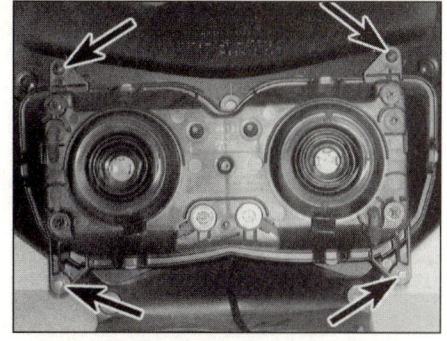

8.2b Headlight mounting screws (arrowed) – XL models

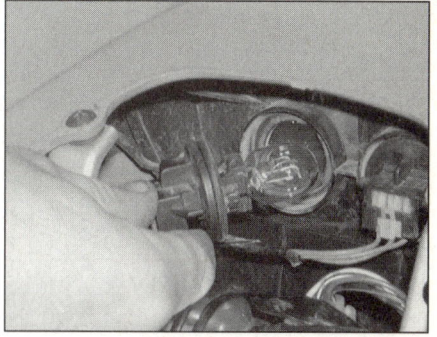

9.2 Remove the bulbholder from the taillight . . .

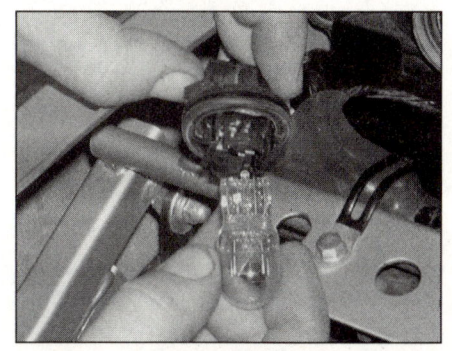

9.3 . . . and the bulb from the holder

9.7a Undo the screws and remove the lens . . .

9.7b . . . then remove the bulb

9 Brake/tail light bulb and licence plate bulb – replacement

Brake/tail light bulb

VTR models and XL-X to XL-6 models

1 Remove the seat (see Chapter 8).
2 Turn the bulbholder anti-clockwise and withdraw it from the tail light **(see illustration)**.

HAYNES HiNT *It is a good idea to use a paper towel or dry cloth when handling the new bulb to prevent injury if the bulb should break and to increase bulb life.*

3 On VTR models, carefully pull the bulb out of the socket **(see illustration)**. Install the new bulb by pushing it into the socket – the bulb can be installed either way round. Check the condition of the rubber seal around the bulbholder and replace the bulbholder with a new one if necessary – the seal is not available separately.
4 On XL models, push the bulb into the holder and twist it anti-clockwise to remove it. Check the socket terminals for corrosion and clean them if necessary. Line up the pins of the new bulb with the slots in the socket, then push the bulb in and turn it clockwise until it locks into place. **Note:** *The pins on the bulb are offset so it can only be installed one way.*

5 Fit the bulbholder into the tail light and turn it clockwise to secure it.
6 Install the seat.

XL-7 models onward

7 Undo the tail light lens screws and remove the lens **(see illustration)**. Push the bulb into the holder and twist it anti-clockwise to remove it **(see illustration)**. Check the socket terminals for corrosion and clean them if necessary. Line up the pins of the new bulb with the slots in the socket, then push the bulb in and turn it clockwise until it locks into place. Fit the tail light lens.

Licence plate light bulb

VTR US models and XL-X to XL-6 models

8 Displace the light from the mudguard – there is no need to disconnect the wiring connector (see Section 10).

9 Unscrew the nuts on the back of the light and detach the lens cover and lens.
10 Push the bulb into the holder and twist it anti-clockwise to remove it. Check the socket terminals for corrosion and clean them if necessary. Line up the pins of the new bulb with the slots in the socket, then push the bulb in and turn it clockwise until it locks into place. **Note:** *It is a good idea to use a paper towel or dry cloth when handling the new bulb to prevent injury if the bulb should break and to increase bulb life.*
11 Install the light (see Section 10).

XL-7 models onward

12 Undo the two screws and remove the cover **(see illustration)**.
13 Pull the bulb out of the socket and replace it with a new one **(see illustration)**.
14 Fit the lens and tighten the screws.
15 Check the operation of the light.

9.12 Undo the screws and remove the cover . . .

9.13 . . . then remove the bulb

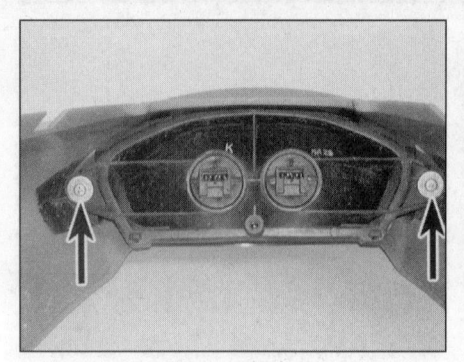

9•8 Electrical system

10.2 The taillight unit is secured by two screws (arrowed)

10.3a Either disconnect the wiring connector . . .

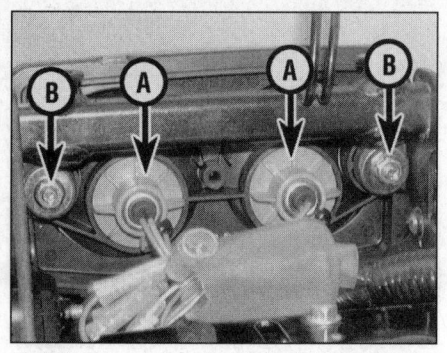

10.3b . . . or remove the bulbholders (A). Taillight mounting nuts (B)

10 Tail light assembly and licence plate light – removal and installation

Removal

Tail light

1 Remove the seat cowling (see Chapter 8, Section 4).
2 On VTR models, remove the screws securing the tail light assembly and carefully withdraw it from the cowling **(see illustration)**. If required and not already done, turn the bulbholders anti-clockwise and withdraw them from the tail light.
3 On XL-X to XL-6 models, either disconnect the tail light wiring connector or turn the bulbholders anti-clockwise and withdraw them from the tail light **(see illustrations)**. Unscrew the nuts securing the tail light assembly and carefully remove it.
4 On XL-7 models onward, disconnect the tail light wiring connector **(see illustration)**. Unscrew the bolts securing the tail light assembly, noting the wiring clamp, and carefully remove it.

Licence plate light – US VTR models and all XL models

5 Remove the seat (see Chapter 8).
6 Trace the wiring and disconnect it at the connector.
7 On US VTR models, unscrew the bolts securing the licence plate bracket and light, then remove them and separate the light from the bracket.
8 On XL-X, Y and 1 to 6 models, unscrew the bolts securing the licence plate light and remove the light **(see illustration)**.
9 On XL-7 models onward, unscrew the nuts on the inside of the rear mudguard and remove the license plate light.

Installation

10 Installation is the reverse of removal. Check the operation of the lights.

11 Turn signal circuit – check

Note: *On US VTR models the front turn signals also function as running lights and have dual filament bulbs. When checking for faults, refer to the wiring diagram at the end of this Chapter.*

1 The battery provides power for operation of the turn signal lights, so if they do not operate, always check the battery voltage first. Low battery voltage indicates either a faulty battery or a defective charging system. Refer to Section 3 for battery checks and Sections 30 and 31 for charging system tests. Also, check the fuse (see Section 5) and the switch (see Section 20).
2 Most turn signal problems are the result of a burned-out bulb or corroded socket. This is especially true when the turn signals function properly in one direction, but fail to flash in the other direction. Check the bulbs and the sockets (see Section 12).
3 If the bulbs and sockets are good, check the relay. On VTR models, the relay is mounted

10.4 Disconnect the wiring connector (A, but hidden), then undo the bolts (B)

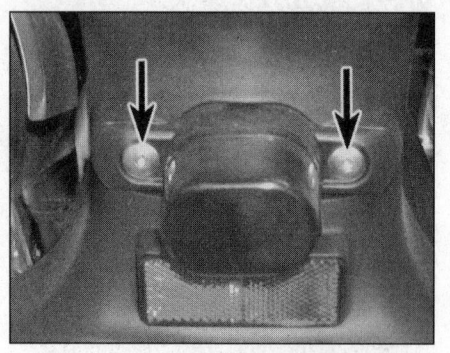

10.8 Licence plate light mounting bolts (arrowed) – XL models

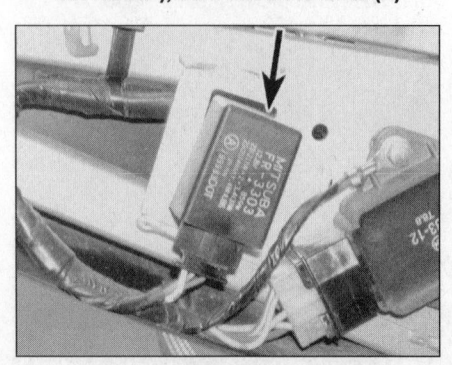

11.3a Turn signal relay (arrowed) – VTR models

11.3b Turn signal relay (arrowed) – XL-X to XL-2 models

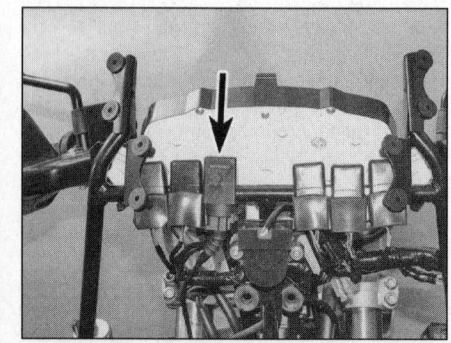

11.3c Turn signal relay (arrowed) – XL-3 models onward

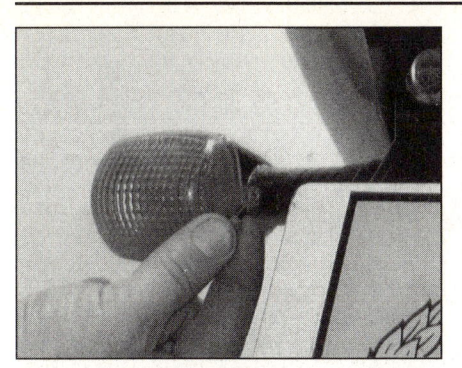

Electrical system 9•9

12.1 Remove the screw and detach the lens...

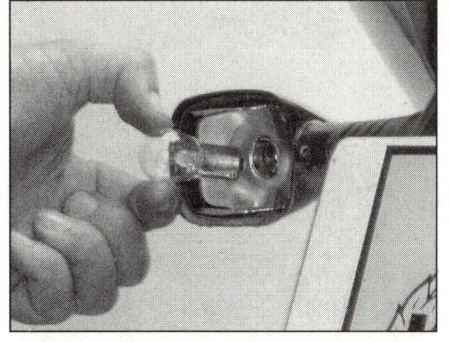

12.2 ...then remove the bulb from the holder

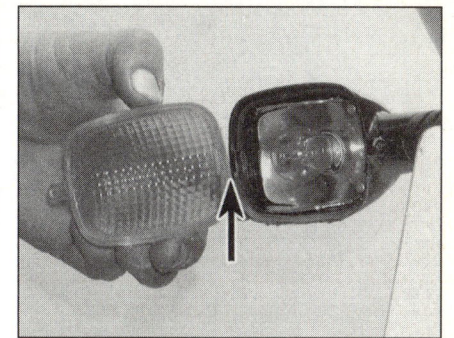

12.3 Locate the tab in the slot in the housing (arrowed)

behind the seat cowling on the right-hand side of the bike **(see illustration)** – remove the cowling for access (see Chapter 8, Section 4). On XL models, the relay is mounted on the fairing bracket **(see illustrations)** – remove the fairing for access (see Chapter 8).
4 Disconnect the relay wiring connector and check for battery voltage at the white/green wire terminal on the loom side of the connector with the ignition ON. Turn the ignition OFF when the check is complete.
5 If no power was present at the relay, check the wiring from the relay to the ignition (main) switch (via the fusebox) for continuity.
6 If power was present at the relay, use the appropriate wiring diagram at the end of this Chapter and check the wiring and connectors between the relay, turn signal switch and turn signal lights for continuity. Also check the green wire for continuity to earth (ground). If the wiring and switch are sound, replace the relay with a new one.
7 On XL-7 models onward if the hazard warning light circuit does not work, short between the red/green and grey wire terminal on the loom side of the relay wiring connector using a jumper wire **(see illustration 11.3c)**. Turn the ignition ON and check the hazard lights – if they work replace the relay with a new one. If not the fault lies in the wiring, switch or connectors.

12 Turn signal bulbs – replacement

1 To replace the bulbs on all turn signals on VTR models and the rear signals on XL-X to XL-6 models, remove the screw securing the lens and detach the lens, noting how it fits **(see illustration)**. Check the lens rubber gasket and renew it if damaged, deformed or deteriorated.
2 Push the bulb into the holder and twist it anti-clockwise to remove it **(see illustration)**. Check the socket terminals for corrosion and clean them if necessary. Line up the pins of the new bulb with the slots in the socket, then push the bulb in and turn it clockwise until it locks into place. **Note:** *It is a good idea to use a paper towel or dry cloth when handling the new bulb to prevent injury if the bulb should break and to increase bulb life.*
3 Fit the lens onto the holder. Use a new rubber gasket if required, and make sure it is properly seated and not pinched by the lens. Locate the tab on the inner end of the lens in the slot in the housing **(see illustration)**.
4 To replace the front turn signal bulbs on XL models: on XL-3 models onward release the trim clips securing the headlight trim panel, then release the tabs and remove the panel **(see illustrations)**. On all XL models release the trim clips securing the inner panel to the fairing side panel and detach the panel, noting how it fits **(see illustrations)**.
5 Turn the bulbholder anti-clockwise and withdraw it from the lens **(see illustration)**. On XL-X, Y, 1 and 2 models carefully pull the bulb out of the socket. On XL-3 models onward push the bulb into the holder and twist it anti-

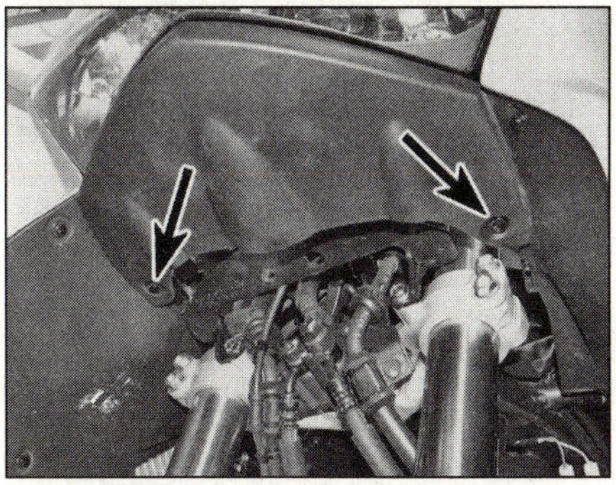

12.4a Release the trim clips (arrowed)...

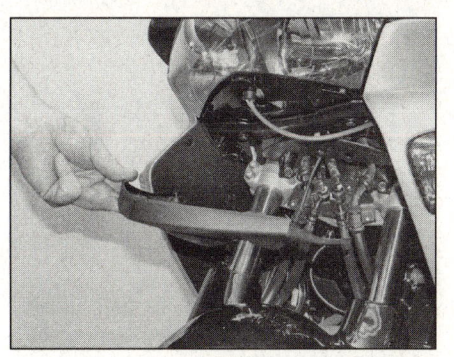

12.4b ...and remove the headlight trim panel

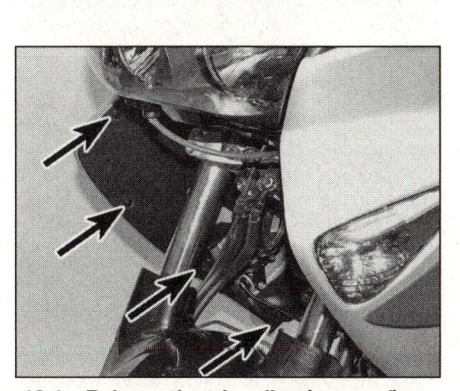

12.4c Release the trim clips (arrowed)...

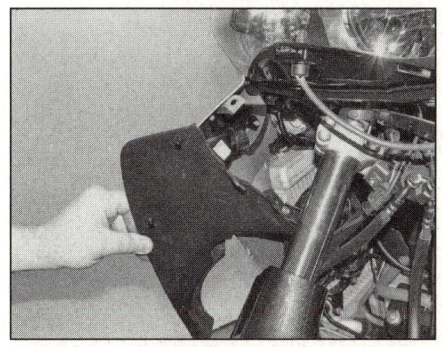

12.4d ...and remove the inner panel

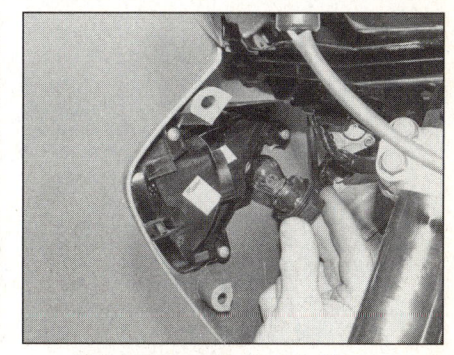

12.5a Release the bulbholder...

9•10 Electrical system

12.5b . . . then remove the bulb

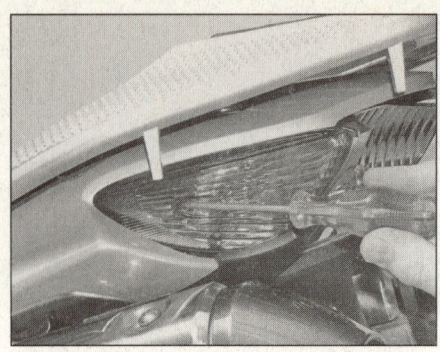

12.7a Undo the screws and remove the lens . . .

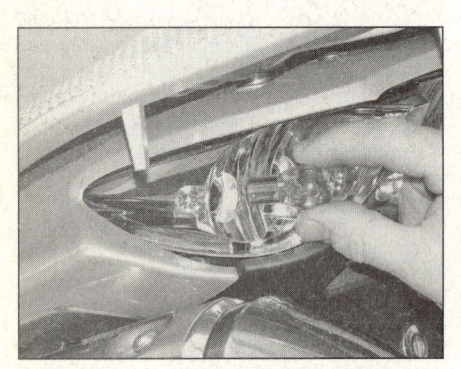

12.7b . . . then remove the bulb

13.1a Front turn signal wiring connectors – VTR models

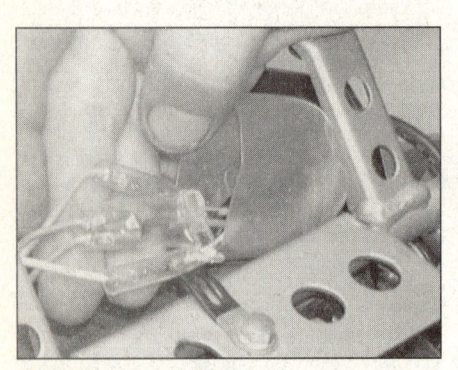

13.1b Rear turn signal wiring connectors – VTR models

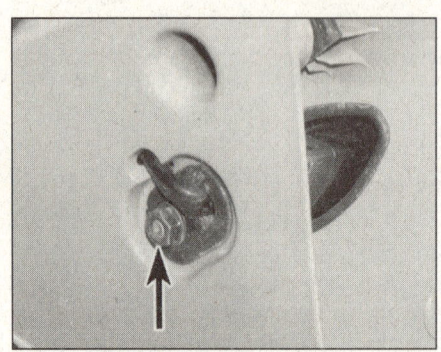

13.2 Front turn signal mounting nut and plate (arrowed) – VTR models

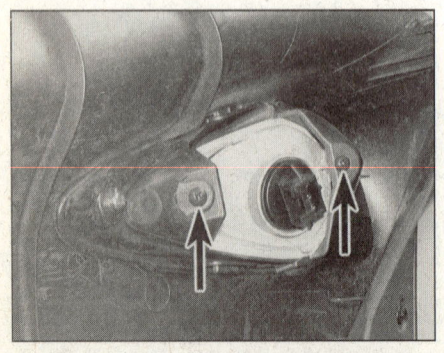

13.3 Front turn signal mounting screws (arrowed) – XL models

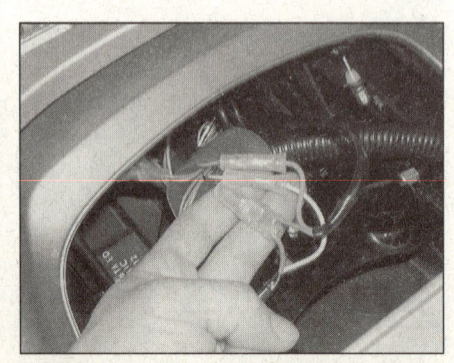

13.4a Rear turn signal wiring connectors – XL models

clockwise to remove it **(see illustration)**. Check the socket terminals for corrosion and clean them if necessary. On XL-X, Y, 1 and 2 models fit the new bulb by pushing it into the socket – the bulb can be installed either way round. On XL-3 models onward line up the pins of the new bulb with the slots in the socket, then push the bulb in and turn it clockwise until it locks into place. Check the condition of the rubber seal around the bulbholder and replace the bulbholder with a new one if necessary – the seal is not available separately.

6 Fit the bulbholder back into the lens, making sure it is securely held, then install the inner panel and fit the trim clips (see Step 4).

7 To replace the rear signal bulbs on XL-7 models onward, undo the tail light lens screws and remove the lens **(see illustration 9.7a)**. Undo the turn signal light lens screw and remove the lens **(see illustration)**. Push the bulb into the holder and twist it anti-clockwise to remove it **(see illustration)**. Check the socket terminals for corrosion and clean them if necessary. Line up the pins of the new bulb with the slots in the socket, then push the bulb in and turn it clockwise until it locks into place. Fit the turn signal lens, then fit the tail light lens.

13 Turn signal assemblies – removal and installation

Removal

VTR models

1 Disconnect the turn signal wiring connectors and draw the wiring through to the stem. On the front turn signals, the connectors are on the inside of the fairing **(see illustration)**. On the rear turn signals, remove the seat (see Chapter 8) – the connectors are inside a rubber boot which is secured by a clip **(see illustration)**.

2 Unscrew the nut securing the stem to either the inside of the fairing or rear mudguard and remove the mounting plate **(see illustration)**. Remove the assembly, noting how it fits. Note the mounting rubbers fitted with the front assemblies.

XL models

3 To remove a front turn signal, remove the fairing side panel (see Chapter 8). Remove the screws securing the turn signal to the inside of the panel and detach the signal, noting how it fits **(see illustration)**. Remove the bulbholder from the lens if not already done.

4 To remove a rear turn signal on XL-X to XL-6 models, remove the seat (see Chapter 8). Disconnect the turn signal wiring connectors – they are inside a rubber boot which is secured by a clip **(see illustration)**. Carefully draw the wiring through to the stem, then

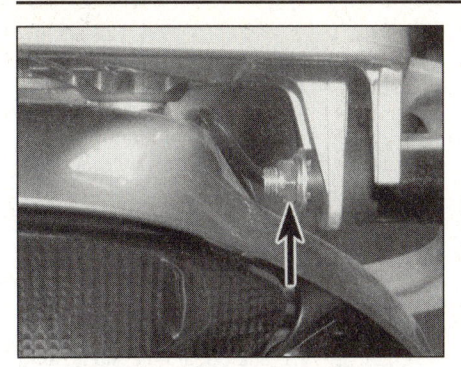

Electrical system 9•11

13.4b Rear turn signal mounting nut (arrowed) – XL models

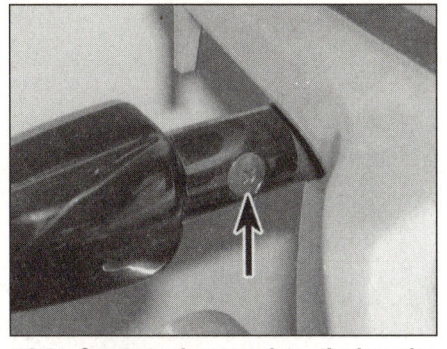

13.4c Separate the stem from the base by removing the screw (arrowed)

14.2 Front brake switch wiring connectors (arrowed) – VTR models

unscrew the nut securing the stem to the luggage rack and remove it, noting the washer and rubber damper **(see illustration)**. If required, separate the turn signal from the mounting base by removing the screw **(see illustration)**.

5 On XL-7 models onward the rear turn signals are an integral part of the tail light unit – refer to Section 10.

Installation

6 Installation is the reverse of removal. Check the operation of the turn signals.

14 Brake light switches – check and replacement

Circuit check

1 Before checking the switches, and if not already done, check the brake light circuit (see Section 6, Step 6).
2 The front brake light switch is mounted on the underside of the brake master cylinder. Disconnect the wiring connectors from the switch **(see illustration)**. Using a continuity tester, connect the probes to the terminals of the switch. With the brake lever at rest, there should be no continuity. With the brake lever applied, there should be continuity. If the switch does not behave as described, replace it with a new one.
3 The rear brake light switch is mounted on the inside of the frame on the right-hand side, above the brake pedal **(see illustrations)**. Remove the seat (VTR models) or right-hand side cover (XL models) to access the wiring connector (see Chapter 8). Trace the wiring from the switch and disconnect it at the connector **(see illustrations)**. On XL models equipped with ABS the rear modulator blocks access to the wiring connector, so you need to displace it (see Chapter 7– there is no need to detach the hoses) **(see illustration)**.
4 Using a continuity tester, connect the probes to the terminals on the switch side of the wiring connector. With the brake pedal at rest, there should be no continuity. With the brake pedal applied, there should be continuity. If the switch does not behave as described, replace it with a new one.
5 If the switches are good, check for voltage at the white/green wire terminal on the connector with the ignition switch ON – there should be battery voltage. If there's no voltage present, check the wiring between the switch and the ignition switch via the fusebox (see the wiring diagrams at the end of this Chapter).

Switch replacement

Front brake lever switch

6 The switch is mounted on the underside of

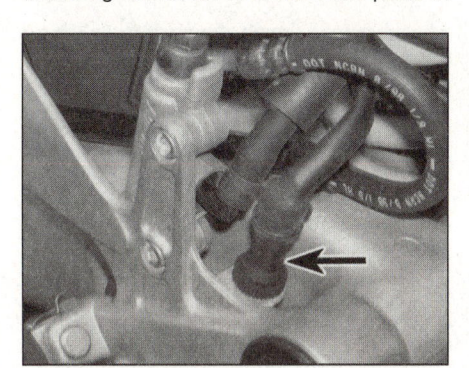

14.3a Rear brake light switch (arrowed) – VTR models

14.3b Rear brake light switch (arrowed) – XL models

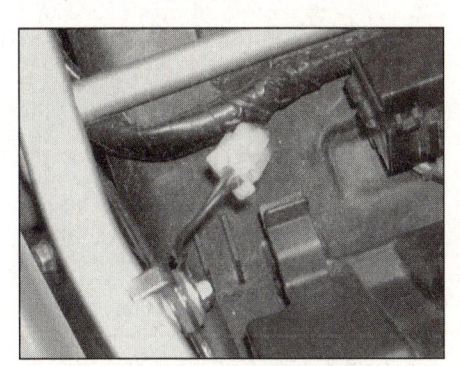

14.3c Rear brake light switch wiring connector – VTR models

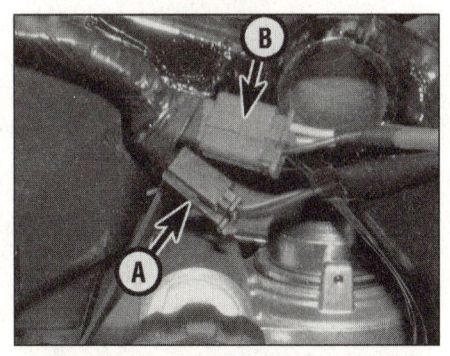

14.3d Rear brake light switch wiring connector (A), speed sensor wiring connector (B) – XL models

14.3e On XL models with ABS displace the rear modulator to access the wiring connector in the rubber boot (arrowed)

9•12 Electrical system

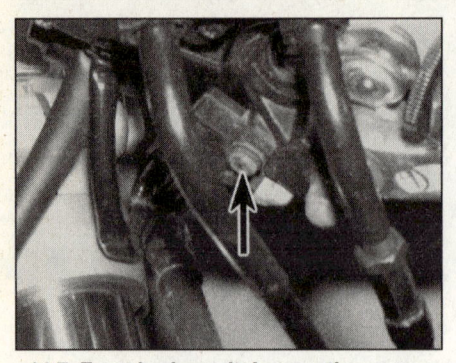

14.7 Front brake switch mounting screw (arrowed) – VTR models

15.2a Unscrew the bolts (arrowed) . . .

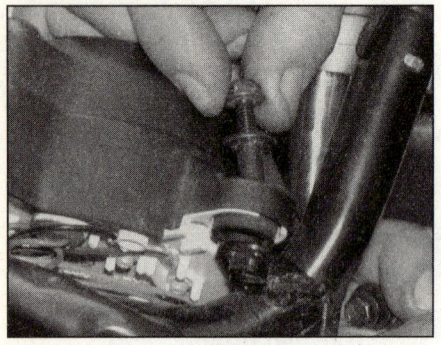

15.2b . . . noting the collars

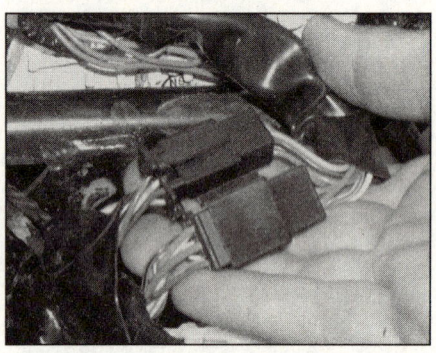

15.3 Disconnect the wiring connectors

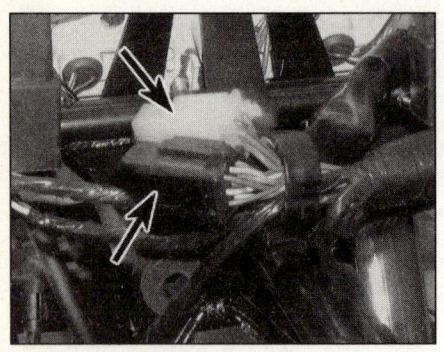

15.5a Disconnect the wiring connectors (arrowed) . . .

15.5b . . . and release the peg from the grommet (arrowed)

15.5c The instrument cluster is secured by two bolts (arrowed)

15.6a Disconnect the wiring connector

the brake master cylinder. Disconnect the wiring connectors from the switch **(see illustration 14.2)**.

7 Remove the single screw securing the switch to the bottom of the master cylinder and remove the switch **(see illustration)**.

8 Installation is the reverse of removal. The switch isn't adjustable.

Rear brake pedal switch

9 The rear brake light switch is mounted on the inside of the frame on the right-hand side, above the brake pedal **(see illustration 14.3a or 14.3b)**. Remove the seat (VTR models) or right-hand side cover (XL models) to access the wiring connector (see Chapter 8). Trace the wiring from the switch and disconnect it at the connector **(see illustration 14.3c or d)**. On XL models equipped with ABS the rear modulator blocks access to the wiring connectors, so you need to displace it (see Chapter 7– there is no need to detach the hoses) **(see illustration 14.3e)**.

10 Detach the lower end of the switch spring from the brake pedal, then release the switch from its mounting and remove it.

11 Installation is the reverse of removal. Make sure the brake light is activated just before the rear brake pedal takes effect. If adjustment is necessary, hold the switch and turn the adjusting ring on the switch body until the brake light is activated when required.

15 Instrument cluster – removal and installation

Removal

VTR models

1 The fairing can remain *in situ*, but to avoid the possibility of damage should a tool slip, remove it (see Chapter 8).

2 Unscrew the three bolts securing the instrument cluster and displace it from the bracket **(see illustration)**. Note the collars fitted in the rubber mounts **(see illustration)**.

3 Disconnect the wiring connectors and remove the instrument cluster **(see illustration)**.

XL models

4 Remove the fairing (see Chapter 8).

5 On XL-X, Y, 1 and 2 models disconnect the wiring connectors and release the wiring from the clip **(see illustration)**. Also release the peg on the back of the cluster from the grommet on the bracket **(see illustration)**. Unscrew the two bolts securing the instrument cluster and remove the cluster **(see illustration)**. Note the collars fitted in the rubber mounts.

6 On XL-3 models onward pull the rubber off the wiring connector, then disconnect the connector **(see illustration)**. Unscrew the two bolts securing the instrument cluster **(see**

Electrical system 9•13

16.5b Free the peg from the grommet

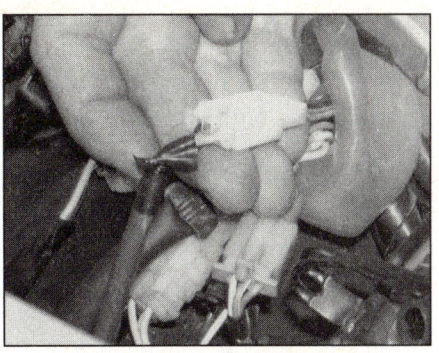

16.2 Speed sensor wiring connector – VTR models

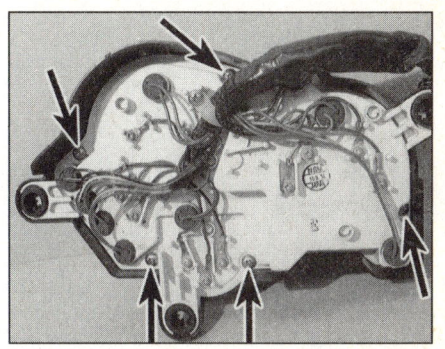

16.5a On VTR models, remove the screws (arrowed) . . .

illustration 15.5c), then free the peg from the grommet and remove the cluster **(see illustration)**. Note the collars fitted in the rubber mounts.

Installation

7 Installation is the reverse of removal. Remove the collars from the rubber mounts and check them for damage, deformation and deterioration. Replace them with new ones if necessary, and install the collars. Make sure that the wiring connectors are correctly routed and secured.

16 Instruments and speed sensor – check and replacement

Speedometer and odometer

Check

1 First check the fuse (see Section 5), and that the battery is fully charged.
2 To check the speedometer, on VTR models, remove the seat (see Chapter 8). On XL models, remove the right-hand side cover (see Chapter 8). Disconnect the speed sensor wiring connector and check for loose or broken connections **(see illustration for VTR models or 14.3d/e for XL models)**. With the ignition switch ON, check for battery voltage between the black/brown and green/black wire terminals on the wiring loom side of the connector. If there is no voltage, refer to the wiring diagrams and check the circuit. If there is voltage, on VTR models displace the instrument cluster (see Section 15), and on XL models remove the fairing (see Chapter 8). Disconnect the instrument cluster wiring connector(s) and check for loose or broken connections, then reconnect it/them **(see illustration 15.3, 15.5a or 15.6a)**. With the ignition switch ON, check for battery voltage between the black/brown and green/black speedometer wire terminals on the back of the instrument cluster. If there is no voltage, refer to the wiring diagrams and check the wiring. If there is voltage, with the ignition switch OFF check for continuity between the pink/green wire terminal on the loom side of the speed sensor wiring connector and the pink/green wire terminal on the rear of the instrument cluster. If there is no continuity, check the circuit for loose or broken connections. If there is continuity, connect a voltmeter between the pink/green and green/black wire terminals on the rear of the instrument cluster. With the machine on an auxiliary stand and the ignition switch ON, turn the rear wheel by hand and check that a fluctuating voltage reading between 0 and 5 volts is obtained. If a reading is obtained, the speedometer is probably faulty. Special instruments are required to properly check the operation of the speedometer. Take the machine to a Honda dealer service department or other qualified repair shop for diagnosis. If no reading is obtained, and the wiring is good, then the sensor is faulty.
3 To check the odometer, on VTR models displace the instrument cluster (see Section 15), and on XL models remove the fairing (see Chapter 8). With the ignition switch OFF, check for battery voltage between the red/green and green/black odometer wire terminals on the back of the instrument cluster. There should be voltage at all times. If no voltage is present, check the wires for continuity and solid connections. If voltage is present, the odometer is probably faulty. Special instruments are required to properly check the operation of the odometer. Take the machine to a Honda dealer service department or other qualified repair shop for diagnosis.

Replacement

4 Remove the instrument cluster (see Section 15).
5 Remove the casing screws from the back of the cluster and lift off the front cover assembly **(see illustrations)**.
6 On VTR-V, W, X and Y models, remove the screws securing the speedometer and its wires and detach the wires, noting which fits

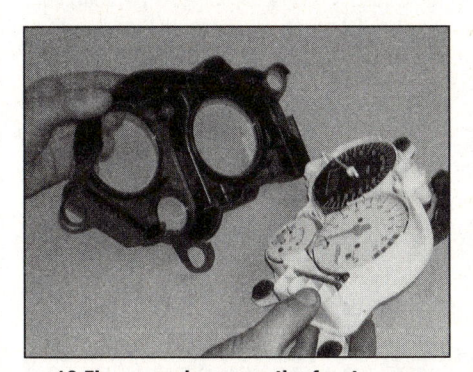

16.5b . . . and remove the front cover

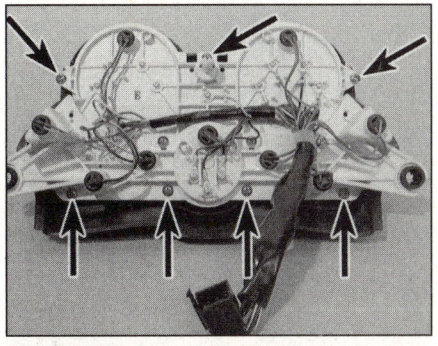

16.5c On XL-X, Y, 1 and 2 models, remove the screws (arrowed) and remove the front cover

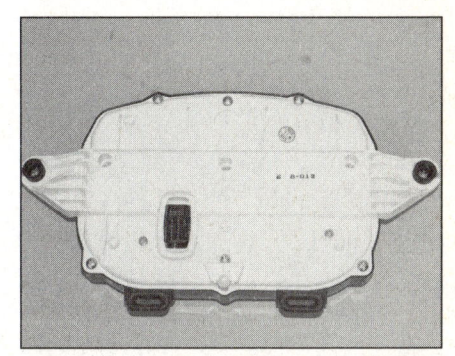

16.5d On XL-3 models onward undo the screws on the back, noting that some screws also secure the PCB in the casing

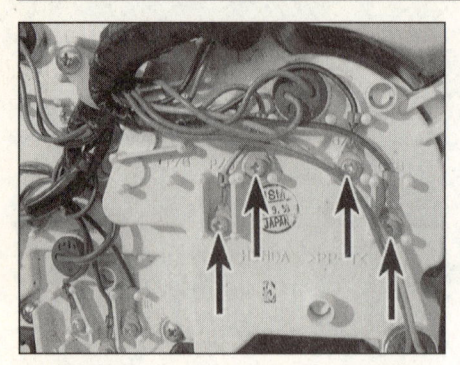

9•14 Electrical system

16.6 Speedometer screws (arrowed) – VTR models

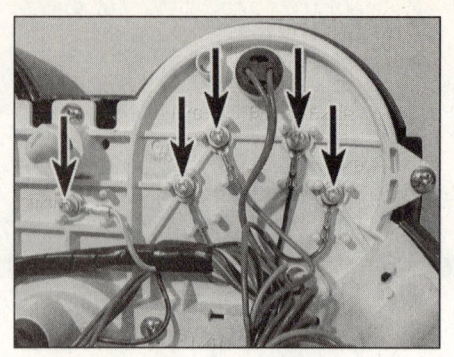

16.7a Speedometer screws (arrowed) – XL-X, Y, 1 and 2 models

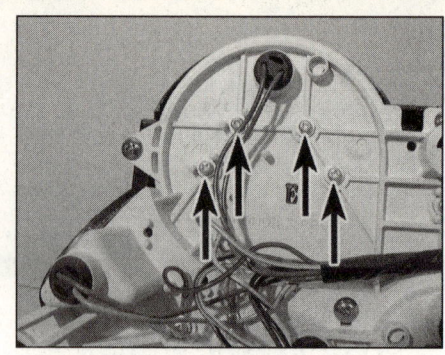

16.7b Tachometer screws (arrowed) – XL-X, Y, 1 and 2 models

where **(see illustration)**. Carefully withdraw the speedometer from the front. On all other VTR models carefully lift the instrument cluster PCB from the housing and replace it with a new one – individual components are not available.

7 On XL models, remove the screws securing the speedometer and its wires and the tachometer and its wires and detach the wires, noting which fits where **(see illustrations)**. Carefully withdraw the speedometer/tachometer assembly from the front.

8 Installation is the reverse of removal. Make sure the wiring is correctly connected. The terminal identification should be marked on the casing.

Speed sensor

Check

9 See Step 2.

Replacement

10 On VTR models, remove the seat (see Chapter 8). On XL models, remove the right-hand side cover (see Chapter 8, Section 4).

11 Trace the wiring from the speed sensor, which is mounted on the crankcase behind the cylinders, and disconnect it at the connector **(see illustration 16.2 or 14.3d)**. On XL models equipped with ABS the rear modulator blocks access to the wiring connector, so you need to displace it (see Chapter 7– there is no need to detach the hoses) **(see illustration 14.3e)**.

12 Unscrew the sensor mounting bolts and remove the sensor, noting the earth strap

secured by the right-hand bolt **(see illustration)**. Remove and discard its O-ring as a new one must be used. Plug the sensor orifice with clean rag to prevent anything falling into the engine.

13 Installation is the reverse of removal, using a new O-ring **(see illustration)**. Do not forget to secure the earth strap with the right-hand bolt **(see illustration)**.

Tachometer

Check – VTR models

14 Displace the instrument cluster (see Section 15), and remove the seat (see Chapter 8). Disconnect the ignition control unit (ICU) wiring connector (see Chapter 5). Check for battery voltage between the black/brown and green/black tachometer wire terminals on the back of the instrument cluster with the ignition ON. If no voltage is present, refer to the wiring diagrams and check the wiring and connectors. Also check for continuity in the yellow/green wire between the ignition control unit wiring connector and its terminal on the back of the instrument cluster. If there is no continuity there is a break in the wire or faulty connector. Refer to the wiring diagrams and trace and rectify the fault. If continuity exists, either the tachometer or the ignition control unit could be faulty. On V, W, X and Y models, with the ignition ON and the kill switch in the RUN position, there should be battery voltage at the yellow/green wire terminal on the back of the cluster. If no voltage is measured and the wire is good, then it is likely the unit is

faulty. If the correct voltage is measured, then it is likely the tachometer is faulty. Take the machine to a Honda dealer service department or other qualified repair shop for further diagnosis. On all other models, with the engine running, there should be an input voltage from the ICU to the tachometer at the yellow/green wire terminal. Special instruments are required to properly check this voltage, and the use of other instruments could lead to false readings. If no voltage is measured and the wire is good, then it is likely the ICU is faulty. If a voltage is measured, then it is likely the tachometer is faulty. Take the machine to a Honda dealer service department or other qualified repair shop for further diagnosis.

Check – XL models

15 Remove the seat and the fairing (see Chapter 8). Disconnect the ignition control unit wiring connector (see Chapter 5). Check for continuity in the yellow/green wire between the ignition control unit wiring connector and its terminal on the back of the instrument cluster. If there is no continuity there is a break in the wire or faulty connector. Refer to the wiring diagrams and trace and rectify the fault. If continuity exists, either the tachometer or the ignition control unit could be faulty. With the engine running, there should be an input voltage from the control unit to the tachometer at the yellow/green wire terminal. Special instruments are required to properly check this voltage, and the use of other instruments could lead to false readings. If no voltage is measured and the wire is good, then it is likely

16.12 Speed sensor mounting bolts (arrowed)

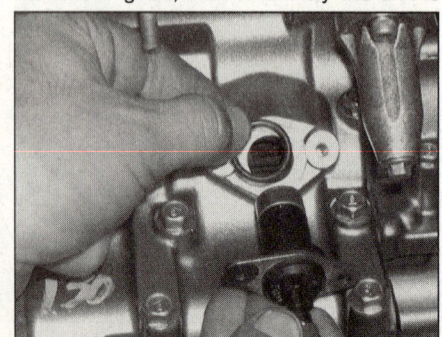

16.13a Install the sensor using a new O-ring

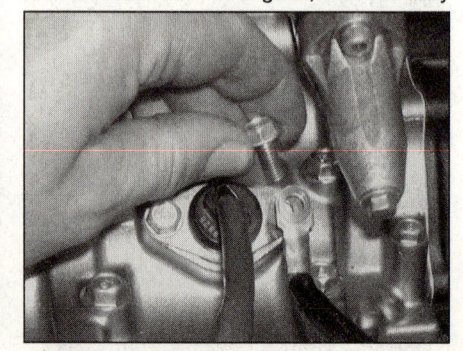

16.13b Secure the earth lead with the right-hand bolt

Electrical system 9•15

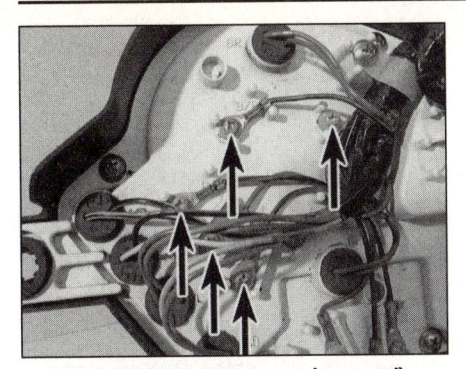

16.18 Tachometer screws (arrowed) – VTR models

the control unit is faulty. If a voltage is measured, then it is likely the tachometer is faulty. Take the machine to a Honda dealer service department or other qualified repair shop for further diagnosis.

Replacement

16 Remove the instrument cluster (see Section 15).
17 Remove the casing screws from the back of the cluster and lift off the front cover assembly **(see illustrations 16.5a and 16.5b or 16.5c or 16.5d)**.
18 On VTR-V, W, X and Y models, remove the screws securing the tachometer and its wires and detach the wires, noting which fits where **(see illustration)**. Carefully withdraw the tachometer from the front. On all other VTR models carefully lift the instrument cluster PCB from the housing and replace it with a new one – individual components are not available.
19 On XL-X, Y, 1 and 2 models, remove the screws securing the speedometer and its wires and the tachometer and its wires and detach the wires, noting which fits where **(see illustrations 16.7a and b)**. Carefully withdraw the speedometer/tachometer assembly from the front. On all later XL models carefully lift the instrument cluster PCB from the housing and replace it with a new one – individual components are not available.
20 Installation is the reverse of removal. Make sure the wiring is correctly connected. The terminal identification for the wiring should be marked on the casing.

Coolant temperature gauge

Check

21 See Chapter 3.

Replacement

22 Remove the instrument cluster (see Section 15).
23 Remove the casing screws from the back of the cluster and lift off the front cover assembly **(see illustrations 16.5a and 16.5b or 16.5c or 16.5d)**.
24 On VTR-V, W, X and Y models and XL-X, Y, 1 and 2 models remove the screws securing the temperature gauge and its wires and detach the wires, noting which fits where **(see illustrations)**. Carefully withdraw the gauge from the front. On all other models carefully lift the instrument cluster PCB from the housing and replace it with a new one – individual components are not available.
25 Installation is the reverse of removal. Make sure the wiring is correctly connected. The terminal identification should be marked on the casing.

Clock – XL-X, Y, 1 and 2 models

Check

26 Remove the fairing (see Chapter 8). With the ignition switch OFF, check for battery voltage between the red/green and green/black clock wire terminals on the back of the instrument cluster. There should be voltage at all times. If no voltage is present, check the wires for continuity and solid connections. If voltage is present, the clock is faulty.

Replacement

27 Remove the instrument cluster (see Section 15).
28 Remove the casing screws from the back of the cluster and lift off the front cover assembly **(see illustration 16.5c)**.
29 Remove the screws securing the speedometer and its wires and the tachometer and its wires and detach the wires, noting which fits where **(see illustration 16.7a and 16.7b)**. Carefully withdraw the speedometer/tachometer assembly from the front. Remove the clock from the tachometer.
30 Installation is the reverse of removal. Make sure the wiring is correctly connected. The terminal identification should be marked on the casing.

Fuel warning light or gauge and level sensor

Check

31 See Chapter 4A.

Replacement

32 On models with a warning light bulb see Section 17 for replacement of the bulb.
33 On VTR-1 to 6 models with a gauge, remove the instrument cluster (see Section 15). Remove the casing screws from the back of the cluster and lift off the front cover assembly **(see illustrations 16.5a and b)**. Carefully lift the instrument cluster PCB from the housing and replace it with a new one – individual components are not available.
34 Installation is the reverse of removal.
35 See Chapter 4A for replacement of the level sensor.

17 Instrument and warning light bulbs – replacement

VTR-V, W, X and Y models and XL-X, Y, 1 and 2 models

1 On VTR models displace the instrument cluster (see Section 15).
2 On XL models remove the fairing (see Chapter 8). Many of the bulbs are accessible with the instrument cluster in place. If access is restricted, release the peg on the back of the cluster from the grommet on the bracket and tilt the cluster away from the bracket **(see illustration 15.5b)**.
3 Gently pull the bulbholder out of the instrument casing, then pull the bulb out of the

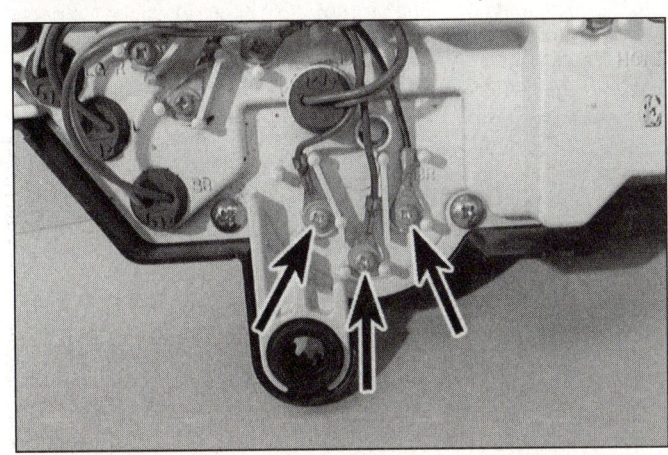

16.24a Coolant temperature gauge screws (arrowed) – VTR models

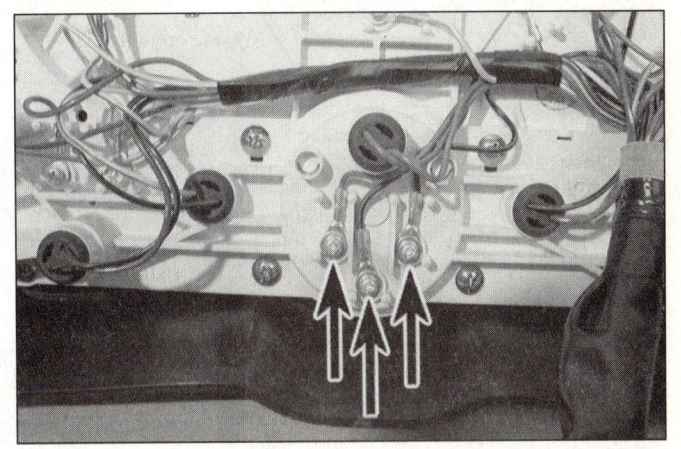

16.24b Coolant temperature gauge screws (arrowed) – XL-X, Y, 1 and 2 models

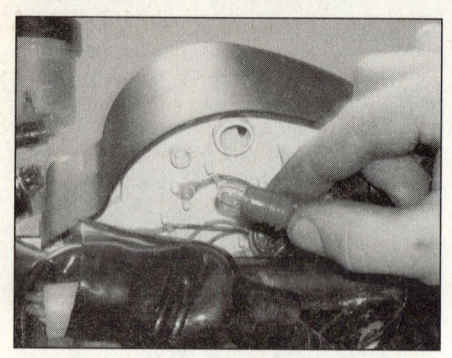

9•16 Electrical system

17.3a Pull the bulbholder out of the instrument ...

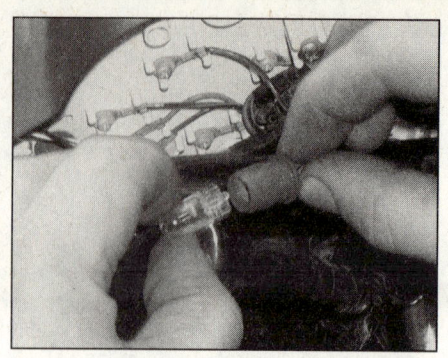

17.3b ... and the bulb out of the holder

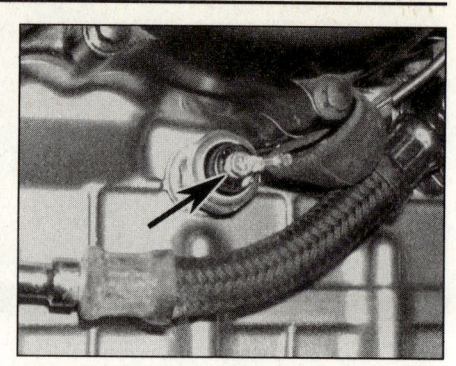

18.3 Pull back the rubber then remove the terminal screw (arrowed) and detach the wiring

bulbholder **(see illustrations)**. If the socket contacts are dirty or corroded, scrape them clean and spray with electrical contact cleaner before a new bulb is installed. Carefully push the new bulb into the holder and install the instrument cluster and fairing, where removed.

VTR-1 to 6 models

4 Remove the casing screws from the back of the cluster and lift off the front cover. Carefully lift the instrument cluster PCB from the housing. Release and withdraw the bulbholder. Pull the bulb out of the holder and replace it with a new one.

XL-3 models onward

5 All the instrument and warning lights are LEDs which are an integral part of the instrument cluster PCB and are not available individually. If an instrument illumination LED fails, first check the instrument cluster wiring connector terminals and wiring. If a warning light LED fails check the component relevant to the warning light (i.e. oil pressure switch, turn signal) then check the wiring and connectors in the circuit, referring to the relevant Section of this Chapter and to the wiring diagrams at the end of it. If all is good, then the instrument cluster PCB must be replaced with a new one (see Sections 15 and 16).

18 Oil pressure switch – check, removal and installation

Check

1 The oil pressure warning light should come on when the ignition (main) switch is turned ON and extinguish a few seconds after the engine is started. If the oil pressure warning light comes on whilst the engine is running, stop the engine immediately and carry out an oil level check, and if the level is correct, an oil pressure check (see Chapter 1).
2 If the oil pressure warning light does not come on when the ignition is turned ON, check the bulb (see Section 17) and fuse (see Section 5).
3 The oil pressure switch is screwed into the crankcase on the left-hand side. On XL models remove the belly-pan for access (see Chapter 8, Section 4). Pull the rubber cover off the switch and remove the screw securing the wiring connector **(see illustration)**. With the ignition switched ON, earth (ground) the wire on the crankcase and check that the warning light comes on. If the light comes on, the switch is defective and must be replaced with a new one.
4 If the light still does not come on, check for voltage at the wire terminal. If there is no voltage present, check the wire between the switch, the instrument cluster and fusebox for continuity (see the wiring diagrams at the end of this Chapter).
5 If the warning light comes on whilst the engine is running, yet the oil pressure is satisfactory, remove the wire from the oil pressure switch. With the wire detached and the ignition switched ON the light should be out. If it is illuminated, the wire between the switch and instrument cluster must be earthed (grounded) at some point. If the wiring is good, the switch must be assumed faulty and replaced.

Removal

6 On XL models, remove the belly-pan (see Chapter 8, Section 4).
7 Pull the rubber cover off the switch and remove the screw securing the wiring connector **(see illustration 18.3)**.
8 Unscrew the oil pressure switch and withdraw it from the crankcase.

Installation

9 Apply a suitable sealant to the upper portion of the switch threads near the switch body, leaving the bottom 3 to 4 mm of thread clean. Install the switch in the crankcase and tighten it to the torque setting specified at the beginning of the Chapter. Attach the wiring connector and secure it with the screw, then fit the rubber cover **(see illustration 18.3)**.
10 Run the engine and check that the switch operates correctly without leakage.
11 On XL models, install the belly-pan (see Chapter 8, Section 4).

19 Ignition (main) switch – check, removal and installation

⚠️ **Warning: To prevent the risk of short circuits, disconnect the battery negative (–ve) lead before making any ignition (main) switch checks.**

Note: Two shear-head bolts mount the ignition switch to the underside of the top yoke – these bolts can only be used once. Obtain new bolts before starting.

Check

1 Trace the wiring from the ignition switch and disconnect it at the connector. On VTR models, either remove the fairing (see Chapter 8) or displace the instrument cluster (see Section 15) – the connector is inside the rubber boot on the right-hand side of the instrument cluster **(see illustration)**. On XL models, remove the left-hand fairing side panel (see Chapter 8) – the connector is inside the rubber boot above the left-hand radiator **(see illustration)**.

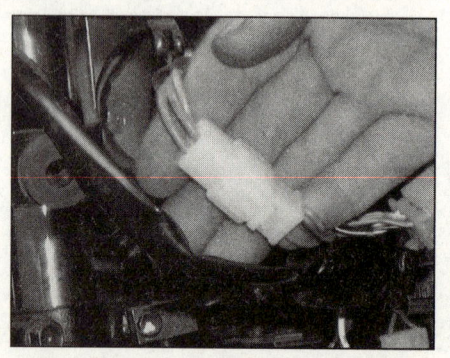

19.1a Ignition switch wiring connector – VTR models

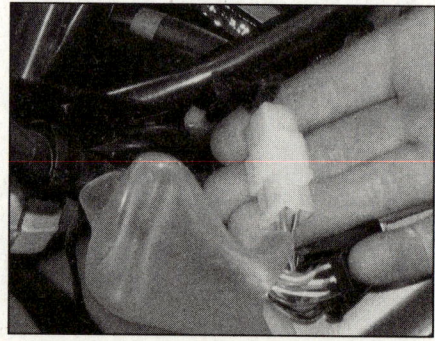

19.1b Ignition switch wiring connector – XL models

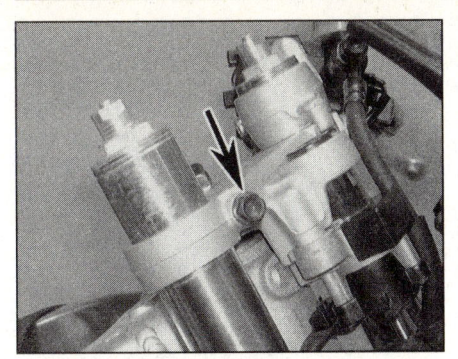

Electrical system 9•17

19.7a Top yoke fork clamp bolt (arrowed) – VTR models

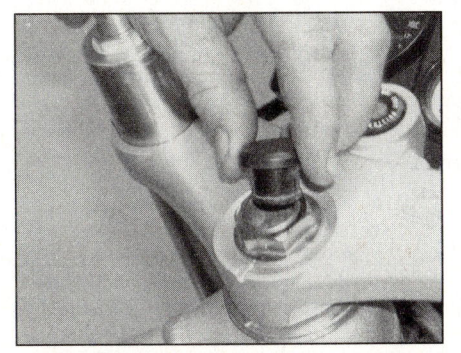

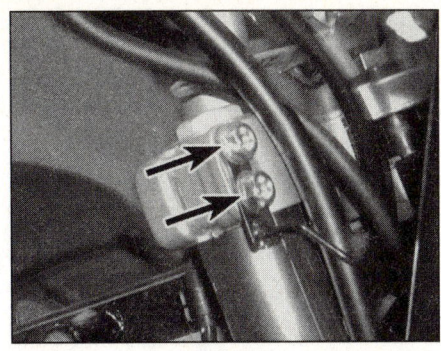

19.7b Top yoke fork clamp bolts (arrowed) – XL models

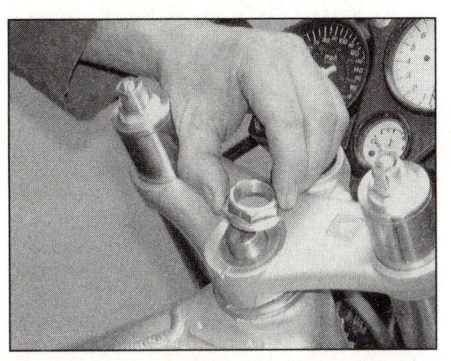

19.8a On VTR models, remove the cap

19.8b Unscrew the steering stem nut...

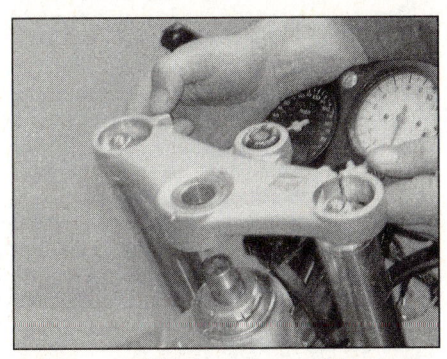

19.9 ...and lift the yoke up off the forks

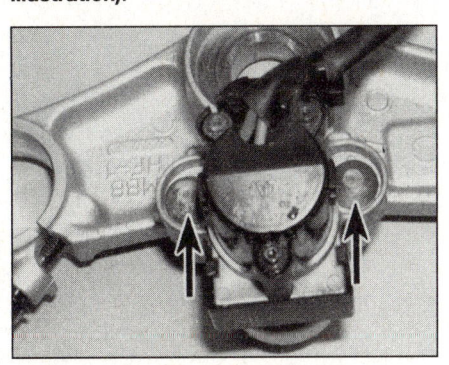

19.10 The ignition switch is secured by two shear-head bolts (arrowed)

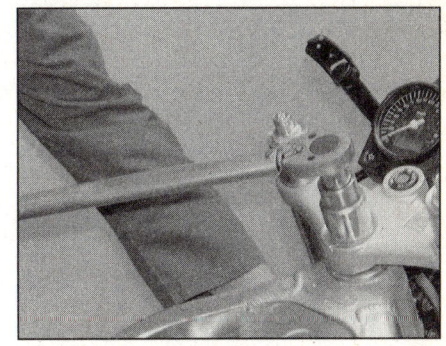

19.12 Tighten the steering stem nut to the specified torque

2 Using an ohmmeter or a continuity tester, check the continuity of the connector terminal pairs (see the wiring diagrams at the end of this Chapter). Continuity should exist between the terminals connected by a solid line on the diagram when the switch is in the indicated position.
3 If the switch fails any of the tests, replace it with a new one.

Removal

4 Remove the fuel tank (see Chapter 4) and the fairing (see Chapter 8). This will prevent the possibility of damage should a tool slip.
5 Trace the wiring from the ignition switch and disconnect it at the connector. On VTR models, the connector is inside the rubber boot on the right-hand end of the fairing bracket (see illustration 19.1a). On XL models, remove the left-hand fairing side panel (see Chapter 8, Section 4) – the connector is inside the rubber boot above the left-hand radiator (see illustration 19.1b). Work back along the harness, freeing it from any clips and ties, noting its correct routing.
6 Displace the handlebars from the top yoke (see Chapter 6). Support them so the master cylinder is upright to prevent the possibility of fluid leakage. There is no need to remove assemblies from the handlebars.
7 Slacken the fork clamp bolts in the top yoke **(see illustrations)**.
8 On VTR models, prise the cap off the steering stem nut **(see illustration)**. Unscrew the nut using a 30 mm socket or spanner, and on XL models remove the washer **(see illustration)**.

9 Gently ease the top yoke up off the fork tubes and remove it **(see illustration)**.
10 Two shear-head bolts mount the ignition switch to the underside of the top yoke **(see illustration)**. The heads of the bolts must be drifted round using a suitable punch or drift, or drilled or ground off, before the switch can be removed. Mount the yoke in a vice equipped with soft jaws and padded out with rags to do this. Remove the bolts and withdraw the switch from the top yoke.

Installation

11 Installation is the reverse of removal. Tighten the new bolts until the heads shear off. Make sure wiring connectors are securely connected and correctly routed.
12 Fit the top yoke onto the steering stem **(see illustration 19.9)**. Install the nut, not forgetting the washer on XL models, and tighten it to the torque setting specified at the beginning of Chapter 6 **(see illustration)**. Now tighten both the fork clamp bolts to the specified torque **(see illustration 19.7a or 19.7b)**. On VTR models, fit the cap over the stem nut **(see illustration 19.8a)**.
13 Install the handlebars (see Chapter 6), the fuel tank (see Chapter 4), the fairing, and on XL models the fairing side panel (see Chapter 8).

20 Handlebar switches – check

1 Generally speaking, the switches are reliable and trouble-free. Most troubles, when they do occur, are caused by dirty or corroded contacts, but wear and breakage of internal parts is a possibility that should not be overlooked. If breakage does occur, the entire switch and related wiring harness will have to be replaced with a new one, as individual parts are not available.
2 The switches can be checked for continuity using an ohmmeter or a continuity test light. Always disconnect the battery negative (–ve) cable, which will prevent the possibility of a short circuit, before making the checks.
3 Trace the wiring harness of the switch in question back to its connector and disconnect it. On VTR models, remove the fairing (see

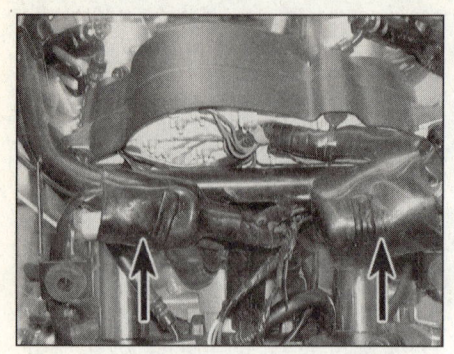

9•18 Electrical system

20.3a On VTR models, the connectors are inside the rubber boots (arrowed)

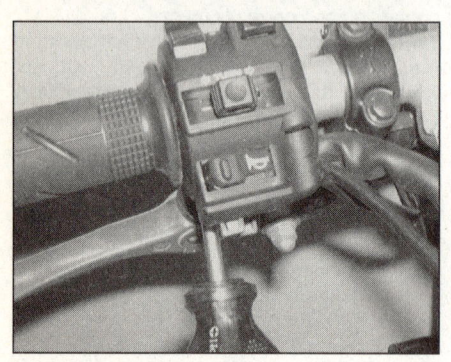

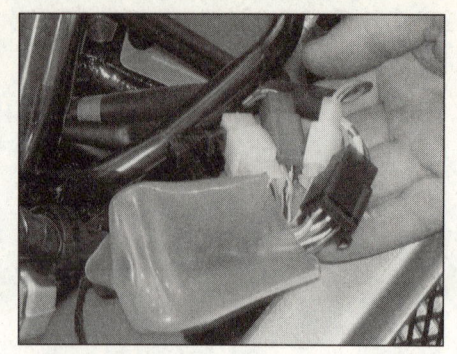

20.3b Switchgear wiring connectors – early XL models

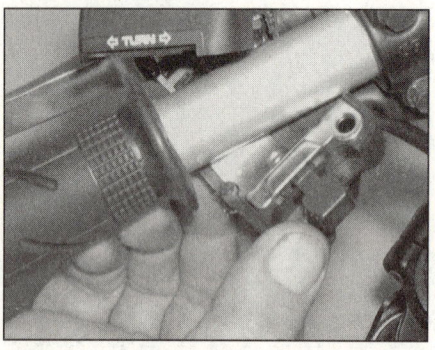

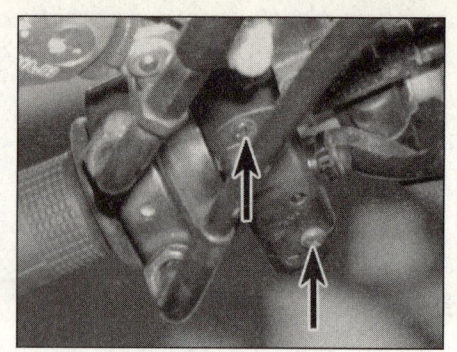

21.3a Right-hand switch screws (arrowed)

21.3b Remove the screws . . .

21.3c . . . and separate the housing halves

21.4 Locate the peg (arrowed) in the hole in the handlebar

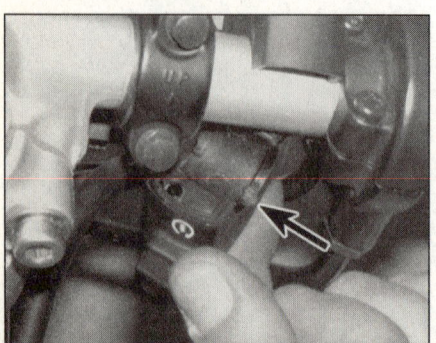

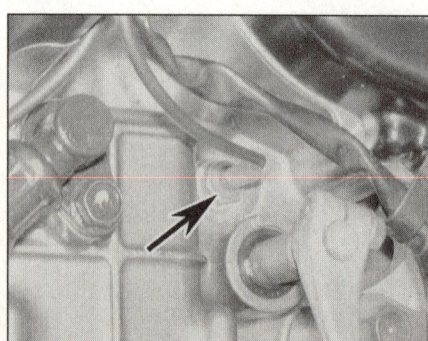

22.2 Neutral switch (arrowed)

fairing bracket **(see illustration 20.3a)**. On XL models, remove the relevant fairing side panel (see Chapter 8) to access the connectors **(see illustration 20.3b)**. Work back along the harness, freeing it from any clips and ties, noting its correct routing.

2 Disconnect the two wires from the brake light switch (if removing the right-hand switch) or the clutch switch (if removing the left-hand switch) **(see illustration 14.2 or 24.2)**.

3 Unscrew the two handlebar switch screws and free the switch from the handlebar by separating the halves **(see illustrations)**.

Installation

4 Installation is the reverse of removal. Make sure the locating pin in the lower half of the switch locates in the hole in the underside of the handlebar **(see illustration)**.

22 Neutral switch – check, removal and installation

Check

1 Before checking the electrical circuit, check the bulb (see Section 17) and fuse (see Section 5).

2 The switch is located in the left-hand side of the transmission casing below the front sprocket cover **(see illustration)**. On XL models, remove the cover to improve access, as it partially covers the switch (see Chapter 6, Section 16). Detach the wiring connector from the switch. Make sure the transmission is in neutral.

3 With the connector disconnected and the ignition switched ON, the neutral light should be out. If not, the wire between the connector and instrument cluster must be earthed (grounded) at some point.

4 Check for continuity between the switch terminal and the crankcase. With the transmission in neutral, there should be continuity. With the transmission in gear, there should be no continuity. If the tests prove otherwise, then the switch is faulty.

5 If the continuity tests prove the switch is good, check for voltage at the wire terminal

Chapter 8) – the connectors for the switchgear are inside the rubber boots on the fairing bracket **(see illustration)**. On XL models, remove the relevant fairing side panel (see Chapter 8) **(see illustration)**.

4 Check for continuity between the terminals of the switch connector with the switch in the various positions (i.e. switch off – no continuity, switch on – continuity) – see the wiring diagrams at the end of this Chapter. Continuity should exist between the terminals connected by a solid line on the diagram when the switch is in the indicated position.

5 If the continuity check indicates a problem exists, refer to Section 21, displace the switch housing and spray the switch contacts with electrical contact cleaner (there is no need to remove the switch completely). If they are accessible, the contacts can be scraped clean with a knife or polished with crocus cloth. If switch components are damaged or broken, it will be obvious when the switch is disassembled.

21 Handlebar switches – removal and installation

Removal

1 If the switch is to be removed from the bike, rather than just displaced from the handlebar, trace the wiring harness of the switch being worked on back to its connector and disconnect it. On VTR models, remove the fairing (see Chapter 8) – the connectors for the switchgear are inside the rubber boots on the

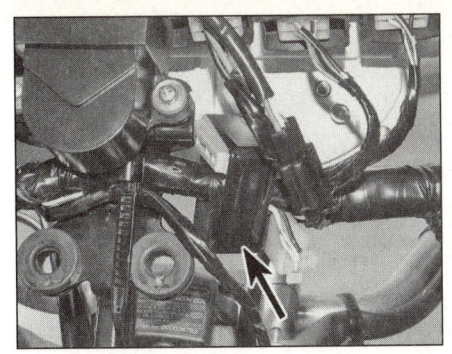

Electrical system 9•19

22.12 Neutral switch diode (arrowed)

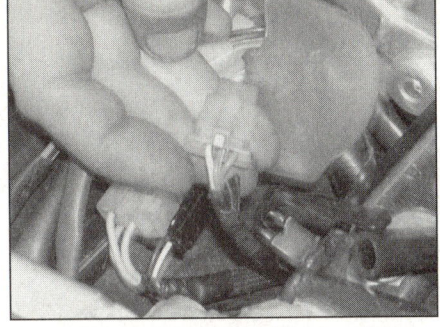

23.2a Sidestand switch wiring connector – VTR models

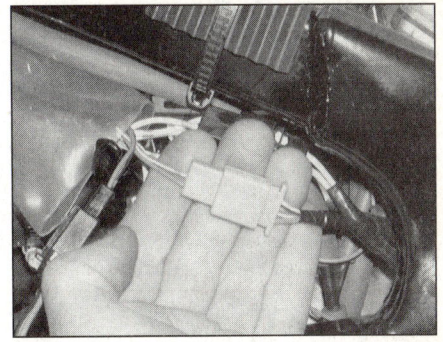

23.2b Sidestand switch wiring connector – XL models

using a test light. If there's no voltage present, check the wire between the switch, the instrument cluster and fusebox (see the wiring diagrams at the end of this Chapter).

Removal

6 The switch is located in the left-hand side of the transmission casing below the front sprocket cover **(see illustration 22.2)**. On XL models, remove the cover to improve access, as it partially covers the switch (see Chapter 6, Section 16).
7 Detach the wiring connector from the switch.
8 Unscrew the switch and withdraw it from the transmission casing. Discard the sealing washer as a new one should be used.

Installation

9 Install the switch using as new washer and tighten it to the torque setting specified at the beginning of the Chapter.
10 Connect the wiring connector and check the operation of the neutral light.
11 On XL models, install the front sprocket cover (see Chapter 6).

Neutral switch diode – XL-7 models onward

Note: *This diode serves to reduce engine idle speed when the transmission is shifted into neutral.*

12 If engine idle speed does not go up when a gear is selected, and reduce again when neutral is reselected, remove the fairing (see Chapter 8). Remove the tape securing the diode to the loom, then disconnect its wiring connector **(see illustration)**. Check that all wires and connector terminals are clean and secure.
13 If engine idle speed does not go up when a gear is selected, measure the resistance between the outer terminal on the shaped side of the diode socket and the centre terminal. There should be approximately 1.2 K-ohms – if not replace the diode with a new one.
14 If engine idle speed does not reduce when neutral is reselected, check for continuity between the outer terminal on the square side of the diode socket and the centre terminal, then reverse the probes and check again.

There should be continuity shown in one direction, but not the other. If the diode doesn't behave as stated, replace it with a new one.

23 Sidestand switch – check and replacement

Check

1 The sidestand switch is mounted on the back of the sidestand. The switch is part of the safety circuit which prevents or stops the engine running if the transmission is in gear whilst the sidestand is down, and prevents the engine from starting if the transmission is in gear unless the sidestand is up and the clutch is pulled in. Before checking the electrical circuit, check the fuse (see Section 5), and on VTR models the warning bulb (see Section 17)
2 On VTR models remove the seat, and on XL models raise or remove the fuel tank (see Chapter 4A). Trace the wiring back from the switch to its connector and disconnect it **(see illustrations)**.
3 Check the operation of the switch using an ohmmeter or continuity test light. Connect the meter between the green/white and green wires on the switch side of the connector. With the sidestand up there should be continuity (zero resistance) between the terminals, and with the stand down there should be no continuity (infinite resistance). On VTR models, now connect the meter to the yellow/black and

23.6 Sidestand switch mounting bolt (arrowed)

green wires on the switch side of the connector. With the sidestand down there should be continuity (zero resistance) between the terminals, and with the stand up there should be no continuity (infinite resistance).
4 If the switch does not perform as expected, it is faulty and must be replaced with a new one.
5 If the switch is good, check the wiring between the various components in the starter safety circuit (see the wiring diagrams at the end of this Chapter).

Replacement

6 The sidestand switch is mounted on the front of the sidestand **(see illustration)**. On VTR models remove the seat, and on XL models raise or remove the fuel tank (see Chapter 4A). Trace the wiring back from the switch to its connector and disconnect it **(see illustration 23.2a or 23.2b)**. Work back along the switch wiring, freeing it from any clips and ties, noting its correct routing.
7 Unscrew the switch bolt and remove the switch from the stand, noting how it fits.
8 Fit the new switch onto the sidestand, making sure the pin locates in the hole in the sidestand, and the lug for the spring on the stand bracket locates into the cut-out in the switch body. Secure the switch with its bolt and tighten it to the torque setting specified at the beginning of the Chapter.
9 Make sure the wiring is correctly routed up to the connector and retained by any clips and ties.
10 Reconnect the wiring connector and check the operation of the sidestand switch.
11 On VTR models install the seat, and on XL models install the fuel tank (see Chapter 4).

24 Clutch switch – check and replacement

Check

1 The clutch switch is mounted on the underside of the clutch master cylinder on VTR models, and on the underside of the clutch lever bracket on XL models. The switch is part of the safety circuit which prevents or

9•20 Electrical system

stops the engine running if the transmission is in gear whilst the sidestand is down, and prevents the engine from starting if the transmission is in gear unless the sidestand is up and the clutch lever is pulled in. The switch isn't adjustable.

2 To check the switch, disconnect the wiring connectors from it **(see illustration)**. Connect the probes of an ohmmeter or a continuity test light to the two switch terminals. With the clutch lever pulled in, continuity should be indicated. With the clutch lever out, no continuity (infinite resistance) should be indicated.

3 If the switch is good, check the other components in the starter circuit as described in the relevant sections of this Chapter. If all components are good, check the wiring between the various components (see the wiring diagrams at the end of this book).

Replacement

4 The clutch switch is mounted on the front of the clutch master cylinder on VTR models, and in the clutch lever bracket on XL models. On XL models, to improve access, unscrew the nut and remove the collar on the underside of the handguard, then unscrew the bolt securing the top of the handguard and remove the guard, noting how it fits.

5 Disconnect the wiring connectors from the switch **(see illustration 24.2)**. Undo the screw and remove the switch, noting how it fits.

6 Installation is the reverse of removal.

25 Diode – check and replacement

Check

1 The diode is a small block that plugs into a connector in the fusebox, which is located under the seat. The diode is part of the safety circuit which prevents or stops the engine running if the transmission is in gear whilst the sidestand is down, and prevents the engine from starting if the transmission is in gear unless the sidestand is up and the clutch lever is pulled in.

2 Remove the seat (see Chapter 8), open the fusebox lid and pull the diode out of its socket **(see illustrations)**.

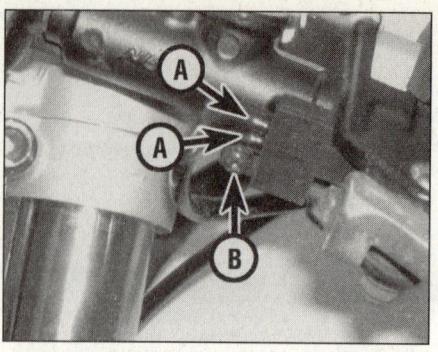

24.2 Clutch switch wiring connectors (A) and mounting screw (B) – VTR models

3 Using an ohmmeter or continuity tester, connect the positive (+ve) probe to one of the outer terminals of the diode and the negative (–ve) probe to the middle terminal of the diode. The diode should show continuity. Now reverse the probes. The diode should show no continuity. Repeat the tests between the other outer terminal and the middle terminal. The same results should be achieved. If it doesn't behave as stated, replace the diode with a new one.

4 If the diode is good, check the other components in the starter circuit as described in the relevant sections of this Chapter. If all components are good, check the wiring between the various components (see the wiring diagrams at the end of this book).

Replacement

5 The diode is a small block that plugs into a connector in the fusebox, which is located under the seat.

6 Remove the seat (see Chapter 8), open the fusebox lid and disconnect the diode out of its socket **(see illustrations 25.2a and 25.2b)**.

26 Horn – check and replacement

Check

1 On VTR models the horn is mounted on the underside of the bottom yoke – remove the fairing for best access. On XL models the horn

25.2a Open the fusebox lid...

is mounted on the inside of the left-hand radiator – remove the left-hand fairing side panel for best access.

2 Unplug the wiring connectors from the horn **(see illustrations)**. Using two jumper wires, apply battery voltage directly to the terminals on the horn. If the horn sounds, check the switch (see Section 20) and the wiring between the switch and the horn (see the wiring diagrams at the end of this Chapter).

3 If the horn doesn't sound, replace it with a new one.

Replacement

4 On VTR models the horn is mounted on the underside of the bottom yoke – remove the fairing for best access. On XL models the horn is mounted on the inside of the left-hand radiator – remove the left-hand fairing side panel for best access.

5 Unplug the wiring connectors from the horn, then unscrew the bolt securing the horn and remove it from the bike **(see illustration 26.2a or 26.2b)**.

6 Install the horn and securely tighten the bolt. Connect the wiring to the horn.

27 Starter relay – check and replacement

Check

1 If the starter circuit is faulty, first check the fuse (see Section 5).

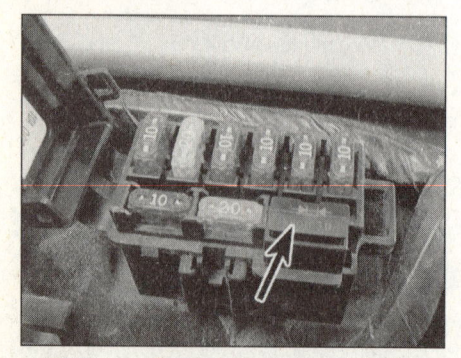

25.2b ...the diode (arrowed) is inside

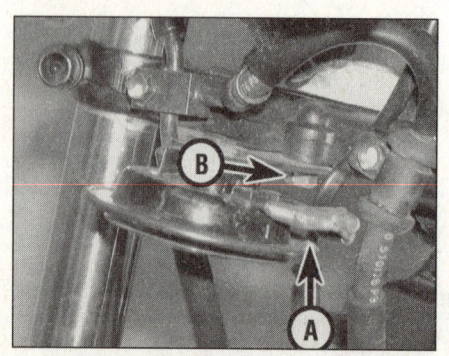

26.2a Horn wiring connectors (A) and mounting bolt (B) – VTR models

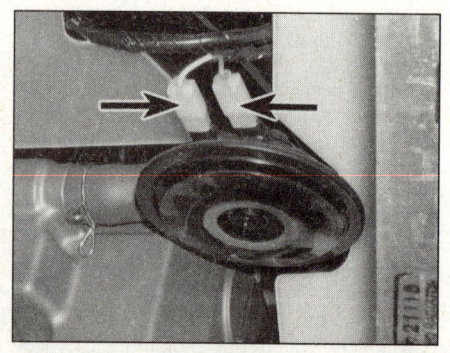

26.2b Horn wiring connectors (arrowed) – XL models

Electrical system 9•21

27.2a Starter relay – VTR models

27.2b Starter relay – XL models

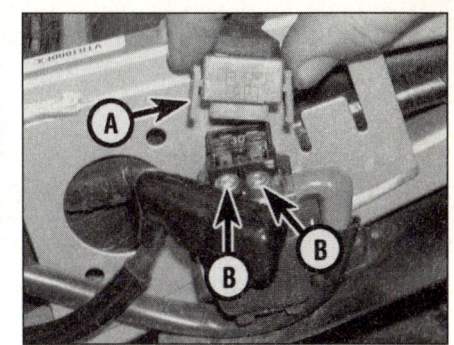

27.3 Relay wiring connector (A) and battery and starter motor leads (B)

2 On VTR models the starter relay is located behind the seat cowling on the left-hand side of the bike **(see illustration)** – remove the seat cowling for access (see Chapter 8, Section 4). On XL models it is located under the seat next to the fusebox **(see illustration)** – remove the seat for access (see Chapter 8.

3 Disconnect the relay wiring connector to provide access to the rear terminals, then lift the rubber terminal cover and unscrew the bolt or nut securing the starter motor lead **(see illustration)**; position the lead away from the relay terminal. Reconnect the wiring connector. With the ignition switch ON, the engine kill switch in the RUN position, the transmission in neutral and the clutch pulled in, press the starter switch. The relay should be heard to click.

4 If the relay doesn't click, switch off the ignition and remove the relay as described below; test it as follows.

5 Set a multimeter to the ohms x 1 scale and connect it across the relay's starter motor and battery lead terminals **(see illustration 27.3)**. Using a fully-charged 12-volt battery and two insulated jumper wires, connect the positive (+ve) terminal of the battery to the yellow/red wire terminal of the relay, and the negative (–ve) terminal to the green/red wire terminal of the relay. At this point the relay should be heard to click and the multimeter read 0 ohms (continuity). If this is the case the relay is proved good. If the relay does not click when battery voltage is applied and indicates no continuity (infinite resistance) across its terminals, it is faulty and must be replaced with a new one.

6 If the relay is good, check for battery voltage at the yellow/red wire when the starter button is pressed. If there is no voltage, check the wiring between the relay wiring connector and the starter button. If voltage is present, check that there is continuity to earth in the green/red wire with the transmission in neutral, the clutch lever pulled in and the sidestand up (note that there will be a very slight resistance due to the diode). If there is no continuity, check the other components in the starter circuit as described in the relevant sections of this Chapter. If all components are good, check the wiring between the various components (see the wiring diagrams at the end of this book).

Replacement

7 On VTR models the starter relay is located behind the seat cowling on the left-hand side of the bike **(see illustration 27.2a)** – remove the seat cowling for access (see Chapter 8, Section 4). On XL models it is located under the seat next to the fusebox **(see illustration 27.2b)** – remove the seat for access (see Chapter 8).

8 Disconnect the battery terminals, remembering to disconnect the negative (–ve) terminal first.

9 Disconnect the relay wiring connector, then lift the insulating cover and unscrew the bolts or nuts securing the starter motor and battery leads to the relay and detach the leads **(see illustration 27.3)**. Remove the relay with its rubber sleeve from its mounting lug on the frame. If the relay is being replaced with a new one, remove the main fuse and its spare from the relay.

10 Installation is the reverse of removal. Make sure the terminal bolts are securely tightened. Do not forget to fit the main fuse and its spare into the relay, if removed. Connect the negative (–ve) lead last when reconnecting the battery.

28 Starter motor – removal and installation

Removal

1 Remove the seat (see Chapter 8). Disconnect the battery negative (–ve) lead. The starter motor is mounted at the front of the engine.

2 Remove the belly-pan (see Chapter 8). On California VTR models, remove the EVAP canister (see Chapter 4A).

3 Peel back the rubber terminal cover on the starter motor **(see illustration)**. Unscrew the nut securing the starter lead to the motor and detach the lead **(see illustrations)**.

4 Unscrew the two bolts securing the starter motor to the crankcase **(see illustration)**. Slide the starter motor out and remove it.

5 Remove the O-ring on the end of the starter motor and discard it as a new one must be used.

28.3a Pull back the terminal cover . . .

28.3b . . . then unscrew the nut and detach the lead

28.4 Unscrew the two bolts and remove the starter motor

9•22 Electrical system

28.6 Fit a new O-ring and lubricate it, then install the starter motor

Installation

6 Fit a new O-ring onto the end of the starter motor, making sure it is seated in its groove **(see illustration)**. Apply a smear of engine oil to the O-ring to aid installation.
7 Manoeuvre the motor into position and slide it into the crankcase. Ensure that the starter motor teeth mesh correctly with those of the starter idle/reduction gear. Install the mounting bolts and tighten them securely.
8 Connect the starter lead to the motor and secure it with the nut **(see illustration 28.3b)**. Fit the rubber cover over the terminal **(see illustration 28.3a)**.
9 On California VTR models, install the EVAP canister (see Chapter 4).
10 Connect the battery negative (–ve) lead and install the belly-pan and the seat (see Chapter 8).

29 Starter motor – disassembly, inspection and reassembly

Disassembly

1 Remove the starter motor (see Section 28) **(see illustration)**.
2 Note the alignment marks between the main housing and the front and rear covers, or make your own if they aren't clear **(see illustration)**.
3 Unscrew the two long bolts then remove the front cover from the motor along with its sealing ring **(see illustration)**. Discard the sealing ring as a new one must be used. Remove the tabbed washer from the cover and slide the insulating washer and shim(s) from the front end of the armature, noting the number of shims and their correct fitted order **(see illustrations)**.
4 Remove the rear cover from the motor along

1 Rear cover
2 Brush plate
3 Brush holder
4 Seal ring
5 Main housing
6 Shims
7 Armature
8 Shims
9 Insulated washer
10 Tabbed washer
11 Front cover

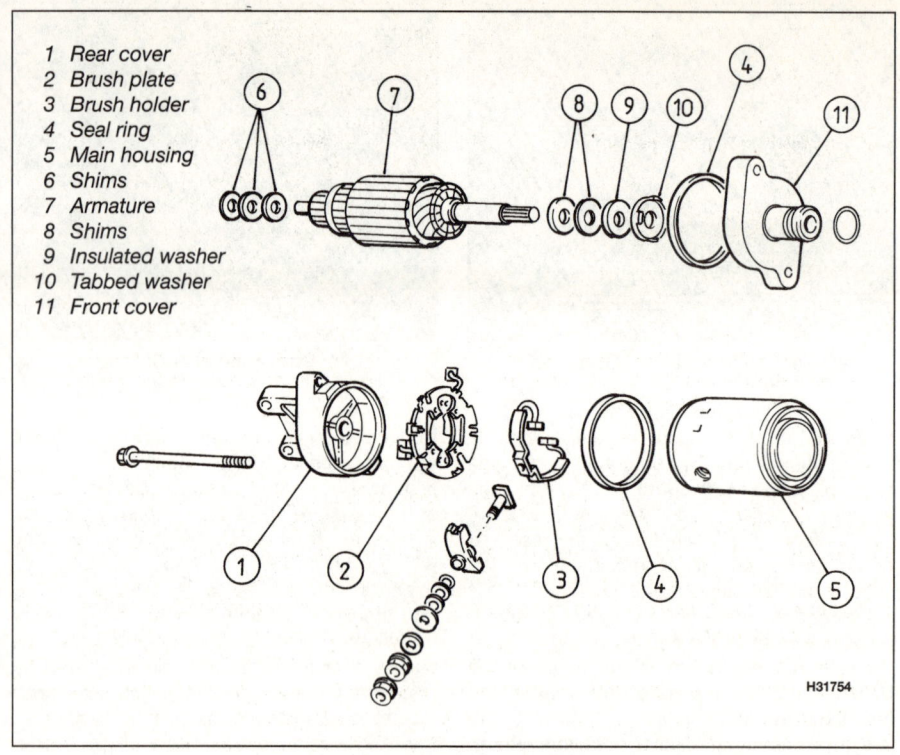

29.1 Starter motor assembly

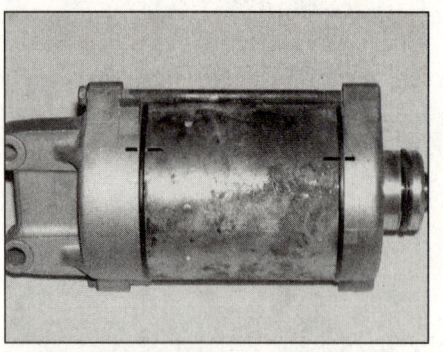

29.2 Note the alignment marks between the housing and the covers

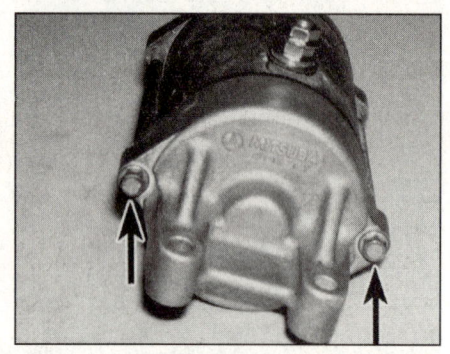

29.3a Unscrew and remove the two bolts (arrowed) . . .

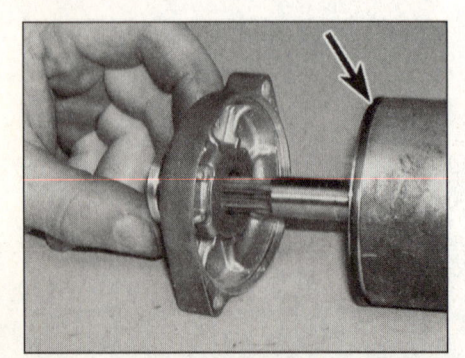

29.3b . . . then remove the front cover and sealing ring (arrowed)

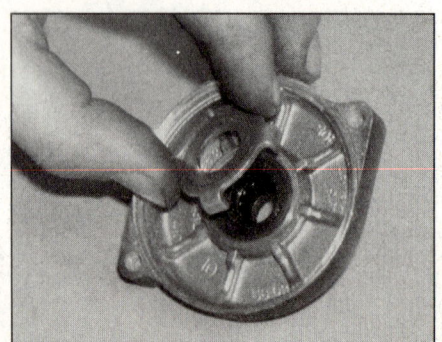

29.3c Remove the tabbed washer . . .

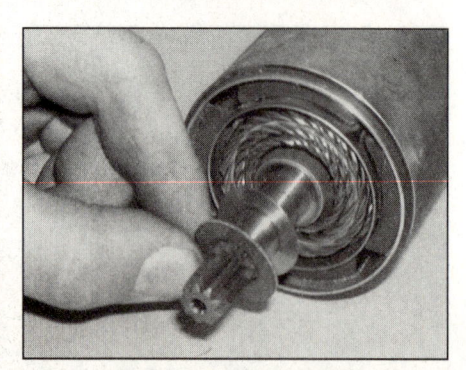

29.3d . . . and the shims

Electrical system 9•23

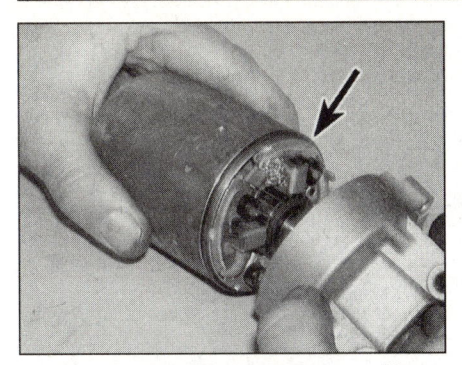

29.4a Remove the front cover and its sealing ring (arrowed)...

29.4b ...and remove the shims

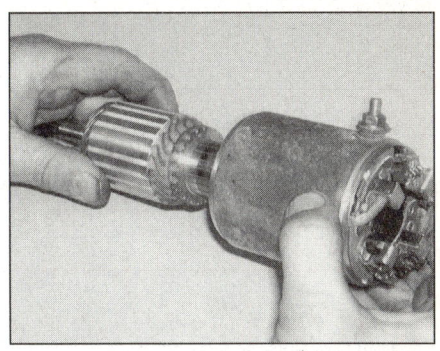

29.5 Withdraw the armature from the housing

with its sealing ring **(see illustration)**. Discard the sealing ring as a new one must be used. Remove the shim(s) from the rear end of the armature noting how many and their correct fitted positions **(see illustration)**.
5 Withdraw the armature from the main housing **(see illustration)**.
6 Lift each brush spring end onto the top of each brush housing and slide the brushes out **(see illustrations)**.
7 At this stage check for continuity between the terminal bolt and the two brushes with yellow insulation. There should be continuity (zero resistance). Check for continuity between the terminal bolt and the housing. There should be no continuity (infinite resistance). Also check for continuity between the brushes with uninsulated wires and the brushplate. There should be continuity (zero resistance). If there is no continuity when there should be or vice versa, identify the faulty component and replace it with a new one.
8 Noting the correct fitted location of each component, unscrew the nut from the terminal bolt and remove the plain washer, the various insulating washers and the rubber O-ring **(see illustration)**. Remove the brushplate assembly and terminal bolt from the main housing, noting how it locates, and recover the insulator **(see illustrations)**.

Inspection

9 The parts of the starter motor that are most likely to require attention are the brushes. Measure the length of each brush and compare the results to the Specifications at

29.6a Place the brush spring ends onto the top of the brush housings...

29.6b ...and slide the brushes out

29.8a Unscrew the nut and remove the washers and O-ring

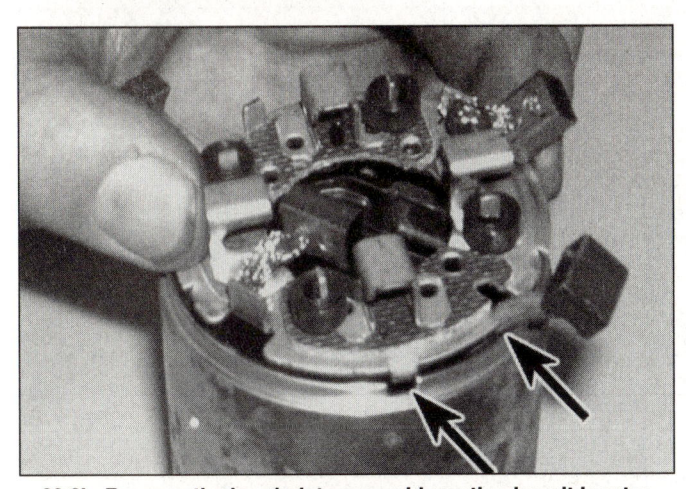

29.8b Remove the brushplate assembly, noting how it locates (arrowed)...

29.8c ...and remove the insulator

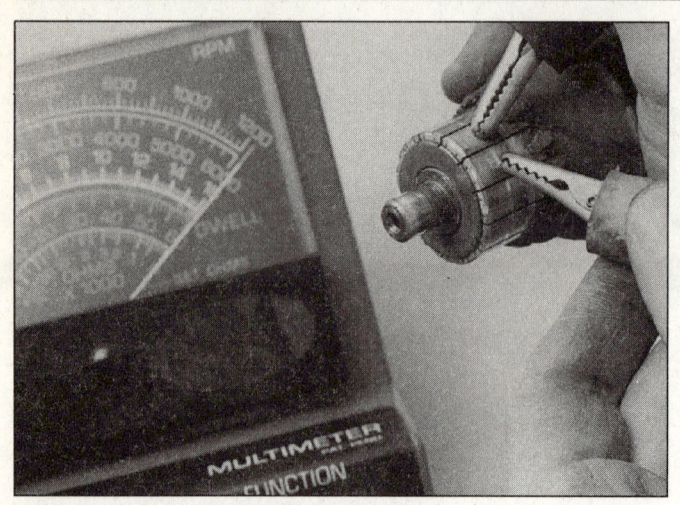

9•24 Electrical system

29.11a Continuity should exist between the commutator bars

29.11b There should be no continuity between the commutator bars and the armature shaft

the beginning of the Chapter. If any of the brushes are worn beyond the service limit, replace the brush holder and/or brushplate assembly with a new one. If the brushes are not worn excessively, nor cracked, chipped, or otherwise damaged, they may be re-used.

10 Inspect the commutator bars on the armature for scoring, scratches and discoloration. The commutator can be cleaned and polished with crocus cloth, but do not use sandpaper or emery paper. After cleaning, wipe away any residue with a cloth soaked in electrical system cleaner or denatured alcohol.

11 Using an ohmmeter or a continuity test light, check for continuity between the commutator bars (see illustration). Continuity should exist between each bar and all of the others. Also, check for continuity between the commutator bars and the armature shaft (see illustration). There should be no continuity (infinite resistance) between the commutator and the shaft. If the checks indicate otherwise, the armature is defective.

12 Check the starter pinion gear for worn, cracked, chipped and broken teeth. If the gear is damaged or worn, replace the starter motor.

13 Inspect the end covers for signs of cracks or wear. Check the needle bearing in the front cover and the bush in the rear cover for wear and damage (see illustration). Inspect the magnets in the main housing and the housing itself for cracks.

14 Inspect the insulating washers, O-ring and front cover oil seal for signs of damage and renew if necessary.

Reassembly

15 Fit the insulator into the main housing (see illustration 29.8c), then install the brush holder and insert the terminal bolt through it and the housing (see illustrations). Slide the rubber O-ring and small insulating washer(s) onto the terminal bolt, followed by the large insulating washer(s) and the plain washer (see illustration 29.8a). Fit the nut onto the terminal bolt and tighten it securely.

16 Install the brushplate assembly, making sure its tab is correctly located in the housing slot, and that each of the insulated brush wires

29.13 There is a needle bearing in the front cover

29.15a Fit the brush holder . . .

29.15b . . . and the terminal bolt

Electrical system 9•25

29.18 Locate the spring ends onto the brushes

29.20 Fit a new sealing ring onto the rear of the housing

sits in its cut-out in the brushplate **(see illustration 29.8b)**.
17 Slide all the brushes back into position in their housings **(see illustration 29.6b)**. Make sure that each brush spring is retained against the top of its housing so that it will not exert any pressure on the brush **(see illustration 29.6a)**.

> **HAYNES HiNT** Lifting the end of the brush spring so that it is against the top of the brush holder and not pressing the brush inwards makes it much easier to install the armature on reassembly.

18 Insert the armature into the front of the housing and locate the brushes on the commutator bars **(see illustration 29.5)**. Slip each brush spring end off the top of the brush housing and onto the brush end **(see illustration)**. Check that each brush is securely pressed against the commutator by its spring and is free to move easily in its housing.
19 Fit the shims onto the rear of the armature shaft **(see illustration 29.4b)**. Apply a smear of grease to the end of the shaft.
20 Fit a new sealing ring onto the rear of the housing **(see illustration)**. Align the rear cover groove with the brushplate outer tab and install the cover – aligning the marks between the cover and housing (Step 2) will help **(see illustration 29.4a)**.
21 Apply a smear of grease to the front cover oil seal lip. Fit the toothed washer into the cover so that its teeth are correctly located with the cover ribs **(see illustration 29.3c)**.
22 Fit a new sealing ring onto the front of the housing **(see illustration)**. Slide the shim(s) onto the front end of the armature shaft then fit the insulating washer **(see illustration 29.3d)**. Slide the front cover into position, aligning the marks made on removal **(see illustration 29.3b)**.
23 Check the marks made on removal are correctly aligned then fit the long bolts and tighten them securely **(see illustration)**.
24 Install the starter motor (see Section 28).

30 Charging system testing – general information and precautions

1 If the performance of the charging system is suspect, the system as a whole should be checked first, followed by testing of the individual components. **Note:** *Before beginning the checks, make sure the battery is fully charged and that all system connections are clean and tight.*
2 Checking the output of the charging system and the performance of the various components within the charging system requires the use of a multimeter (with voltage, current and resistance checking facilities).
3 When making the checks, follow the procedures carefully to prevent incorrect connections or short circuits, as irreparable damage to electrical system components may result if short circuits occur.
4 If a multimeter is not available, the job of checking the charging system should be left to a Honda dealer.

29.22 Fit a new sealing ring onto the front of the housing

29.23 Fit the long bolts and tighten them securely

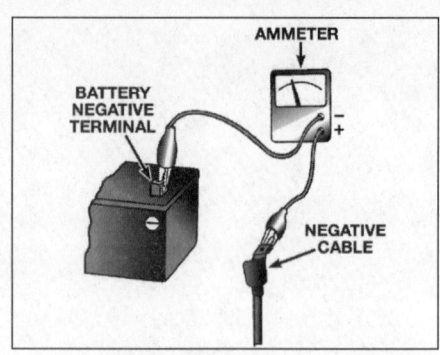

9•26 Electrical system

31.3 Checking the charging system leakage rate – connect the meter as shown

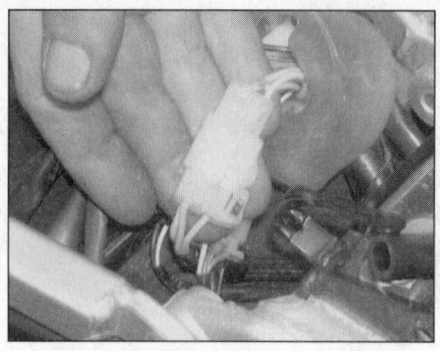

32.2a Alternator wiring connector – VTR models

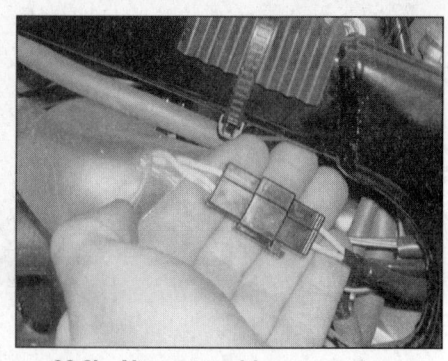

32.2b Alternator wiring connector – XL models

31 Charging system – leakage and output test

1 If the charging system of the machine is thought to be faulty, remove the seat (see Chapter 8) and perform the following checks.

Leakage test

Caution: Always connect an ammeter in series, never in parallel with the battery, otherwise it will be damaged. Do not turn the ignition ON or operate the starter motor when the ammeter is connected – a sudden surge in current will blow the meter's fuse.

2 Turn the ignition switch OFF and disconnect the lead from the battery negative (–ve) terminal.
3 Set the multimeter to the amps function and connect its negative (–ve) probe to the battery negative (–ve) terminal, and positive (+ve) probe to the disconnected negative (–ve) lead **(see illustration)**. Always set the meter to a high amps range initially and then bring it down to the mA (milliamps) range; if there is a high current flow in the circuit it may blow the meter's fuse.
4 If the current leakage indicated exceeds the amount specified at the beginning of the Chapter, there is probably a short circuit in the wiring. Use the wiring diagrams at the end of this Chapter and systematically disconnect individual electrical components until the source is identified.
5 Disconnect the meter and connect the negative (–ve) lead to the battery, tightening it securely.

Output test

6 Start the engine and warm it up to normal operating temperature. Remove the seat (see Chapter 8).
7 To check the voltage output, allow the engine to idle and connect a multimeter set to the 0 to 20 volts dc scale (voltmeter) across the terminals of the battery (positive (+ve) lead to battery positive (+ve) terminal, negative (–ve) lead to battery negative (–ve) terminal). Slowly increase the engine speed to 5000 rpm and note the reading obtained. The regulated voltage should be as specified at the beginning of the Chapter. If the voltage is outside these limits, check the alternator and the regulator (see Sections 32 and 33).

HAYNES HINT *Clues to a faulty regulator are constantly blowing bulbs, with brightness varying considerably with engine speed, and battery overheating.*

32 Alternator – check, removal and installation

Check

1 On VTR models remove the seat (see Chapter 8), on XL-X, Y, 1 and 2 models raise or remove the fuel tank (see Chapter 4A), and on XL-3 models onward remove the left-hand side cover (see Chapter 8).
2 Trace the wiring back from the alternator cover on the left-hand side of the engine and disconnect it at the connector containing the three yellow wires **(see illustrations)**.
3 Using a multimeter set to the ohms x 1 (ohmmeter) scale measure the resistance between each of the yellow wires on the alternator side of the connector, taking a total of three readings, then check for continuity between each terminal and earth (ground). If the stator coil windings are in good condition the three readings should be within the range shown in the Specifications at the start of this Chapter and there should be no continuity (infinite resistance) between any of the terminals and earth (ground). If not, the alternator stator coil assembly is at fault and should be replaced with a new one. **Note:** *Before condemning the stator coils, check the fault is not due to damaged wiring between the connector and the coils.*

Removal

4 On VTR models remove the seat and the fairing (see Chapter 8), and displace the clutch release cylinder (see Chapter 2). On XL-X, Y, 1 and 2 models remove the fuel tank (see Chapter 4A) and on XL-3 models onward remove the left-hand side cover (see Chapter 8). On all XL models remove the belly-pan (see Chapter 8).
5 Trace the wiring back from the alternator cover on the left-hand side of the engine and disconnect it at the connector containing the three yellow wires **(see illustration 32.2a or 32.2b)**. Free the wiring from any clips or guides and feed it through to the alternator cover.
6 Working in a criss-cross pattern, evenly slacken the alternator cover bolts **(see illustration)**. Lift the cover away from the engine, noting that it will be restrained by the force of the rotor magnets, and being prepared to catch any residual oil. Remove the gasket and discard it. Remove the dowels from either the cover or the crankcase if they are loose. On XL-3 models onward remove the oil jet

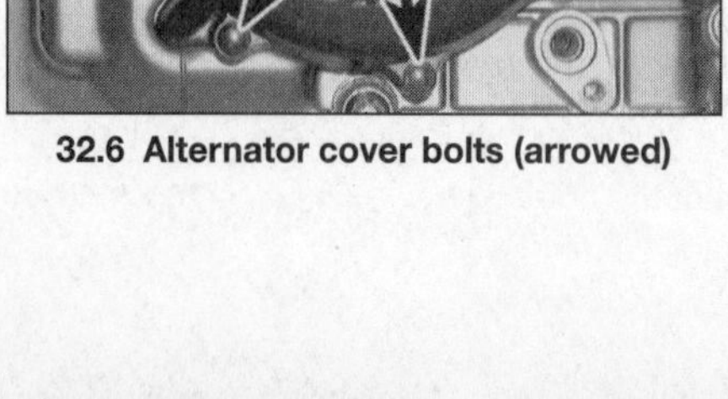

32.6 Alternator cover bolts (arrowed)

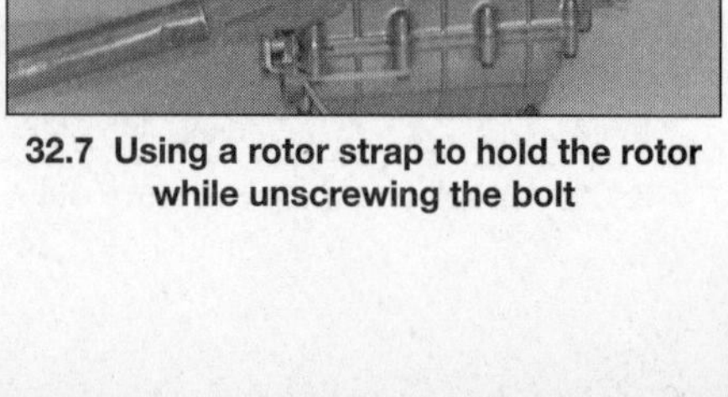

32.7 Using a rotor strap to hold the rotor while unscrewing the bolt

Electrical system 9•27

32.8a Using a puller to remove the rotor

32.8b Remove the Woodruff key (arrowed) if it is loose

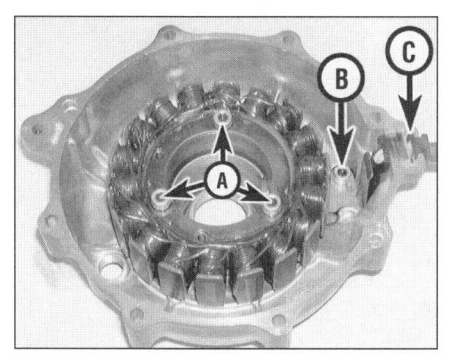

32.9 Unscrew the stator bolts (A) and the wiring clamp bolt (B) and free the grommet (C)

with its two O-rings – new O-rings should be used on installation.

7 To remove the rotor bolt it is necessary to stop the rotor from turning. The best way is to use a commercially available rotor strap **(see illustration)**. If one is not available, try placing the transmission in gear and having an assistant apply the rear brake hard, then unscrew the bolt. Note the washer fitted with the bolt.

8 To remove the rotor from the shaft it is necessary to use a rotor puller. Thread the rotor puller into the centre of the rotor and turn it until the rotor is displaced from the shaft **(see illustration)**. Remove the Woodruff key from its slot in the crankcase if it is loose **(see illustration)**. Note how the starter driven gear

on the starter clutch on the back of the rotor meshes with the idle/reduction gear in the crankcase. Separate the starter clutch from the rotor if required (see Chapter 2).

9 To remove the stator from the cover, unscrew the bolts securing the stator, and the bolt securing the wiring clamp, then remove the assembly, noting how the rubber wiring grommet fits **(see illustration)**.

Installation

10 Fit the stator into the cover, aligning the rubber wiring grommet with the groove **(see illustration 32.9)**. Apply a suitable non-permanent thread locking compound to the stator bolt threads, then install the bolts

and tighten them to the torque setting specified at the beginning of the Chapter. Apply a suitable sealant to the wiring grommet, then press it into the cut-out in the cover. Secure the wiring with its clamp and tighten the bolt securely.

11 If separated, fit the starter clutch onto the back of the rotor (see Chapter 2). Apply some oil to the needle bearing in the starter clutch.

12 Clean the tapered end of the crankshaft and the corresponding mating surface on the inside of the rotor with a suitable solvent. Fit the Woodruff key into its slot in the crankshaft if removed **(see illustration 32.8b)**. Make sure that no metal objects have attached themselves to the magnet on the inside of the rotor. Slide the rotor onto the shaft, making sure the groove on the inside of the rotor is aligned with and fits over the Woodruff key, and that the teeth on the starter driven gear mesh correctly with those of the idle/reduction gear **(see illustration)**. Make sure the Woodruff key does not become dislodged when installing the rotor.

13 Apply some clean oil to the rotor bolt threads and the underside of the head. Install the rotor bolt with its washer and tighten it to the torque setting specified at the beginning of the Chapter, using the method employed on removal to prevent the rotor from turning **(see illustrations)**.

14 Apply a smear of suitable sealant to the area around the crankcase joints. Fit the dowels into the crankcase if removed. On XL-3 models onward clean the oil jet and blow it through, then fit new O-rings smeared with oil into the grooves and fit the jet into its hole. Install the alternator cover using a new gasket, making sure they locate onto the dowels **(see illustration)**. Tighten the cover bolts evenly in a criss-cross sequence.

15 Reconnect the wiring at the connector and secure it with any clips or ties **(see illustration 32.2a or 32.2b)**.

16 On VTR models install the clutch release cylinder (see Chapter 2), the seat and the fairing (see Chapter 8). On XL models install the fuel tank (see Chapter 4A) and, if removed, the belly pan (see Chapter 8).

32.12 Slide the rotor onto the shaft, aligning the groove (arrowed) with the Woodruff key

32.13a Install the bolt with its washer . . .

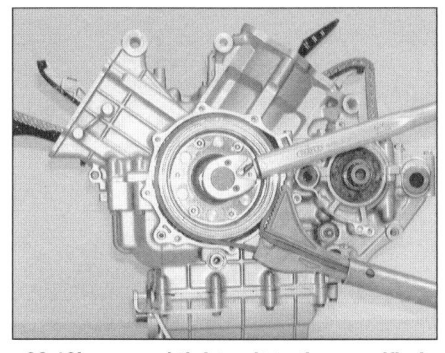

32.13b . . . and tighten it to the specified torque

32.14 Install the cover using a new gasket

9•28 Electrical system

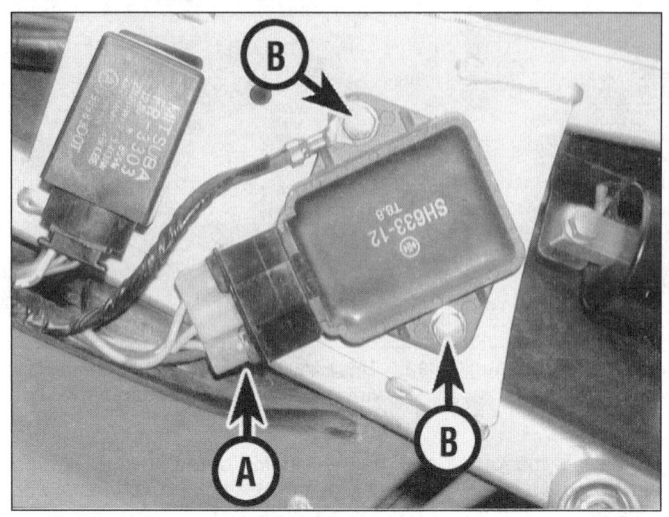

33.1a Regulator/rectifier wiring connector (A) and mounting bolts (B) – VTR models

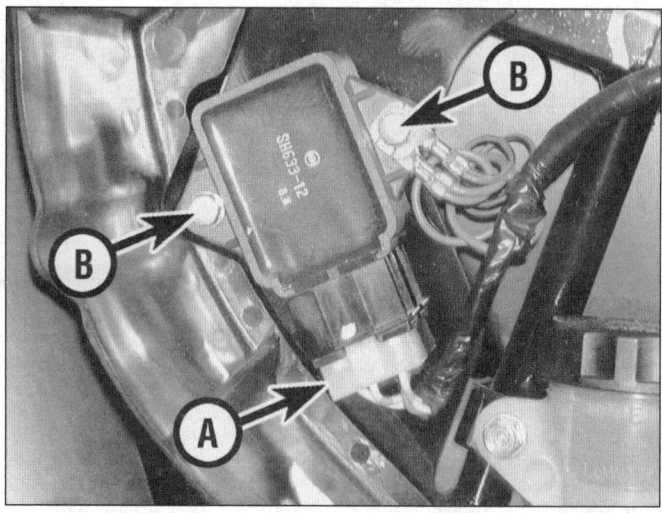

33.1b Regulator/rectifier wiring connector (A) and mounting bolts (B) – early XL models

33 Regulator/rectifier – check and replacement

Check

1 On VTR models remove the seat cowling, on XL-X, Y, 1 and 2 models remove the right-hand side cover, and on XL-3 models onward remove the left-hand side cover (see Chapter 8). The regulator/rectifier is mounted on the right-hand side on all VTR models and XL-X, Y and 1 to 6 models, and under the rear undertray on all ABS equipped models and non-ABS XL-7 models onward **(see illustrations)**. Disconnect the wiring connector(s) and check for loose, damaged or corroded terminals.

2 Set the multimeter to the 0 to 20 dc volts setting. Connect the meter positive (+ve) probe to the red/white terminal and the negative (–ve) probe to a suitable earth (ground) point and check for voltage. Full battery voltage should be present at all times.

3 Switch the multimeter to the resistance (ohms) scale. Check for continuity in the green wire between the terminal in the wiring connector and earth (ground). There should be continuity.

4 Set the multimeter to the ohms x 1 (ohmmeter) scale and measure the resistance between each of the yellow wires on the alternator side of the connector, taking a total of three readings, then check for continuity between each terminal and earth (ground). The three readings should be within the range shown in the Specifications for the alternator stator coil at the start of this Chapter, and there should be no continuity (infinite resistance) between any of the terminals and earth (ground).

5 If the above checks do not provide the expected results check the wiring and connectors between the battery, regulator/rectifier and alternator for shorts, breaks, and loose or corroded terminals (see the wiring diagrams at the end of this book).

6 If the wiring checks out, the regulator/rectifier unit is probably faulty. Honda provide no test data for the unit itself. Take it to a Honda dealer for confirmation of its condition before replacing it with a new one.

Replacement

7 On VTR models remove the seat cowling, on XL-X, Y, 1 and 2 models remove the right-hand side cover, and on XL-3 to 8 models remove the left-hand side cover (see Chapter 8). The regulator/rectifier is mounted on the right-hand side on all VTR models and XL-X, Y and 1 to 6 models, and under the rear undertray on all ABS equipped models and non-ABS XL-7 models onward. Disconnect the wiring connector(s) **(see illustrations 33.1a or b, or c and d)**.

8 Unscrew the two bolts securing the regulator/rectifier and remove it, noting the earth wire(s) secured by one of the bolts where present.

9 Install the new unit and tighten its bolts securely, not forgetting the earth wire(s) where detached. Connect the wiring connector(s).

10 Install the seat cowling (VTR models) or side cover (XL models) (see Chapter 8).

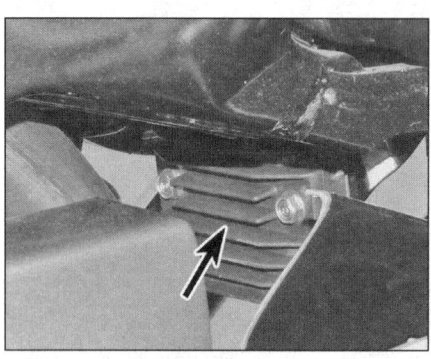

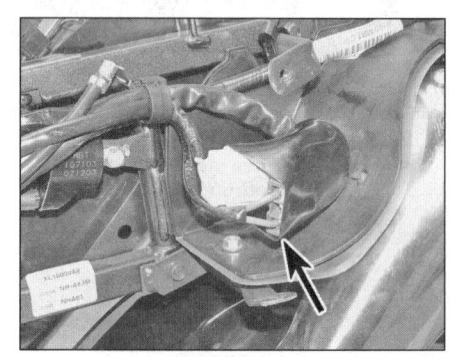

33.1c Regulator/rectifier (arrowed) . . .

33.1d . . . and its wiring connectors – XL-7 models onward

Electrical system 9•29

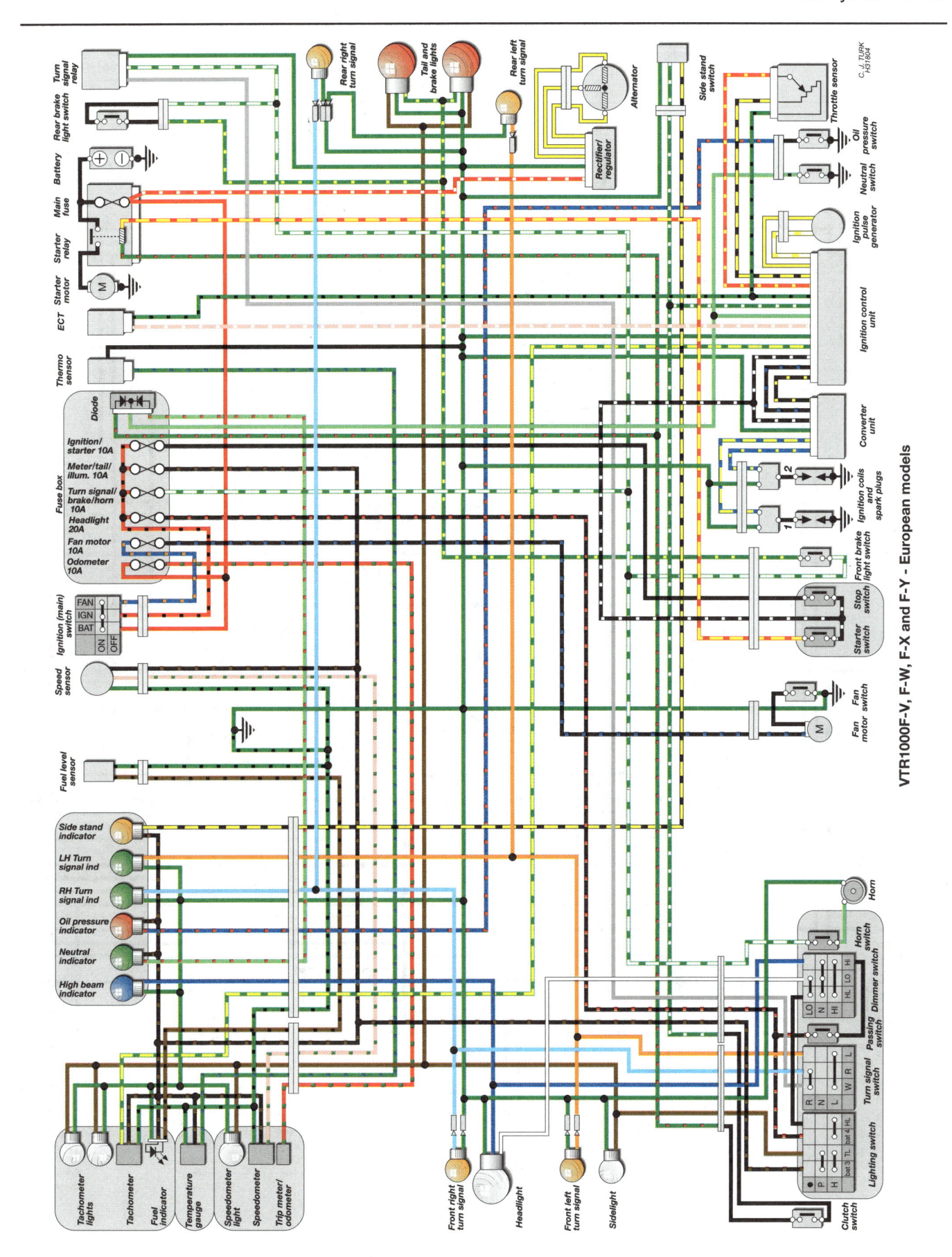

VTR1000F-V, F-W, F-X and F-Y - European models

9•30 Electrical system

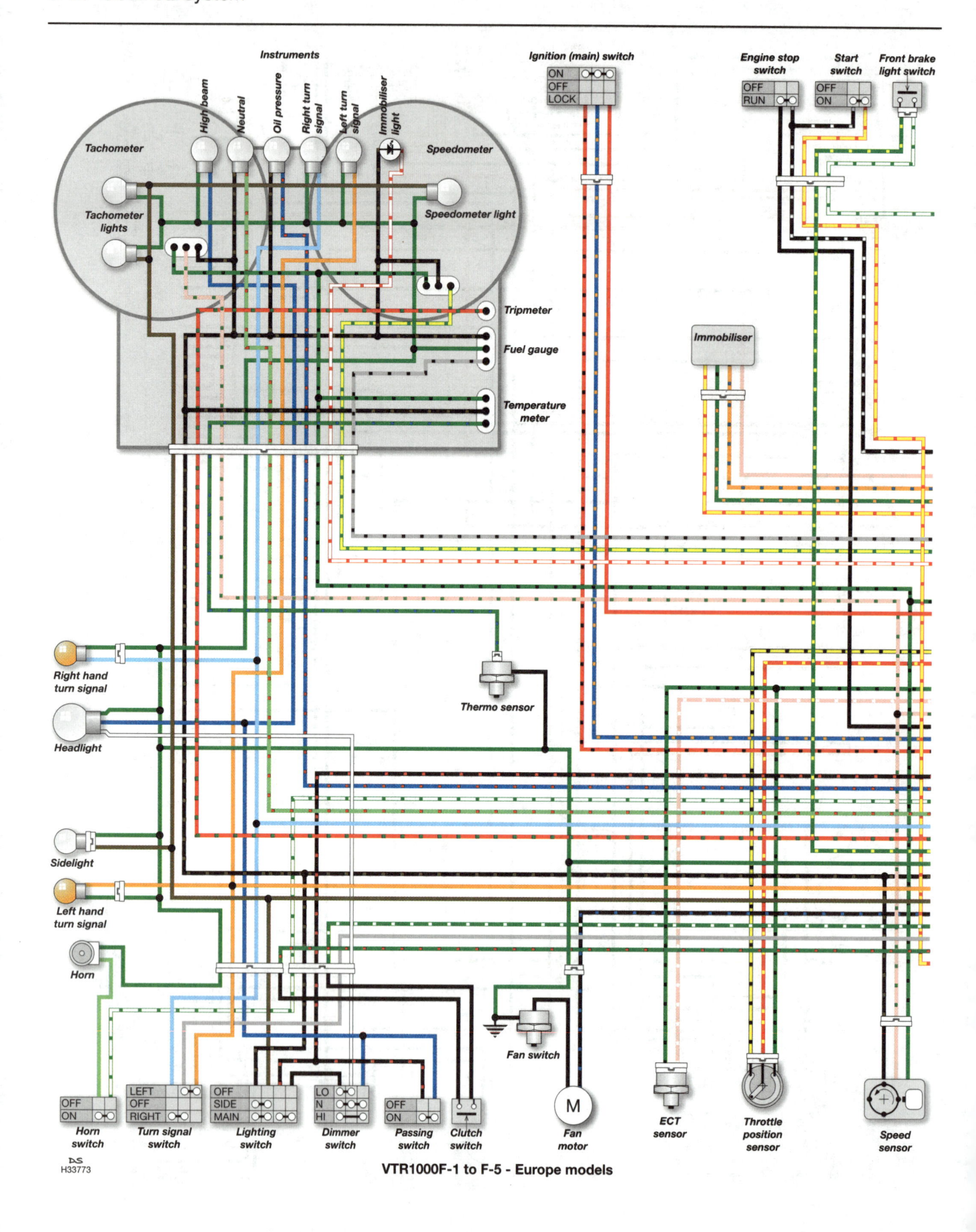

VTR1000F-1 to F-5 - Europe models

Electrical system 9•31

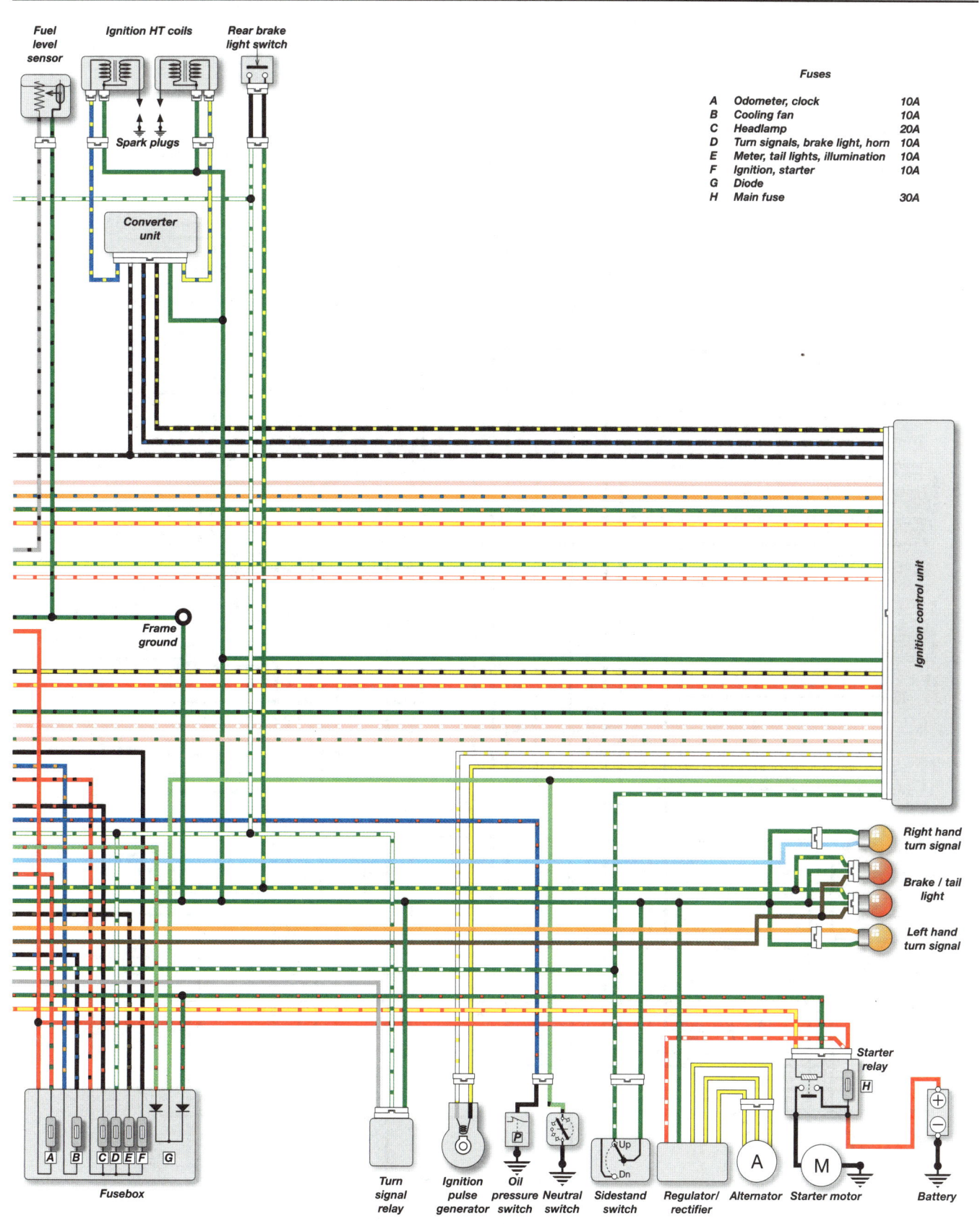

Fuses

A	Odometer, clock	10A
B	Cooling fan	10A
C	Headlamp	20A
D	Turn signals, brake light, horn	10A
E	Meter, tail lights, illumination	10A
F	Ignition, starter	10A
G	Diode	
H	Main fuse	30A

VTR1000F-1 to F-5 - Europe models

H33773

9•32 Electrical system

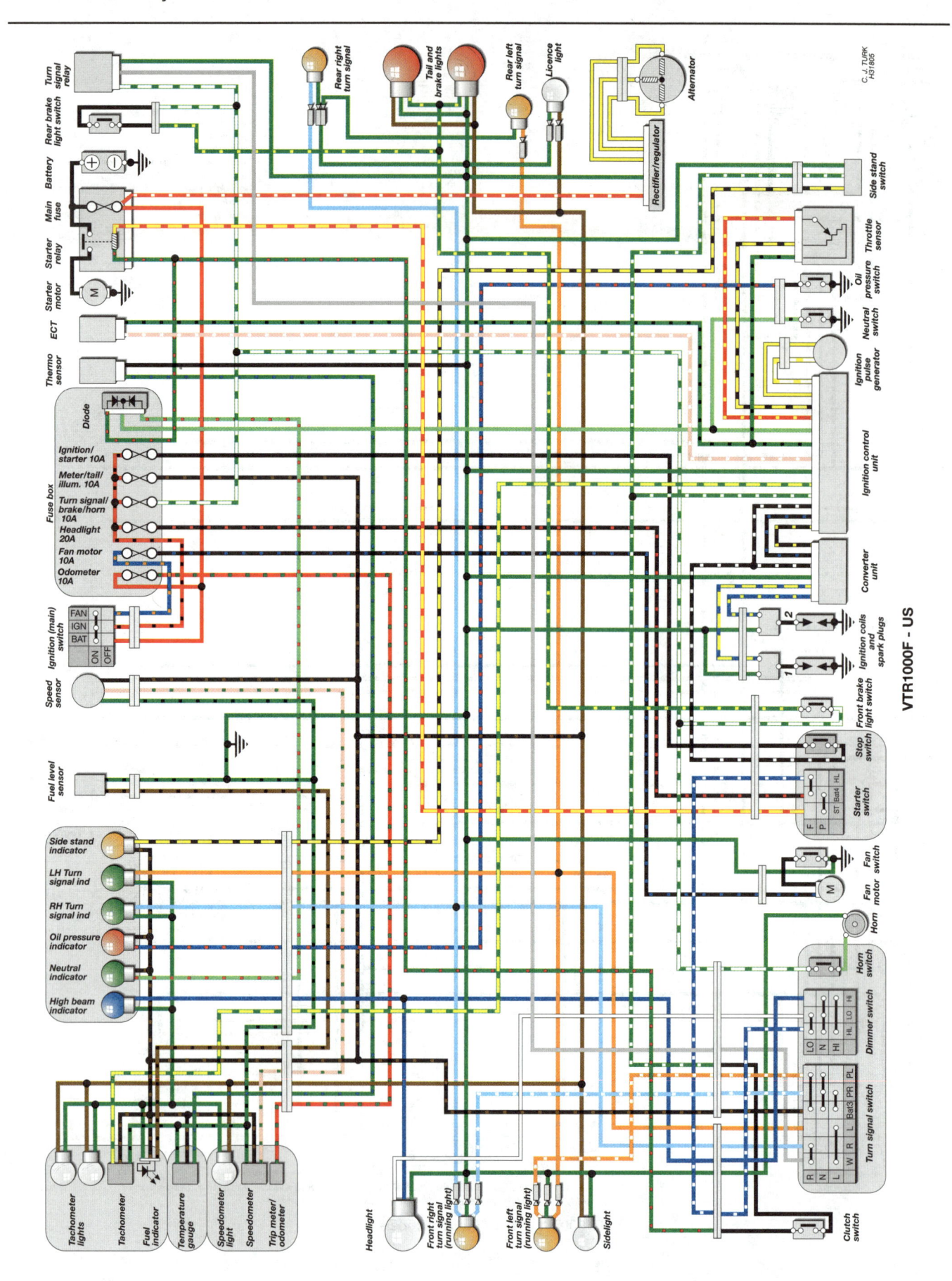

VTR1000F - US

Electrical system 9•33

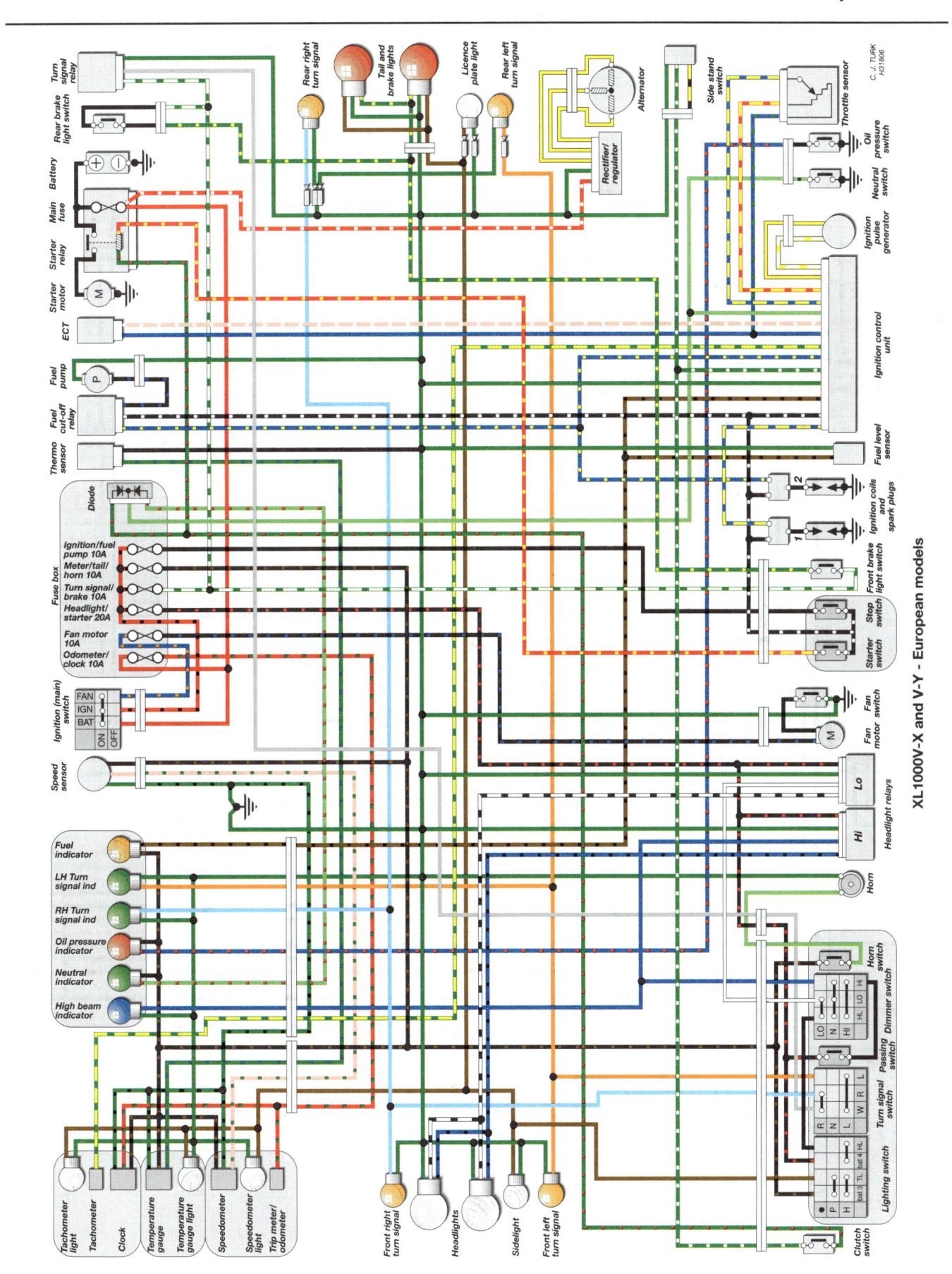

XL1000V-X and V-Y - European models

9•34 Electrical system

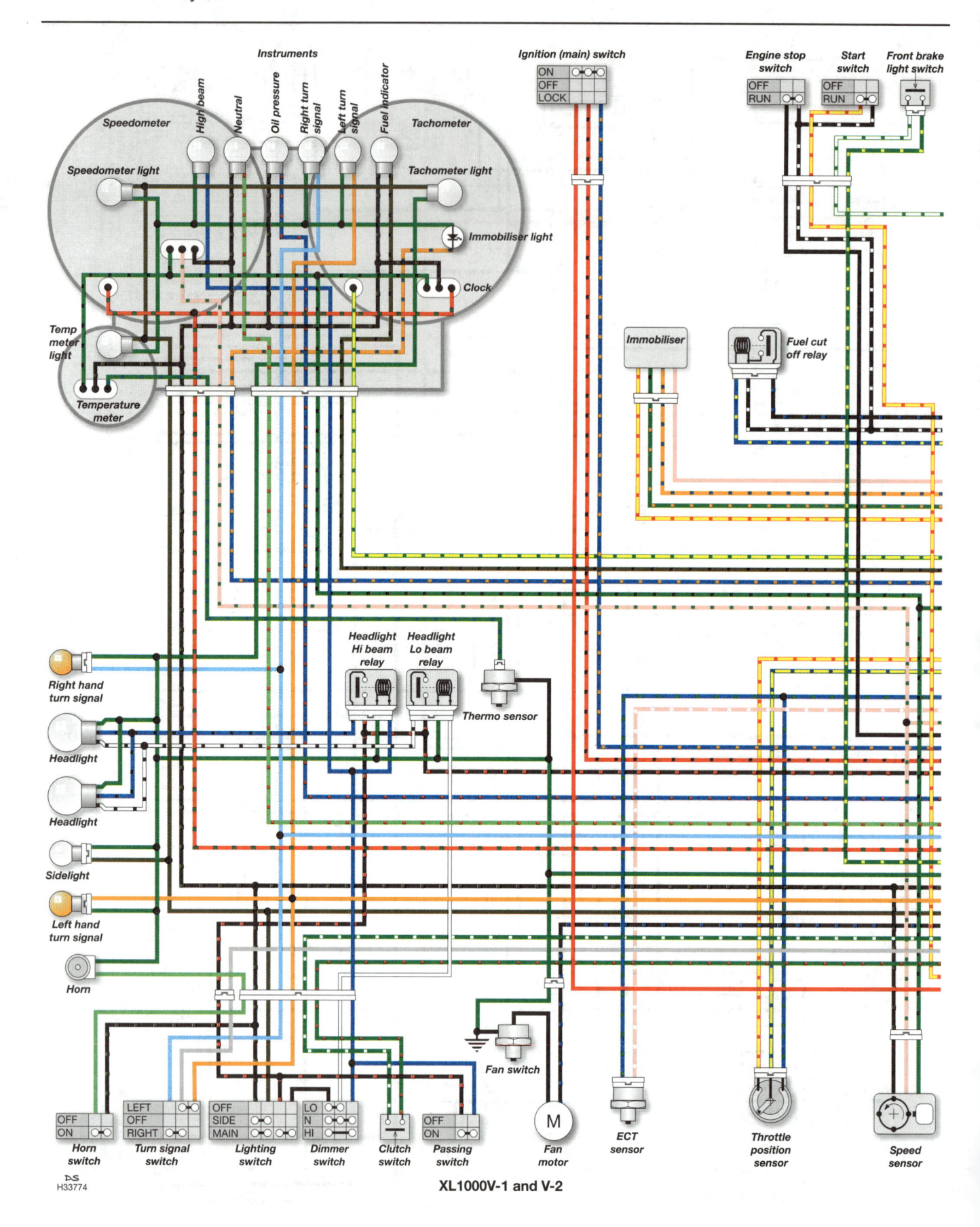

XL1000V-1 and V-2

Electrical system 9•35

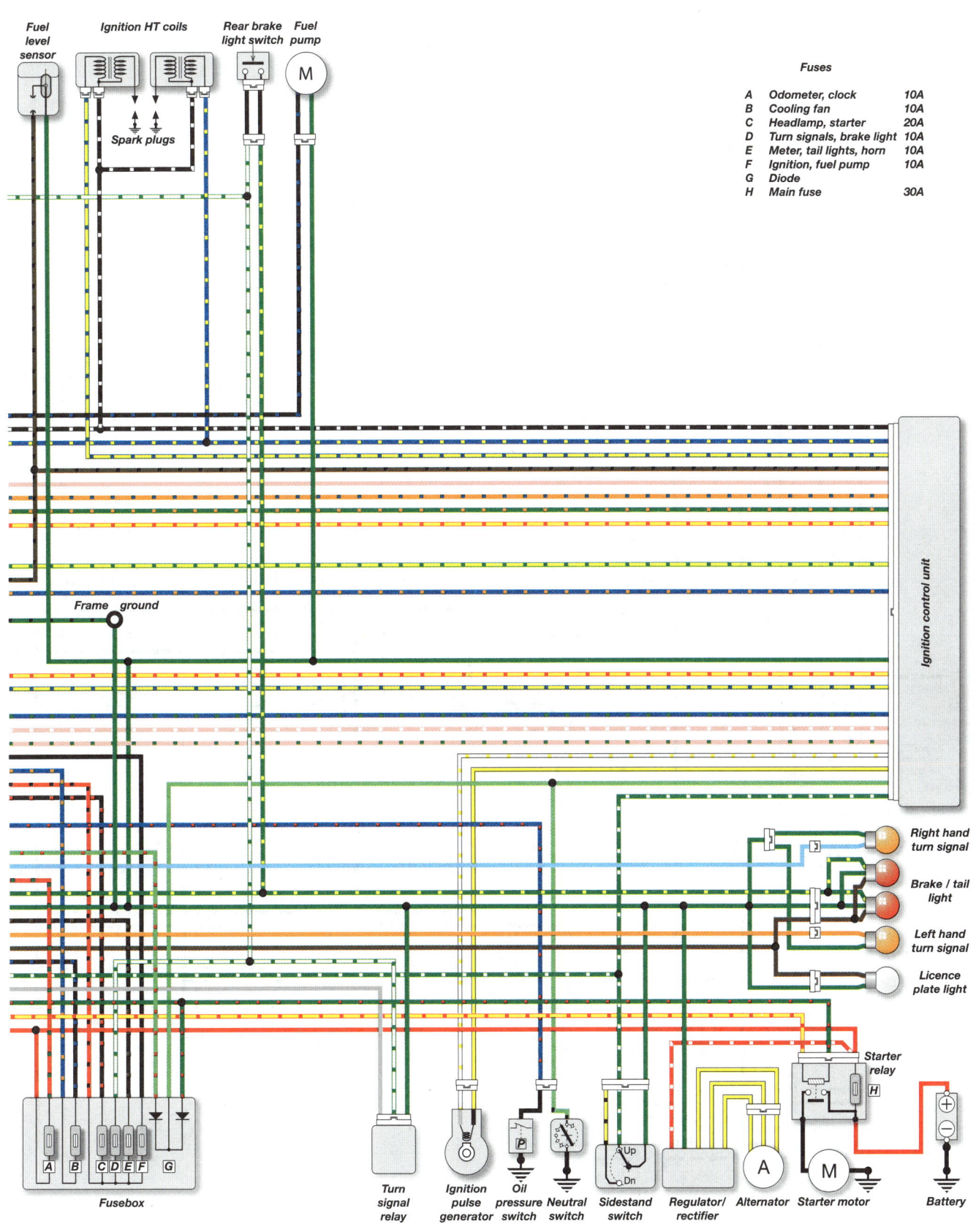

	Fuses	
A	Odometer, clock	10A
B	Cooling fan	10A
C	Headlamp, starter	20A
D	Turn signals, brake light	10A
E	Meter, tail lights, horn	10A
F	Ignition, fuel pump	10A
G	Diode	
H	Main fuse	30A

XL1000V-1 and V-2

H33774

9•36 Electrical system

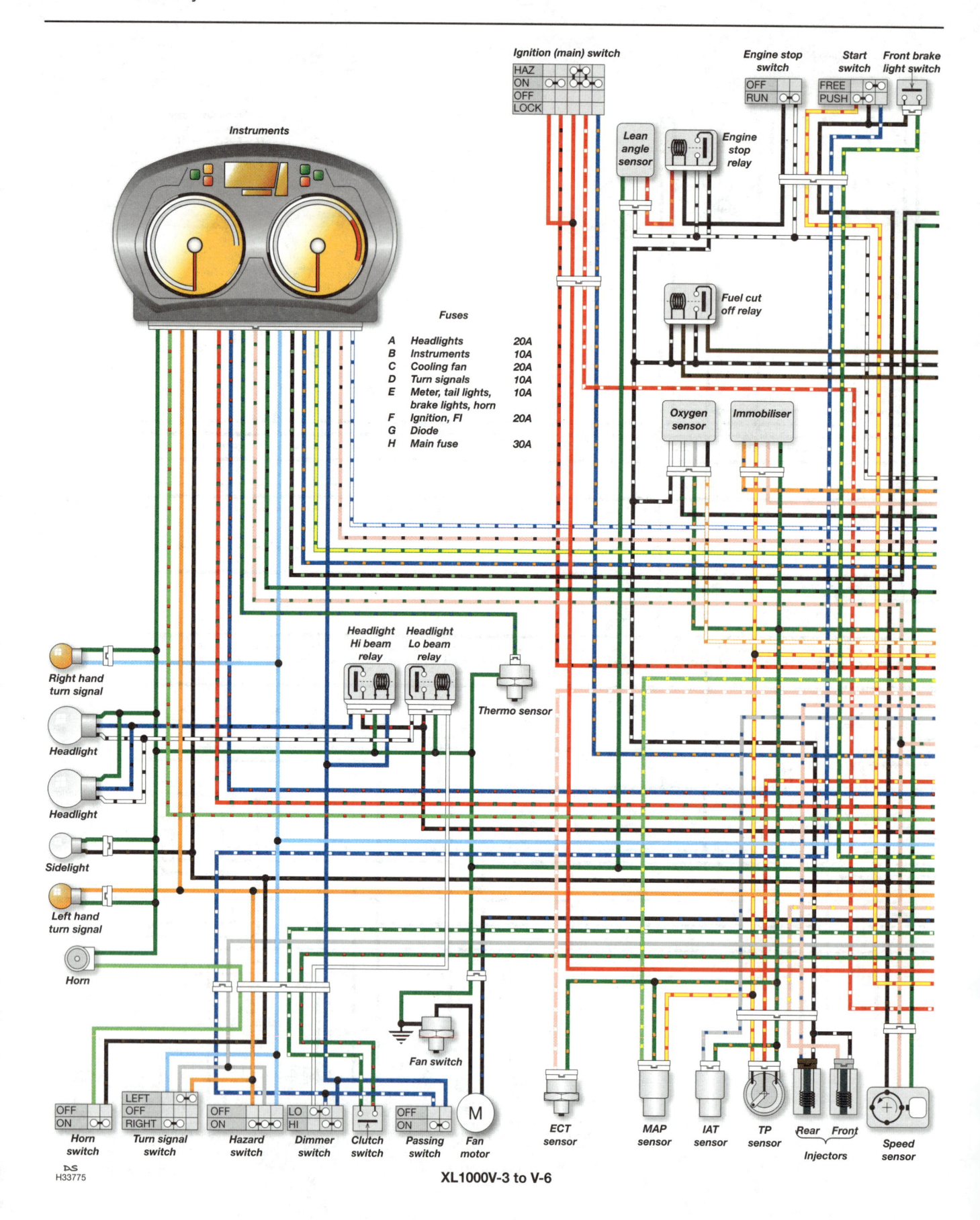

XL1000V-3 to V-6

Electrical system 9•37

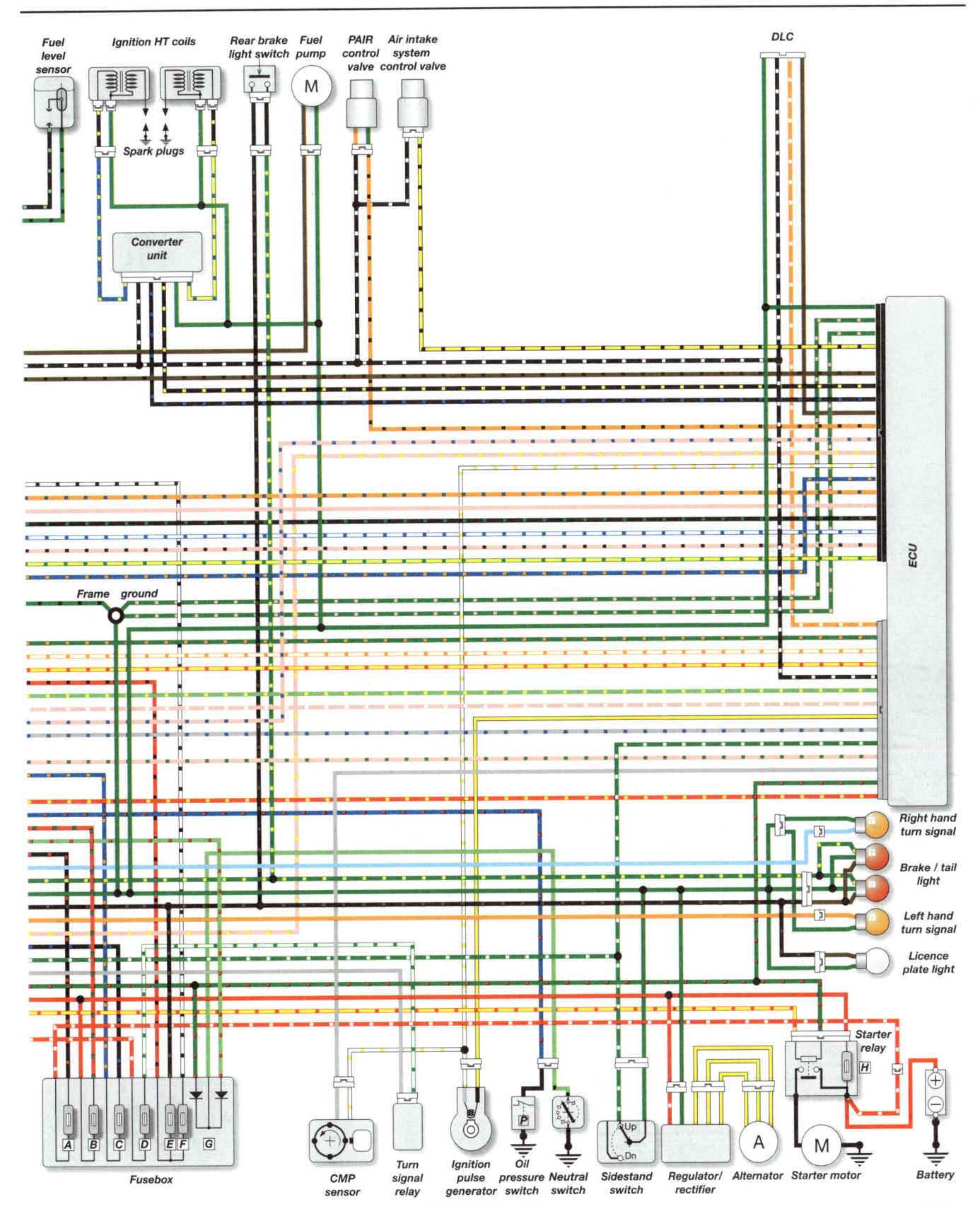

XL1000V-3 to V-6

9•38 Electrical system

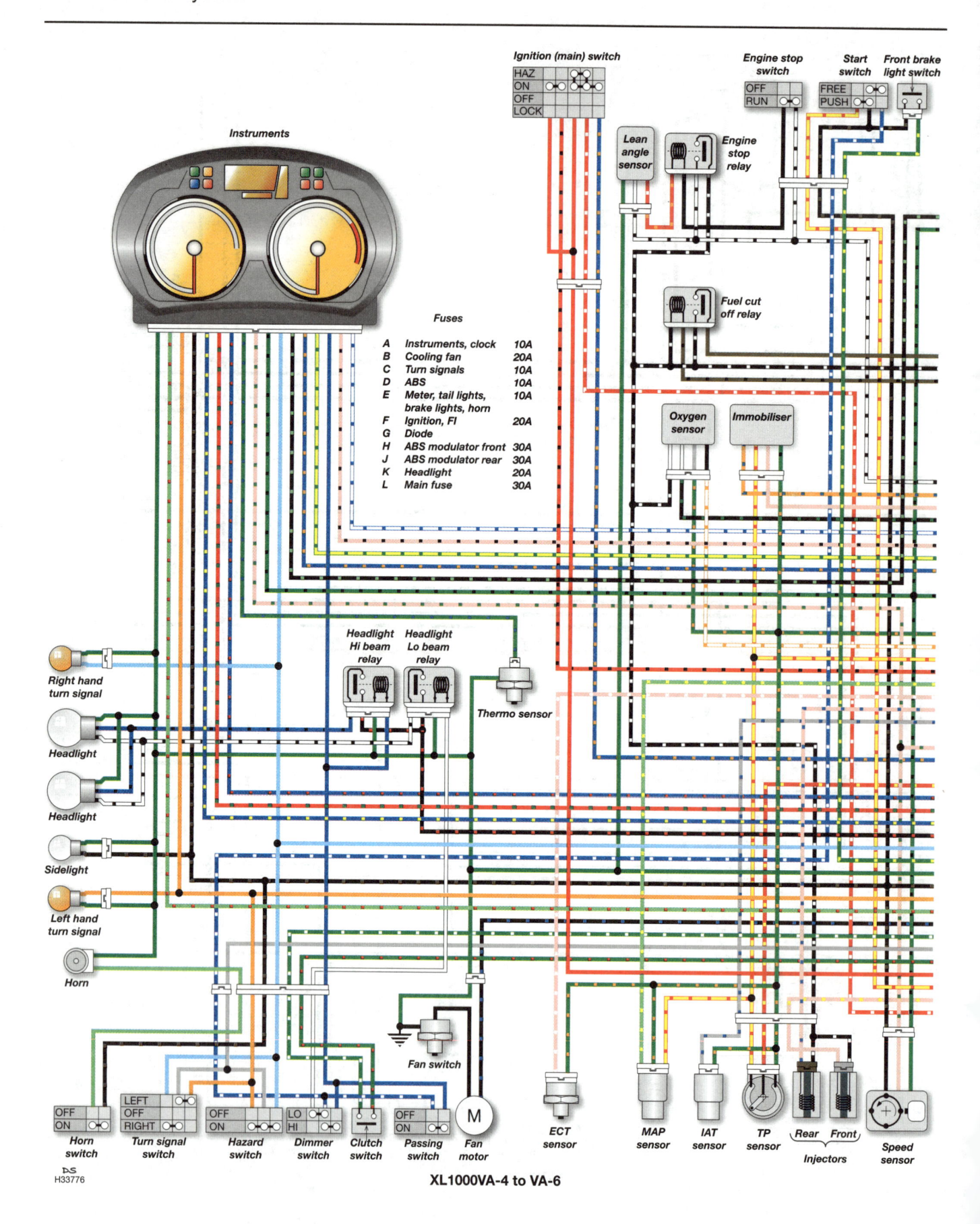

XL1000VA-4 to VA-6

Electrical system 9•39

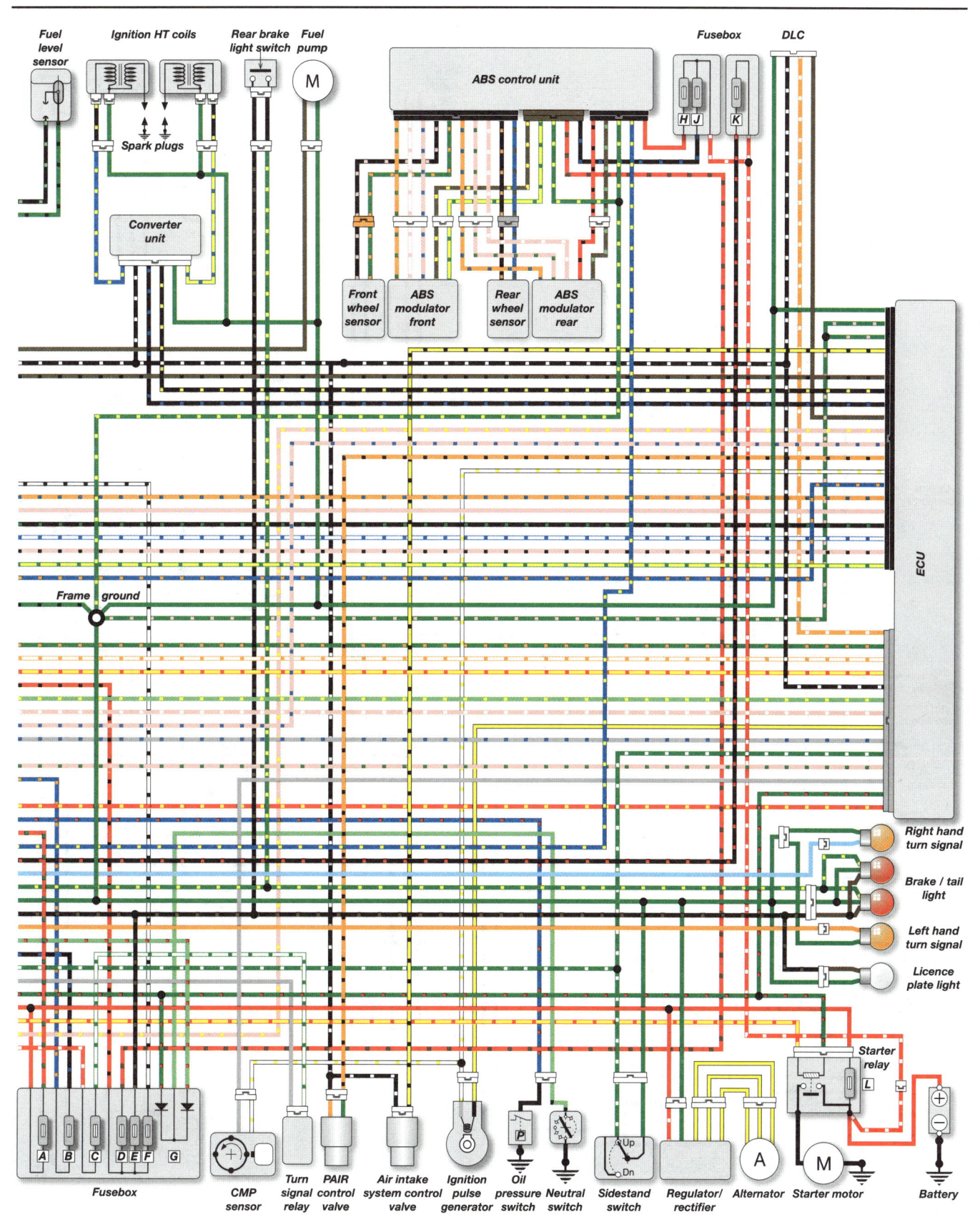

XL1000VA-4 to VA-6

9•40 Electrical system

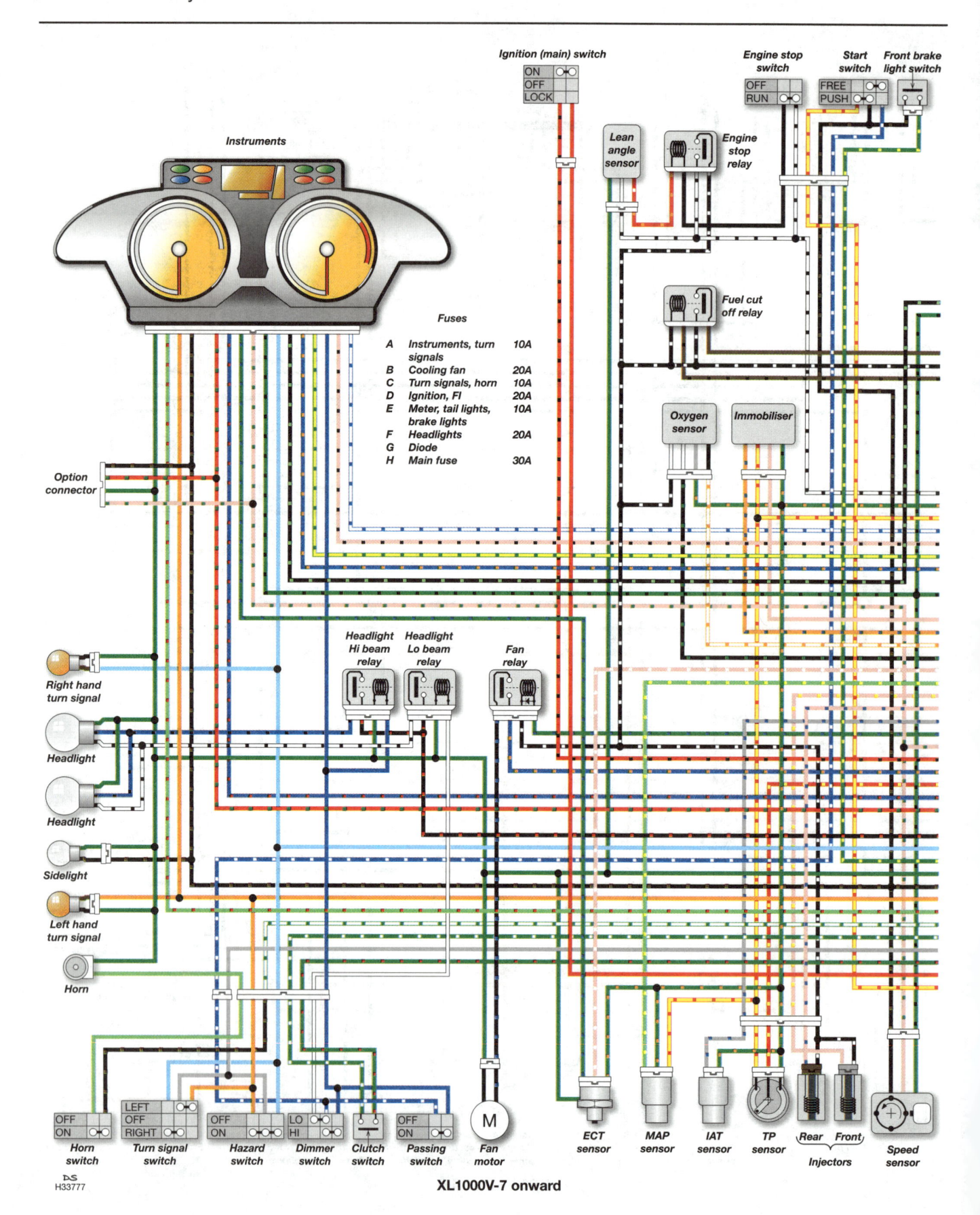

XL1000V-7 onward

Fuses:
- A Instruments, turn signals — 10A
- B Cooling fan — 20A
- C Turn signals, horn — 10A
- D Ignition, FI — 20A
- E Meter, tail lights, brake lights — 10A
- F Headlights — 20A
- G Diode
- H Main fuse — 30A

Electrical system 9•41

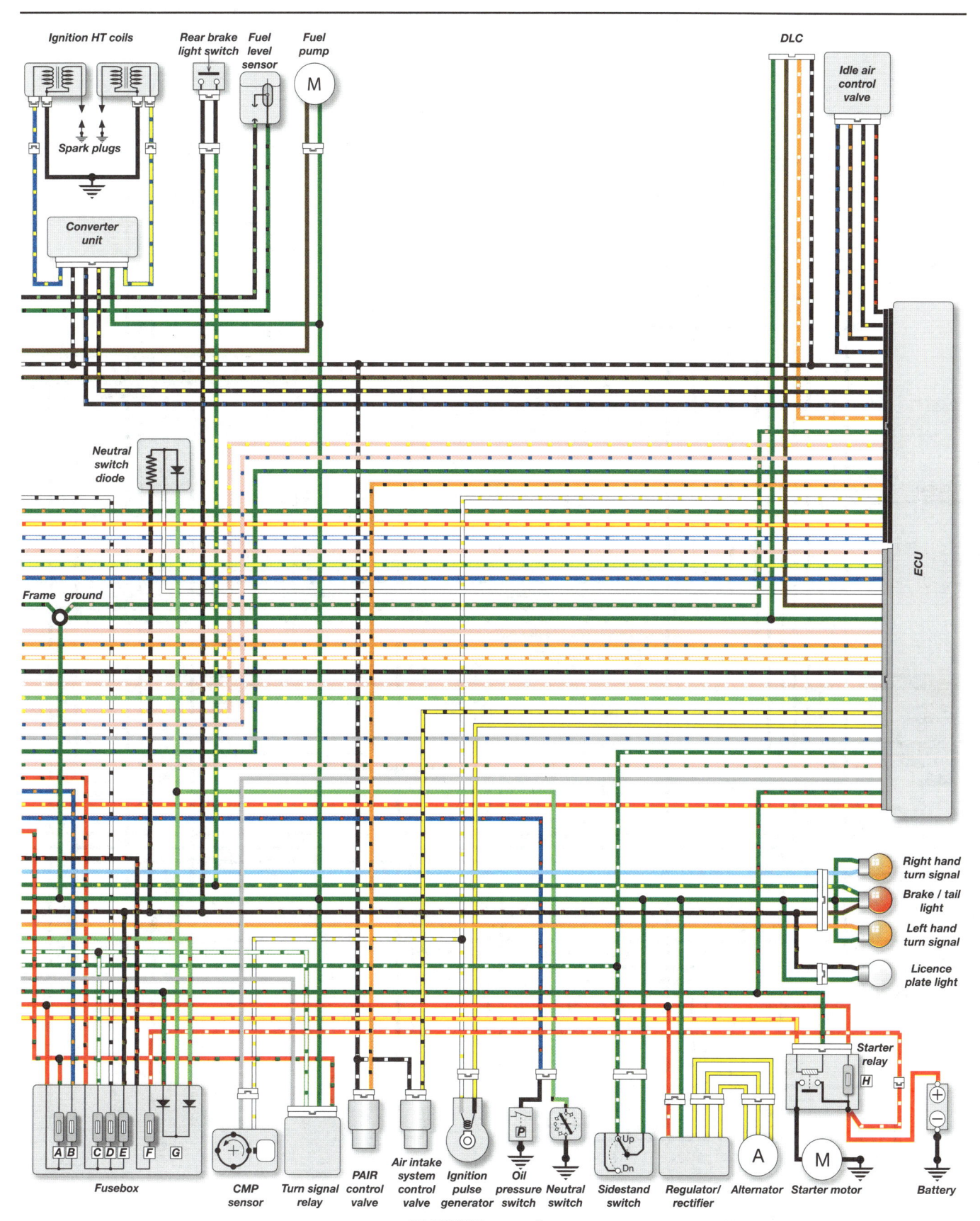

XL1000V-7 onward

9•42 Electrical system

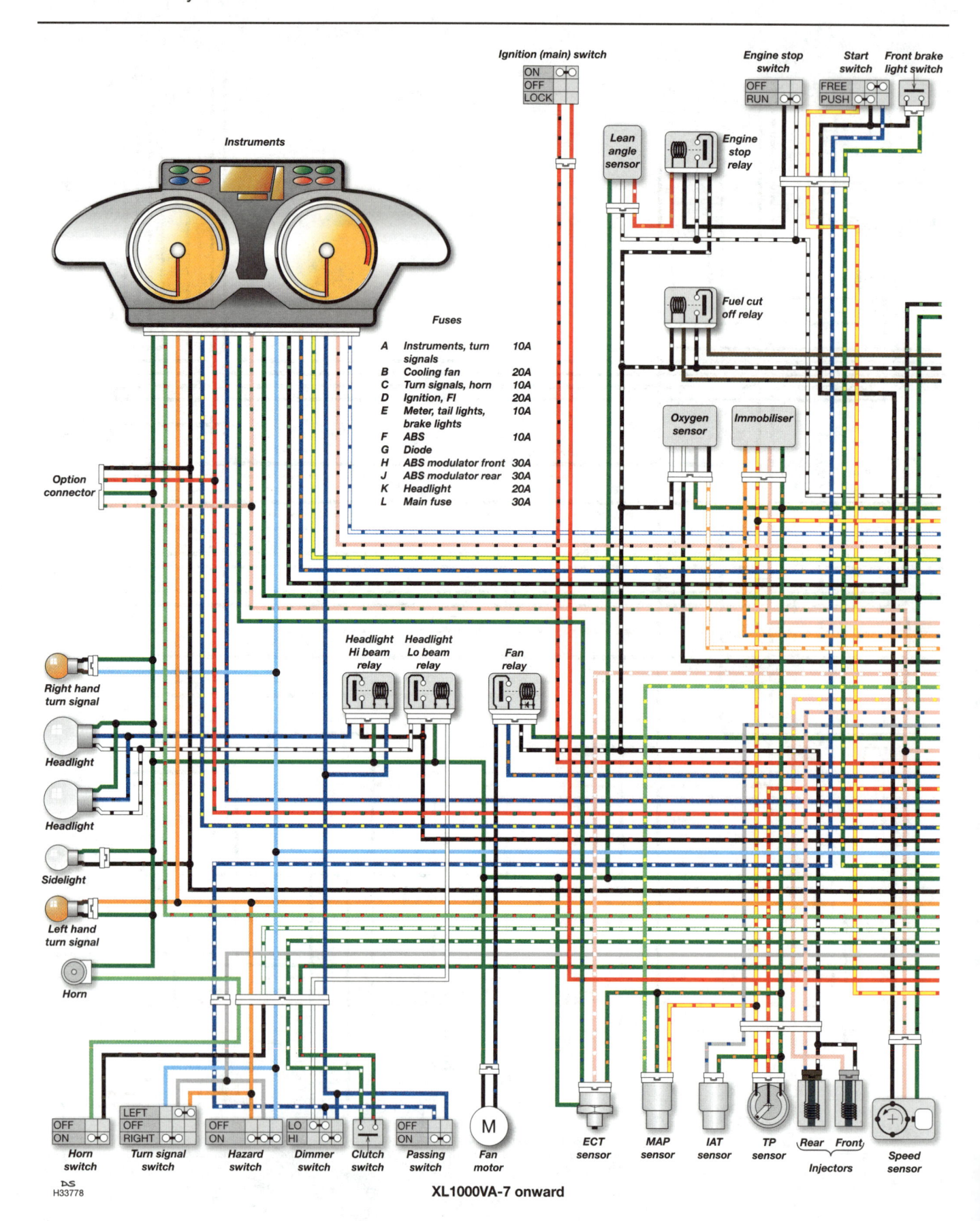

Electrical system 9•43

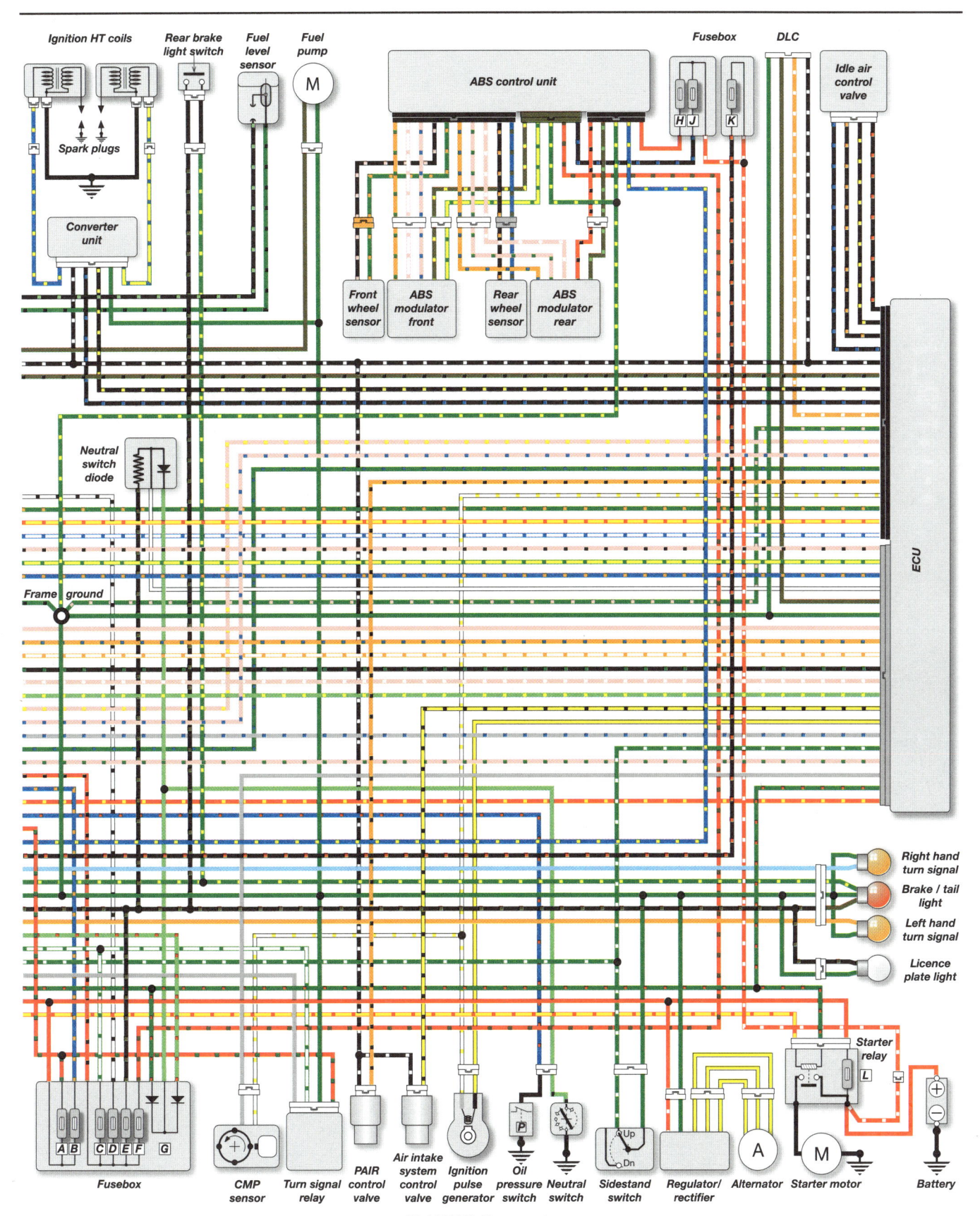

XL1000VA-7 onward

Notes

Reference REF•1

Dimensions and Weights	**REF•1**	Storage	**REF•29**
Tools and Workshop Tips	**REF•2**	Fault Finding	**REF•32**
Lubricants and fluids	**REF•20**	Fault Finding Equipment	**REF•41**
Conversion Factors	**REF•23**	Technical Terms Explained	**REF•45**
MOT Test Checks	**REF•24**	Index	**REF•49**

Dimensions and weights

VTR1000F
Wheelbase .... 1430 mm
Overall length .... 2050 mm
Overall width .... 710 mm
Overall heigh .... 1155 mm
Seat height .... 810 mm
Footrest height .... 377 mm
Ground clearance .... 135 mm
Weight (dry)
    European models .... 192 kg
    US 49 States and Canada models .... 193 kg
    California models .... 194 kg

XL1000V-X, Y, 1 and 2 models
Wheelbase .... 1560 mm
Overall length .... 2295 mm
Overall width .... 880 mm
Overall height .... 1460 mm
Seat height .... 845 mm
Footrest height .... 334 mm
Ground clearance .... 195 mm
Weight (dry) .... 220 kg

XL1000V-3, 4, 5 and 6 models
Wheelbase .... 1559 mm
Overall length .... 2292 mm
Overall width .... 924 mm
Overall height .... 1465 mm
Seat height .... 843 mm
Footrest height .... 338 mm
Ground clearance .... 181 mm
Weight (dry) .... 245 kg

XL1000V-7 models onward
Wheelbase .... 1555 mm
Overall length .... 2305 mm
Overall width .... 925 mm
Overall height
    windshield lowered .... 1465 mm
    windshield raised .... 1505 mm
Seat height .... 844 mm
Footrest height .... 338 mm
Ground clearance .... 177 mm
Weight (dry) .... 250 kg

REF•2 Tools and Workshop Tips

Buying tools

A toolkit is a fundamental requirement for servicing and repairing a motorcycle. Although there will be an initial expense in building up enough tools for servicing, this will soon be offset by the savings made by doing the job yourself. As experience and confidence grow, additional tools can be added to enable the repair and overhaul of the motorcycle. Many of the specialist tools are expensive and not often used so it may be preferable to hire them, or for a group of friends or motorcycle club to join in the purchase.

As a rule, it is better to buy more expensive, good quality tools. Cheaper tools are likely to wear out faster and need to be renewed more often, nullifying the original saving.

> **Warning: To avoid the risk of a poor quality tool breaking in use, causing injury or damage to the component being worked on, always aim to purchase tools which meet the relevant national safety standards.**

The following lists of tools do not represent the manufacturer's service tools, but serve as a guide to help the owner decide which tools are needed for this level of work. In addition, items such as an electric drill, hacksaw, files, soldering iron and a workbench equipped with a vice, may be needed. Although not classed as tools, a selection of bolts, screws, nuts, washers and pieces of tubing always come in useful.

For more information about tools, refer to the Haynes *Motorcycle Workshop Practice Techbook* (Bk. No. 3470).

Manufacturer's service tools

Inevitably certain tasks require the use of a service tool. Where possible an alternative tool or method of approach is recommended, but sometimes there is no option if personal injury or damage to the component is to be avoided. Where required, service tools are referred to in the relevant procedure.

Service tools can usually only be purchased from a motorcycle dealer and are identified by a part number. Some of the commonly-used tools, such as rotor pullers, are available in aftermarket form from mail-order motorcycle tool and accessory suppliers.

Maintenance and minor repair tools

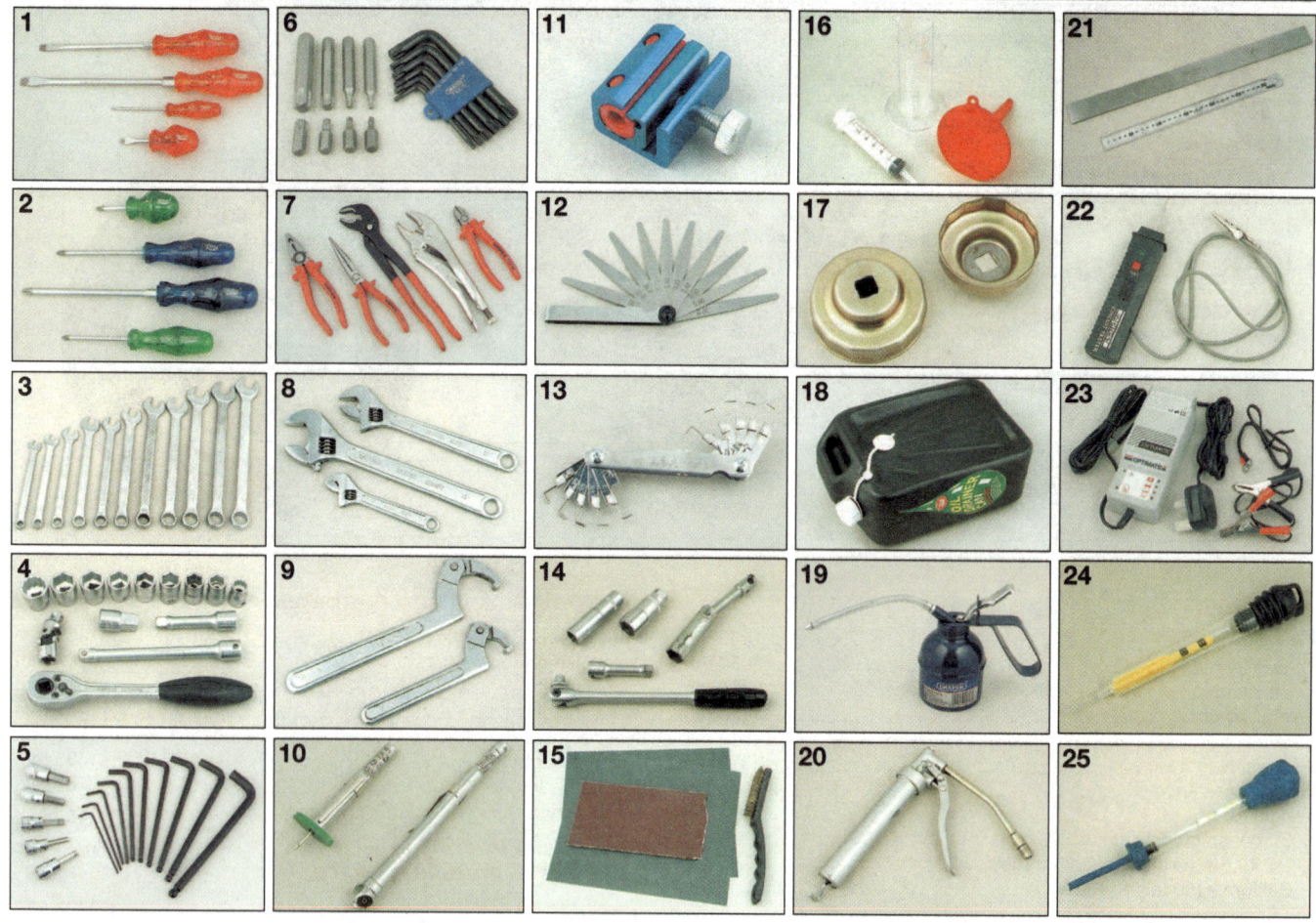

1. Set of flat-bladed screwdrivers
2. Set of Phillips head screwdrivers
3. Combination open-end and ring spanners
4. Socket set (3/8 inch or 1/2 inch drive)
5. Set of Allen keys or bits
6. Set of Torx keys or bits
7. Pliers, cutters and self-locking grips (Mole grips)
8. Adjustable spanners
9. C-spanners
10. Tread depth gauge and tyre pressure gauge
11. Cable oiler clamp
12. Feeler gauges
13. Spark plug gap measuring tool
14. Spark plug spanner or deep plug sockets
15. Wire brush and emery paper
16. Calibrated syringe, measuring vessel and funnel
17. Oil filter adapters
18. Oil drainer can or tray
19. Pump type oil can
20. Grease gun
21. Straight-edge and steel rule
22. Continuity tester
23. Battery charger
24. Hydrometer (for battery specific gravity check)
25. Anti-freeze tester (for liquid-cooled engines)

Tools and Workshop Tips REF•3

Repair and overhaul tools

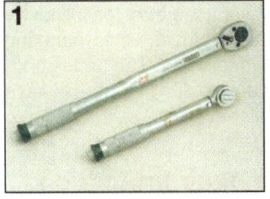

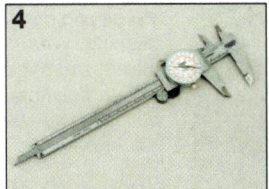

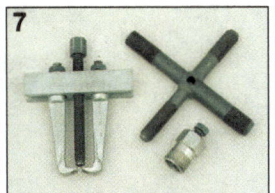

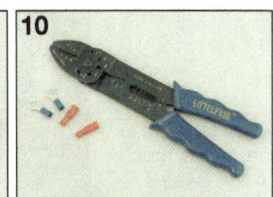

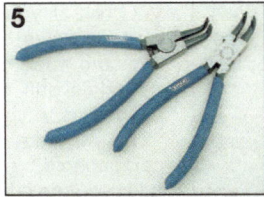

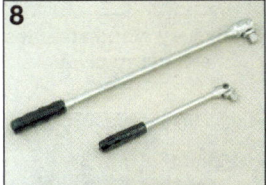

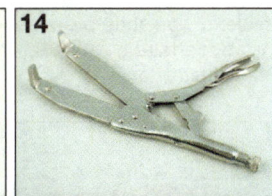

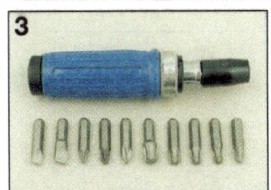

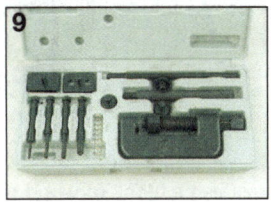

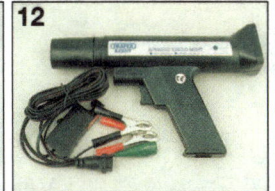

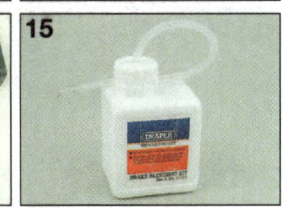

1 Torque wrench
  (small and mid-ranges)
2 Conventional, plastic or
  soft-faced hammers
3 Impact driver set
4 Vernier gauge
5 Circlip pliers (internal and
  external, or combination)
6 Set of cold chisels
  and punches
7 Selection of pullers
8 Breaker bars
9 Chain breaking/
  riveting tool set
10 Wire stripper and
   crimper tool
11 Multimeter (measures
   amps, volts and ohms)
12 Stroboscope (for
   dynamic timing checks)
13 Hose clamp
   (wingnut type shown)
14 Clutch holding tool
15 One-man brake/clutch
   bleeder kit

Specialist tools

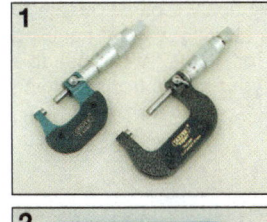

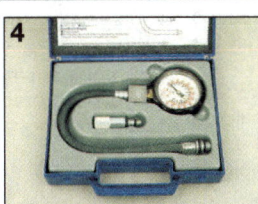

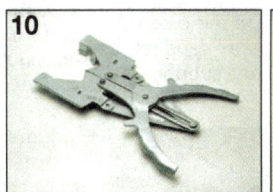

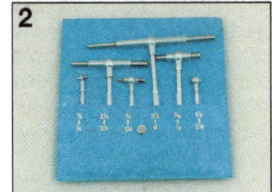

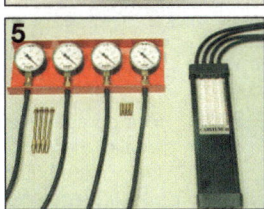

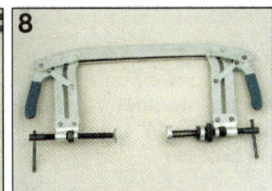

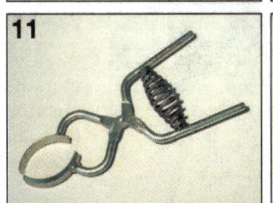

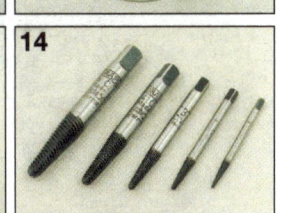

1 Micrometers
  (external type)
2 Telescoping gauges
3 Dial gauge
4 Cylinder
  compression gauge
5 Vacuum gauges (left) or
  manometer (right)
6 Oil pressure gauge
7 Plastigauge kit
8 Valve spring compressor
  (4-stroke engines)
9 Piston pin drawbolt tool
10 Piston ring removal and
   installation tool
11 Piston ring clamp
12 Cylinder bore hone
   (stone type shown)
13 Stud extractor
14 Screw extractor set
15 Bearing driver set

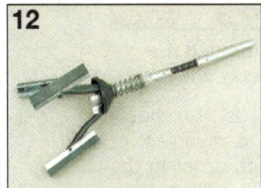

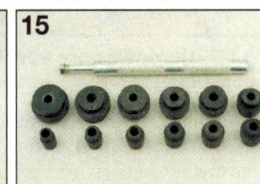

REF•4 Tools and Workshop Tips

1 Workshop equipment and facilities

The workbench

● Work is made much easier by raising the bike up on a ramp - components are much more accessible if raised to waist level. The hydraulic or pneumatic types seen in the dealer's workshop are a sound investment if you undertake a lot of repairs or overhauls **(see illustration 1.1)**.

1.1 Hydraulic motorcycle ramp

● If raised off ground level, the bike must be supported on the ramp to avoid it falling. Most ramps incorporate a front wheel locating clamp which can be adjusted to suit different diameter wheels. When tightening the clamp, take care not to mark the wheel rim or damage the tyre - use wood blocks on each side to prevent this.

● Secure the bike to the ramp using tie-downs **(see illustration 1.2)**. If the bike has only a sidestand, and hence leans at a dangerous angle when raised, support the bike on an auxiliary stand.

1.2 Tie-downs are used around the passenger footrests to secure the bike

● Auxiliary (paddock) stands are widely available from mail order companies or motorcycle dealers and attach either to the wheel axle or swingarm pivot **(see illustration 1.3)**. If the motorcycle has a centrestand, you can support it under the crankcase to prevent it toppling whilst either wheel is removed **(see illustration 1.4)**.

1.3 This auxiliary stand attaches to the swingarm pivot

1.4 Always use a block of wood between the engine and jack head when supporting the engine in this way

Fumes and fire

● Refer to the Safety first! page at the beginning of the manual for full details. Make sure your workshop is equipped with a fire extinguisher suitable for fuel-related fires (Class B fire - flammable liquids) - it is not sufficient to have a water-filled extinguisher.

● Always ensure adequate ventilation is available. Unless an exhaust gas extraction system is available for use, ensure that the engine is run outside of the workshop.

● If working on the fuel system, make sure the workshop is ventilated to avoid a build-up of fumes. This applies equally to fume build-up when charging a battery. Do not smoke or allow anyone else to smoke in the workshop.

Fluids

● If you need to drain fuel from the tank, store it in an approved container marked as suitable for the storage of petrol (gasoline) **(see illustration 1.5)**. Do not store fuel in glass jars or bottles.

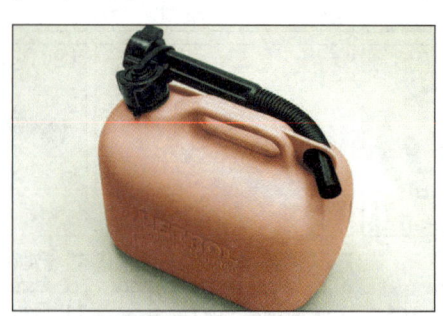

1.5 Use an approved can only for storing petrol (gasoline)

● Use proprietary engine degreasers or solvents which have a high flash-point, such as paraffin (kerosene), for cleaning off oil, grease and dirt - never use petrol (gasoline) for cleaning. Wear rubber gloves when handling solvent and engine degreaser. The fumes from certain solvents can be dangerous - always work in a well-ventilated area.

Dust, eye and hand protection

● Protect your lungs from inhalation of dust particles by wearing a filtering mask over the nose and mouth. Many frictional materials still contain asbestos which is dangerous to your health. Protect your eyes from spouts of liquid and sprung components by wearing a pair of protective goggles **(see illustration 1.6)**.

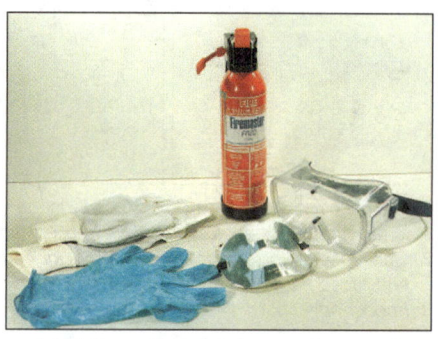

1.6 A fire extinguisher, goggles, mask and protective gloves should be at hand in the workshop

● Protect your hands from contact with solvents, fuel and oils by wearing rubber gloves. Alternatively apply a barrier cream to your hands before starting work. If handling hot components or fluids, wear suitable gloves to protect your hands from scalding and burns.

What to do with old fluids

● Old cleaning solvent, fuel, coolant and oils should not be poured down domestic drains or onto the ground. Package the fluid up in old oil containers, label it accordingly, and take it to a garage or disposal facility. Contact your local authority for location of such sites or ring the oil care hotline.

OIL CARE
0800 66 33 66
www.oilbankline.org.uk

Note: It is antisocial and illegal to dump oil down the drain. To find the location of your local oil recycling bank, call this number free.

In the USA, note that any oil supplier must accept used oil for recycling.

Tools and Workshop Tips REF•5

2 Fasteners - screws, bolts and nuts

Fastener types and applications

Bolts and screws

● Fastener head types are either of hexagonal, Torx or splined design, with internal and external versions of each type **(see illustrations 2.1 and 2.2)**; splined head fasteners are not in common use on motorcycles. The conventional slotted or Phillips head design is used for certain screws. Bolt or screw length is always measured from the underside of the head to the end of the item **(see illustration 2.11)**.

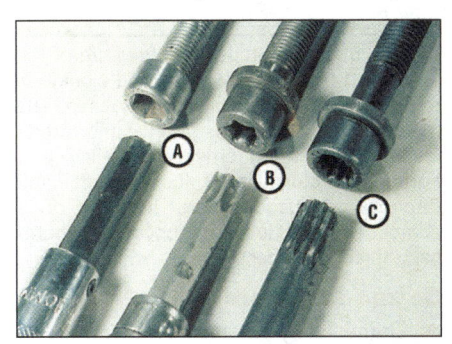

2.1 Internal hexagon/Allen (A), Torx (B) and splined (C) fasteners, with corresponding bits

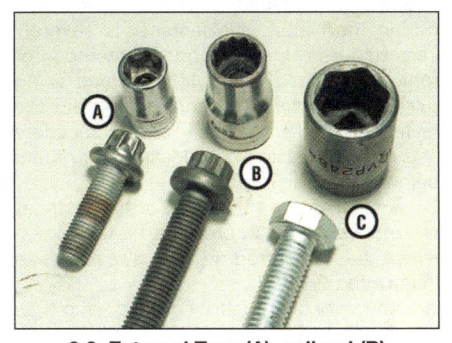

2.2 External Torx (A), splined (B) and hexagon (C) fasteners, with corresponding sockets

● Certain fasteners on the motorcycle have a tensile marking on their heads, the higher the marking the stronger the fastener. High tensile fasteners generally carry a 10 or higher marking. Never replace a high tensile fastener with one of a lower tensile strength.

Washers (see illustration 2.3)

● Plain washers are used between a fastener head and a component to prevent damage to the component or to spread the load when torque is applied. Plain washers can also be used as spacers or shims in certain assemblies. Copper or aluminium plain washers are often used as sealing washers on drain plugs.

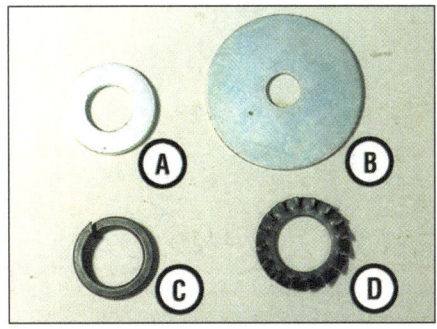

2.3 Plain washer (A), penny washer (B), spring washer (C) and serrated washer (D)

● The split-ring spring washer works by applying axial tension between the fastener head and component. If flattened, it is fatigued and must be renewed. If a plain (flat) washer is used on the fastener, position the spring washer between the fastener and the plain washer.
● Serrated star type washers dig into the fastener and component faces, preventing loosening. They are often used on electrical earth (ground) connections to the frame.
● Cone type washers (sometimes called Belleville) are conical and when tightened apply axial tension between the fastener head and component. They must be installed with the dished side against the component and often carry an OUTSIDE marking on their outer face. If flattened, they are fatigued and must be renewed.
● Tab washers are used to lock plain nuts or bolts on a shaft. A portion of the tab washer is bent up hard against one flat of the nut or bolt to prevent it loosening. Due to the tab washer being deformed in use, a new tab washer should be used every time it is disturbed.
● Wave washers are used to take up endfloat on a shaft. They provide light springing and prevent excessive side-to-side play of a component. Can be found on rocker arm shafts.

Nuts and split pins

● Conventional plain nuts are usually six-sided **(see illustration 2.4)**. They are sized by thread diameter and pitch. High tensile nuts carry a number on one end to denote their tensile strength.

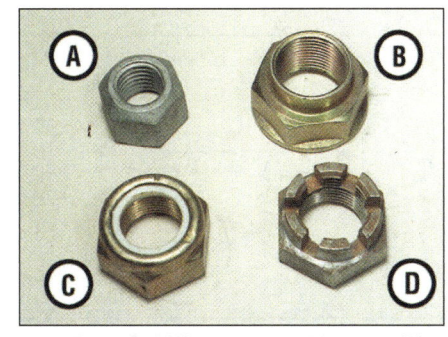

2.4 Plain nut (A), shouldered locknut (B), nylon insert nut (C) and castellated nut (D)

● Self-locking nuts either have a nylon insert, or two spring metal tabs, or a shoulder which is staked into a groove in the shaft - their advantage over conventional plain nuts is a resistance to loosening due to vibration. The nylon insert type can be used a number of times, but must be renewed when the friction of the nylon insert is reduced, ie when the nut spins freely on the shaft. The spring tab type can be reused unless the tabs are damaged. The shouldered type must be renewed every time it is disturbed.
● Split pins (cotter pins) are used to lock a castellated nut to a shaft or to prevent slackening of a plain nut. Common applications are wheel axles and brake torque arms. Because the split pin arms are deformed to lock around the nut a new split pin must always be used on installation - always fit the correct size split pin which will fit snugly in the shaft hole. Make sure the split pin arms are correctly located around the nut **(see illustrations 2.5 and 2.6)**.

2.5 Bend split pin (cotter pin) arms as shown (arrows) to secure a castellated nut

2.6 Bend split pin (cotter pin) arms as shown to secure a plain nut

Caution: If the castellated nut slots do not align with the shaft hole after tightening to the torque setting, tighten the nut until the next slot aligns with the hole - never slacken the nut to align its slot.

● R-pins (shaped like the letter R), or slip pins as they are sometimes called, are sprung and can be reused if they are otherwise in good condition. Always install R-pins with their closed end facing forwards **(see illustration 2.7)**.

REF•6 Tools and Workshop Tips

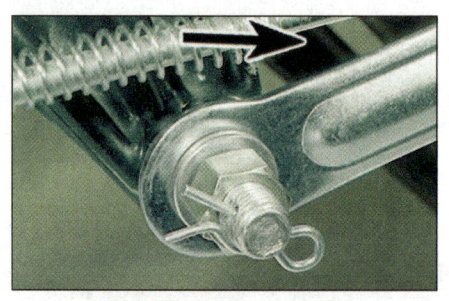

2.7 Correct fitting of R-pin. Arrow indicates forward direction

Circlips (see illustration 2.8)

● Circlips (sometimes called snap-rings) are used to retain components on a shaft or in a housing and have corresponding external or internal ears to permit removal. Parallel-sided (machined) circlips can be installed either way round in their groove, whereas stamped circlips (which have a chamfered edge on one face) must be installed with the chamfer facing away from the direction of thrust load **(see illustration 2.9)**.

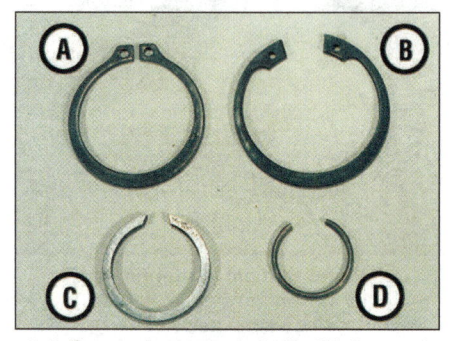

2.8 External stamped circlip (A), internal stamped circlip (B), machined circlip (C) and wire circlip (D)

● Always use circlip pliers to remove and install circlips; expand or compress them just enough to remove them. After installation, rotate the circlip in its groove to ensure it is securely seated. If installing a circlip on a splined shaft, always align its opening with a shaft channel to ensure the circlip ends are well supported and unlikely to catch **(see illustration 2.10)**.

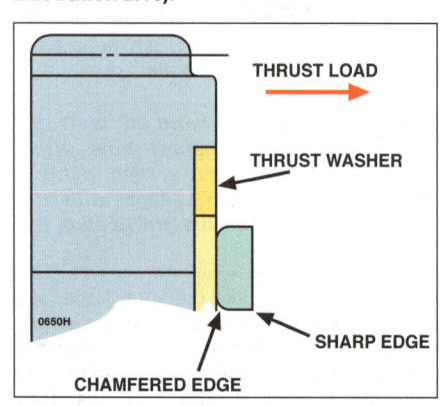

2.9 Correct fitting of a stamped circlip

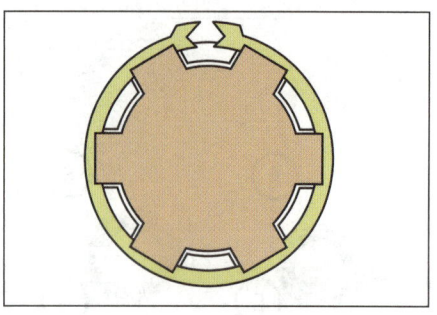

2.10 Align circlip opening with shaft channel

● Circlips can wear due to the thrust of components and become loose in their grooves, with the subsequent danger of becoming dislodged in operation. For this reason, renewal is advised every time a circlip is disturbed.

● Wire circlips are commonly used as piston pin retaining clips. If a removal tang is provided, long-nosed pliers can be used to dislodge them, otherwise careful use of a small flat-bladed screwdriver is necessary. Wire circlips should be renewed every time they are disturbed.

Thread diameter and pitch

● Diameter of a male thread (screw, bolt or stud) is the outside diameter of the threaded portion **(see illustration 2.11)**. Most motorcycle manufacturers use the ISO (International Standards Organisation) metric system expressed in millimetres, eg M6 refers to a 6 mm diameter thread. Sizing is the same for nuts, except that the thread diameter is measured across the valleys of the nut.

● Pitch is the distance between the peaks of the thread **(see illustration 2.11)**. It is expressed in millimetres, thus a common bolt size may be expressed as 6.0 x 1.0 mm (6 mm thread diameter and 1 mm pitch). Generally pitch increases in proportion to thread diameter, although there are always exceptions.

● Thread diameter and pitch are related for conventional fastener applications and the accompanying table can be used as a guide. Additionally, the AF (Across Flats), spanner or socket size dimension of the bolt or nut **(see illustration 2.11)** is linked to thread and pitch specification. Thread pitch can be measured with a thread gauge **(see illustration 2.12)**.

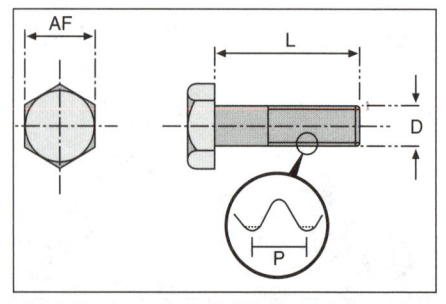

2.11 Fastener length (L), thread diameter (D), thread pitch (P) and head size (AF)

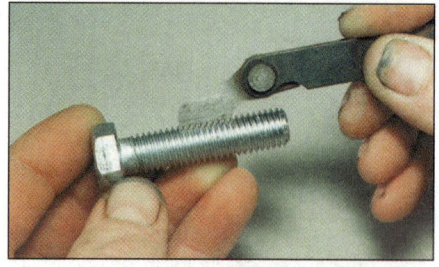

2.12 Using a thread gauge to measure pitch

AF size	Thread diameter x pitch (mm)
8 mm	M5 x 0.8
8 mm	M6 x 1.0
10 mm	M6 x 1.0
12 mm	M8 x 1.25
14 mm	M10 x 1.25
17 mm	M12 x 1.25

● The threads of most fasteners are of the right-hand type, ie they are turned clockwise to tighten and anti-clockwise to loosen. The reverse situation applies to left-hand thread fasteners, which are turned anti-clockwise to tighten and clockwise to loosen. Left-hand threads are used where rotation of a component might loosen a conventional right-hand thread fastener.

Seized fasteners

● Corrosion of external fasteners due to water or reaction between two dissimilar metals can occur over a period of time. It will build up sooner in wet conditions or in countries where salt is used on the roads during the winter. If a fastener is severely corroded it is likely that normal methods of removal will fail and result in its head being ruined. When you attempt removal, the fastener thread should be heard to crack free and unscrew easily - if it doesn't, stop there before damaging something.

● A smart tap on the head of the fastener will often succeed in breaking free corrosion which has occurred in the threads **(see illustration 2.13)**.

● An aerosol penetrating fluid (such as WD-40) applied the night beforehand may work its way down into the thread and ease removal. Depending on the location, you may be able to make up a Plasticine well around the fastener head and fill it with penetrating fluid.

2.13 A sharp tap on the head of a fastener will often break free a corroded thread

Tools and Workshop Tips REF•7

- If you are working on an engine internal component, corrosion will most likely not be a problem due to the well lubricated environment. However, components can be very tight and an impact driver is a useful tool in freeing them **(see illustration 2.14)**.

2.14 Using an impact driver to free a fastener

- Where corrosion has occurred between dissimilar metals (eg steel and aluminium alloy), the application of heat to the fastener head will create a disproportionate expansion rate between the two metals and break the seizure caused by the corrosion. Whether heat can be applied depends on the location of the fastener - any surrounding components likely to be damaged must first be removed **(see illustration 2.15)**. Heat can be applied using a paint stripper heat gun or clothes iron, or by immersing the component in boiling water - wear protective gloves to prevent scalding or burns to the hands.

2.15 Using heat to free a seized fastener

- As a last resort, it is possible to use a hammer and cold chisel to work the fastener head unscrewed **(see illustration 2.16)**. This will damage the fastener, but more importantly extreme care must be taken not to damage the surrounding component.

Caution: Remember that the component being secured is generally of more value than the bolt, nut or screw - when the fastener is freed, do not unscrew it with force, instead work the fastener back and forth when resistance is felt to prevent thread damage.

2.16 Using a hammer and chisel to free a seized fastener

Broken fasteners and damaged heads

- If the shank of a broken bolt or screw is accessible you can grip it with self-locking grips. The knurled wheel type stud extractor tool or self-gripping stud puller tool is particularly useful for removing the long studs which screw into the cylinder mouth surface of the crankcase or bolts and screws from which the head has broken off **(see illustration 2.17)**. Studs can also be removed by locking two nuts together on the threaded end of the stud and using a spanner on the lower nut **(see illustration 2.18)**.

2.17 Using a stud extractor tool to remove a broken crankcase stud

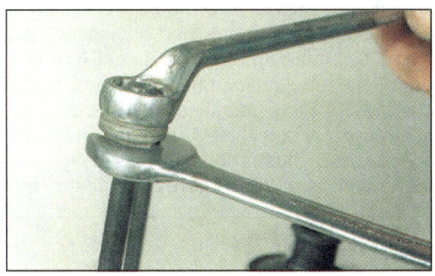

2.18 Two nuts can be locked together to unscrew a stud from a component

- A bolt or screw which has broken off below or level with the casing must be extracted using a screw extractor set. Centre punch the fastener to centralise the drill bit, then drill a hole in the fastener **(see illustration 2.19)**. Select a drill bit which is approximately half to three-quarters the

2.19 When using a screw extractor, first drill a hole in the fastener . . .

diameter of the fastener and drill to a depth which will accommodate the extractor. Use the largest size extractor possible, but avoid leaving too small a wall thickness otherwise the extractor will merely force the fastener walls outwards wedging it in the casing thread.

- If a spiral type extractor is used, thread it anti-clockwise into the fastener. As it is screwed in, it will grip the fastener and unscrew it from the casing **(see illustration 2.20)**.

2.20 . . . then thread the extractor anti-clockwise into the fastener

- If a taper type extractor is used, tap it into the fastener so that it is firmly wedged in place. Unscrew the extractor (anti-clockwise) to draw the fastener out.

> ⚠ **Warning: Stud extractors are very hard and may break off in the fastener if care is not taken - ask an engineer about spark erosion if this happens.**

- Alternatively, the broken bolt/screw can be drilled out and the hole retapped for an oversize bolt/screw or a diamond-section thread insert. It is essential that the drilling is carried out squarely and to the correct depth, otherwise the casing may be ruined - if in doubt, entrust the work to an engineer.

- Bolts and nuts with rounded corners cause the correct size spanner or socket to slip when force is applied. Of the types of spanner/socket available always use a six-point type rather than an eight or twelve-point type - better grip

REF•8 Tools and Workshop Tips

2.21 Comparison of surface drive ring spanner (left) with 12-point type (right)

is obtained. Surface drive spanners grip the middle of the hex flats, rather than the corners, and are thus good in cases of damaged heads **(see illustration 2.21)**.

- Slotted-head or Phillips-head screws are often damaged by the use of the wrong size screwdriver. Allen-head and Torx-head screws are much less likely to sustain damage. If enough of the screw head is exposed you can use a hacksaw to cut a slot in its head and then use a conventional flat-bladed screwdriver to remove it. Alternatively use a hammer and cold chisel to tap the head of the fastener around to slacken it. Always replace damaged fasteners with new ones, preferably Torx or Allen-head type.

> **HAYNES HiNT**
> A dab of valve grinding compound between the screw head and screwdriver tip will often give a good grip.

Thread repair

- Threads (particularly those in aluminium alloy components) can be damaged by overtightening, being assembled with dirt in the threads, or from a component working loose and vibrating. Eventually the thread will fail completely, and it will be impossible to tighten the fastener.
- If a thread is damaged or clogged with old locking compound it can be renovated with a thread repair tool (thread chaser) **(see illustrations 2.22 and 2.23)**; special thread

2.22 A thread repair tool being used to correct an internal thread

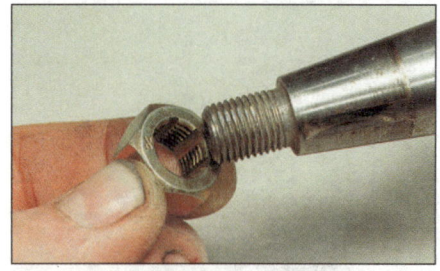

2.23 A thread repair tool being used to correct an external thread

chasers are available for spark plug hole threads. The tool will not cut a new thread, but clean and true the original thread. Make sure that you use the correct diameter and pitch tool. Similarly, external threads can be cleaned up with a die or a thread restorer file **(see illustration 2.24)**.

2.24 Using a thread restorer file

- It is possible to drill out the old thread and retap the component to the next thread size. This will work where there is enough surrounding material and a new bolt or screw can be obtained. Sometimes, however, this is not possible - such as where the bolt/screw passes through another component which must also be suitably modified, also in cases where a spark plug or oil drain plug cannot be obtained in a larger diameter thread size.
- The diamond-section thread insert (often known by its popular trade name of Heli-Coil) is a simple and effective method of renewing the thread and retaining the original size. A kit can be purchased which contains the tap, insert and installing tool **(see illustration 2.25)**. Drill out the damaged thread with the size drill specified **(see illustration 2.26)**. Carefully retap the thread **(see illustration 2.27)**. Install the

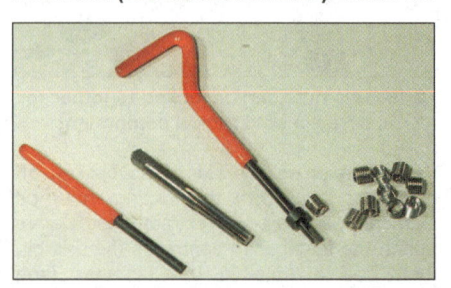

2.25 Obtain a thread insert kit to suit the thread diameter and pitch required

2.26 To install a thread insert, first drill out the original thread . . .

2.27 . . . tap a new thread . . .

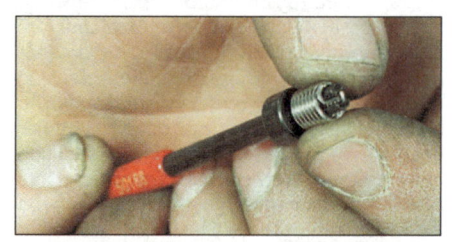

2.28 . . . fit insert on the installing tool . . .

2.29 . . . and thread into the component . . .

2.30 . . . break off the tang when complete

insert on the installing tool and thread it slowly into place using a light downward pressure **(see illustrations 2.28 and 2.29)**. When positioned between a 1/4 and 1/2 turn below the surface withdraw the installing tool and use the break-off tool to press down on the tang, breaking it off **(see illustration 2.30)**.

- There are epoxy thread repair kits on the market which can rebuild stripped internal threads, although this repair should not be used on high load-bearing components.

Tools and Workshop Tips   REF•9

Thread locking and sealing compounds

● Locking compounds are used in locations where the fastener is prone to loosening due to vibration or on important safety-related items which might cause loss of control of the motorcycle if they fail. It is also used where important fasteners cannot be secured by other means such as lockwashers or split pins.

● Before applying locking compound, make sure that the threads (internal and external) are clean and dry with all old compound removed. Select a compound to suit the component being secured - a non-permanent general locking and sealing type is suitable for most applications, but a high strength type is needed for permanent fixing of studs in castings. Apply a drop or two of the compound to the first few threads of the fastener, then thread it into place and tighten to the specified torque. Do not apply excessive thread locking compound otherwise the thread may be damaged on subsequent removal.

● Certain fasteners are impregnated with a dry film type coating of locking compound on their threads. Always renew this type of fastener if disturbed.

● Anti-seize compounds, such as copper-based greases, can be applied to protect threads from seizure due to extreme heat and corrosion. A common instance is spark plug threads and exhaust system fasteners.

3 Measuring tools and gauges

Feeler gauges

● Feeler gauges (or blades) are used for measuring small gaps and clearances **(see illustration 3.1)**. They can also be used to measure endfloat (sideplay) of a component on a shaft where access is not possible with a dial gauge.

● Feeler gauge sets should be treated with care and not bent or damaged. They are etched with their size on one face. Keep them clean and very lightly oiled to prevent corrosion build-up.

3.1 Feeler gauges are used for measuring small gaps and clearances - thickness is marked on one face of gauge

● When measuring a clearance, select a gauge which is a light sliding fit between the two components. You may need to use two gauges together to measure the clearance accurately.

Micrometers

● A micrometer is a precision tool capable of measuring to 0.01 or 0.001 of a millimetre. It should always be stored in its case and not in the general toolbox. It must be kept clean and never dropped, otherwise its frame or measuring anvils could be distorted resulting in inaccurate readings.

● External micrometers are used for measuring outside diameters of components and have many more applications than internal micrometers. Micrometers are available in different size ranges, eg 0 to 25 mm, 25 to 50 mm, and upwards in 25 mm steps; some large micrometers have interchangeable anvils to allow a range of measurements to be taken. Generally the largest precision measurement you are likely to take on a motorcycle is the piston diameter.

● Internal micrometers (or bore micrometers) are used for measuring inside diameters, such as valve guides and cylinder bores. Telescoping gauges and small hole gauges are used in conjunction with an external micrometer, whereas the more expensive internal micrometers have their own measuring device.

External micrometer

Note: *The conventional analogue type instrument is described. Although much easier to read, digital micrometers are considerably more expensive.*

● Always check the calibration of the micrometer before use. With the anvils closed (0 to 25 mm type) or set over a test gauge (for

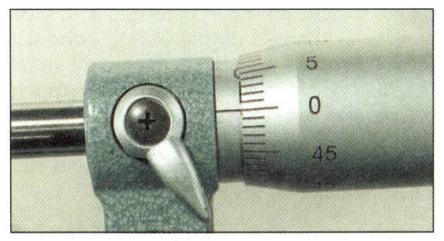

3.2 Check micrometer calibration before use

the larger types) the scale should read zero **(see illustration 3.2)**; make sure that the anvils (and test piece) are clean first. Any discrepancy can be adjusted by referring to the instructions supplied with the tool. Remember that the micrometer is a precision measuring tool - don't force the anvils closed, use the ratchet (4) on the end of the micrometer to close it. In this way, a measured force is always applied.

● To use, first make sure that the item being measured is clean. Place the anvil of the micrometer (1) against the item and use the thimble (2) to bring the spindle (3) lightly into contact with the other side of the item **(see illustration 3.3)**. Don't tighten the thimble down because this will damage the micrometer - instead use the ratchet (4) on the end of the micrometer. The ratchet mechanism applies a measured force preventing damage to the instrument.

● The micrometer is read by referring to the linear scale on the sleeve and the annular scale on the thimble. Read off the sleeve first to obtain the base measurement, then add the fine measurement from the thimble to obtain the overall reading. The linear scale on the sleeve represents the measuring range of the micrometer (eg 0 to 25 mm). The annular scale

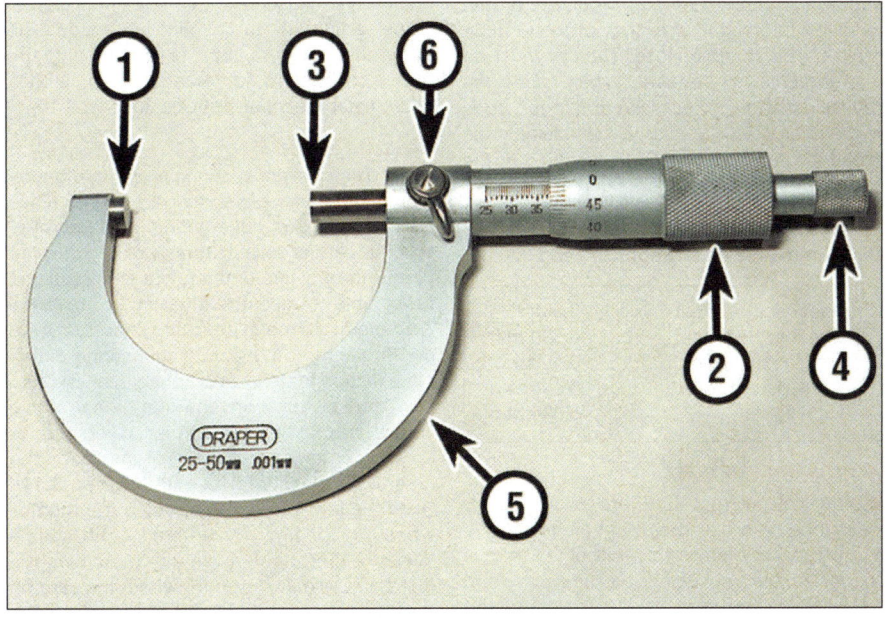

3.3 Micrometer component parts

| 1 Anvil | 3 Spindle | 5 Frame |
| 2 Thimble | 4 Ratchet | 6 Locking lever |

REF•10 Tools and Workshop Tips

on the thimble will be in graduations of 0.01 mm (or as marked on the frame) - one full revolution of the thimble will move 0.5 mm on the linear scale. Take the reading where the datum line on the sleeve intersects the thimble's scale. Always position the eye directly above the scale otherwise an inaccurate reading will result.

In the example shown the item measures 2.95 mm (see illustration 3.4):

Linear scale	2.00 mm
Linear scale	0.50 mm
Annular scale	0.45 mm
Total figure	**2.95 mm**

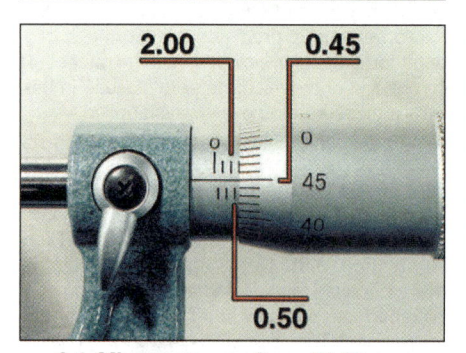

3.4 Micrometer reading of 2.95 mm

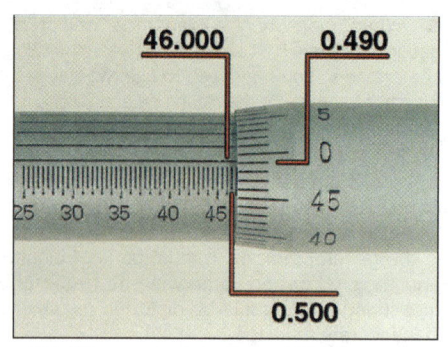

3.5 Micrometer reading of 46.99 mm on linear and annular scales . . .

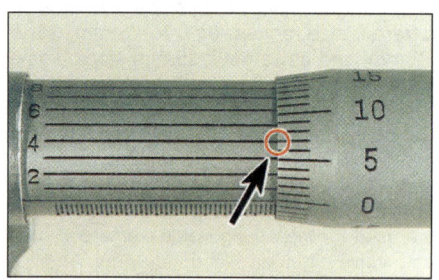

3.6 . . . and 0.004 mm on vernier scale

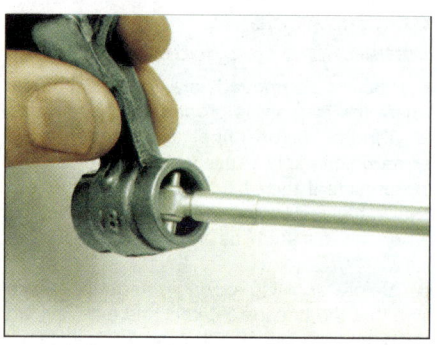

3.7 Expand the telescoping gauge in the bore, lock its position . . .

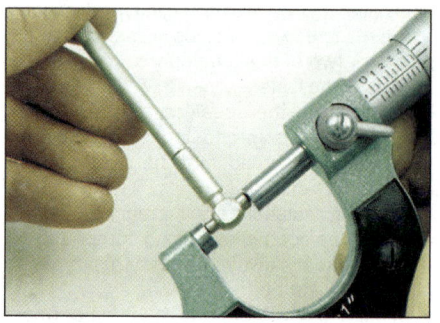

3.8 . . . then measure the gauge with a micrometer

Most micrometers have a locking lever (6) on the frame to hold the setting in place, allowing the item to be removed from the micrometer.
● Some micrometers have a vernier scale on their sleeve, providing an even finer measurement to be taken, in 0.001 increments of a millimetre. Take the sleeve and thimble measurement as described above, then check which graduation on the vernier scale aligns with that of the annular scale on the thimble **Note:** *The eye must be perpendicular to the scale when taking the vernier reading - if necessary rotate the body of the micrometer to ensure this.* Multiply the vernier scale figure by 0.001 and add it to the base and fine measurement figures.

In the example shown the item measures 46.994 mm (see illustrations 3.5 and 3.6):

Linear scale (base)	46.000 mm
Linear scale (base)	00.500 mm
Annular scale (fine)	00.490 mm
Vernier scale	00.004 mm
Total figure	**46.994 mm**

Internal micrometer

● Internal micrometers are available for measuring bore diameters, but are expensive and unlikely to be available for home use. It is suggested that a set of telescoping gauges and small hole gauges, both of which must be used with an external micrometer, will suffice for taking internal measurements on a motorcycle.
● Telescoping gauges can be used to measure internal diameters of components. Select a gauge with the correct size range, make sure its ends are clean and insert it into the bore. Expand the gauge, then lock its position and withdraw it from the bore (see illustration 3.7). Measure across the gauge ends with a micrometer (see illustration 3.8).
● Very small diameter bores (such as valve guides) are measured with a small hole gauge. Once adjusted to a slip-fit inside the component, its position is locked and the gauge withdrawn for measurement with a micrometer (see illustrations 3.9 and 3.10).

Vernier caliper

Note: *The conventional linear and dial gauge type instruments are described. Digital types are easier to read, but are far more expensive.*
● The vernier caliper does not provide the precision of a micrometer, but is versatile in being able to measure internal and external diameters. Some types also incorporate a depth gauge. It is ideal for measuring clutch plate friction material and spring free lengths.
● To use the conventional linear scale vernier, slacken off the vernier clamp screws (1) and set its jaws over (2), or inside (3), the item to be measured (see illustration 3.11). Slide the jaw into contact, using the thumbwheel (4) for fine movement of the sliding scale (5) then tighten the clamp screws (1). Read off the main scale (6) where the zero on the sliding scale (5) intersects it, taking the whole number to the left of the zero; this provides the base measurement. View along the sliding scale and select the division which

3.9 Expand the small hole gauge in the bore, lock its position . . .

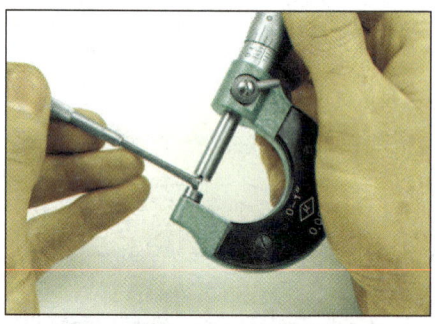

3.10 . . . then measure the gauge with a micrometer

lines up exactly with any of the divisions on the main scale, noting that the divisions usually represents 0.02 of a millimetre. Add this fine measurement to the base measurement to obtain the total reading.

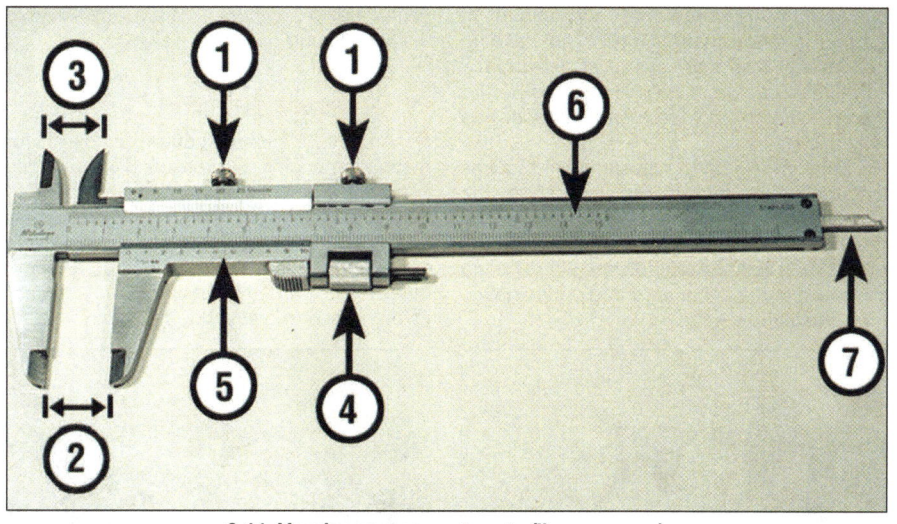

Tools and Workshop Tips   REF•11

Plastigauge

● Plastigauge is a plastic material which can be compressed between two surfaces to measure the oil clearance between them. The width of the compressed Plastigauge is measured against a calibrated scale to determine the clearance.

● Common uses of Plastigauge are for measuring the clearance between crankshaft journal and main bearing inserts, between crankshaft journal and big-end bearing inserts, and between camshaft and bearing surfaces. The following example describes big-end oil clearance measurement.

● Handle the Plastigauge material carefully to prevent distortion. Using a sharp knife, cut a length which corresponds with the width of the bearing being measured and place it carefully across the journal so that it is parallel with the shaft (see illustration 3.15). Carefully install both bearing shells and the connecting rod. Without rotating the rod on the journal tighten its bolts or nuts (as applicable) to the specified torque. The connecting rod and bearings are then disassembled and the crushed Plastigauge examined.

3.11 Vernier component parts (linear gauge)

1 Clamp screws
2 External jaws
3 Internal jaws
4 Thumbwheel
5 Sliding scale
6 Main scale
7 Depth gauge

In the example shown the item measures 55.92 mm (see illustration 3.12):

Base measurement	55.00 mm
Fine measurement	00.92 mm
Total figure	**55.92 mm**

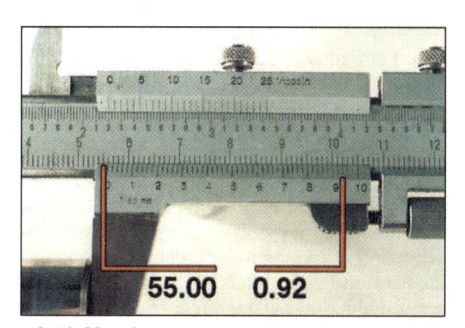

3.12 Vernier gauge reading of 55.92 mm

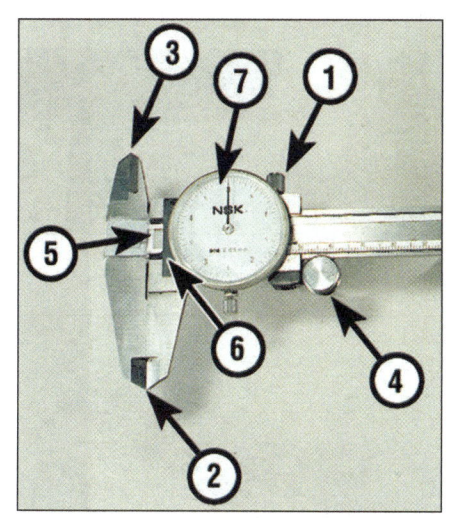

● Some vernier calipers are equipped with a dial gauge for fine measurement. Before use, check that the jaws are clean, then close them fully and check that the dial gauge reads zero. If necessary adjust the gauge ring accordingly. Slacken the vernier clamp screw (1) and set its jaws over (2), or inside (3), the item to be measured (see illustration 3.13). Slide the jaws into contact, using the thumbwheel (4) for fine movement. Read off the main scale (5) where the edge of the sliding scale (6) intersects it, taking the whole number to the left of the zero; this provides the base measurement. Read off the needle position on the dial gauge (7) scale to provide the fine measurement; each division represents 0.05 of a millimetre. Add this fine measurement to the base measurement to obtain the total reading.

In the example shown the item measures 55.95 mm (see illustration 3.14):

Base measurement	55.00 mm
Fine measurement	00.95 mm
Total figure	**55.95 mm**

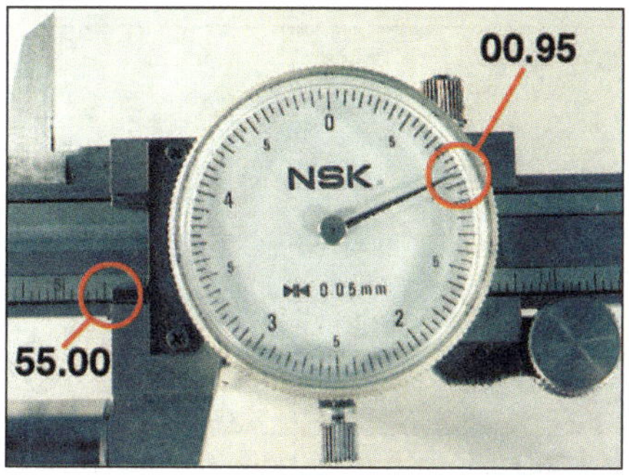

3.13 Vernier component parts (dial gauge)

1 Clamp screw
2 External jaws
3 Internal jaws
4 Thumbwheel
5 Main scale
6 Sliding scale
7 Dial gauge

3.14 Vernier gauge reading of 55.95 mm

3.15 Plastigauge placed across shaft journal

● Using the scale provided in the Plastigauge kit, measure the width of the material to determine the oil clearance (see illustration 3.16). Always remove all traces of Plastigauge after use using your fingernails.

Caution: Arriving at the correct clearance demands that the assembly is torqued correctly, according to the settings and sequence (where applicable) provided by the motorcycle manufacturer.

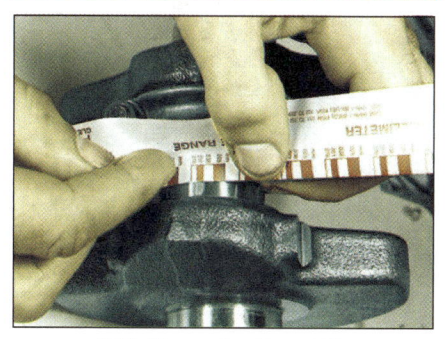

3.16 Measuring the width of the crushed Plastigauge

Tools and Workshop Tips

Dial gauge or DTI (Dial Test Indicator)

● A dial gauge can be used to accurately measure small amounts of movement. Typical uses are measuring shaft runout or shaft endfloat (sideplay) and setting piston position for ignition timing on two-strokes. A dial gauge set usually comes with a range of different probes and adapters and mounting equipment.

● The gauge needle must point to zero when at rest. Rotate the ring around its periphery to zero the gauge.

● Check that the gauge is capable of reading the extent of movement in the work. Most gauges have a small dial set in the face which records whole millimetres of movement as well as the fine scale around the face periphery which is calibrated in 0.01 mm divisions. Read off the small dial first to obtain the base measurement, then add the measurement from the fine scale to obtain the total reading.

In the example shown the gauge reads 1.48 mm (see illustration 3.17):

Base measurement	1.00 mm
Fine measurement	0.48 mm
Total figure	**1.48 mm**

3.17 Dial gauge reading of 1.48 mm

● If measuring shaft runout, the shaft must be supported in vee-blocks and the gauge mounted on a stand perpendicular to the shaft. Rest the tip of the gauge against the centre of the shaft and rotate the shaft slowly whilst watching the gauge reading **(see illustration 3.18)**. Take several measurements along the length of the shaft and record the maximum gauge reading as the amount of runout in the shaft. **Note:** *The reading obtained will be total runout at that point - some manufacturers specify that the runout figure is halved to compare with their specified runout limit.*

● Endfloat (sideplay) measurement requires that the gauge is mounted securely to the surrounding component with its probe touching the end of the shaft. Using hand pressure, push and pull on the shaft noting the maximum endfloat recorded on the gauge **(see illustration 3.19)**.

3.19 Using a dial gauge to measure shaft endfloat

● A dial gauge with suitable adapters can be used to determine piston position BTDC on two-stroke engines for the purposes of ignition timing. The gauge, adapter and suitable length probe are installed in the place of the spark plug and the gauge zeroed at TDC. If the piston position is specified as 1.14 mm BTDC, rotate the engine back to 2.00 mm BTDC, then slowly forwards to 1.14 mm BTDC.

Cylinder compression gauges

● A compression gauge is used for measuring cylinder compression. Either the rubber-cone type or the threaded adapter type can be used. The latter is preferred to ensure a perfect seal against the cylinder head. A 0 to 300 psi (0 to 20 Bar) type gauge (for petrol/gasoline engines) will be suitable for motorcycles.

● The spark plug is removed and the gauge either held hard against the cylinder head (cone type) or the gauge adapter screwed into the cylinder head (threaded type) **(see illustration 3.20)**. Cylinder compression is measured with the engine turning over, but not running - carry out the compression test as described in *Fault Finding Equipment*. The gauge will hold the reading until manually released.

Oil pressure gauge

● An oil pressure gauge is used for measuring engine oil pressure. Most gauges come with a set of adapters to fit the thread of the take-off point **(see illustration 3.21)**. If the take-off point specified by the motorcycle manufacturer is an external oil pipe union, make sure that the specified replacement union is used to prevent oil starvation.

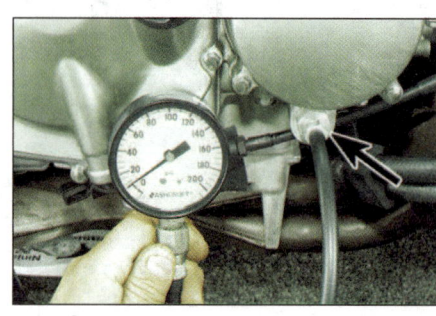

3.21 Oil pressure gauge and take-off point adapter (arrow)

● Oil pressure is measured with the engine running (at a specific rpm) and often the manufacturer will specify pressure limits for a cold and hot engine.

Straight-edge and surface plate

● If checking the gasket face of a component for warpage, place a steel rule or precision straight-edge across the gasket face and measure any gap between the straight-edge and component with feeler gauges **(see illustration 3.22)**. Check diagonally across the component and between mounting holes **(see illustration 3.23)**.

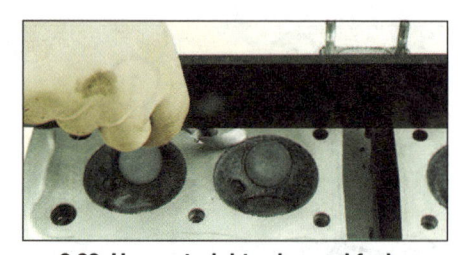

3.22 Use a straight-edge and feeler gauges to check for warpage

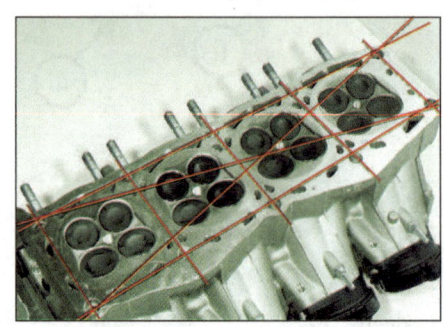

3.18 Using a dial gauge to measure shaft runout

3.20 Using a rubber-cone type cylinder compression gauge

3.23 Check for warpage in these directions

Tools and Workshop Tips   REF•13

- Checking individual components for warpage, such as clutch plain (metal) plates, requires a perfectly flat plate or piece or plate glass and feeler gauges.

4 Torque and leverage

What is torque?

- Torque describes the twisting force about a shaft. The amount of torque applied is determined by the distance from the centre of the shaft to the end of the lever and the amount of force being applied to the end of the lever; distance multiplied by force equals torque.
- The manufacturer applies a measured torque to a bolt or nut to ensure that it will not slacken in use and to hold two components securely together without movement in the joint. The actual torque setting depends on the thread size, bolt or nut material and the composition of the components being held.
- Too little torque may cause the fastener to loosen due to vibration, whereas too much torque will distort the joint faces of the component or cause the fastener to shear off. Always stick to the specified torque setting.

Using a torque wrench

- Check the calibration of the torque wrench and make sure it has a suitable range for the job. Torque wrenches are available in Nm (Newton-metres), kgf m (kilograms-force metre), lbf ft (pounds-feet), lbf in (inch-pounds). Do not confuse lbf ft with lbf in.
- Adjust the tool to the desired torque on the scale (see illustration 4.1). If your torque wrench is not calibrated in the units specified, carefully convert the figure (see Conversion Factors). A manufacturer sometimes gives a torque setting as a range (8 to 10 Nm) rather than a single figure - in this case set the tool midway between the two settings. The same torque may be expressed as 9 Nm ± 1 Nm. Some torque wrenches have a method of locking the setting so that it isn't inadvertently altered during use.

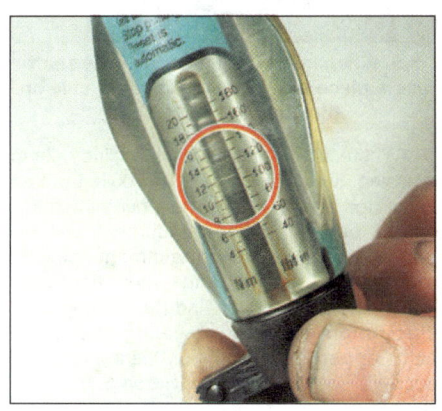

4.1 Set the torque wrench index mark to the setting required, in this case 12 Nm

- Install the bolts/nuts in their correct location and secure them lightly. Their threads must be clean and free of any old locking compound. Unless specified the threads and flange should be dry - oiled threads are necessary in certain circumstances and the manufacturer will take this into account in the specified torque figure. Similarly, the manufacturer may also specify the application of thread-locking compound.
- Tighten the fasteners in the specified sequence until the torque wrench clicks, indicating that the torque setting has been reached. Apply the torque again to double-check the setting. Where different thread diameter fasteners secure the component, as a rule tighten the larger diameter ones first.
- When the torque wrench has been finished with, release the lock (where applicable) and fully back off its setting to zero - do not leave the torque wrench tensioned. Also, do not use a torque wrench for slackening a fastener.

Angle-tightening

- Manufacturers often specify a figure in degrees for final tightening of a fastener. This usually follows tightening to a specific torque setting.
- A degree disc can be set and attached to the socket (see illustration 4.2) or a protractor can be used to mark the angle of movement on the bolt/nut head and the surrounding casting (see illustration 4.3).

4.2 Angle tightening can be accomplished with a torque-angle gauge . . .

4.3 . . . or by marking the angle on the surrounding component

Loosening sequences

- Where more than one bolt/nut secures a component, loosen each fastener evenly a little at a time. In this way, not all the stress of the joint is held by one fastener and the components are not likely to distort.
- If a tightening sequence is provided, work in the REVERSE of this, but if not, work from the outside in, in a criss-cross sequence (see illustration 4.4).

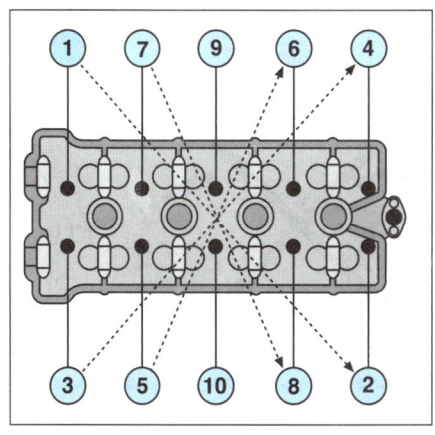

4.4 When slackening, work from the outside inwards

Tightening sequences

- If a component is held by more than one fastener it is important that the retaining bolts/nuts are tightened evenly to prevent uneven stress build-up and distortion of sealing faces. This is especially important on high-compression joints such as the cylinder head.
- A sequence is usually provided by the manufacturer, either in a diagram or actually marked in the casting. If not, always start in the centre and work outwards in a criss-cross pattern (see illustration 4.5). Start off by securing all bolts/nuts finger-tight, then set the torque wrench and tighten each fastener by a small amount in sequence until the final torque is reached. By following this practice,

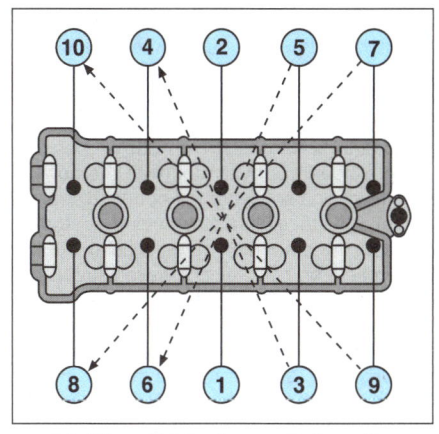

4.5 When tightening, work from the inside outwards

Tools and Workshop Tips

the joint will be held evenly and will not be distorted. Important joints, such as the cylinder head and big-end fasteners often have two- or three-stage torque settings.

Applying leverage

● Use tools at the correct angle. Position a socket wrench or spanner on the bolt/nut so that you pull it towards you when loosening. If this can't be done, push the spanner without curling your fingers around it **(see illustration 4.6)** - the spanner may slip or the fastener loosen suddenly, resulting in your fingers being crushed against a component.

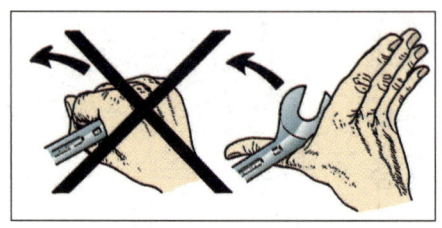

4.6 If you can't pull on the spanner to loosen a fastener, push with your hand open

● Additional leverage is gained by extending the length of the lever. The best way to do this is to use a breaker bar instead of the regular length tool, or to slip a length of tubing over the end of the spanner or socket wrench.
● If additional leverage will not work, the fastener head is either damaged or firmly corroded in place (see *Fasteners*).

5 Bearings

Bearing removal and installation

Drivers and sockets

● Before removing a bearing, always inspect the casing to see which way it must be driven out - some casings will have retaining plates or a cast step. Also check for any identifying markings on the bearing and if installed to a certain depth, measure this at this stage. Some roller bearings are sealed on one side - take note of the original fitted position.
● Bearings can be driven out of a casing using a bearing driver tool (with the correct size head) or a socket of the correct diameter. Select the driver head or socket so that it contacts the outer race of the bearing, not the balls/rollers or inner race. Always support the casing around the bearing housing with wood blocks, otherwise there is a risk of fracture. The bearing is driven out with a few blows on the driver or socket from a heavy mallet. Unless access is severely restricted (as with wheel bearings), a pin-punch is not recommended unless it is moved around the bearing to keep it square in its housing.

● The same equipment can be used to install bearings. Make sure the bearing housing is supported on wood blocks and line up the bearing in its housing. Fit the bearing as noted on removal - generally they are installed with their marked side facing outwards. Tap the bearing squarely into its housing using a driver or socket which bears only on the bearing's outer race - contact with the bearing balls/rollers or inner race will destroy it **(see illustrations 5.1 and 5.2)**.
● Check that the bearing inner race and balls/rollers rotate freely.

5.1 Using a bearing driver against the bearing's outer race

5.2 Using a large socket against the bearing's outer race

Pullers and slide-hammers

● Where a bearing is pressed on a shaft a puller will be required to extract it **(see illustration 5.3)**. Make sure that the puller clamp or legs fit securely behind the bearing and are unlikely to slip out. If pulling a bearing off a gear shaft for example, you may have to locate the puller behind a gear pinion if there is no access to the race and draw the gear pinion off the shaft as well **(see illustration 5.4)**.

Caution: Ensure that the puller's centre bolt locates securely against the end of the shaft and will not slip when pressure is applied. Also ensure that puller does not damage the shaft end.

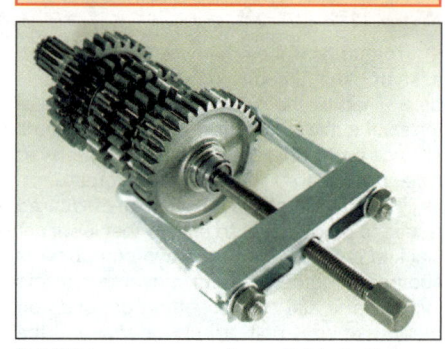

5.4 Where no access is available to the rear of the bearing, it is sometimes possible to draw off the adjacent component

● Operate the puller so that its centre bolt exerts pressure on the shaft end and draws the bearing off the shaft.
● When installing the bearing on the shaft, tap only on the bearing's inner race - contact with the balls/rollers or outer race with destroy the bearing. Use a socket or length of tubing as a drift which fits over the shaft end **(see illustration 5.5)**.

5.5 When installing a bearing on a shaft use a piece of tubing which bears only on the bearing's inner race

● Where a bearing locates in a blind hole in a casing, it cannot be driven or pulled out as described above. A slide-hammer with knife-edged bearing puller attachment will be required. The puller attachment passes through the bearing and when tightened expands to fit firmly behind the bearing **(see illustration 5.6)**. By operating the slide-hammer part of the tool the bearing is jarred out of its housing **(see illustration 5.7)**.
● It is possible, if the bearing is of reasonable weight, for it to drop out of its housing if the casing is heated as described opposite. If this

5.3 This bearing puller clamps behind the bearing and pressure is applied to the shaft end to draw the bearing off

Tools and Workshop Tips REF•15

5.6 Expand the bearing puller so that it locks behind the bearing . . .

5.7 . . . attach the slide hammer to the bearing puller

method is attempted, first prepare a work surface which will enable the casing to be tapped face down to help dislodge the bearing - a wood surface is ideal since it will not damage the casing's gasket surface. Wearing protective gloves, tap the heated casing several times against the work surface to dislodge the bearing under its own weight **(see illustration 5.8)**.

5.8 Tapping a casing face down on wood blocks can often dislodge a bearing

- Bearings can be installed in blind holes using the driver or socket method described above.

Drawbolts

- Where a bearing or bush is set in the eye of a component, such as a suspension linkage arm or connecting rod small-end, removal by drift may damage the component. Furthermore, a rubber bushing in a shock absorber eye cannot successfully be driven out of position. If access is available to a engineering press, the task is straightforward. If not, a drawbolt can be fabricated to extract the bearing or bush.

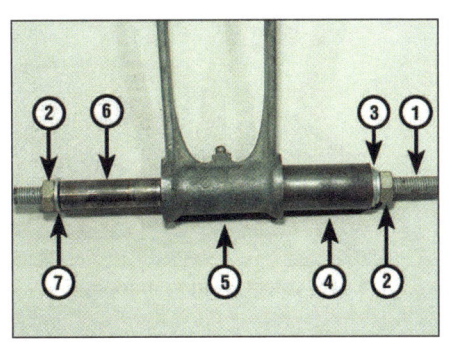

5.9 Drawbolt component parts assembled on a suspension arm

1. Bolt or length of threaded bar
2. Nuts
3. Washer (external diameter greater than tubing internal diameter)
4. Tubing (internal diameter sufficient to accommodate bearing)
5. Suspension arm with bearing
6. Tubing (external diameter slightly smaller than bearing)
7. Washer (external diameter slightly smaller than bearing)

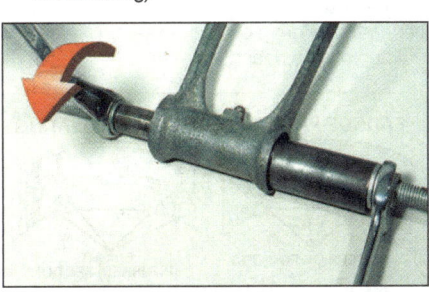

5.10 Drawing the bearing out of the suspension arm

- To extract the bearing/bush you will need a long bolt with nut (or piece of threaded bar with two nuts), a piece of tubing which has an internal diameter larger than the bearing/bush, another piece of tubing which has an external diameter slightly smaller than the bearing/bush, and a selection of washers **(see illustrations 5.9 and 5.10)**. Note that the pieces of tubing must be of the same length, or longer, than the bearing/bush.
- The same kit (without the pieces of tubing) can be used to draw the new bearing/bush back into place **(see illustration 5.11)**.

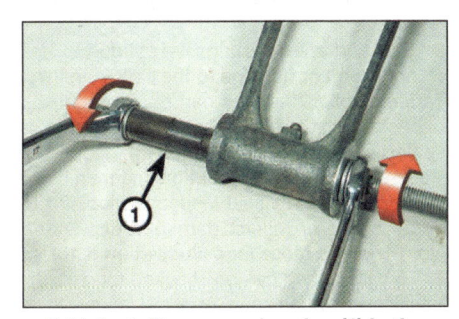

5.11 Installing a new bearing (1) in the suspension arm

Temperature change

- If the bearing's outer race is a tight fit in the casing, the aluminium casing can be heated to release its grip on the bearing. Aluminium will expand at a greater rate than the steel bearing outer race. There are several ways to do this, but avoid any localised extreme heat (such as a blow torch) - aluminium alloy has a low melting point.
- Approved methods of heating a casing are using a domestic oven (heated to 100°C) or immersing the casing in boiling water **(see illustration 5.12)**. Low temperature range localised heat sources such as a paint stripper heat gun or clothes iron can also be used **(see illustration 5.13)**. Alternatively, soak a rag in boiling water, wring it out and wrap it around the bearing housing.

> ⚠ **Warning:** All of these methods require care in use to prevent scalding and burns to the hands. Wear protective gloves when handling hot components.

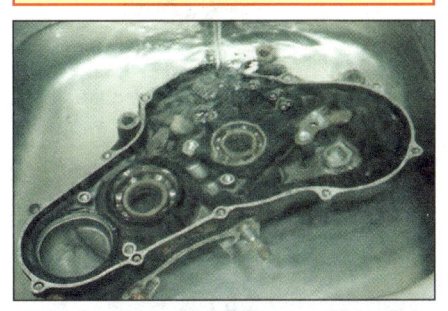

5.12 A casing can be immersed in a sink of boiling water to aid bearing removal

5.13 Using a localised heat source to aid bearing removal

- If heating the whole casing note that plastic components, such as the neutral switch, may suffer - remove them beforehand.
- After heating, remove the bearing as described above. You may find that the expansion is sufficient for the bearing to fall out of the casing under its own weight or with a light tap on the driver or socket.
- If necessary, the casing can be heated to aid bearing installation, and this is sometimes the recommended procedure if the motorcycle manufacturer has designed the housing and bearing fit with this intention.

REF•16 Tools and Workshop Tips

- Installation of bearings can be eased by placing them in a freezer the night before installation. The steel bearing will contract slightly, allowing easy insertion in its housing. This is often useful when installing steering head outer races in the frame.

Bearing types and markings

- Plain shell bearings, ball bearings, needle roller bearings and tapered roller bearings will all be found on motorcycles **(see illustrations 5.14 and 5.15)**. The ball and roller types are usually caged between an inner and outer race, but uncaged variations may be found.

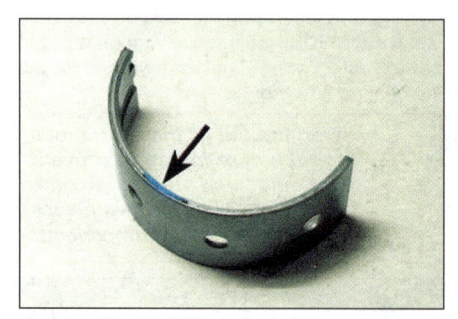

5.14 Shell bearings are either plain or grooved. They are usually identified by colour code (arrow)

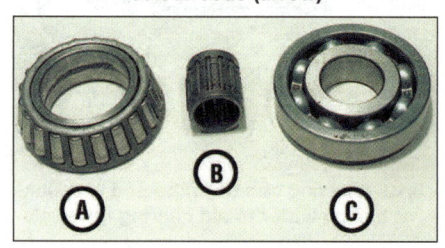

5.15 Tapered roller bearing (A), needle roller bearing (B) and ball journal bearing (C)

- Shell bearings (often called inserts) are usually found at the crankshaft main and connecting rod big-end where they are good at coping with high loads. They are made of a phosphor-bronze material and are impregnated with self-lubricating properties.
- Ball bearings and needle roller bearings consist of a steel inner and outer race with the balls or rollers between the races. They require constant lubrication by oil or grease and are good at coping with axial loads. Taper roller bearings consist of rollers set in a tapered cage set on the inner race; the outer race is separate. They are good at coping with axial loads and prevent movement along the shaft - a typical application is in the steering head.
- Bearing manufacturers produce bearings to ISO size standards and stamp one face of the bearing to indicate its internal and external diameter, load capacity and type **(see illustration 5.16)**.
- Metal bushes are usually of phosphor-bronze material. Rubber bushes are used in suspension mounting eyes. Fibre bushes have also been used in suspension pivots.

5.16 Typical bearing marking

Bearing fault finding

- If a bearing outer race has spun in its housing, the housing material will be damaged. You can use a bearing locking compound to bond the outer race in place if damage is not too severe.
- Shell bearings will fail due to damage of their working surface, as a result of lack of lubrication, corrosion or abrasive particles in the oil **(see illustration 5.17)**. Small particles of dirt in the oil may embed in the bearing material whereas larger particles will score the bearing and shaft journal. If a number of short journeys are made, insufficient heat will be generated to drive off condensation which has built up on the bearings.

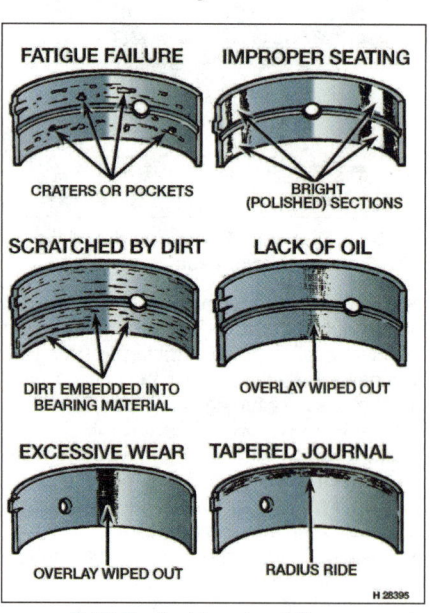

5.17 Typical bearing failures

- Ball and roller bearings will fail due to lack of lubrication or damage to the balls or rollers. Tapered-roller bearings can be damaged by overloading them. Unless the bearing is sealed on both sides, wash it in paraffin (kerosene) to remove all old grease then allow it to dry. Make a visual inspection looking to dented balls or rollers, damaged cages and worn or pitted races **(see illustration 5.18)**.
- A ball bearing can be checked for wear by listening to it when spun. Apply a film of light oil to the bearing and hold it close to the ear - hold the outer race with one hand and spin the inner race with the other hand **(see illustration 5.19)**. The bearing should be almost silent when spun; if it grates or rattles it is worn.

5.18 Example of ball journal bearing with damaged balls and cages

5.19 Hold outer race and listen to inner race when spun

6 Oil seals

Oil seal removal and installation

- Oil seals should be renewed every time a component is dismantled. This is because the seal lips will become set to the sealing surface and will not necessarily reseal.
- Oil seals can be prised out of position using a large flat-bladed screwdriver **(see illustration 6.1)**. In the case of crankcase seals, check first that the seal is not lipped on the inside, preventing its removal with the crankcases joined.

6.1 Prise out oil seals with a large flat-bladed screwdriver

- New seals are usually installed with their marked face (containing the seal reference code) outwards and the spring side towards the fluid being retained. In certain cases, such as a two-stroke engine crankshaft seal, a double lipped seal may be used due to there being fluid or gas on each side of the joint.

Tools and Workshop Tips   REF•17

● Use a bearing driver or socket which bears only on the outer hard edge of the seal to install it in the casing - tapping on the inner edge will damage the sealing lip.

Oil seal types and markings

● Oil seals are usually of the single-lipped type. Double-lipped seals are found where a liquid or gas is on both sides of the joint.
● Oil seals can harden and lose their sealing ability if the motorcycle has been in storage for a long period - renewal is the only solution.
● Oil seal manufacturers also conform to the ISO markings for seal size - these are moulded into the outer face of the seal **(see illustration 6.2)**.

6.2 These oil seal markings indicate inside diameter, outside diameter and seal thickness

7 Gaskets and sealants

Types of gasket and sealant

● Gaskets are used to seal the mating surfaces between components and keep lubricants, fluids, vacuum or pressure contained within the assembly. Aluminium gaskets are sometimes found at the cylinder joints, but most gaskets are paper-based. If the mating surfaces of the components being joined are undamaged the gasket can be installed dry, although a dab of sealant or grease will be useful to hold it in place during assembly.
● RTV (Room Temperature Vulcanising) silicone rubber sealants cure when exposed to moisture in the atmosphere. These sealants are good at filling pits or irregular gasket faces, but will tend to be forced out of the joint under very high torque. They can be used to replace a paper gasket, but first make sure that the width of the paper gasket is not essential to the shimming of internal components. RTV sealants should not be used on components containing petrol (gasoline).
● Non-hardening, semi-hardening and hard setting liquid gasket compounds can be used with a gasket or between a metal-to-metal joint. Select the sealant to suit the application: universal non-hardening sealant can be used on virtually all joints; semi-hardening on joint faces which are rough or damaged; hard setting sealant on joints which require a permanent bond and are subjected to high temperature and pressure. **Note:** *Check first if the paper gasket has a bead of sealant impregnated in its surface before applying additional sealant.*
● When choosing a sealant, make sure it is suitable for the application, particularly if being applied in a high-temperature area or in the vicinity of fuel. Certain manufacturers produce sealants in either clear, silver or black colours to match the finish of the engine. This has a particular application on motorcycles where much of the engine is exposed.
● Do not over-apply sealant. That which is squeezed out on the outside of the joint can be wiped off, whereas an excess of sealant on the inside can break off and clog oilways.

Breaking a sealed joint

● Age, heat, pressure and the use of hard setting sealant can cause two components to stick together so tightly that they are difficult to separate using finger pressure alone. Do not resort to using levers unless there is a pry point provided for this purpose **(see illustration 7.1)** or else the gasket surfaces will be damaged.
● Use a soft-faced hammer **(see illustration 7.2)** or a wood block and conventional hammer to strike the component near the mating surface. Avoid hammering against cast extremities since they may break off. If this method fails, try using a wood wedge between the two components.

Caution: If the joint will not separate, double-check that you have removed all the fasteners.

7.1 If a pry point is provided, apply gently pressure with a flat-bladed screwdriver

7.2 Tap around the joint with a soft-faced mallet if necessary - don't strike cooling fins

Removal of old gasket and sealant

● Paper gaskets will most likely come away complete, leaving only a few traces stuck on the sealing faces of the components. It is imperative that all traces are removed to ensure correct sealing of the new gasket.
● Very carefully scrape all traces of gasket away making sure that the sealing surfaces are not gouged or scored by the scraper **(see illustrations 7.3, 7.4 and 7.5)**. Stubborn deposits can be removed by spraying with an aerosol gasket remover. Final preparation of

> **HAYNES HINT** 
>
> *Most components have one or two hollow locating dowels between the two gasket faces. If a dowel cannot be removed, do not resort to gripping it with pliers - it will almost certainly be distorted. Install a close-fitting socket or Phillips screwdriver into the dowel and then grip the outer edge of the dowel to free it.*

7.3 Paper gaskets can be scraped off with a gasket scraper tool . . .

7.4 . . . a knife blade . . .

7.5 . . . or a household scraper

REF•18 Tools and Workshop Tips

7.6 Fine abrasive paper is wrapped around a flat file to clean up the gasket face

7.7 A kitchen scourer can be used on stubborn deposits

the gasket surface can be made with very fine abrasive paper or a plastic kitchen scourer **(see illustrations 7.6 and 7.7)**.

● Old sealant can be scraped or peeled off components, depending on the type originally used. Note that gasket removal compounds are available to avoid scraping the components clean; make sure the gasket remover suits the type of sealant used.

8 Chains

Breaking and joining final drive chains

● Drive chains for all but small bikes are continuous and do not have a clip-type connecting link. The chain must be broken using a chain breaker tool and the new chain securely riveted together using a new soft rivet-type link. Never use a clip-type connecting link instead of a rivet-type link, except in an emergency. Various chain breaking and riveting tools are available, either as separate tools or combined as illustrated in the accompanying photographs - read the instructions supplied with the tool carefully.

Warning: The need to rivet the new link pins correctly cannot be overstressed - loss of control of the motorcycle is very likely to result if the chain breaks in use.

● Rotate the chain and look for the soft link. The soft link pins look like they have been deeply centre-punched instead of peened over like all the other pins **(see illustration 8.9)** and its sideplate may be a different colour. Position the soft link midway between the sprockets and assemble the chain breaker tool over one of the soft link pins **(see illustration 8.1)**. Operate the tool to push the pin out through the chain **(see illustration 8.2)**. On an O-ring chain, remove the O-rings **(see illustration 8.3)**. Carry out the same procedure on the other soft link pin.

Caution: Certain soft link pins (particularly on the larger chains) may require their ends to be filed or ground off before they can be pressed out using the tool.

● Check that you have the correct size and strength (standard or heavy duty) new soft link - do not reuse the old link. Look for the size marking on the chain sideplates **(see illustration 8.10)**.

● Position the chain ends so that they are engaged over the rear sprocket. On an O-ring

8.1 Tighten the chain breaker to push the pin out of the link . . .

8.2 . . . withdraw the pin, remove the tool . . .

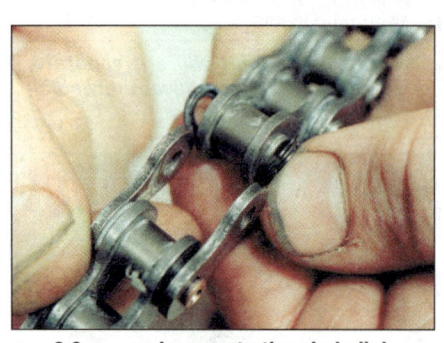

8.3 . . . and separate the chain link

8.4 Insert the new soft link, with O-rings, through the chain ends . . .

8.5 . . . install the O-rings over the pin ends . . .

8.6 . . . followed by the sideplate

chain, install a new O-ring over each pin of the link and insert the link through the two chain ends **(see illustration 8.4)**. Install a new O-ring over the end of each pin, followed by the sideplate (with the chain manufacturer's marking facing outwards) **(see illustrations 8.5 and 8.6)**. On an unsealed chain, insert the link through the two chain ends, then install the sideplate with the chain manufacturer's marking facing outwards.

● Note that it may not be possible to install the sideplate using finger pressure alone. If using a joining tool, assemble it so that the plates of the tool clamp the link and press the sideplate over the pins **(see illustration 8.7)**. Otherwise, use two small sockets placed over

8.7 Push the sideplate into position using a clamp

Tools and Workshop Tips   REF•19

8.8 Assemble the chain riveting tool over one pin at a time and tighten it fully

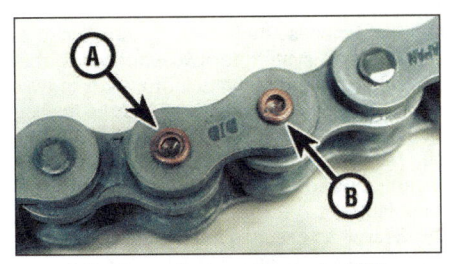

8.9 Pin end correctly riveted (A), pin end unriveted (B)

the rivet ends and two pieces of the wood between a G-clamp. Operate the clamp to press the sideplate over the pins.

● Assemble the joining tool over one pin (following the maker's instructions) and tighten the tool down to spread the pin end securely **(see illustrations 8.8 and 8.9)**. Do the same on the other pin.

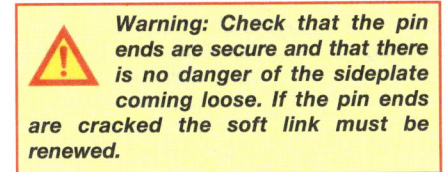

> **Warning:** Check that the pin ends are secure and that there is no danger of the sideplate coming loose. If the pin ends are cracked the soft link must be renewed.

Final drive chain sizing

● Chains are sized using a three digit number, followed by a suffix to denote the chain type **(see illustration 8.10)**. Chain type is either standard or heavy duty (thicker sideplates), and also unsealed or O-ring/X-ring type.

● The first digit of the number relates to the pitch of the chain, ie the distance from the centre of one pin to the centre of the next pin **(see illustration 8.11)**. Pitch is expressed in eighths of an inch, as follows:

8.10 Typical chain size and type marking

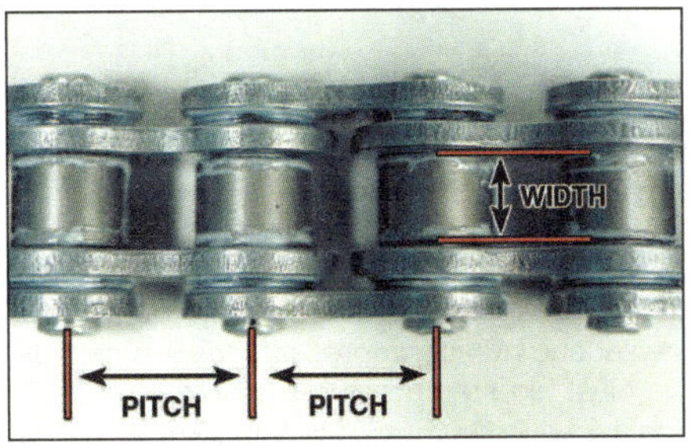

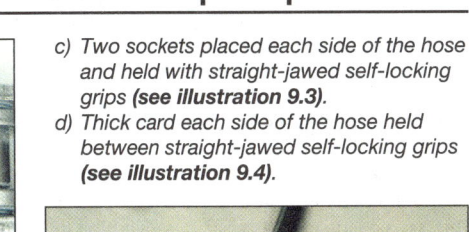

8.11 Chain dimensions

| Sizes commencing with a 4 (eg 428) have a pitch of 1/2 inch (12.7 mm) |
| Sizes commencing with a 5 (eg 520) have a pitch of 5/8 inch (15.9 mm) |
| Sizes commencing with a 6 (eg 630) have a pitch of 3/4 inch (19.1 mm) |

● The second and third digits of the chain size relate to the width of the rollers, again in imperial units, eg the 525 shown has 5/16 inch (7.94 mm) rollers **(see illustration 8.11)**.

9 Hoses

Clamping to prevent flow

● Small-bore flexible hoses can be clamped to prevent fluid flow whilst a component is worked on. Whichever method is used, ensure that the hose material is not permanently distorted or damaged by the clamp.

a) A brake hose clamp available from auto accessory shops **(see illustration 9.1)**.
b) A wingnut type hose clamp **(see illustration 9.2)**.
c) Two sockets placed each side of the hose and held with straight-jawed self-locking grips **(see illustration 9.3)**.
d) Thick card each side of the hose held between straight-jawed self-locking grips **(see illustration 9.4)**.

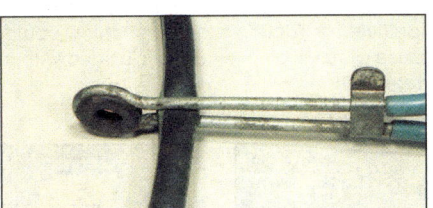

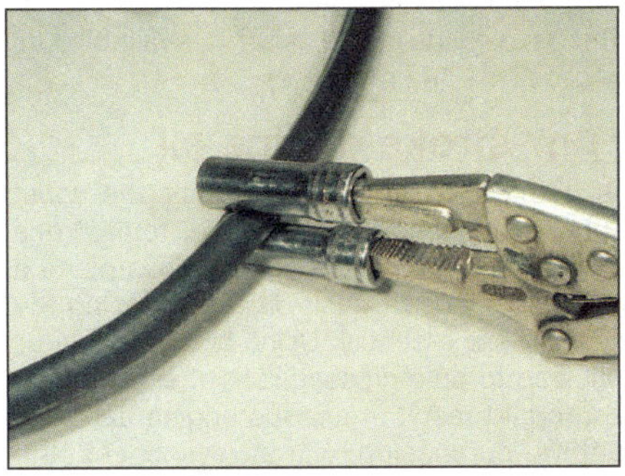

9.1 Hoses can be clamped with an automotive brake hose clamp . . .

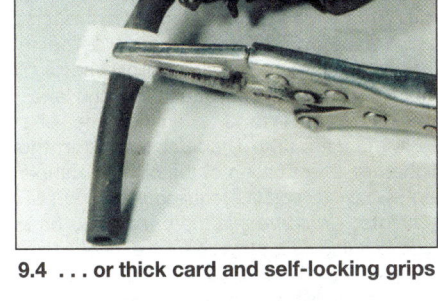

9.2 . . . a wingnut type hose clamp . . .

9.3 . . . two sockets and a pair of self-locking grips . . .

9.4 . . . or thick card and self-locking grips

Freeing and fitting hoses

● Always make sure the hose clamp is moved well clear of the hose end. Grip the hose with your hand and rotate it whilst pulling it off the union. If the hose has hardened due to age and will not move, slit it with a sharp knife and peel its ends off the union **(see illustration 9.5)**.

● Resist the temptation to use grease or soap on the unions to aid installation; although it helps the hose slip over the union it will equally aid the escape of fluid from the joint. It is preferable to soften the hose ends in hot water and wet the inside surface of the hose with water or a fluid which will evaporate.

9.5 Cutting a coolant hose free with a sharp knife

Lubricants and fluids

A wide range of lubricants, fluids and cleaning agents is available for motor-cycles. This is a guide as to what is available, its applications and properties.

Four-stroke engine oil

- Engine oil is without doubt the most important component of any four-stroke engine. Modern motorcycle engines place a lot of demands on their oil and choosing the right type is essential. Using an unsuitable oil will lead to an increased rate of engine wear and could result in serious engine damage. Before purchasing oil, always check the recommended oil specification given by the manufacturer. The manufacturer will state a recommended 'type or classification' and also a specific 'viscosity' range for engine oil.
- The oil 'type or classification' is identified by its API (American Petroleum Institute) rating. The API rating will be in the form of two letters, e.g. SG. The S identifies the oil as being suitable for use in a petrol (gasoline) engine (S stands for spark ignition) and the second letter, ranging from A to J, identifies the oil's performance rating. The later this letter, the higher the specification of the oil; for example API SG oil exceeds the requirements of API SF oil. **Note:** *On some oils there may also be a second rating consisting of another two letters, the first letter being C, e.g. API SF/CD. This rating indicates the oil is also suitable for use in a diesel engines (the C stands for compression ignition) and is thus of no relevance for motorcycle use.*
- The 'viscosity' of the oil is identified by its SAE (Society of Automotive Engineers) rating. All modern engines require multigrade oils and the SAE rating will consist of two numbers, the first followed by a W, e.g. 10W/40. The first number indicates the viscosity rating of the oil at low temperatures (W stands for winter – tested at –20ºC) and the second number represents the viscosity of the oil at high temperatures (tested at 100ºC). The lower the number, the thinner the oil. For example an oil with an SAE 10W/40 rating will give better cold starting and running than an SAE 15W/40 oil.
- As well as ensuring the 'type' and 'viscosity' of the oil match the recommendations, another consideration to make when buying engine oil is whether to purchase a standard mineral-based oil, a semi-synthetic oil (also known as a synthetic blend or synthetic-based oil) or a fully-synthetic oil. Although all oils will have a similar rating and viscosity, their cost will vary considerably; mineral-based oils are the cheapest, the fully-synthetic oils the most expensive with the semi-synthetic oils falling somewhere in-between. This decision is very much up to the owner, but it should be noted that modern synthetic oils have far better lubricating and cleaning qualities than traditional mineral-based oils and tend to retain these properties for far longer. Bearing in mind the operating conditions inside a modern, high-revving motorcycle engine it is highly recommended that a fully synthetic oil is used. The extra expense at each service could save you money in the long term by preventing premature engine wear.
- As a final note always ensure that the oil is specifically designed for use in motorcycle engines. Engine oils designed primarily for use in car engines sometimes contain additives or friction modifiers which could cause clutch slip on a motorcycle fitted with a wet-clutch.

Two-stroke engine oil

- Modern two-stroke engines, with their high power outputs, place high demands on their oil. If engine seizure is to be avoided it is essential that a high-quality oil is used. Two-stroke oils differ hugely from four-stroke oils. The oil lubricates only the crankshaft and piston(s) (the transmission has its own lubricating oil) and is used on a total-loss basis where it is burnt completely during the combustion process.
- The Japanese have recently introduced a classification system for two-stroke oils, the JASO rating. This rating is in the form of two letters, either FA, FB or FC – FA is the lowest classification and FC the highest. Ensure the oil being used meets or exceeds the recommended rating specified by the manufacturer.
- As well as ensuring the oil rating matches the recommendation, another consideration to make when buying engine oil is whether to purchase a standard mineral-based oil, a semi-synthetic oil (also known as a synthetic blend or synthetic-based oil) or a fully-synthetic oil. The cost of each type of oil varies considerably; mineral-based oils are the cheapest, the fully-synthetic oils the most expensive with the semi-synthetic oils falling somewhere in-between. This decision is very much up to the owner, but it should be noted that modern synthetic oils have far better lubricating properties and burn cleaner than traditional mineral-based oils. It is therefore recommended that a fully synthetic oil is used. The extra expense could save you money in the long term by preventing premature engine wear, engine performance will be improved, carbon deposits and exhaust smoke will be reduced.

Lubricants and fluids

- Always ensure that the oil is specifically designed for use in an injector system. Many high quality two-stroke oils are designed for competition use and need to be pre-mixed with fuel. These oils are of a much higher viscosity and are not designed to flow through the injector pumps used on road-going two-stroke motorcycles.

Transmission (gear) oil

- On a two-stroke engine, the transmission and clutch are lubricated by their own separate oil bath which must be changed in accordance with the Maintenance Schedule.
- Although the engine and transmission units of most four-strokes use a common lubrication supply, there are some exceptions where the engine and gearbox have separate oil reservoirs and a dry clutch is used.
- Motorcycle manufacturers will either recommend a monograde transmission oil or a four-stroke multigrade engine oil to lubricate the transmission.
- Transmission oils, or gear oils as they are often called, are designed specifically for use in transmission systems. The viscosity of these oils is represented by an SAE number, but the scale of measurement applied is different to that used to grade engine oils. As a rough guide a SAE90 gear oil will be of the same viscosity as an SAE50 engine oil.

Shaft drive oil

- On models equipped with shaft final drive, the shaft drive gears are will have their own oil supply. The manufacturer will state a recommended 'type or classification' and also a specific 'viscosity' range in the same manner as for four-stroke engine oil.
- Gear oil classification is given by the number which follows the API GL (GL standing for gear lubricant) rating, the higher the number, the higher the specification of the oil, e.g. API GL5 oil is a higher specification than API GL4 oil. Ensure the oil meets or exceeds the classification specified and is of the correct viscosity. The viscosity of gear oils is also represented by an SAE number but the scale of measurement used is different to that used to grade engine oils. As a rough guide an SAE90 gear oil will be of the same viscosity as an SAE50 engine oil.
- If the use of an EP (Extreme Pressure) gear oil is specified, ensure the oil purchased is suitable.

Fork oil and suspension fluid

- Conventional telescopic front forks are hydraulic and require fork oil to work. To ensure the forks function correctly, the fork oil must be changed in accordance with the Maintenance Schedule.
- Fork oil is available in a variety of viscosities, identified by their SAE rating; fork oil ratings vary from light (SAE 5) to heavy (SAE 30). When purchasing fork oil, ensure the viscosity rating matches that specified by the manufacturer.
- Some lubricant manufacturers also produce a range of high-quality suspension fluids which are very similar to fork oil but are designed mainly for competition use. These fluids may have a different viscosity rating system which is not to be confused with the SAE rating of normal fork oil. Refer to the manufacturer's instructions if in any doubt.

Brake and clutch fluid

- All disc brake systems and some clutch systems are hydraulically operated. To ensure correct operation, the hydraulic fluid must be changed in accordance with the Maintenance Schedule.
- Brake and clutch fluid is classified by its DOT rating with most motorcycle manufacturers specifying DOT 3 or 4 fluid. Both fluid types are glycol-based and can be mixed together without adverse effect; DOT 4 fluid exceeds the requirements of DOT 3 fluid. Although it is safe to use DOT 4 fluid in a system designed for use with DOT 3 fluid, never use DOT 3 fluid in a system which specifies the use of DOT 4 as this will adversely affect the system's performance. The type required for the system will be marked on the fluid reservoir cap.
- Some manufacturers also produce a DOT 5 hydraulic fluid. DOT 5 hydraulic fluid is silicone-based and is not compatible with the glycol-based DOT 3 and 4 fluids. Never mix DOT 5 fluid with DOT 3 or 4 fluid as this will seriously affect the performance of the hydraulic system.

Coolant/antifreeze

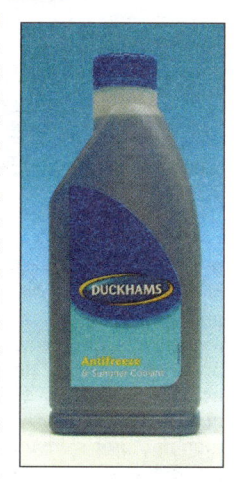

- When purchasing coolant/antifreeze, always ensure it is suitable for use in an aluminium engine and contains corrosion inhibitors to prevent possible blockages of the internal coolant passages of the system. As a general rule, most coolants are designed to be used neat and should not be diluted whereas antifreeze can be mixed with distilled water to provide a coolant solution of the required strength. Refer to the manufacturer's instructions on the bottle.
- Ensure the coolant is changed in accordance with the Maintenance Schedule.

Chain lube

- Chain lube is an aerosol-type spray lubricant specifically designed for use on motorcycle final drive chains. Chain lube has two functions, to minimise friction between the final drive chain and sprockets and to prevent corrosion of the chain. Regular use of a good-quality chain lube will extend the life of the drive chain and sprockets and thus maximise the power being transmitted from the transmission to the rear wheel.
- When using chain lube, always allow some time for the solvents in the lube to evaporate before riding the motorcycle. This will minimise the amount of lube which will

Lubricants and fluids

'fling' off from the chain when the motorcycle is used. If the motorcycle is equipped with an 'O-ring' chain, ensure the chain lube is labelled as being suitable for use on 'O-ring' chains.

Degreasers and solvents

- There are many different types of solvents and degreasers available to remove the grime and grease which accumulate around the motorcycle during normal use. Degreasers and solvents are usually available as an aerosol-type spray or as a liquid which you apply with a brush. Always closely follow the manufacturer's instructions and wear eye protection during use. Be aware that many solvents are flammable and may give off noxious fumes; take adequate precautions when using them (see Safety First!).
- For general cleaning, use one of the many solvents or degreasers available from most motorcycle accessory shops. These solvents are usually applied then left for a certain time before being washed off with water.

Brake cleaner is a solvent specifically designed to remove all traces of oil, grease and dust from braking system components. Brake cleaner is designed to evaporate quickly and leaves behind no residue.

Carburettor cleaner is an aerosol-type solvent specifically designed to clear carburettor blockages and break down the hard deposits and gum often found inside carburettors during overhaul.

Contact cleaner is an aerosol-type solvent designed for cleaning electrical components. The cleaner will remove all traces of oil and dirt from components such as switch contacts or fouled spark plugs and then dry, leaving behind no residue.

Gasket remover is an aerosol-type solvent designed for removing stubborn gaskets from engine components during overhaul. Gasket remover will minimise the amount of scraping required to remove the gasket and therefore reduce the risk of damage to the mating surface.

Spray lubricants

- Aerosol-based spray lubricants are widely available and are excellent for lubricating lever pivots and exposed cables and switches. Try to use a lubricant which is of the dry-film type as the fluid evaporates, leaving behind a dry-film of lubricant. Lubricants which leave behind an oily residue will attract dust and dirt which will increase the rate of wear of the cable/lever.
- Most lubricants also act as a moisture dispersant and a penetrating fluid. This means they can also be used to 'dry out' electrical components such as wiring connectors or switches as well as helping to free seized fasteners.

Greases

- Grease is used to lubricate many of the pivot-points. A good-quality multi-purpose grease is suitable for most applications but some manufacturers will specify the use of specialist greases for use on components such as swingarm and suspension linkage bushes. These specialist greases can be purchased from most motorcycle (or car) accessory shops; commonly specified types include molybdenum disulphide grease, lithium-based grease, graphite-based grease, silicone-based grease and high-temperature copper-based grease.

Gasket sealing compounds

- Gasket sealing compounds can be used in conjunction with gaskets, to improve their sealing capabilities, or on their own to seal metal-to-metal joints. Depending on their type, sealing compounds either set hard or stay relatively soft and pliable. 
- When purchasing a gasket sealing compound, ensure that it is designed specifically for use on an internal combustion engine. General multi-purpose sealants available from DIY stores may appear visibly similar but they are not designed to withstand the extreme heat or contact with fuel and oil encountered when used on an engine (see 'Tools and Workshop Tips' for further information).

Thread locking compound

- Thread locking compounds are used to secure certain threaded fasteners in position to prevent them from loosening due to vibration. Thread locking compounds can be purchased from most motorcycle (and car) accessory shops. Ensure the threads of the both components are completely clean and dry before sparingly applying the locking compound (see 'Tools and Workshop Tips' for further information).

Fuel additives

- Fuel additives which protect and clean the fuel system components are widely available. These additives are designed to remove all traces of deposits that build up on the carburettors/injectors and prevent wear, helping the fuel system to operate more efficiently. If a fuel additive is being used, check that it is suitable for use with your motorcycle, especially if your motorcycle is equipped with a catalytic converter.

- Octane boosters are also available. These additives are designed to improve the performance of highly-tuned engines being run on normal pump-fuel and are of no real use on standard motorcycles.

Conversion Factors REF•23

Length (distance)
Inches (in)	x 25.4	= Millimetres (mm)	x 0.0394	=	Inches (in)
Feet (ft)	x 0.305	= Metres (m)	x 3.281	=	Feet (ft)
Miles	x 1.609	= Kilometres (km)	x 0.621	=	Miles

Volume (capacity)
Cubic inches (cu in; in³)	x 16.387	= Cubic centimetres (cc; cm³)	x 0.061	=	Cubic inches (cu in; in³)
Imperial pints (Imp pt)	x 0.568	= Litres (l)	x 1.76	=	Imperial pints (Imp pt)
Imperial quarts (Imp qt)	x 1.137	= Litres (l)	x 0.88	=	Imperial quarts (Imp qt)
Imperial quarts (Imp qt)	x 1.201	= US quarts (US qt)	x 0.833	=	Imperial quarts (Imp qt)
US quarts (US qt)	x 0.946	= Litres (l)	x 1.057	=	US quarts (US qt)
Imperial gallons (Imp gal)	x 4.546	= Litres (l)	x 0.22	=	Imperial gallons (Imp gal)
Imperial gallons (Imp gal)	x 1.201	= US gallons (US gal)	x 0.833	=	Imperial gallons (Imp gal)
US gallons (US gal)	x 3.785	= Litres (l)	x 0.264	=	US gallons (US gal)

Mass (weight)
Ounces (oz)	x 28.35	= Grams (g)	x 0.035	=	Ounces (oz)
Pounds (lb)	x 0.454	= Kilograms (kg)	x 2.205	=	Pounds (lb)

Force
Ounces-force (ozf; oz)	x 0.278	= Newtons (N)	x 3.6	=	Ounces-force (ozf; oz)
Pounds-force (lbf; lb)	x 4.448	= Newtons (N)	x 0.225	=	Pounds-force (lbf; lb)
Newtons (N)	x 0.1	= Kilograms-force (kgf; kg)	x 9.81	=	Newtons (N)

Pressure
Pounds-force per square inch (psi; lbf/in²; lb/in²)	x 0.070	= Kilograms-force per square centimetre (kgf/cm²; kg/cm²)	x 14.223	=	Pounds-force per square inch (psi; lbf/in²; lb/in²)
Pounds-force per square inch (psi; lbf/in²; lb/in²)	x 0.068	= Atmospheres (atm)	x 14.696	=	Pounds-force per square inch (psi; lbf/in²; lb/in²)
Pounds-force per square inch (psi; lbf/in²; lb/in²)	x 0.069	= Bars	x 14.5	=	Pounds-force per square inch (psi; lbf/in²; lb/in²)
Pounds-force per square inch (psi; lbf/in²; lb/in²)	x 6.895	= Kilopascals (kPa)	x 0.145	=	Pounds-force per square inch (psi; lbf/in²; lb/in²)
Kilopascals (kPa)	x 0.01	= Kilograms-force per square centimetre (kgf/cm²; kg/cm²)	x 98.1	=	Kilopascals (kPa)
Millibar (mbar)	x 100	= Pascals (Pa)	x 0.01	=	Millibar (mbar)
Millibar (mbar)	x 0.0145	= Pounds-force per square inch (psi; lbf/in²; lb/in²)	x 68.947	=	Millibar (mbar)
Millibar (mbar)	x 0.75	= Millimetres of mercury (mmHg)	x 1.333	=	Millibar (mbar)
Millibar (mbar)	x 0.401	= Inches of water (inH$_2$O)	x 2.491	=	Millibar (mbar)
Millimetres of mercury (mmHg)	x 0.535	= Inches of water (inH$_2$O)	x 1.868	=	Millimetres of mercury (mmHg)
Inches of water (inH$_2$O)	x 0.036	= Pounds-force per square inch (psi; lbf/in²; lb/in²)	x 27.68	=	Inches of water (inH$_2$O)

Torque (moment of force)
Pounds-force inches (lbf in; lb in)	x 1.152	= Kilograms-force centimetre (kgf cm; kg cm)	x 0.868	=	Pounds-force inches (lbf in; lb in)
Pounds-force inches (lbf in; lb in)	x 0.113	= Newton metres (Nm)	x 8.85	=	Pounds-force inches (lbf in; lb in)
Pounds-force inches (lbf in; lb in)	x 0.083	= Pounds-force feet (lbf ft; lb ft)	x 12	=	Pounds-force inches (lbf in; lb in)
Pounds-force feet (lbf ft; lb ft)	x 0.138	= Kilograms-force metres (kgf m; kg m)	x 7.233	=	Pounds-force feet (lbf ft; lb ft)
Pounds-force feet (lbf ft; lb ft)	x 1.356	= Newton metres (Nm)	x 0.738	=	Pounds-force feet (lbf ft; lb ft)
Newton metres (Nm)	x 0.102	= Kilograms-force metres (kgf m; kg m)	x 9.804	=	Newton metres (Nm)

Power
Horsepower (hp)	x 745.7	= Watts (W)	x 0.0013	=	Horsepower (hp)

Velocity (speed)
Miles per hour (miles/hr; mph)	x 1.609	= Kilometres per hour (km/hr; kph)	x 0.621	=	Miles per hour (miles/hr; mph)

Fuel consumption*
Miles per gallon (mpg)	x 0.354	= Kilometres per litre (km/l)	x 2.825	=	Miles per gallon (mpg)

Temperature
Degrees Fahrenheit = (°C x 1.8) + 32   Degrees Celsius (Degrees Centigrade; °C) = (°F - 32) x 0.56

It is common practice to convert from miles per gallon (mpg) to litres/100 kilometres (l/100km), where mpg x l/100 km = 282

REF•24 MOT Test Checks

About the MOT Test

In the UK, all vehicles more than three years old are subject to an annual test to ensure that they meet minimum safety requirements. A current test certificate must be issued before a machine can be used on public roads, and is required before a road fund licence can be issued. Riding without a current test certificate will also invalidate your insurance.

For most owners, the MOT test is an annual cause for anxiety, and this is largely due to owners not being sure what needs to be checked prior to submitting the motorcycle for testing. The simple answer is that a fully roadworthy motorcycle will have no difficulty in passing the test.

This is a guide to getting your motorcycle through the MOT test. Obviously it will not be possible to examine the motorcycle to the same standard as the professional MOT tester, particularly in view of the equipment required for some of the checks. However, working through the following procedures will enable you to identify any problem areas before submitting the motorcycle for the test.

It has only been possible to summarise the test requirements here, based on the regulations in force at the time of printing. Test standards are becoming increasingly stringent, although there are some exemptions for older vehicles. More information about the MOT test can be obtained from the TSO publications, *How Safe is your Motorcycle* and *The MOT Inspection Manual for Motorcycle Testing*.

Many of the checks require that one of the wheels is raised off the ground. If the motorcycle doesn't have a centre stand, note that an auxiliary stand will be required. Additionally, the help of an assistant may prove useful.

Certain exceptions apply to machines under 50 cc, machines without a lighting system, and Classic bikes - if in doubt about any of the requirements listed below seek confirmation from an MOT tester prior to submitting the motorcycle for the test.

Check that the frame number is clearly visible.

Electrical System

Lights, turn signals, horn and reflector

✔ With the ignition on, check the operation of the following electrical components. **Note:** The electrical components on certain small-capacity machines are powered by the generator, requiring that the engine is run for this check.

a) *Headlight and tail light.* Check that both illuminate in the low and high beam switch positions.
b) *Position lights.* Check that the front position (or sidelight) and tail light illuminate in this switch position.
c) *Turn signals.* Check that all flash at the correct rate, and that the warning light(s) function correctly. Check that the turn signal switch works correctly.
d) *Hazard warning system (where fitted).* Check that all four turn signals flash in this switch position.
e) *Brake stop light.* Check that the light comes on when the front and rear brakes are independently applied. Models first used on or after 1st April 1986 must have a brake light switch on each brake.
f) *Horn.* Check that the sound is continuous and of reasonable volume.

✔ Check that there is a red reflector on the rear of the machine, either mounted separately or as part of the tail light lens.
✔ Check the condition of the headlight, tail light and turn signal lenses.

Headlight beam height

✔ The MOT tester will perform a headlight beam height check using specialised beam setting equipment **(see illustration 1)**. This equipment will not be available to the home mechanic, but if you suspect that the headlight is incorrectly set or may have been maladjusted in the past, you can perform a rough test as follows.

✔ Position the bike in a straight line facing a brick wall. The bike must be off its stand, upright and with a rider seated. Measure the height from the ground to the centre of the headlight and mark a horizontal line on the wall at this height. Position the motorcycle 3.8 metres from the wall and draw a vertical line up the wall central to the centreline of the motorcycle. Switch to dipped beam and check that the beam pattern falls slightly lower than the horizontal line and to the left of the vertical line **(see illustration 2)**.

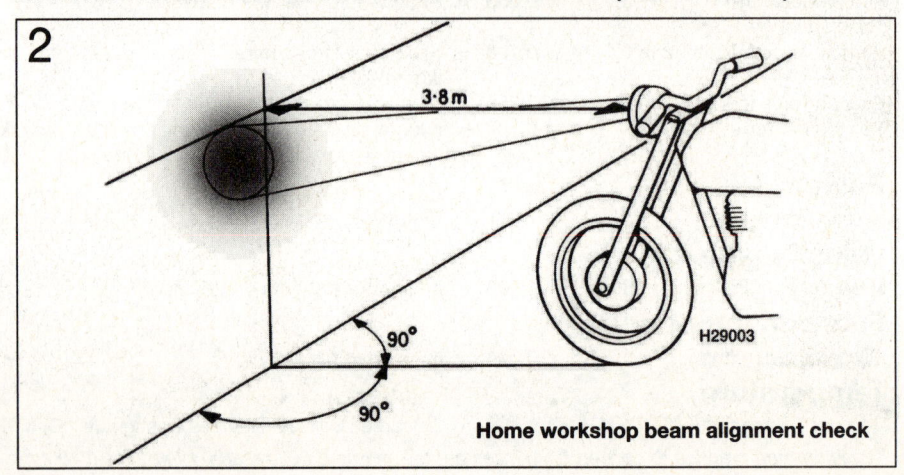

Headlight beam height checking equipment

Home workshop beam alignment check

MOT Test Checks REF•25

Exhaust System and Final Drive

Exhaust

✔ Check that the exhaust mountings are secure and that the system does not foul any of the rear suspension components.
✔ Start the motorcycle. When the revs are increased, check that the exhaust is neither holed nor leaking from any of its joints. On a linked system, check that the collector box is not leaking due to corrosion.

✔ Note that the exhaust decibel level ("loudness" of the exhaust) is assessed at the discretion of the tester. If the motorcycle was first used on or after 1st January 1985 the silencer must carry the BSAU 193 stamp, or a marking relating to its make and model, or be of OE (original equipment) manufacture. If the silencer is marked NOT FOR ROAD USE, RACING USE ONLY or similar, it will fail the MOT.

Final drive

✔ On chain or belt drive machines, check that the chain/belt is in good condition and does not have excessive slack. Also check that the sprocket is securely mounted on the rear wheel hub. Check that the chain/belt guard is in place.
✔ On shaft drive bikes, check for oil leaking from the drive unit and fouling the rear tyre.

Steering and Suspension

Steering

✔ With the front wheel raised off the ground, rotate the steering from lock to lock. The handlebar or switches must not contact the fuel tank or be close enough to trap the rider's hand. Problems can be caused by damaged lock stops on the lower yoke and frame, or by the fitting of non-standard handlebars.
✔ When performing the lock to lock check, also ensure that the steering moves freely without drag or notchiness. Steering movement can be impaired by poorly routed cables, or by overtight head bearings or worn bearings. The tester will perform a check of the steering head bearing lower race by mounting the front wheel on a surface plate, then performing a lock to lock check with the weight of the machine on the lower bearing (see illustration 3).
✔ Grasp the fork sliders (lower legs) and attempt to push and pull on the forks (see illustration 4). Any play in the steering head bearings will be felt. Note that in extreme cases, wear of the front fork bushes can be misinterpreted for head bearing play.
✔ Check that the handlebars are securely mounted.
✔ Check that the handlebar grip rubbers are secure. They should by bonded to the bar left end and to the throttle cable pulley on the right end.

Front wheel mounted on a surface plate for steering head bearing lower race check

Front suspension

✔ With the motorcycle off the stand, hold the front brake on and pump the front forks up and down (see illustration 5). Check that they are adequately damped.

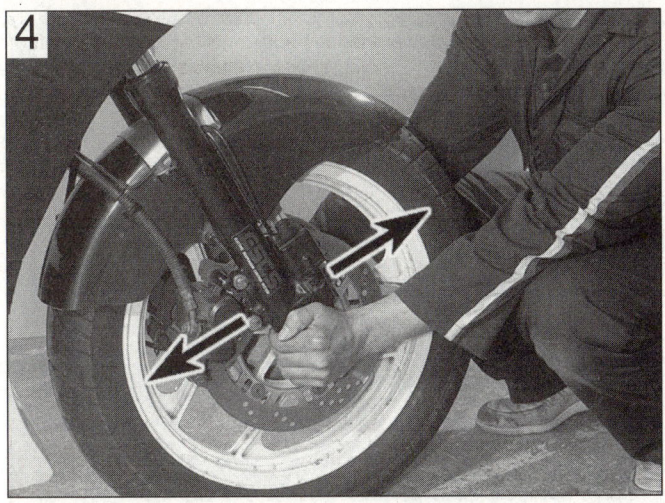

Checking the steering head bearings for freeplay

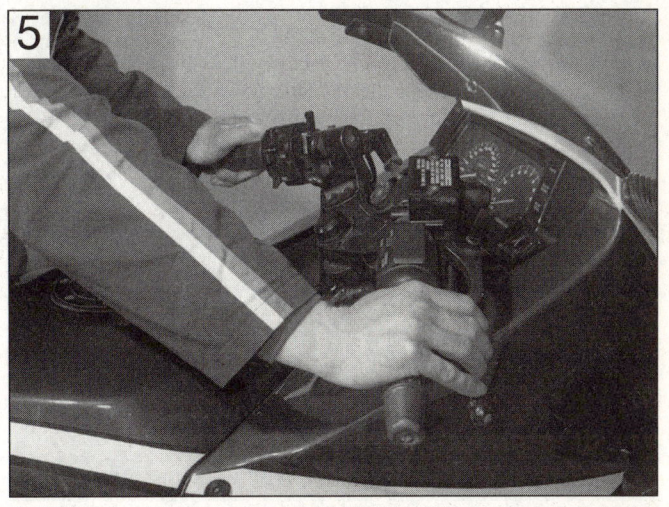

Hold the front brake on and pump the front forks up and down to check operation

REF•26 MOT Test Checks

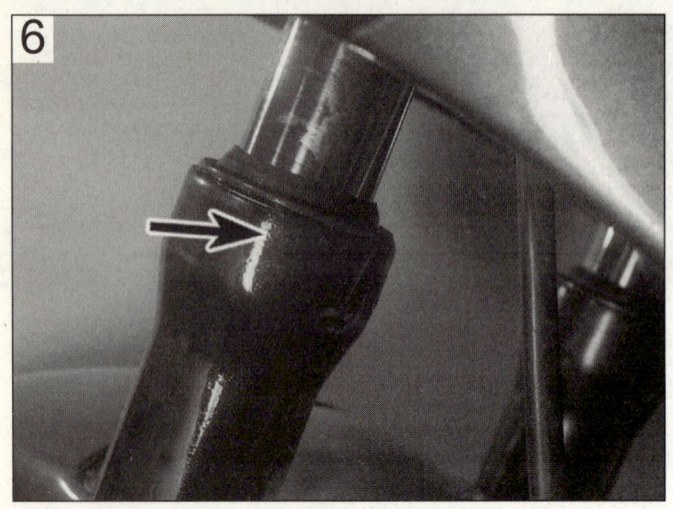

6 Inspect the area around the fork dust seal for oil leakage (arrow)

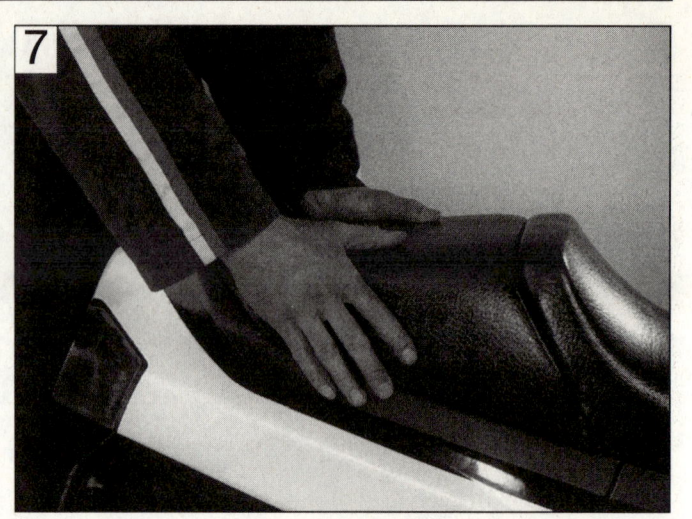

7 Bounce the rear of the motorcycle to check rear suspension operation

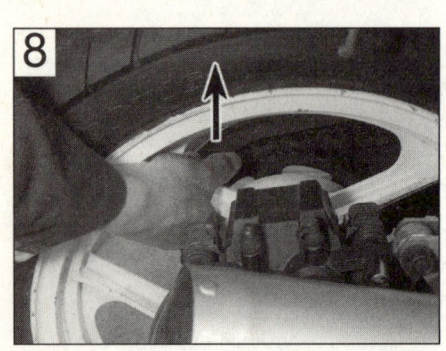

8 Checking for rear suspension linkage play

✔ Inspect the area above and around the front fork oil seals **(see illustration 6)**. There should be no sign of oil on the fork tube (stanchion) nor leaking down the slider (lower leg). On models so equipped, check that there is no oil leaking from the anti-dive units.

✔ On models with swingarm front suspension, check that there is no freeplay in the linkage when moved from side to side.

Rear suspension

✔ With the motorcycle off the stand and an assistant supporting the motorcycle by its handlebars, bounce the rear suspension **(see illustration 7)**. Check that the suspension components do not foul on any of the cycle parts and check that the shock absorber(s) provide adequate damping.

✔ Visually inspect the shock absorber(s) and check that there is no sign of oil leakage from its damper. This is somewhat restricted on certain single shock models due to the location of the shock absorber.

✔ With the rear wheel raised off the ground, grasp the wheel at the highest point and attempt to pull it up **(see illustration 8)**. Any play in the swingarm pivot or suspension linkage bearings will be felt as movement. **Note:** *Do not confuse play with actual suspension movement.* Failure to lubricate suspension linkage bearings can lead to bearing failure **(see illustration 9)**.

✔ With the rear wheel raised off the ground, grasp the swingarm ends and attempt to move the swingarm from side to side and forwards and backwards - any play indicates wear of the swingarm pivot bearings **(see illustration 10)**.

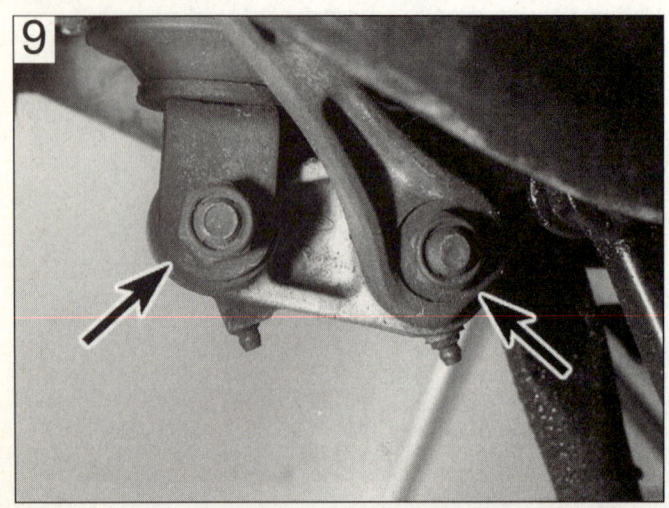

9 Worn suspension linkage pivots (arrows) are usually the cause of play in the rear suspension

10 Grasp the swingarm at the ends to check for play in its pivot bearings

MOT Test Checks REF•27

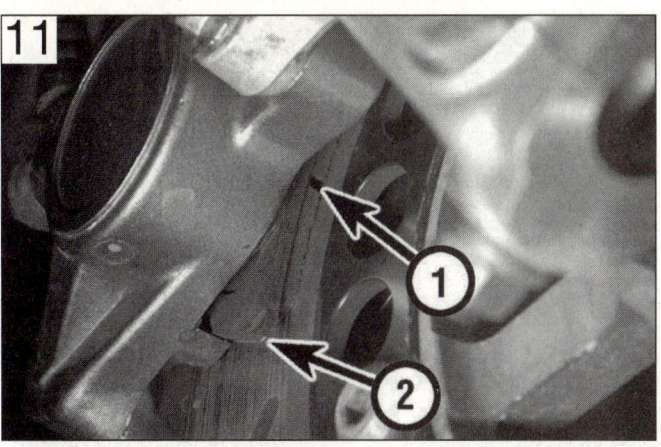

Brake pad wear can usually be viewed without removing the caliper. Most pads have wear indicator grooves (1) and some also have indicator tangs (2)

On drum brakes, check the angle of the operating lever with the brake fully applied. Most drum brakes have a wear indicator pointer and scale.

Brakes, Wheels and Tyres

Brakes

✔ With the wheel raised off the ground, apply the brake then free it off, and check that the wheel is about to revolve freely without brake drag.
✔ On disc brakes, examine the disc itself. Check that it is securely mounted and not cracked.
✔ On disc brakes, view the pad material through the caliper mouth and check that the pads are not worn down beyond the limit **(see illustration 11)**.
✔ On drum brakes, check that when the brake is applied the angle between the operating lever and cable or rod is not too great **(see illustration 12)**. Check also that the operating lever doesn't foul any other components.
✔ On disc brakes, examine the flexible hoses from top to bottom. Have an assistant hold the brake on so that the fluid in the hose is under pressure, and check that there is no sign of fluid leakage, bulges or cracking. If there are any metal brake pipes or unions, check that these are free from corrosion and damage. Where a brake-linked anti-dive system is fitted, check the hoses to the anti-dive in a similar manner.
✔ Check that the rear brake torque arm is secure and that its fasteners are secured by self-locking nuts or castellated nuts with split-pins or R-pins **(see illustration 13)**.
✔ On models with ABS, check that the self-check warning light in the instrument panel works.
✔ The MOT tester will perform a test of the motorcycle's braking efficiency based on a calculation of rider and motorcycle weight. Although this cannot be carried out at home, you can at least ensure that the braking systems are properly maintained. For hydraulic disc brakes, check the fluid level, lever/pedal feel (bleed of air if its spongy) and pad material. For drum brakes, check adjustment, cable or rod operation and shoe lining thickness.

Wheels and tyres

✔ Check the wheel condition. Cast wheels should be free from cracks and if of the built-up design, all fasteners should be secure. Spoked wheels should be checked for broken, corroded, loose or bent spokes.
✔ With the wheel raised off the ground, spin the wheel and visually check that the tyre and wheel run true. Check that the tyre does not foul the suspension or mudguards.
✔ With the wheel raised off the ground, grasp the wheel and attempt to move it about the axle (spindle) **(see illustration 14)**. Any play felt here indicates wheel bearing failure.

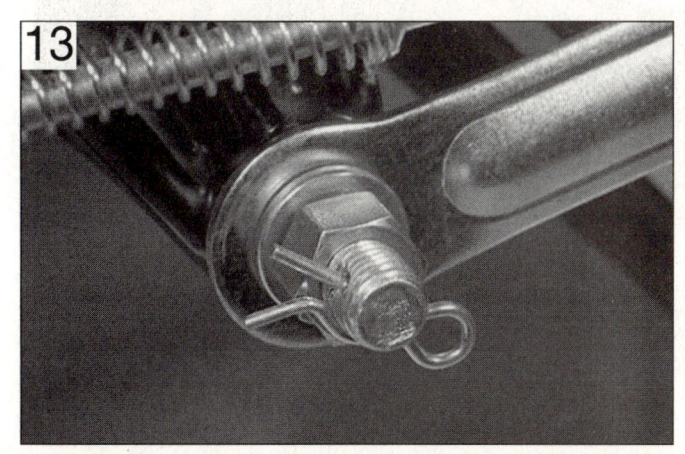

Brake torque arm must be properly secured at both ends

Check for wheel bearing play by trying to move the wheel about the axle (spindle)

REF•28 MOT Test Checks

Checking the tyre tread depth

Tyre direction of rotation arrow can be found on tyre sidewall

Castellated type wheel axle (spindle) nut must be secured by a split pin or R-pin

Two straightedges are used to check wheel alignment

✔ Check the tyre tread depth, tread condition and sidewall condition **(see illustration 15)**.
✔ Check the tyre type. Front and rear tyre types must be compatible and be suitable for road use. Tyres marked NOT FOR ROAD USE, COMPETITION USE ONLY or similar, will fail the MOT.

✔ If the tyre sidewall carries a direction of rotation arrow, this must be pointing in the direction of normal wheel rotation **(see illustration 16)**.
✔ Check that the wheel axle (spindle) nuts (where applicable) are properly secured. A self-locking nut or castellated nut with a split-pin or R-pin can be used **(see illustration 17)**.
✔ Wheel alignment is checked with the motorcycle off the stand and a rider seated. With the front wheel pointing straight ahead, two perfectly straight lengths of metal or wood and placed against the sidewalls of both tyres **(see illustration 18)**. The gap each side of the front tyre must be equidistant on both sides. Incorrect wheel alignment may be due to a cocked rear wheel (often as the result of poor chain adjustment) or in extreme cases, a bent frame.

General checks and condition

✔ Check the security of all major fasteners, bodypanels, seat, fairings (where fitted) and mudguards.

✔ Check that the rider and pillion footrests, handlebar levers and brake pedal are securely mounted.

✔ Check for corrosion on the frame or any load-bearing components. If severe, this may affect the structure, particularly under stress.

Sidecars

A motorcycle fitted with a sidecar requires additional checks relating to the stability of the machine and security of attachment and swivel joints, plus specific wheel alignment (toe-in) requirements. Additionally, tyre and lighting requirements differ from conventional motorcycle use. Owners are advised to check MOT test requirements with an official test centre.

Storage REF•29

Preparing for storage

Before you start

If repairs or an overhaul is needed, see that this is carried out now rather than left until you want to ride the bike again.

Give the bike a good wash and scrub all dirt from its underside. Make sure the bike dries completely before preparing for storage.

Engine

● Remove the spark plug(s) and lubricate the cylinder bores with approximately a teaspoon of motor oil using a spout-type oil can **(see illustration 1)**. Reinstall the spark plug(s). Crank the engine over a couple of times to coat the piston rings and bores with oil. If the bike has a kickstart, use this to turn the engine over. If not, flick the kill switch to the OFF position and crank the engine over on the starter **(see illustration 2)**. If the nature on the ignition system prevents the starter operating with the kill switch in the OFF position, remove the spark plugs and fit them back in their caps; ensure that the plugs are earthed (grounded) against the cylinder head when the starter is operated **(see illustration 3)**.

⚠️ **Warning: It is important that the plugs are earthed (grounded) away from the spark plug holes otherwise there is a risk of atomised fuel from the cylinders igniting.**

HAYNES HiNT *On a single cylinder four-stroke engine, you can seal the combustion chamber completely by positioning the piston at TDC on the compression stroke.*

● Drain the carburettor(s) otherwise there is a risk of jets becoming blocked by gum deposits from the fuel **(see illustration 4)**.

● If the bike is going into long-term storage, consider adding a fuel stabiliser to the fuel in the tank. If the tank is drained completely, corrosion of its internal surfaces may occur if left unprotected for a long period. The tank can be treated with a rust preventative especially for this purpose. Alternatively, remove the tank and pour half a litre of motor oil into it, install the filler cap and shake the tank to coat its internals with oil before draining off the excess. The same effect can also be achieved by spraying WD40 or a similar water-dispersant around the inside of the tank via its flexible nozzle.

● Make sure the cooling system contains the correct mix of antifreeze. Antifreeze also contains important corrosion inhibitors.

● The air intakes and exhaust can be sealed off by covering or plugging the openings. Ensure that you do not seal in any condensation; run the engine until it is hot,

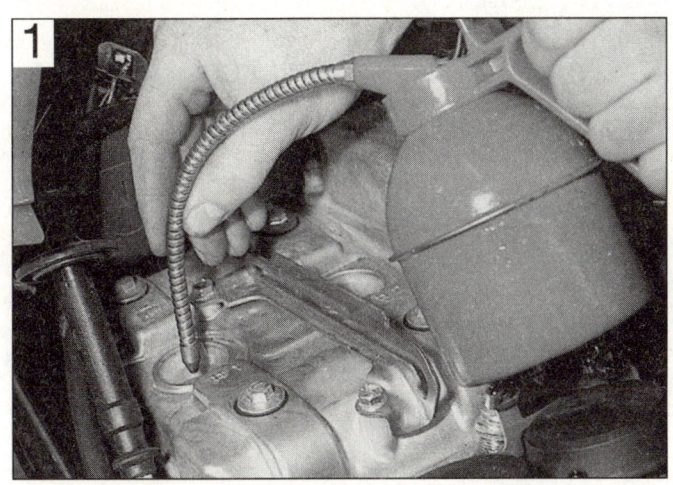

1 Squirt a drop of motor oil into each cylinder

2 Flick the kill switch to OFF . . .

3 . . . and ensure that the metal bodies of the plugs (arrows) are earthed against the cylinder head

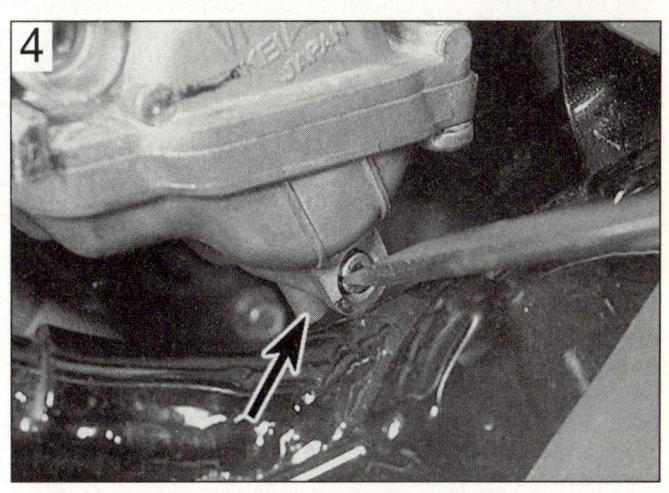

4 Connect a hose to the carburettor float chamber drain stub (arrow) and unscrew the drain screw

Storage

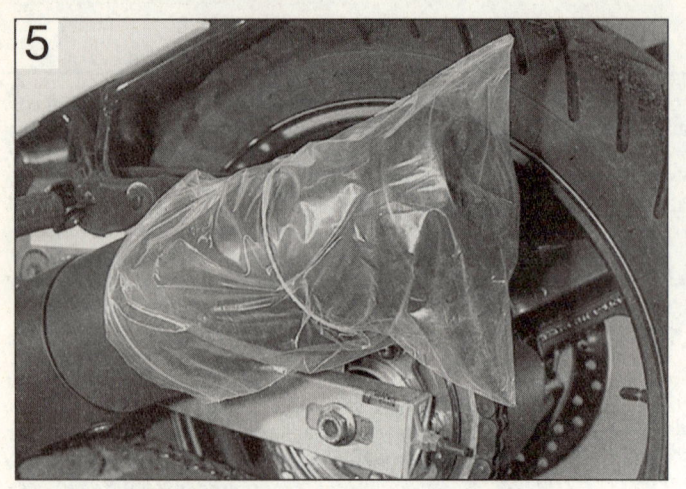

Exhausts can be sealed off with a plastic bag

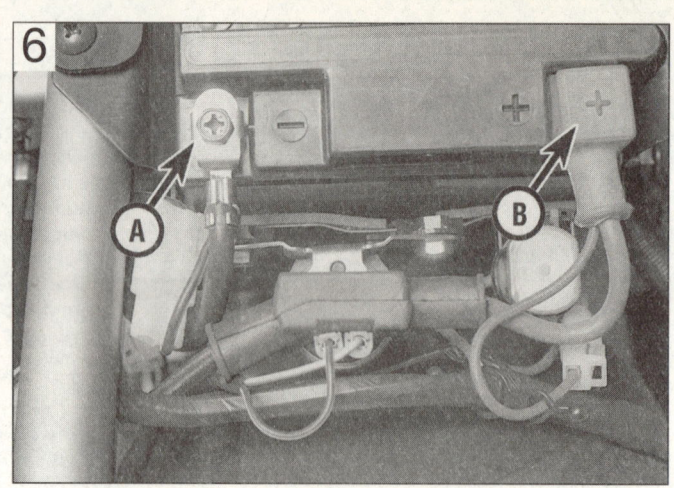

Disconnect the negative lead (A) first, followed by the positive lead (B)

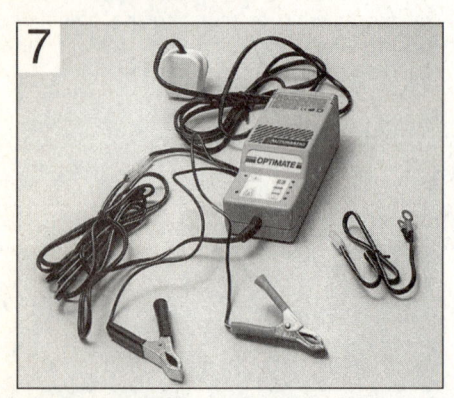

Use a suitable battery charger - this kit also assess battery condition

then switch off and allow to cool. Tape a piece of thick plastic over the silencer end(s) **(see illustration 5)**. Note that some advocate pouring a tablespoon of motor oil into the silencer(s) before sealing them off.

Battery

● Remove it from the bike - in extreme cases of cold the battery may freeze and crack its case **(see illustration 6)**.

● Check the electrolyte level and top up if necessary (conventional refillable batteries). Clean the terminals.
● Store the battery off the motorcycle and away from any sources of fire. Position a wooden block under the battery if it is to sit on the ground.
● Give the battery a trickle charge for a few hours every month **(see illustration 7)**.

Tyres

● Place the bike on its centrestand or an auxiliary stand which will support the motorcycle in an upright position. Position wood blocks under the tyres to keep them off the ground and to provide insulation from damp. If the bike is being put into long-term storage, ideally both tyres should be off the ground; not only will this protect the tyres, but will also ensure that no load is placed on the steering head or wheel bearings.
● Deflate each tyre by 5 to 10 psi, no more or the beads may unseat from the rim, making subsequent inflation difficult on tubeless tyres.

Pivots and controls

● Lubricate all lever, pedal, stand and footrest pivot points. If grease nipples are fitted to the rear suspension components, apply lubricant to the pivots.
● Lubricate all control cables.

Cycle components

● Apply a wax protectant to all painted and plastic components. Wipe off any excess, but don't polish to a shine. Where fitted, clean the screen with soap and water.
● Coat metal parts with Vaseline (petroleum jelly). When applying this to the fork tubes, do not compress the forks otherwise the seals will rot from contact with the Vaseline.
● Apply a vinyl cleaner to the seat.

Storage conditions

● Aim to store the bike in a shed or garage which does not leak and is free from damp.
● Drape an old blanket or bedspread over the bike to protect it from dust and direct contact with sunlight (which will fade paint). This also hides the bike from prying eyes. Beware of tight-fitting plastic covers which may allow condensation to form and settle on the bike.

Getting back on the road

Engine and transmission

● Change the oil and replace the oil filter. If this was done prior to storage, check that the oil hasn't emulsified - a thick whitish substance which occurs through condensation.
● Remove the spark plugs. Using a spout-type oil can, squirt a few drops of oil into the cylinder(s). This will provide initial lubrication as the piston rings and bores comes back into contact. Service the spark plugs, or fit new ones, and install them in the engine.

● Check that the clutch isn't stuck on. The plates can stick together if left standing for some time, preventing clutch operation. Engage a gear and try rocking the bike back and forth with the clutch lever held against the handlebar. If this doesn't work on cable-operated clutches, hold the clutch lever back against the handlebar with a strong elastic band or cable tie for a couple of hours **(see illustration 8)**.
● If the air intakes or silencer end(s) were blocked off, remove the bung or cover used.
● If the fuel tank was coated with a rust

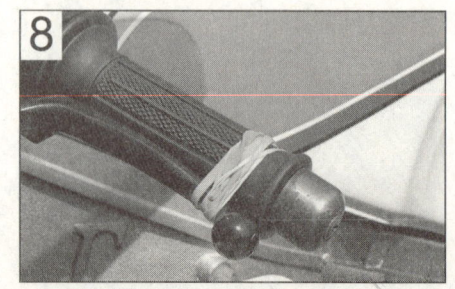

Hold clutch lever back against the handlebar with elastic bands or a cable tie

Storage REF•31

preventative, oil or a stabiliser added to the fuel, drain and flush the tank and dispose of the fuel sensibly. If no action was taken with the fuel tank prior to storage, it is advised that the old fuel is disposed of since it will go off over a period of time. Refill the fuel tank with fresh fuel.

Frame and running gear

● Oil all pivot points and cables.
● Check the tyre pressures. They will definitely need inflating if pressures were reduced for storage.
● Lubricate the final drive chain (where applicable).
● Remove any protective coating applied to the fork tubes (stanchions) since this may well destroy the fork seals. If the fork tubes weren't protected and have picked up rust spots, remove them with very fine abrasive paper and refinish with metal polish.
● Check that both brakes operate correctly. Apply each brake hard and check that it's not possible to move the motorcycle forwards, then check that the brake frees off again once released. Brake caliper pistons can stick due to corrosion around the piston head, or on the sliding caliper types, due to corrosion of the slider pins. If the brake doesn't free after repeated operation, take the caliper off for examination. Similarly drum brakes can stick due to a seized operating cam, cable or rod linkage.
● If the motorcycle has been in long-term storage, renew the brake fluid and clutch fluid (where applicable).
● Depending on where the bike has been stored, the wiring, cables and hoses may have been nibbled by rodents. Make a visual check and investigate disturbed wiring loom tape.

Battery

● If the battery has been previously removal and given top up charges it can simply be reconnected. Remember to connect the positive cable first and the negative cable last.
● On conventional refillable batteries, if the battery has not received any attention, remove it from the motorcycle and check its electrolyte level. Top up if necessary then charge the battery. If the battery fails to hold a charge and a visual checks show heavy white sulphation of the plates, the battery is probably defective and must be renewed. This is particularly likely if the battery is old. Confirm battery condition with a specific gravity check.
● On sealed (MF) batteries, if the battery has not received any attention, remove it from the motorcycle and charge it according to the information on the battery case - if the battery fails to hold a charge it must be renewed.

Starting procedure

● If a kickstart is fitted, turn the engine over a couple of times with the ignition OFF to distribute oil around the engine. If no kickstart is fitted, flick the engine kill switch OFF and the ignition ON and crank the engine over a couple of times to work oil around the upper cylinder components. If the nature of the ignition system is such that the starter won't work with the kill switch OFF, remove the spark plugs, fit them back into their caps and earth (ground) their bodies on the cylinder head. Reinstall the spark plugs afterwards.
● Switch the kill switch to RUN, operate the choke and start the engine. If the engine won't start don't continue cranking the engine - not only will this flatten the battery, but the starter motor will overheat. Switch the ignition off and try again later. If the engine refuses to start, go through the fault finding procedures in this manual. **Note:** *If the bike has been in storage for a long time, old fuel or a carburettor blockage may be the problem. Gum deposits in carburettors can block jets - if a carburettor cleaner doesn't prove successful the carburettors must be dismantled for cleaning.*
● Once the engine has started, check that the lights, turn signals and horn work properly.
● Treat the bike gently for the first ride and check all fluid levels on completion. Settle the bike back into the maintenance schedule.

Fault Finding

This Section provides an easy reference-guide to the more common faults that are likely to afflict your machine. Obviously, the opportunities are almost limitless for faults to occur as a result of obscure failures, and to try and cover all eventualities would require a book. Indeed, a number have been written on the subject.

Successful troubleshooting is not a mysterious 'black art' but the application of a bit of knowledge combined with a systematic and logical approach to the problem. Approach any troubleshooting by first accurately identifying the symptom and then checking through the list of possible causes, starting with the simplest or most obvious and progressing in stages to the most complex.

Take nothing for granted, but above all apply liberal quantities of common sense.

The main symptom of a fault is given in the text as a major heading below which are listed the various systems or areas which may contain the fault. Details of each possible cause for a fault and the remedial action to be taken are given, in brief, in the paragraphs below each heading. Further information should be sought in the relevant Chapter.

1 Engine doesn't start or is difficult to start
- [ ] Starter motor doesn't rotate
- [ ] Starter motor rotates but engine does not turn over
- [ ] Starter works but engine won't turn over (seized)
- [ ] No fuel flow
- [ ] Engine flooded
- [ ] No spark or weak spark
- [ ] Compression low
- [ ] Stalls after starting
- [ ] Rough idle

2 Poor running at low speed
- [ ] Spark weak
- [ ] Fuel/air mixture incorrect
- [ ] Compression low
- [ ] Poor acceleration

3 Poor running or no power at high speed
- [ ] Firing incorrect
- [ ] Fuel/air mixture incorrect
- [ ] Compression low
- [ ] Knocking or pinging
- [ ] Miscellaneous causes

4 Overheating
- [ ] Engine overheats
- [ ] Firing incorrect
- [ ] Fuel/air mixture incorrect
- [ ] Compression too high
- [ ] Engine load excessive
- [ ] Lubrication inadequate
- [ ] Miscellaneous causes

5 Clutch problems
- [ ] Clutch slipping
- [ ] Clutch not disengaging completely

6 Gearchange problems
- [ ] Doesn't go into gear, or lever doesn't return
- [ ] Jumps out of gear
- [ ] Overshifts

7 Abnormal engine noise
- [ ] Knocking or pinging
- [ ] Piston slap or rattling
- [ ] Valve noise
- [ ] Other noise

8 Abnormal driveline noise
- [ ] Clutch noise
- [ ] Transmission noise
- [ ] Final drive noise

9 Abnormal frame and suspension noise
- [ ] Front end noise
- [ ] Shock absorber noise
- [ ] Brake noise

10 Oil pressure indicator light comes on
- [ ] Engine lubrication system
- [ ] Electrical system

11 Excessive exhaust smoke
- [ ] White smoke
- [ ] Black smoke
- [ ] Brown smoke

12 Poor handling or stability
- [ ] Handlebar hard to turn
- [ ] Handlebar shakes or vibrates excessively
- [ ] Handlebar pulls to one side
- [ ] Poor shock absorbing qualities

13 Braking problems
- [ ] Brakes are spongy, don't hold
- [ ] Brake lever or pedal pulsates
- [ ] Brakes drag

14 Electrical problems
- [ ] Battery dead or weak
- [ ] Battery overcharged

Fault Finding REF•33

1 Engine doesn't start or is difficult to start

Starter motor doesn't rotate
- [ ] Engine kill switch OFF.
- [ ] Fuse blown. Check main fuse and starter circuit fuse (Chapter 9).
- [ ] Battery voltage low. Check and recharge battery (Chapter 9).
- [ ] Starter motor defective. Make sure the wiring to the starter is secure. Make sure the starter relay clicks when the start button is pushed. If the relay clicks, then the fault is in the wiring or motor.
- [ ] Starter relay faulty. Check it according to the procedure in Chapter 9.
- [ ] Starter switch not contacting. The contacts could be wet, corroded or dirty. Disassemble and clean the switch (Chapter 9).
- [ ] Wiring open or shorted. Check all wiring connections and harnesses to make sure that they are dry, tight and not corroded. Also check for broken or frayed wires that can cause a short to ground (earth) (see wiring diagram, Chapter 9).
- [ ] Ignition (main) switch defective. Check the switch according to the procedure in Chapter 9. Replace the switch with a new one if it is defective.
- [ ] Engine kill switch defective. Check for wet, dirty or corroded contacts. Clean or replace the switch as necessary (Chapter 9).
- [ ] Faulty neutral, side stand or clutch switch. Check the wiring to each switch and the switch itself according to the procedures in Chapter 9.

Starter motor rotates but engine does not turn over
- [ ] Starter clutch defective. Inspect and repair or replace (Chapter 2).
- [ ] Damaged idle/reduction or starter gears. Inspect and replace the damaged parts (Chapter 2).

Starter works but engine won't turn over (seized)
- [ ] Seized engine caused by one or more internally damaged components. Failure due to wear, abuse or lack of lubrication. Damage can include seized valves, followers, camshafts, pistons, crankshaft, connecting rod bearings, or transmission gears or bearings. Refer to Chapter 2 for engine disassembly.

No fuel flow
- [ ] No fuel in tank.
- [ ] Fuel tank breather hose obstructed.
- [ ] Fuel tap filter or in-line filter (XL models) clogged. Remove the tap and clean it and the filter (Chapter 4A).
- [ ] Fuel tap vacuum hose split or detached (VTR models). Check the hose.
- [ ] Fuel tap diaphragm split (VTR models). Remove the tap and check the diaphragm (Chapter 4A).
- [ ] Fuel line clogged. Pull the fuel line loose and carefully blow through it.
- [ ] Float needle valve clogged (carburetor models). For both valves to be clogged, either a very bad batch of fuel with an unusual additive has been used, or some other foreign material has entered the tank. Many times after a machine has been stored for many months without running, the fuel turns to a varnish-like liquid and forms deposits on the inlet needle valves and jets. The carburettors should be removed and overhauled if draining the float chambers doesn't solve the problem (Chapter 4A).
- [ ] Fuel pump or relay faulty (XL models). Check the fuel pump and relay (Chapter 4A or B).

Engine flooded
- [ ] Float height too high (carburettor models). Check as described in Chapter 4A.
- [ ] Float needle valve worn or stuck open (carburetor models). A piece of dirt, rust or other debris can cause the valve to seat improperly, causing excess fuel to be admitted to the float chamber. In this case, the float chamber should be cleaned and the needle valve and seat inspected. If the needle and seat are worn, then the leaking will persist and the parts should be replaced with new ones (Chapter 4A).
- [ ] Starting technique incorrect. Under normal circumstances (i.e., if all the carburettor functions are sound) the machine should start with little or no throttle. When the engine is cold, the choke should be operated and the engine started without opening the throttle. When the engine is at operating temperature, only a very slight amount of throttle should be necessary. If the engine is flooded, turn the fuel tap OFF and hold the throttle open while cranking the engine. This will allow additional air to reach the cylinders. Remember to turn the fuel tap back ON after the engine starts.

No spark or weak spark
- [ ] Ignition switch OFF.
- [ ] Engine kill switch turned to the OFF position.
- [ ] Battery voltage low. Check and recharge the battery as necessary (Chapter 9).
- [ ] Spark plugs dirty, defective or worn out. Locate reason for fouled plugs using spark plug condition chart and follow the plug maintenance procedures (Chapter 1).
- [ ] Spark plug caps or secondary (HT) wiring faulty. Check condition. Replace either or both components if cracks or deterioration are evident (Chapter 5).
- [ ] Spark plug caps not making good contact. Make sure that the plug caps fit snugly over the plug ends.
- [ ] ICU/ECU defective. Check the unit, referring to Chapter 5 for details.
- [ ] Pulse generator defective. Check the unit, referring to Chapter 5 for details.
- [ ] Ignition HT coils defective. Check the coils, referring to Chapter 5.
- [ ] Ignition or kill switch shorted. This is usually caused by water, corrosion, damage or excessive wear. The switches can be disassembled and cleaned with electrical contact cleaner. If cleaning does not help, replace the switches (Chapter 9).
- [ ] Wiring shorted or broken between:
  a) Ignition (main) switch and engine kill switch (or blown fuse)
  b) ICU/ECU and engine kill switch
  c) Ignition control unit, converter unit (VTR models) and ignition HT coils. ECU and HT coils (fuel injection models)
  d) Ignition HT coils and spark plugs
  e) ICU/ECU and pulse generator
- [ ] Make sure that all wiring connections are clean, dry and tight. Look for chafed and broken wires (Chapters 5 and 9).

Compression low
- [ ] Spark plugs loose. Remove the plugs and inspect their threads. Reinstall and tighten to the specified torque (Chapter 1).
- [ ] Cylinder heads not sufficiently tightened down. If a cylinder head is suspected of being loose, then there's a chance that the gasket or head is damaged if the problem has persisted for any length of time. The head bolts should be tightened to the proper torque in the correct sequence (Chapter 2).
- [ ] Incorrect valve clearance. This means that the valve is not closing completely and compression pressure is leaking past the valve. Check and adjust the valve clearances (Chapter 1).
- [ ] Cylinder and/or piston worn. Excessive wear will cause compression pressure to leak past the rings. This is usually accompanied by worn rings as well. A top-end overhaul is necessary (Chapter 2).
- [ ] Piston rings worn, weak, broken, or sticking. Broken or sticking piston rings usually indicate a lubrication or carburation problem that causes excess carbon deposits to form on the pistons and rings. Top-end overhaul is necessary (Chapter 2).
- [ ] Piston ring-to-groove clearance excessive. This is caused by excessive wear of the piston ring lands. Piston replacement is necessary (Chapter 2).

Fault Finding

1 Engine doesn't start or is difficult to start (continued)

- [ ] Cylinder head gasket damaged. If a head is allowed to become loose, or if excessive carbon build-up on the piston crown and combustion chamber causes extremely high compression, the head gasket may leak. Retorquing the head is not always sufficient to restore the seal, so gasket replacement is necessary (Chapter 2).
- [ ] Cylinder head warped. This is caused by overheating or improperly tightened head bolts. Machine shop resurfacing or head replacement is necessary (Chapter 2).
- [ ] Valve spring broken or weak. Caused by component failure or wear; the springs must be replaced (Chapter 2).
- [ ] Valve not seating properly. This is caused by a bent valve (from over-revving or improper valve adjustment), burned valve or seat (improper carburation) or an accumulation of carbon deposits on the seat (from carburation or lubrication problems). The valves must be cleaned and/or replaced and the seats serviced if possible (Chapter 2).

Stalls after starting

- [ ] Improper choke action. On carburettor engines, make sure the choke linkage shaft is getting a full stroke and staying in the out position (Chapter 4A). On fuel injected engines, check the operation of the fast idle cable and starter valves (XL-3 to 6 models) or intake air control valve on later models (Chapter 4B).
- [ ] Ignition malfunction. See Chapter 5.
- [ ] Carburettor or fuel injection malfunction. See Chapter 4A or B according to model.
- [ ] Fuel contaminated. The fuel can be contaminated with either dirt or water, or can change chemically if the machine is allowed to sit for several months or more. Drain the tank and float chambers (Chapter 4A). Also check that the fuel flows freely and is not being restricted.
- [ ] Intake air leak. On carburettor models, check for loose carburettor-to-intake manifold connections, loose or missing vacuum gauge adapter screws or hoses, or loose carburettor tops (Chapter 4A). On fuel injected models, check the throttle body-to-inlet adaptor joints are air-tight and that all hoses are intact (Chapter 4B).
- [ ] Engine idle speed incorrect. On all except XL-7 models onward it can be adjusted (Chapter 1).

Rough idle

- [ ] Ignition malfunction. See Chapter 5.
- [ ] Idle speed incorrect. On all except XL-7 models onward it can be adjusted. See Chapter 1.
- [ ] Carburettors not synchronised. Adjust carburettors with vacuum gauge or manometer set as described in Chapter 1.
- [ ] Throttle body starter valves not synchronised on XL-3 to 6 models (Chapter 4B).
- [ ] Carburettor or fuel injection malfunction. See Chapter 4A or B according to model.
- [ ] Fuel contaminated. The fuel can be contaminated with either dirt or water, or can change chemically if the machine is allowed to sit for several months or more. Drain the tank and float chambers (Chapter 4A).
- [ ] Intake air leak. Check for loose carburettor-to-intake manifold connections, loose or missing vacuum gauge adapter screws or hoses, or loose carburettor tops (Chapter 4A). On fuel injection models, check for air leaks at the throttle body-to-intake adaptor joints (Chapter 4B).
- [ ] Air filter clogged. Replace the air filter element (Chapter 1).

2 Poor running at low speeds

Spark weak

- [ ] Battery voltage low. Check and recharge battery (Chapter 9).
- [ ] Spark plugs fouled, defective or worn out. Refer to Chapter 1 for spark plug maintenance.
- [ ] Spark plug cap or HT wiring defective. Refer to Chapters 1 and 5 for details on the ignition system.
- [ ] Spark plug caps not making contact.
- [ ] Incorrect spark plugs. Wrong type, heat range or cap configuration. Check and install correct plugs listed in Chapter 1.
- [ ] Ignition control unit (ICU) defective on carburettor models. See Chapter 5.
- [ ] Engine control unit (ECU) defective on fuel injected models. See Chapter 4B.
- [ ] Pulse generator defective. See Chapter 5.
- [ ] Ignition HT coils defective. See Chapter 5.

Fuel/air mixture incorrect (carburetor models)

- [ ] Pilot screws out of adjustment (Chapter 4A).
- [ ] Pilot jet or air passage clogged. Remove and overhaul the carburettors (Chapter 4A).
- [ ] Air bleed holes clogged. Remove carburettor and blow out all passages (Chapter 4A).
- [ ] Air filter clogged, poorly sealed or missing (Chapter 1).
- [ ] Air filter housing poorly sealed. Look for cracks, holes or loose clamps and replace or repair defective parts.
- [ ] Fuel level too high or too low. Check the float height (Chapter 4A).
- [ ] Fuel tank breather hose obstructed.
- [ ] Carburettor intake manifolds loose. Check for cracks, breaks, tears or loose clamps. Replace the rubber intake manifold joints if split or perished.

Compression low

- [ ] Spark plugs loose. Remove the plugs and inspect their threads. Reinstall and tighten to the specified torque (Chapter 1).
- [ ] Cylinder heads not sufficiently tightened down. If a cylinder head is suspected of being loose, then there's a chance that the gasket and head are damaged if the problem has persisted for any length of time. The head bolts should be tightened to the proper torque in the correct sequence (Chapter 2).
- [ ] Incorrect valve clearance. This means that the valve is not closing completely and compression pressure is leaking past the valve. Check and adjust the valve clearances (Chapter 1).
- [ ] Cylinder and/or piston worn. Excessive wear will cause compression pressure to leak past the rings. This is usually accompanied by worn rings as well. A top-end overhaul is necessary (Chapter 2).
- [ ] Piston rings worn, weak, broken, or sticking. Broken or sticking piston rings usually indicate a lubrication or carburation problem that causes excess carbon deposits to form on the pistons and rings. Top-end overhaul is necessary (Chapter 2).
- [ ] Piston ring-to-groove clearance excessive. This is caused by excessive wear of the piston ring lands. Piston replacement is necessary (Chapter 2).
- [ ] Cylinder head gasket damaged. If a head is allowed to become loose, or if excessive carbon build-up on the piston crown and combustion chamber causes extremely high compression, the head gasket may leak. Retorquing the head is not always sufficient to restore the seal, so gasket replacement is necessary (Chapter 2).
- [ ] Cylinder head warped. This is caused by overheating or improperly tightened head bolts. Machine shop resurfacing or head replacement is necessary (Chapter 2).

Fault Finding REF•35

2 Poor running at low speeds (continued)

- ☐ Valve spring broken or weak. Caused by component failure or wear; the springs must be replaced (Chapter 2).
- ☐ Valve not seating properly. This is caused by a bent valve (from over-revving or improper valve adjustment), burned valve or seat (improper carburation) or an accumulation of carbon deposits on the seat (from carburation, lubrication problems). The valves must be cleaned and/or replaced and the seats serviced if possible (Chapter 2).

Poor acceleration

- ☐ Carburettors leaking or dirty. Overhaul the carburettors (Chapter 4A).

- ☐ Timing not advancing. The pulse generator or the ICU/ECU may be defective. If so, they must be replaced with new ones, as they can't be repaired.
- ☐ Carburettors not synchronised. Adjust them with a vacuum gauge set or manometer (Chapter 1).
- ☐ Throttle body starter valves not synchronised on XL-3 to 6 models (Chapter 4B).
- ☐ Engine oil viscosity too high. Using a heavier oil than that recommended in 'Daily (pre-ride) checks' can damage the oil pump or lubrication system and cause drag on the engine.
- ☐ Brakes dragging. Usually caused by debris which has entered the brake piston seals, or from a warped disc or bent axle. Repair as necessary (Chapter 7).

3 Poor running or no power at high speed

Firing incorrect

- ☐ Air filter restricted. Clean or replace filter (Chapter 1).
- ☐ Spark plugs fouled, defective or worn out. See Chapter 1 for spark plug maintenance.
- ☐ Spark plug caps or HT wiring defective. See Chapters 1 and 5 for details of the ignition system.
- ☐ Spark plug caps not in good contact. See Chapter 5.
- ☐ Incorrect spark plugs. Wrong type, heat range or cap configuration. Check and install correct plugs listed in Chapter 1.
- ☐ ICU/ECU defective. See Chapter 5.
- ☐ Ignition HT coils defective. See Chapter 5.

Fuel/air mixture incorrect (carburetor models)

- ☐ Main jet clogged. Dirt, water or other contaminants can clog the main jets. Clean the fuel tap filter, the in-line filter, the float chamber area, and the jets and carburettor orifices (Chapter 4A).
- ☐ Main jet wrong size. The standard jetting is for sea level atmospheric pressure and oxygen content.
- ☐ Throttle shaft-to-carburettor body clearance excessive. Refer to Chapter 4A for inspection and part replacement procedures.
- ☐ Air bleed holes clogged. Remove and overhaul carburettors (Chapter 4A).
- ☐ Air filter clogged, poorly sealed, or missing (Chapter 1).
- ☐ Air filter housing poorly sealed. Look for cracks, holes or loose clamps, and replace or repair defective parts.
- ☐ Fuel level too high or too low. Check the float height (Chapter 4A).
- ☐ Fuel tank breather hose obstructed.
- ☐ Carburettor intake manifolds loose. Check for cracks, breaks, tears or loose clamps. Replace the rubber intake manifolds if they are split or perished (Chapter 4A).

Compression low

- ☐ Spark plugs loose. Remove the plugs and inspect their threads. Reinstall and tighten to the specified torque (Chapter 1).
- ☐ Cylinder heads not sufficiently tightened down. If a cylinder head is suspected of being loose, then there's a chance that the gasket and head are damaged if the problem has persisted for any length of time. The head bolts should be tightened to the proper torque in the correct sequence (Chapter 2).
- ☐ Incorrect valve clearance. This means that the valve is not closing completely and compression pressure is leaking past the valve. Check and adjust the valve clearances (Chapter 1).
- ☐ Cylinder and/or piston worn. Excessive wear will cause compression pressure to leak past the rings. This is usually accompanied by worn rings as well. A top-end overhaul is necessary (Chapter 2).
- ☐ Piston rings worn, weak, broken, or sticking. Broken or sticking piston rings usually indicate a lubrication or carburation problem that causes excess carbon deposits or seizures to form on the pistons and rings. Top-end overhaul is necessary (Chapter 2).

- ☐ Piston ring-to-groove clearance excessive. This is caused by excessive wear of the piston ring lands. Piston replacement is necessary (Chapter 2).
- ☐ Cylinder head gasket damaged. If a head is allowed to become loose, or if excessive carbon build-up on the piston crown and combustion chamber causes extremely high compression, the head gasket may leak. Retorquing the head is not always sufficient to restore the seal, so gasket replacement is necessary (Chapter 2).
- ☐ Cylinder head warped. This is caused by overheating or improperly tightened head bolts. Machine shop resurfacing or head replacement is necessary (Chapter 2).
- ☐ Valve spring broken or weak. Caused by component failure or wear; the springs must be replaced (Chapter 2).
- ☐ Valve not seating properly. This is caused by a bent valve (from over-revving or improper valve adjustment), burned valve or seat (improper carburation) or an accumulation of carbon deposits on the seat (from carburation or lubrication problems). The valves must be cleaned and/or replaced and the seats serviced if possible (Chapter 2).

Knocking or pinking

- ☐ Carbon build-up in combustion chamber. Use of a fuel additive that will dissolve the adhesive bonding the carbon particles to the crown and chamber is the easiest way to remove the build-up. Otherwise, the cylinder heads will have to be removed and decarbonized (Chapter 2).
- ☐ Incorrect or poor quality fuel. Old or improper grades of fuel can cause detonation. This causes the piston to rattle, thus the knocking or pinking sound. Drain old fuel and always use the recommended fuel grade.
- ☐ Spark plug heat range incorrect. Uncontrolled detonation indicates the plug heat range is too hot. The plug in effect becomes a glow plug, raising cylinder temperatures. Install the proper heat range plug (Chapter 1).
- ☐ Improper air/fuel mixture. This will cause the cylinders to run hot, which leads to detonation. Clogged jets or an air leak can cause this imbalance on carburettor engines. See Chapter 4A.

Miscellaneous causes

- ☐ Throttle valve doesn't open fully. Adjust the throttle grip freeplay (Chapter 1).
- ☐ Clutch slipping. May be caused by loose or worn clutch components. Refer to Chapter 2 for clutch overhaul procedures.
- ☐ Timing not advancing.
- ☐ Engine oil viscosity too high. Using a heavier oil than the one recommended in 'Daily (pre-ride) checks' can damage the oil pump or lubrication system and cause drag on the engine.
- ☐ Brakes dragging. Usually caused by debris which has entered the brake piston seals, or from a warped disc or bent axle. Repair as necessary.

Fault Finding

4 Overheating

Engine overheats
- [ ] Coolant level low. Check and add coolant (Daily (pre-ride) checks).
- [ ] Leak in cooling system. Check cooling system hoses and radiator for leaks and other damage. Repair or replace parts as necessary (Chapter 3).
- [ ] Thermostat sticking open or closed. Check and replace as described in Chapter 3.
- [ ] Faulty radiator cap. Remove the cap and have it pressure tested.
- [ ] Coolant passages clogged. Have the entire system drained and flushed, then refill with fresh coolant.
- [ ] Water pump defective. Remove the pump and check the components (Chapter 3).
- [ ] Clogged radiator fins. Clean them by blowing compressed air through the fins from the rear.
- [ ] Cooling fan or fan switch/relay fault (Chapter 3).

Firing incorrect
- [ ] Spark plugs fouled, defective or worn out. See Chapter 1 for spark plug maintenance.
- [ ] Incorrect spark plugs.
- [ ] ICU/ECU defective. See Chapter 5.
- [ ] Faulty ignition HT coils (Chapter 5).

Fuel/air mixture incorrect (carburettor models)
- [ ] Main jet clogged. Dirt, water and other contaminants can clog the main jets. Clean the fuel tap filter, the fuel pump in-line filter, the float chamber area and the jets and carburettor orifices (Chapter 4A).
- [ ] Main jet wrong size. The standard jetting is for sea level atmospheric pressure and oxygen content.
- [ ] Air filter clogged, poorly sealed or missing (Chapter 1).
- [ ] Air filter housing poorly sealed. Look for cracks, holes or loose clamps and replace or repair.
- [ ] Fuel level too low. Check float height (Chapter 4A).
- [ ] Fuel tank breather hose obstructed.
- [ ] Carburettor intake manifolds loose. Check for cracks, breaks, tears or loose clamps. Replace the rubber intake manifold joints if split or perished.

Compression too high
- [ ] Carbon build-up in combustion chamber. Use of a fuel additive that will dissolve the adhesive bonding the carbon particles to the piston crown and chamber is the easiest way to remove the build-up. Otherwise, the cylinder heads will have to be removed and decarbonized (Chapter 2).
- [ ] Improperly machined head surface or installation of incorrect gasket during engine assembly.

Engine load excessive
- [ ] Clutch slipping. Can be caused by damaged, loose or worn clutch components. Refer to Chapter 2 for overhaul procedures.
- [ ] Engine oil level too high. The addition of too much oil will cause pressurisation of the crankcase and inefficient engine operation. Check Specifications and drain to proper level (Chapter 1 and Daily (pre-ride) checks).
- [ ] Engine oil viscosity too high. Using a heavier oil than the one recommended in 'Daily (pre-ride) checks' can damage the oil pump or lubrication system as well as cause drag on the engine.
- [ ] Brakes dragging. Usually caused by debris which has entered the brake piston seals, or from a warped disc or bent axle. Repair as necessary.

Lubrication inadequate
- [ ] Engine oil level too low. Friction caused by intermittent lack of lubrication or from oil that is overworked can cause overheating. The oil provides a definite cooling function in the engine. Check the oil level (Daily (pre-ride) checks).
- [ ] Poor quality engine oil or incorrect viscosity or type. Oil is rated not only according to viscosity but also according to type. Some oils are not rated high enough for use in this engine. Check the Specifications section and change to the correct oil (Daily (pre-ride) checks).

Miscellaneous causes
- [ ] Modification to exhaust system. Most aftermarket exhaust systems cause the engine to run leaner, which make them run hotter. When installing an accessory exhaust system, always rejet the carburettors.

5 Clutch problems

Clutch slipping
- [ ] Insufficient clutch cable freeplay (XL models). Check and adjust (Chapter 1).
- [ ] Friction plates worn or warped. Overhaul the clutch assembly (Chapter 2).
- [ ] Plain plates warped (Chapter 2).
- [ ] Clutch springs broken or weak. Old or heat-damaged (from slipping clutch) springs should be replaced with new ones (Chapter 2).
- [ ] Clutch release mechanism defective. Replace any defective parts (Chapter 2).
- [ ] Clutch centre or housing unevenly worn. This causes improper engagement of the plates. Replace the damaged or worn parts (Chapter 2).
- [ ] Use of an engine oil designed for car engines. Such oils contain friction modifiers which can cause clutch slip when used in a 'wet clutch' engine. Use an engine oil packaged for motorcycle use.

Clutch not disengaging completely
- [ ] Excessive clutch cable freeplay (XL models). Check and adjust (Chapter 1).
- [ ] Air in hydraulic release system (VTR models). Bleed the system (see Chapter 2).
- [ ] Clutch plates warped or damaged. This will cause clutch drag, which in turn will cause the machine to creep. Overhaul the clutch assembly (Chapter 2).
- [ ] Clutch spring tension uneven. Usually caused by a sagged or broken spring. Check and replace the springs as a set (Chapter 2).
- [ ] Engine oil deteriorated. Old, thin, worn out oil will not provide proper lubrication for the plates, causing the clutch to drag. Replace the oil and filter (Chapter 1).
- [ ] Engine oil viscosity too high. Using a heavier oil than recommended in Chapter 1 can cause the plates to stick together, putting a drag on the engine. Change to the correct weight oil (Daily (pre-ride) checks).
- [ ] Clutch housing guide seized on mainshaft. Lack of lubrication, severe wear or damage can cause the guide to seize on the shaft. Overhaul of the clutch, and perhaps transmission, may be necessary to repair the damage (Chapter 2).
- [ ] Clutch release mechanism defective. Overhaul the clutch cover components (Chapter 2).
- [ ] Loose clutch centre nut. Causes housing and centre misalignment putting a drag on the engine. Engagement adjustment continually varies. Overhaul the clutch assembly (Chapter 2).

Fault Finding REF•37

6 Gearchange problems

Doesn't go into gear or lever doesn't return
- [ ] Clutch not disengaging. See above.
- [ ] Selector fork(s) bent or seized. Often caused by dropping the machine or from lack of lubrication. Overhaul the transmission (Chapter 2).
- [ ] Gear(s) stuck on shaft. Most often caused by a lack of lubrication or excessive wear in transmission bearings and bushings. Overhaul the transmission (Chapter 2).
- [ ] Selector drum binding. Caused by lubrication failure or excessive wear. Replace the drum and bearing (Chapter 2).
- [ ] Gearchange lever return spring weak or broken (Chapter 2).
- [ ] Gearchange lever broken. Splines stripped out of lever or shaft, caused by allowing the lever to get loose or from dropping the machine. Replace necessary parts (Chapter 2).
- [ ] Gearchange mechanism stopper arm broken or worn. Full engagement and rotary movement of selector drum results. Replace the arm (Chapter 2).
- [ ] Stopper arm spring broken. Allows arm to float, causing sporadic selector operation. Replace spring (Chapter 2).

Jumps out of gear
- [ ] Selector fork(s) worn. Overhaul the transmission (Chapter 2).
- [ ] Gear groove(s) worn. Overhaul the transmission (Chapter 2).
- [ ] Gear dogs or dog slots worn or damaged. The gears should be inspected and replaced. No attempt should be made to service the worn parts.

Overshifts
- [ ] Stopper arm spring weak or broken (Chapter 2).
- [ ] Gearchange shaft return spring post broken or distorted (Chapter 2).

7 Abnormal engine noise

Knocking or pinking
- [ ] Carbon build-up in combustion chamber. Use of a fuel additive that will dissolve the adhesive bonding the carbon particles to the piston crown and chamber is the easiest way to remove the build-up. Otherwise, the cylinder heads will have to be removed and decarbonized (Chapter 2).
- [ ] Incorrect or poor quality fuel. Old or improper fuel can cause detonation. This causes the pistons to rattle, thus the knocking or pinking sound. Drain the old fuel and always use the recommended grade fuel.
- [ ] Spark plug heat range incorrect. Uncontrolled detonation indicates that the plug heat range is too hot. The plug in effect becomes a glow plug, raising cylinder temperatures. Install the proper heat range plug (Chapter 1).
- [ ] Improper fuel/air mixture (carburettor models). This will cause the cylinders to run hot and lead to detonation. Clogged jets or an air leak can cause this imbalance on carburettor engines. See Chapter 4A.

Piston slap or rattling
- [ ] Cylinder-to-piston clearance excessive. Caused by improper assembly. Inspect and overhaul top-end parts (Chapter 2).
- [ ] Connecting rod bent. Caused by over-revving, trying to start a badly flooded engine or from ingesting a foreign object into the combustion chamber. Replace the damaged parts (Chapter 2).
- [ ] Piston pin or piston pin bore worn or seized from wear or lack of lubrication. Replace damaged parts (Chapter 2).
- [ ] Piston ring(s) worn, broken or sticking. Overhaul the top-end (Chapter 2).
- [ ] Piston seizure damage. Usually from lack of lubrication or overheating. Replace the pistons and rebore the cylinders, as necessary (Chapter 2).
- [ ] Connecting rod upper or lower end clearance excessive. Caused by excessive wear or lack of lubrication. Replace worn parts.

Valve noise
- [ ] Incorrect valve clearances. Adjust the clearances by referring to Chapter 1.
- [ ] Valve spring broken or weak. Check and replace weak valve springs (Chapter 2).
- [ ] Camshaft or cylinder head worn or damaged. Lack of lubrication at high rpm is usually the cause of damage. Insufficient oil or failure to change the oil at the recommended intervals are the chief causes. Since there are no replaceable bearings in the head, the head itself will have to be replaced if there is excessive wear or damage (Chapter 2).

Other noise
- [ ] Cylinder head gasket leaking.
- [ ] Exhaust pipe leaking at cylinder head connection. Caused by improper fit of pipe(s) or loose exhaust flange. All exhaust fasteners should be tightened evenly and carefully. Failure to do this will lead to a leak.
- [ ] Crankshaft runout excessive. Caused by a bent crankshaft (from over-revving) or damage from an upper cylinder component failure. Can also be attributed to dropping the machine on either of the crankshaft ends.
- [ ] Engine mounting bolts loose. Tighten all engine mounting bolts (Chapter 2).
- [ ] Crankshaft bearings worn (Chapter 2).
- [ ] Camshaft drive gear assembly defective. Replace according to the procedure in Chapter 2.

REF•38 Fault Finding

8 Abnormal driveline noise

Clutch noise
☐ Clutch outer drum/friction plate clearance excessive (Chapter 2).
☐ Loose or damaged clutch pressure plate and/or bolts (Chapter 2).

Transmission noise
☐ Bearings worn. Also includes the possibility that the shafts are worn. Overhaul the transmission (Chapter 2).
☐ Gears worn or chipped (Chapter 2).
☐ Metal chips jammed in gear teeth. Probably pieces from a broken clutch, gear or selector mechanism that were picked up by the gears. This will cause early bearing failure (Chapter 2).
☐ Engine oil level too low. Causes a howl from transmission. Also affects engine power and clutch operation (Daily (pre-ride) checks).

Final drive noise
☐ Chain not adjusted properly (Chapter 1).
☐ Front or rear sprocket loose. Tighten fasteners (Chapter 6).
☐ Sprockets worn. Renew sprockets (Chapter 6).
☐ Rear sprocket warped. Renew sprockets (Chapter 6).
☐ Rubber dampers in rear wheel hub worn. Check and renew (Chapter 7).

9 Abnormal frame and suspension noise

Front end noise
☐ Low fluid level or improper viscosity oil in forks. This can sound like spurting and is usually accompanied by irregular fork action (Chapter 6).
☐ Spring weak or broken. Makes a clicking or scraping sound. Fork oil, when drained, will have a lot of metal particles in it (Chapter 6).
☐ Steering head bearings loose or damaged. Clicks when braking. Check and adjust or replace as necessary (Chapters 1 and 6).
☐ Fork yokes loose. Make sure all clamp pinch bolts are tightened to the specified torque (Chapter 6).
☐ Fork tube bent. Good possibility if machine has been dropped. Replace tube with a new one (Chapter 6).
☐ Front axle bolt or axle clamp bolts loose. Tighten them to the specified torque (Chapter 7).
☐ Loose or worn wheel bearings. Check and replace as needed (Chapter 7).

Shock absorber noise
☐ Fluid level incorrect. Indicates a leak caused by defective seal. Shock will be covered with oil. Replace shock or seek advice on repair from a suspension specialist (Chapter 6).
☐ Defective shock absorber with internal damage. This is in the body of the shock and can't be remedied. The shock must be replaced with a new one (Chapter 6).
☐ Bent or damaged shock body. Replace the shock with a new one (Chapter 6).
☐ Loose or worn suspension linkage components. Check and replace as necessary (Chapter 6).

Brake noise
☐ Squeal caused by pad shim not installed or positioned correctly (where fitted) (Chapter 7).
☐ Squeal caused by dust on brake pads. Usually found in combination with glazed pads. Clean using brake cleaning solvent (Chapter 7).
☐ Contamination of brake pads. Oil, brake fluid or dirt causing brake to chatter or squeal. Clean or replace pads (Chapter 7).
☐ Pads glazed. Caused by excessive heat from prolonged use or from contamination. Do not use sandpaper, emery cloth, carborundum cloth or any other abrasive to roughen the pad surfaces as abrasives will stay in the pad material and damage the disc. A very fine flat file can be used, but pad replacement is suggested as a cure (Chapter 7).
☐ Disc warped. Can cause a chattering, clicking or intermittent squeal. Usually accompanied by a pulsating lever and uneven braking. Replace the disc (Chapter 7).
☐ Loose or worn wheel bearings. Check and replace as needed (Chapter 7).

10 Oil pressure indicator light comes on

Engine lubrication system
☐ Engine oil pump defective, blocked oil strainer gauze or failed relief valve. Carry out an oil pressure check (Chapter 1).
☐ Engine oil level low. Inspect for leak or other problem causing low oil level and add recommended oil (Daily (pre-ride) checks).
☐ Engine oil viscosity too low. Very old, thin oil or an improper weight of oil used in the engine. Change to correct oil (Daily (pre-ride) checks).
☐ Camshaft or journals worn. Excessive wear causing drop in oil pressure. Replace cam and/or cylinder head. Abnormal wear could be caused by oil starvation at high rpm from low oil level or improper weight or type of oil.
☐ Crankshaft and/or bearings worn. Same problems as above. Check and replace crankshaft and/or bearings (Chapter 2).

Electrical system
☐ Oil pressure switch defective. Check the switch according to the procedure in Chapter 9. Replace it if it is defective.
☐ Oil pressure indicator light circuit defective. Check for pinched, shorted, disconnected or damaged wiring (Chapter 9).

Fault Finding REF•39

11 Excessive exhaust smoke

White smoke
- [ ] Piston oil ring worn. The ring may be broken or damaged, causing oil from the crankcase to be pulled past the piston into the combustion chamber. Replace the rings with new ones (Chapter 2).
- [ ] Cylinders worn, cracked, or scored. Caused by overheating or oil starvation. The cylinders will have to be rebored and new pistons installed.
- [ ] Valve oil seal damaged or worn. Replace oil seals with new ones (Chapter 2).
- [ ] Valve guide worn. Perform a complete valve job (Chapter 2).
- [ ] Engine oil level too high, which causes the oil to be forced past the rings. Drain oil to the proper level (Daily (pre-ride) checks).
- [ ] Head gasket broken between oil return and cylinder. Causes oil to be pulled into the combustion chamber. Replace the head gasket and check the head for warpage (Chapter 2).
- [ ] Abnormal crankcase pressurisation, which forces oil past the rings. Clogged breather is usually the cause.

Black smoke (carburettor engines)
- [ ] Air filter clogged. Clean or replace the element (Chapter 1).
- [ ] Main jet too large or loose. Compare the jet size to the Specifications (Chapter 4A).
- [ ] Choke cable or linkage shaft stuck, causing fuel to be pulled through choke circuit (Chapter 4A).
- [ ] Fuel level too high. Check and adjust the float height(s) as necessary (Chapter 4A).
- [ ] Float needle valve held off needle seat. Clean the float chambers and fuel line and replace the needles and seats if necessary (Chapter 4A).

Brown smoke (carburettor engines)
- [ ] Main jet too small or clogged. Lean condition caused by wrong size main jet or by a restricted orifice. Clean float chambers and jets and compare jet size to Specifications (Chapter 4A).
- [ ] Fuel flow insufficient. Float needle valve stuck closed due to chemical reaction with old fuel. Float height incorrect. Restricted fuel line. Clean line and float chamber and adjust floats if necessary.
- [ ] Carburettor intake manifold clamps loose (Chapter 4A).
- [ ] Air filter poorly sealed or not installed (Chapter 1).

12 Poor handling or stability

Handlebar hard to turn
- [ ] Steering head bearing adjuster nut too tight. Check adjustment as described in Chapter 1.
- [ ] Bearings damaged. Roughness can be felt as the bars are turned from side-to-side. Replace bearings and races (Chapter 6).
- [ ] Races dented or worn. Denting results from wear in only one position (e.g., straight ahead), from a collision or hitting a pothole or from dropping the machine. Replace races and bearings (Chapter 6)
- [ ] Steering stem lubrication inadequate. Causes are grease getting hard from age or being washed out by high pressure car washes. Disassemble steering head and repack bearings (Chapter 6).
- [ ] Steering stem bent. Caused by a collision, hitting a pothole or by dropping the machine. Replace damaged part. Don't try to straighten the steering stem (Chapter 6).
- [ ] Front tyre air pressure too low (Daily (pre-ride) checks).

Handlebar shakes or vibrates excessively
- [ ] Tyres worn or out of balance (Chapter 7).
- [ ] Swingarm bearings worn. Replace worn bearings (Chapter 6).
- [ ] Wheel rim(s) warped or damaged. Inspect wheels for runout (Chapter 7).
- [ ] Wheel bearings worn. Worn front or rear wheel bearings can cause poor tracking. Worn front bearings will cause wobble (Chapter 7).
- [ ] Handlebar clamp bolts loose (Chapter 6).
- [ ] Fork yoke bolts loose. Tighten them to the specified torque (Chapter 6).
- [ ] Engine mounting bolts loose. Will cause excessive vibration with increased engine rpm (Chapter 2).

Handlebar pulls to one side
- [ ] Frame bent. Definitely suspect this if the machine has been dropped. May or may not be accompanied by cracking near the bend. Replace the frame (Chapter 6).
- [ ] Wheels out of alignment. Caused by improper location of axle spacers or from bent steering stem or frame (Chapter 6).
- [ ] Swingarm bent or twisted. Caused by age (metal fatigue) or impact damage. Replace the arm (Chapter 6).
- [ ] Steering stem bent. Caused by impact damage or by dropping the motorcycle. Replace the steering stem (Chapter 6).
- [ ] Fork tube bent. Disassemble the forks and replace the damaged parts (Chapter 6).
- [ ] Fork oil level uneven. Check and add or drain as necessary (Chapter 6).

Poor shock absorbing qualities
- [ ] Too hard:
    a) Fork oil level excessive (Chapter 6).
    b) Fork oil viscosity too high. Use a lighter oil (see the Specifications in Chapter 6).
    c) Fork tube bent. Causes a harsh, sticking feeling (Chapter 6).
    d) Shock shaft or body bent or damaged (Chapter 6).
    e) Fork internal damage (Chapter 6).
    f) Shock internal damage (Chapter 6).
    g) Tyre pressure too high (Daily (pre-ride) checks).
- [ ] Too soft:
    a) Fork or shock oil insufficient and/or leaking (Chapter 6).
    b) Fork oil level too low (Chapter 6).
    c) Fork oil viscosity too light (Chapter 6).
    d) Fork springs weak or broken (Chapter 6).
    e) Shock internal damage or leakage (Chapter 6).

REF•40 Fault Finding

13 Braking problems

Brakes are spongy, don't hold

- ☐ Air in brake line. Caused by inattention to master cylinder fluid level or by leakage. Locate problem and bleed brakes (Chapter 7).
- ☐ Pad or disc worn (Chapters 1 and 7).
- ☐ Brake fluid leak. Locate problem and replace the faulty components (Chapter 7).
- ☐ Contaminated pads. Caused by contamination with oil, grease, brake fluid, etc. Renew pads. Clean disc thoroughly with brake cleaner (Chapter 7).
- ☐ Brake fluid deteriorated. Fluid is old or contaminated. Drain system, replenish with new fluid and bleed the system (Chapter 7).
- ☐ Master cylinder internal parts worn or damaged causing fluid to bypass (Chapter 7).
- ☐ Master cylinder bore scratched by foreign material or broken spring. Repair or replace master cylinder (Chapter 7).
- ☐ Disc warped. Replace disc (Chapter 7).

Brake lever or pedal pulsates

- ☐ Disc warped. Replace disc (Chapter 7).
- ☐ Axle bent. Replace axle (Chapter 7).
- ☐ Brake caliper bolts loose (Chapter 7).
- ☐ Brake caliper sliders damaged or sticking (XL models and VTR rear caliper), causing caliper to bind. Lubricate the sliders or replace them if they are corroded or bent (Chapter 7).
- ☐ Wheel warped or otherwise damaged (Chapter 7).
- ☐ Wheel bearings damaged or worn (Chapter 7).

Brakes drag

- ☐ Master cylinder piston seized. Caused by wear or damage to piston or cylinder bore (Chapter 7).
- ☐ Lever balky or stuck. Check pivot and lubricate (Chapter 7).
- ☐ Brake caliper binds on bracket (XL models and VTR rear caliper). Caused by inadequate lubrication or damage to caliper sliders (Chapter 7).
- ☐ Brake caliper piston seized in bore. Caused by wear or ingestion of dirt past deteriorated seal (Chapter 7).
- ☐ Brake pad damaged. Pad material separated from backing plate. Usually caused by faulty manufacturing process or from contact with chemicals. Replace pads (Chapter 7).
- ☐ Pads improperly installed (Chapter 7).

ABS indicator light comes on

- ☐ If the light comes on when riding or remains on after start-up, carry out the fault code procedure as described in Chapter 7, Section 17.

14 Electrical problems

Battery dead or weak

- ☐ Battery faulty. Caused by sulphated plates which are shorted through sedimentation. Also, broken battery terminal making only occasional contact (Chapter 9).
- ☐ Battery cables making poor contact (Chapter 9).
- ☐ Load excessive. Caused by addition of high wattage lights or other electrical accessories.
- ☐ Ignition (main) switch defective. Switch either grounds (earths) internally or fails to shut off system. Replace the switch (Chapter 9).
- ☐ Regulator/rectifier defective (Chapter 9).
- ☐ Alternator stator coil open or shorted (Chapter 9).
- ☐ Wiring faulty. Wiring grounded (earthed) or connections loose in ignition, charging or lighting circuits (Chapter 9).

Battery overcharged

- ☐ Regulator/rectifier defective. Overcharging is noticed when battery gets excessively warm (Chapter 9).
- ☐ Battery defective. Replace battery with a new one (Chapter 9).
- ☐ Battery amperage too low, wrong type or size. Install manufacturer's specified amp-hour battery to handle charging load (Chapter 9).

Fault Finding Equipment   REF•41

Checking engine compression

● Low compression will result in exhaust smoke, heavy oil consumption, poor starting and poor performance. A compression test will provide useful information about an engine's condition and if performed regularly, can give warning of trouble before any other symptoms become apparent.
● A compression gauge will be required, along with an adapter to suit the spark plug hole thread size. Note that the screw-in type gauge/adapter set up is preferable to the rubber cone type.
● Before carrying out the test, first check the valve clearances as described in Chapter 1.

1 Run the engine until it reaches normal operating temperature, then stop it and remove the spark plug(s), taking care not to scald your hands on the hot components.
2 Install the gauge adapter and compression gauge in No. 1 cylinder spark plug hole **(see illustration 1)**.

Screw the compression gauge adapter into the spark plug hole, then screw the gauge into the adapter

3 On kickstart-equipped motorcycles, make sure the ignition switch is OFF, then open the throttle fully and kick the engine over a couple of times until the gauge reading stabilises.
4 On motorcycles with electric start only, the procedure will differ depending on the nature of the ignition system. Flick the engine kill switch (engine stop switch) to OFF and turn the ignition switch ON; open the throttle fully and crank the engine over on the starter motor for a couple of revolutions until the gauge reading stabilises. If the starter will not operate with the kill switch OFF, turn the ignition switch OFF and refer to the next paragraph.
5 Install the plugs back in their caps and arrange the plug electrodes so that their metal bodies are earthed (grounded) against the cylinder head; this is essential to prevent damage to the ignition system **(see illustration 2)**. Position the plugs well away from the plug holes otherwise there is a risk of

All spark plugs must be earthed (grounded) against the cylinder head

atomised fuel escaping from the plug holes and igniting. As a safety precaution, cover the cylinder head covers with rag and on XV1000V models disconnect the fuel pump wiring connector (see Chapter 4A or 4B). Turn the ignition switch and kill switch ON, open the throttle fully and crank the engine over on the starter motor for a couple of revolutions until the gauge reading stabilises.
6 After one or two revolutions the pressure should build up to a maximum figure and then stabilise. Take a note of this reading and on multi-cylinder engines repeat the test on the remaining cylinders.
7 The correct pressures are given in Chapter 1 Specifications. If the results fall within the specified range and on multi-cylinder engines all are relatively equal, the engine is in good condition. If there is a marked difference between the readings, or if the readings are lower than specified, inspection of the top-end components will be required.
8 Low compression pressure may be due to worn cylinder bores, pistons or rings, failure of the cylinder head gasket, worn valve seals, or poor valve seating.
9 To distinguish between cylinder/piston wear and valve leakage, pour a small quantity of oil into the bore to temporarily seal the piston rings, then repeat the compression tests **(see illustration 3)**. If the readings show

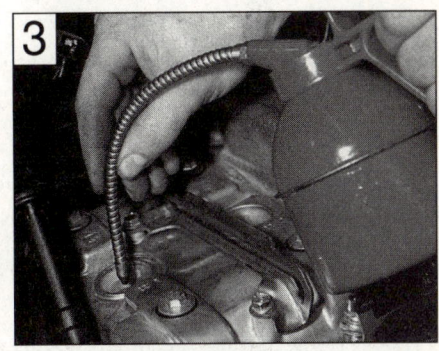

Bores can be temporarily sealed with a squirt of motor oil

a noticeable increase in pressure this confirms that the cylinder bore, piston, or rings are worn. If, however, no change is indicated, the cylinder head gasket or valves should be examined.
10 High compression pressure indicates excessive carbon build-up in the combustion chamber and on the piston crown. If this is the case the cylinder head should be removed and the deposits removed. Note that excessive carbon build-up is less likely with the used on modern fuels.

Checking battery open-circuit voltage

⚠️ *Warning: The gases produced by the battery are explosive - never smoke or create any sparks in the vicinity of the battery. Never allow the electrolyte to contact your skin or clothing - if it does, wash it off and seek immediate medical attention.*

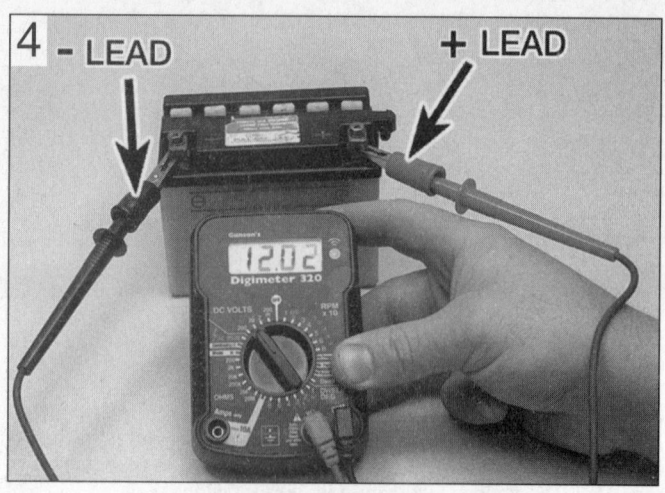

REF•42 Fault Finding Equipment

Measuring open-circuit battery voltage

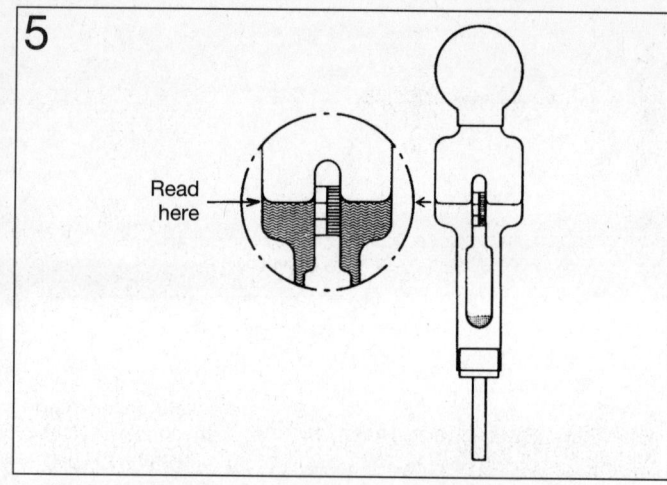

Float-type hydrometer for measuring battery specific gravity

- Before any electrical fault is investigated the battery should be checked.
- You'll need a dc voltmeter or multimeter to check battery voltage. Check that the leads are inserted in the correct terminals on the meter, red lead to positive (+ve), black lead to negative (-ve). Incorrect connections can damage the meter.
- A sound fully-charged 12 volt battery should produce between 12.3 and 12.6 volts across its terminals (12.8 volts for a maintenance-free battery). On machines with a 6 volt battery, voltage should be between 6.1 and 6.3 volts.

1 Set a multimeter to the 0 to 20 volts dc range and connect its probes across the battery terminals. Connect the meter's positive (+ve) probe, usually red, to the battery positive (+ve) terminal, followed by the meter's negative (-ve) probe, usually black, to the battery negative terminal (-ve) **(see illustration 4)**.

2 If battery voltage is low (below 10 volts on a 12 volt battery or below 4 volts on a six volt battery), charge the battery and test the voltage again. If the battery repeatedly goes flat, investigate the motorcycle's charging system.

Checking battery specific gravity (SG)

⚠️ *Warning: The gases produced by the battery are explosive - never smoke or create any sparks in the vicinity of the battery. Never allow the electrolyte to contact your skin or clothing - if it does, wash it off and seek immediate medical attention.*

- The specific gravity check gives an indication of a battery's state of charge.
- A hydrometer is used for measuring specific gravity. Make sure you purchase one which has a small enough hose to insert in the aperture of a motorcycle battery.
- Specific gravity is simply a measure of the electrolyte's density compared with that of water. Water has an SG of 1.000 and fully-charged battery electrolyte is about 26% heavier, at 1.260.
- Specific gravity checks are not possible on maintenance-free batteries. Testing the open-circuit voltage is the only means of determining their state of charge.

1 To measure SG, remove the battery from the motorcycle and remove the first cell cap. Draw

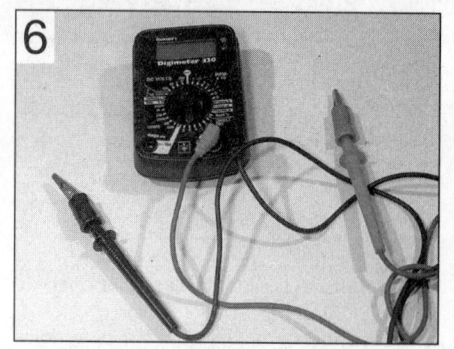

Digital multimeter can be used for all electrical tests

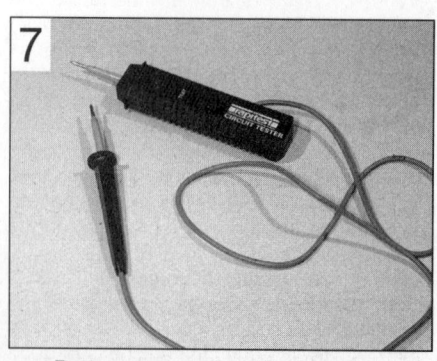

Battery-powered continuity tester

some electrolyte into the hydrometer and note the reading **(see illustration 5)**. Return the electrolyte to the cell and install the cap.

2 The reading should be in the region of 1.260 to 1.280. If SG is below 1.200 the battery needs charging. Note that SG will vary with temperature; it should be measured at 20°C (68°F). Add 0.007 to the reading for every 10°C above 20°C, and subtract 0.007 from the reading for every 10°C below 20°C. Add 0.004 to the reading for every 10°F above 68°F, and subtract 0.004 from the reading for every 10°F below 68°F.

3 When the check is complete, rinse the hydrometer thoroughly with clean water.

Checking for continuity

- The term continuity describes the uninterrupted flow of electricity through an electrical circuit. A continuity check will determine whether an **open-circuit** situation exists.
- Continuity can be checked with an ohmmeter, multimeter, continuity tester or battery and bulb test circuit **(see illustrations 6, 7 and 8)**.

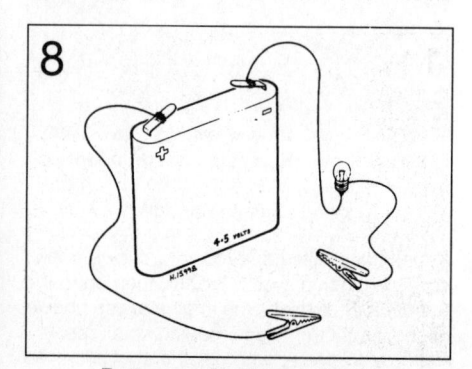

Battery and bulb test circuit

Fault Finding Equipment   REF•43

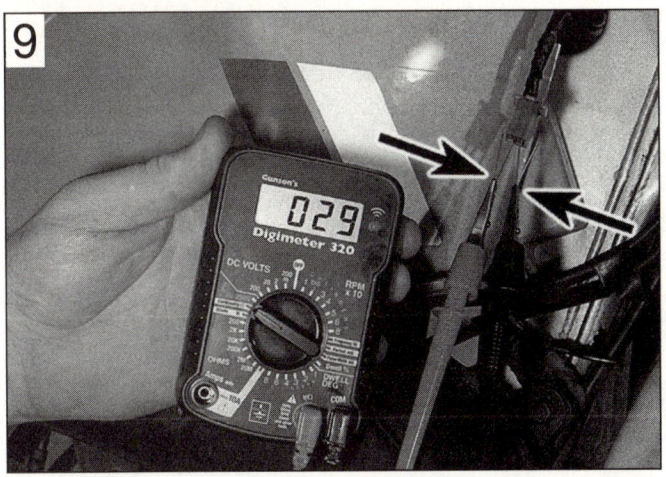

Continuity check of front brake light switch using a meter - note split pins used to access connector terminals

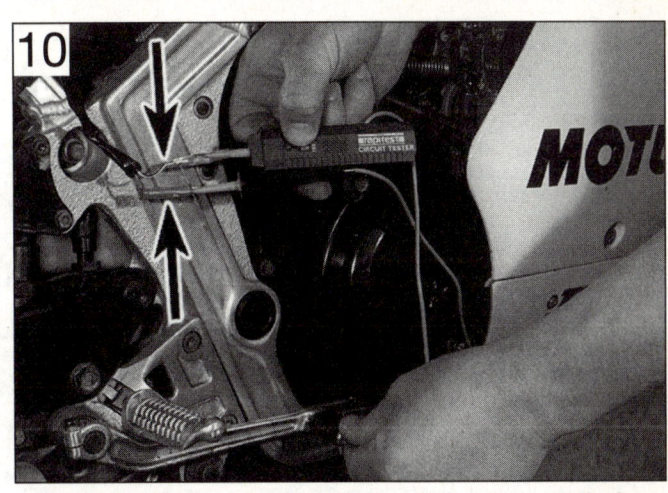

Continuity check of rear brake light switch using a continuity tester

- All of these instruments are self-powered by a battery, therefore the checks are made with the ignition OFF.
- As a safety precaution, always disconnect the battery negative (-ve) lead before making checks, particularly if ignition switch checks are being made.
- If using a meter, select the appropriate ohms scale and check that the meter reads infinity (∞). Touch the meter probes together and check that meter reads zero; where necessary adjust the meter so that it reads zero.
- After using a meter, always switch it OFF to conserve its battery.

Switch checks

1 If a switch is at fault, trace its wiring up to the wiring connectors. Separate the wire connectors and inspect them for security and condition. A build-up of dirt or corrosion here will most likely be the cause of the problem - clean up and apply a water dispersant such as WD40.

2 If using a test meter, set the meter to the ohms x 10 scale and connect its probes across the wires from the switch **(see illustration 9)**. Simple ON/OFF type switches, such as brake light switches, only have two wires whereas combination switches, like the ignition switch, have many internal links. Study the wiring diagram to ensure that you are connecting across the correct pair of wires. Continuity (low or no measurable resistance - 0 ohms) should be indicated with the switch ON and no continuity (high resistance) with it OFF.

3 Note that the polarity of the test probes doesn't matter for continuity checks, although care should be taken to follow specific test procedures if a diode or solid-state component is being checked.

4 A continuity tester or battery and bulb circuit can be used in the same way. Connect its probes as described above **(see illustration 10)**. The light should come on to indicate continuity in the ON switch position, but should extinguish in the OFF position.

Wiring checks

- Many electrical faults are caused by damaged wiring, often due to incorrect routing or chaffing on frame components.
- Loose, wet or corroded wire connectors can also be the cause of electrical problems, especially in exposed locations.

1 A continuity check can be made on a single length of wire by disconnecting it at each end and connecting a meter or continuity tester across both ends of the wire **(see illustration 11)**.

2 Continuity (low or no resistance - 0 ohms) should be indicated if the wire is good. If no continuity (high resistance) is shown, suspect a broken wire.

Checking for voltage

- A voltage check can determine whether current is reaching a component.
- Voltage can be checked with a dc voltmeter, multimeter set on the dc volts scale, test light or buzzer **(see illustrations 12 and 13)**. A meter has the advantage of being able to measure actual voltage.
- When using a meter, check that its leads are inserted in the correct terminals on the meter, red to positive (+ve), black to negative (-ve). Incorrect connections can damage the meter.
- A voltmeter (or multimeter set to the dc volts scale) should always be connected in parallel (across the load). Connecting it in series will not harm the meter, but the reading will not be meaningful.
- Voltage checks are made with the ignition ON.

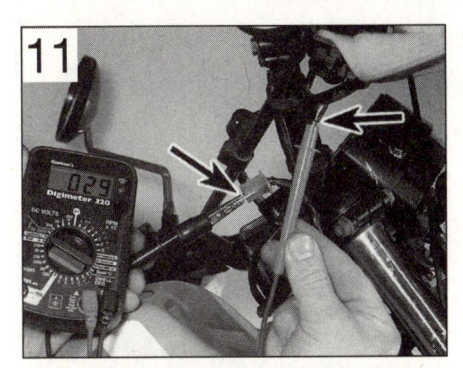

Continuity check of front brake light switch sub-harness

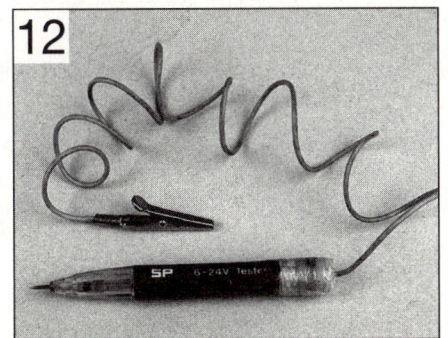

A simple test light can be used for voltage checks

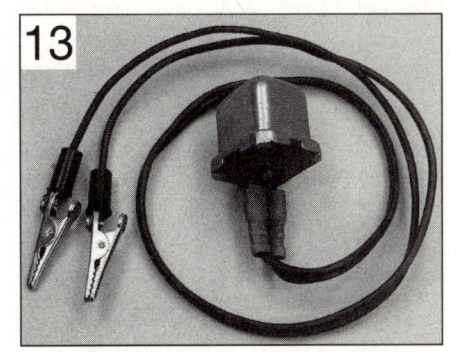

A buzzer is useful for voltage checks

REF•44 Fault Finding Equipment

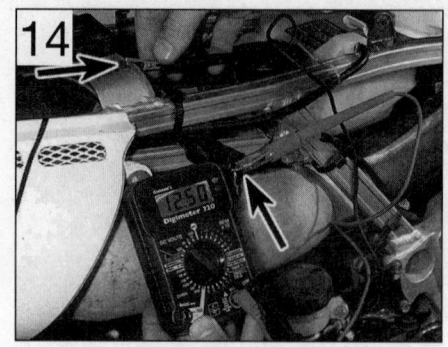

Checking for voltage at the rear brake light power supply wire using a meter . . .

1 First identify the relevant wiring circuit by referring to the wiring diagram at the end of this manual. If other electrical components share the same power supply (ie are fed from the same fuse), take note whether they are working correctly - this is useful information in deciding where to start checking the circuit.

2 If using a meter, check first that the meter leads are plugged into the correct terminals on the meter (see above). Set the meter to the dc volts function, at a range suitable for the battery voltage. Connect the meter red probe (+ve) to the power supply wire and the black probe to a good metal earth (ground) on the motorcycle's frame or directly to the battery negative (-ve) terminal **(see illustration 14)**. Battery voltage should be shown on the meter

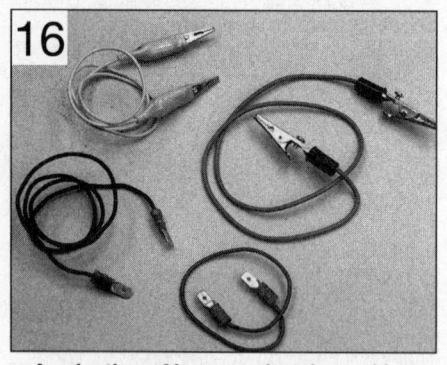

A selection of jumper wires for making earth (ground) checks

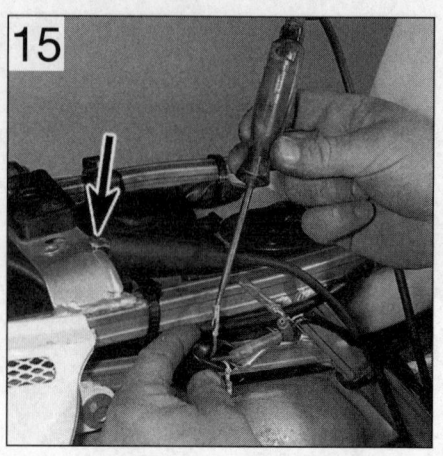

. . . or a test light - note the earth connection to the frame (arrow)

with the ignition switched ON.

3 If using a test light or buzzer, connect its positive (+ve) probe to the power supply terminal and its negative (-ve) probe to a good earth (ground) on the motorcycle's frame or directly to the battery negative (-ve) terminal **(see illustration 15)**. With the ignition ON, the test light should illuminate or the buzzer sound.

4 If no voltage is indicated, work back towards the fuse continuing to check for voltage. When you reach a point where there is voltage, you know the problem lies between that point and your last check point.

Checking the earth (ground)

● Earth connections are made either directly to the engine or frame (such as sensors, neutral switch etc. which only have a positive feed) or by a separate wire into the earth circuit of the wiring harness. Alternatively a short earth wire is sometimes run directly from the component to the motorcycle's frame.
● Corrosion is often the cause of a poor earth connection.
● If total failure is experienced, check the security of the main earth lead from the negative (-ve) terminal of the battery and also the main earth (ground) point on the wiring harness. If corroded, dismantle the connection and clean all surfaces back to bare metal.

1 To check the earth on a component, use an insulated jumper wire to temporarily bypass its earth connection **(see illustration 16)**. Connect one end of the jumper wire between the earth terminal or metal body of the component and the other end to the motorcycle's frame.

2 If the circuit works with the jumper wire installed, the original earth circuit is faulty. Check the wiring for open-circuits or poor connections. Clean up direct earth connections, removing all traces of corrosion and remake the joint. Apply petroleum jelly to the joint to prevent future corrosion.

Tracing a short-circuit

● A short-circuit occurs where current shorts to earth (ground) bypassing the circuit components. This usually results in a blown fuse.

● A short-circuit is most likely to occur where the insulation has worn through due to wiring chafing on a component, allowing a direct path to earth (ground) on the frame.

1 Remove any bodypanels necessary to access the circuit wiring.

2 Check that all electrical switches in the circuit are OFF, then remove the circuit fuse and connect a test light, buzzer or voltmeter (set to the dc scale) across the fuse terminals. No voltage should be shown.

3 Move the wiring from side to side whilst observing the test light or meter. When the test light comes on, buzzer sounds or meter shows voltage, you have found the cause of the short. It will usually shown up as damaged or burned insulation.

4 Note that the same test can be performed on each component in the circuit, even the switch.

Technical Terms Explained   REF•45

A

ABS (Anti-lock braking system) A system, usually electronically controlled, that senses incipient wheel lockup during braking and relieves hydraulic pressure at wheel which is about to skid.
Aftermarket Components suitable for the motorcycle, but not produced by the motorcycle manufacturer.
Allen key A hexagonal wrench which fits into a recessed hexagonal hole.
Alternating current (ac) Current produced by an alternator. Requires converting to direct current by a rectifier for charging purposes.
Alternator Converts mechanical energy from the engine into electrical energy to charge the battery and power the electrical system.
Ampere (amp) A unit of measurement for the flow of electrical current. Current = Volts ÷ Ohms.
Ampere-hour (Ah) Measure of battery capacity.
Angle-tightening A torque expressed in degrees. Often follows a conventional tightening torque for cylinder head or main bearing fasteners **(see illustration)**.

Angle-tightening cylinder head bolts

Antifreeze A substance (usually ethylene glycol) mixed with water, and added to the cooling system, to prevent freezing of the coolant in winter. Antifreeze also contains chemicals to inhibit corrosion and the formation of rust and other deposits that would tend to clog the radiator and coolant passages and reduce cooling efficiency.
Anti-dive System attached to the fork lower leg (slider) to prevent fork dive when braking hard.
Anti-seize compound A coating that reduces the risk of seizing on fasteners that are subjected to high temperatures, such as exhaust clamp bolts and nuts.
API American Petroleum Institute. A quality standard for 4-stroke motor oils.
Asbestos A natural fibrous mineral with great heat resistance, commonly used in the composition of brake friction materials. Asbestos is a health hazard and the dust created by brake systems should never be inhaled or ingested.
ATF Automatic Transmission Fluid. Often used in front forks.
ATU Automatic Timing Unit. Mechanical device for advancing the ignition timing on early engines.
ATV All Terrain Vehicle. Often called a Quad.
Axial play Side-to-side movement.
Axle A shaft on which a wheel revolves. Also known as a spindle.

B

Backlash The amount of movement between meshed components when one component is held still. Usually applies to gear teeth.
Ball bearing A bearing consisting of a hardened inner and outer race with hardened steel balls between the two races.
Bearings Used between two working surfaces to prevent wear of the components and a build-up of heat. Four types of bearing are commonly used on motorcycles: plain shell bearings, ball bearings, tapered roller bearings and needle roller bearings.
Bevel gears Used to turn the drive through 90°. Typical applications are shaft final drive and camshaft drive **(see illustration)**.

Bevel gears are used to turn the drive through 90°

BHP Brake Horsepower. The British measurement for engine power output. Power output is now usually expressed in kilowatts (kW).
Bias-belted tyre Similar construction to radial tyre, but with outer belt running at an angle to the wheel rim.
Big-end bearing The bearing in the end of the connecting rod that's attached to the crankshaft.
Bleeding The process of removing air from an hydraulic system via a bleed nipple or bleed screw.
Bottom-end A description of an engine's crankcase components and all components contained there-in.
BTDC Before Top Dead Centre in terms of piston position. Ignition timing is often expressed in terms of degrees or millimetres BTDC.
Bush A cylindrical metal or rubber component used between two moving parts.
Burr Rough edge left on a component after machining or as a result of excessive wear.

C

Cam chain The chain which takes drive from the crankshaft to the camshaft(s).
Canister The main component in an evaporative emission control system (California market only); contains activated charcoal granules to trap vapours from the fuel system rather than allowing them to vent to the atmosphere.
Castellated Resembling the parapets along the top of a castle wall. For example, a castellated wheel axle or spindle nut.
Catalytic converter A device in the exhaust system of some machines which converts certain pollutants in the exhaust gases into less harmful substances.
Charging system Description of the components which charge the battery, ie the alternator, rectifier and regulator.
Circlip A ring-shaped clip used to prevent endwise movement of cylindrical parts and shafts. An internal circlip is installed in a groove in a housing; an external circlip fits into a groove on the outside of a cylindrical piece such as a shaft. Also known as a snap-ring.
Clearance The amount of space between two parts. For example, between a piston and a cylinder, between a bearing and a journal, etc.
Coil spring A spiral of elastic steel found in various sizes throughout a vehicle, for example as a springing medium in the suspension and in the valve train.
Compression Reduction in volume, and increase in pressure and temperature, of a gas, caused by squeezing it into a smaller space.
Compression damping Controls the speed the suspension compresses when hitting a bump.
Compression ratio The relationship between cylinder volume when the piston is at top dead centre and cylinder volume when the piston is at bottom dead centre.
Continuity The uninterrupted path in the flow of electricity. Little or no measurable resistance.
Continuity tester Self-powered bleeper or test light which indicates continuity.
Cp Candlepower. Bulb rating commonly found on US motorcycles.
Crossply tyre Tyre plies arranged in a criss-cross pattern. Usually four or six plies used, hence 4PR or 6PR in tyre size codes.
Cush drive Rubber damper segments fitted between the rear wheel and final drive sprocket to absorb transmission shocks **(see illustration)**.

Cush drive rubbers dampen out transmission shocks

D

Degree disc Calibrated disc for measuring piston position. Expressed in degrees.
Dial gauge Clock-type gauge with adapters for measuring runout and piston position. Expressed in mm or inches.
Diaphragm The rubber membrane in a master cylinder or carburettor which seals the upper chamber.
Diaphragm spring A single sprung plate often used in clutches.
Direct current (dc) Current produced by a dc generator.

Technical Terms Explained

Decarbonisation The process of removing carbon deposits - typically from the combustion chamber, valves and exhaust port/system.
Detonation Destructive and damaging explosion of fuel/air mixture in combustion chamber instead of controlled burning.
Diode An electrical valve which only allows current to flow in one direction. Commonly used in rectifiers and starter interlock systems.
Disc valve (or rotary valve) A induction system used on some two-stroke engines.
Double-overhead camshaft (DOHC) An engine that uses two overhead camshafts, one for the intake valves and one for the exhaust valves.
Drivebelt A toothed belt used to transmit drive to the rear wheel on some motorcycles. A drivebelt has also been used to drive the camshafts. Drivebelts are usually made of Kevlar.
Driveshaft Any shaft used to transmit motion. Commonly used when referring to the final driveshaft on shaft drive motorcycles.

E

Earth return The return path of an electrical circuit, utilising the motorcycle's frame.
ECU (Electronic Control Unit) A computer which controls (for instance) an ignition system, or an anti-lock braking system.
EGO Exhaust Gas Oxygen sensor. Sometimes called a Lambda sensor.
Electrolyte The fluid in a lead-acid battery.
EMS (Engine Management System) A computer controlled system which manages the fuel injection and the ignition systems in an integrated fashion.
Endfloat The amount of lengthways movement between two parts. As applied to a crankshaft, the distance that the crankshaft can move side-to-side in the crankcase.
Endless chain A chain having no joining link. Common use for cam chains and final drive chains.
EP (Extreme Pressure) Oil type used in locations where high loads are applied, such as between gear teeth.
Evaporative emission control system Describes a charcoal filled canister which stores fuel vapours from the tank rather than allowing them to vent to the atmosphere. Usually only fitted to California models and referred to as an EVAP system.
Expansion chamber Section of two-stroke engine exhaust system so designed to improve engine efficiency and boost power.

F

Feeler blade or gauge A thin strip or blade of hardened steel, ground to an exact thickness, used to check or measure clearances between parts.
Final drive Description of the drive from the transmission to the rear wheel. Usually by chain or shaft, but sometimes by belt.
Firing order The order in which the engine cylinders fire, or deliver their power strokes, beginning with the number one cylinder.
Flooding Term used to describe a high fuel level in the carburettor float chambers, leading to fuel overflow. Also refers to excess fuel in the combustion chamber due to incorrect starting technique.

Free length The no-load state of a component when measured. Clutch, valve and fork spring lengths are measured at rest, without any preload.
Freeplay The amount of travel before any action takes place. The looseness in a linkage, or an assembly of parts, between the initial application of force and actual movement. For example, the distance the rear brake pedal moves before the rear brake is actuated.
Fuel injection The fuel/air mixture is metered electronically and directed into the engine intake ports (indirect injection) or into the cylinders (direct injection). Sensors supply information on engine speed and conditions.
Fuel/air mixture The charge of fuel and air going into the engine. See **Stoichiometric ratio**.
Fuse An electrical device which protects a circuit against accidental overload. The typical fuse contains a soft piece of metal which is calibrated to melt at a predetermined current flow (expressed as amps) and break the circuit.

G

Gap The distance the spark must travel in jumping from the centre electrode to the side electrode in a spark plug. Also refers to the distance between the ignition rotor and the pickup coil in an electronic ignition system.
Gasket Any thin, soft material - usually cork, cardboard, asbestos or soft metal - installed between two metal surfaces to ensure a good seal. For instance, the cylinder head gasket seals the joint between the block and the cylinder head.
Gauge An instrument panel display used to monitor engine conditions. A gauge with a movable pointer on a dial or a fixed scale is an analogue gauge. A gauge with a numerical readout is called a digital gauge.
Gear ratios The drive ratio of a pair of gears in a gearbox, calculated on their number of teeth.
Glaze-busting see **Honing**
Grinding Process for renovating the valve face and valve seat contact area in the cylinder head.
Gudgeon pin The shaft which connects the connecting rod small-end with the piston. Often called a piston pin or wrist pin.

H

Helical gears Gear teeth are slightly curved and produce less gear noise that straight-cut gears. Often used for primary drives.

Installing a Helicoil thread insert in a cylinder head

Helicoil A thread insert repair system. Commonly used as a repair for stripped spark plug threads (see illustration).
Honing A process used to break down the glaze on a cylinder bore (also called glaze-busting). Can also be carried out to roughen a rebored cylinder to aid ring bedding-in.
HT (High Tension) Description of the electrical circuit from the secondary winding of the ignition coil to the spark plug.
Hydraulic A liquid filled system used to transmit pressure from one component to another. Common uses on motorcycles are brakes and clutches.
Hydrometer An instrument for measuring the specific gravity of a lead-acid battery.
Hygroscopic Water absorbing. In motorcycle applications, braking efficiency will be reduced if DOT 3 or 4 hydraulic fluid absorbs water from the air - care must be taken to keep new brake fluid in tightly sealed containers.

I

Ibf ft Pounds-force feet. An imperial unit of torque. Sometimes written as ft-lbs.
Ibf in Pound-force inch. An imperial unit of torque, applied to components where a very low torque is required. Sometimes written as in-lbs.
IC Abbreviation for Integrated Circuit.
Ignition advance Means of increasing the timing of the spark at higher engine speeds. Done by mechanical means (ATU) on early engines or electronically by the ignition control unit on later engines.
Ignition timing The moment at which the spark plug fires, expressed in the number of crankshaft degrees before the piston reaches the top of its stroke, or in the number of millimetres before the piston reaches the top of its stroke.
Infinity (∞) Description of an open-circuit electrical state, where no continuity exists.
Inverted forks (upside down forks) The sliders or lower legs are held in the yokes and the fork tubes or stanchions are connected to the wheel axle (spindle). Less unsprung weight and stiffer construction than conventional forks.

J

JASO Quality standard for 2-stroke oils.
Joule The unit of electrical energy.
Journal The bearing surface of a shaft.

K

Kickstart Mechanical means of turning the engine over for starting purposes. Only usually fitted to mopeds, small capacity motorcycles and off-road motorcycles.
Kill switch Handebar-mounted switch for emergency ignition cut-out. Cuts the ignition circuit on all models, and additionally prevent starter motor operation on others.
km Symbol for kilometre.
kmh Abbreviation for kilometres per hour.

L

Lambda (λ) sensor A sensor fitted in the exhaust system to measure the exhaust gas oxygen content (excess air factor).

Technical Terms Explained REF•47

Lapping see **Grinding**.
LCD Abbreviation for Liquid Crystal Display.
LED Abbreviation for Light Emitting Diode.
Liner A steel cylinder liner inserted in a aluminium alloy cylinder block.
Locknut A nut used to lock an adjustment nut, or other threaded component, in place.
Lockstops The lugs on the lower triple clamp (yoke) which abut those on the frame, preventing handlebar-to-fuel tank contact.
Lockwasher A form of washer designed to prevent an attaching nut from working loose.
LT Low Tension Description of the electrical circuit from the power supply to the primary winding of the ignition coil.

M

Main bearings The bearings between the crankshaft and crankcase.
Maintenance-free (MF) battery A sealed battery which cannot be topped up.
Manometer Mercury-filled calibrated tubes used to measure intake tract vacuum. Used to synchronise carburettors on multi-cylinder engines.
Micrometer A precision measuring instrument that measures component outside diameters **(see illustration)**.

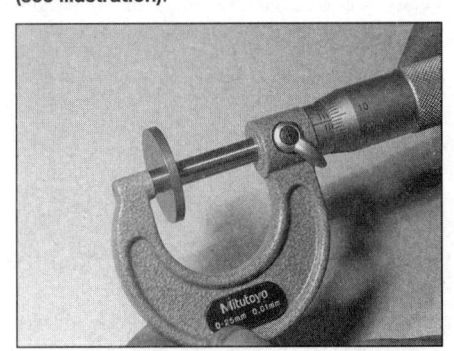

Tappet shims are measured with a micrometer

MON (Motor Octane Number) A measure of a fuel's resistance to knock.
Monograde oil An oil with a single viscosity, eg SAE80W.
Monoshock A single suspension unit linking the swingarm or suspension linkage to the frame.
mph Abbreviation for miles per hour.
Multigrade oil Having a wide viscosity range (eg 10W40). The W stands for Winter, thus the viscosity ranges from SAE10 when cold to SAE40 when hot.
Multimeter An electrical test instrument with the capability to measure voltage, current and resistance. Some meters also incorporate a continuity tester and buzzer.

N

Needle roller bearing Inner race of caged needle rollers and hardened outer race. Examples of uncaged needle rollers can be found on some engines. Commonly used in rear suspension applications and in two-stroke engines.
Nm Newton metres.
NOx Oxides of Nitrogen. A common toxic pollutant emitted by petrol engines at higher temperatures.

O

Octane The measure of a fuel's resistance to knock.
OE (Original Equipment) Relates to components fitted to a motorcycle as standard or replacement parts supplied by the motorcycle manufacturer.
Ohm The unit of electrical resistance. Ohms = Volts ÷ Current.
Ohmmeter An instrument for measuring electrical resistance.
Oil cooler System for diverting engine oil outside of the engine to a radiator for cooling purposes.
Oil injection A system of two-stroke engine lubrication where oil is pump-fed to the engine in accordance with throttle position.
Open-circuit An electrical condition where there is a break in the flow of electricity - no continuity (high resistance).
O-ring A type of sealing ring made of a special rubber-like material; in use, the O-ring is compressed into a groove to provide the sealing action.
Oversize (OS) Term used for piston and ring size options fitted to a rebored cylinder.
Overhead cam (sohc) engine An engine with single camshaft located on top of the cylinder head.
Overhead valve (ohv) engine An engine with the valves located in the cylinder head, but with the camshaft located in the engine block or crankcase.
Oxygen sensor A device installed in the exhaust system which senses the oxygen content in the exhaust and converts this information into an electric current. Also called a Lambda sensor.

P

Plastigauge A thin strip of plastic thread, available in different sizes, used for measuring clearances. For example, a strip of Plastigauge is laid across a bearing journal. The parts are assembled and dismantled; the width of the crushed strip indicates the clearance between journal and bearing.
Polarity Either negative or positive earth (ground), determined by which battery lead is connected to the frame (earth return). Modern motorcycles are usually negative earth.
Pre-ignition A situation where the fuel/air mixture ignites before the spark plug fires. Often due to a hot spot in the combustion chamber caused by carbon build-up. Engine has a tendency to 'run-on'.
Pre-load (suspension) The amount a spring is compressed when in the unloaded state. Preload can be applied by gas, spacer or mechanical adjuster.
Premix The method of engine lubrication on older two-stroke engines. Engine oil is mixed with the petrol in the fuel tank in a specific ratio. The fuel/oil mix is sometimes referred to as "petroil".
Primary drive Description of the drive from the crankshaft to the clutch. Usually by gear or chain.
PS Pfedestärke - a German interpretation of BHP.
PSI Pounds-force per square inch. Imperial measurement of tyre pressure and cylinder pressure measurement.
PTFE Polytetrafluroethylene. A low friction substance.

Pulse secondary air injection system A process of promoting the burning of excess fuel present in the exhaust gases by routing fresh air into the exhaust ports.

Q

Quartz halogen bulb Tungsten filament surrounded by a halogen gas. Typically used for the headlight **(see illustration)**.

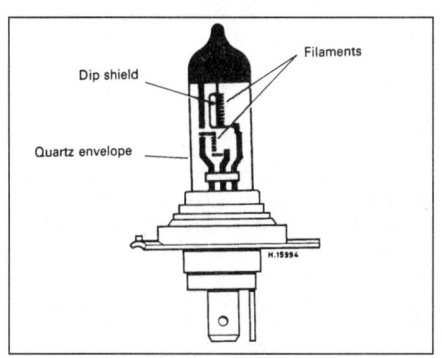

Quartz halogen headlight bulb construction

R

Rack-and-pinion A pinion gear on the end of a shaft that mates with a rack (think of a geared wheel opened up and laid flat). Sometimes used in clutch operating systems.
Radial play Up and down movement about a shaft.
Radial ply tyres Tyre plies run across the tyre (from bead to bead) and around the circumference of the tyre. Less resistant to tread distortion than other tyre types.
Radiator A liquid-to-air heat transfer device designed to reduce the temperature of the coolant in a liquid cooled engine.
Rake A feature of steering geometry - the angle of the steering head in relation to the vertical **(see illustration)**.

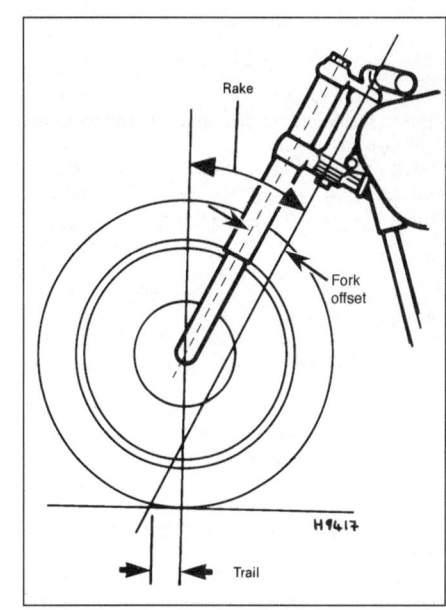

Steering geometry

Technical Terms Explained

Rebore Providing a new working surface to the cylinder bore by boring out the old surface. Necessitates the use of oversize piston and rings.
Rebound damping A means of controlling the oscillation of a suspension unit spring after it has been compressed. Resists the spring's natural tendency to bounce back after being compressed.
Rectifier Device for converting the ac output of an alternator into dc for battery charging.
Reed valve An induction system commonly used on two-stroke engines.
Regulator Device for maintaining the charging voltage from the generator or alternator within a specified range.
Relay A electrical device used to switch heavy current on and off by using a low current auxiliary circuit.
Resistance Measured in ohms. An electrical component's ability to pass electrical current.
RON (Research Octane Number) A measure of a fuel's resistance to knock.
rpm revolutions per minute.
Runout The amount of wobble (in-and-out movement) of a wheel or shaft as it's rotated. The amount a shaft rotates `out-of-true'. The out-of-round condition of a rotating part.

S

SAE (Society of Automotive Engineers) A standard for the viscosity of a fluid.
Sealant A liquid or paste used to prevent leakage at a joint. Sometimes used in conjunction with a gasket.
Service limit Term for the point where a component is no longer useable and must be renewed.
Shaft drive A method of transmitting drive from the transmission to the rear wheel.
Shell bearings Plain bearings consisting of two shell halves. Most often used as big-end and main bearings in a four-stroke engine. Often called bearing inserts.
Shim Thin spacer, commonly used to adjust the clearance or relative positions between two parts. For example, shims inserted into or under tappets or followers to control valve clearances. Clearance is adjusted by changing the thickness of the shim.
Short-circuit An electrical condition where current shorts to earth (ground) bypassing the circuit components.
Skimming Process to correct warpage or repair a damaged surface, eg on brake discs or drums.
Slide-hammer A special puller that screws into or hooks onto a component such as a shaft or bearing; a heavy sliding handle on the shaft bottoms against the end of the shaft to knock the component free.
Small-end bearing The bearing in the upper end of the connecting rod at its joint with the gudgeon pin.
Spalling Damage to camshaft lobes or bearing journals shown as pitting of the working surface.
Specific gravity (SG) The state of charge of the electrolyte in a lead-acid battery. A measure of the electrolyte's density compared with water.
Straight-cut gears Common type gear used on gearbox shafts and for oil pump and water pump drives.
Stanchion The inner sliding part of the front forks, held by the yokes. Often called a fork tube.

Stoichiometric ratio The optimum chemical air/fuel ratio for a petrol engine, said to be 14.7 parts of air to 1 part of fuel.
Sulphuric acid The liquid (electrolyte) used in a lead-acid battery. Poisonous and extremely corrosive.
Surface grinding (lapping) Process to correct a warped gasket face, commonly used on cylinder heads.

T

Tapered-roller bearing Tapered inner race of caged needle rollers and separate tapered outer race. Examples of taper roller bearings can be found on steering heads.
Tappet A cylindrical component which transmits motion from the cam to the valve stem, either directly or via a pushrod and rocker arm. Also called a cam follower.
TCS Traction Control System. An electronically-controlled system which senses wheel spin and reduces engine speed accordingly.
TDC Top Dead Centre denotes that the piston is at its highest point in the cylinder.
Thread-locking compound Solution applied to fastener threads to prevent slackening. Select type to suit application.
Thrust washer A washer positioned between two moving components on a shaft. For example, between gear pinions on gearshaft.
Timing chain See **Cam Chain**.
Timing light Stroboscopic lamp for carrying out ignition timing checks with the engine running.
Top-end A description of an engine's cylinder block, head and valve gear components.
Torque Turning or twisting force about a shaft.
Torque setting A prescribed tightness specified by the motorcycle manufacturer to ensure that the bolt or nut is secured correctly. Undertightening can result in the bolt or nut coming loose or a surface not being sealed. Overtightening can result in stripped threads, distortion or damage to the component being retained.
Torx key A six-point wrench.
Tracer A stripe of a second colour applied to a wire insulator to distinguish that wire from another one with the same colour insulator. For example, Br/W is often used to denote a brown insulator with a white tracer.
Trail A feature of steering geometry. Distance from the steering head axis to the tyre's central contact point.
Triple clamps The cast components which extend from the steering head and support the fork stanchions or tubes. Often called fork yokes.
Turbocharger A centrifugal device, driven by exhaust gases, that pressurises the intake air. Normally used to increase the power output from a given engine displacement.
TWI Abbreviation for Tyre Wear Indicator. Indicates the location of the tread depth indicator bars on tyres.

U

Universal joint or U-joint (UJ) A double-pivoted connection for transmitting power from a driving to a driven shaft through an angle. Typically found in shaft drive assemblies.
Unsprung weight Anything not supported by the bike's suspension (ie the wheel, tyres, brakes, final drive and bottom (moving) part of the suspension).

V

Vacuum gauges Clock-type gauges for measuring intake tract vacuum. Used for carburettor synchronisation on multi-cylinder engines.
Valve A device through which the flow of liquid, gas or vacuum may be stopped, started or regulated by a moveable part that opens, shuts or partially obstructs one or more ports or passageways. The intake and exhaust valves in the cylinder head are of the poppet type.
Valve clearance The clearance between the valve tip (the end of the valve stem) and the rocker arm or tappet/follower. The valve clearance is measured when the valve is closed. The correct clearance is important - if too small the valve won't close fully and will burn out, whereas if too large noisy operation will result.
Valve lift The amount a valve is lifted off its seat by the camshaft lobe.
Valve timing The exact setting for the opening and closing of the valves in relation to piston position.
Vernier caliper A precision measuring instrument that measures inside and outside dimensions. Not quite as accurate as a micrometer, but more convenient.
VIN Vehicle Identification Number. Term for the bike's engine and frame numbers.
Viscosity The thickness of a liquid or its resistance to flow.
Volt A unit for expressing electrical "pressure" in a circuit. Volts = current x ohms.

W

Water pump A mechanically-driven device for moving coolant around the engine.
Watt A unit for expressing electrical power. Watts = volts x current.
Wear limit see **Service limit**
Wet liner A liquid-cooled engine design where the pistons run in liners which are directly surrounded by coolant (see illustration).

Wet liner arrangement

Wheelbase Distance from the centre of the front wheel to the centre of the rear wheel.
Wiring harness or loom Describes the electrical wires running the length of the motorcycle and enclosed in tape or plastic sheathing. Wiring coming off the main harness is usually referred to as a sub harness.
Woodruff key A key of semi-circular or square section used to locate a gear to a shaft. Often used to locate the alternator rotor on the crankshaft.
Wrist pin Another name for gudgeon or piston pin.

Index REF•49

Note: *References throughout this index are in the form – "Chapter number" • "page number"*

A

ABS
  checks – 7•25
  component removal and installation – 7•29
  control unit – 7•30
  front modulator – 7•29
  operation and fault finding – 7•24
  rear modulator – 7•30
Air filter – 1•20
Air filter housing (carburettor models) – 4A•5
Air filter housing and intake system (fuel injection models) – 4B•3
Alternator – 9•26

B

Battery
  charging – 9•4
  check – 1•13
  removal and installation – 9•3
Bearings
  main and connecting rod bearings – 2•48
  sprocket coupling bearing – 7•23
  steering head bearings – 1•18, 1•26, 6•18
  swingarm and suspension linkage – 1•26, 6•23
  transmission shafts and bearings – 2•56
  wheel – 1•25
Bodywork – 8•1 *et seq*
  belly pan – 8•3, 8•5, 8•8
  fairing and body panels – 8•2, 8•4, 8•6, 8•9
  front mudguard – 8•9
  general information – 8•1
  seat – 8•2
  seat cowl – 8•3, 8•5, 8•6, 8•9
  side covers – 8•5, 8•6, 8•8
  rear view mirror – 8•2
Brake
  bleeding – 7•17
  brake light bulb – 9•7
  caliper – 1•26, 7•6, 7•13
  CBS (combined brake system) – 1•17, 7•12
  discs – 7•9
  fault finding – REF•40
  fluid change – 1•21
  fluid level – 0•12
  general information – 7•3
  hoses – 1•26, 7•17
  light bulb – 9•7
  light switch – 9•11
  master cylinder – 1•26, 7•10, 7•15
  pads – 1•8, 7•3
  pedal – 6•3
  system check – 1•16
Bulbs – 9•2, 9•4

C

Cables
  choke – 1•13, 4A•14
  clutch – 1•8, 2•38
  fast idle – 4B•13
  throttle – 1•13, 4A•13
Carburettor
  disassembly, cleaning and inspection – 4A•7
  general information – 4A•6
  reassembly and float height – 4A•11
  removal and installation – 4A•6
  separation and joining – 4A•10
  specifications – 4A•1
  synchronisation – 1•14
Cam chain tensioners – 2•15
Cam chain, tensioner blade and guide blades – 2•22
Camshaft and followers – 2•17
Camshaft position sensor – 4B•10
Catalytic converter – 4B•16
Charging system testing – 9•25
Clock – 9•15
Clutch (VTR models)
  bleeding – 2•37
  check and adjustment – 1•8
  fluid change – 1•21
  fluid level – 0•14
  fault finding – REF•36
  hose – 1•26
  master cylinder – 1•26, 2•35
  lever – 6•6
  release cylinder – 1•26, 2•36
  removal, inspection and installation – 2•30
  switch – 9•19
Clutch (XL models)
  cable – 1•8, 2•38
  check and adjustment – 1•8
  lever – 6•7
  release mechanism – 2•38
  removal, inspection and installation – 2•30
Component locations – 1•4
Connecting rods – 2•49
Conversion factors – REF•23
Coolant level – 0•15
Coolant temperature gauge – 9•15
Coolant temperature sensor – 4B•7, 5•7
Cooling system
  check – 1•15
  coolant reservoir – 3•2
  coolant temperature gauge and thermosensor – 3•4
  coolant hoses – 3•9
  cooling fan and fan switch – 3•3
  draining, flushing and refilling – 1•24
  fault finding – REF•36
  general information – 3•2
  radiator pressure cap – 3•2
  radiators – 3•6
  thermostat and housing – 3•5
  water pump – 3•7
Crankcase halves – 2•46, 2•48
Crankshaft and main bearings – 2•54
Cylinder
  bores – 2•48
  compression – 1•25
  heads – 2•23
  heads and valves – 2•24

D

Delay valve and proportional control valve – 7•12
Dimensions and weights – REF•1
Diode – 9•19, 9•20
Discs – 7•9
Drive chain and sprockets – 1•6, 6•24
Dual combined braking system components – 7•12

Index

E

Electrical system – 9•1 et seq
  alternator – 9•26
  battery – 9•3
  brake light/tail light and licence plate bulb – 9•7
  brake light switches – 9•11
  charging system testing – 9•25
  clock – 9•15
  clutch switch – 9•19
  coolant temperature gauge – 9•15
  diode – 9•20
  general information – 9•3
  fault finding – 9•3, REF•40
  fuel warning light or gauge and level sensor – 9•15
  fuses – 9•4
  handlebar switches – 9•17
  headlight assembly – 9•6
  headlight bulb and sidelight bulb – 9•5
  horn – 9•20
  ignition (main) switch – 9•16
  instrument and speed sensor – 9•13
  instrument and warning light bulbs – 9•15
  instrument cluster – 9•12
  lighting system check – 9•5
  neutral switch – 9•18
  oil pressure switch – 9•16
  regulator/rectifier – 9•28
  sidestand switch – 9•19
  starter motor – 9•21
  starter relay – 9•20
  tachometer – 9•14
  tail light assembly – 9•9
  turn signal assemblies – 9•10
  turn signal bulbs – 9•9
  turn signal circuit – 9•8
  wiring diagrams – 9•29 to 9•43
Engine – 2•1 et seq
  camshaft and followers – 2•17
  cam chain tensioners – 2•15
  cam chain, tensioner blade and guide blades – 2•22
  connecting rods – 2•49
  crankcase halves – 2•46, 2•48
  crankshaft and main bearings – 2•54
  cylinder bores – 2•48
  cylinder compression – 1•25
  cylinder heads – 2•23
  cylinder heads and valves – 2•24
  disassembly and reassembly – 2•13
  fault finding – REF•33
  general information – 2•8
  main and connecting rod bearings – 2•48
  oil change and filter – 1•11
  oil cooler and pipes – 2•14
  oil level – 0•11
  oil pressure – 1•25
  oil pressure switch – 9•16
  oil pump – 2•40
  oil sump, strainer and pressure relief valve – 2•39
  piston rings – 2•53
  pistons – 2•51
  radiators – 3•6
  removal and installation – 2•9
  starter clutch – 2•28
  valve covers – 2•14
  valve/valve seats/valve guides – 2•24
Engine control unit (ECU) – 4B•11
Engine number – 0•9
Engine stop relay – 4B•11
Evaporative emission control (EVAP) system – 1•20, 4A•19
Exhaust system – 4A•14

F

Fairing and body panels – 8•2, 8•4, 8•6
Fast idle cable – 4B•13
Fault finding – REF•32 to REF•40
Fault finding equipment – REF•41
Footrests – 6•3
Front forks
  check – 1•18
  disassembly, inspection and reassembly – 6•9
  front forks oil change – 1•26
  removal and installation – 6•8
Frame
  fault finding – REF•38
  inspection and repair – 6•3
  number – 0•9
Front brake
  calipers – 7•6
  discs – 7•9
  lever – 6•6
  master cylinder – 7•10
  pads – 1•8, 7•6
Front mudguard – 8•9
Front wheel – 7•19
Fuel system (carburettor models)
  carburettors – 1•14, 4A•6 to 4A•11
  general information – 1•12, 4A•2
  pump and relay – 4A•16
  tank and fuel tap – 4A•3
Fuel system (injection models)
  cut-off relay – 4B•11
  fault finding – 4B•5
  fuel injection and engine management system components – 4B•7
  general information – 1•12, 4B•5
  pressure check – 4B•15
  pump – 4B•15
  rail and injectors – 4B•8
  tank and fuel tap – 4A•3
Fuel warning light or gauge and level sensor – 4A•17, 9•15
Fuses – 9•2, 9•4

G

Gearbox – 2•5, 2•56, 2•59
Gearchange
  fault finding – REF•37
  lever – 6•4
  mechanism – 2•44

H

Handlebars and levers – 6•5
Handlebar switches – 9•17
Headlight aim – 1•17
Headlight bulb – 9•5
Horn – 9•20
Hoses
  brake – 1•26, 7•17
  clutch – 1•26
  coolant – 3•9
  fuel – 1•26, 4B•16
HT coils – 5•3

I

Idle fuel/air mixture – 4A•6
Idle speed – 1•7
Ignition (main) switch – 9•16
Ignition system – 5•1 et seq
  check – 5•2
  coils – 5•3
  control unit (carburettor models) – 5•6
  control unit (fuel injection models) – 4B•11
  general information – 5•2
  pulse generator – 5•5
  switch – 9•16
  timing – 5•6
  throttle position sensor – 4B•7, 5•7
Immobiliser system – 5•8
Initial start-up – 2•66
Instrument and warning light bulbs – 9•15
Instrument cluster – 9•12
Intake air control valve (IACV) – 4B•14
Intake air temperature (IAT) sensor – 4B•8
Introduction – 0•4

L

Lean angle sensor – 4B•10
Levers
  brake – 6•6
  clutch – 6•6
Licence plate light – 9•7
Lighting system check – 9•5
Lubricants and fluids – 1•2, REF•20

M

Main and connecting rod bearings – 2•48
Maintenance schedule – 1•3
Manifold absolute pressure (MAP) sensor – 4B•7
Master cylinder – 7•10, 7•15
Model development – 0•9
MOT test checks – REF•24
Mudguard (front) – 8•9

N

Neutral switch – 9•18
Neutral switch diode – 9•19
Nuts and bolts – 1•20

O

Oil (engine)
  change and filter (engine) – 1•11
  cooler and pipes – 2•14
  level check – 0•11
  pressure check – 1•25
  pressure switch – 9•16
  pump – 2•40
  sump, strainer and pressure relief valve (engine) – 2•39

Index

Oil change (forks) – 1•26
Oxygen sensor – 4B•10

P

Pads – 1•8, 7•3
Piston rings – 2•53
Pistons – 2•51
Pulse secondary air injection (PAIR) system – 1•20, 4A•18
Pump
　fuel – 4A•16, 4B•15
　oil – 2•40
　water – 3•7

R

Radiators – 3•6
Radiator pressure cap – 3•2
Rear brake
　caliper – 7•13
　disc – 7•9
　master cylinder – 7•15
　pads – 6•3
Rear shock absorber – 6•19
Rear sprocket coupling/rubber dampers – 6•26
Rear suspension linkage – 6•20
Rear view mirrors – 8•2
Rear wheel – 7•20
Regulator/rectifier – 9•28
Running-in procedure – 2•66

S

Safety first – 0•10
Seat – 8•2
Seat cowling – 8•3, 8•5, 8•6, 8•9
Selector drum and forks – 2•64
Sensors
　camshaft position sensor – 4B•10
　engine coolant temperature (ECT) sensor – 4B•7, 5•7
　fuel warning light and senor – 4A•17
　instrument and speed sensor – 9•13
　intake air temperature (IAT) sensor – 4B•8
　lean angle sensor – 4B•10
　manifold absolute pressure (MAP) sensor – 4B•7
　oxygen sensor – 4B•10
　speed sensor – 4B•8, 9•13
　thermosensor – 3•4
　throttle position (TP) sensor – 4B•7, 5•7
Side covers – 8•5, 8•6, 8•8
Sidelight bulb – 9•5
Sidestand – 1•10, 1•18, 6•5
Sidestand switch – 9•19
Spark plugs – 1•9
Specifications – 1•1, 2•2, 3•1, 4A•1, 4B•1, 5•1, 6•1, 7•1, 9•1
Speed sensor – 4B•8, 9•13
Sprockets – 1•6, 6•24, 7•23
Starter clutch – 2•28
Starter motor – 9•21
Starter relay – 9•20
Starter valves and fast idle cable – 4B•13
Steering head bearings – 1•18, 6•18
Steering stem – 6•15
Storage – REF•29
Suspension
　adjustments – 6•20
　check – 0•14, 1•18
　fault finding – REF•39
　rear shock absorber – 6•19
　rear suspension linkage – 6•20
Swingarm
　inspection and bearing replacement – 6•23
　removal and installation – 6•22
Swingarm and suspension linkage bearings – 1•26
Switches
　brake light – 9•11
　clutch – 9•19
　cooling fan – 3•3
　handlebar – 9•6
　ignition – 9•16
　neutral – 9•18
　oil pressure – 9•16
　sidestand – 9•19

T

Tachometer – 9•14
Tail light – 9•7
Tail light assembly – 9•9
Technical terms explained – REF•45
Timing rotor and primary drive gear – 2•45
Thermostat and housing – 3•5
Throttle bodies – 4B•12
Throttle and choke cables – 1•13, 4A•13
Throttle position sensor – 4B•7, 5•7
Tools and workshop tips – REF•2 to REF•19
Torque settings – 1•2, 2•7, 3•1, 4A•2, 4B•2, 5•2, 6•2, 7•2, 9•2
Transmission shafts and bearings – 2•56, 2•59
Turn signal assemblies – 9•10
Turn signal bulbs – 9•9
Turn signal circuit – 9•8
Tyres – 0•16, 1•20, 7•24

V

Valve
　clearances – 1•22
　covers – 2•14
　intake air control valve (IACV) – 4B•14
　seats and guides – 2•24

W

Water pump – 3•7
Wheel
　alignment – 7•18
　bearings – 1•25, 7•21
　front – 7•19
　general information – 1•20
　inspection and repair – 7•18
　rear – 7•20
Wiring diagrams – 9•29 to 9•43

Notes

Haynes Motorcycle Manuals – The Complete List

Title	Book No
APRILIA RS50 (99 - 06) & RS125 (93 - 06)	4298
Aprilia RSV1000 Mille (98 - 03)	♦ 4255
Aprilia SR50	4755
BMW 2-valve Twins (70 - 96)	♦ 0249
BMW F650	♦ 4761
BMW K100 & 75 2-valve Models (83 - 96)	♦ 1373
BMW R850, 1100 & 1150 4-valve Twins (93 - 04)	♦ 3466
BMW R1200 (04 - 06)	♦ 4598
BSA Bantam (48 - 71)	0117
BSA Unit Singles (58 - 72)	0127
BSA Pre-unit Singles (54 - 61)	0326
BSA A7 & A10 Twins (47 - 62)	0121
BSA A50 & A65 Twins (62 - 73)	0155
Chinese Scooters	4768
DUCATI 600, 620, 750 and 900 2-valve V-Twins (91 - 05)	♦ 3290
Ducati MK III & Desmo Singles (69 - 76)	◊ 0445
Ducati 748, 916 & 996 4-valve V-Twins (94 - 01)	♦ 3756
GILERA Runner, DNA, Ice & SKP/Stalker (97 - 07)	4163
HARLEY-DAVIDSON Sportsters (70 - 08)	♦ 2534
Harley-Davidson Shovelhead and Evolution Big Twins (70 - 99)	♦ 2536
Harley-Davidson Twin Cam 88 (99 - 03)	♦ 2478
HONDA NB, ND, NP & NS50 Melody (81 - 85)	◊ 0622
Honda NE/NB50 Vision & SA50 Vision Met-in (85 - 95)	◊ 1278
Honda MB, MBX, MT & MTX50 (80 - 93)	0731
Honda C50, C70 & C90 (67 - 03)	0324
Honda XR80/100R & CRF80/100F (85 - 04)	2218
Honda XL/XR 80, 100, 125, 185 & 200 2-valve Models (78 - 87)	0566
Honda H100 & H100S Singles (80 - 92)	0734
Honda CB/CD125T & CM125C Twins (77 - 88)	◊ 0571
Honda CG125 (76 - 07)	◊ 0433
Honda NS125 (86 - 93)	◊ 3056
Honda CBR125R (04 - 07)	4620
Honda MBX/MTX125 & MTX200 (83 - 93)	◊ 1132
Honda CD/CM185 200T & CM250C 2-valve Twins (77 - 85)	◊ 0572
Honda XL/XR 250 & 500 (78 - 84)	0567
Honda XR250L, XR250R & XR400R (86 - 04)	2219
Honda CB250 & CB400N Super Dreams (78 - 84)	0540
Honda CR Motocross Bikes (86 - 01)	2222
Honda CRF250 & CRF450 (02 - 06)	2630
Honda CBR400RR Fours (88 - 99)	◊ ♦ 3552
Honda VFR400 (NC30) & RVF400 (NC35) V-Fours (89 - 98)	◊ ♦ 3496
Honda CB500 (93 - 02) & CBF500 03 - 08	◊ 3753
Honda CB400 & CB550 Fours (73 - 77)	0262
Honda CX/GL500 & 650 V-Twins (78 - 86)	0442
Honda CBX550 Four (82 - 86)	◊ 0940
Honda XL600R & XR600R (83 - 08)	♦ 2183
Honda XL600/650V Transalp & XRV750 Africa Twin (87 to 07)	◊ ♦ 3919
Honda CBR600F1 & 1000F Fours (87 - 96)	♦ 1730
Honda CBR600F2 & F3 Fours (91 - 98)	♦ 2070
Honda CBR600F4 (99 - 06)	♦ 3911
Honda CB600F Hornet & CBF600 (98 - 06)	◊ ♦ 3915
Honda CBR600RR (03 - 06)	♦ 4590
Honda CB650 sohc Fours (78 - 84)	0665
Honda NTV600 Revere, NTV650 and NT650V Deauville (88 - 05)	◊ ♦ 3243
Honda Shadow VT600 & 750 (USA) (88 - 03)	2312
Honda CB750 sohc Four (69 - 79)	0131
Honda V45/65 Sabre & Magna (82 - 88)	0820
Honda VFR750 & 700 V-Fours (86 - 97)	♦ 2101
Honda VFR800 V-Fours (97 - 01)	♦ 3703
Honda VFR800 V-Tec V-Fours (02 - 05)	♦ 4196
Honda CB750 & CB900 dohc Fours (78 - 84)	0535
Honda VTR1000 (FireStorm, Super Hawk) & XL1000V (Varadero) (97 - 08)	♦ 3744
Honda CBR900RR FireBlade (92 - 99)	♦ 2161
Honda CBR900RR FireBlade (00 - 03)	♦ 4060
Honda CBR1000RR Fireblade (04 - 07)	♦ 4604
Honda CBR1100XX Super Blackbird (97 - 07)	♦ 3901
Honda ST1100 Pan European V-Fours (90 - 02)	♦ 3384
Honda Shadow VT1100 (USA) (85 - 98)	2313
Honda GL1000 Gold Wing (75 - 79)	0309
Honda GL1100 Gold Wing (79 - 81)	0669
Honda Gold Wing 1200 (USA) (84 - 87)	2199
Honda Gold Wing 1500 (USA) (88 - 00)	2225
KAWASAKI AE/AR 50 & 80 (81 - 95)	1007
Kawasaki KC, KE & KH100 (75 - 99)	1371
Kawasaki KMX125 & 200 (86 - 02)	◊ 3046
Kawasaki 250, 350 & 400 Triples (72 - 79)	0134
Kawasaki 400 & 440 Twins (74 - 81)	0281
Kawasaki 400, 500 & 550 Fours (79 - 91)	0910
Kawasaki EN450 & 500 Twins (Ltd/Vulcan) (85 - 07)	2053
Kawasaki EX500 (GPZ500S) & ER500 (ER-5) (87 - 08)	♦ 2052
Kawasaki ZX600 (ZZ-R600 & Ninja ZX-6) (90 - 06)	♦ 2146
Kawasaki ZX-6R Ninja Fours (95 - 02)	♦ 3541
Kawasaki ZX-6R (03 - 06)	♦ 4742
Kawasaki ZX600 (GPZ600R, GPX600R, Ninja 600R & RX) & ZX750 (GPX750R, Ninja 750R)	♦ 1780
Kawasaki 650 Four (76 - 78)	0373
Kawasaki Vulcan 700/750 & 800 (85 - 04)	♦ 2457
Kawasaki 750 Air-cooled Fours (80 - 91)	0574
Kawasaki ZR550 & 750 Zephyr Fours (90 - 97)	♦ 3382
Kawasaki Z750 & Z1000 (03 - 08)	♦ 4762
Kawasaki ZX750 (Ninja ZX-7 & ZXR750) Fours (89 - 96)	♦ 2054
Kawasaki Ninja ZX-7R & ZX-9R (94 - 04)	♦ 3721
Kawasaki 900 & 1000 Fours (73 - 77)	0222
Kawasaki ZX900, 1000 & 1100 Liquid-cooled Fours (83 - 97)	♦ 1681
KTM EXC Enduro & SX Motocross (00 - 07)	♦ 4629
MOTO GUZZI 750, 850 & 1000 V-Twins (74 - 78)	0339
MZ ETZ Models (81 - 95)	◊ 1680
NORTON 500, 600, 650 & 750 Twins (57 - 70)	0187
Norton Commando (68 - 77)	0125
PEUGEOT Speedfight, Trekker & Vivacity Scooters (96 - 08)	◊ 3920
PIAGGIO (Vespa) Scooters (91 - 06)	◊ 3492
SUZUKI GT, ZR & TS50 (77 - 90)	◊ 0799
Suzuki TS50X (84 - 00)	◊ 1599
Suzuki 100, 125, 185 & 250 Air-cooled Trail bikes (79 - 89)	0797
Suzuki GP100 & 125 Singles (78 - 93)	◊ 0576
Suzuki GS, GN, GZ & DR125 Singles (82 - 05)	◊ 0888
Suzuki GSX-R600/750 (06 - 09)	♦ 4790
Suzuki 250 & 350 Twins (68 - 78)	0120
Suzuki GT250X7, GT200X5 & SB200 Twins (78 - 83)	◊ 0469
Suzuki GS/GSX250, 400 & 450 Twins (79 - 85)	0736
Suzuki GS500 Twin (89 - 06)	♦ 3238
Suzuki GS550 (77 - 82) & GS750 Fours (76 - 79)	0363
Suzuki GS/GSX550 4-valve Fours (83 - 88)	1133
Suzuki SV650 & SV650S (99 - 08)	♦ 3912
Suzuki GSX-R600 & 750 (96 - 00)	♦ 3553
Suzuki GSX-R600 (01 - 03), GSX-R750 (00 - 03) & GSX-R1000 (01 - 02)	♦ 3986
Suzuki GSX-R600/750 (04 - 05) & GSX-R1000 (03 - 06)	♦ 4382
Suzuki GSF600, 650 & 1200 Bandit Fours (95 - 06)	♦ 3367
Suzuki Intruder, Marauder, Volusia & Boulevard (85 - 06)	♦ 2618
Suzuki GS850 Fours (78 - 88)	0536
Suzuki GS1000 Four (77 - 79)	0484
Suzuki GSX-R750, GSX-R1100 (85 - 92), GSX600F, GSX750F, GSX1100F (Katana) Fours	♦ 2055
Suzuki GSX600/750F & GSX750 (98 - 02)	♦ 3987
Suzuki GS/GSX1000, 1100 & 1150 4-valve Fours (79 - 88)	0737
Suzuki TL1000S/R & DL1000 V-Strom (97 - 04)	♦ 4083
Suzuki GSF650/1250 (05 - 09)	♦ 4798
Suzuki GSX1300R Hayabusa (99 - 04)	♦ 4184
Suzuki GSX1400 (02 - 07)	♦ 4758
TRIUMPH Tiger Cub & Terrier (52 - 68)	0414
Triumph 350 & 500 Unit Twins (58 - 73)	0137
Triumph Pre-Unit Twins (47 - 62)	0251
Triumph 650 & 750 2-valve Unit Twins (63 - 83)	0122
Triumph Trident & BSA Rocket 3 (69 - 75)	0136
Triumph Bonneville (01 - 07)	4364
Triumph Daytona, Speed Triple, Sprint & Tiger (97 - 05)	♦ 3755
Triumph Triples and Fours (carburettor engines) (91 - 04)	♦ 2162
VESPA P/PX125, 150 & 200 Scooters (78 - 06)	0707
Vespa Scooters (59 - 78)	0126
YAMAHA DT50 & 80 Trail Bikes (78 - 95)	◊ 0800
Yamaha T50 & 80 Townmate (83 - 95)	◊ 1247
Yamaha YB100 Singles (73 - 91)	◊ 0474
Yamaha RS/RXS100 & 125 Singles (74 - 95)	0331
Yamaha RD & DT125LC (82 - 95)	◊ 0887
Yamaha TZR125 (87 - 93) & DT125R (88 - 07)	◊ 1655
Yamaha TY50, 80, 125 & 175 (74 - 84)	◊ 0464
Yamaha XT & SR125 (82 - 03)	◊ 1021
Yamaha YBR125	4797
Yamaha Trail Bikes (81 - 00)	2350
Yamaha 2-stroke Motocross Bikes 1986 - 2006	2662
Yamaha YZ & WR 4-stroke Motocross Bikes (98 - 08)	2689
Yamaha 250 & 350 Twins (70 - 79)	0040
Yamaha XS250, 360 & 400 sohc Twins (75 - 84)	0378
Yamaha RD250 & 350LC Twins (80 - 82)	0803
Yamaha RD350 YPVS Twins (83 - 95)	1158
Yamaha RD400 Twin (75 - 79)	0333
Yamaha XT, TT & SR500 Singles (75 - 83)	0342
Yamaha XZ550 Vision V-Twins (82 - 85)	0821
Yamaha FJ, FZ, XJ & YX600 Radian (84 - 92)	2100
Yamaha XJ600S (Diversion, Seca II) & XJ600N Fours (92 - 03)	♦ 2145
Yamaha YZF600R Thundercat & FZS600 Fazer (96 - 03)	♦ 3702
Yamaha FZ-6 Fazer (04 - 07)	♦ 4751
Yamaha YZF-R6 (99 - 02)	♦ 3900
Yamaha YZF-R6 (03 - 05)	♦ 4601
Yamaha 650 Twins (70 - 83)	0341
Yamaha XJ650 & 750 Fours (80 - 84)	0738
Yamaha XS750 & 850 Triples (76 - 85)	0340
Yamaha TDM850, TRX850 & XTZ750 (89 - 99)	◊ ♦ 3540
Yamaha YZF750R & YZF1000R Thunderace (93 - 00)	♦ 3720
Yamaha FZR600, 750 & 1000 Fours (87 - 96)	♦ 2056
Yamaha XV (Virago) V-Twins (81 - 03)	♦ 0802
Yamaha XVS650 & 1100 Drag Star/V-Star (97 - 05)	♦ 4195
Yamaha XJ900F Fours (83 - 94)	♦ 3239
Yamaha XJ900S Diversion (94 - 01)	♦ 3739
Yamaha YZF-R1 (98 - 03)	♦ 3754
Yamaha YZF-R1 (04 - 06)	♦ 4605
Yamaha FZS1000 Fazer (01 - 05)	♦ 4287
Yamaha FJ1100 & 1200 Fours (84 - 96)	♦ 2057
Yamaha XJR1200 & 1300 (95 - 06)	♦ 3981
Yamaha V-Max (85 - 03)	♦ 4072

ATVs

Title	Book No
Honda ATC70, 90, 110, 185 & 200 (71 - 85)	0565
Honda Rancher, Recon & TRX250EX ATVs	2553
Honda TRX300 Shaft Drive ATVs (88 - 00)	2125
Honda Foreman (95 - 07)	2465
Honda TRX300EX, TRX400EX & TRX450R/ER ATVs (93 - 06)	2318
Kawasaki Bayou 220/250/300 & Prairie 300 ATVs (86 - 03)	2351
Polaris ATVs (85 - 97)	2302
Polaris ATVs (98 - 06)	2508
Yamaha YFS200 Blaster ATV (88 - 06)	2317
Yamaha YFB250 Timberwolf ATVs (92 - 00)	2217
Yamaha YFM350 & YFM400 (ER and Big Bear) ATVs (87 - 03)	2126
Yamaha Banshee and Warrior ATVs (87 - 03)	2314
Yamaha Kodiak and Grizzly ATVs (93 - 05)	2567
ATV Basics	10450

TECHBOOK SERIES

Title	Book No
Twist and Go (automatic transmission) Scooters Service and Repair Manual	4082
Motorcycle Basics TechBook (2nd Edition)	3515
Motorcycle Electrical TechBook (3rd Edition)	3471
Motorcycle Fuel Systems TechBook	3514
Motorcycle Maintenance TechBook	4071
Motorcycle Modifying	4272
Motorcycle Workshop Practice TechBook (2nd Edition)	3470

◊ = not available in the USA   ♦ = Superbike

The manuals on this page are available through good motorcycle dealers and accessory shops.
In case of difficulty, contact: **Haynes Publishing**
(UK) +44 1963 442030   (USA) +1 805 498 6703
(SV) +46 18 124016
(Australia/New Zealand) +61 3 9763 8100

MCL24.08/09

Preserving Our Motoring Heritage

The Model J Duesenberg Derham Tourster. Only eight of these magnificent cars were ever built – this is the only example to be found outside the United States of America

Almost every car you've ever loved, loathed or desired is gathered under one roof at the Haynes Motor Museum. Over 300 immaculately presented cars and motorbikes represent every aspect of our motoring heritage, from elegant reminders of bygone days, such as the superb Model J Duesenberg to curiosities like the bug-eyed BMW Isetta. There are also many old friends and flames. Perhaps you remember the 1959 Ford Popular that you did your courting in? The magnificent 'Red Collection' is a spectacle of classic sports cars including AC, Alfa Romeo, Austin Healey, Ferrari, Lamborghini, Maserati, MG, Riley, Porsche and Triumph.

A Perfect Day Out

Each and every vehicle at the Haynes Motor Museum has played its part in the history and culture of Motoring. Today, they make a wonderful spectacle and a great day out for all the family. Bring the kids, bring Mum and Dad, but above all bring your camera to capture those golden memories for ever. You will also find an impressive array of motoring memorabilia, a comfortable 70 seat video cinema and one of the most extensive transport book shops in Britain. The Pit Stop Cafe serves everything from a cup of tea to wholesome, home-made meals or, if you prefer, you can enjoy the large picnic area nestled in the beautiful rural surroundings of Somerset.

John Haynes O.B.E., Founder and Chairman of the museum at the wheel of a Haynes Light 12.

The 1936 490cc sohc-engined International Norton – well known for its racing success

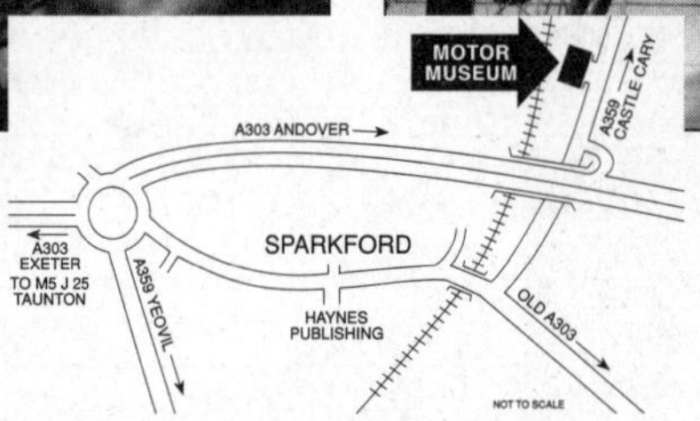

The Museum is situated on the A359 Yeovil to Frome road at Sparkford, just off the A303 in Somerset. It is about 40 miles south of Bristol, and 25 minutes drive from the M5 intersection at Taunton.
Open 9.30am - 5.30pm (10.00am - 4.00pm Winter) 7 days a week, *except Christmas Day, Boxing Day and New Years Day*
Special rates available for schools, coach parties and outings Charitable Trust No. 292048